Ti

MW01679532

The Professionalization of the American Magazine

BEITRÄGE
ZUR ENGLISCHEN UND AMERIKANISCHEN LITERATUR

Im Auftrag der Görres-Gesellschaft herausgegeben von
Bernd Engler und Kurt Müller

in Verbindung mit Rüdiger Ahrens, Ulrich Broich,
Willi Erzgräber †, Armin Paul Frank,
Roland Hagenbüchle, Hubertus Schulte-Herbrüggen,
Karl Josef Höltgen, Karl Heinz Göller, Franz Link †,
Klaus Lubbers, Christian Mair,
Heinz Joachim Müllenbrock,
Theodor Wolpers und Waldemar Zacharasiewicz

Band 33

TIM LANZENDÖRFER

The Professionalization of the American Magazine

Periodicals, Biography, and Nationalism in the Early Republic

2013

Ferdinand Schöningh
Paderborn · München · Wien · Zürich

Umschlagabbildung:
Port Folio, März 1807
(Courtesy of Library Company of Philadelphia)

Bibliographische Information der Deutschen Nationalbibliothek

Die Deutsche Nationalbibliothek verzeichnet diese Publikation in der Deutschen Nationalbibliografie; detaillierte bibliografische Daten sind im Internet über http://dnb.d-nb.de abrufbar.

Alle Rechte vorbehalten. Dieses Werk sowie einzelne Teile desselben sind urheberrechtlich geschützt. Jede Verwertung in anderen als den gesetzlich zugelassenen Fällen ist ohne vorherige schriftliche Zustimmung des Verlags nicht zulässig.

© 2013 Ferdinand Schöningh, Paderborn
(Verlag Ferdinand Schöningh GmbH & Co. KG, Jühenplatz 1, D-33098 Paderborn)

Internet: www.schoeningh.de

Einbandgestaltung: Evelyn Ziegler, München
Printed in Germany
Herstellung: Ferdinand Schöningh GmbH & Co. KG, Paderborn

ISBN 978-3-506-77773-7

Contents

Acknowledgements

I have incurred a number of debts over the course of writing this book and the dissertation which it developed from. First and foremost, my thanks to Prof. Dr. Oliver Scheiding, my dissertation advisor. Without his encouragement, ready knowledge, and interest in the progress of my work, as well as his unceasing support even when I insisted on doing things differently, this dissertation could not have been written. Thanks also to Prof. Dr. Alfred Hornung for his valuable support as a reader of the dissertation. The German Research Foundation (DFG) funded the project "Life Writing im Spiegel der frühen amerikanischen Zeitschriftenliteratur 1790-1830" (SCHE1616-4-1) within which I was gainfully employed for two years, permitting me to concentrate on work related to my dissertation, an impossibility without the DFG's generous support. Thanks are also in order to Görres Society's generous sponsoring of the printing of this book.

Several people were especially helpful in the process of writing and thinking about this book. My colleagues in American Studies were a great help, especially Matthias Köhler and Clemens Spahr. The fellows of the doctoral college "Life Writing" at Johannes Gutenberg University, as well as my other fellow doctoral candidates in the years of writing, were a valuable sounding board. Anette Vollrath has always been helpful. Thanks to Jared Gardner and Elizabeth Hewitt, too, for their stimulating conversation and help with various bits and pieces of this study during their stay at Mainz in the summer of 2011. The staffs of the Historical Society of Pennsylvania, the Library Company of Philadelphia, Houghton Library of Harvard University, the Massachusettts Historial Society, the American Antiquarian Society, and the Library of Congress were everything a researcher could hope for, and made the dry archival days a joy. A similar thanks to the reproductions departments for their quick aid in getting high quality images for this book.

For proofreading parts of the final manuscript of this study, my thanks go to Damien Schlarb and Clemens Spahr (again), whose sharp eyes caught many of the errors which I had missed. Whatever errors remain they failed to catch, but then I did not pay them, either, so there.

Ein ganz persönlicher Dank gilt meiner Familie: meiner Mutter und meinem Vater, meiner Stiefmutter und meinem Stiefvater und meinen Großmüttern, für die vielen Jahre, in denen sie mein Studium und meine Promotion begleitet und unterstützt haben. Ohne sie wäre es nicht gegangen.

Lastly, none of this would have been possible without the support and love, and the final full read-through which caught so many mistakes, of my wife Anselma, to whom this book is dedicated. Thank you so very much for everything.

Introduction

The real value of a thing
Is as much money as 'twill bring.

Pennsylvania Magazine 1775, 53

This study offers a re-reading of the history of American magazines in the Early Republic. I argue that we must understand the history of American periodicals in the first two decades of the 1800s as an evolutionary process in which a growing acceptance of the existence of the periodical in a market system was mirrored by a professionalization of the periodical business—a history of continuities, in other words, in which the periodical as a market-oriented publishing venture steadily came to the fore, even as very few of its individual constitutive parts were ultimately new. In the bluntest sense, my argument is thus precisely the inverse of recent scholarship, which has frequently suggested that in the history of American magazines, in comparing the situation in the 1790s with that of the 1820s, "the differences were ultimately more meaningful than the continuities" (Gardner 2012, 170). The periodicals were shaped in response to the market in which they were produced, rather than according to ideological formations that resulted in recognizably distinct periods, 'befores' and 'afters.' This continuous response to the market took shape most importantly in an increasing openness about and readiness to accept the heteronomy of economic conditions which underlay the production of periodicals in the Early Republic. Whether it is the question of paid contributions or merely the recognition that magazines were produced for a paying audience: there was nothing new under the sun of 1825, nothing being done that magazines had not been doing, on a smaller scale and perhaps slightly less overtly, at least since 1790, and perhaps, as the *Pennsylvania Magazine*'s pithy note suggests, as early as 1775.

What I will be showing in the following is precisely that heteronomy in a history which I will ultimately argue is a history of the growing professionalization of periodical production. I speak of professionalization here with some timidity. As Leon Jackson has discussed in his seminal study of authorship in the antebellum era, the concepts of professionals and amateurs are difficult to apply in the early 1800s, and this is emphatically true for the periodical field. Jackson has argued that it would be better to speak of a "disembedding of the economy" of authorship, a process through which the centrality of "[s]ocial relations came to be replaced by commercialized and impersonal ones" (2008, 48). While I am not following Jackson's suggestion to abandon use of the term professionalization outright, I recognize the need to be clear about its use in my analysis. I mean to have it understood in the broadest possible sense, and as an unfinished process that led towards, but did not yet end in, anything approaching today's specialization of editorial, publishing, and printing functions. Rather, for the purposes of this study it is best understood as shorthand for a process of laying open the economic determinants and goals of the periodical market to both consumers and producers, a process by which what might be termed the 'fantasy' of disinterested virtue was replaced by a growing penetration of periodical production by the demands of the market, and an increasing openness in all corners of the periodical field about those demands.

I do not suggest that this process occurred simultaneously and indiscriminately with all magazines, or even that the aspects of professionalization that I identify appeared exclusively during the narrow timeframe I am discussing. The best example to see that these processes stretch beyond timeframe of this study is Mathew Carey, who as early as 1787 employed editors and paid contributors for the *Columbian Magazine*, a publication that was not the publisher's central business, but rather one among many ventures (cf. Wood 1949, 17-9). But even though Carey saw his magazine as a professional enterprise, the aspects I will emphasize were much more structurally relevant factors for the journals under consideration here. I am suggesting that a broadly conceived process of increasing professionalization and open display of the commodity character of periodicals is the most adequate way of describing the changes which occurred between about 1795 and 1825 in much of the American periodical business. The aspects of this conception of professionalization include the greater frequency of a functional split between, first, editor and publisher/printer, and then also between publisher and printer; the increasing willingness of magazine publishers to pay contributors for submissions, and those publisher's growing tendency to actively demand particular kinds of submissions; a tighter control over the distribution process and the hiring of additional staff (beyond a single editor) to help organize that process; the growing tendency to make one's living solely of the production of one or several well-regarded and successful magazines; and a more frequent rotation of editors at a magazine remaining otherwise under the same publisher's control. These functional aspects of professionalization interacted with an increased awareness of the importance of the readership as a market. My analysis seeks to foreground this increasing awareness of and consequently the increasing adaption of the entire complex field of periodical production to what Robert Gross has called a "world where print supplied not what an elite deemed best but what the people desired most" (2010, 517).

Since I speak in the following of professionalization as a process devoid of a definite beginning or a definite end, I second Jackson's belief that to suggest that one could, for example, fix 1850 as the point where things usually had 'become professional' is a conceptual misunderstanding (cf. 2008, 22). What I ultimately consider professionalization is a process by which certain features of the periodical business became increasingly prominent and public. This process was neither directed at any definite point of conclusion, nor were its features more 'advanced' or 'better' than previous modes of operation. And, in fact, no single periodical in the period I am discussing managed to fully incorporate all of these features. Still, their increase over time speaks to the evolution of the American periodical away from a loss leader whose publication was often couched in terms of civic duty towards an appreciation and increasingly an open admission that a well-organized periodical could and indeed should make significant profit for its proprietors.[1]

If my overarching goal, then, is to offer a re-evaluation of the history of the American periodical, my approach is necessarily restricted to analyzing a slice of that history only, and I draw my larger conclusions from that smaller slice. In particular, I want to discuss three interwoven issues: the ways in which periodicals were produced, the usages of the genre of biography in magazines, and their discussion of American nationalism. These three topics are not only related but complexly interwoven, and it is precisely this interwoven relationship that allows us to draw larger conclusions about the periodical market. On the one hand, I hold that a clearer and fuller appreciation of any of the three topics—magazine production, biographical writings, and Early Republic nationalism—depends on seeing them in connection with each other. That is to say: we cannot speak about Early Republic biography without looking carefully at magazine biographies; we cannot discuss nationalism in the Early Republic without looking at the ways in which periodicals discussed it; and while we could look at the production of periodicals in the Early Republic without necessarily looking at biography and questions of nationalism in particular, the two topics allow us to see both the market-dependent limitations of periodical writings in the Early Republic as well as their occasional potential to exceed, or at least go to the very boundaries of, those very limitations. On the other hand, I suggest that the three topics are so tightly interwoven that they allow us to come to broader conclusions about the complex system of American periodical production. The perspective I have chosen for this study, precisely because it shows the ways in which production side, genre, and ideology interacted, allows us to see in miniature the heteronomy of the entire system—but also the momentary opportunities to escape that heteronomy.

A reading such as this, with its emphasis on the market of periodicals, stands in some contrast to readings which have foregrounded the periodical's role in the creation of alternative "forums of citizenship," to adopt Catherine O'Donnell Kaplan's felicitous but misleading phrase, such as Kaplan's work itself, Michael Warner's "res publica of letters" in his seminal *The Letters of the Republic* (1991), or Jared Gardner's "virtual coffeehouse of the periodical" (2012, 47). Warner's suggestions on the constitutiveness of print for the production of the republic of letters, in which print produced an abstract, because disembodied public united in potential readership, "an audience that was real but in principle not identifiable" (1991, 62), are, somewhat puzzlingly, countered by the nature of the periodical: in principle, but probably not in reality given the problems which the subscription system had

1 Indeed, it would even be wrong to suggest that a return to previous forms of doing business might not also be 'more professional,' as the modern day example of the return to subscription prior to publication via such internet-based services as Kickstarter suggests. With Kickstarter, individuals can promise start-up businesses (publishers among them!) money which they will only pay upon the actual conclusion of the project, a system very much alike to the types of book publishing prevalent in the 1790s to 1820s.

with keeping track of customers, it was possible to identify precisely the audience of the periodical—certainly, at any rate, the paying audience, given the small size any such audience attained. There is good reason to be wary of the idea that any coherent ideological community was created by periodicals in the Early Republic. The kind of broad-based readership which echoed through so many of the magazines' self-conceptions, the limited participation of individuals in the preparation of content, and the centrality of variations of amusement in content over a clear ideological line—which would imply a certain lack of variation—makes readings of periodicals as vehicles of public ideologies difficult. Magazines, magazine editors, and magazine publishers might well claim that they sought particular ulterior goals for their magazines, yet ultimately, they recurred to the simple equation in which success on the periodical market, a secure position in the periodical field, trumped any ideology.

My answers to the questions I am asking—how did the production of periodicals work? What was the status of biography in Early Republic periodicals? What can biography tell us about how these periodicals worked? What was the role of the periodical in the construction of American nationalism? What was the role of biography in the construction of American nationalism?—are not meant to suggest that we should reduce our study of texts to the contexts of their production (that is to say the entirety of the process by which a periodical came to be, from the writing of articles, the purchase of paper and type, printing, distribution, editing, etc.), but rather that we must account for something more closely approaching the totality of periodical production, not just individual essays; this, we can only do by appreciating the complexity of the periodical form in its relation to the market. My central argument boils down to this: periodicals in the Early Republic were primarily meant to make money for their editors and publishers. To understand periodicals as mainly concerned with making money in a complex market situation ultimately results in a reappraisal of their relationship to their content.

Part of my argument then is a rejection of the neatness which a reliance on ideological readings of the periodical brings in explaining the workings of periodicals. This problem manifests specifically in arguments which ascribe an idealistic motivation to periodical publication, such as Bruce Weiner's with regard to the printers and publishers of periodicals in the Early Republic. "My contention is," says Weiner, "that their enterprise was idealistic and ambivalent [...] devoted to the idea that periodical publication—especially monthly magazines—were the best means of realizing in printed form republican principles of freedom and social equality" (2009, 102). Weiner correctly notes that "[i]t is easy to dismiss the rhetorical flourishes" with which magazines stated their ideals, while one cannot deny the fact of the rhetoric's persistence (109). In a sense, Weiner's thesis may just not be strong enough: printers and publishers and editors were not 'ambivalent' about the role of the periodical, they were downright contradictory, readily able to keep before the public a variety of idealistic motivations which successfully (if in complicity with their readers) erected a façade of idealism beneath which lay little more than the desire to make a profit. They performed their part in a mutually-accepted fantasy of disinterested virtue.

The centrality of the periodical in the period I discuss needs little emphasis. "[P]eriodical publications," wrote Thomas Green Fessenden, editor of the *Weekly Inspector* in his prospectus in 1806, "are multiplied beyond all precedent" (*WI* 1806, 1). In 1813, the editors of the *Olio* admitted that it was necessary to give "some account [...] of the motives which have induced them to add another paper to a list thought by many already too large" (O 1813, 1). Not all of the magazines on this too-large list, of course, lasted; indeed, the average life of a magazine was a mere fourteen months (cf. Kaplan 2007, 140). Despite this short life-span, periodicals were a booming market in the Early Republic. Indeed, by one count, as many as 600 different magazines appeared in the United States between 1800 and 1825 (cf. Mott 1957a, 120-1), and numerous of those were recognized by their contemporaries as important parts of the American literary landscape. Scott Casper has highlighted the importance of biography as a genre in the early nineteenth century (1999); and the study of Early Republic nationalism has a long tradition (cf. inter alia Waldstreicher 1997; but cf. ch. 3). But is there a necessary connection between periodicals, biography, and nationalism? There is not, of course: yet there is an actual connection between them, a connection which I will trace in this study. In offering an analysis of the three complex subjects of periodical production, biography, and nationalism in the Early Republic, I argue that we greatly benefit both from this synthetic approach as well as from a close attention to the production processes which underlay the publication of the various magazines I discuss in the following. The vast number of sources which I have consulted, many of which have not been studied before in any detail, suggests that there is still a significant side of the periodical in the Early Republic which scholarship has so far ignored. At the same time, my approach offers ways through which scholarship may tackle the problems incipient in periodical research by suggesting that synthetic studies are possible, combining attention to production, form, genre, and individual text on a limited but representative scale.

In trying to come to terms with Early Republic periodicals, I advocate a closer look at the complex and often hard to reconstruct relationships between publisher, editor, audience, genre, and content, among other issues. I do not wish to be understood as completely dismissing the impact of idealistic considerations and motivations, and their ability to trump, from time to time, other editorial and publishing considerations. Joseph Dennie, the *Port Folio* editor from 1801-1812, is still a central figure in Chapter 2, and of course he was an unabashed conservative, vociferous anti-republican, and a "malcontent," as he called himself in a letter to his mother. He told her in April 1797 that "[h]ad it not been for the selfish patriotism of that hoary traitor, Adams [...] I might now, perhaps, in a Literary Diplomatic, or lucrative Situation been in the service of my rightful King and instead of shivering in the bleakness of the United States, felt the genial sunshine of a Court." But at the same time, I argue that we are not helped by ignoring that he also recognized that "[i]n my Editorial capacity, I am obliged to the nauseous task of flattering republicans" (in Pedder 1936, 159). Dennie was quite capable of distinguishing between public moral and more private financial editorial obligations and readily acted on the latter even while loudly proclaiming the centrality of his own political opinions. Indeed, the ability to simultaneously do both was the foundation upon which the continued success of the *Port Folio*, and of any long-lived magazine in the Early Republic, ultimately rested.

All this forces us to make some methodological modifications in periodical scholarship. Instead of focusing on content, on analyzing that content with the tools of literary scholarship looking for themes or even entirely coherent ideologies such as republican virtue or the advancement of a national agenda, we must appreciate said content's role in the complex of relations between the various elements that constituted the periodical business. A general overview over the production of periodicals in the Early Republic, such as I offer in Chapter 1, can help us identify the large network of interrelations that shaped the nature of the Early Republic magazine. I have selected the genre of biography to more clearly elaborate on the consequences of these relations because biography can be understood as an exemplary genre for periodicals, capable of being adapted into a great variety of roles in the periodical, and showing clearly the ways in which content was subordinated under the heteronomous demands of the periodical—a process I discuss in greater detail in Chapter 2. I claim that we can most easily trace the controlling influence of this heteronomy by concentrating on this one genre's engagement with one frequently and critically foregrounded idealistic purpose of periodicals, American nationalism, and by identifying the extent to which it was possible to offer a more autonomous reaction to the strictures of the periodical market. I will do that in Chapter 3.

The reasons for my selective approach to the study of Early Republic periodicals through one genre and one issue in particular stem from the problems identified in scholarly literature with the studies of periodicals, and the solutions which have been suggested, and I will briefly sketch some critical assumptions and concerns below. More importantly, however, I will suggest what concerns drove my own research, and how I intend to frame this study. In emphasizing the constraints under which the producers of Early American periodicals labored, I hope to suggest the need to expand our study of Early American periodicals: ultimately, the value of any interpretation of what American periodicals published depends on the validity of our assumptions on why it was published.

The Nature of Periodical Research

Although periodical research has been ongoing for decades, the question of how we should look at periodicals has gone largely unanswered. Although some attempts have been made to locate periodical studies in an interdisciplinary field (cf. Lee 2006), these attempts have not yielded a coherent theoretical framework with which to approach periodical studies, a fact which is owed primarily to the diversity of the field. The most important publication on periodical research theory is still a 1989 special issue of the British journal *Victorian Periodical Research*, a journal devoted to the study of British magazines, a fact which foregrounds again the lack of a theoretical discussion in the context of American periodicals in particular. The *VPR* issue was devoted entirely to the question of theory. Among its concerns were the problem of authorship and its relation to the periodical, as well as the approaches to be employed in reading Victorian periodicals. Tellingly, even this theory issue struggled with the question of a method of periodical study. In one of the most ambitious and earliest statements of what periodical research should be doing, Michael Wolff has suggested that an "adequate description"—here, of one of the key changes diagnosed for British journalism between 1815 and 1840—would require an approach that covered almost every detail periodical production and consumption:

> We would need to know the range and type of newspaper and magazine publication in both 1815 and 1840; we would need to know a lot about circulation and content, and about the writers, editors, and proprietors, and their attitudes towards the hoped-for readership, including for example, whether the object of each periodical was to make money or to influence people or, if both, in what proportion—and these factors would have to be seen not just at a given moment but dynamically through the runs of the serials. We would need to know something, perhaps a good deal, about the readership for the various publications, who bought what, what was distributed for free to whom, what clubs or places of entertainment made what available, and what sort of reading aloud or word-of-mouth extension of news and opinion took place, and, finally and most difficult of all to recapture, how seriously particular publications were read or listened to and how their actual influence might be measured. (Wolff 1971, 14)

Wolff's enumeration of the many issues which periodical research needs to deal with in order to come to an "adequate description" of its fields hinges, of course, on the assumption that we are looking for a kind of totality in our understanding: looking, as it were, not to cover a single aspect of the whole, but to understand the entirety of periodical production in its large shifts and turns, a project which in the case Wolff was addressing required the researcher to investigate the writings in one hundred English journals in 1815 and 1840. As Lyn Pickett has noted, Wolff's plan seems to call for "the super-scholar […] of such awesome erudition that one fears that they would sink under the burden they carry" (1989, 101). Despite the seemingly overwhelming amount of connections which a study of magazines would require scholars to make, the idea that periodicals are best understood in context, using what Judith Yaross Lee has called a "holistic approach," has continued to be seen as valid and necessary. Like Wolff, Lee emphasizes the importance of

> exploring the means of production characterizing serial publication: the confluence of editors, writers, publishers, advertisers, investors, agents, and readers who collaboratively construct the editorial policy of a successful magazine, journal, or newspaper in an environment created in part by other economic stakeholders, including printers, distributors, postmasters, legislators, politicians, and other forces ranging from transportation and communication technologies to economic and social factors. (2005, 198)

In the final analysis, however, neither Lee's nor Wolff's essays offer a fully formed methodology. Somewhat more helpful in that regard is Lyn Pykett's own approach in *Victorian Periodicals Research.* It does not deny Wolff's suggestion of what is needed in periodical studies as much as it emphasizes the centrality of (poststructuralist) theory in structuring the mass of knowledge it is possible to attain, as well as the necessity for the periodical researcher to be aware of the methodological models and patterns he uses (cf. 1989, 101). Notably, Pykett does not end up suggesting a single methodology of periodical research. Rather, she highlights the interdisciplinarity and plurality of method that periodical studies permit.[2] The central question for all discussion of periodicals, Pykett suggests, is "how, and within what structures and frameworks, we should attempt to contextualize" the periodical text (105). Tellingly, Pykett's own attempt at suggesting methods and approaches does not negate the basic fact of Lee's and Wolff's lists of things that periodical researchers need to know in order to come to terms with their subject. Pykett's concern is to add to this list more questions: not just what researchers need to know, but "how we need to know it, [...] what kinds of knowledge we need, what models we use, and what patterns we construct" (101).

In Brian Maidment's words, also written in the context of periodical research, the idea is, therefore, to "view expressed opinion not in isolation from but rather in complex relation to formal and generic aspects of periodical publication," and to depart from efforts to read periodical texts (indeed the same could be said about biography) as "pre-eminently [illustrating] ideological formations widely perceived in other kinds of economic and cultural formations" (1984, 86). Such efforts include, despite several nods to larger, non-ideological concerns, Michael Warner's *The Letters of the Republic*, with its emphasis on reading ideological positions into a print discourse, "printing defined as a technology of publicity, having an essentially civic and emancipatory character" (1990, 9), as well as Scott Casper's *Constructing*

2 Pykett takes from cultural and media studies the belief that periodicals need to be addressed in an interdisciplinary fashion that refuses to privilege text over context, but reads them as "indivisible elements" (103). Pykett's methodological pluralism acknowledges the possibilities offered by a wide-range of structuralist and poststructuralist approaches to periodicals, and the need to stress the "historical specificities of 19th-century culture and society, and the conditions of [media] production" (104). She offers the example of John Stuart Mill's mid-1820s reflections on the periodical press as an example of a poststructuralist reading *avant la lettre*, a reading which emphasizes not so much the periodical text as a mirror of the times as the ideological purpose of the periodical and the role of the periodical in a Foucauldian discourse community, as well as a reflection on reader-response approaches to periodicals. Pykett situates the periodical in its times, interacting with its cultural context rather than mirroring it. Her reading of Mill's text as unconscious poststructuralism reveals the possibilities of poststructuralist readings of periodicals, offering "an approach [which] would avoid the colonization of periodicals study by a purely literary or formal methodology, while, at the same time, it would challenge those historians who refuse to regard the history of cultural forms, such as writing and its particular genres, as a central part of 'general history'" (107).

American Lives, which reads biography for its idealistic content but rarely makes forays into considerations of materiality. But the actual texts produced in the periodicals cannot be read solely as expressions of authorial intent, or even just for content, as texts alone.

In his recent study on the *Rise and Fall of Early American Magazine Culture*, Jared Gardner has called the Early Republic magazine a "motley and cacophonous" type of literature, one which, to the literary scholar, offers a problematic array of "contradictory evidence and ambiguous conclusions" (2012, 3). Gardner has concisely formulated the central problem which scholarship has identified as critical for our engagement with periodicals. Scholars of periodicals, note Sean Latham and Robert Scholes, "are rarely in a position to say much about the periodical as a whole. As a consequence, we have often been too quick to see magazines merely as containers of discrete bits of information rather than autonomous objects of study" (2006, 517-8); and at the same time, the "periodical as a whole" offers an almost unmanageably large mass of material of an ununifiable heterogeneity. Because of the overwhelming mass of material, any study can only cover a limited amount of ground. A study of the entire *Port Folio*, for example, even if it were limited to the texts contained within the magazine itself and were to refuse to look at correspondence, historical context, or into tracing sources, would amount to reading and analyzing on the order of 50 volumes (one for each year between 1801 and 1806, two for every year between 1807 and 1827, though the last years are more complicated) of between four hundred and five hundred pages each—at a conservative estimate, some 22,000 pages of primary material that spans a huge gamut of genres and topics. Consequentially, most work hitherto published on periodicals has "focused on small magazines with short print runs or on single themes or motifs in larger periodicals" (Latham and Scholes 2006, 529). Such periodical theory as there is does not in fact make matters easier: the theory of periodical studies, instead of providing convenient access points for an analysis of periodicals, stresses the ways in which periodicals cannot be read autonomously, but need to be contextualized. Even the 22,000 pages of the *Port Folio* are not enough: they become merely the center of a reading project which would need to include a vast amount of material surrounding the text proper, such as the editorial correspondence where available, business records and histories of the development of printing and entrepreneurial publishing.

The problem, then, is clear: we cannot hope to be able to read 'the individual magazine,' much less 'the Early Republic periodical,' a mass too vast to cope with. Nor can we expect to come to terms with it through an analysis of single texts tracing a single motif, since we end up excluding the contradictions and ambiguities which even a casual survey of a broader selection of material necessarily presses into the foreground. In the following, I choose to encounter this issue by using a more functional approach than the suggestions outlined above, focusing on specific case studies while at the same time recognizing the need to embed those case studies in the larger production context of periodicals.

As Judith Lee has noted, "periodicals differ substantially from other publications" (Lee 2005, 197), and Sean Latham and Robert Scholes have similarly asserted that this distinction has frequently either escaped scholars or has been ignored: scholars "continue to see [periodicals] essentially as aggregations of otherwise autonomous works, similar to literary anthologies" (2006, 519). But, of course, they were nothing of the sort. Rather, Early Republic periodicals themselves were highly heteronomous, their content, in turn, was determined by the contingencies and strictures under which the production of periodicals as a whole labored. The field of periodical productions in the Early Republic left little room for autonomy, either for periodicals as cohesive units or for their individual articles, neither for their editors, nor for their authors.

The terms I use above—"field," "heteronomy," "autonomy"—reveal something of a debt in formulating my conception of the production of periodicals in the Early Republic to the ideas of Pierre Bourdieu. I follow Leon Jackson's investigation of antebellum authorship here in making use of aspects of Pierre Bourdieu's influential notion of the "field," to which the other two terms belong, if only as a useful heuristic for the discussion of periodical production in the Early Republic. Key to my adaptation of Bourdieu's concept of the field is his overarching concern for the structural relations between social positions and his comparative neglect of the individual's agency even as he does not in the end completely exclude the effects of agency (cf. 1993a, 29). For Bourdieu, "fields," sets of objective relations within structural spaces possessing specific resources or interests, are the basis of any social formation (cf. Bourdieu 2003a, 6). Within them, agents compete for available positions in relation to precisely those resources. Among those fields which Bourdieu himself identifies is the literary field, which most closely approximates the field of periodical production. The most important distinction which Bourdieu draws, at least for the purposes of this study, is the distinction between the field's two divergent poles, towards which producers of literature may orient themselves along a sliding scale: the heteronomous pole, "favourable to those who dominate the field economically and politically," and the autonomous pole, at which the economic and political influences decline and it becomes possible for producers to create works of art solely for themselves and others at the same location in the field (1993, 40). The consequence for producers at the autonomous pole, as Bourdieu is well aware, is that they may obtain critical success among their peers, but remain poor economically; in Bourdieu's terms, they amass cultural or symbolic capital even as they fail to gain economic capital.

Yet, as Bourdieu emphasizes, "economic capital is at the root of all the other types of capital and that these transformed, disguised forms of economic capital, never entirely reducible to that definition, produce their most specific effects only to the extent that they conceal (not least from their possessors) the fact that economic capital is at their root, in other words—but only in the last analysis—at the root of their effects" (2011, 89). It is important to recognize the centrality of the economic in Bourdieu's theory since even Jackson's sociological model neglects that fact, and it is a crucial aspect of my adaptation here. While Jackson points out that each of the forms of capital which Bourdieu identifies "circulates within a discrete economy" (2008, 32), he is more ambivalent about the fact that the basis of the exchange is economic capital, even though individual 'transactions' may be better explained by reference to other types of capital. More crucially, I foreground the economic in the following because it was ultimately the particular systematic expression of economic relationships—in increasing marketization and capitalization of the economic systems in which periodicals were produced—that drove the process of professionalization which I describe.

I suggest that we read the production of periodicals in the Early Republic analogously, as taking place in the 'field of periodical production,' in which the production of different forms of capitals, mainly economic and symbolic, plays a significant role. Such an analogy can, of course, only go so far: it must be stressed that there are significant obstacles to employing Bourdieu's concepts on the literary and cultural fields as well as the idea of convertible forms of capitals to periodical writing and production. Bourdieu, of course, discusses a literary field, and this concept must be adapted to the specific 'field' of the periodical, based on the empirical evidence I assemble below. Bourdieu's argument suggests that the literary field constitutes "a world apart, subject to its own laws" (1995, 48), where autonomous literary production stood in direct opposition to something approaching a 'popular' literary culture in which "the most common literary works" figured prominently owing to the favor they were in with press and bourgeois readers and buyers (58-9). Not for nothing does Bourdieu entitle the chapter laying down his principle formulations on the literary field "The Conquest of Autonomy:" for Bourdieu, a disillusionment with the existing opportunities of literary expression and a determined resistance to the forces shaping the existing marketplace for literary products induced some artists to break away from external demands—political and economic—and bourgeois art and strive for a conception of 'art for art's sake' (cf. 1995, 50-112).[3] It is extremely difficult, indeed impossible, to reconcile Bourdieu's ultimate expression of authorial autonomy, an indifference to politics, economy, and morality, and a total dedication to the "norms specific to one's art" (1996, 76-7), with the actuality of the production of magazines in the Early Republic. This may suggest a more fundamental difference between literature as Bourdieu conceives it and the periodical form, in

3 As the repeated use here of the word "bourgeois" indicates, Bourdieu traces the emergence of the literary field in 1840s and 1850s France; certainly, conditions in France at that time differed considerably from those we encounter in the Early Republic United States, and the authorial economies of the novelists which Bourdieu discusses share only moderate similarities with the magazine editors and publishers which I discuss. While some efforts were made to produce monthly magazines without the help of contributors even when these magazines contained for the most part selected matter copied from other magazines, they hardly ever lasted long. Bourdieu's notion of "producers who produce for other producers" (1993a, 39) is therefore complicated: are we talking about editors producing magazines for other editors? Contributors contributing to magazines for other contributors? Indeed, this question is not the only problem that arises with Bourdieu's theories of the literary field when blindly adopted to the field of periodicals; other questions, such as where one would identify the habitus, are similarly problematical—but a discussion of this question would no doubt be out of place here.

which autonomy ultimately was impossible.[4] The consequence of a Bourdieuan authorial autonomy, in the last analysis, is a kind of genteel poverty, where authorial success, unmeasured in money but rather in critical acclaim, is not necessarily capable of sustaining authorial life.[5] The sustenance of financial profitability was, however, ultimately the chief concern for the producers of periodicals, and increasingly also for contributors.

I believe that several aspects of Bourdieu's notion of the field lend themselves to adoption in a study of the Early Republic magazine, even though it is probably not useful to offer a genuinely Bourdieuan reading.[6] My use of the Bourdieuan terms involves, for one thing, a reversal of his trajectory of authorial occupation—a 'conquest of heteronomy,' as it were: Bourdieu's maxim 'art for art's sake' most nearly approximates authorial and periodical autonomy in the early period of American magazine production which still most clearly shows suggestions of such authorial and periodical autonomy in voluntary contributions, minimal editorial oversight, and the collusion of editors and proprietors in one person, capable if they were willing of making editorial decisions absent of monetary concerns. By no means all early magazines, and probably not even most of them, operated on the basis of such autonomy, of course. Yet most if not all of them were willing to claim the essential disinterestedness of their actions as marker of the ultimate detachment of magazine production from the monetary economy (cf. Bourdieu 1996, 142). It is precisely the modest expression, both in terms of overt claims and in underlying structures, of such an autonomy that we see diminish during the period here under consideration: the voluntary contributions by anonymous writers are replaced by an ever increasing number of commissioned contributions, and editors beholden only to their own beliefs became hired hands to profit-oriented publishers. Central among the features I suggest are those of a growing professionalization of the periodical business is thus the distribution of the functions of editor, publisher, printer, and contributors. The most the important of these is certainly the differentiation between the role of publisher and editor, between the person chiefly responsible for the business side of the periodical and the person responsible for the selection

4 It may be helpful in this case to compare Jared Gardner's approach in his *The Rise and Fall of the Early American Magazine*, which explicitly parallels the developments of novel and periodical (cf. 7); such a parallel reading reveals interesting and perhaps indeed periodical-like aspects of the Early Republic novel, but ultimately must be considered problematical, given the wholly different production conditions of these two kinds of writing.

5 The author whose life history might be said to most closely approach the kind of authorial poverty in service of art in the United States, certainly in popular estimation, may be Edgar Allen Poe. Significantly, however, for Poe, the periodical was always his means of being able to escape the poverty of authorship.

6 Jackson (2008) is one such reading for a later period, and Günter Leypoldt (2009) is a Bourdieuan study of the mid-1800s, especially of Walt Whitman, that shows the possibilities of the approach in an era much closer to the one Bourdieau himself had studied, and in a field much more likely to yield similar results.

of content, increasingly within a larger framework or agenda, based on publishing considerations, set by the publisher. No less important is periodicals' shift towards an authorial economy that saw the production of an increasing number of commissioned articles, rather than the voluntary contributions of the earlier periods. At the same time, editorial autonomy decreased as more and more publishers sought hired editors for their periodical ventures.

Ultimately, in a structural view of the periodical business, general historical trends were more crucial for periodical writing than the individual beliefs of authors and editors, but I would go one step further still: more important than the general historical developments are the specific economic conditions of the periodicals which I discuss. As Stephen Shapiro has suggested, "[t]he modern shape of the United States emerges throughout the 1790s, and economic, rather than political, history explains this transformation" (2008, 106); the periodical 'emerged,' that is, was continuously transformed, similarly through the economic conditions of its production. Such an approach thus reframes the narrative of periodical history in the Early Republic away from considerations of individuals and of overarching ideologies. Critical studies of the periodical in the Early Republic have largely centered their narratives on individual agency, and mostly approached their objects via the figure of the periodical editor.

To be sure, this is already a significant shift away from a focus on authors, as Jared Gardner points out (cf. 2012, 74); yet it unduly privileges the editor as an autonomous agent. Perhaps the most extreme expression of this view is Neal Edgar's emphatic suggestion that "[a] magazine's success depends largely upon the ability of its editor, and its pages reflect his personality, character and individuality" (1975, 11). Tellingly, Edgar subscribes to the erroneous view that Washington Irving was responsible for the "innovation" of the naval biographies published in the *Analectic Magazine*, of which Irving was editor—a myth that I will attempt to correct in Chapter 3 (cf. 46). Likewise, Randolph C. Randall, in his essay on Joseph Dennie's literary attitudes, suggests that Dennie intended the *Port Folio* "to serve [his] political views" (1973, 57). His argument that Dennie ceased being able of "good writing" in late 1808 because the only explanation for the 'sudden' inclusion in the *Port Folio* after 1808 of essays on bridges and sheep was that Dennie could not write or edit the magazine himself anymore (cf. 86) is particularly unhelpful. That Randall never touches a single piece of writing from after 1809, despite Dennie's continuance in the editor's chair in those years, highlights critics' desire to see the editor's figure as autonomous.

Even more explicitly devoted to this agenda are John Tebbel and Mary Zuckermann who, adopting an almost hagiographic tone, note of the *Port Folio* that above it "hovered the Spirit of Dennie himself, a write of wit and incisiveness, a superb critic, and a man of taste—a charismatic figure" (1991, 9).[7] Such views

7 Such interpretations of the editorial role in the periodical business are descended from historical forebears, of course. Albert H. Smyth (1892) at least acknowledges that the *Port Folio* required the writings of its contributors or its success and that it was founded not by Dennie alone, but

have permeated the study of American periodicals, and, more problematically, have led to an unfortunate short hand in studies that do not primarily deal with periodicals as such. Albrecht Koschnik's *Let a Common Interest Bind Us Together*, thus, suggests in severe reduction of the actual events that "Dennie used his political connections and good name as a partisan writer to start his own magazine" (2007, 162). As I will spell out in detail in Chapter 2, in actuality, things were much less politicized and much more complicated.[8] The problem with such interpretations is not that they examine the question of ideology as it can be traced in American magazines, as those ideologies certainly exist. The problem is rather that such ideologies are treated as autonomous ideas that were printed regardless of economic considerations

rather in conjunction with Asbury Dickins (cf. 92); Ellis Oberholtzer's *Literary History of Philadelphia* suggests that the *Port Folio*'s "editor continued on his way boldly and fearlessly with no master but his own cultivated spirit" (1906, 168), and Algernon Tassin's groundbreaking early study *The Magazine in America* saw the editor in general as someone who "thought of himself as a torch-bearer" to "popularize literature in the States," and someone who felt he had a "high calling" (1916, 9) and celebrated the men who "entered the arena and shouted smilingly, 'We who are about to die salute you!'" (26). James Wood's *Magazines in the United States* (1949) continued this trend to see editors as the only crucial figures for magazines.

8 Some more recent studies have successfully managed to transfer at least some of the attention away from the figure of the editor and the idea of the nationalizing function of the American magazine. The earliest counter-example is Benjamin Lewis's *Introduction to American Magazines 1800-1810*. While it is too short to actually investigate more deeply the relationships between printers, publishers, and editors which it outlines (cf. 6), at least it points to the existence of a broader field of relationships, all of which played a role in the periodical business. Robb Haberman's 2009 dissertation, "Periodical Publics: Magazines and Literary Networks in Post-Revolutionary America," argues that early post-revolutionary magazine efforts such as those undertaken by Matthew Carey and Isaiah Thomas created regional publics and helped publishers by offering them a chance to advertise, to socialize, and otherwise relate themselves to a larger public. Yet Haberman also suggests that "magazines arose out of the sociable activities of literary-minded men and women and demonstrated their politeness, sophistication, intellect, and civic pride" (8)—in other words, that despite clear monetary interests, forms of idealism, broadly virtuous behavior, underlay such hard-calculating publishers' decision to offer their readers magazines. A similar view, also with an emphasis on the immediate post-revolutionary era until about 1800, is offered by Jared Gardner. But his study *The Rise and Fall of Early American Magazine Culture* (2012), while it admirably broadens our understanding of the relationships between publishers, editors, and readers in the 1790s, again resorts to focusing his attention on the persons of Charles Brockden Brown, Susanna Rowson, and Washington Irving for its short analysis of the nineteenth century. In doing so, he ignores Irving's service as editor of the *Analectic Magazine* in 1813-15. Despite Gardner's recurrence to a more abstract 'editorial function,' the autonomous editor still remains. Catherine O'Donnell Kaplan, while she convincingly suggests the importance of the concept of sociability for understanding the relationships between men of letters, foregrounds the person of Joseph Dennie in her analyses of the *Farmer's Weekly Museum* and the *Port Folio*.

and motivations. And even this might not be such a crucial issue if critics did not draw general conclusions about the nature of the magazine enterprise and even American society from an exclusively ideological vantage point.

Connected to the view of the autonomous editor is the belief that he was driven by essentially idealistic motivations in his editorial and his contributors in their authorial decisions, or that, at the very least, an editor was writing to an audience of likeminded men. Thus Theodore Greene suggests that magazines were written "by gentlemen, for gentlemen, and contain[ed] biographies about gentlemen" (1970, 33) who had "some motivation beyond the desire for monetary gain" (24). This interpretation has more recently been upheld (with caveats) by Robert Gross, who sees magazines as the translation of "the ethos of the private club into a public periodical" (2010, 520). Gross is essentially echoing Michael Warner's thesis of the *res publica* of letters which laid the emphasis on the notion that private-cum-national virtues determined content, that dedicated and essentially disinterested men published journals in a quest for the imagined community of "a virtual salon" (Gardner 2012, 170), more generally of the public sphere of alternative citizenship, and other transcending goals (cf. Warner 1991, Kaplan 2007, Weiner 2009).[9] Studies such as Catherine O'Donnell Kaplan's *Men of Letters in the Early Republic* (2007) have reinforced this view.

Two main beliefs have supported the argument from ideology. The first is a quasi-empirical, but fallaciously selective one, which points out how periodicals themselves have frequently highlighted their political and philosophical bases. I tackle this argument in some detail below, since it is ultimately founded on a narrow choice of essays among a plethora of texts which really do not support the belief that there inhered a chiefly ideological function in periodicals. Instead, the vast majority of texts published in periodicals, and a quite significant number of conceptual statements made by publishers, editors, and readers suggests the opposite, namely that politics were accepted to some extent but failed to fulfill the chief purpose of the magazine as those participants in the field of periodicals perceived it.

The second belief which has sustained the idea of the ideological basis of periodical production is founded on another empirical fact: the sad demise of the vast majority of magazine enterprises in the Early Republic before their second birthday. As Luther Mott points out, "only three magazines of all those started in the closing years of the eighteenth century outlasted two years" (1957a, 120). Why, the argument goes, would right-thinking, economically-savvy publishers and editors be willing to risk debt, business failure, and bankruptcy on such an uncertain venture, if not for the sake of their fervent belief in the necessity to advance republicanism, Federalism, nationalism, or some other ideology? Yet the somewhat unsurprising fact is that there was very little special about the financial success and failure of magazines. Their economic careers were necessarily public, making it perhaps

9 Warner's argument is based on Jürgen Habermas's notion of the public sphere, for which cf. Habermas (1989). Stephen Shapiro's critique of Habermas and the applicability of his theory is found in Shapiro (2008, 68, 189-93), and well worth reading.

more readily apparent how fragile any kind of economic venture in the Early Republic was. As Bruce Mann points out, the "increasingly commercial economies of the eighteenth century created new opportunities for success. They also multiplied the risk of failure" (2002, 35; cf. also Rilling 2006, 320). The increasing number of magazines published was as much an artifact of a general increase in American prosperity in the last decade of the eighteenth century as anything else, of what Mann calls a

> tide that reflected the confidence of prosperity as farmers and planters, artisans and shopkeepers, traders and merchants borrowed against anticipated profits to finance the undertakings that they knew—not hoped, but knew—would create them. Their dreams and ambitions took flight on wings of entrepreneurial indebtedness, more enticingly known as investment. Not surprisingly, some faltered while others soared. Crops fail, prices fall, ships sink, warehouses burn, owners die, partners steal, pirates pillage, wars ravage, and people simply make mistakes. In highly leveraged, largely uninsured economies, even single misfortunes can bring ruin. (36)

It was not just magazine publishers who faced financial failure, then: Robert Morris, the 'financier of the Revolution,' ended up in debtor's prison because of failed real-estate speculations (cf. Chamberlain 33)—yet real-estate speculation still flourished. Newspapers regularly carried announcements of bankruptcy proceedings begun after the failure of an individual business venture, especially after the passing of the Bankruptcy Act in 1800.[10] Magazine publication was not a sure investment; but neither was anything else, and, as Rosalind Remer has established, publishing—whether of books or magazines—"offered a chance at financial success" (1996, 48), and concomittant risks. As with all those other failing enterprises, the chances of failure existed, but so did the chance for profit; and just as it is unlikely that a grocer or merchant ultimately found himself in need of ideological justifications for his business, neither is it necessary to postulate such justifications for magazine publishers.[11]

The perception that idealistic conceptions lay at the heart of the magazine is also the reason for the false impression of the role that magazines played, whether consciously or unconsciously, in nationalizing public discourse; a related claim is

10 An example from before 1800 is in the *Federal Gazette* 1791, 5.754, [1] (bankruptcy of a grocery store owner); after 1800, the amount of bankruptcy proceedings announced in newspapers is far too big to even selectively cite. The majority of people whose profession is indicated were merchants, traders, or brokers.

11 Unfortunately, studies of the economy of the United States are usually not so detailed as to discuss the question of small-scale enterprise and its dangers (cf. Robertson (1973), Engerman and Gallman (2000), Seavoy (2006), Walton and Rockoff (2010) for general surveys of the United States economy; cf. Sellers (1991), Stokes and Conway (1996), Gilje (1997), Balleisen (2001), and Matson (2006) for studies concentrating more particularly on the United States between 1776 and the Civil War). Perhaps the most useful study of small-scale entrepreneurship is Rilling (2006), but Remer (1996) is also helpful.

that there was a genuinely 'American' magazine not as a geographic marker but as a particular kind of ideologically conceived text (cf. Gardner 2012). This is the view which Tebbel and Zuckerman have offered, for example, in claiming that "a new medium was being born in America after the Revolution" and in searching for "distinctively American" character traits in that new medium (1991, 5), something, in fact, of a self-fulfilling prophesy, and indeed something of a circular argument. Most recently, the two interpretations from idealism have been combined by Andie Tucher: "Throughout the eighteenth century most American magazines had been inspired by their editors' conviction—or perhaps their hope—that America was just as capable as Britain of producing, supporting, and enjoying a sophisticated literary culture" (2010, 397). As much as this view often squares with at least the publically professed beliefs of editors, as frequently is it a view in need of revision. As a correspondent to the *Monthly Anthology* wrote in 1805, "[a]s to our periodical publications I could wish them adorned with transatlantick silk and fine-twined linen; and not with tow-cloth, merely because it is homespun" (405). Nationalist goals were in fact no more frequently highlighted by editorial commentary or readers' comments than, for example, the periodicals' ability to spread literary but also technical and vocational information among the populace. This is not to say, of course, that information and national sentiment could not be spread by periodicals, but to caution against deducing any general motivations, and suggesting that any particular idealistic motivation was more important than any other.

American magazines more often publically proclaimed an interest in nationalizing literature than they actively worked for such a national literature—an aspect which I will discuss with attention to its reflection in the writing and publishing of periodical biography. For periodicals, Scott Casper has suggested, biography served precisely the purpose of 'Americanizing' the United States: "magazines shared the [...] goals [of] preserving American worthies from oblivion, announcing American glory to the world, and inculcating the Revolutionary fathers' virtues in the next generation" (1999, 40); for Casper, the only critic to have extensively engaged with biography in the Early Republic, the central feature of American biography was that it was "didactic and nationalistic" (4). Implicitly, Casper's view of American biography in the Early Republic is static and unshaped by external events (cf. 37). Casper's focus on American biography, understood as lives of Americans, written by Americans and for Americans, justifies some of this limitation, but, as I will argue in great detail, it is precisely this limitation to American biography that ultimately cannot fully explain biography, especially as used in the periodicals. This difficulty, in fact, is most pronounced in Casper's abridged version of his book on biography, published in the recent second volume of *A History of the Book in America, An Extensive Republic* (2010). Here, the contradictions of an essentially idealistic reading of biography come strikingly to the fore: biography "aimed to build a national culture" (2010, 458), but was "far more [often] read across national boundaries and for a multitude of reasons" (459); collective biographies were the "hallmark biographical form" of the new republic but "resembled similar English publications," even though the American context of democracy gave "particular resonance of the "collective form"

(459-60). These paradoxes suggest that we should seek explanations for the forms biography took in the Early Republic, especially in the vast amount of biography published in periodicals, in something else than republican or national ideology.

Implicitly, most of these studies recur to Benedict Anderson's notion of the 'imagined' community in advancing the belief that print culture, whether manifested in biography or periodicals in general, can nationalize a public by offering them a community of readers sharing their experience of reading. It is striking that proponents of the periodical-as-imagined community usually forget to mention Anderson's insistence on the market. Quoting the French historians Lucien Febvre and Henri-Jean Martin, Anderson notes that "[n]aturally, 'booksellers were primarily concerned to make a profit and to sell their products, and consequently they sought out first and foremost those works which were of interest to the largest possible number of their contemporaries'" (2006, 38). For Anderson, print capitalism, with the emphasis on 'capitalism,' remains the inescapable precondition of the imagined community: "never forget that behind print stand printers and publishing firms" (44n). Behind biography, behind nationalism, behind the periodicals' engagement with any of these, too, stand the printers and publishers which seek to make money.

In emphasizing the constraints under which the producers of Early American periodicals labored, I hope to suggest the need to expand our study of Early American periodicals. In my reading, to emphasize the point again, the value of any interpretation of what American periodicals published depends on the validity of our assumptions on why it was published. This should not be a controversial point, given that previous studies have regularly assumed editorial intentions to be reflected in idealistic public statements. On the other hand, a closer look at what was published suggests that idealism cannot be the answer to the question of why this material was published. My answer to the question of why, stemming from a survey of contents which do not easily fit into ideological niches, of production processes which belie the idea that virtuous disinterest underlay the periodical business, and of public and private communications which emphasize a common interest in profits, thus suggests that we must ultimately recur to the market in which periodicals operated. Leon Jackson's point is well taken, and must be emphasized for its explanatory value: those who participate in literary economies "are apt to misrecognize or misrepresent the nature of the transactions in which they engage" (2008, 36). Indeed, when publishers, editors, readers and contributors to Early Republic periodicals framed their work in terms of voluntary disinterest, this was precisely a form of misrecognition and misrepresentation, the creation of a fantasy about periodical production shared between the participants. "Individuals," as Jackson points out, "often fabricated accounts of what they thought they were up to, or what they wished they were up to, or what they wanted others to think they were up to, when they engaged in the business of letters" (37). This point has also been noted by Stephen Shapiro, who suggests that Charles Brockden Brown's address to the readers of his *Literary Magazine* "might be read as evidencing an anxiety about the onset of a fully commercialized marketplace"—even for periodicals. Whereas I do not believe that there was in fact much anxiety about the growing commercialization of periodical production, certainly not in Charles Brockden Brown's case, its growing openness in periodical production is what I foreground in much of this study: in Shapiro's words again, the increasing willingness "to handle the risk in the capitalist marketplace, despite their penchant for exclaiming the reverse" (2008, 153), and a growing openness about the commercial nature of the periodical products that were created.

I am much in agreement with Leon Jackson, therefore, when he suggests that any public accounts of the nature of the transactions behind periodicals must be read symptomatically. Where I part ways with Jackson is in my interest not just in the "authorial economies" which underlay the relationships between authors and the people for whom they produced works, but also in the works themselves and their role in the structural relations of periodical production. As much as we cannot ignore the production conditions and the marketplace in an analysis of periodicals' content, neither can we ultimately discuss those conditions divorced from the content which they resulted in. To understand either side, it is necessary to read both complementarily; the image which emerges from such a complimentary reading is one in which an increasing openness towards the demands of the periodical market emerges as the central marker or professionalization.

The Structure of This Book

I will approach this argument in three parts, each of which builds on the foregoing. Chapter 1 offers a general overview of the nature of periodical production in the Early Republic, in an attempt to understand its general conditions. Both contemporary periodicals and scholars engaging with them have emphasized the idea of moral instruction as central to the conception of the periodical in the Early Republic, suggesting perhaps a greater autonomy than my theoretical paradigm would allow for. As I will show in the following, however, the adoption of the Horacian dictum of literature's "instructive and amusing" ideal by Early Republic periodicals was a thoroughly conventional trope, itself as much, if not more, grounded in economic considerations as in a genuine interest in the autonomous idealism of readers and producers. Ultimately, conceptions of readership, instruction and amusement, and the strictures of periodical production combined to emphasize the role of periodicals as vehicles for amusing variety, rather than for the promotion of an idealistic discourse. It is in this context that the chapter will approach one genre, biography, and suggest that its role in the periodical's quest for amusing variety can be read as an example for the process by which all content was ultimately selected in periodicals. What becomes evident in this analysis is the interconnectedness of the various factors which influenced the periodical in the Early Republic: the roles of inherited conceptions of periodical literature in structuring the general layout of the periodical as well as the particular demands placed on individual realizations of this general layout—that is to say, the content of individual magazines and even individual issues—by the heteronomities under which publishers, editors, and authors worked.

Chapter 2 recognizes that the heteronomy of periodical production forces us to consider in greater detail how these conditions affected even those magazines which were the most influential, and in this sense, due to a relatively large contributor base and editorial independence, perhaps the most 'autonomous' magazines. It thus builds upon the foundational knowledge about the details and difficulties of periodical production, which become evident through a closer look at biography as the exemplary genre. It presents a diachronic case study of one of the most financially and critically successful periodicals, the Philadelphia *Port Folio* (1801-1827). The choice of the *Port Folio* is perhaps obvious in this instance. Not only is it the longest-lived of the early magazines (with the exception of *Niles' Weekly Register*, a magazine started too late to offer a truly panoramic view of the critical period of 1800-1820), but its particular publication history, with all its changes and vicissitudes, foregrounds representatively the heteronomous demands on the magazine and the consequences of such demands on the content. The *Port Folio*'s wide ranging network of contributors, especially of contributors whose names have survived for identification today, is also immensely helpful—as is the comparatively large corpus of archival material that was not yet been collected, and in some case not even been appreciated for its importance to the *Port Folio*'s history. The *Port Folio*'s first editor, Joseph Dennie, had previously published the *Farmer's Weekly Museum*, which also included a number of biographical pieces, and cross-examinations of these texts with those from the *Port Folio* proper reveal the similarities in the production process over many years. Furthermore, the business structure of the *Port Folio* changed frequently over its twenty-six year history, with a frequently-changing array of printers, publishers, and finally even editors and proprietors, and different publication formats. At the same time, the *Port Folio* made biography a central part of its textual production, and showed marked changes in the choices it made on which biography it published. Beneath the superficial changes of owner- and editorship, however, the *Port Folio* is representative of the increasing professionalization of the magazine business and highlights the constancy of the underlying economic constraints and financial considerations. Ultimately, then, the *Port Folio* shows that textual production in the periodicals of the Early Republic was not an autonomous intellectual endeavor, but was firmly bound by considerations of economy, and that a genre like biography was made to serve such considerations. Or, in the rather more poetic if no less clear phrase of Joseph Dennie: "Who goeth a warfare, at any time, at his own charges? Who planteth a vineyard, and eateth not of the fruit thereof" (*PF* 1808 2, 239)?

Chapter 3 considers the consequences of the recognition that it is clearly not enough to suggest that economic factors in general played a key part in the shaping of the American magazine in the Early Republic. Once this point has been established, it is also necessary to examine how it helps us understand the ways in which editors addressed and dealt with the conditions of periodical production at a particular historical moment. For this reason, the third part of this study will offer a synchronic view of periodical biography around the War of 1812 with an emphasis on periodical biography's role in contestations of American national identities. Nationalism, in all its possible and often vague meanings, has frequently been highlighted as one of the central literary preoccupations of the Early Republic. The third chapter thus seeks to combine a reading of the production of the periodical, as in Chapter 1, and an analysis of the role of a particular exemplary genre within the periodical, as in Chapter 2, with a discussion of the possibilities and limits of ideological statements in periodicals. Chapter 3 thereby builds upon the foundations of the previous two chapters while adding a third layer to the discussion. Its synchronic perspective and the previous diachronic perspectives necessarily complement each other. Unlike the diachronic study of Chapter 2, which focuses on the mutations gone through by one magazine through its lifespan, the synchronic study of periodical biography (especially naval biography) around the War of 1812 covers a somewhat broader range of publications. The synchronic approach allows the study of the reactions which were caused by the events of the War of 1812, reactions of some interest where the field of biography, and especially its nationalistic bent, is concerned.

The synchronic study complements the diachronic study by recognizing that, at least in this instance, changes which occurred in the publication of biography in one magazine—the *Port Folio*—were not unique to it, and rather must be read in a wider context of political and social implications, but also in the context of a different market. Perhaps somewhat counter-intuitively given my interest in structural relations, Chapter 3 offers an example of how periodical biography deserves to be analyzed on its own merits. Especially around the War of 1812, periodical biography deserves a closer look: when O'Neill claims, for example, that Irving "waves the flag and makes the eagle scream" (1935, 25), he misses the ways in which Irving's constructions of American nationalism complicate straightforward readings of what biographies in the Early Republic could do; and by limiting their readings of periodical biography to the productions of a few, well-known authors, scholars have missed the ways in which other biographies around the same time offer different answers to the same question of what the war and its naval victories, symbolized by the men who won them, meant for the struggling nationalist impulse of the American republic. Here, some of American literature's early rising stars contributed complex meditations on political events, biography, and the American political system. The biographies which were published around the War of 1812 were the first sustained batch of periodical biographies written by American authors specifically for the American market, and have often been critically dismissed. Edward O'Neill's *History of American Biography 1800-1935* (1935) briefly and largely dismissively discusses the four biographies of naval officers which Irving contributed to the *Analectic Magazine* in 1813-14, calling them "average apprentice work," and remains silent about the rest of American periodical biography (1935, 25). For Elsie West, the four biographies which Irving penned were also-rans in a list dominated by Irving's biographical monographs (cf. 1993, 199). Scott Casper recognizes them as the "best known" (1999, 22) of biographies in magazines, a curiously descriptive statement which avoids any discussion of their literary or economic value. Contrary to these dismissive interpretations, I will suggest that in the particular historical moment of the War of 1812, biography's momentary relative autonomy permitted the writing of literarily complex texts, suggesting different visions of American national identity not necessarily demanded by the structural relations of periodical production. Ultimately, however, even this relative autonomy of content can not detract from the fact that biography fulfilled a market purpose, was tailored with the express desire to profit off of external events. Rather than trying to understand the nationalist sentiments variously expressed by periodical biography as a major force in shaping American nationalism, as some studies would have it, I will suggest that we must understand it as a market response to "a *pre-existing demand*, and in *pre-established forms*" (Bourdieu 1996, 142, original emphasis), in which nationalism as a motive for biography was picked up from a general upswing in national sentiment. This is not to argue that it was inconsequential, of course. Not the least of its important influences on the periodical field, I argue, is the way in which the genre of naval biography predicated a change in the business model of the periodical, one of the first attempts, as far as I can tell, to sell individual issues of magazines instead of utilizing subscription alone, and one of the first sustained efforts to recruit paid writers specifically to write nationalist naval biography. The popularity of naval biography, advanced by the existence of momentary nationalist sentiments, thus impacted the very shape of the periodical. If this impact was not lasting (importantly, neither was the upsurge in American nationalism), it was nonetheless yet another way marker on the road of professionalization. Three of the main issues connected with the professionalization of the magazine business around the War of 1812 conclude Chapter 3: firstly, the relationship between publishers and editors, increasingly one which saw publishers hire editors to run magazines for them, even as the publisher made any particular magazine venture just one business among many; secondly, an increasing willingness to pay contributors for specific texts, here, not coincidentally, naval biographies, and an increasing openness on the part of publishers and editors about this practice, to the extent that by the end of the War of 1812, it was possible to actively advertise payments for contributions; and thirdly, the possibility of selling magazines by the issue, rather than by subscription alone.

The complementary diachronic and synchronic studies of periodicals through the lens of biography, grounded in a understanding of the general conditions of the periodical market, revises our understanding of the periodical business: while individual texts can be amenable to literary interpretation, to offer such textual interpretations without a solid grounding in the production context of the periodicals under discussions leads to misinterpretations, especially when we seek to draw larger ideological conclusions about the role of the magazine from the content of its articles alone. Conversely, to study the production of periodicals alone without also looking at the opportunities for authors, editors, and publishers to develop a relatively autonomous response to the political moment is too narrow a framework. By emphasizing the need to do both, but to weigh carefully the relative importance of either aspect at specific historical moments, it becomes possible both to understand the continuities of the periodical market in a process of professionalization with decreasing opportunities for authorial and editorial autonomy and a consequent increase in the importance of heteronomous factors in the production of periodicals, including the selection and creation of their content; and it similarly becomes possible to trace more clearly the moments when a relative autonomy in periodical content permits us to read texts as literary artifacts. It is this dual perspective which ultimately allows us to more clearly appreciate the history of the Early Republic magazine.

1 The Production of Periodicals and the Uses of Biography

> Many […] are ardently thanked for their communications, literary and pecuniary. Both are essential to the success of a periodical publication […].
>
> *Port Folio* 1807, 240

In 1811, Boston's *Monthly Anthology* folded. In their editorial address, the editors, William Smith Shaw and James Savage, members of the Boston Athenaeum, also sang the swan song on the kind of publishing in which "magazines […] tended to resemble gentlemen's clubs rather than business enterprises" (Greene 1970, 21). The editors lamented that "[a]fter having for so many years found, in preparing materials for this work, the amusement and solace of our leisure hours" (*MA* 1811, 261), they would now need to cease publication of the *Anthology*.

Why did the magazine, a staple of American magazine culture since its takeover by the Anthology Society in 1805, fold? The editors had a number of reasons. Their editorial business was conducted by a committee, meaning "nothing was published without the consent of the [Anthology] society" which was the primary source of authorial and editorial labor for the magazine (Tudor 1821, 2), and from 1807, the duty of bringing manuscripts to print had devolved on two or three members of the superintending committee (cf. Mott 1957a, 253). By 1811, that process was clearly not working anymore. It had always been, in the words of Lewis Simpson, "an enterprise in magazine-making so clumsy and uncertain" (1954, 168) that it was a small wonder the *Anthology* had lasted as long as it did anyway; now, few Athenaeum members were available to the editorial team and even those which had not left or died felt themselves unable to afford time away from the pressing duties of their professions—they needed to make money as lawyers, doctors, and clergymen. The *Anthology*, simply put, just did not pay for itself, and much less did it pay for the kind of supervision it would have required to operate with financial success. Its gentleman-editors had gone into 1811 on the lookout for a "permanent editor" for whom they had more or less advertised in their magazine, hoping to be "relieved from" some of the "inconveniences" connected with the business. But no-one had volunteered: "we have been disappointed, from the inadequacy of receipts of the Anthology to repay the labour of any gentleman to whom we should be willing to confide it" (*MA* 1811, 264). This can hardly have been a surprise: at 440 subscribers in 1805 (cf. Mott 1957a, 258), the *Anthology* "never gave enough to pay the moderate expense of [...] suppers" for the contributors (Tudor 1821, 4).[1]

The *Monthly Anthology* was certainly not alone in assuming that the duties of editor could be handled by gentlemen already employed in making their money elsewhere. As Benjamin Lewis has noted, a large number of periodicals in the first decade of the nineteenth century was edited by committee (cf. Lewis 1961, 7). Tellingly, however, none of these magazines lasted—indeed, the *Monthly Anthology* itself was the most successful of them. The demise of the *Monthly Anthology* did not as such spell the end of magazines conducted on a small scale and with an amateur editorship, as religious magazines especially continued to be conducted in this fashion, like Boston's *Panoplist* (cf. Mott 1957a, 262).[2] But by coincidence, in the same month of June 1811 that the *Monthly Anthology* put out its last issue, in Baltimore a prospectus advertised a periodical "on a plan entirely new" (*WR* 1811, 2), that was to become Hezekiah Niles's *Weekly Register*—perhaps the most successful of all periodical publications in the Early Republic, running for an astonishing 38 years and, at its height, distributing some 4.500 copies per week (cf. Luxon 1970, 6-7). Printer, publisher and editor in one, Hezekiah Niles was prototypical of the professional entrepreneur periodical producer in an arrangement which sharply contrasted with the *Monthly Anthology*'s haphazard set up. The *Weekly Register*'s title pages proudly proclaimed "printed and published by H. Niles [...] at 5$ per annum," payable in advance in every year except the first (cf. *WR* 1811, 2), a rate which was capable of sustaining Niles's paper for the entirety of its run—indeed, in 1848, shortly before its demise under a different editor, the rate was lowered to 4$ (cf. Luxon 1970, 7-8). Niles's paper was, in the words of Norval Luxon, "virtually a one-man publication" (1970, 2), a type of publication which Niles could probably keep up largely because his paper was a miscellany with little original copy besides the editor's announcements; its circulation, far beyond that of any other periodical, covered the entire United States and its territories, as well as subscribers abroad (cf. 1970, 8).

The *Monthly Anthology* and *Niles' Weekly Register* are extremes in the U.S. periodical market, to be sure. The *Anthology*'s leisured, non-professional editors, apparently not on the lookout for monetary gain, contrasted sharply with Hezekiah Niles's operation, in which the roles of editor, publisher and printer were conflated

1 For a short history of the *Monthly Anthology* and the Boston Athenaeum, and the principles on which the *Anthology* was conducted, cf. Kaplan (2007, 184-215). Further details on its financial operations will be discussed below.

2 Another exception was the *North American Review*, which ran, largely supported by a club of unpaid professionals, for over five years until the function of owner and editor became consolidated during Jared Sparks's second run as editor in 1824. Sparks's editorship was exemplary of the kind of activity that successful owners brought to their magazines. Like Hezekiah Niles, he worked with great zeal at advertising his magazine. "Sparks had promoted it at every opportunity during his years in Baltimore, and later, on his travels through the South for historical research, he called on the Review's agents to stimulate their quest for new subscribers" (Cappon 1978, 11). On the history of the *North American Review*, cf. Mott (1957b, 219-261).

and became more professionalized in one basic sense at least: Niles's profession, the major source of his income, was the *Weekly Register*. Between these extreme poles lay various other arrangements. As in point is the *Literary Tablet*, whose first address to its readers, courtesy of publisher Moses Davis, noted that that the person engaged to perform the editor's duty "will devote a few leisure hours he can steal from professional pursuits and necessary avocations" (*LT* 1803, 1; cf. Lewis 1961, 7-8). Tellingly, the man Davis chose to hire would not be able to devote his entire energy to the job: instead, he was a professional man who devoted some of his leisure time to the editorship. Davis, printer-publisher of the magazine, did not wish to take over the editorial duties, but neither did he wish to pay a professional editor. That this was problematical became clear very quickly. On September 17, 1803, four weeks into the *Literary Tablet*'s life, the editor noted that typographical errors in the previous number were due to "a series of engagements, which, at that time had a higher claim to his attention" (*LT* 1803, 15). If the remuneration Davis's editor is impossible to find out, at the very least it was apparently not high enough to afford the editor relief from his other work, to the detriment of the magazine. From the publisher's perspective at least, the *Literary Tablet* was clearly a business venture first, and the person of the editor and consequently the editorial principles were dependent on the publisher at the very least in so far as any employee is dependent on his employer. If the precise distribution of tasks between Davis and his editor is not at all clear, Davis certainly retained control over financial matters—or so the *Literary Tablet* informed its readers on May 21, 1806, requesting delinquent subscribers to make "immediate payment to the Printer" (*LT* 1806, 71). Such financial matters also stretched into the question of where the appropriate cut-off point for the first volume should be: on August 9, 1804, a note "To the Public" began by stating that "[t]he Proprietor, contemplating an enlargement of the Tablet, deems it proper to close the first volume with the present number [...] The publication will be suspended until the 19th of September next, that proper arrangements may be made." It was Davis's choice to enlarge the *Tablet* (though precisely how the magazine was enlarged is unclear—its first issue of the second volume, like all previous issues, contained four quarto pages), and it was Davis's choice to delay further publications for almost a month. At the same time, intriguingly, Davis's first choice of editor retired. Although the extent of his comment on the matter was that he was "resigning the care of the Tablet," it may be more than coincidental (*LT* 1804, 103). Davis's suggestion that he was "contemplating" enlarging the magazine could very well have been a means of buying time while he was looking for a new editor—the "proper arrangements" that needed to be made.

At any rate, the *Tablet*'s next issue really was not until September 19, and the editorship now lay with the possibly pseudonymous Nicholas Orlando, who would continue to handle editorial matters for the duration of the magazine's life. Orlando, like his predecessor, was not a professional editor. That meant that he was frequently absent: either because of sickness, against which even a fully-engaged editor would not have been proof, or due to being "unexpectedly called to remove his residence from this place [Hanover, NH]" (*LT* 1806, 71). To the editor's chagrin, his temporary replacement was not all that could be wished for. Moses Davis's magazine venture required a professional editor, but it was characteristic of the time that to have a salaried editor, even if that editor ran the magazine in his spare time, contrasted with the proceedings around him.

The examples of *Niles' Weekly Register*, the *Monthly Anthology*, and the *Literary Tablet* illustrate some of the peculiarities of magazine publishing in the Early Republic—periodicals could be social efforts as well as business ventures, run by capable professionals as well as overambitious and overwhelmed amateurs—men and women whose editorial work came second to their actual professions—and successful in the long run as well as speedily defunct. None of the magazines published in the Early Republic could ignore the challenges which the periodical market posed.

Instruction and Amusement: The Purpose of Periodicals

Even a superficial glance at American periodicals in the Early Republic must suggest the importance that the concept of instruction and amusement, and its various paraphrases, had in the minds of editors, publishers, and readers. The *Royal American Magazine*, the *New London Magazine*, the *Lady's Monthly Museum*, the *United States Magazine*—they all carried the terms in their subtitles. Periodicals were constructed with a general idea of instruction and amusement guiding both readers' expectations and editors' self-conceptions, a point which readers and editors both agreed on. A correspondent with the *Nightingale*, a short-lived Boston literary magazine, noted, for instance, that upon reading the magazine's prospectus, he had "placed [his] name among the subscribers with the greatest cheerfulness, and promised [himself] instruction and entertainment" (*N* 1796, 57). He was merely one of a vast number of readers and correspondents, editors, publishers, and critics whose public avowals foregrounded the idea of the instructive and amusing periodical.

Yet the Horacian notion of art's entertaining utily, the *utile dulci*, was perhaps nothing more than an example of the "superficial and pervasive" (Heilbronn 1996, 344) Latinate influence on Americans in the Early Republic, an influence which, while it infected all walks of life, rarely resulted in practical consequences. To be instructing and amusing, or useful and entertaining, was a charge that was laid on all kinds of literature—indeed it was a charge that any cultural or societal event, from the arts to evening discussions, was expected to conform to, a *sine qua non* of cultural production at the same as it was an empty demand by its very proliferation. It was not necessary, either for Horace or for his Early Republic periodical disciples, to combine the two in any individual text—Horace had made clear earlier that "[p]oets aim either to do good or to give pleasure—or, thirdly, to say things which are both pleasing and serviceable to life" (Horace 2010, 130), giving authors and other cultural producers great leeway to amuse, or instruct, or to do both. Especially the neo-classicists of the early eighteenth century had held with Horace's third poetical option; thus Alexander Pope noted in his translation of the

Odyssey that "History is chiefly for instruction: but a Poet takes another method, and disposes every circumstance arbitrarily; he chuses or rejects, as suits best with his principal design, and in such a manner as to give at once delight and instruction" (1796, 11). To commentators in the Early Republic, however, such fine distinctions between the arts no longer held water. Whether it was 'instruction and amusement,' 'useful and entertaining,' or any number of similar constructions, any kind of writing was made to fit the premise, or perhaps more accurately, was argued to already fulfill the premise, without regard to its actual content. Periodical commentators used the phrase to announce their approbation of books of history, biology, or geography, of plays and their authors, of poetry, poets, dancing, singers and song, of anecdotes, novels, and of tales, of describing the social aptitude of random characters, of fossils, or the Bible. Neither the most beneficent means of feeding cattle nor the history and propriety of swearing escaped the all-encompassing need to be 'instructive and amusing.' Editors claimed 'instruction and amusement' as the goal of their miscellanies, both in their prospectuses and the subsequent obituaries for their magazines; correspondents found 'useful and entertaining' a handy phrase with which to compliment the work of editors.

The term "utility," especially as Early Republic writers understood it, covered a broad spectrum, and it was never entirely clear were the boundaries of the useful lay. Certainly, the ubiquitous quest for public and private virtue played a central role: the conventional assumption was that useful pieces would strengthen readers' virtue. But at the same time, quite pedestrian profit might be drawn from useful pieces in magazines. As a correspondent to the *Weekly Magazine* noted, "I think a corner of your Magazine might very properly be set aside for useful questions and answers" such as: "What is the best method of getting rid of cockroaches" (*WM* 1798, 140-1). Horace, it may be assumed, would have been puzzled by this particular application of the *utile*.[3]

3 Or would he? If periodicals delighted in repeating their assurance that their business was in the utile dulci, they wisely did not stress that for Horace as for them, ulterior motives lay behind their services, and behind the sweetly instructive. "[H]ic meret aera liber Sosiis, hic et mare transit / et longum noto scriptori prorogat aeuum," Horace had written in the two lines following his oft-quoted encouragement to poets: it was valuable to produce works that were pleasing and instructive both, "[because] this is the book that earns money for the Sosii [booksellers], goes overseas and gives your celebrated writer a long lease of fame" (different translations of this line read "Sosius and Son, Booksellers;" the Sosii were not merely bookseller, an anachronistic term anyhow, but also ran a scriptorium, in which copies of manuscripts were made (cf. Richter 2007, 83)). If Americans in the Early Republic frequently found their political ideals in republican Romans, first and foremost Cincinnatus, they made their poetic ideal in the Augustan poet-critic Horace. Horace's dictum was bound on both sides by the financial interests and audience proclivities he detected: while the Greeks, he wrote, wrote for "praise," Romans had cultivated a "rust and care for cash" (Horace 2010, 130). Could there still be poetry? Horace held that there could, but also that the question had a different answer than it had had for the Greeks. It was the booksellers' business which determined what ended up in publication,

It would be easy but fallacious to conclude that periodical editors published their magazines for readers seeking instruction and amusement both, and only both together. As readers differed, so did their interest in magazines: not everybody sought instruction, nor did everybody necessarily agree on the definition of amusement. The constant paralleling of instruction and amusement, usefulness and entertainment, did not prevent editors from understanding that if their articles did combine both, readers might still be reading for one thing or the other. The problem was that editors perceived their periodicals to be written for two disparate kinds of readers. The *Floriad*, its editors believed,

> might be interesting to two classes of readers. We could not doubt but literary characters, especially those who have ever had any connection with this institution, must when unbending their minds from their more weighty avocations, take a pleasure in viewing the first openings of those blossoms which are to ripen into fruit, when they themselves shall be nipt by the frost of years, withered and fallen to the earth. *This class of readers we surely could have little hopes of instructing*. But there is another and more numerous class, to whom we were in hopes of affording something practically useful. There are many who have neither time nor opportunity to pursue any systematic or extensive course of reading, and whose affluence is not such as will enable them to take the larger and more expensive literary productions of the day. To those many of the compositions written in col-

in circulation, and in high regard. Of course, booksellers sold, and authors wrote, what readers wished to read, suggesting an interrelation between content, sales, between readers' demand and authors' supply. Far more than a mere poetics, far more even than a manual of good writing, Horace's *Ars Poetica* explicitly embedded the question of what should be written within the framework of what could be 'sold,' both literally and figuratively. Appreciative of his audience, Horace enjoined his correspondent to "be brief" and to be aware that "elder citizens chase things off the stage if there's no good meat in them, and the high-spirited youngsters won't vote for dry poetry" (Horace 2010, 130). Horace understood readers and audiences: among other things, he advocated the iambic foot because it was "able to subdue the shouts of the mob" (124). The echoes of Horace that can be traced in Early Republic periodicals far exceed the hoary dictum of the instructive and amusing—aware of their inscription in the marketplace, readily perceptive of the interaction between audience expectation and the author's freedom, and mindful that genius only goes so far in any business which is addressed to the masses, the production of periodicals always involved the question of how ideas might be transported to readers, but as importantly, which ideas, that is to say, what content, could be sold to readers. For the vast majority of Early Republic periodicals, as perhaps for Horace, it turned out, what could be sold to readers was not instruction, but amusement. (But cf. David H. Richter for a slightly more charitable reading of Horace's concepts, highlighting that Horace likely considered himself "not a private man, put a public servant" (2007, 83) in his role as a poet, and conceived of monetary gain as a secondary effect profiting the booksellers, whose services he needed for his own private aim, fame. Here, too, we find echoes in the public personae of several Early Republic editors, notably Joseph Dennie (cf. ch. 3)).

> lege, tinctured as they always are with the sentiments of other authors, *will afford amusement for a leisure hour, and perhaps impart some pleasing or useful information*. (*F* 1811, 4, my emphasis)

Aside from the *Floriad*'s peculiar insistence, owing to its origin in two student literary societies at Union College in Schenectady, on the benefits to be had from offering young writers an outlet for their prose, so as to try themselves in the court of public literary opinion, the editors' defense of the magazine's usefulness is probably not far from the general conception of the time.[4] Although like all of its contemporaries, it stresses the instructive and amusing function of periodical writings, it makes clear that in the end, which of these separate functions a periodical fulfilled depended on the reader, and indeed even those readers whom it hoped to be able to instruct, it could reach only through the amusement of a leisure hour. Strikingly, the kind of reader which most scholarly accounts consider to be the primary readership of periodicals, the *Floriad* suggests, reads periodicals merely for amusement. Theodore Greene's suggestion that "magazines were produced by the few for the few" (1970, 19), by which he meant the educated elites, runs afoul of the *Floriad*'s encompassing conception of itself for the "many [...] whose affluence is not such as will enable them" to join in with those readers who could afford expensive publications. The *Floriad* conceived itself for a comparatively broad audience who, significantly, did not necessarily share in either the editors' educational background or its monetary status.

Beyond merely subscribing to the foreshortened trope of *utile dulci*, periodicals in the Early Republic recognized these practical elements as crucial to their financial success, too, even if they often studiously avoided the appearance of paying too close attention to it. The desire for money, or perhaps more charitably phrased, the "imperatives of commercial enterprise," as Joyce Appelby has argued (2000, 250), was becoming ever stronger in the course of the first decades of the nineteenth century. Just as Horace had identified in the Roman republicans their talent for arithmetic with an economically calculating type of poetical writing, James Hall suggested that arithmetic "comes by instinct among this guessing, reckoning, expecting, and calculating people" (in Appleby 2000, 250)—an intriguing parallel. Yet American periodicals did not, as Appleby also suggests, conceive of their marketplace as being at "odds with traditional mores and aesthetics" (253); rather, their traditional mores had already explicitly included the mores of the new marketplace,

4 The *Floriad* was not the only college-connected literary magazine which saw its major purpose in offering an outlet for its students' literary productions. The Yale-based *Literary Cabinet*, which was published 1806-7, was similar in conception. Seven years after its demise, Yale's faculty and students launched the *Athenaeum* with the same purpose, "the improvement of the students of this seminary in the art of writing" (A 1814, 1). Indeed, even magazines which were not tied to educational facilities sometimes shared in the sentiment. The *Philadelphia Monthly Magazine* suggested in 1798 that a talent for writing was a prerequisite for careful thought, leading it to recommend the writing of essays for periodicals as a means of exercising this talent; cf. LC 1806,1; PMM 1798, 71-4.

and tied aesthetics to the question of economic success. If, as David H. Richter suggests in his introduction to Horace's *Ars Poetica*, the "poet must understand [different upper class] demands—and even those of the middle classes, the 'roast-beans-and-chestnuts crowd' who applaud what is simple and exciting" (2007, 83), this, as I will further elaborate in the following, was precisely what American periodical productions also constantly kept in mind.

The *Monthly Anthology*, too, saw the difficulties of periodical publications in providing content tuned to the tastes of its readers. In a lengthy review of the *Literary Miscellany* of Boston, the *Anthology* suggested the rival paper's flaw to be "that it is deficient in exciting interest or affording amusement" (*MA* 1805, 170). Here, as in the *Floriad*, instruction is of minor importance when compared to amusement, and novelty is prized above all (cf. *MA* 1805, 170), while instruction from periodicals is reserved for the learned. Advice, which might have seemed to be a possible interpretation of the "instruction" that magazines wrote about, is dismissed as "in general sufficiently disgusting" (172). Perhaps the most intriguing example of this polarity was offered in a recounting of a probably fictional conversation overheard by a correspondent of Charles Brockden Brown's, concerning the editor's *Monthly Magazine*. The conversation might have contained "hints for [the magazine's] improvement," as the correspondent "Philomuthos" suggested (*MM* 1800, 96), but most importantly, it emphasized the different readers envisaged by Early Republic periodicals. "Edward" was favorably disposed to the *Monthly Magazine*, and a reader who thought "instruction of more importance than amusement," a "grave man" whom "grave things" suited best. All the same, it "would not displease [him] to see some of the more serious pieces omitted, to make room for a larger portion of wit and merriment" if that were to the taste of more readers (96-7). "William," on the other hand, found fault with the *Magazine*, and his reasons are telling: "I read such things chiefly for amusement, when I am tired of the toils of business, or of systematic reading." So, he suggested, does the greater part of the readership: "[Y]ou know mankind: they must be amused and diverted, or they will never attend to you. What are all their remarks on *Walstein's School of History*—on *Astringency*—and on *American Population*, worth? I don't read these things;—and not one in fifty reads them" (97, original emphasis). Despite Edward's exasperated astonishment, this remained the final statement on the question.

I do not wish to overemphasize the connection between Horace and the American periodical of the Early Republic beyond seeing it as a useful parallel and to highlight what Horace still emphasized—namely that the instructive and amusing was very much a business necessity, as well as desirable in and of itself—and what the Early Republic periodical usually did not stress quite as much—that its own desire to prove instructive and amusing was a rhetorical trope that ultimately merely meant to suggest its own ability to succeed in the periodical market. Instruction and amusement were keys to the locks that opened the periodical market.[5] The

5 Bruce Weiner has suggested that "[t]he paucity of entertaining material in their magazines makes these claims seem perfunctory, but again I would argue that magazine publishers were seeking to

Horacian notion of the *utile dulci* thus was one of the many abstract universals which permeated the conception of the periodical of the time and whose importance stemmed not so much from the fact that it meant anything in particular as that it could mean something to everybody.

The Periodical Business

Whatever "odes to friendship" and "high-minded thoughts" literary clubs and their publications produced in the Early Republic, the bottom line, in virtually all instances of periodical publications, was whether or not editors and publishers produced one thing: "saleable copy" (Gross 2010, 520) capable of sustaining the periodical business in the long term. In arguing my case that, to quote the epigraph of this chapter again, "the real value of a thing is as much money as 'twill bring," I am not even arguing that, on a subordinate level, idealistic motivations could never play a role, and occasionally even a decisive role, in shaping periodical content. Certainly political and occasionally philosophical motivations informed editorial behavior, and no doubt some magazines were indeed conducted with, as Theodore Greene has argued, "some motivation beyond the desire for monetary gain" (1970, 24). But neither is Greene's interpretation a general truth, nor do such essentially idealistic readings as Scott Casper's belief that magazines were invested in the promulgation of American glory and revolutionary virtue (cf. 1999, 40) do justice to the complicated nature of publishing a periodical in the Early Republic, or the role which biographies played in this larger context.

Bound in a network of economic and material constraints, editors of periodicals in the Early Republic were hardly autonomous agents, free to publish exactly the matter that would best serve some overarching ideal. The diverse nature of the magazines which they submitted to the reading public was intimately connected to these constraints. Editors were at once more restricted in editing their publications and more successful in their role of shaping the content of magazines within those restrictions than has hitherto been suggested. They were bound to their subscribers and their contributors, to their printers and publishers, to their editorial conceptions and to the materials they could obtain, as well as to their own ability to manage the disparate requirements of these aspects. Above all, periodical publications were for the largest number of producers a business venture, meant to sustain the livelihoods of at the very least their editors, and often enough of an editor-publisher team. Few editors put it as clearly

mediate in the culture wars, such as they were, of the new republic. They proposed to amuse readers but with forms of 'rational entertainment'" (2009, 110). Certainly, the vast mass of material which appeared in Early Republic periodicals would not have figured on *Saturday Night Live*, and, from our own perspective, is rather more tedious than amusing to the reader. Weiner's suggestion, however, that contemporaries felt likewise, seems ill-supported by the evidence.

as the *Emporium of Arts & Sciences*'s second editor, Thomas Cooper: "I must not forget, that for a book to be useful, it must be saleable" (*EAS* 1813, 7).

To an extent, Cooper here suggests a point that has also largely escaped notice: not only did whatever idea about American glory periodical editors may have wanted to promote have to be sold to be influential; but conversely, a readership interested in particular ideology—whether concepts of biography or American nationalism—was also a market. There is a remarkable correlation between the periodicals' output of 'American' biography and a boost in nationalist feelings and, consequently, interest in texts which highlight American virtues, as the texts conceived them. But it was national sentiment which preceded interest in American biography, as the biographies themselves make unmistakably clear: rather than writing in order to create, to paraphrase Henry Adams, the spirit that they lacked, biographies were far more often written for an already receptive market place. Biography's ideological functions, such as the creating of a national pantheon or national identity, were often far submerged under the necessity and opportunity of making money. Three groups of people on the production side of periodicals stood to make money off of them: editors, publishers, and printers. There is less information about the relationship between editors, publishers, and printers than would be desirable. Yet we can discover significant information about the convoluted relations between these three groups, information that is of immeasurable importance in any discussion of the production of periodicals.

While in some cases, as with Hezekiah Niles or Isaiah Thomas, all three functions were filled by one person, the usual case was that they were split at least between an editor and a publisher-printer. Printing houses may indeed have considered periodicals a "promising way to utilize costly facilities" (Greene 1970, 21) when these were not otherwise in use. Alternatively, printers sometimes found it expedient to purchase the property of a magazine in order to profit from its further publication under their own imprint. Moses Thomas's purchase of the *Select Review*, the Philadelphia miscellany which he turned into the *Analectic Magazine*, is a case in point, but perhaps the most telling story lies behind the *Monthly Anthology* of Boston.

The *Monthly Anthology* had started out as a private venture of editor David P. Adams and publisher/printer E. Lincoln in 1803. After the quick demise of their effort, the publishing firm of Munroe & Francis took the magazine over. They engaged the Reverend William Emerson to run the magazine, whose friends and colleagues eventually formed the Anthology Society to support it. In due course, Munroe & Francis turned to the Society as editors for the *Monthly Anthology*. The terms of this engagement reveal a lot about the distribution of responsibility in running the *Monthly Anthology*. The publishers agreed to pay the Anthology Society for their work in running the magazine, but expected it to show results. They kept control over subscriber lists and consequently received the entire income of the magazine, except for the sum they had agreed to pay out. They expected the Anthology Society to deliver subscribers, complaining in July 1806 about the low number of 440 subscribers which the editors had succeeded in convincing to subscribe to the magazine. Business between the two parts of the magazine grew tedious, so that the Anthology Society sought a new publisher. Munroe & Francis refused to release the subscription list to the firms of Snelling and Simons and Hastings, Etheridge and Bliss, which had offered the Society one thousand dollars a year for the privilege of publishing the magazine—in other words, an editorial salary to a group of editors. Due to the difficulties of obtaining the subscriber list, by 1809 the Society had to settle for 500 dollars annually from Hastings, Etheridge and Bliss for a period of three years. Even this, however, did not come to pass. The publisher failed, leaving the *Monthly Anthology* to migrate, now for 450 dollars a year for three, and then 500 a year for two years, to the firm of Thomas B. Wait. Early in 1811, the end was getting closer. Wait, presumably because he was not making money off of the *Monthly Anthology*, refused payment, and eventually concluded publication of the final volume without any further payment to the Anthology Society (cf. Simpson 1954, 170, 180-3).

Despite the critical attention paid to the editorial principles put forward by the editors of the *Monthly Anthology*, the most striking aspect of this history is that what can be nonchalantly summarized as "troubles with many publishers" (Mott 1957a, 258) was in fact a complicated entanglement of interests. Mott's suggestion that "friends of the infant magazine prevailed upon William Emerson" (253) to edit the magazine obscures the fact that those friends, Munroe & Francis, were a publishing firm with a vested financial interest, who were indeed willing to pay the Anthology Society for their editorship—but only if they managed to achieve results. It was these results that the Anthologists did not manage to deliver, but despite the failure, publishers other than the firm of Munroe & Francis remained interested in the venture, even to the extent of offering a considerable sum of money for the editorial staff and the property of the *Anthology*. What these publishers were bargaining for, apparently, was the subscriber list, a list which Munroe & Francis were loath to part with, unless paid the entirety of their outstanding claims on the Anthology Society (presumably printing costs; cf. Simpson 1954, 181). Notably, the money which the Anthology Society obtained for the publication rights to the *Monthly Anthology*, after initially being offered a thousand dollars, was just half that without the subscriber list. Publishers, quite clearly, realized the monetary potentials of the magazines they chose to purchase and develop. Of course, as with any business venture, the possibility of failure was always present; but at the same time, publishers were business men, attempting to calculate the relationship between potential gain and necessary risk.

Of the three roles I differentiate above, printer, editor, and publisher, perhaps the least likely to be involved actively in the periodical business—beyond, as it were, *printing* periodicals—after 1800 or so was the printer. Indeed, earlier periods would have seen the printer also as the publisher of a periodical, and many printers became publishers and booksellers in due course. Hugh Maxwell, Joseph Dennie's publisher at the *Port Folio*, was one such man; Samuel Bradford, Dennie's later publisher, came from the influential Bradford family of printers, the first of whom, Andrew, had been Benjamin Franklin's competitor back in the 1740s.

Rosalind Remer identifies ten individuals who "made the transition from printer to publisher most completely" (1996, 70), and a number of individuals, Maxwell among them, who never completely gave up the printer's trade.[6] Printing a periodical was a way to something of a regular income, if the magazine turned out a success. When it did not, printers often found themselves stuck not just with the cost for their journeymen printers, their time, and their ink, but also with the paper which they had to buy. It was a rare printer who permitted his customer, the publisher, to pay him as the publisher himself was paid, in yearly installments. As the *Panoplist* put it in an 1812 letter to its readers, its costs were various and needed immediate attention.

> In the first place, the Printer makes contracts for paper, to a large amount, which he expects, and ought, punctually to fulfil. His journeymen, also, must be paid every Saturday night to furnish their families with bread; not to mention the reward of his own labor and payment for the use of his types and presses. Secondly, the Editor expects a suitable remuneration for the time which he devotes to the work. (*PN* 1812, 200-1)

What the *Panoplist* rightly concludes is that publishers' indebtedness to their printers trumped their own need to make money—that, in other words, paying the printers came before their own profits—though perhaps not always, as Nathaniel Chapman's 1806 memorandum indicates, suggesting that the *Port Folio* was owing two paper makers 1700$ total.[7] Maxwell, for example, while still the printer for the *Port Folio*, handed in half-monthly bills to Asbury Dickins, and was paid, usually in cash, by Dennie in regular, usually something like weekly, installments, and additional money went to Maxwell from William Fry while the latter was publisher.[8]

Hugh Maxwell's transition from mere printer to publisher and printer ended with financial disaster for him, although the *Port Folio* was only tangentially involved in this (cf. ch. 2), and Maxwell made a return as a bookseller and stationer. But, as Remer has established, the diversification of the printing and publishing trade was one of the hallmarks of development in the business in the first decades of the 1800s. Printers steadily moved outside the central city districts, publisher/booksellers moved closer to the thoroughfares to sell book. The consequence of the division between the printing and publishing businesses was the creation of two distinct classes, one essentially commercial and the other essen-

6 The *Port Folio* after 1812 was printed by James Maxwell, presumably a relation of Hugh's. The Philadelphia city directory in 1810 listed Maxwell as a "late printer," presumably because he had passed on his business to his relative and himself had moved on to mainly work as a bookseller (as indicated by his entry in the directory for 1808).

7 Cf. Nathaniel Chapman Memorandum, January 28, 1806. Historical Society of Pennsylvania, Meredith Family Papers 1509, Box 99.

8 William Fry Account Sheet for the *Port Folio*, Historical Society of Pennsylvania, Meredith Family Papers 1509, Box 99

tially artisanal. This process of diversification, then, was also one of professionalization, delimiting more clearly the spheres in which each individual acted.

Functional differentiation was frequently the consequence of a failure to survive in the magazine business of endeavors in which the roles were not split. When the *Philadelphia Repertory* ended its run after two years, editor and publisher/printer Dennis Heartt had no qualms about stating clearly his reasons. He stopped publication of his magazine because of the "want of patronage sufficient to remunerate him for his labour and afford him that moderate profit without which it would be imprudent and impossible for him to proceed" (*PRP* 1812, 399). But despite this financial failure, Heartt was undaunted in the belief that periodical publications could yield money, though possibly not with him at the editorial helm and as printer/publisher both. Heartt thus reduced his own involvement to the printing trade. He was even then acting as printer for Stephen Carpenter's new *Bureau*, which, Heartt suggested, was the "superior enterprise." Singing the *Bureau*'s praises, Heartt advertised the product he was putting out as cheaper and more content-rich than comparable ventures, while entreating his subscribers to change their allegiance from the *Philadelphia Repertory* to the *Bureau*: "D. Heartt would fain persuade himself that there is not one of the subscribers to the Repertory who will not follow him with their subscription to the Bureau." But of course, no one could really "follow" Heartt. Heartt did not act as the editor of the different venture, although he made sure only to claim that he was "engaged" in the new magazine. Whoever read the *Philadelphia Repertory* for Heartt's editorship would not easily find a new home in the *Bureau*. Following Heartt to the *Bureau* meant paying more (if for a larger magazine), a fact which Heartt knew and addressed: even "exclusive of the quality of the composition of the Bureau, the quantity exceeds that of the Repertory in proportion to the increase in price. For the *Mirror of Taste* edited by the same person, the subscription was eight dollars a year, while the Bureau which fixed at five only contains more reading matter in the ratio of thirteen to nine" (*PRP* 1812, 399). Again, despite the fundamentally reasonable and detached tone used by Heartt, his argument is structured in such a way as to prejudice the reader's choice. The *Bureau* was more expensive than the *Philadelphia Repertory* (for which subscribers paid four dollars a year), so readers wishing to "follow" Heartt would have to pay more, for which, in turn, they would receive more content that would at the same time be better than what the *Repertory* offered. Yet the comparison with Carpenter's *Mirror of Taste* (a magazine published, incidentally, by Bradford & Inskeep, also the publishers of the *Port Folio*) was calculated to prejudice the reader. The *Mirror of Taste*'s focus on drama criticism and history was clearly different from the *Bureau*'s pedestrian content of reviews, chronicles, and miscellaneous articles. While the *Bureau* was aimed at a general audience, the *Mirror of Taste* could not but appeal to a minority, which in turn justified its higher price. The comparison which Heartt offered, although ostensibly based on the fact that Stephen Carpenter was editor of both, was then primarily calculated to highlight the lower price of the *Bureau*, thus neatly negating the increase in price from the *Philadelphia Repertory*. Behind all this stood Heartt's interest as the printer of the new magazine, obscured by all the talk of superior content and comparable cheapness for a venture which bore, in the final analysis, little resemblance to the cancelled *Repertory*.

The diversification of the roles of editor, publisher, and printer was a process which increasingly demanded a clearly delineation of the constitutive elements of these roles, and something of a hierarchical structure in which clear lines of responsibility could be drawn. With a mixture of irony and self-effacement, in May 1813, the *Polyanthos* suggested that one might compare a periodical with a mail coach: proprietors of both required the selection of "horses" which had "seen their best days, and acquired discretion to submit to their necessary task." It was no use to hire editor-horses who were too volatile to submit to the fatiguing duties expected of them daily. Fortunately, as the short note maliciously suggested, there was no shortage of failed authors who would be ready to "subject talents worthy of a better employment, to whatever task a bookseller shall be pleased to dictate" (*P* 1813 1, 64). That this short note was not meant as a serious analysis of the role and the general position of the editor in American periodicals does not mean, of course, that it did not contain a grain of truth. Most importantly, the *Polyanthos* recognized, as early as 1813, that a growing number of editors were effectively being held on a very short leash by their publishers (often booksellers, as we have seen), and by implication that editorial virtue alone could hardly determine periodical content.

The editorial position was, ultimately, one of responsibility for the selection of content, even if it was in actuality more circumscribed than editors might have liked. While the interference of business-oriented publishers like Moses Thomas often signally restricted editorial control, the final responsibility to the reader was the editor's—a fact recognized by both the editors and the readers. In 1809, Joseph Dennie, always a stickler for his editorial rights, announced that "he must be the *sole executive*." If he then seemed to downplay this claim to absolutism—"The casting vote is often his, and he must often determine, and pretty absolutely too, *in the last resort*. Without this sort of power, and this right of judgment, any man, however endowed, is but the outside, the outline, the shadow, the *mockery* of an Editor" (*PF* 1809 2, 175-6, original emphasis)—it would be a mistake to assume that underlying the editorial service at the *Port Folio* was any sort of democracy, with the editor but the deciding vote in an otherwise undecided editorial staff; rather, Dennie's point was that the editor needed to enforce his editorial guidelines even against the majority opinion, if he meant to keep regarding himself as an actual editor—even as Dennie's own editorial freedom had been sharply circumscribed by his publishers. Readers recognized that the editor himself was ultimately responsible to them for the content selected, and this was the relationship which Dennie encouraged. As a correspondent wrote Dennie in April 1801, in a letter Dennie published without comment and might thus have implicitly supported, "although it may be urged on your behalf, that you are not the writer of all that appears in your paper—yet, are you supposed to sanction, by your approbation, the sentiments offered to the public, through that medium" (*PF* 1801, 123). It was the logical corollary of the long process by which the relationship between editor and readership was stabilized—

his frequent contact with his readers through correspondence and printed answers, the promissory prospectus, and others—that readers would consider the editorial role as more than merely caretaking. Within the boundaries of ideology and content that the prospectuses set up, the editor's privilege of deciding the particulars of the content meant that he was justifiably considered to be, unless otherwise noted, implicitly in favor of sentiments proposed, statements made, and views aired. This was most readily apparent where editors made sure that their views did not coincide with the texts they published. Thus, for example, Joseph Dennie took care to note that a biography of Charles Fox, published in March 1809, did not mean that he was "one of his partizans" (*PF* 1809 1, 359), and Washington Irving, in 1813, excised "several passages of a political nature" (*AM* 1813 2, 70) of James Paulding's life of Jacob Jones because the *Analectic Magazine*'s stance was in the party-political sense apolitical. This, of course, was a determination that was not Irving's, but which had been made by the publisher, Moses Thomas. Irving served, as well as he could, the interests of his publisher in avoiding any material, even if written by his best friends, that could give offense to the broad national audience which Thomas envisaged (cf. ch. 3).

A short note about the various financial arrangements which were possible can be provided here, using the example of the *Port Folio*. Asbury Dickins, the first publisher, shared profits with Dennie while serving as its publisher; Dickins's eventual successor, William Fry, deducted 75$ from the *Port Folio*'s account with him in 1802 for his "services," presumably his work as publisher. Fry was more of a glorified clerk. From his accounts, it is clear that for much of early 1802, when he was publisher for the city of Philadelphia, he mainly paid the carrier and assorted paraphernalia, such as a carrying case, and a book into which to enter the subscribers' names. When, later in the year, he became publisher also for the rest of the country, postage and twine for binding the packages was added. Fry seems not to have felt his job as publisher to be an undue burden and was very cheap for Dennie to pay; when Hugh Maxwell succeeded him, and ended up in 1805 charging the *Port Folio* 500$, Dennie's attorney William Meredith became suitably exasperated (cf. ch. 2). Maxwell himself took a more direct interest in the venture, but was not a success as publisher. Neither was Dennie himself, when he took over as publisher in 1807: the regulating of finances was a burden which Dennie was ill-fitted to bear. But despite this failure, Dennie defended his proprietorship with zeal. In October 1807, he felt pushed by an anonymous report that "the property of The Port folio had passed into other hands, and that for more than two years, the Editor had merely lent his name to assist the sale of that work" (*PF* 1807 2, 284), to issue a strict denial, double spaced with occasional italics and capitals, in his column "To Readers and Correspondents". Clearheaded about his own worth, Dennie considered the claim "pernicious," because he believed that both his dependence on subscribers and his dependence on the income generated by the *Port Folio* necessitated his disavowal of having become a figurehead. In a revealing passage, he emphasizes "that MANY who would willingly patronize the work, have withheld their names, from a persuasion that they were only advancing the interest of some venal mechanic, who walked abroad with a vizor mask, disgracefully borrowed from the Editor" (*PF* 1807 2, 284, original emphasis).

Distribution, managing subscriptions, paying printers and other assorted peripheral tasks took up a lot of time and energy, and were not, indeed, questions of editorship. But the distinction between the editor responsible for the content of the magazine and the publisher and proprietor who dealt with business matters was only slow to come—as indeed was the distinction between professional editor-publisher, whose business it was to put out a regular paper and who lived off the proceeds of the endeavor, and the gentleman-editor who, in the words of Theodore Greene, "found personal satisfaction along with some social usefulness [...] and who generally had some other occupation to help sustain them" (1970, 24). Joseph Dennie certainly presented himself in his editorial persona as precisely this kind of "volunteer-editor" (*PF* 1801 Prospectus 1). In calling himself a volunteer, Dennie played on the idea that he was offering the *Port Folio* more as a public service, noting that "[a]t an early season of life, he voluntarily forsook the path of ordinary business, for a lowly seat in the Muses' bower" (5). By 1809, however, he had become a salaried editor for a profit-oriented publisher, Bradford & Inskeep, with branches in New York and Philadelphia. Dennie's earnings of 800$ annually were on the lower end of the editorial pay scale—both his successor Nicholas Biddle, at 2500$, and his near contemporary Washington Irving, at 1500$, earned much more (cf. ch. 3)—there was no way to hide that overall control was slipping from his hands. While communications were still supposed to go to him if they concerned topics dealing with the content of the magazine, "[e]very communication, touching the pecuniary concerns the Port Folio, must be directed to his publishers" (*PF* 1811 1, 87), as he informed his readers in the January edition of 1811. In January 1812, shortly before his death, Dennie yet again reaffirmed what he considered his central role in the *Port Folio*'s endeavor, noting in a rambling essay on his illness the previous months that "no deputy editor [...] can possibly, at all times, supply the place of the Principal. From the very nature of his office, the latter must have more experience in editing, and more technical knowledge, with respect to the details of literary labour" (*PF* 1812 1, 96). The recognition of this fact explains the note in Joseph Dennie's final address to his readers in the *Port Folio* in January 1812. Ill for a long time in the winter of 1811, Dennie noted that despite his "illness and rustication," despite the time that he had to beg off working on the *Port Folio*, "the interest of the proprietors of The Port Folio has not been affected. The subscription list has increased, is increasing, and shall not be diminished" (*PF* 1812, 92). Dennie may here have been reassuring himself as much as his readers, who might be expected to have been somewhat puzzled to be informed at length about the subscription list of the *Port Folio*: that, certainly, was not much of their concern. It was, however, a measurable way of Dennie's success as an editor, something that was directly relevant to his continued service for the publishers.

If Joseph Dennie and Washington Irving, certainly the best-known editors of their day, were still in many ways amateurs at their tasks, their careers still signify the steps taken towards a professionalization of the editor's function early in the 1810s. Indeed, that the editor was becoming more of a 'function,' in the sense that he was replaceable, rather than a central figure, is itself an indication of that professionalization. Crucially, these professionalizing steps were taken at the behest of publishers, who sought to recruit precisely those figures whose recruitment would most directly translate into sales, and they were willing to pay considerable sums for such editors. As John Queenan has established, by 1811, with Dennie no longer in chief control and the controlling interest of the *Port Folio* having passed to the publishing house of Bradford & Inskeep of Philadelphia, the *Port Folio* realized a profit of 6000$ per year, and the publishers were secure enough in their belief that it would remain profitable on this order that they offered a half-share in the magazine with a guaranteed profit of 1500$ each of two prospective buyers if they were also going to become editors (cf. Queenan 1955, 44-5; cf. ch. 3). Hezekiah Niles felt himself compelled to admit that although he was not growing rich, he was "so far independent as to be enabled to act purely from the dictates of his own conscience," although the necessity of commingling editorship with being publisher and proprietor caused him to spend too much time "occupied at [the desk] in the counting house" (*WR* 1820 2, 449). Despite this complaint, however, the experience of the *Port Folio*, *Niles' Weekly Register* and the *Analectic Magazine* in particular show the importance of professionalization to the magazine business.

Critical acclaim could devolve on magazines on the basis of their content alone; but financial success, measured in profits, in lastingness, and not least in publishers' interest to take over when their predecessors ran into trouble, required more. Unsurprisingly, the most enduring and successful magazines of the age combined a strong subscriber base with a potent force of contributors and a clear-eyed publisher with a capable, though not necessarily superlative editor. Even then, the question of money was a difficult one, and to solve it the major issue in periodical production in the Early Republic.

That magazines were out to make money for their editors and publishers was not a fact often openly communicated to the public. Editors, who often corresponded at great frequency with their readers through the letter columns of their magazines, preferred to consider themselves publically "volunteer-editors," like Joseph Dennie in the prospectus to the *Port Folio*, offering something very much akin to a public service. More importantly, they desired to be considered so: being volunteers, they could assure readers that their services would not depend on something as mundane as commercial considerations. But privately, they could be straightforward about their hopes and dreams. In a letter to his mother, Joseph Dennie noted that "[m]y reputation as a man of letters is now producing me property. *This is everything*, and soon it will render me independent" (in Pedder 1936, 154, my emphasis). For Dennie, this may reflect something of a mild trauma, as he indicated in a later letter: noting that he had been "animated with expectation of realizing fortune and fame from the Tablet," a periodical he had set out to edit in Boston, that magazine's quick demise was a bit of a shock. He connected this failure not with a lack of literary talent, however, but suggested that "if I had been in possession of property, neither the waywardness of the times, the dullness of the Bostonians, nor, the infancy of my *savage* Country would have repressed the growth of my miscellany" (in Pedder 1936, 157, original emphasis).

Despite the multitude of complaints about not being paid by subscribers and a refusal to print advertisements, the basic fact remains and must not be ignored that good money could be made off magazines, even if editors were generally loath to admit it. Charles Brockden Brown, without a cent to his name and with no other occupation to fill his time or purse, found it necessary to note in the editor's address to the public prefacing his *Literary Magazine and American Register*:

> The project is not a mercenary one. Nobody relies for subsistence on its success, nor does the editor put any thing but his reputation at stake. At the same time, he cannot but be desirous of an ample subscription, not merely because pecuniary profit is acceptable, but because this is the best proof which he can receive that his endeavours to amuse and instruct have not been unsuccessful. (*LM* 1803, 3)

Such prose was heartwarming but disingenuous. As William Dunlap, a close friend of Brown's and his first if generally derided biographer noted, Brown and Elihu Hubbard Smith, editor of the *Medical Repository*, were "under the necessity of being economists" while all three were members of the Friendly Club in New York. Dunlap noted that Brown "*acted* as if he had no use for money" but, although he does not spell it out, clearly implied in the contrast with the "systematically" (1822, 56, my emphasis) calculating Smith that he was not able to avoid debt. Whatever background of monetary needs there was, Brown's later effort at a magazine, the *American Register*, apparently yielded him the considerable sum of 1,500$ a year, probably as a salary from his publishers, the Conrad brothers (cf. Shapiro 2008, 165).

Among those editors who, like Thomas Cooper of the *Emporium of Arts & Sciences*, were straightforward about their priorities was, predictably, Hezekiah Niles. In early 1819, the *Weekly Register*'s publisher asked his readers' support in extending the circulation of the magazine, for three objects:

> 1st, a diffusion of the facts that belong to the proceedings of our own and other governments, among the *people*, on which they may reflect and conclude for themselves; 2d, in enabling the editor to make his work more and more valuable, by an increased ability to give a greater quantity of matter for the sum received; and 3d—which comes home to him, *that his profits may be increased!* (*WR* 1819 1, 2, original emphasis).

Niles's enumeration, not a little strikingly, emphasizes his own potential benefits far more than those which would accrue to his readers. Certainly, to increase the circulation (Niles obviously was speaking about the number of subscribers, rather than the circulation of already-sold numbers) meant that more people would benefit from the democratic privilege of free information on public affairs—one of the common declarations of public spiritedness in magazines, and not surprisingly Niles's first point of interest. Even in turning to his second point, however, Niles's reasoning becomes ambivalent. Certainly, the public's benefit in receiving more information at the same price plays again to the notion, popular with editors' public personae, that they were primarily in the service of an idea. Yet it would also in a very direct sense become "more and more valuable." More valuable to readers, certainly, but more valuable also to Niles: a paper with more content, saleable at the same price, meant the potential for more satisfied customers, thus the potential for a higher number of subscribers and in the final analysis higher profits for Niles. That he emphasized his profits again in particular in his third point cannot hide the fact that even reasons which seem idealistic enough in Early Republic publishing are all too often stark business, a means of making money. Niles gets credit for putting it quite bluntly, continuing his suggestion about the need to increase his profits by noting that "[a]fter all, this is the main-spring that causes the most of us to exert ourselves […]" (*WR* 1819 1, 2). For the men (and very few women) who did the often tedious job of editor, money was the object for which they worked. The central problem that most magazines faced in this endeavor was the limited number of possibly avenues to follow in obtaining the money they needed.

Between Dennie's 1795 experience with the *Tablet* and Niles's 1819 comment lay twenty-five years in which magazines increasingly became more open about the role of the market and more generally of commerce in their business, and increasingly made open use of the commercial argument in hiring editors and contributors. Niles's comment, therefore, might be read as a sign post on the road of the professionalization of the American magazine which I identify as an underlying narrative of the periodical field in the Early Republic. This does not mean that Niles stood at the end point of a telos of professionalization; rather, that we can gain a glimpse at the crucial changes that slowly transformed the periodical field in this era by looking at various sign posts along the road.

Magazines made money primarily by two means: selling subscriptions and selling advertisement space. Of the two, the problems of subscription remained far more pressing for editors, and their discussion needs to be postponed a little here. Advertisements, on the other hand, were seemingly straightforward: magazines did not want advertisements. Directly or indirectly, however, magazines certainly profited from marketing schemes, others or their own, throughout the Early Republic. Not a few of those advertisement schemes connected with biography.

Unlike magazines, Early Republic newspapers made the major part of their income through the sale of advertisements, and advertisements could have been a profitable way of stretching meager resources, even for magazines (cf. Steffen 2003, 402-9).[9] That they were not, by and large, as predominant in magazines, editors and publishers argued, was mostly by choice. Thomas Green Fessenden, editor of the *Weekly Inspector*, recognized that "the profits of periodical publications are prin-

9 But cf. Jackson (2008, 149), who suggests that it is by no means clear that advertisements really amounted to the larger part of newspapers' revenue. Contemporaries, it seems, at least thought it useful to suggest that newspapers and magazines differed in this regards, the truth of the matter notwithstanding.

cipally derived" (*WI* 1806, 81) from advertisements, but did not desire to take any advertisements on himself. Advertisements, he had noted in his prospectus, were a necessity to which newspapers devoted a great deal of space. At the same time, newspapers were full of "falsehood and sophistry" (*WI* 1806, 1-2)—not necessarily the kind of reputation which magazine publishers sought. Refusals to burden their magazines with advertisements were common for Early Republic magazines. Hezekiah Niles reminded readers bluntly that "[a]dvertisements of all sorts are excluded" (*WR* 1816, 381). Joseph Dennie made the point in one of his periodical philippics to subscribers, noting that he "neither derives, nor can derive, any support from the lucrative aid of advertisements; WHICH NEVER HAS BEEN, NOR NEVER SHALL be a source of emolument to its proprietor" (*PF* 1803, 167, original emphasis). Magazine editors distanced themselves from newspapers through refusing, or claiming to refuse, to print advertisements, and restricted themselves to obtaining their income from their readers.

However, not all evidence points necessarily to this refusal being part of a larger ideological critique of newspapers per se. The always shrewd Joseph Dennie pinpointed one of the possible defects of advertisements to magazines which aspired to more than mere local circulation. The kind of very localized advertising which took place in newspapers would be entirely uninteresting to subscribers farther away, so that the *Port Folio*, "vacant of advertisements, must be peculiarly desirable to remote residents." But when Dennie spoke of a vacancy from advertisements, his language was not entirely devoid of sophistry itself. Dennie merely meant advertisements in the body of the text—in the form that contemporary newspapers would print them, interspersed with other items of interest—as his prospectus also made quite clear. Merchants and booksellers, whose wares Dennie might expect to be potentially useful even to distant subscribers and who, at the same time, might be interested in obtaining access to the kind of high-brow subscribers that Dennie envisaged, were specifically enjoined to offer their advertisements. Publishing in Philadelphia, one of the major inlets for foreign books and for the various luxury goods that were imported into the country, Dennie recognized that such advertisements could easily find interest even in the far-flung readership he hoped to have. Rather than appearing in the body of the *Port Folio*, they would be "conspicuously printed on a separate sheet, which will serve as an useful envelope to the Port Folio" (*PF* 1801 Prospectus, 6, original emphasis), a "blue wrapper [which] will prove very convenient for advertising" (5; cf. fig. 1). By refusing to print advertisements in the body of his magazine, Dennie could claim a certain necessary distance from, especially, weekly newspapers, which might be expected to consist to a large part of advertisements. Dennie's eight-page *Port Folio* would thus carry additional material of actual literary interest. Merchants' disappointment at being denied the prominence of typographic inclusion in the magazine was allayed by the conspicuousness of the color of the wrapper. At the same time, Dennie rendered the inclusion of advertisements as a public service: the wrapper not only served the purpose of keeping out advertisements from the paper, but it was also "useful" as an envelope, a sort of basic utilitarianism which was in uneasy but nonetheless tangible alliance with the benefits the wrapper had for merchants and other advertisers, and for Dennie himself. The editor did not handle the business of negotiating with potential advertisers—advertisers he envisaged to consist of "[m]erchants, booksellers, auctioneers, &c.[...] [v]enders of fashionable goods, milliners, perfumers, &c." but resolutely refused place to "quack doctors [...] gibberish bills of jugglers, tumblers, rope-dancers, French mountebanks, &c." (*PF* 1801, 23)—but referred them to Asbury Dickens, his publisher, who would receive the advertisements.

That advertisements, despite the care which Dennie took to make them appear marginal, were still a valuable source of additional income to the fledgling magazine the editor made clear late in January 1801, when he placed a request in the *Port Folio* noting that "[s]everal *promised* advertisements" were still wanted, even before "more *City* Subscriptions" (*PF* 1801, 39, emphasis in the original). The request clearly indicates that advertisements not only become available quickly for inclusion in the *Port Folio*, or at least that there was interest in putting advertisements in the *Port Folio*, but also that Dennie and his publisher Asbury Dickins calculated with them. Just like city subscriptions (which, not needing postage, were considerably cheaper for the publisher to deliver), advertisements were a significant part of the business, no matter what Dennie just as publically and

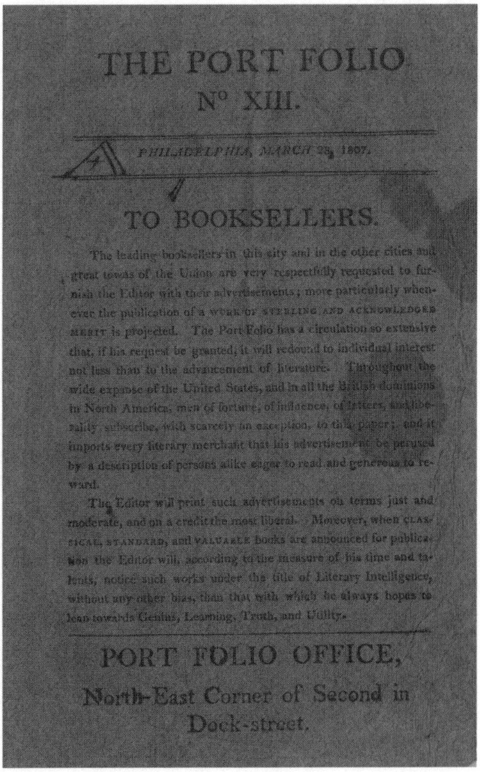

THE PORT FOLIO

N° XIII.

PHILADELPHIA, MARCH 28, 1807.

TO BOOKSELLERS.

The leading booksellers in this city and in the other cities and great towns of the Union are very respectfully requested to furnish the Editor with their advertisements; more particularly whenever the publication of a WORK OF STERLING AND ACKNOWLEDGED MERIT is projected. The Port Folio has a circulation so extensive that, if his request be granted, it will redound to individual interest not less than to the advancement of literature. Throughout the wide expanse of the United States, and in all the British dominions in North America, men of fortune, of influence, of letters, and liberality subscribe, with scarcely an exception, to this paper; and it imports every literary merchant that his advertisement be perused by a description of persons alike eager to read and generous to reward.

The Editor will print such advertisements on terms just and moderate, and on a credit the most liberal. Moreover, when CLASSICAL, STANDARD, and VALUABLE books are announced for publication the Editor will, according to the measure of his time and talents, notice such works under the title of Literary Intelligence, without any other bias, than that with which he always hopes to lean towards Genius, Learning, Truth, and Utility.

PORT FOLIO OFFICE,

North-East Corner of Second in Dock-street.

FIG. 1: The now badly-faded, once blue wrapper of the March 1807 *Port Folio* carries a prominent advertisement: its own readiness to accept booksellers' advertisements, particularly for works of "sterling and acknowledged merit"—noting also that time permitting, he would be glad to review such works in the "Literary Intelligence" section, no doubt with great impartiality. Cf. Appendix 1 for a larger version of this image.
Courtesy of the Library Company of Philadelphia.

just as repeatedly claimed. "A literary paper," Dennie wrote in December 1802, "without the gainful aid of advertisements," by which he meant the *Port Folio*, "relies for its support upon distant subscribers, a general circulation, and regular receipts" (*PF* 1802, 383). For Dennie, the lack of advertisements publically circumscribed the role, indeed the commitments, of his subscribers: because he offered them a paper free from advertisements, he was owed more than usual attentiveness to punctual payments. But could he really not "derive support," make money off of advertisements? Even in public, Dennie was ambivalent about this. In a note of February 1806, he apologized "for the non-appearance of several advertisements, which are omitted for want of room" (*PF* 1806, 109), and in 1807, he noted that he had published an advertisement for a proposed publication by Samuel Bradford. The available data on advertisements is spotty (cf. Queenan 1955, 18), but the repeated appearance of commentary on advertisements, or the advertisements themselves throughout the entire run of the *Port Folio* make it most likely that they remained a significant part of the *Port Folio*'s income. Bradford & Innskeep, Dennie's publishers after 1809, frequently made use of the advertising space in the front and back of the magazine to market their own books and publications, and it was not until 1818, under the editorship of John Hall and while the magazine was being published by the Hall family, that advertisements encroached upon the primary spaces of the magazine, and then included the usual variety of harped wares, from books to steam engines to ladies' seminaries.

It must appear slightly puzzling to see Dennie's repeated insistence on the absence of advertisements contrasted with nearly as frequent referrals to precisely those advertisements. Dennie clearly distinguished between the body of his magazine and its margins. The body of the magazine was sacrosanct, as far as advertising was concerned. To put advertisements in the magazine proper was too much like the business of newspapers, a qualitatively minor form of writing in Dennie's opinion. Dennie could be quite scathing when the issue came to that: in 1807, in one of his exchanges with his readers, Dennie mocked John Russell of the *Boston Gazette*, joking that "in a dearth of news, or of advertisements, the Editor found a place for a clever political paragraph" (*PF* 1807 I, 127), suggesting clearly the priorities which Dennie believed newspapers to have—probably not overly unfairly. Advertisements were newspaper fare, and more: newspapers were carriers, primarily, of advertisements, rather than valuable literary productions. In this complaint, Dennie echoed others. When the *Weekly Inspector* failed in mid-1807, it complained of the readiness with which advertisements preempted the inclusion of more worthy materials, and indirectly also pinpointed the reason for its own demise: "[L]et A, have a hogshead of Molasses to advertise, and B. an elegant Essay, and we should be glad to know which would find the most ready insertion in our newspapers" (*WI* 1807, 415). Implicitly, many magazine editors connected advertisements with newspapers. Hezekiah Niles's prospectus for the *Weekly Register* explicitly noted that the new magazine would have "about *one fourth more* reading than is compressed in the *largest* of our newspapers, outside and inside—Advertisements will not be admitted" (*WR* 1811, 2, original emphasis), a juxtaposition which clearly emphasized the dominance which advertisements had in the newspapers of the day.[10]

The wrapper was indeed the most prominent place where advertisements could be placed—and itself the place for the editor to ask for such advertisements in the first place. The wrapper to the March 28, 1807 edition of the *Port Folio*, to pick just one example, had Dennie ask booksellers for advertisements for their books, especially if they should have great merit, for which the *Port Folio*, with its "circulation so extensive," and including such "men of fortune, of influence, of letters, and liberality," that booksellers could not be expected to forego this chance to advertise their wares (cf. fig. 1, and Appendix 1). Most frequently, these covers ended up running the publishers' own advertisements, of future publications and current stock.

Magazines did make use of outside advertising in different forms, though, not all of them as obvious as the *Port Folio*'s. The most common form of marketing was not the attempt to stimulate the purchase of other people's products, but to advertise the contents and the success of the magazines themselves or the products which the publisher/booksellers also sold. Studying the wrappers of extant individual numbers of the *Analectic Magazine*, for example, the incidence of advertisements of books published by Moses Thomas is striking, for example.[11] Editors informed their readers of articles which remained in their possession for future inclusion in their magazine, of articles which had been commissioned from outside sources or promised by contributors, and also otherwise made sure that subscribers were well aware of the quality of the product they were holding in their hands. In April 1816, Hezekiah Niles, never shy to celebrate himself in the service of sales, printed five letters from readers received, as Niles emphasizes, in the course of a single day. The letters overflowed with adjectives such as "valuable," "admirable," "patriotic," and other terms of praise of Niles. In January 1816, he had already, with the somewhat cheeky note that he was "opposed to the system of puffing," placed a letter in praise of the *Register* from Oliver Hazard Perry, victor of the Battle of Lake Erie, in the 9th volume supplement (cf. *WR* 1816 1, 381). Similarly, even if outside the pages of the magazine proper, Joseph Dennie kept the *Port Folio* prospectus of 1800 in circulation through at least three editions, the third of which was printed in October 1803, and which Dennie supplied to his agents in the country "*gratis*, with copies for distribution" (*PF* 1803, 319, original emphasis), i.e. so that agents could pass them on to interested people who might become subscribers. Subscription and self-adver-

10 Surprisingly, not all commentators regarded newspaper advertisements as a negative aspect of those papers. As the *Gleaner* noted in 1809, "advertisements, moreover, which [newspapers] daily contain respecting new books, projects, inventions, discoveries and improvements, are well calculated to enlarge and enlighten the public mind, and are worthy of being enumerated among the many methods of awakening and maintaining the popular attention, with which more modern times, beyond all preceding example, abound." (499-500). This notion of public service through advertisements, however, seems to have been rather unique.

11 Examples of these can be seen in the collection of the Library Company of Philadelphia.

tising were intimately connected. Future content was also a frequently used means of advertising indirectly the quality of one's magazine, one in which biography often played a significant role. In 1806, the *Polyanthos* announced to its readers that it had in production, for inclusion at a later point, eight biographies and engravings (cf. *P* 1806, 144), and throughout the War of 1812, the periodicals which produced naval biography repeatedly used forthcoming biographical texts for the purpose of advertising the value of their periodicals. Most prominently perhaps Hezekiah Niles used biography as a central element in advertising his 5th volume supplement in 1814; both the *Port Folio* and the *Analectic* utilized engravings to advertise biographies which would be published in a subsequent issue, and also directly addressed their readers with notices of biographies to come (cf. ch. 3). Such forms of self-advertising did not, of course, bring immediate profit in the sense of revenues. Rather, it emphasized the value of subscription by indicating what was to come, and that what was to come was part of a coherent plan for the magazine.

More important and more central to the financial success of the magazine than the sale of advertisements was the sale of the magazine itself, done in the Early Republic almost entirely by way of subscription. It was in the nature of the periodical to be ephemeral, and more likely to be read than bought, as was frequently ruefully acknowledged. "Those publications which are sought for, rather to be consulted than studied, have now become so numerous, that few would purchase them, who could otherwise obtain their use [...] Among books of [this] description, may be ranked almost all the periodical publications of Great Britain and of the United States," an advertisement for a lending library suggested in 1805 (*PF* 1805, 277). The system of distribution thus became key: how to make enough people pay for the privilege of reading the magazine to render it a profitable venture. In principle, subscription was a safe way of ensuring at least a year's worth of profit, workable even with comparatively few actual subscribers. Charles Brockden Brown has frequently been mocked for his suggestion, made on launching the *Monthly Magazine* in 1799, that "[f]our hundred subscribers will repay the annual expence of sixteen hundred dollars. As soon as this number is obtained, the printers will begin and trust to the punctual payment of these for reimbursement. All above found hundred will be a clear profit for me..." (in Tassin 1915, 23). Algernon Tassin dismissed Brown's calculation as self-interestedly optimistic (cf. 1915, 23), and Theodore Greene considered it evidence of Brown's "considerable optimism" (1970, 21). But in fact, these kinds of calculations were both necessary and accurate enough, and probably not even particularly optimistic. More problematic than the mere calculation of profit was actually obtaining the money. Joseph Dennie indirectly pointed out the more crucial flaw in Brown's calculation: "It is not the extent of subscription," wrote Dennie in the May 1, 1802 edition of the *Port Folio*, "but very general and prompt payments, that must support this paper" (135). Another factor becomes clear in Brown's calculation: subscriber lists were insurance policies for printers, whose layout of money was considerable. As the *Panoplist* noted in its already-quoted request for punctual payment of subscriptions, printers bought paper at their own expense and themselves employed journeymen printers. All of these were expenses that had to be considered, and considered before any question of personal profit or of reimbursement for the loss of time and the use of his facilities could be entertained (cf. *PN* 1812, 199). And even if all this could be paid, the publisher and editor had not yet made a single cent in profit. The peril of subscription, then, was that it placed subscribers and publishers in a mutual dependency, the financial burden of which lay on the publisher's side: if no money was forthcoming, he was likely to have contracted for a printing job much larger than would ultimately be paid for.

Publishing by subscription was not unique to magazines and had a long history. Printers, who for the most part also functioned as publishers of books, looked to subscription to lessen the entrepreneurial risks they ran. This form of publishing, which had been popular in America for nearly a century before the Revolution, depended on publishers' clear statement of the contents of any proposed work. Periodical editors and publishers usually required payment in advance for their publications, a method of publication which defrayed the initial outlay of capital for paper, ink, and delivery, but which required either an established name in the business to accredit the proposed magazine, or a clear outline of the principles upon which the magazine would be conducted. Periodicals in the Early Republic did so in the form of prospectuses, more or less lengthy statements which included a clear delineation of the content of the proposed magazine, its price, publication mode, and editorial conception. So doing was both traditional, as many prospectuses themselves noted, and shrewd business: prospectuses laid out their content to attract readers.[12] Few where quite as clear about it as the outspoken Stephen Carpenter in offering the public the prospectus of his 1812 *Bureau*, but Carpenter no doubt echoed the reasoning through which editors and publishers resorted to the prospectus:

12 More basic issues also found mention in magazine prospectuses; above all, the quality of printing. The *Philadelphia Repertory*'s prospectus, for instance, advertised its "handsome type on fine paper" (*PRP* 1810, 224); the *Floriad* "good paper and [...] good type" (*F* 1811); the *Weekly Register*'s original prospectus noted the "fine super-royal paper with a nonpareil or brevier type" (*WR* 1811, 2), and the *Port Folio* merely pointed to its prospectus and noted that it was "a specimen of the size and quality of the paper, and of the typographical execution" (*PF* 1801 Prospectus, 5) while mocking the apparently prevailing tendency to advertise rather the materiality than the content of periodicals: "The paper is neither wire-woven, nor hot-pressed, and it certainly, in more sense than one, shall not be cream-coloured" (*PF* 1801 Prospectus, 1). Such reassurances not only helped justify the high price of periodical publications, they also took part in a complicated interplay between the care taken with the form of publication and the publication itself. As Elizabeth Reilly and David Hall suggest, the "materialities of every text—the quality of paper, the spacing of the lines of text, the nature of the binding (if bound at all)—[...] conveyed how it should be read" (2000, 404). If we cannot entirely illuminate how these interactions worked, the general notion that better paper and more attractive typefaces corresponded to a more genteel journal, or at least a magazine for which the market would seem to offer a financially more attractive audience, is clear.

> Were it possible to dispense with the ceremonial of a prospectus on the present occasion, the editor would most gladly decline one: but since, of a work which is to be published in successive parts, and which, from its nature, cannot be put at once into the hands of the public, the scheme can be made known only by a premonition of this kind, the editor finds it necessary to break through the obstructions that present themselves and to lay open that prospect to which he hopes to attract the attention. (*PRP* 1812, 400)

The very nature of the periodical publications made it necessary to clearly lay out the contents in a prospectus, the more so since publishers required payment in advance of the subscriber's ever receiving anything to read. The contractual nature of the prospectus was always implicit; Joseph Dennie made it explicit in his *Port Folio* prospectus: he "makes his public contract" (*PF* Prospectus 1801, 1) with his readers, a contract with includes both a negative part—a list of things he will not print—as well as a "*promisory* part," in which he "engages that *attempts* will be made (2, original emphasis). This remained a constant throughout the *Port Folio*'s dealings with its customers. The 1806 prospectus readily reaffirmed that readers might well take its enumeration of prospective contents in the new series as "promissory notes, to be paid every six months" (*PF* Prospectus 1806, [5]), and in 1809, in an advertisement which preceded the *Port Folio*'s reorganization after its sale to Bradford & Inskeep, Dennie emphatically stressed again that his forthcoming prospectus constituted "a frank pledge for the faithful execution of whatever it may stipulate" (*NYCA* 1809, 12.4256, [3]). Seriality obviously played a major role in the promises of prospectuses by highlighting the ways in which reader tastes would be gratified over the course of a number of issues. As Martin Christadler suggests, it was one of the basic differences between the American and the British periodical markets that what he calls the "single essay periodical" never managed to gain a safe foothold in the United States. Americans preferred essay series, reflecting again the prospectus' desire to outline continuities and seriality in their conception of new periodical ventures (cf. 1965, 76).[13]

Not all periodicals offered their readers a fully streamlined mode of publication. But it is striking that when they did, they insisted on the subscription model, notwithstanding the problems subscription brought with it. Subscription remained the dominant form of periodical publication throughout the period under discussion here—so much so that some periodicals found themselves in a position to explicitly deny other options of selling their papers. Hezekiah Niles spoke for periodical editors and publishers when he noted, barely two months after the commencement of the *Weekly Register*, that "[f]requent applications has [sic] been made at this office to purchase [back] numbers of the Register [...]—the public are respectfully informed that this paper cannot be sold, or given away, except to regular subscribers, under any pretense whatsoever" (*WR*

13 It is suggestive that Christadler emphasizes the market viability of the essay series over seriality's role in creating new forms of narrative.

1811, 240). Niles refused the sale of individual numbers, that is to say, the weekly editions. Editors and publishers were in agreement that the value of the periodical lay not so much in the separate issues which the reader received, but in the entirety of the scheme. Stephen Carpenter conceived, at least publicly, of the *Bureau* as a "work […] in successive parts" in his prospectus. In so framing the *Bureau*, Carpenter justified the need for a yearly subscription by suggesting that the *Bureau* could only be conceived of in an artificial entirety. At least publically, the work Carpenter was producing was the annual run of the *Bureau*, rather than the individual issues composing it: That the *Bureau* was available only through subscription, rather than, for example, by applying for individual issues to the printer, or making them available in bookstores, was necessary for the integrity of the project. At the same time, Niles, and many other publishers, not only allowed sales of back volumes, that is to say half-yearly runs of numbers, but actively encouraged them. As Hugh Maxwell apprised Joseph Dennie before the initial publication of the *Port Folio*:

> A magazine may be so conducted as to form a kind of history of our country during the period in which it was conducted, so that at a future day the work may become estimable, and the copies which remain on hand be sold to advantage. In this lies the great profit of a magazine. Without this advantage it is never worth prosecuting.[14]

The emphasis which editors and publishers placed on the volumes of periodicals might have seemed an obstacle to some subscribers, who may have wished to obtain a subscription outside of the semiannual turn of volumes, but would then have been forced to forego part of the volume during whose run they were subscribing. Here again, Hezekiah Niles proved to be one of the more cunning publishers of the age. In his able hands, publication by volume became a way for the publisher to sell more papers to subscribers. The start of any volume, Niles noted, "offers a good opportunity to others who design to give us their support" (*WR* 1817, 432), and he realized and told his customers that "[e]veryone should […] begin with a volume." But should, to a salesman like Niles, could never become must, and so "any gentleman may commence at such time as he pleases—provided he pays one year in advance" (*WR* 1818, xiv). Gentlemen who did do so were then free to obtain from Niles the entire run of the *Register* "from the beginning," at the cost of the yearly subscription of five dollars per issue. But while subscribers to the magazine received gratuitously (an emphasis that Niles was fond of repeating often) the annual supplements containing various papers that Niles had not been able to fit in any of the year's numbers, back-ordered by new subscribers these cost a dollar each, plus three dollars for the General Index.

The assumption which Hezekiah Niles printed into the prospectus for his *Weekly Register*, that "every subscriber will carefully file his numbers, under an assurance

14 Hugh Maxwell to Joseph Dennie, February 25, 1800. Historical Society of Pennsylvania, Meredith Family Papers 1509, Box 99. The full text of this letter is in Lanzendörfer (2012).

that they will always be worth the first cost," and for which "[w]ith the last number each volume will be delivered a minute index and general title, free of expense" (*WR* Prospectus, in *WR* 1811, 2) was not his alone. Editors conceived of their periodicals as repositories of lasting influence, and virtually all of them put out semiannual or annual indices and cover sheets so that readers could have their loose-bound weeklies or monthlies bound safely and lastingly as books. Indeed, editors firmly believed that their volumes would make lasting a useful addition to libraries, and to offer repositories for the safeguarding of material useful to later historians (cf. *WI* 1806, 81). "[S]tanding as a permanent record of all the public transactions of the time," as the *Monthly Register*'s prospectus advertised (in *BCR* 1804, 293), was but one of the reasons why magazines were conceived of as a lasting investment for the consumer. At least some subscribers agreed with the general notion of editors and publishers that the magazines were written to last. A correspondent of Joseph Dennie's noted in March 1801 (the *Port Folio* was barely three months old and still in its newspaper-sized weekly format) that he considered the *Port Folio* no ordinary newspaper, but held it worthy of lasting fame. Subscribers, he noted, "are desirous of preserving it in its original shape, for the amusement and instruction of their grand children," on a level with Addison's *Spectator* (the benchmark of so many periodical publications in the Early Republic). The writer's grandiloquent pronouncement led him to wonder if Dennie might not "after wrapping round each number a small piece of paper, inscribed with the name of its owner, [...] pack up all directed to one post-office together, in a cover of strong paper" (*PF* 1801, 83). Though it may seem trivial, a concern for the delivery of their magazines seems not to have left subscribers. Hezekiah Niles was careful to address the concerns of "several subscribers to the Register" that the *Weekly Register* reached them folded, which Niles suggested was unavoidable, but could easily be remedied by the simple expedient of "plac[ing] it, for a very short time, between two books, or any other even surfaces" (*WR* 1812 1, 47). Niles assured his readers, however, that he would soon make available wrapping paper for such postal deliveries.

Readers' concern for the condition of their papers spoke to their desire to make them last, and editors and publishers catered to them whenever they could. Back issues of the *Port Folio* were available as early as October 1803, when Joseph Dennie advised subscribers that "sets from the commencement of the work" had been re-printed, available via his regular mailing address (*PF* 1803, 319). With greater salesmanship, Hezekiah Niles, who had been publically chary about seeming to be advertising his agents' list, was far less reticent about promoting the sale of his back issues. In November 1815, Niles printed a complimentary note from "a gentleman who has filled one of the high offices of the republic," who noted that the *Register* "rises in merit as it progresses. Like sound Madeira, it improves by age." With this anonymous praise still ringing in readers' ears, Niles appended a none-too-subtle sales pitch for "complete files of the *Weekly Register*, bound or in sheets." The work, Niles noted, was "not in the market, nor is it *likely* to be" (original emphasis). But most importantly,

> Its number is counted, and those now in hand are all that ever will be offered to the public. The stock is daily diminishing; and she [sic] only reason that exists for inviting gentlemen, at present, to purchase what they may hereafter desire and not be able to obtain, is simply this—that the capital invested in them is heavier than is convenient—and, that the money, for a part of them, could be advantageously used to give ease to the editor and his business; for he has no apprehension that they will long remain on his hands, and certainly believes that twice the number he has will be demanded in a very few years. [...] Gentlemen, also, may find it more expedient to take the files now, than suffer them to grow up to a value that may serious check the desire to have them. (*WR* 1815, 205)

Ensuring readers both of the limited supply of the offer as well as its inherent desirability, Niles also offered readers the option of getting their (usually looseleaf) copies delivered already bound, and more: contrary to his suggestion that there was anything like a fixed stock, Niles also offered readers the "[c]urrent year in advance to Sept[ember] 1816" (*WR* 1815, 205), in other words, issues which he had not even yet printed. Selling the next years' run at five dollars, then, Niles conflated the desirable sale of back issues with the regular subscription to future issues, and the perhaps real danger to subscribers of missing out on material which they could, indeed, not otherwise get, with the not-quite-as-real danger of missing out on Niles's future productions. As noted in the discussion of Stephen Carpenter's *Bureau* prospectus, the public façade which stressed the integrity of the entire yearly run of a magazine, or at least the integrity of the half-yearly volumes into which the periodical were usually structured, owed much to editors' desire to justify their refusal of selling individual numbers. This stricture certainly had its roots in the lack of a well-organized alternative distribution system, but of course it also tied subscribers to magazines.

Despite repeated assurances by publishers, subscription was not the only way by which interested readers could obtain magazines. For most magazines, however, subscription was the predominant way to go, despite the serious problems which the system had. Perusing the editorial commentary of Early Republic magazines, it seems that when editors were not praising their contributors, they were haranguing their subscribers for not paying. The failure to find a large enough subscription base was frequently fatal for aspiring magazine editors, such as William Allen, whose editor- and proprietorship of the *Merrimack Miscellany* ended in October 1805 because of "the limited subscription he has received" (MMS 1805, 71) and which caused him to transfer the ownership of the magazine to two successors. Even for magazines which obtained enough subscribers to survive, if not to prosper, the subscription system was problematical. Payment mores were, at least as far as the editors' and publishers' perspectives were concerned, decidedly lax. Thus Joseph Dennie, in March 1808, pointedly thanked his "*punctual* Patrons" (original emphasis) and then went on to say that

> the expense of the establishment is much heavier than its friends generally imagine [...] it is obvious, without a rigid punctuality on the part of Patrons, the finances of

> the concern must be always embarrassed, and the Editor a malecontent [sic], with Industry interrupted, with Zeal baffled, and with Enterprize overthrown. (*PF* 1808 1, 160, original emphasis)

Seven months later, Dennie suggested that he was "a claimant upon his subscription list to the bona fide amount of Ten Thousand Dollars" (*PF* 1808 2, 239), the same amount which John Hall claimed for the same magazine's outstanding subscriptions after eighteen months' editorial tenure in July 1817 (cf. *PF* 1817 2, 2). A month later, Hezekiah Niles felt himself so overburdened by outstanding payments that he went entirely to advance payment. It actually behooved him little: in October 1820, the *Register* again included the by-now familiar lament of defaulting subscribers, and repeated it in July 1822.

A February 1822 phillipic published in the *Port Folio* stood out among this litany of complaints about subscribers. Not content with the genteel reminder to the anonymous subscribership which informed Dennie's usual way of addressing the concern of outstanding subscription moneys, and not prepared to restrict itself even to Hezekiah Niles's increasingly forward notes requesting delinquent subscribers to pay, John E. Hall now directed his ire at one particular, identifiable subscriber. "Let *delinquent subscribers* be held up by name to scorn and derision," he thundered, "and our editors may then devote themselves to their profession, without aching hearts and distracted heads." He then made an example of "Mr. Lewis A. Fowler, of *Poughkeepsie*, N.Y., [who] two years ago [...] communicated his wish to be considered as a subscriber to the Port Folio, and promised to transmit the price of it, as soon as he was apprized of the amount. The magazine has been regularly sent," but Hall did not, at any point, receive money—Fowler was a subscriber to a number of other papers which fared similarly, as Hall was ready to point out (*PF* 1822 1, 169, original emphasis).

One of the major faults of the subscriber system was its inherent costliness and the complicated logistic and interpersonal relationships it set up. In theory, as Luther Mott has noted, in addition to the price of the periodical proper, subscribers were supposed to pay postage when mailing in their money, certainly no cheap matter, especially for recipients far from Philadelphia, New York or Boston, the publishing hubs of the age. At two cents a sheet for magazine postage over two hundred miles, mailing a sixteen-page paper such as the early *Port Folio* added another four cents per weekly issue for the subscriber; the yearly postage surcharge was roughly a dollar even after the *Port Folio* went to monthly publication in 1809 (cf. Mott 1957a, 120). Posting magazines was not a right: postmasters were within their rights to decline service to senders of magazines if the posts would find it a burden (cf. John 1995, 39-40); there is no contemporary evidence, however, of a systematic postal problem in getting far-off subscribers their magazines. Hezekiah Niles offered a defense when confronted with complaints from his readers, stating categorically that neither he nor the Baltimore post office were to be blamed for delays in reception. "All papers," he noted, "are packed up for the various mails that leave this place on the day of their publication, and are sent by them, except, sometimes, from their quantity and the pre-occupancy of the portmanteaus, a few bundles for the south lay over until the succeeding day" (*WR* 1812, 47). Despite the cautionary note of the Postal Acts, the "size of the mail" (Kielbowicz 1983, 268) could only very rarely have prevented the distribution of magazines via mail: in fact, as Richard John points out, "newspapers made up the vast bulk of the mail" (1995, 154), and magazines were only a small part of the postal burden.

Beyond the question of how to mail their magazines, however, it appears that postage was yet another aspect of the periodical business in which publishers could easily lose money. Addressing his readers in October 1803, an exasperated Joseph Dennie noted that his readers seemed to "mistake [the *Port Folio*'s] conditions. The postage of letters is not always paid" (*PF* 1803, 319), a complaint which indicates that distribution was not always as easy as is sometimes assumed by critics. Although correspondents were enjoined to send their letters post-paid so as to spare Dennie the cost of correspondence, evidently the *Port Folio* was distributed post-paid as well, neatly cancelling out any benefit he obtained. Indeed, the postal system privileged magazines considerably compared to letters, a fact which contributed to the financial problem with receiving mailed subscription payments. If a magazine cost two cents per sheet long-distance, letters over three hundred miles cost twenty-five cents a page, including whatever enclosures could be counted as pages (cf. John 1995, 159).[15] That meant that the usual way of paying for a subscription long-distance, via a bank bill drawn on one of the numerous local banks (cf. *PF* 1803, 343, with Dennie specifically requesting bank bills), could cost the recipient fifty cents: 25 for the sheet in which the bill was enclosed and 25 for the bill itself. Indeed, most people avoided pre-paying their letters, unwilling to pay for an as-yet unperformed service (cf. John 1995, 160). When Dennie took over again as publisher of the *Port Folio* in 1807, he therefore enjoined his "remote" subscribers: "were the Editor, unjustly, obliged to pay the postage of only one half the letters received in the course of a year, the profits of publication would be below his regard" (*PF* 1807, [4]; though it is telling that there still would be profits!). Hezekiah Niles, too, was at his most annoyed when speaking of the costs he incurred in receiving letters. He first broached the subject in late 1811, suggesting that "to individuals the amount of the postage of their letters is a mere trifle, but to him, in the aggregate, a heavy expense" (*WR* 1811, 175). Nothing much can have come of the complaint, for in 1815, he was still harping on the subject, noting that to grant favors and receive one dollar in payment via the mails, he had paid "taxes"—outstanding postage—of a dollar and two and a half cents (cf. *WR* 1815, 235). By 1820, he had given up, telling subscribers to send their due rates at his own expense and risk, if they thought it wise (cf. *WR* 1820, 449).

These costs must have contributed to editors' and publishers' desire to establish a system of agents in the country which could consolidate bills of payment and send

15 Postage calculations were by sheet for magazines and newspapers, each sheet of paper making sixteen octavo pages. By contrast, letters were somewhat illiberally charged per page; cf. Mott 1957a, 120.

out larger single payments. City subscribers, as Joseph Dennie had noted earlier, were a valuable commodity to a magazine, largely because, as the *Panoplist*, a Boston religious magazine had it, "subscribers in large towns generally [...] give no cause of complaint" (1812, 199). City subscribers, which could pay for their magazines in person at the printer's office or bookshops, saved on postage, but were also in a more direct personal relationship with the people whom they, by not paying, would have defrauded. They also received their magazines by carrier, and thus it was comparatively easy both to communicate with them as well as to withhold papers. Agents offered a way of establishing similarly personal relationships in far-flung locales; they also seemed a possible way of easing the editor-publisher's work load by devolving some of the business of handling subscriptions on designated locals, as well as providing local addressees for larger bundles of magazines. By 1812, for example, the *Weekly Register* granted that it would be possible to send larger bundles to such places where twenty or more subscribers lived, for distribution through the post office, whose postmaster would function as Niles's agent (cf. *WR* 1812, 47). The way these agents were organized grew progressively more elaborate. In 1797, Philip Freneau had suggested to his rural readers that if they wished to obtain copies of the *Time Piece*, they might "find themselves best served by appointing some person resident in town as agent for the purpose of handing in & attending to their subscriptions" (*TP* 1797, 1), for which service they might obtain a free copy for every fifteen subscribed. Voluntary, essentially unpaid agents remained a fixture of most distribution systems, especially for the more wide-spread and successful magazines. But instead of relying on the self-organization of readers, editors and publishers went forward and obtained agents for their periodicals. By June 1802, Joseph Dennie had obtained partners across the United States to facilitate his business operations. Agents in Boston, Salem, New-York, Baltimore, Norfolk and Charleston were charged with taking in subscription money, and subscribers were enjoined to direct their correspondence about debts and future subscriptions to those agents.

Dennie started with six agents, but both he and later papers extended into a broad network. A new list of agents published three times in successive issues in February 1803 contained forty names (and the office of the Washington *Federalist*), of whom three were in Canada (cf. *PF* 1803, 55), and another list printed twice in May 1803 had seventy-six agents throughout North America, including one in Natchez and one in Cincinnati (cf. *PF* 1803, 167).[16] Similarly, Hezekiah Niles, barely two months after the initial number of his *Weekly Register* had appeared, reported to his readers that he had been "often requested to publish the names of the gentlemen who have kindly consented to act as agents for the Weekly Register," and appended what he called an "incomplete" list of agents in the United States. The list still comprised several dozen names in all states of the Union as well as the Indiana, Illinois, and Louisiana territories.

16 This list was considerably reduced in 1807, when Dennie himself took over as publisher of the *Port Folio*. The new list of agents included many long time correspondents, mostly booksellers, so that Dennie may have culled the list in favor of fewer but more reliable persons.

Both Niles and Dennie were well aware of the possible advertising value of this list. Dennie's triple and double reprints of his agents' lists was cheap and effective advertising, couched in the respectability of doing subscribers a service by enumerating for them options for payment. Niles noted "some resemblance to an advertisement, though immediately connected with the business of the paper"—and although chary of admitting it, was no doubt willing to have readers recognize that the large number of agents and their wide distribution must signify something about the quality of the product. Niles's list was, in addition, printed in one of the many supplements which Niles published gratis—as "a free-will offering to the liberality of the public" (*WR* 1811, 175)—in yet another example of the unique craftsmanship of the professional editor-publisher.

Agencies did not solve all the financial troubles of editors and publishers. David Johnson, a Portland subscriber, wrote Joseph Dennie in 1806 that "the agent for Portland [...] for one or two years has been much disordered in his mind."[17] In 1817, despite the success of the agencies, Niles went to advance payment for the *Weekly Register* and temporarily suspended agencies until all agents' accounts—at some of which, by his own accounting, up to 700$ were due—were settled, which, as he indicated, would save him "at least 1000 dollars a year for clerk-hire and other cash expenses incident to keeping and collecting the accounts" (*WR* 1817, 369). But Niles made sure to note that the suspension would be temporary, and there is every indication that agents continued to play a significant role in the distribution system of the *Weekly Register*. In August 1818, he noted that the previous year's accounts from his agents were due and requested his readers, at Niles's own expense, to send the money for their subscriptions to him, if they had not paid an agent (*WR* 1818, xiv).

Apart from the agents system, booksellers and printers (who often ran bookshops on the side) were sometimes part of an unofficial distribution system. Granted that we have only a few glimpses into this system, it more closely resembles modern periodical sales. As the subscribers lists of several magazines indicate, it was not uncommon for booksellers to subscribe to a larger number of copies of a magazine, presumably for local sale, rather than for distribution to other subscribers. The *Medical Repository* of New York carried a subscriber list in January 1797 which listed bookseller Jabez Denison of Newport, Rhode Island, for three copies, Isaac Beers of New Haven, Connecticut for six, James Rice of Baltimore, Maryland, and the store of Freneau & Paine in Charleston, South Carolina, for twelve each, Boston bookseller Ebenezer Larkin as having subscribed for 36 copies, and Thomas Dobson of Philadelphia for fifty (*MER* 1797, 9-15). All of these booksellers were outside of the city limits of New York. As Catherine O'Donnell Kaplan has noted, Elihu Hubbard Smith, the *Repository*'s editor, "urged [...] booksellers to stock the periodical, hoping that [Smith's reform impulse] and the quest for profit could serve each other" (2007, 95).

17 David Johnson to Joseph Dennie, September 7, 1806. Historical Society of Pennsylvania, Meredith Family Papers 1509, Box 99.

A similar mode of distribution was used by the *Emporium of Arts & Sciences*. It unhelpfully does not list booksellers specifically in its April 1813 list of subscribers. On its list, however, the names of R. & T. Patterson, printers and booksellers, stand out—they subscribed to 33 copies of the magazine. Similarly, booksellers Hale & Hosmer, of Hartford, Connecticut at 22 copies, printer-bookseller James Webster of Philadelphia at 24 copies, and a number of subscribers to between twelve and two copies subscribed with the apparent intention of resale or further distribution. All those numbers pale, however, besides the number of copies ordered by Samuel Wood of New York and Charles Williams of Boston, who subscribed respectively to 227 and 400 copies. The *Emporium* had no further subscribers in either New York or Massachusetts, leaving the obvious conclusion that readers of the *Emporium* in those states were required to obtain their copies through the local distributor (cf. *EAS* 1813, i-iv; cf. Appendix 2 for book sellers listed on title pages). The *Emporium*'s conditions made no mention of this variant for obtaining the magazine, so that some final doubts may remain as to how it was supposed to work.

The subscriber system had a major influence on the shape of the periodical in the Early Republic, much beyond the financial problems it frequently brought. Often enough, publishers' and editors' claims on their subscribers for large sums were as indicative of the well-being of the periodical as of its problems—as when Hezekiah Niles could suggest that he had ten thousand dollars outstanding subscription monies, and yet kept publishing his magazine at a regular rate and to some evident profit for year after year. Nor, as Leon Jackson has convincingly pointed out, was subscribers' indebtedness to publishers unexpected by publishers or necessarily crippling. "Debt, it turns out, was both widespread and widely socially accepted" (2008, 151), a system in which the expectation was that momentarily incurred debt might not be relieved immediately, but would eventually be repaid. At some points in the process, it could become inevitable that some debts were paid at once so that people further down the line might themselves be paid—witness the *Panoplist*'s insistence at the beginning of this chapter on the need for the journeymen to have bread for their families. This was the ultimate end point, perhaps, of a system where punctuality was something that concerned the publisher and editor not so much as it did those whose labor produced the immediate raw materials of the publication: printers and paper makers. To be sure, punctuality of payment was something that editors in the public pronouncements strongly encouraged—in this sense it is probably necessary to expand Jackson's analysis to understand that the general social acceptability of debt and the impossibility for publishers to actually do something about those debts did not mean that they would not have much preferred to have their subscribers pay timely. Yet, as Jackson also points out, the crucial pressure to refuse to accept subscribers' debt came with the increasing need to capital in the paper-making industry in the 1840s (cf. 175-7).

More importantly, perhaps, the various paraphernalia of the subscription system shaped periodical content. Prospectuses did not in detail determine but did in general terms lay out the content of periodicals, and while often phrased vaguely enough to allow almost any content to serve, could be prohibitive. Thus, the *Port*

Folio's post-1809 prospectuses, explicitly disavowing concerns of party, remained a significant limit as well as an important promise for the magazine. Article series, not least among them particular biographies—American biography, lives of painters, lives of authors—gave periodicals a sense of seriality and continuity, and offered readers an idea of what they were in for as they tethered themselves for a least a year to a particular magazine. The exclusivity of the subscription system came to be slowly undermined as early as the 1810s by offers to put up individual magazine issues for sale; subscription had prepared this new route (which did not ultimately succeed in American periodical publishing until much later in the century) of selling magazines by advertising contents for prospective subscribers, beyond the general promises of the prospectuses (cf. ch. 3).

Subscribers were the life blood of Early Republic magazines; its contributors were nearly as important, but a far smaller group of people. Original contributions were the only assurance magazines had that they would be able to produce the kind of novel writings that they felt would lastingly attract readers. Contributors also submitted their own scraps from foreign magazines, a less helpful approach for some of the larger magazines with good access to periodicals (such as the *Port Folio*, or the *Monthly Anthology*) but no doubt a help to smaller, perhaps more rural magazines that did not readily have such access.

None of the major magazines of the period was produced without outside contributions (usually unpaid), and nearly all made their dependence on contributions clear from the outset. Calls for contributors filled the first installments and prospectuses of magazines as regularly as stern reminders to defaulting subscribers did the later numbers, and, as the *Merrimack Miscellany*'s suggestion to its readers and correspondents suggests, such contributors were often regarded as crucially important to the success of a magazine. The *Miscellany* was certainly not alone in its belief. In 1805, the *Polyanthos* "respectfully solicit[ed] the assistance of the classical and refined scholar, the entertaining biographer, and the instructive historian" (*P* 1806 1, iii) in its equivalent of a prospectus. Six months later, its regular column "To Readers and Correspondents" again carried a specially-marked note soliciting "Biographical and Historical Anecdotes, Criticisms, Theatrical Information, &c" (*P* 1806 1, 144), while at the same time noting the successes which the magazine had had in obtaining articles. These are only two examples for what was almost a continual refrain asking for contributors.

Contributors frequently were recruited from various kinds of voluntary associations which flourished in the Early Republic. The Friendly Club of New York supported Charles Brockden Brown's *Monthly Magazine*; the Athenaeum's Anthology Society was behind the Boston *Monthly Anthology*; the Tuesday Club lent its help to the *Port Folio*; the Lads of Kilkenny of New York were active in *Salmagundi* and the *Analectic Magazine*; and Baltimore's Delphian Club supported the *Portico*.[18] Yet if anything, the relationship between magazines and voluntary

18 Cf. Waterman 2007, 46-8, the *Journal of the Proceedings of the Anthology Society*, Koschnik 2007, 164-6; Burstein 2007, 51-6; Mott 1957a, 293-6; cf. also ch. 4.

groups of supporters was tenuous, and ultimately incapable of lastingly supporting a magazine. The Tuesday Club's contributions started off strong in 1801-3, then slowly petered out until, by Dennie's death, it had been supplanted by a far less voluntary group of contributors (cf. ch. 2 & 3); by the middle of Nicholas Biddle's editorship of the *Port Folio* (1812-14), it had probably been entirely replaced, at least as a major contributor, by paid-for contributions from commissioned writers. The *Monthly Anthology*'s demise was directly traceable, as we have seen above, to the lack of interest and time of the Athenaeum's members; the Friendly Club never managed to get the *Monthly Magazine* off the ground; and while the Lads of Kilkenny proved capable of sustaining their satirical *Salmagundi* for two years on their own, by the time they wrote for the *Analectic*, they too were being paid for their contributions (cf. ch. 3).

For a while, it was still possible to run periodicals on the basis of voluntary contributions. John E. Hall's files indicate, however, how many people were required to sustain a periodical for any length of time. More than 90 outside contributors, some who submitted just one piece, some who wrote dozens, are listed for the *Port Folio*, mostly for the years 1801 to 1804 (cf. Randall 1940). This was certainly not the whole number of people who wrote for the *Port Folio* in these years, as Dennie no doubt received submission whose writers Hall was not able to reconstruct after the fact. Especially the poetical department was hardly ever lacking for contributions—yet it could not, of course, fill the magazine, especially given the oft-voiced need for variety. And the novelty of contributing to the *Port Folio* tended to wear off quickly. John Quincy Adams, whose brutally boring "Journal of a Tour Through Silesia" and translation of Juvenal's third satire occupied much of the early numbers of the *Port Folio*, soon seriously curtailed his contributions. On the one hand, he certainly found himself overwhelmed with other things to do, but his example matches those of others in the Hall files. Indeed, few contributors were regulars: rather, most submitted one or two texts, then retired, and consequently, as we will see below, editors, despite their varying attitudes and aptitudes for constructive criticism of their contributors, were usually not overly discriminating in their acceptance of unsolicited material.

Some magazines found from the very beginning that depending upon contributors was a dangerous if necessary game. The *American Review, and Literary Journal* concluded its first "Preface" with an apologetic note admitting that despite its prospectus's promises, "original essays on moral, literary and scientific subjects; and biographical memoirs and anecdotes of remarkable and eminent persons" (*AR* 1802, v) were not forthcoming in the foreseeable future, unless, of course, contributors would step forward and supply these articles. Similarly, the editor of the *New York Magazine*, a magazine which did not even manage to last a year in 1814, noted that he would never undertake the project but for his certainty of outside support (*NYM* 1814, 1), and the *Portico*'s prospectus showed the magazine publishers' awareness that while they, too, depended on outside contributions, the extent of that dependence was critically important: readers, the *Portico* suggested, might well ask the editors "whether they possess more exhaustless materials, and are less dependent on casual supplies and external accidents, for the permanence of their design, and the success of their undertaking, than their predecessors" (*PO* 1816, 1). It explicitly noted the dangers of overly relying on outside contributions:

> To depend on adventitious aid for success, is to invite miscarriage; to reject it when it may be obtained, is to refuse the gift of perfection because it emanates from another. The Editors purpose to pursue a middle track, that will lead to splendid acquisitions. While they solicit, and firmly hope to receive, much substantial support from extraneous channels; they do not mean to waste the hours in expectations that may be disappointed, nor indulge in languid supinity on the promises of others. (2)

The *Portico*'s ultimate demise was more frequently attributed to the dearth of subscription in its hometown of Baltimore, rather than the lack of submissions; but its outline is suggestive of the difficulties with which magazines had to cope. Periodicals could neither expect to supply themselves wholly from the pen(s) of their editor(s), and neither could they bank on the lasting support even of organized associations which stood behind them. The ultimate solution were arrangements which professionalized the contribution to periodicals, namely paid writing of commissioned papers on specific, editorially determined content (cf. ch. 4).

If the *Portico*'s announcement fell into the timeframe when paid contributions came to make increasing inroads into American magazines, for much of the earlier period, contributors were a valuable resource to periodicals. Recognizing their value, editors groomed their contributors with fulsome praise. Joseph Dennie commented on one of his correspondents, "[i]f he thought proper, he might become a celebrated votary of the miscellaneous Muse" (*PF* 1809, 89), and this was just one of many instances when the *Port Folio* explicitly praised its contributors individually. Dennie for his part was as stringent in his criticism, often bitingly sarcastic; but ultimately, editorial influence on the quality and quantity of submissions was slight. In this regard, voluntary contribution was probably the most evidently autonomous aspect of periodical production in the Early Republic. Writers could submit just about anything they pleased to the editors in whose magazines they sought inclusion, and, as the editorial addresses to the readership as well as private correspondence indicates, quite frequently did so. The limits of this autonomy were reached, however, on the editor's desk. There, submissions which failed to interest the editor, which failed to suit the conception of the magazine, or which exceeded restrictions of length, soon found themselves excluded from publication. Thus, the *Boston Weekly Magazine* rejected submissions, even corrected submissions, as "too puerile [sic] and incorrect for insertion" (1803, 91); recognizing perhaps that to wait for the perfect submission was to wait a long time, it later, somewhat more charitably, edited poems which it received or included at least parts of them (cf. 1804 2, 19). The *Polyanthos* likewise rejected submissions out of hand to substance and style, if with more tact (cf. *P* 1806 1, 72). This list might be endlessly prolonged if one were so inclined, but it will probably suffice to say that contributions to a magazine were by no means in the ultimate analysis autonomous. The *Omnium Gatherum* suggested as much in May, 1810: commenting on a contribution from a "*Juvenile Traveller*," the magazine noted that if he avoided the topic of love in his future poetry, his submissions might be interesting to the magazine's readership, and "profitable to—*ourselves*" (336, original emphasis). It was this profitability which ultimately determined what happened to contributions. They might, if the occasion demanded, be postponed while other more deserving, or in any case more various productions were inserted before; they might also be declined as unfitting the principles outlined in prospectuses or as the taste of the editor determined.

Contributors were often plentiful, but they did not submit all kinds of texts in equal number, or in quality. As Joseph Dennie had cause to complain in 1809, he had a large mass of submissions to consider for the *Port Folio*, but much of that mass was, in his words, "trash" (*PF* 1809 2, 579), and much of it, too much in fact, was poetry. One of the problems of voluntary contribution was the clear lack of control over submissions which were held in the publishers' and editors' hands. Partially for this reason, and partially because submissions might often be plentiful, but rarely plentiful enough to fill issue after issue of a magazine, all magazines remained in dire need of either editorial writings to supplement their content, or more frequently the inclusion of selected matter from other periodicals. Dennie himself recognized as much, as an example from 1809 shows. He trusted his subscribers, he suggested, that they would not suppose the *Port Folio* to be able to print original matter only, and roundly blamed the country he was working in for that fault (cf. *PF* 1809 1, 93). Other magazines found similarly that readers should not expect them to be able to be exclusively original.

The ultimate quest, of course, was not for contributions as much as for readers. Contributors were to be sure usually also readers; readers, by and large, were not contributors. But readers were usually subscribers. Their wishes, their concerns, and their interests therefore to a large degree determined the content of American periodicals. Investigating the readership, both actual and ideal, of American periodicals, therefore, offers us a much clearer idea of what aspects influenced the production of periodicals in the Early Republic. Readerships and reading practices are among the most difficult to establish aspects of the Early Republic magazine business, and yet one of the most critical. Frequently assumed to have been solely members of the cultural elite, not least because of what are often regarded as prohibitively high prices for subscription, magazines of the Early Republic in fact had a remarkably broad readership. This broad readership included non-subscribers as well as subscribers, and all social classes. What united readers in the eyes of publishers and editors was not just their recognition of the usefulness of periodicals, but also their requirement of something that they could read at leisure. This requirement of the periodical followed from periodicals' conception of their readership, a readership which thus already hints at the changes which were slowly occurring in the urban markets of the periodicals (cf. Sellers 1991, 12).

Magazine editors themselves were publically certain, of course, that their magazines served a useful societal purpose. As Stephen Carpenter had it in the *Monthly Register*'s prospectus, "[e]verything which contributes to innocent pleasure, and can preserve the mind from the mischiefs of idleness, should be considered as worthy of cultivation" (*BCR* 1804, 293) in a periodical. What the *Massachusetts Magazine* supposed to be true in 1795, that the "utility of periodical publications when well conducted, judiciously selected, and generally circulated, is sufficiently obvious" (*MAM* 1795, 3), the *New-York Magazine* agreed was still the case in 1814: "The utility of the publications commonly called Magazines, when conducted on a judicious and impartial plan, is so well known, as to render it almost unnecessary to advance a single argument in their favor" (*NYM* 1814, 1). Despite their recurring readiness to assume readers' cheerful acquiescence to the fact of periodical utility, many periodicals attempted to offer those obvious reasons for periodicals' usefulness that the *Massachusetts Magazine* and the *New-York Magazine* cavalierly presupposed. Periodical publications were variously held to support the instruction of youth or the generalization of knowledge, help aspiring writers by showing them the great variety of possible writings or by giving them room to exercise their own fledgling talents. At the same time, they provided a wide variety of subject matter and were comparatively inexpensive. Yet while all periodicals agreed that some form of instruction was possible through magazines, they did not agree on what kind of instruction was the periodical's primary aim (mere generalized "virtue," or perhaps genuine vocational training?). And all too frequently, this self-conception collided with the knowledge that virtuous instruction was perhaps not what readers actually sought when they subscribed to a magazine.

The key issue with regard to which periodicals shaped their contents, thus, was their appraisal of their readership. What did readers believe periodicals should look like, and consequently, what did editors offer them? Perhaps the most telling suggestion was offered by a correspondent to the New York *Theological Magazine*. In his "Remarks on the Several Classes of Readers," the writer suggested that readers in general fall into three classes, those who read for improvement in knowledge, those who read for improvement in knowledge and virtue, and those who read merely for the sake of amusement. The *Theological Magazine*, he notes, seemed too metaphysical to some; that was because they read for amusement only, and were too indolent for the exertion which the acquisition of knowledge and virtue required, while they would always find fault with the layout of any magazine they subscribed to. The solution which the correspondent offered was simple:

> If the Theological Magazine is calculated to promote knowledge and virtue, you may not expect, in my opinion, but few who will like it; perhaps ten or fifteen hundred through the whole continent of America. Still, for their sakes, the labour and expence necessary to print and circulate it, ought to be submitted to with the greatest cheerfulness. For the good, which may accrue to them from perusing it, may be a mean [sic] to the highest good of many thousands in future generations. (*TM* 1796, 33)

The writer's belief in there being as few as a thousand people in the whole of the North American continent interested in a magazine which was not only publically devoted to knowledge and virtue but also exclusively published such writings was, of course, not based on empirical research; still, the statement gives an indication of the limited level of support that might be expected even by people whose livelihoods were not on the line in the venture, and who might be less inclined to be careful about their estimates. It was certainly one thing for an otherwise uninvolved letter writer to suggest that people should devote money and time to the effort regardless of the size of the audience, but it was hardly to be expected that publishers would find the argument particularly persuasive.

A significant number of magazines understood and foregrounded that instruction was hardly the most critical aspect of the texts they published. "In all periodical publications," the *Lancaster Hive* noted in 1803, "originality is sought for—and destitute of which, works of this nature will instruct little, muss less will they amuse. Novelty to the gay and volitile [sic] is gratifying—to the serious interesting, inasmuch as it may afford instruction" (1803, 18). The *Monthly Anthology*, itself not necessarily devoted to the light and frivolous, likewise held that periodicals were "eagerly read" precisely "for their novelty" in a review of the (second) *Literary Miscellany*, which it felt forced to proclaim "deficient in exciting interest or affording amusement" (*MA* 1805, 107). Novelty, amusement, interest—those were the central concepts which underlay, in general terms, the production of periodicals. A periodical "may afford instruction"—or it may not; to the *Lancaster Hive*, it was really all the same. Instruction, as many examples of editorial commentary could attest, was always regarded to have a far more limited scope than amusement, and as ultimately subordinate: as the *Floriad* suggested in its prospectus, while it hoped by its literary productions to please both the old and the young, both the learned writer and the up-and-coming author, it did not hope to instruct the old; yet, it averred, there were "many who have neither time nor opportunity to pursue any systematic or extensive course of reading" for whom the *Floriad*'s essays "will afford amusement for a leisure hour, and perhaps impart some pleasing or useful information" (*F* 1811, 5). The *Floriad*'s prose indicates the comparative value which ultimately almost all magazines attached to the two points of instruction and amusement—and indicates what readership the magazines expected, and which we will follow in greater detail below. The *Floriad* believed it could be entertaining to all its readers, instructive to some, but even then only "perhaps," and even relegated this "useful"ness to second place behind mere pleasure. As the *Monthly Anthology* pithily put it: "Advice is in general sufficiently disgusting" without it also being boring (*MA* 1805, 172).

What kinds of readerships did periodicals expect, therefore? Perhaps somewhat surprisingly, given the often-voiced assumption especially of critics that the readership which periodicals catered to was strictly limited by class, this was probably not so. Both in their public pronouncements and in their actual readerships, periodicals in the Early Republic frequently showed a fairly broadly based distribution of readers among different classes and professions. These varieties of readership help explain the highly miscellaneous nature of their content, as well. In 1813, the *Olio* published a letter concerning the utility of periodical publications which stressed a number of advantages of the periodical which reflected upon the magazine's readership. The *Olio*'s correspondent noted the magazines' comparatively great variety at a comparatively low price, and emphasized that "they generally circulate through a greater number of hands, in a shorter time, than voluminous and costly works do; particularly among the lower classes, who cannot afford to pay for expensive volumes" (1813, 19). Like the *Floriad* two years earlier, the *Olio* felt it was not just available to subscribers of small means, but also that readership was not solely excluded to the subscribers of any people, but rather that there existed a circulation beyond mere subscribership. Periodicals, editors and readers agreed, deserved a broad reception, or as the *Philadelphia Monthly Magazine* put it, they must be "communicated to the public at large" (1798 1, 72). The same magazine also emphasized the great differences between readers of a periodical, who nonetheless shared one central feature. Every reader of a periodical was seeking something else:

> Their brevity allures the indolent, locality the curious; their wit is a relief to the learned, and the most vinegar aspect, or torpid risibility, will relax into a smile, at the redundancy of genuine humour, so often found in them; while the universality of matter becomes an irresistible inducement to them all. (1798 2, 7)

Indeed, many editors conceived of periodicals as at heart egalitarian. Unlike expensive books, available only to the very affluent and leisured, periodicals could provide even those with a more modest income with access to the public sphere. "[T]hough apparently a humble kind of writings," wrote the *Polyanthos*'s editor in the first number of the magazine, periodicals brought together "[m]en of all ranks, and of all nations, however widely disjoined each other [...] to converse at ease" (*P* 1806 1, 23-24). Periodical publications promised to diffuse education among the populace, an aspect which religious magazines especially applauded, but whose benefits other magazines likewise praised. "Learning is no longer confined within the retreats of academics," noted the *Christian Observer*, "but it is diffused among all ranks and classes of men" (*CO* 1802, 120), and the *Massachusetts Missionary Magazine* agreed that to reach "all classes of people [...] in promoting any important public cause [and to] make it appear worthy of universal attention and pursuits," no means "promise greater success, than Periodical Publications" (*MMM* 1803, 3). Yet the idea of reaching a wide audience with their content engaged periodicals far beyond religious messages. The *Olio*'s praise for periodicals' access to the poor was expanded by the *Miscellany* of Trenton emphatically pronouncing it to be "not the scholar only who enjoys the advantages of weekly or monthly publications," but also the "mechanic or farmer" (*M* 1805, 2) if articles catering to their particular interests were provided by magazines. This, of course, was an artificial limitation based on the assumption that there were particular kinds of texts with which farmers might be interested in a periodical: indeed, it is more likely that such groups, too, were perfectly interested in the kinds of amusing variety that magazines naturally produced. The *Philadelphia Monthly Magazine* noted that periodicals communicated information "to the people at large," and in particular noted the leveling propensities of the periodicals in the realm of essay writing. Communal reading, too, helped the cause of periodicals to prosper in a wide variety of settings. "There is scarcely a village of country post office in the United States, particularly if it be kept in a tavern or store, in which newspapers are not as free to all comers, as to the persons to whom they rightfully belong," wrote a commentator in the *National Intelligencer* in 1822 (in John 1995, 154-5), and some postal clerks even established reading rooms for the most current periodical productions (cf. John 1995, 155).

There is some evidence that editors' ideas about their readership were reasonably accurate. David Nord's analysis of the readership of the *New-York Magazine* establishes convincingly that despite a magazine's pretension to culture and refinement, qualities which may be more associated with the professional, or even the leisured classes, its readership could comprise all classes. The *New-York Magazine*'s subscribers were split about equally between professionals and merchants on the one hand, people who, within the society of the day, were most likely to be considered upper class; and artisans and shopkeepers on the other hand, who would be unlikely to be mistaken for men of leisure (cf. Nord 1988). If Nord's reclassification of the magazine's purpose as being a "republican literature" for "a republican readership" merely shifts the old idealist discourse—magazines as being "by the few, for the few"—into a major key—his argument, ultimately, is about the broad range of addressees for the republican idealism he finds is central to the *New-York Magazine*—it is a very useful attempt to discover who read magazines.

An attempt similar to Nord's can be made for two Philadelphia journals about two decades apart. The short-lived *Literary Miscellany* (1795) not only had among its readers a plethora of names which at that time or later were involved in the periodical and literary businesses—Charles Brockden Brown, Matthew Carey, William Cobbett, Asbury Dickins, Hugh Maxwell, and Parson Mason Weems—but offers other interesting insights into readerships. Of its 225 named subscribers, a list of whom the magazine published in its first number (cf. *LMS* 1795, 23), 54 were women—both married and unmarried. Several subscribers took large numbers of issues, probably for resale—Weems took 90 copies, a Dublin subscriber 50, and several booksellers throughout the country took from two to fifty copies each. But what is most notable is the great variety in subscribers which the *Miscellany* attracted. The magazine's bi-weekly numbers sold for 12½¢ each; it is unclear whether subscription was a requirement (cf. *PG* 1795 12.1944, 3 for an advertisement of the new magazine), but a yearly subscription would have cost 3,25$ at that rate. The *Miscellany* was exclusively a literary journal, carrying poetry and prose by Oliver Goldsmith, Thomas Gray, and other notable English authors. Despite this narrow focus on literature, however, its subscribers included almost the entire social spectrum of Philadelphia, from Pennsylvania Governor Thomas Mifflin and naval officer Captain Thomas Truxtun down through leisured "gentlemen," public servants, lawyers, doctors, schoolmasters, and merchants. But apart from these men (and women), the *Miscellany* also attracted an audience that was, in today's term, solidly middle or even lower class. Among the Philadelphians identifiable through the *Philadelphia Directory* for 1795 (cf. Hogan 1795) are an innkeeper, several tailors, storekeepers, and artisans: carpenters, hosiers, upholsterers, and sugar refiners. There are also, however, even more lowly workers: two scriveners, John Woodside and Jacob Hoffman; a skindresser, Martin Gilman; a painter, John Stock; a watchman, Samuel Carter; and a blacksmith, John Carter. Only about ten to fifteen percent of the names in the subscription list can be readily identified—the *Philadelphia Directory* is obviously incomplete, as can be deduced from known Philadelphians not in the *Directory*, and in several cases, the information contained in the subscribers list is insufficient. But the majority of those subscribers which could be identified were solidly middle class, rather than the leisured gentlemen so often imagined as the most numerous class of magazine readers.

The second opportunity to investigate readership structures is offered by the *Emporium of Arts & Sciences*; using 1810 directory data for Philadelphia and the 1813 list of subscribers (cf. *EAS* 1813, 481-484; Robinson 1810). There are 259 subscribers in Philadelphia, of whom 39 can be tentatively identified throught the 1810 directory and five could be two or more people. Both the small sample size and the high price and specific content of the *Emporium* make a general evaluation of the readership difficult, but the *New-York Magazine*'s trend can be identified here, too. While learned professionals—in this case, mainly doctors—make up a large part of the subscriber base, and there are a number of both "gentlemen" without any profession at all, as well as merchants of various description, the identified subscribers include at least nine people engaged in the book trade, printers, engravers, and booksellers, as well as artisans of various description, such as a chandler, a combmaker, and a coachmaker, as well as two laborers, a gardener and a mariner. The *Emporium* charged seven dollars per annum for a subscription, making it one of the most expensive magazines around, but given that Philadelphia artisans might make as much as 700$ a year, and possibly more (cf. Rilling 2006, 326), this was not too large a sum, evidently, to deter even middle-class subscribers. That its subscribership included such a great social variety speaks to the chances for a wide dissemination of periodical texts even without the possibilities opened by lending libraries, by the simple sharing of reading materials within households or between friends, and other ways of obtaining access to magazines.

This short evaluation of the possible breadth of readership is echoed by the experiences abroad as well. Jan Fergus's thorough study of English rural reading audiences in the English Midlands during the late eighteenth century convincingly argues that magazine readers were a highly diverse group, including men and women, the landed gentry, professionals, laborers, and even schoolboys. Her study of the *Lady's Magazine* not only reveals the ostensibly gender-specific periodical to have been bought and read by male readers; it also establishes, and this is perhaps a greater surprise, that "farmers and tradesmen altogether surpass professional men as subscribers" (2006, 209).[19] Fergus's reconstruction reveals rather a remarkable rural readership. Whether English or American, lower class subscribers to magazines could expect to pay about a weekly wage for the subscription.[20] That they were well willing to do so is attested to by Fergus's findings—she identifies, among others, a draper's servant and a labourer as paying subscribers to a literary magazine—and her approval of Roger Chartier's carefully phrased note that to "a greater extent than has been though, widely distributed texts and books crossed social boundaries and drew readers from very different social and economic levels" (in Fergus 2011, 208) is certainly valid for the United States as well. As Fergus points out, especially in the lower classes of readership, it is more likely that subscription also meant active readership, as a subscriber had "little disposable income to squander monthly on print that he did not read" (2011, 208). The similarities between the print markets in Britain and the United States make it somewhat likely that analogous reading practices may have prevailed in both. Stephen Colclough's investigation into reading practices is focused on Great Britain, but contains a number of interesting observations from which we may be able to deduce more about American practice. His chief source for the 1790s, Joseph Hunter, kept a diary of his reading at age 15, when he was apprenticed to a Sheffield merchant. An avid reader, Hunter both frequented libraries and purchased books. Besides books, the circle of friends and family in which Hunter lived "bought mainly periodicals and newspapers" (2010, 99), and did so "collectively" —that is to say, there was shared access and a sharing of costs between at least three people, none of which were family—suggesting that "regular access to new texts came at a cost that

19 Indeed, as I suggest in Chapter 2, the *Lady's Magazine* was one of the sources from which Joseph Dennie obtained many of his biographies for the *Farmer's Weekly Museum*, hinting at a readership not only crossed gender barriers, but was also transatlantic.

20 A caveat is necessary in any analysis which compares the rural British practice in the 1770s with the American practice in the 1790s and 1800s. The *Lady's Magazine* cost 6s 6d a year, about one third of a pound. The pound traded roughly at 4,50$ in 1790 (the closest approximate date we have data for), making the yearly subscription to the *Lady's Magazine* about 1.50$ per year. This was decidedly at the low end of the scale for American magazines, most of which cost around 5-6. Average weekly earnings for British laborers in the cotton industry in the 1770s were about 6s 11d (cf. Broadberry and Gupta 2008, 35), or about 1.80$, whereas the weekly income of a Massachusetts laborer, working six days a week, came to about 6,45$ in 1798 (when Joseph Hunter was a subscriber to the *Lady's Magazine*; cf. Wright 1885, 60. The average of wages in1798 gives 4,9s per day, 29,4s per week—this corresponds to 1,47£, or 6,45$ at 1798 exchange rates; cf. Officer 2010). In other words, at least as far as such a rough estimate and cross-comparison between decades and countries can reveal, subscription to a magazine cost either British or American laborers about a week's salary. The problems with such a rough comparison, indeed the problems in wage estimates, are evident if one compares this particular one to others. Adams (1986, 633) suggests, for example, and average daily wage in the 1790s for a Massachusetts agricultural worker to be 62¢ and for a Maryland agricultural worker to be 44¢; whereas Wright's data would roughly suggest an average of 70¢ for Massachusetts. This 12% difference in estimates makes for about 77¢ at the estimated weekly wage of 6,45$.

was still beyond the means of the majority of readers," given the middle-class background of Colclough's source (99-100).[21] Hunter, his friends and family, Colclough suggests, found periodical reading a ubiquitous part of their daily lives, and supposes that "it was not simply regarded as an ephemeral publication" (99). Rather, "periodicals were at the centre of [Hunter's] reading experience" (100) a belief supported by the broad range of periodicals which his circle subscribed to and traces of which can be found in his diary. Likewise, as Colclough notes, Hunter's library borrowing leaned heavily towards the miscellaneous readings offered by periodicals:

> his reading was dominated by texts from the imprecise category 'Moral and Miscellaneous'. This contained any prose fiction that could not be included in the 'Novels' section of the catalogue and the majority of monthly periodicals. Of the items borrowed from this category three can be reclassified as fiction, but the majority were current issues of periodicals such as the *European Magazine*. (103)

Without doubt, Joseph Hunter's reading experience was idiosyncratic, and does not permit major conclusions to be drawn about the generality of reading practices, especially when we attempt to transfer his experiences across the Atlantic.

> Hunter's diaries reveal the interaction of the reader with available networks of distribution, and confirm that it was possible for a young middle-class reader to access texts with apparent ease from a number of different institutions, including both subscription and circulating libraries. (Colclough 2010, 104)

Yet Hunter's experience was decidedly urban, if not metropolitan. While Philadelphia, New York and Boston were home to circulating libraries of the kind which Hunter used to gain access to expensive books and the broad range of periodicals he read, more rural sections of Great Britain, as well as most of the United States, would not offer such opportunities.[22] What the example of Joseph Hunter

21 Colclough's limited empirical basis should be emphasized, however, and his conclusion weighed against other options: that sharing the costs reduced them no matter if the subscribers could have afforded the papers separately, while still granting each of them access. In other words, we cannot conclude from the fact that people shared subscriptions that they needed to share them; perhaps it was a matter of convenience more than of necessity.

22 Despite some efforts at publication in the South and West of the country, magazine publication was a metropolitan affair, and even the southern metropolis of Charleston could not long support a monthly. Having started his endeavor in January of 1805, by December 1806, the *Monthly Register*'s Stephen C. Carpenter had removed himself and his magazine to New York. Addressing his readers, Carpenter noted that "his residence in, and his publishing the work in a comparatively remote part of the union, where the mechanical operations requisite to introduce it to the world, must, unavoidably, from the nature of its climate, and the very constitution of its society, be carried on with tardiness and want of vigour, and must labour under all those manifold and various disadvantages, which, are necessarily attendant upon its distance from the centre of the nation" (*MR* 1806 1, 1).

gives ample evidence for, however, is the many possible avenues of obtaining access to periodical writings, and the great interest which the form had for contemporaries. Whether through a shared subscription, through libraries, through family, or through friends, the circle of readers could easily expand far from the individual subscribers listed in periodical subscription lists.

We should be careful, however, not to interpret too much into this socioeconomic variety in the readership. Jared Gardner has suggested that this variety indicated that "periodical editors were at least partially successful getting across their message that magazine reading was a vital form of participatory democracy" (2012, 104). Yet none of the studies I have cited above or those which I have myself undertaken ultimately reveals anything about the motivations for becoming a periodical reader; if the suggestion is, in turn, merely that to read magazines was automatically to participate in a democratic polity, the question becomes how meaningful this kind of democracy ultimately is.

Reading periodicals was a leisure activity that did not amount to proper 'study,' and catered to those among the public who were already gainfully employed. Readers were expected to be busy during the day, and attend to their reading at night: "men engaged in active occupations," as the *American Review* had it, "may gradually acquire a degree of intellectual cultivation and improvement, without any infringement of the time allotted to their customary and necessary concerns" (*AR* 1801, ii). What was customary and necessary—business, in other words—could not be expected to be delayed on account of leisure activities such as periodical reading. Periodicals, however, were a form that at least fit that limited leisure time which people still had, at any level of society. Thus the *Christian Observer* suggested: "[T]he bulk of readers, whether of the higher or lower orders in society, are debarred by their business, their pleasures, or their indolence, from the perusal of large and abstruse disquisitions. A Newspaper, a Magazine, or a Review, is, therefore, exactly the publication suited to their case" (*CO* 1802, 120).

This sentiment was echoed in many publications. Few went as far as Philadelphia's *Evening Fire-Side*, a magazine which carried the expectation of when and where it would be perused by the readership in its very title, but most would agree with its sentiment that "[w]hen the toils of the day have been gone through, and the hours of honest industry spun out, it is pleasing to sit down and contemplate the comforts that result" (*EF* 1804, 1), comforts that no doubt included the time and leisure to finally address oneself to the pleasures of a periodical. None of this, of course, was very surprising: as David and Jeanne Heidler have noted, "[t]he majority of Americans worked six days a week" (2004, 96) and "[l]eisure activities during the early Republic [...] usually took second place to work" (95). Even their only day off work, Sunday, was usually a day reserved for church attendance, but at least offered a chance to grasp some minutes for non-essential pursuits. Joseph Dennie's prospectus for the *Port Folio* noted how desirable its weekly publication date of Saturday must have seemed to those of "retired leisure" whom Dennie addressed. Importantly, 'leisure' attained on a Saturday or

Sunday, which, Dennie notes, "is generally found, or *made* on that day" (*PF* 1801 Prospectus 1, my emphasis), was different from the kind of leisure which went hand-in-hand with "opulence" (*PMM* 1798 2, 7). As Dennie hints, periodical readers were expected to have to make their leisure, that is to say, they had to actively take time off from other possible ways of occupying their time, rather than having the luxury of more time than possible employment. "[T]rue relaxation," as David and Jeanne Heidler have it, "only the very young and the very rich could indulge in" (2004, 95). Leisure needed to be made, and magazines competed with other potential pursuits—social visits, the theater, sports, or going to the tavern—for this short timeframe.[23] "Candidus," Charles Brockden Brown's early and very probably fake correspondent in the *Monthly Magazine*, emphasized this conception of the busy and critical subscriber: "I doubt not but that I shall find amusement in your work. I trust to my own candour, and to the variety, at least, of your collections for that." (*MM* 1799, 1). "I am a plain man, and have little leisure, but some of that leisure, if you behave well, I have no objection to bestow upon you" (*MM* 1799, 2). The periodicals' market was not just that in which they competed for the money of subscribers against each other, but also one in which they were in constant battle for readers' limited amount of spare time. Brevity was therefore frequently stressed as one of the most important characteristics of periodical texts precisely because such texts would not overly tax the reader or impinge too much upon his time. As Elihu Hubbard Smith had it, "[t]o these the man of business can recur, while he waits for an unexpected guest, lingers at an ill-attended appointment, or patiently submits to the operations of his hairdresser. From these, even the self-complacent beau, & the fashionable fair-one, may catch an unexpected ray of knowledge, while they sip their morning coffee, or their evening tea" (in Waterman 2007, 48). (Precisely how one waits for a guest one does not expect we must leave to Smith's imagination.)

Magazine editors were well aware that they catered to a variegated reading public. In contrast to book authors, their direct contact with readers through subscription allowed them insight into who was willing to pay for the writings which they published. But at least implicitly, they also realized that those who paid were unlikely to be the only ones who read their magazines. To admit as much openly might perhaps have been counterproductive, yet there can be little doubt that subscribers gladly passed on and even circulated their magazines, although, by and large, they would ultimately collect them again for later binding. As Elihu Hubbard Smith wrote to Joseph Dennie in March of 1797, the boarding house in which he lived was entertained each week by a single subscription taken by one of the renters, though Smith was willing to take a second subscription for himself (cf. Cronin 1973, 299). Such readership communities at the microlocal level surely existed in different other places. At least implicitly, magazine editors recognized that

23 Heidler and Heidler devote only one paragraph to magazine reading (cf. 113), and do not differentiate between social classes in this particular question, but otherwise offer a serviceable summary of leisure in the Early Republic; cf. 2004, 95-118.

reading a magazine was a different process from reading a monograph, and that the readership also did not entirely overlap. Although some readers, particularly those who possessed the means to subscribe to the periodicals, were assumed to have both the wherewithal and the inclination to read issues from cover to cover, editors also recognized that a large number of potential readers would read selectively.

The opportunity to be read cursorily was a key aspect of the miscellaneous departments that so many of the periodicals of the Early Republic advertised. Precisely because, as the *Philadelphia Monthly Magazine* had it, "[u]nmethodized reading is adapted to the many; regular study is confined to the few" (*PMM* 1798 2, 7), periodicals prepared their contents with a mind to the unmethodized reading of the many. "When a student sits down to a system, he expects the formality and method of the schools, but how frequent would be the yawn, if periodical writings resembled Locke's essay on understanding," asked the *Tablet* in 1795, and answered its own rhetorical question to note that in "works intended for amusement, the essence is sprightliness and variety" (*T* 1795, 1). Not only did the *Tablet*, then, admit its ultimate aim of "amusing" its readers—rather than instructing them—it understood that it was operating within a discourse which clearly proscribed roles to readers and magazines. Readers expected lightness from the *Tablet*, rather than schooling; conversely, the *Tablet* acknowledged, and thus reproduced, this particular idea about periodicals. The ability to select from a broad variety of texts only those which were interesting to the individual reader was central to the form of the periodical, and readers clearly exercised their privilege to do so, as evidence of contemporary reading patterns shows: extant unbound issues of the *Port Folio*, *Portico*, and *Analectic Magazine* indicate the selective reading of subscribers through the number of uncut pages that remain in their editions. The tops of the pages were frequently still folded together when they were delivered, and readers would have to cut the folds open in order to peruse the essays on them. Yet, as the issues show, they sometimes did not do so, and thus could hardly have read the texts.

"In the very nature of Reviews," the *Christian Observer* believed, were "many things adapted to render them popular. They charm by their variety, their brevity, and their aptitude to furnish matter for general conversation" (*CO* 1802, 120). While the *Observer* credited the periodical's nature in general with these characteristics, clearly the task of the individual writer for a periodical (whether he was himself also the editor or merely a contributor, paid or unpaid) was to write in such a fashion as to make the "Review" as a whole produce these 'charms'. As the *Literary Magazine* averred, it was the "duty of periodical essayists" to "diffuse a taste for useful and ornamental learning, in the engaging form of short and popular essays, which may be perused without much effort of intellect, and without encroaching on the engagements of the higher or stated employments of the middle classes of society" (*LM* 1806, 265). It seemed to some magazines that even such minor claims to the diffusion of learning as the *Literary Magazine*'s were off the mark when contrasted with the realities under which magazines labored. A correspondent of David Hogan's *Philadelphia Repository* compared Hogan's paper with the local *Minerva*, and somewhat scathingly suggested that the *Minerva*'s readership, the "leves mentes" (Latin for "feeble minds") did "not read for instruction or profit, but to 'kill time.'" This practice was more than common, suggested the correspondent, so that the practical benefit of submitting to the public material suitable for the killing of time—chiefly such types of stories as would today be called adventure, crime, and horror—was immense. "[T]here-fourths of the community" (*Philadelphia Repository* 1802 2.33, 261), the correspondent estimated, were among this class of readership. In consequence, suggested the *Literary Miscellany*, "[a] work conducted on proper principles, is calculated to do infinite service, among those more especially who are incapable of thinking for themselves, and who by habit acquire the sentiments that perpetually meet their eyes and amuse their vacant hours." (*Literary Miscellany* 1811, 38; the original of this article was published in the London *Juvenile Olio*, in 1795). The *Miscellany* realized that such "proper principles" were going to be hard to come by in any individual magazine, and suggested that it was only by reading a variety of different magazines that periodical readings would ultimately be rendered beneficial—that, in other words, leisure hours could be made to amusing and thereby, but as an afterthought, instructive. This self-conception of magazines differed from some of the conceptions offered by some critics. Michael Warner, for example, has argued that people like Benjamin Rush, interested in the dissemination of literacy, believed the educative potential of newspapers and magazines would yield leisure for its readers (cf. Warner 1991, 131). As becomes clear in the examples cited above, however, the magazines themselves who, unlike Rush, could not be content with potentialities and republican idealism, recognized that their readerships did not yet have extensive leisure time to spend, and that thus the educative potential of the readings they offered depended in large part on being light reading. A proposal for a monthly work of natural historical engravings, published in the *Port Folio*, thus suggested that its target audience, the "juvenile mind," required an agreeable format for its information, and the proposed monthly magazine, "in preference to a dull, monotonous, and frigid regularity of method, adopted the pleasing variety" common to periodical publications (*PF* 1805, 75). Still more to the point was the *Polyanthos*: "Our principle object has been to amuse those, who are not too wise to be amused" (*P* 1806 2, 72). Yet it was not just learning as such which the periodicals resisted, or rather, sought to subsume under the broader hope to amuse their readers. By imagining their readers as at heart a slothful, leisure and pleasure-seeking group, magazines probably were not far from the mark; more importantly, this particular conception of the reader suggested the importance of variety for Early Republic magazines.

Periodicals' diversity of audience certainly did not make the task of editing them easier. Having to cope with a wider range of possible readers, editors realized that they could not possibly hope to reach everyone with the same subject matter. "[T]he learned it will not instruct, and the ignorant it will not amuse" (*MA* 1805, 172) was probably the worst that could be said of any article, but it highlights the possibility that the learned might be instructed without the amusement of the ignorant, and vice versa. Key to even this modest fulfillment of the Horacian dictum of the *utile dulci*, as much as it was possible and desirable, was the editorial insistence on variety. From the beginning of periodical writings in the early eighteenth century, variety was considered one of the cornerstones of a good magazine. In 1712, Joseph Addison suggest in the *Spectator No. 412* that variety was the crucial ingredient of a periodical, "where the mind is every instant called off to something new, and the attention not suffered to dwell too long, and waste itself on any particular object" (278).[24] American magazines took their cue of this, their most famous forebear. American periodicals and periodical readers had shared sentiments on the question of variety. A correspondent to the *Nightingale* told the editor: "I know much address and variety will be necessary, in order to suit the different tastes of the people, who look to you for entertainment [...] The above hints I have ventured to sug-

24 Enlightenment aestheticians, very incidentally, also agreed on the necessity of variety: Francis Hutcheson, the Scottish philosopher, had announced in his study on the ideas of beauty and virtue that beauty depended on "Uniformity amidst Variety" (1746, 17). For Hutcheson, beauty hinged in no small part on the measured combination of regularity with variety, whether in geometry, in architecture, or in music; indeed, he suggested "the pleasant sensation" (29) required it. Hutcheson stressed that while uniformity and variety were both pleasing, both beautiful, they increased each other's beauty: "where the Uniformity of Bodys [sic] is equal, the Beauty is as the Variety; and where the Variety is equal, the Beauty is as the Uniformity" (17; original emphasis). This measured approach to beauty was not shared by everybody: In 1768, William Gilpin, the celebrated theorist of art, referring to the art of prints, suggested that "sameness [...] will always disgust the eye" (7), and praised variety throughout as artistically desirable. The British artist William Hogarth also differed slightly from Hutcheson in his conception of variety as an ingredient of beauty. Hogarth too considered variety an essential aspect of beauty, but suggested that it is was "more pleasing than uniformity, where the same end is answered by both" (22) even as he cautioned that relief could be found "in a certain degree of sameness" when "the eye is glutted with a succession of variety" (16), so that it "becomes a check upon itself when overdone" (43). Neither Hutcheson, nor Gilpin, nor Hogarth found beauty in periodical literature—at least, their treatises did not discuss it; and certainly neither of them intended to offer a philosophy of the periodical. But their conceptions of the value of variety in the arts indicates that Early Republic periodicals recurred to a long philosophical and material history in which variety, usefulness, the sensibility of experienced pleasures, and rational utility combined to form objects worthy of contemplation. "I mean here, and every where indeed, a composed variety; for variety uncomposed, and without design, is confusion and deformity," (17) wrote William Hogarth. If Early Republic magazines did not, either consciously or subconsciously, wish to evoke enlightenment aesthetics, as a background these aesthetics suggest why the Early Republic's periodicals and their readerships were insistent on the value of the prospectus and a well thought out plan. Prospectuses promised to supply Francis Hutcheson's call for "uniformity amidst variety," clearly delineating the materials that would find inclusion in a magazine, lending order and structure to what might otherwise easily be seen as a disjointed collection of miscellaneous writings, a 'farrago,' as the common epithet was. I have already outlined the blunt market considerations for prospectuses above, to which this aesthetic consideration forms a complement, something which rendered acceptable the ultimately market-driven idea of variety for the sake of a more general amusement of a broader readership.

gest for the improvement of a paper, which I verily think promises more useful entertainment, than any before attempted [...]" (*N* 1796, 57-8). Candidus highlighted both the urgent need as well as the possible dangers of variety in his letter to Charles Brockden Brown: "By the variety and multiplicity of your objects, you seem aware that the approbation of a few will not answer your purpose, and, what is much more questionable, you seem to think that the taste of all may be gratified" (*MM* 1799, 1). Candidus was obviously embarrassed by the idea of gratifying everybody's tastes, notwithstanding not just Brown's but indeed most periodicals' sincere hope. The *Lady's Weekly Miscellany*'s editor reified this position by noting that the "object of a literary miscellany should be to collect pieces on different subjects and of different styles, that by variety pleasure may be diversified:"

> [The *Lady's Weekly Miscellany's*] plan is most likely to yield universal gratification; for among the various matter which fills it, some will be found agreeable to every taste—a piece which would be rejected by one, would be read with avidity by another. On Saturday's [sic] we call on our subscribers to suspend for a moment their customary labours and listen to the lessons of the moral sage, to the pathetic narrative of the novelist, and the enchanting numbers of the poet. (*LWM* 1808, 253).

So did the Boston *Polyanthos*, noting in 1806 that it made its selections precisely so that "every one of our patrons might find something to his taste" (1806 2, 72). Nor could editors hope to escape censure from their readership when they failed to offer substantial variety in their magazines, or forgot about the requirement for amusement. As the *Western Gleaner*'s editor had to admit in 1814, his quest to be "essentially useful" has caused him to have "frequently selected subjects which will scarcely afford any pleasurable sensation to the mere lounger." Thus, he finds to his chagrin, it "has been remarked by some that [the *Gleaner*] was deficient both in variety and novelty, the two first requisites of every periodical work" (*WG* 1814 2, 52). The consequence, as he readily admits, is easy to draw: "It will be consequently, in future, one of his first concerns, to write for their satisfaction, and not for his own" (55). That to satisfy the public desire for variety was not an easy task as clear—Charles Caldwell in 1815 complained about the requirement of periodical editorship to "make up a sprightly variety out of articles which present nothing but a dull uniformity" (*PF* 1815 1, 99)—but it was the central task of the periodical editor at large.

Variety was a question of seriality as much as it concerned the individual issue of any magazine. One article could not fill too much of the space of one issue of a magazine, as the frequent practice of splitting an article between two, three, or even more issues of a periodical indicates—but likewise, any long-running series of articles, biography included, tended to be seen as problematical because it failed to offer the variety expected of periodicals (an example of this in the *Port Folio* can be seen in Chapter 2). Likewise, more modestly-sized weeklies recognized that they might not be able to offer the variety that readers sought. Thus the New York *Prospect* commented that the "number and size of the pages will not admit of great variety of matter for each week; this variety must sought for and exhibited in successive numbers" (1803, 8). Whether this was in any sense a real problem or not—the *Port Folio*, for example, managed to diversify its content well even on sixteen pages by printing short articles and anecdotes—it certainly reflected the periodicals' continual concern to provide variety either serially or internally. It was chiefly this which made biography the quintessential genre of American periodicals. Few other texts promised on the one hand a readily available supply, often of novel texts never before printed in the United States, and on the other hand the kind of "sprightly variety" which Charles Caldwell found so difficult to achieve.

Biography in Early Republic Periodicals

Biography in the periodicals of the Early Republic must be seen in connection with the complicated network of editor-publisher-printer relationships, of distribution and advertisement, of readers' expectations and expected readers, of genre considerations and general assumptions about the nature of periodicals. Biography's place in American periodicals of the Early Republic was a strong one. Uncounted and probably uncountable thousands of biographical articles appeared in the Early Republican magazines; few magazines of the period managed without it. By one count, only poetry and book reviews were published in larger numbers than biography (cf. Casper 1999, 22); certainly the share which biography had in the periodical publications of the Early Republic was great enough to be remarked upon by contemporary commentators (cf. *AMU* 1815, 177).

Periodical biography attracted some of America's early literary giants: Charles Brockden Brown, Joseph Dennie, Washington Irving, and James K. Paulding all wrote biographies specifically for publication in Early Republic magazines. Notable men of letters who never quite made it into the upper echelons of literary fame likewise tried their hand at biography, men such as Gulian Verplanck, Charles Caldwell, and one man whose political fame certainly trumped his literary, John Quincy Adams. Besides these men, numerous others wrote pieces of biography anonymously. Their interest in writing periodical biography, an interest which might well have had a large ideological component, was not however the only reason for the success which biography attained in American periodicals—nor was it necessarily the strongest. Biographies were published in Early American magazines not just, perhaps not even mainly, because they had "the power to shape individuals' lives and character and to help define America's national character" (Casper 1999, 2), but because biography was a genre which proved eminently suitable to periodical production at a time when the periodical—not just the newspaper, but also weekly, monthly and quarterly magazines—saw a tremendous rise in popularity.

Nor did this periodical biography necessary remain in periodicals only: the republication of James Fenimore Cooper's series of American naval officers' biographies from *Graham's Magazine* in book form (1846) is just one late example of a publication route which several biographies had earlier gone, indicating the large market for biography which existed in the Early Republic. In the years after 1810, the War of 1812 was the cause of the publication of a large number of war-related biographical compendia drawing much of their material from periodicals, like Benjamin Folsom's compilation of *Biographical Sketches of Distinguished Officers in the American Navy* (1814), Isaac Bailey's *American Naval Biography* (1815), James McBride's *Naval Biography* (1815), and Thomas Wilson's *Biography of the Principal American Military and Naval Heroes* (1819). Conversely, neither did the discussion of biography in periodicals exclude discussion of non-periodical biography and biographical theory. It is this broader conception of biography inside and outside the periodical that must necessarily engage us first.

Writing in the middle of 1815, the *Port Folio*'s correspondent wondered: "We have heard of the golden age, the silver age, the iron age, the age of chivalry, with, God knows, how many more. I don't know whether we may not call this the age of Biography" (*PF* 1815 2, 195). Not only was he not alone in his estimation—two years later, the trend having apparently no abated, the *Port Folio*'s editor John Hall suggested in one of his periodical miscellaneous ramblings in "An Author's Evenings" that there was a "present rage for biography" (*PF* 1817, 29)—but there was considerable cause to consider biography one of the predominant forms of writing of the age. Among the major monograph publications, John Marshall's mammoth five-volume *Life of Washington* (1805-7), which sold on the order of seven thousand copies across the country, had pride of place both for sales and scope, but many other notable books also saw publication. In the final decade of the eighteenth century, Jeremy Belknap had published his *American Biography* (1794-8), a two-volume compendium of notable people connected with the United States (even if distantly: Belknap's first biography was of "Biron," Bjarni Herjolfsson, allegedly the first man to sight the American mainland), and in the first ten years of the nineteenth century, biographical publications included Mason Locke Weems's *The Life of Washington* (1800) and his *Life of General Francis Marion* (1805), the biographical anthologies of John Wilmer's *American Nepos* and William Allen's *American Biographical Dictionary* (1809), and many more local biographies. Biography, whether in the short form of periodicals or in the long form of monographs and anthologies, sold.

Attempts to understand this explosion of biographical production in the Early Republic have been few, and, as the study of periodical biography will show, are perhaps all too ready to accept neat answers that do not tell the whole story. The most seminal work on the topic is Scott Casper's *Constructing American Lives: Biography and Culture in Nineteenth-Century America* (1999). In Casper's analysis, American biography engaged in two "potentially contradictory" practices: biography in the vein of the renowned English biographer and critic Samuel Johnson (1709-1784), and, in his wake, Johnson's own biographer, James Boswell (1740-1795). For Johnson, biography was a matter of obtaining a view of the "essential person" (Altick 1965, 48), and biography's chief virtue the depiction of exemplary lives:

> Those parallel circumstances, and kindred images to which we readily conform our minds, to be found in narratives of the lives of particular persons; and therefore no species of writings seems more worthy of cultivation than biography, since none can be more delightful or more useful, none can more certainly enchain the heart by irresistible interest, or more *widely diffuse instruction to every diversity of condition.* (Johnson 1793, 36; my emphasis)

For Johnsonian biography, it was imperative that the biographer experience his subject first hand, that he obtain negative and positive character traits alike, that he show vice in order to condemn vice. In the case of Boswell's biography of Johnson, this led to a surfeit of biographical detail frequently ridiculed by contemporaries, but the Johnsonian biographical paradigm proved one of the lasting conceptions of the genre well into the Early Republic. Nor did this form of biography necessarily have to be of great men: as Johnson noted, actual proof of character could only be obtained in "the minute details of daily life, where exterior appendages are cast aside, and men excel each other only by prudence and virtue" (38). What this meant in practical terms was that biography's relationship with history, with great men, could be dissolved: all lives could become instructive to the writers of Johnsonian biography.

Against this model of Johnson's, Casper sets one which was "founded on American patriotism and republican ideas of citizenship," and which "appeared in most of the biographies" (31). Casper's suggestion is that while critics favored Johnsonian biography, biographers produced nationalist biographies of great men because in them, they found the images they needed for the furthering of the ulterior goal of American nationalism and republican civil virtue. While it is true that for certain periods and certain biographical productions, a clear interest in the goals Casper sees can be established, the broad variety of periodical biography requires a more balanced view. Casper's suggestion that "[p]articularly in magazines that ran their own series of 'American biographies,' the rhetoric of American assertion was more prominent than the language of Johnson" (40) may or may not be correct (Casper does not, unfortunately, suggest which journals in particular he means); but as will be seen, not only could and did magazines print American biography side by side with British, French, or other lives:. They also were engaged in a marketplace in which the emphasis on American nationalism versus the private character was almost a necessary consequence of public interest. Periodical biography did not just oscillate between Johnson and nationalism, but also between periods were it could be more or less arbitrarily selected and periods where it became in the interest of a magazine to pursue a particular kind of biographical writing.[25] If I have suggested above that a large number of authors contributed their own biographical short texts to magazines,

25 Helpful surveys of biographical theory are Oates (1986), Klein (2002 and 2009), Parke (2002), Fetz and Schweiger (2006), Fetz (2009), Caine (2010), Fetz and Hemecker (2011); American biography in particular is usefully explored in Merrill (1932/1957), O'Neill (1935/1961), Garraty (1957), Greene (1970), Hankins (1975), Kirsch (1982), Harris (1985), Lawson (1998).

the vast majority of these texts were produced around the War of 1812, and nearly all of the American biographies published in magazines were clustered around that time—a time with which I will deal in detail in Chapter 3. Far more biography was stripped from contemporary British magazines, from biographical compendia and the biographical prefaces of collected works, and other sources.

Periodical biography, even in the more elaborate treatment which Casper has offered, is either ignored, or dismissed on the grounds that it is not worthy of closer—literary—attention. To be sure, in their dismissive attitude towards periodical biography, O'Neill, West, and Casper as quoted above to an extent merely echo complaints which contemporaries had about Early Republic biography. FAG, the *Port Folio* critic who had wondered about calling his era the age of biography, was not full of praise for the development: "swarms of new lives, new memoirs, and new histories […] What are they but catalogues of private spleen and folly and scandal?" (*PF* 1815, 196). Biography had become predictable, commonplace, and utterly uninteresting; why not spare authors, those "good, honest, dull fellow[s]" (197) the need for research into the lives of people about whom nothing useful, nothing interesting could be said in reality, FAG asked. His sarcastic solution was a syllabus, a simple guideline by which authors could find "that class of [biography] to which his proposed subject belongs, and he will find his life and opinions ready written to his hand" (197). To some observers, evidently, biography was a genre in which, in the last analysis, the specifics of the subject did not matter in particular.

FAG never got around to providing the "specimen [which] will do better than a page of description" (197). But his description of the situation spoke volumes already: biography, "though […] the most useful and amusing department of literature" (196), had proliferated to such an extent that it was ripe for satire, and deserving of critical dismissiveness. Biography, noted editor Joseph Dennie in an editorial comment for the *Port Folio* in 1809, "has not been very often pursued in this country," and he did not "remember many names, who have distinguished themselves in this delightful department of composition" (*PF* 1809, 21). Dennie's memory, indeed, extended only to John Marshall and Jeremy Belknap. Even these works, to some contemporaries, had certainly not heralded an age of biography. In 1810, William Tudor suggested of Belknap's *American Biography*, which had been sold by subscription at the high rate of 6$ per volume, that it was written "rather for [his] posterity than for [his] contemporaries" (*MA* 1810 2, 156). Marshall's biography came in for similarly harsh criticism: not all reviewers agreed with the *Monthly Anthology*'s belief that that Marshall was "completely justified in interweaving with his biography a history of the American revolution" (*MA* 1808, 260), and preferred to join the Boston-based magazine's conclusion that there was "too little biography" in Marshall's work. If these books were the heralds of the age of biography, perhaps FAG had a little cause for satire.

Studies of biography in America have been studies of American biography: works such as Scott Casper's explicitly speak of American biography, that is to say, American-written lives of Americans, under the assumption that "[w]hen critics talked of 'American biography,' […] they meant […] lives of individuals clearly associated with the history of what had become the United States" (1999, 21). Reviewers often engaged critically with the penchant of writers of biography to provide lives which were only distantly valuable to the republic. Jeremy Belknap's *American Biography* started out with the life of a Norman sailor of almost mythical connection to America; it included the lives of a Welshman and a Venetian, whose connection with the United States was likewise both remote and anecdotal. This fact enraged a reviewer in Charles Brockden Brown's *Monthly Magazine*: why were these men "introduced in so conspicuous a manner into a work of American Biography, when neither of them was ever in America, nor ever distinguished by any remarkable discoveries of achievements connected with this country" (*MM* 1799, 282)? Americans disagreed on what American biography meant, but more importantly, American biography was not the only biography which Americans published and consumed: non-American lives made it into a work like Jeremy Belknap's explicitly entitled *American Biography*, and to an even larger extent, they found their way into the periodicals, where ancient Romans and contemporary English and Frenchmen shared the biographical space with 'genuine' American lives, and indeed were dominant for at least the first decade here under consideration. As Joseph Dennie among other editors discovered, it was a noble goal to provide readers with American biography, but a goal which neither his resources nor the interest of his contributors could readily achieve. FAG's unfulfilled promise of a "specimen" of the kind of biographical text he envisaged is symptomatic of the problems under which American magazines labored. However much they would have wanted to publish the anonymous author's satire, if it was not forthcoming, it could not be put in print. A work like Theodore Greene's *American Heroes: The Changing Models of Success in American Magazines* (1970), still the only scholarly volume on magazine biography, falls short of explaining the role of periodical biography because it does not take into account the vast number of biographies which are not of Americans, not of "heroes," and not written by Americans. Still, these texts found a way into American periodicals, and their presence in them needs explanation.

What this also points to is the need to stress the general differences between the ways in which biography functioned as a commodity in magazines versus the way that monographs and biographical anthologies were produced and sold. Magazine publication occurred in a dense web of interrelations that inevitably had an influence on the form, meaning, and uses of magazine biographies. Biography was always merely one part among many which together constituted a periodical issue. Readers did not expect to be pleased at all times by all of the content of a periodical, and this general rule held true for biography as well. Readers did not buy periodicals or subscribe to them for biography alone, at least by and large. Although periodicals, like books, sold by subscription, a subscriber to Belknap's *American Biography*, Marshall's *Life of Washington*, or Delaplaine's *Repository of the Lives of Distinguished Americans* was actively engaged in obtaining biography, and a very specific kind of biography at that; a subscriber to a magazine had to accept whatever biography his weekly or monthly issue contained.

Biography's inherent popularity may have made it an obvious choice for inclusion in periodical productions anyway, but the wide range of possible subjects, and the ready availability of biographical compendia (not necessarily American) from which to cull them, made it even more useful to periodical producers. In biography, they had a text genre which combined ready variety—as already noted, biographies published in Early Republic periodicals stretched from ancient Roman statesmen to contemporary teenage British actors—with the predictability of being a recurrent genre. In the last analysis, of course, this system of periodical production was largely self-perpetuating. Biographies were considered the epitome of the useful and instructive periodical text because publishers and editors did not tire to emphasize that it was. Biographies were held to be useful and instructive by a discerning readership because they were constantly claimed to be useful and instructive by the editors, and editors and publishers did not tire to re-emphasize biography as useful and instructive because they realized that the readership desired it. Like so much else about periodicals, periodical biography was based on a useful mutual fantasy of instructiveness which was hardly based on the empirical reality of the biographies actually printed.

In the contested periodical market, biography was one of the genres which possessed the greatest importance for magazines. Their quest for variety led most periodicals to publish texts in a great number of different genres, not just the reviews, poems and biographies which formed the most popular triad of texts, but also essays, histories, drama criticism, scientific reports, and a host of others. Within this context, biography was a genre particularly suitable to fulfilling all requirements of periodical texts. Their focus could and did lie on any number of people. There were biographies of lawyers, for lawyers; biographies of clergymen, for the clergy; and numberless biographies considered to be of general interest to a reading public which was expected to find profit and amusement in all of these publications.

Periodicals provided a unique context for biography, a context which created pressures and opportunities that other kinds of publications did not have. In the particular field of periodical production, the "cultural purposes" which Scott Casper has made out for biography (1999, 3), the ways in which the content of biography, the selection of biographees, and the choices which writers made with regard to the biographical theory they wished to employ, tell just part of the story. Yet these purposes cannot fully come to terms with the kind of biography which periodicals provided their readers. "Biography in these early magazines," Theodore Greene claims, "catered to no frivolous purposes. Editors did not proclaim an intention to enliven their pages with 'human interest' accounts of the great or the notorious. Writers did not concern themselves with actresses or celebrated tavern keepers" (38). They most certainly did concern themselves with actresses, with actors, and other less-than-great men and women, even if no actual life of a tavern keeper has been discovered so far. Underlying Greene's misconception is an assumption, probably false, but certainly falling short of complete explanatory validity for periodical biography: that "American editors in this period accentuated the normal nationalistic function of biographies," an "admirable means for stimulating moral impulses as well as inspiring national pride among Americans" (39-40). In fact, periodical publishers and periodical editors saw much less idealistic, much more concrete benefits in publishing biographical short texts in their magazines.

Scott Casper has suggested that "[c]ritics and biographers alike argued that biography's chief virtue was its extraordinary combination of 'instruction and amusement'" (1999, 31). This was certainly true: yet as we have already seen, a closer look at the business of periodicals reveals the conventionality of the claim that biography was instructive and amusing, as well as the relevance of the claim for periodicals as a whole. Biography excelled as a periodical genre not because of its value for instruction and amusement, often foregrounded by writers but hardly an exclusive feature of the genre in the Early Republic. Instead, it was chiefly its capacity for variety, the most important single value which periodical texts could have, made it so useful to American periodicals. It was the *Polyanthos* which drove home the point in 1805, in a biography of Jeremy Belknap. "Biographical sketches, or memoirs of person who have adorned their own characters by their virtues, are useful in every form they are given to the public." The *Polyanthos* then went on to reframe biography for magazines in particular: "They are peculiarly calculated for periodical productions, by affording an agreeable variety, and making a few pages very interesting to those who know the character; and instructive to many who read only pass away a few leisure hours" (*P* 1806 1, 5). The *Polyanthos* thus neatly formulated the reasons for biography's suitability, indeed its exemplariness, for periodical short texts. First and foremost, the *Polyanthos* put biography's capacity for variety. Producers of periodicals sought to strike a "balance between predictability and novelty," as Judith Yaross Lee has correctly pointed out (2005, 198-9), and biography proved to be a genre of immense usefulness in this endeavor. Like very few other types of text, biography promised an easy compromise capable of meeting the interests of the variegated readership of Early Republic periodicals. In the *Portico*'s words, biography was a "agreeable to every taste and fitted to every capacity," capable, "through variety of character," to both merely delight the reader with good, "captivating" stories and to provide the "lessons of experience" that would secure instruction for those who sought it (*PO* 1816 1, 2).

Biography's variety thus did not just extend to the obviously copious amount of different biographees that could be and were chosen by American periodicals for inclusion: these ranged from ancient Greeks and Romans through medieval figures, Renaissance painters, artists and politicians to contemporary soldiers, statesmen, and other figures of greater or lesser prominence. At the same time, biography also encompassed a rather wide array of different styles, lengths, and arguments, from essentially historical surveys of military campaigns in which individual soldiers could be presented through more intimate character studies, from half a page to half an issue (and more, as biographies were often serialized across issues). The benefit of biography, to slightly emendate the *Portico*, was not that each and every piece of biographical writing was agreeable to everybody, and suitable to everyone's capacity, but rather that the aggregate of biographies ultimately ended up being thus agreeable and made to fit. And not the least, as the *Portico* also suggested, biography could lay a reliable claim to the mantle of the instructive by offering the "lessons of experience" to readers while telling captivating, that is to say amusing, stories. As the *Observer* put it, "[b]iography is a study to which every reader is indebted for the amusement of many an hour, and its fascination is so powerful, that Pliny's opinion of History may be applied to it with equal truth: It is always pleasing, write as you will" (*Observer* Prospectus 1806, 3). This sentiment was also shared, in Joseph Dennie's typically flowery style, by the *Port Folio.* Commenting on its resumption of the biography of Captain Edward Preble, it put a similar spin on the topic in 1810:

> The duty, which it imposes upon the biographer, is high and solemn, the delight it yields to the reader is, perhaps, of the very first class of our literary pleasures. We are so enthralled ourselves by this bewitching species of composition, and so thoroughly persuaded by old Experience [footnote: Milton] that biography is not less beautiful in the eyes of others than in our own, that it is determined to devote to her airs and graces a very liberal share of this Journal. [...] What liberal scholar is ignorant of the Biographia Britannica? What philosophical student has not turned over the curious pages of Bayle? What lounger has not been amused by the literary gossiping of Boswell, and what lady who is not entertained by the gay vivacity of Thrale? Dr. Aikin delights us more by his biographies, modeled after the best manner of Addison and Goldsmith, than by any other class of his composition; and what judicious critic is ignorant that Johnson's lives are the most pleasing of all his productions? [...] His canvas may be ill chosen, his colours faint, and his pencil heavy; he picture may be unskillfully disposed, and its light and shade blended with all the awkwardness of a pupil; yet, nevertheless, from the public partiality for such designs, he is confident they will not be viewed with emotions of absolute indifference. (*PF* 1810 2, 528-9).

Here, the belief that biography was a delightful genre was directly projected onto the reader, but more than that: the *Port Folio* clearly spelled out the broad basis of interest which it conceived for biography and the relative importance (just counting the frequency of adjectives) of entertainment over instruction: many more people could be entertained, delighted, amused, and pleased than could be instructed. As importantly, the *Port Folio* agreed with the *Observer*, if in somewhat sharper terms, that biography need not even be well-written to be cheerfully received: in the metaphor of painting, even a mediocre sketch might, just because of the public's well-known interest in the genre, be expected to be a success.

Crucially perhaps in light of the above-voiced complaint that instruction could be a severely dull thing to have to suffer through, biography could be regarded as instruction, as it were, en passant. This quality was frequently remarked upon by contemporaries. The *Theological Magazine*, noting specifically the relevance to itself of religious figures, suggested that "[t]he principal design of publishing memoirs of men, eminent in knowledge and piety, is the benefit of survivors, through the influence of examples" (*TM* 1795, 5), and, in more detail, the *Universal Asylum* claimed even earlier:

> To instruct and amuse are the two grand objects intended by authors. Without novelty, or something to amuse and captivate the attention, the most salutary in-

> struction soon tires. Writings, which combine the useful with the pleasing, are, therefore, the most acceptable, and the most beneficial. It is, perhaps, for this reason, that Biography has been a favourite species of writing in all ages, and in all countries. The life of most men affords something to amuse, and the history of their vices and their virtues, and the consequences of them, will excite us to avoid the one, and to imitate the other. (*UACM* 1790, 268)

Through amusement, then, biography could be hoped to transport instruction by showing the results of actions, without necessarily spelling out in details what the lessons to be learned were. Even this modest conception of the instructional value of biography was not followed if readers' entertainment beckoned. Yet it helped justify, in the larger system of periodical production, the prominence of biography as a genre.

Biography, Scott Casper has argued, "entertained by creating relationships between subject and reader" (1999, 31). That these relationships were often unclear was a realization with which editors specifically sought to cope, indeed realized they had to cope, by suggesting to readers precisely the ways in which particular lives could be useful and entertaining to them. Texts which would not, offhand, seem to fit the categories or concerns which had been previously voiced by editors could thus be retrofitted, as it were, by emphasizing their peculiar value for entertainment and instruction—indeed, I will show that this was the *Port Folio*'s primary mode of justifying the inclusion of biographical short texts during much of its existence. Precisely because few periodicals bothered to conclusively define what they meant by 'virtue,' and precisely because they kept the possible 'lessons of experience' allegedly dwelling in every biographical account vague, biographies could be actively tailored by editorial commentary to fit both the prospectuses' promises of the regular appearance of biography as a genre, as well as its pretensions to amusing and instructing the readership. Even such men and women who were, ultimately, not examples of virtuous behavior could be made into epitomes of how *not* to behave—if the editorials made clear as much. Similarly, biographies that highlighted the importance of the private character of the biographee might be followed by those which emphasized their public deeds (and indeed, as we will see in Chapter 2, they often were), with no regard to biographical theories of any kind. Biography thus had the advantage of being variegated and of being able to be easily made to seem variegated by editorial fiat, making it eminently useful to editors.

The Production of American Magazines in Summary

The production of periodicals in the Early Republic was a complex endeavor, in which the capabilities as well as the sensibilities of a number of actors needed to be weighed as much as basic practical, chiefly economic, considerations. The result was a system in which success and failure were unpredictable and contingent, dependent on vagaries such as the amount of submissions from unpaid contributors, the number of subscribers attracted to any particular venture, those subscribers' readiness to pay their dues on time, and so on. Positioning a new periodical, to come back to Bourdieu's terminology, meant entering an ever more crowded field with often fairly indistinguishable competitors. The prospectuses which were produced as the opening gambits in the struggle for a safe position highlighted the awareness of publishers and editors that they were entering an ever more fully occupied field, but rarely affirmed that that this must of needs result in a commercial struggle. To win a safe position, in the sense of a continued existence, in this commercial struggle was impossible, or at least extremely difficult, from a position of autonomy vis-à-vis the controlling forces of the periodical market. Recognizing the heteronomy which determined the success of a periodical, periodicals couched their position in terms that suggested a much stronger ideological, that is to say, more autonomous, basis for their content than they ultimately really possessed. In other words: neither periodical authors, nor the periodicals themselves, could hope to produce, as it were, 'periodicals for periodicals' sake,' or even 'periodicals for the sake of readers' instruction,' with any hope of long-term survival. Rather, they needed to submit to the periodical market, a market which honored the description of virtuous aims through such ubiquitous but empty signifiers as 'instruction and amusement' even as it ultimately demanded that the periodicals produce for the most part the kind of amusing variety that could attract a significant enough subscribership to make them financially viable. As we shall see in the following chapter, it was quite possible to cope with some of the difficulties which would, almost certainly, be encountered by any particular periodical venture. From the beginning, the *Port Folio*'s business side, for example, expected significant financial outlays—1000$ per annum—just to occur, without the money paying for anything in particular. In this, the *Port Folio* established a margin of safety precisely for defaulting subscribers, rises in print and paper costs, increased postage rates, and other contingencies in a periodical's life. It is hard to say whether this caution paid off in particular, but the *Port Folio* survived for two decades, indicating that not everything it did financially was quite a disaster.

2 The *Port Folio*, the Market, and Periodical Biography

> The truth is, he has been so long accustomed to use his pen at intervals when the fit of bright inspiration was on him, that he groans beneath the necessity of the kind of clerkship he now endures, and finds his muse not as easily confined eight hours a day to the desk, as he is himself.
>
> Gertrude Meredith to William Meredith, June 8, 1809[1]

Two Days in the Life of Joseph Dennie, Esq.

It never was too early in the morning when Joseph Dennie, editor of the Philadelphia magazine *Port Folio*, arrived at his editorial office, given his penchant for staying up late and carousing with friends. But work called—unless it was summer and Dennie fled the unhealthy streets of Philadelphia for more temperate, less feverish climes—and it required his attention. The *Port Folio*'s editorial office was in a bookstore, well stocked already with materials from which Dennie could select such texts as would fit into his magazine, liberally cutting them out and pasting them into his own magazine. Of course, Dennie himself possessed books, not a few of them biographical compendia. Yet being housed in a bookstore—and ever since he had partnered with Asbury Dickins, the *Port Folio* had never been published out of anything but a bookstore—permitted Dennie a far broader selection of material than he would have otherwise have easy access to, and a central working place where all the materials could reach him—such newspapers, five of which he received daily, and which he searched for material every day. Every month or so, as the incoming ships delivered them, he would scour the British periodicals for articles that he deemed useful for inclusion in the *Port Folio*, assiduously clipping articles from them. Dozens of such magazines, some already stocked by his publisher, a local bookseller, some sent to him by virtue of his friendly connections, were available to him. From London alone came 46 different newspapers and magazines (cf. *PF* 1805, 118)—not all of which Dennie read, as he would freely admit when asked, but all of which were potentially available to him, vast treasure-troves of selectable material. When he turned up something of interest in either

1 Historical Society of Pennsylvania, Meredith Family Papers 1509, Box 99.

these magazines or newspapers, or in the books which he read privately, he would make a note of it, or, if the occasion was right, immediately place a text in the *Port Folio*; magazine articles usually found early insertion, as the editor was careful of preserving the novelty of the texts he published (at least he attempted to be), but other texts went in a file for later reference. This file also included the backlog of voluntary contributions which the editor received: not all of them, to be sure, but those he deemed fundamentally worthy of inclusion in the *Port Folio*. Not all of those texts would necessarily have been something Dennie himself found interesting, and conversely, the most vitriolic texts hounding the Jefferson administration were, as Dennie recognized, a bit strong even for the *Port Folio*. Material, anyway, there was always enough.

Dennie settled at the desk. Here lay scrap paper and scissors, stood paste and ink pot. From the pocket of his coat he drew a sheet of paper, on which he had written out a passage from the *Life of Edmund Burke* which he had been reading, and stuck it into the file for later use. Then, he began arranging the content for the new issue of the magazine. Few would accuse him of being overly methodological in this. Some of the prospective content was immediately obvious: there was a biography which had not fully fit the previous issue, and which needed to be continued, and Dennie had already prepared a note to Readers and Correspondents which reminded them that payment for the next year should be speedily arranged. But much of everything else was still open. Of course Dennie had guidelines: his prospectus gave suggestions for content, his previous issues gave hints at things to avoid for the sake of variety. John E. Hall had written him an essay for the "American Lounger" series, delayed for some time, which nicely helped out here, even though its topic was somewhat obscure—but this was the "Lounger's" role: the various indulgences of contributors could find their common denominator under the broad "Lounger" rubric. The deficits of any particular piece (unless they were grave) did not matter: such things could be rectified editorially. Dennie hastily wrote an introduction proclaiming the precise ways in which this text was instructive and amusing, not that he believed that Hall had really written a good essay here. His files held a large poetry selection to draw one, which Dennie did, taking more care to fill pages than to make the selection neat. A review filled more space, and Dennie felt the subject worthwhile of editorial commentary praising both the judiciousness of the reviewer as well as the reviewed volume itself—a volume whose publisher upon occasion saw fit to advertise in the *Port Folio*. But still there was some space to fill. Back to scissors and paste-pot: the section "Variety" required attention, and Dennie scrambled through the file of short humorous anecdotes, four of five lines each, until he had found a half-dozen or so that made a neat selection, but more importantly, neatly filled out the paper. By now, it was getting late in the day, and Dennie passed on the sheet, on which his own handwriting mingled with cut-and-pasted printing from half a dozen magazines, to the printer's journeymen. Typesetting was quickly done; but there was some place to fill yet, if very little time, so Dennie went to compose directly at the press. To his trained editorial eye, a longish editorial note suddenly appeared to be necessary for the biographical text: "We take this opportunity of resuming our life of Mr. X," the note read, "to reaffirm our belief in the utility of biography. Nothing is more likely to amuse and instruct the reader..."

At this time, Dennie was still unquestioned as the final editorial instance of the *Port Folio*: nobody controlled him but his audience, his prospectus, his awareness of what the *Port Folio* could publish and what it had better not. Yet by late 1811, the daily efforts at the *Port Folio*, or for that matter the *Analectic Magazine*, would have looked much different. Now, letters went back and forth between publisher and editor, discussing possible engravings and articles, suggesting contributors; these contributors were addressed directly, commissioned to write articles, and paid for their services; and the growing readiness to publically present periodicals as commodities had sown the seeds for publisher's hopes to actually sell by issue, rather than subscription, the increasingly popular magazines they printed. Now, four men were sitting around the table at the back of the bookstore of Samuel Bradford: Joseph Dennie, still haggard-looking from his long illness, still editor, but with reduced authority; Nicholas Biddle and Paul Allen, the editorial assistants on whom so much work had devolved these past months; and Samuel Bradford himself, the publisher. It was a Monday morning in mid-December, and the men had met to discuss the upcoming issue of the *Port Folio*, and to discuss future concerns of the magazine. Of primary importance, Dennie, Biddle, Allen, and Bradford agreed, was the reassurance of the readership that Dennie was again back on board. Dennie's months of absence in the country had not gone unnoticed by the readership, and Bradford was adamant: however glad he was that Dennie was back, the readership needed to be reinsured that the *Port Folio* was preparing for the next season of Dennie's absence, which all present realized was sure to come. Dennie proposed a long statement to the public, openly declaring his sickness during the previous year and Allen's help, and also that Biddle was on board (Biddle suggested to leave out his name, and Dennie acceeded). That was not enough for Bradford. He needed Dennie to do more: assure readers that he was back as full time editor, but also that he would do again an even better job than Allen and Biddle, or else why should Bradford go to the lengths of bringing him back and paying him 1000$ a year. In no uncertain terms, Bradford made sure Dennie understood that his name must pay for itself. Tell people everything is fine, and bound to get even better, Bradford demanded: this was the way in which the *Port Folio* could prosper through 1812. Tell people that John Inskeep, Bradford's mostly silent partner, was in London, ready to supply the *Port Folio* with the latest literary news—tell people!

And Bradford set another agenda: the *Port Folio* would henceforward pay for submissions. The group of people, drafted from the Tuesday Club and other circles of friends, which Bradford had motivated in 1809 and 1810 to supply the magazine with texts had fallen apart, and it was time to make sure people knew. Bradford told Dennie to draft a note for the Readers and Correspondents section to the effect. What should the *Port Folio* be ready to pay for? Dennie spoke up: no riddles, no poems about dead girls. Laughingly, the other men agreed, realizing that Dennie would offer no real resistance to the plan of paying for publications. The *Port Folio*'s January edition would be put out in the most collegial fashion possible, and then, perhaps, 1812 would be another profitable year for the magazine's proprietors.

Joseph Dennie and the Editorship of the *Port Folio*

The two evidently fantastical days in the life of Joseph Dennie I have just presented are, of course, conjectural, yet they exhibit the relative dependencies of the early period of the *Port Folio*, and the period around the War of 1812. I offer it so we can more clearly imagine the ways in which periodicals were produced, through an account of how an editorial day in the office of the *Port Folio* might have looked, or rather, since the actual process would have exceeded the length of a day, what we may imagine the process of creating an issue of that work might have been like if contracted to the course of one, now metaphorical, day. Such a fantasy, which we might call metafactual, must necessarily be based on inference and deduction—and, to some minds, may seem somewhat fanciful. Yet it seems to me beneficial to reiterate by this means a possible way of conceiving of the editorial role as narrowly circumscribed by the contingencies of periodical production. While the details of this fantasy are invented, they conform with what we know about the editor's role.

Its early reliance on irregular submissions, chance finds in other magazines, and the editor's ability to cobble together an acceptable paper week after week left much to the hazards of fortune, and in the particular case of the *Port Folio*, to Joseph Dennie's often dilatory work ethic. By 1811, the professional supervision offered by Samuel Bradford had managed to smoothen greatly the process by which the *Port Folio* was created. While we cannot imagine the staff meeting I have outlined above as a regular occurrence (if only because we have evidence for only one such meeting, and that occurring without Dennie present), it is a significant turn from the haphazard editorial procedures which underlay the *Port Folio* in its earlier years, and speaks towards the diminished role which the editor assumed in the complex of relations that finally produced each individual issue of the magazine. In the intervening years, the editor's position at the *Port Folio* had diminished, not as a consequence of the personal sunset of Joseph Dennie, as William Dowling has suggested, but rather as a consequence of the increasing market-orientation of the periodical field as a whole, and of the process of professionalization. This is the story that I will unfold in this chapter.

The *Port Folio* was, by far, the most critically successful of Early Republic magazines. For twenty-six years the periodical appeared in Philadelphia, first as a weekly, then, from 1809 to 1820, as a monthly publication. It was a quarterly journal in 1820 and 1821, and ended its career as a monthly again. The man who edited it for the most successful part of its life—the magazine appeared from 1801 until

1827[2]—became himself famous as the 'American Addison,' the best-known literary editor of his time: Joseph Dennie. In this chapter, I will offer an evaluation of the respective roles of Dennie as editor, and the various men with whom he divided the task of putting out a weekly, and later monthly, magazine: his printers and publishers, some of whom left extensive correspondence with Dennie (though most of them did not). What I will attempt to highlight in the following chapter is the strictures under which Dennie, despite high hopes, labored during the dozen years he lived in Philadelphia: his struggles with the availability of material, with subscribers, his printers and publishers, his contributors, and, not least, himself. Dennie stands front center in this narrative, but this chapter will seek to place him firmly in an ensemble cast.

By putting Dennie's editorial work in the larger context of periodical production, and ways in which changes in this larger context shaped the nature of the magazine, it is possible to identify the movement towards a greater openness about the financial aims of the magazine, especially after 1809. At the same time, it becomes possible to identify the centrality which economic considerations played at each step of the *Port Folio*'s existence. Dennie's role in the *Port Folio* was, without a doubt, crucial; but at the same time, this chapter will offer a necessary corrective to a prevailing view of the *Port Folio*'s editor as the decisive, indeed perhaps the only, actor in the shaping of the magazine. Dennie's role as the spokesperson, the front man, and the chief voice of the *Port Folio*, his position allowing him direct access to the reader, the opportunity for voicing his thoughts directly on the page, and consequently, the preservation and availability of this material to scholars, has made him the object of much research into the *Port Folio*. His position as editor was prominent, and has caused Dennie to remain prominent for scholars today. This chapter corrects that view: Dennie's, or rather, his editorial persona Oliver Oldschool's prominence should not obscure the other factors which influenced the form, style, and content, as well as the success, of the *Port Folio*. I, too, am using Dennie's name for the most part in the discussion of editorial pronouncements below, but I would like to offer a caution here to reflect my suggestion that public pronouncements by the editor and his motivations as revealed by his private correspondence and the actual workings of the magazines he edited need to be understood as functions of the split between the actual person of Joseph Dennie and the editorial persona he offered. Joseph Dennie needed to eat, to drink, fell sick, and had to cope with the demands of his publishers and other extrinsic problems. Oliver Oldschool did not eat: he could project precisely that façade which best mirrored what the editor conceived of as the most attractive version of himself to the audience, with all the shifts that this version ultimately needed to go through as the audience's interests and composition changed. If I write "Dennie wrote" below, therefore, readers should be aware that while Dennie wrote, readers read Oliver Oldschool.

Biography functioned as a central genre in the *Port Folio*, and the analysis of the magazine's use of it, its choice of sources and its hopes and desires for the genre

2 Possibly 1828; cf. Queenan 1955, 91.

as voiced in editorial commentary and as implied by its selection of biographies, as well as the ways in which editorial efforts were spent to justify the inclusion of biography, suggests interpretations more generally about the ways in which periodicals worked in the 1800s. Biography's prominence throughout the years, and the comparative ease with which it is possible to trace sources, the amount of editorial commentary it engendered, and the serious shifts in content which it experienced make it an exemplary genre in the *Port Folio*; but, as this chapter will also argue, for the largest part of the eleven years of *Port Folio* history which this chapter will mainly cover (1801-1811), it was not a genre that lends itself to the forms of literary interpretation that seek to elucidate greater ideological ideas behind periodical texts. This is one of the reasons, I argue, why it is exemplary, and why it allows us to see more clearly the ways in which periodicals worked with texts. Selected from a broad range of sources, with little attention to political and ideological meanings except for what retroactively could be applied to them, the vast majority of the biographies, and indeed, of all texts in the *Port Folio*, were material without a message beyond the hope of finding a receptive audience by providing them with light, often frivolous, entertainment. Rather than discussing biographies as artistic texts, this chapter will discuss biographies in the *Port Folio* as functional texts: texts which did not in the last analysis form the core of a message, or participated in a greater ideological quest, but rather texts which allowed the *Port Folio*'s editor to fulfill the requirements which had filled the various prospectuses which the magazine offered during its lifetime. Even this indicates the close interlinks between the various persons involved in the periodical: the *Port Folio*'s prospectus, although, as far as we can tell, always written by Joseph Dennie, was the brainchild of many, publisher, editor, and indeed in 1801 even the printer. I argue that we can deduce much about the professionalization processes which the *Port Folio* underwent by looking at the changes in relationship between these figures over the course of its history. The first prospectus was very much a communal effort. This in itself must be noted, as it indicates that Joseph Dennie, often loudly proclaiming publically his editorial independence, had bound himself to a proposed structure and to contents which he had not the ultimate control over. But more importantly, by 1809, the writing of the new series' prospectus was decidedly less collegial, and in 1812, it became clear that the publishers were calling the shots on the kinds of texts to be produced for the *Port Folio*. Such subtle shifts in the power structures of the magazine, I suggest, are indicative of the growing professionalization of the periodical trade, and the *Port Folio* offers a fascinating case study of the process.

The *Port Folio*'s history did not end with Dennie's death in 1812. Under the editorships of Nicholas Biddle, Charles Caldwell, and John E. Hall—whose brother Harrison was also the final owner of the magazine—the *Port Folio* continued to be published. The *Port Folio*'s history after 1816, when the Halls took over, requires an acknowledgment again that professionalization as I conceive it is not a teleological process. Some of the steps towards a professionalization of its production were reversed under the Halls: their close familial ties were un-

FIG. 2 Joseph Dennie, pastel on paper, a portrait by James Sharples, ca. 1790. This is the only known portrait of Joseph Dennie. There exists besides a silhouette taken at a later date.

like the business-only relationship between Dennie and Bradford & Inskeep, and the proliferation of materials that were composed by John Hall was a departure from the external submissions which filled the *Port Folio* earlier, for example. Between the death of Joseph Dennie and the purchase of the *Port Folio* property by Harrison Hall lay, however, one of the most interesting periods of the magazine's history, the editorships of Nicholas Biddle and Charles Caldwell, and the War of 1812. Here, even as we still do well to emphasize the heteronomity of periodical writing, biography suddenly, and unexpectedly, surged as a genre capable of absorbing artistic, literary writing, and thus to highlight the possible extent of authorial autonomy in Early Republic periodicals.

Just as we must trace the fortunes of the magazine under different editors and ownerships, we can understand much about the uses of biography in the *Port Folio* by looking at one of Dennie's earlier editorships in some detail, because it reveals continuities that allow us to identify at least some of the principles underlying the production of magazines in the Early Republic, if, as Dennie himself suggest, "in a minor form." I thus, perhaps slightly counter-intuitively, will start the chapter on the *Port Folio* with a glance at a different magazine: The *Farmer's Weekly Museum*,[3] a village paper of little repute published in the backwoods of New Hampshire.

3 The *Farmer's Weekly Museum* operated under a number of names from 1793 until Dennie's departure in 1799: *The New Hampshire and Vermont Journal: Or, The Farmer's Weekly Museum* (1794-1797), *The Farmer's Weekly Museum: Newhampshire and Vermont Journal* (1797-1799), and *Farmer's Museum, of Lay Preacher's Gazette* (1799-1800); for the final decade it is simply the *Farmer's Museum*. The name changes did not, however, affect the numbering of the journal, and for reasons of simplicity, I have chosen to quote all variants of the journal as "*FWM*" for *Farmer's Weekly Museum*.

Prologue: The *Farmer's Weekly Museum* of Walpole, N.H.

The young man who, sometime in April 1796, took over direction of the two-year-old Walpole weekly, the *New Hampshire and Vermont Journal: Or, the Farmer's Weekly Museum*, published by the local printer David Carlisle in a joint venture with the noted Boston publisher Isaiah Thomas,[4] could not have been the most obviously auspicious choice. Joseph Dennie, a Harvard-educated lawyer, had been the co-editor and chief contributor to a Boston magazine, the *Tablet*, in 1795. His chief claim to fame were his *Farrago* essays, which had first appeared in a Vermont newspaper and then migrated to the New Hampshire-based *Eagle*, and the productions of the "Shop of Colon and Spondee," poems and light prose which he composed with Royall Tyler (cf. Ellis 1971, 43-80; Christadler 1968, 206). An indifferent lawyer, Joseph Dennie's interest clearly lay in literary production, from which he sought to obtain money and repute. "[F]ame and fortune," Dennie wrote to his mother in April, 1797, had been his "expectation" when he said down to write for the *Tablet*, but its life was cut excruciatingly short: it lasted a mere thirteen issues (Ellis 1971, 83). From Boston, Dennie moved to Walpole, where Roger Vose, a friend of Dennie's from Harvard days, lived and practiced law. Dennie, too, planned to open his own practice at Walpole. But more than in his law practice, Dennie was interested in the *New Hampshire Journal*, and which he figured would be an opportunity to wield his pen once more, fully realizing, or at least strongly suspecting, the value which his productions would bring to the rural paper. From the start of his meteoric rise to the prominence of being America's foremost magazine editor, then, Dennie recognized that there existed a symbiotic relationship between writers and those who published their works: Dennie, the writer, who wanted to live off his writing, could only do so if his publications would yield additional sales—or subscribers—to his publishers. As he wrote his mother in a letter summarizing his experiences since the demise of the *Tablet*, he "determined, by the agency of my pen, to convince [Carlisle] that I could be useful [...] I was sure he would encourage me when his own *interest* was the prompter" (Dennie's emphasis). Dennie's initial plan was to "be useful, by exhibiting truths in a plain dress to the common people" (in Pedder 1936, 158), by contributing essays to the paper, rather than to run it as editor. On October 12, 1795, the *New Hampshire Journal* carried its first contribution by Dennie, an essay by the "Lay Preacher," which was to become his most successful authorial persona and would form a large part of the later success of his work at the Walpole paper.

Not too long after Dennie's arrival in Walpole, on April 5, 1796, the *New Hampshire Journal* announced changes in its ownership structure. Isaiah Thomas left the part-

4 In fact, David Carlisle had been an apprentice of Thomas's in Worcester and was a Walpole local sent to his hometown specifically to open a branch of the Thomas business there; the *Museum* was part of that venture. Clifford Shipton's short note on Dennie's service for the *Museum* is otherwise unserviceable and wrong (cf. Shipton 1948, 61).

nership he had established with David Carlisle, leaving the journal entirely in the hands of the Walpole printer. At that point, Dennie had been a contributor to the magazine for half a year, but precisely what role he played in the paper is still unclear. Ellis's suggestion, based on Dennie's own epistolary claims, that he had become the "conductor," whatever that might mean in detail, as soon as he had arrived in Walpole, is difficult to verify independently (cf. Ellis 1971, 86), but circumstantial evidence points to Dennie's assumption of the role as editor in both name and practice by early April, 1796. In his message announcing Isaiah Thomas's departure from the venture, Carlisle mentioned both the journal's "editor" and its "publisher," without clearly distinguishing between the two, and without truly indicating if he still assumed both roles. Around this time, however, as Dennie wrote to his mother another four months later, "my Printer made me pecuniary proposals which I accepted" (Ellis 1971, 86), including the annual payment of 110£ (about 470$[5]), payable every first of April. Between Thomas's departure from the venture and Carlisle's opportunity to hire an editor who, if not successfully, had previously managed a paper and had contributed significant material to the magazine already, this early April 1796 date seems the most likely point for Dennie to have started editing Carlisle's magazine in earnest.[6] Carlisle's paper remained political—the publisher

5 Cf. Officer, Lawrence H. "Exchange Rate Between the United States Dollar and the British Pound, 1791-2004." *Economic History Services*. URL: http://www.eh.net/hmit/exchangerates/pound.php. Accessed April 18, 2011. In 1796, the currency system of the United States still included a variety of state currencies (some denominated in pound, others in dollars), a national currency, and the use of various foreign coins, especially Spanish dollars. The exchange rate here offered is for British pounds, although the possibility that New Hampshire pounds were used exists (supposed to have been phased out in 1792, but no doubt still in circulation, respectively still used by entrepreneurs accustomed to them, in 1797). Conversion rates for the New Hampshire pound were about 3,30$ per pound. However, it bears pointing out that the conversion rates fluctuated widely. For example, Donald R. Hickey, concerned with the War of 1812, has noted that the average conversion rate between the British pound and the U.S. dollar during the war years was $3,87 per pound, while for the years 1793-1815, it was $4,37 (2006, xxix). Thus, in 1797, Dennie would have earned 489$ at the average yearly exchange rate; at its lowest during Dennie's employment with the *Museum*, he would have made 450$. As a comparison, a journeyman printer working for Isaiah Thomas in Boston made 100£ in 1792, not as an annual salary but in consequence of work done, being paid by the token (cf. Shipton 1948, 65).

6 Whenever Dennie actively assumed the editorship of the magazine, by mid-April 1796, his voice is unmistakable: in a short note entitled "Acknowledgment to Correspondents," Dennie's gratefulness to "Simon Spunkey" (Thomas Green Fessenden; cf. Clapp 1880, 28) for his Hudibrastic verse precedes the acerbic commentary devolving on three correspondents who did not make Dennie's editorial cut: "The fair authoress, ignorant of orthography, guessing at grammer [sic] and a stranger, even to the names of the muses, we advise to suspend her poetical studies, to exercise the broom, instead of the pen, and to make puddings rather than verses" (*FWM* 1796, 4.159, 3). From this rubric would evolve Dennie's "To Readers and Correspondents," a feature which he would continue throughout his tenure as editor of the *Museum*, and take with him into the *Port Folio* later.

felt himself obliged "to avow the firmness of his federalism" (*FWM* 1796, 4.157, 1)—but now projected a radically different image of itself to the reading public. It had set out three years earlier with a primary focus on information, and information, at that, well suitable to the rural audience Thomas and Carlisle envisaged in New Hampshire, in an area "remote from the seat of government" and devoid of a printing office. "[U]seful discoveries and improvements in agriculture" lead the initial list of things which the then-*New Hampshire Journal* would supply. As the initial address to the public also made clear, however, it was Isaiah Thomas who supplied "extensive correspondence, in the line of publick information," as he "has long been established in business in a neighbouring State" (*FWM* 1793, 1.1, 1). Thomas's departure opened a hole in this arrangement, because Carlisle, a former apprentice of Thomas's, did not have his master's connections. Dennie, young, energetic, and connected beyond Walpole through his studies at Harvard and residence in Boston, and prepared to expend much energy to make more literary acquaintances throughout the United States, must have been considered a more than suitable replacement in this regard.

Joseph Dennie's Conception of the Editor

Changes to the paper, whether solely related to Dennie's editorial choices or the interaction between publisher and editor, started at once upon Dennie's arrival in the editor's chair. The first edition under the new management, published on April 5, 1797, already highlighted changes in the offing: for three years, the headnote had quoted Benjamin Franklin's "Where liberty is, there is my country—Franklin" and separately, if without great creativity, proclaimed "The Liberty of the Press is essential to the Rights of Man." Now, it changed to the rather lighter if badly near-rhymed "Ho, every one, that thirsteth for novelty-come" (*FWM* 1796, 4.156, 4.157). If, as David Jaffee has suggested, recurring to Benedict Anderson's concept of the imagined community, the Franklin quote "indicated how the newspapers achieved a community or readers" in which "[v]illagers could imagine a new nation" (1999, 226), the new motto spelled a difference in the conception of the paper after Dennie's ascension to the editorship. The Franklin quote had highlighted, almost in the form of self-justification, the ways in which newspaper publishing stood for the exercise of fundamental rights, but at the same time, it had implicitly defined the role of the reader, and even more so the subscriber who paid for the papers: by giving his money for the paper, he reaffirmed the unalienable rights of Americans, and by extension, aided the cause of American liberty.

Publishing under this motto became a form of mutual reinforcement, in which the publisher's provision of useful and entertaining material to the reading public was not a central determinant for the value of the product, because that product had an inherent value in promoting American liberty, merely by existing. The motto which Carlisle and Thomas had chosen for the *Museum* displayed an interest, perhaps, in what Michael Warner has suggested was "a market strategy [which] articulates a republican reading of general public discourse, rather than a leisurely consumption of luxury goods" (1991, 125). It is especially in contrast to Warner's argument that the new motto becomes significant. It highlighted not only the new relationship between editor and subscriber which Dennie's editorial announcements would later also stress. Its cheerful lightness already promised change: the hailing "ho" indicated that the new version of the *Museum* would be reaching out to its subscribers, and the rest of the motto followed suit. The 'thirst for novelty' that the motto promised to quench in its readers was both a recognition of publishing realities as well as a marked shift in outlook. No longer was there the sense of a mutual service to the republican nation in which readers and publisher shared; rather, the motto made clear that it was the service to the reader that would take center stage from now on. What Warner calls the "diffusion" of "the kind of nationalism appropriate to print, and the kind of print appropriate to the nation" (1991, 123), precisely that form of republican idealism which held that the dissemination of knowledge was the foremost guard against tyranny, took a backseat. The 'thirst for novelty' was recognized—or at least hypothesized—as the driving force which impelled prospective readers to become active subscribers to the paper. At the same time, it is clear that this also bound Dennie and Carlisle to provide novelty, something of a departure from Dennie's epistolary claim that in his service in Walpole he wanted chiefly to be "useful," and the final lines of the editorial comment made clear that Dennie's job would be more to provide things that "will amuse the imagination" than otherwise: the "short Sermons of the Lay Preacher, the fantastick Farrago, and small parcels of the fancy goods of Mess. Colon and Spondee" were prominently advertised (*FWM* 1796, 4.157, 1). In this short note, Dennie succinctly summarized the periodical's mission: brevity fit for the casual reader and the fantastically entertaining flights of literary fancy that would delight him.[7]

7 It is worth pointing out in this connection that when the *Museum* went on a still different plan in April 1797 and changed its name from *The New Hampshire and Vermont Journal: Or, the Farmer's Weekly Museum* to *The Farmer's Weekly Museum: Newhampshire and Vermont Journal*, this too was more than a mere innocent change of name. It reflected the relative importance of the new national aspirations and the title's affirmation of the paper's rural origins. This became even clearer in early 1799, when the *Museum* lost all geographical reference and instead adopted the alternative title of *Lay Preacher's Gazette*. Dennie fabulously successful Lay Preacher essays were promissory of the universal value of the magazine, but also of its growing emphasis on the fine arts. The change of view coincided, again, with a change of motto in April 1797—now, the *Museum*'s head note was a quote from John Bunyan's author's apology prefacing *The Pilgrim's Progress*: "would'st though remember / From New Year's Day to the Last of December? / Then read." Bunyan's verse in the original went on to celebrate the innocuous pleasure that his book would yield readers: "Would'st thou divert thyself from Melancholy? / Would'st though be pleasant, yet be far from folly? / Would'st though read Riddles, and their Explanation? / Or else be drowned in thy contemplation? […] Would'st though lose thyself, and catch no harm, / And find thyself again without a charm?" In his apology, Bunyan stressed the interaction between harmless entertainment and not so much the positive benefits but the avoidance of negative

The changes effected in April 1796 worked to increase the circulation of the *Farmer's Weekly Museum* beyond its rural surroundings: As early as October 1796, the *Museum* could be read, in excerpts, as far south as North Carolina, where Hodge's *North-Carolina Almanack* republished its "useful and amusing Articles," including several "Lay Preachers" and the sketch of Thomas Topham (discussed in more detail below; cf. *North Carolina Journal* 223, October 24, 1796, [4]). In addition, Carlisle had from the start promised his readers that he was "making arrangements to establish an extensive correspondence with Political and Literary characters, in various parts of the United States" (*FWM* 1796, 4.157, 1), and indeed Carlisle's new editor Dennie was very active in courting submissions from friends in Boston, New York, and elsewhere.

An example from early 1797 is especially interesting for what it reveals about the interactions between editors. Sometime in February, Dennie solicited Elihu Hubbard Smith's support for the *Museum*. Smith, a New York physician and intellectual and a member of the Friendly Club, in which he met and adopted as protégés such future and current literary luminaries as Charles Brockden Brown and William Dunlap, was also well known as an author of some talent; and it must have been chiefly on the strength of his fame as a writer that Dennie contacted him through Jeremiah Mason. Even so, his initial missive to Smith did not apparently mention a desire for contributions from his part, or else Smith ignored the request—probably the former, as Smith wrote Dennie on March 5 that "I shall shew your Proposal's [sic] & Address to such persons as may be likely to subscribe;

consequences. The *Museum*'s excerpt, with its emphasis on memory, seems virtually unintelligible in this regard, but played off of reader's knowledge on how to place the quote, and to understand its allusions to the more descriptive and clear later parts of the apology. *Pilgrim's Progress* had been a staple of reading in American at least since 1681 (cf. Amory 2000, 104), and the *Museum* of course aided its readers considerably in identifying the source of the quotation. The final shift of motto under Dennie's editorship came in April 1799, when the *Museum* faked an Oliver Goldsmith quote: "Hither, each week, the peasant shall repair / To sweet oblivion of its daily care; / Again the farmer's news, the barber's tale / Again the woodman's ballad shall prevail." Compare this to the original, from Goldsmith's *The Deserted Village* (1770): "Thither no more the peasant shall repair / To sweet oblivion of his daily care / No more the farmer's news, the barber's tale /No more the woodman's ballad shall prevail;" (cf. Goldsmith 1770, 14). Where Goldsmith lamented the loss of village life in England, the *Museum* crafted its own encomium, suggesting not only that the well-known English poet had, in some way, shape, or form, endorsed periodical productions; it also again highlighted the very mundane emphasis which underlay the conception of the *Museum*'s contents: news, tales, ballads, all encouraging the weekly reader's immersion for the "oblivion" of his everyday business. If it now may have seemed to emphasize again republican ideals by emphasizing the wide distribution among the working classes, this should be regarded as an artifact of the Goldsmith poem which it was playing off of, rather than a political or ideological statement; as, indeed, we should probably understand the reference to the "peasant" not as a voucher of interest in a agriculturally-based readership, but rather as a general support of the idea of a life that did not stress industry and commerce.

& may, perhaps, obtain a few name for you. This, I presume, is all that you expected. You must be too well acquainted with the state of society here, to have any expectations of obtaining literary aid" (Cronin 1973, 299). But Smith kindly asked Dennie to subscribe him to the *Museum*, even though he boarded with Thomas Green Fessenden, who already was a subscriber and contributor, and offered a number of well-meant hints on conducting the paper (cf. Cronin 1973, 299-300). In his reply, Dennie apparently directly broached the subject of contributions by Smith, but Smith, himself heavily engaged in publishing and editing the *Medical Repository*, declined to be of service to Dennie. Writing to Dennie in July, 1797, he stated plainly: "In regard to original communications, I must again assure you, that it will be wholly out of my power to do you any personal service." He did, however, suggest that he could offer the help of a friend, if Dennie was willing to pay for the writings. This friend was Charles Brockden Brown, failed lawyer and at this time probably hard at work on his novels *Wieland* and *Arthur Mervyn*, as well as, in Smith's words, "poor: absolutely destitute. His pen is his only support" (Cronin 1973, 336).[8] It could not surprise, therefore, that Brown "relishe[d] the proposal of writing for the New Hampshire paper" (1930, 124), as William Dunlap quoted from correspondence with Elihu Hubbard Smith. Smith was sanguine that Dennie would be able to pay him "a very moderate compensation," and be "certain of one or two weekly essays, critical, literary, or moral; either in a continued series,

8 The identity of Charles Brockden Brown as the anonymous friend of Smith's can be established from a number of hints in Smith's letters. Smith notes that his friend was "not in New York at present"—Brown had moved back to Philadelphia earlier in the decade, but visited on occasion. Not long after his letter to Dennie, Smith wrote one directed to Brown: "I have just written to Dennie, & shall probably be able to send you his terms in the course of a month or three weeks." Dennie, not uncharacteristically, did not reply to Smith's letter, and on September 7, Smith wrote again to Dennie, slightly impatiently, repeating his offer and suggesting that his friend "leaves the terms wholly to us; & has sent me a manuscript as a specimen of what he may do, provided you think proper to engage his pen" (Cronin 1973, 357). Dennie apparently did not see fit to hire Brown (whether, as Kaplan stresses, he never replied to Smith's offer, not even the second one, is impossible to prove: certainly, there is no surviving letter to indicate he did; cf. Kaplan 2007, 125). Note, however, Stephen Shapiro's analysis of the nature of Brown's literary endeavors and financial status: in Shapiro's recounting, "Brown's family was never in real financial distress," and "Brown seems to have been entirely supported by his parents or extended family until he was nearly thirty years old" (in 1801; 2008, 164-5); Smith's letter might thus be understood as creating a much more dire outlook for Brown than was warranted, in hopes of getting him a job with Dennie. A second item of note might be added here, apropos of Brown and Smith. The *Monthly Magazine*, so often described as "Brown's" (in this study, too!), is much more properly seen as Smith's, given the involvement which Smith had in its conception and nascence. The Friendly Club heavily supported Brown during his editorship, a position which he probably, as Smith's correspondence with Dennie indicates, owed much to Smith's protection, rather than his own editorial brilliance. Cf. Waterman 2007, 47-8, for notes on Smith's role in the conception of the *Monthly Magazine*.

or under different titles and signatures, as you should deem best" (Cronin 1973, 336). Dennie was not interested: perhaps he "knew that he could get contributions for free and so remained silent in the face of Smith's suggestions" (2007, 126), as Catherine Kaplan has suggested. But it is clear that Dennie was in fact willing to pay for the contributions he received, just as he was prepared to be paid for the contributions he himself later offered to other magazines. In a letter to Royall Tyler, just a month after Smith's missive had reached him, Dennie scolded his friend for inactivity and suggested to Tyler, whose novel *The Algerine Captive* had just been published by David Carlisle, that he might rethink his writing. "If you wish to compose another novel," Dennie wrote, "[rather] compile an Annual Register, or be concerned in a magazine or Review, you can sell for a liberal price your copy, or be well remunerated for your contributions" (in Pedder 1936, 165). Like Smith, he recognized the business practices as they existed, and even made use of them in harrying his subscribers about money. In February 1799, when he once more announced a major change to the *Museum*, he also once again held forth on the need for his subscribers to pay their subscriptions. Part of the reason they should do so, among outlays for paper, printing costs, and shipping, Dennie noted his "many originals, procured by pecuniary compensation" (*FWM* 1799, 6.306, 4). If Dennie could get some contributions for free, most importantly the snippets of foreign magazines that correspondence frequently forwarded him, his desire to publish original matter beyond his own productions apparently did require him to pay. Certainly, in this case, he had very little reason to be misinforming his audience: apart from possibly inspiring his subscribers to punctual payment, there was no profit to be had from admitting that he—or rather, publisher Isaiah Thomas—was paying for submissions. Rather to the contrary: if the *Museum* was perceived, and supposed to be perceived, as a form of "intellectual and even artisanal companionship" (Kaplan 2007, 128) in which readers could "understand themselves [...] as links in a chain of information, emotion, and judgments" (127), such an admission had the potential of being dangerous, given that it certainly cheapened the voluntary submissions still requested by Dennie.[9]

9 I am indebted to Jared Gardner for suggesting that the opposite might be true: claiming to have to pay for contributions may have indicated that the contributors were, at least sometimes, men of literary standing—ergo, that the *Museum* was in fact more valuable for having these contributions, and Dennie was effectively advertising. This may have been true for Jeremy Belknap, whom Matthew Carey paid for contributions to his *American Museum*, who had previously worked for pay for the *Columbian Magazine*, and who was a well-known writer at the time; but the question remains whether Belknap's association with the *Museum* was well known enough to make it likely that Carey profited from the name, rather than from the quality of Belknap's productions (cf. Kirsch 1982, 158-62). As I will show in Chapter 3, when magazines began, in the course of and after the War of 1812, to more frequently offer contributors remuneration, there was considerable critical opposition to the idea; and it will become evident that advertising with famous figures, in this case, Washington Irving, tended to be a less roundabout and more straightforward business.

Smith's letter is both revealing and remarkable for the way in which the New Yorker was hawking his friend Brown. With a fellow man of letters, obviously, Smith saw no need to hem and haw about the processes behind the publication of a magazine: Brown's services were for sale, and the author prepared—indeed, in Smith's telling, anxious—to produce at Dennie's request whatever his paper needed. In Smith's recounting, what Catherine O'Donnell Kaplan has termed "the quest for Shaftesburian fellowship" (2007, 53), the sense of belonging to a community of dedicated men of letters involving themselves in the intellectual betterment both of themselves and their peers and readers, becomes a matter of business alone. Smith makes Brown a hack: a writer whom Dennie could hire for service as required, notably capable of improvising on subjects literary or moral both. But it is possible to go even further: Smith's suggestion indicates, if it does not comment on Dennie's, at least Smith's own willingness to forego what Kaplan has called the "marker of cultural community" and "coveted evidence of their own activities and communities" (2007, 127) by faking different signatures.[10] Like the knowledge that Dennie was paying for submissions, knowledge of being led to assume a community of like-minded authors where there was in fact potentially just one hired writer had the latent capability to disrupt part of the façade which Dennie gave the *Museum*.

These details of Dennie's editorial business cannot detract from the remarkable success the paper attained under his editorship. By December 1797, Dennie could proudly proclaim that circulation had reached more than two thousands subscribers and spread as far south as Georgia and as far west as the "banks of the Ohio" (*FWM* 1797, 5.244, 3). In the same announcement to "Readers and Correspondents," Dennie also showed some of the editorial work that he was engaged in. He declined the printing of some submissions and actively solicited others by (pen)name; he commented favorably on his own choice of the biography of Edmund Burke ("entirely novel, in this country") and asked his readers to use their own reading to discover interesting "fugitive good things" for Dennie, so he would be able to publish them in his paper. "[W]hatsoever things are lovely and of good reports," he announced, would easily find itself in the *Museum*. But at the same time, he announced that there would be more changes in the new year: a higher price (owed, as Dennie noted, to the difficulties of obtaining outstanding debts from far-away subscribers) remained the only concrete promise he made, however.

Two months later, momentous changes did indeed occur: Isaiah Thomas, who had left the partnership with David Carlisle two years earlier, became the paper's proprietor again, after a failure of Carlisle's business (cf. *FWM* 1797, 5.255, 3). It meant no major change for Dennie—he remained editor, if at a reduced salary—but gave him the chance to once more offer his personal reading of the editorial business. He would, Dennie said, make a "full attempt, by variegated Literature, and pure Politicks, to interest the numerous readers, by whose patronage he is

10 Smith may be making explicit what Dennie condoned quietly: it is possible that the Lay Preacher itself, Dennie's most saleable persona at the *Museum*, may have sometimes been written by his friend Roger Vose.

honoured." But, he added, the problem of punctual payment remained: without it, Dennie could not remain "animate" and "on his course". Here, he presented himself as an "industrious workman" like any other: "he has a right to *bread*," and sometimes, to write "all cheerily," he "ought to have *wine*. The incumbrance of excessive wealth is," he continued, "scarcely to be dreaded by an author, but for the decent recompence of literary labour he has an importunate claim. If the Publick will merely *compensate* that labour, the task shall be fulfilled by the Editor, with his best possible exertions" (*FWM* 1797, 5.255, 3, original emphasis). Dennie styled himself an artisan here rather than an artist, a servant, and a servant for whom the slight hope of recompense—not profit—was the driving force behind his editorial labors. It seems unlikely that Dennie was nearly as poorly off as he suggested in this note: in Carlisle's failure earlier in the year, he had lost a considerable amount of money, for sure, but the work for the *Museum* sufficed to sustain him even as it allowed him to save money. That Dennie suggested a correlation between the readiness of the public to pay promptly for their paper and his own compensation may strike us as odd, considering that Dennie was employed for annual wages by Thomas as much as he had been for Carlisle. While ultimately, that salary was certainly tied if not to the actual level of success of the paper or at least to its survival, Dennie's plea ignored such distinctions and offered readers a far more direct relationship than was practically the case. Dennie was creating for himself an editorial persona that tied his readers more closely to him than otherwise possible. For the purpose of animating his subscribers to pay, he was willing to ignore the actual business relations underlying his service in Walpole, realizing, no doubt, that the personal relationship which he was building with his subscribers through editorial commentary and letters was more likely to yield a response than any suggestion could which would have advanced Isaiah Thomas's claims on the subscribers.

The public persona which Dennie exhibited in the *Museum* fluctuated between the pleading for money to subsist and the acknowledgment that more than mere competence was his goal, between repeated assertions that he, the editor, would be in chief control of the magazine, and timid assurances of public servitude: in December 1797, he assured his correspondents of the importance of their affirmations of his editorship: as editor, he wished not to include a piece apparently anti-Federalist, and so did "an immense majority of his readers;" his own essay in criticism in the issue, he noted to his readers, would be his last if readers felt he had misjudged his aim and done injury to "the ingenious and the wealthy" (*FWM* 1797, 5.244, 3). For Dennie, editing the *Museum* was a permanent exercise in setting what material he had in the best possible light, a constant struggle to sell not just magazines, but also the appropriateness of the inclusion of individual texts.

Dennie's conception of his editorial role at the *Farmer's Weekly Museum*, not coincidentally, found its reflection in commentary on biography. On October 22, 1798, he published a biography of Nicholas Chamfort, a French writer, and preceded the piece with an introduction which precisely outlined his editorial thinking. "As a Traiteur, whose shop is frequented by epicures, is studious of the brightness of his wine, and the flavour of his partridge," Dennie wrote, "so an Editor, a similar caterer for the public, should provide things rare and in request, if he wish to have custom, profit and praise" (*FWM* 1798, 6.290, 1). Here is one of the few outright statements of editorial policy which Dennie made in the *Museum*. The list of editorial desires is commendably straightforward: custom and profit go hand in hand, of course, as increased custom must translate into increased profit. Although he provides a service—he fulfills requests—the end of this service is not some ulterior goal, the education of the populace, the furthering of Republican virtue, or the improvement of the republic of letters. Rather, it is at once ultimately selfish, concerned only with the benefit of the editor, and mundane.

Dennie's conception of himself as being "like a Traiteur," at once highlights his hopes for a genteel readership capable of appreciating the fineness of his metaphorical literary wines and his recognition of providing a service that is ultimately an unessential and fleeting luxury. Dennie envisaged his readership less in terms of people on the search for self-improvement than as an audience for whom his paper was a distraction in their leisure time—"fugitive sheets and pamphlets [...] to cheat lingering moments." He felt, he noted, "a constant solicitude to give *interest* to a paper, which is [at most] very generally *glanced* over by curious and critical eyes" (*FWM* 1798, 6.290, 1, original emphasis). Biography, he suggested, was especially useful for his journal under these conditions, because "he has remarked that the lives of extraordinary personages ever excite the liveliest attention." Couching this observation in terms of empirical fact, rather than normative claim, Dennie highlighted, if it was even still necessary, the ways in which he constituted his journal not on the basis of ideological considerations, but as the result of the success he attained. Only a paper which could capture the attention of the reader would proliferate, but again the choice of words is auspicious: it is not usefulness that is important, it is not even interest which concerns Dennie, but rather, "attention" is critical, the catching of the reader's eye, the fleeting moments in which the leisured reader, drinking "the coffee of the morning" or seeking something "to charm away the shades of night," might be attracted by the offerings of the *Museum*. In the final analysis, then, if the productions with which he filled his paper were successful in attracting readers, this was sufficient reason to continue them, as this translated directly into monetary profit. We need not take, therefore, Dennie's praise for biography as a genre at face value, any more than we need to consider his choice of printing the biography of Chamfort in any way "extraordinary," or assume that there was a good reason to suspect his readers' attention would be excited by the biography of Chamfort specifically. As Appendix 3 shows, his source for the biography was one from which, before and after, he extracted a great number of biographies, all of which were at least as "extraordinary" to his American customers as that of Chamfort—some perhaps more so. But Dennie's sales pitch for the biography indicates the importance which he ascribed to offering variety in his magazine, even when, for all practical purposes, he did not vary his sources or his subjects very much. The claim of offering a "strange" biography implied its extraordinariness.

Like the biography of the Queen of France with which Dennie had leavened a monotonous weekly fare of British poets' lives earlier, the biography as such was not at all out of the ordinary; what made it extraordinary was only Dennie's pitching of it as extraordinary. Whenever possible, he emphasized particular biographies' status as new or interesting: in December 1797, he proudly noted that the biography of Robert Burns in the same issue was "entirely novel, in this country, and is written with fidelity and elegance" (*FWM* 1797, 5.244, 3): novelty's centrality and the aesthetic appeal of the individual pieces is once more highlighted. In May 1797, he advertised to the public a biography of Shakespeare he had drawn from a recently published American edition of the Bard's plays. Other biographies, such as were commonly seen in other editions of the plays, Dennie noted in one of his editorial asides, were "lamely written," "penuriously exhibited," and "imperfectly told." But Dennie, "ever anxious to exhibit the curious and the new, presents his patrons with a more lucid account of a matchless poet, than has yet appeared. He claims no merit except for making perhaps a grateful oblation to the public. That public is indebted to some Southern man of letters for what of information or amusement is comprised in the following sketch" of Shakespeare (*FWM* 1798, 6.268, 1). In a similar vein, a biography of William Enfield was announced editorially with the note that beside "the ordinary stimulus of curiosity," the fact that the text was written by a gentlemen of acknowledged literary skill would render it a delightful read (*FWM* 1798, 6.292, 1). What is striking here is the recognition implicit in the praise of the biographies that they were not, in any way, useful. Nowhere does Dennie suggest that Shakespeare's or Burns's lives could form the template from which readers could shape their own literary endeavors towards the excellence of these English and Scottish authors, or that of Chamfort. If Chamfort's depiction in the biography as one who had "steered a steady course through the revolutionary storm […] openly protesting an equal hatred of priests and nobles, and of Marat and the rest of the men of blood" (*FWM* 1798, 6.290, 2) must have appealed to Dennie's fundamental opposition of Jacobinism both French and American, nearly half the biography consists of the sensationalist depiction of Chamfort's demise at his own hands, a badly bungled suicide attempt which left him disfigured and in constant pain until his death a year later. Where could instruction lie in such a life—when almost certainly Dennie did not mean to instruct his readers in the art of suicide? What inspired the choice of Chamfort, apart from the ready availability of the life in the volumes from which he had already poached, was manifestly not the *utile* part of the Horacian dictum. Chamfort's life could, however, be as "attention"-grabbing and interesting as was necessary for Dennie's paper.

Biography and the *Farmer's Weekly Museum*

Implicit in the changes instituted in the paper under Dennie's editorship, then, was a change of outlook. To be useful to Carlisle's mostly rural subscribership, the paper had required precisely the kind of article that Carlisle and Thomas had advertised in their initial prospectus and filled their paper with in the previous years: agricultural news and local events. These considerations are well reflected, certainly, in the small number of biographies published before April 1796.

Biography heavily reflected the rural nature of the eponymous readership of the *Farmer's Weekly Museum* prior to Dennie's tenure as editor, and the original conception of the journal as a repository for "[i]nformation from the various parts of this extensive continent," but notably of "useful discoveries and improvements in Agriculture, to which [readers] will be particularly attentive." In their initial announcement for the *Museum*, the publishers Thomas and Carlisle had made quite clear that they were establishing, first and foremost, "a Printing Office in this place" which "will essentially serve the inhabitants of *this part of the country*" (*FWM* 1793 1.1, 1, my emphasis). Perhaps the *Farmer's Weekly Museum* in this scheme played the role of filler for those times when the new printing office's pressed lay idle. At any rate, biography played a negligible role for this determinedly rural paper; when, in March 1795, the *Museum* published its first biography, a piece copied from the *Connecticut Gazette*, it conformed entirely to the prospectus's claim for local applicability. Entitled "Useful Biography," it was a character piece, written about a "man not very remotely known, but of a character so exemplary that we was one of the few whose life and death deserve to be publicly commemorated." This exemplary, and nameless, person was "a labourer in husbandry," possessed of "industry," "cheerful, and, at fit times, jocose," "[i]n short, he was a very extraordinary pattern of Industry and of the whole train of virtues that usually attend on her" (*FWM* 1795, 2.102, 1). Here was the exemplary farmer, couched in the genre of biography, and clearly not a candidate for the wide dissemination of the kind of literary journal which Dennie would come to guide later, but no doubt eminently suitable for the local distribution then still prevalent. A year later, in February 1796, the magazine printed a biography of Robert Bakewell, the "most successful and celebrated experimental farmer ever known in England," and only recently deceased in October 1795. The biography was an extract from a London paper, and had already been published in several other papers, most recently in the *Federal Orrery* of Boston, a paper run by Dennie's friend Robert Treat Paine, Jr.[11] Bakewell's exploits as a sheep farmer had already caught the attention of American magazines and newspapers before his death, but even in his posthumous biography, much attention was lavished by the English biographer on his professional exploits. It followed the style of the life and character biography typical of the times, especially in Britain, giving a summary of his professional life and concluding in a paragraph in which his kindness to the animals under his care was especially highlighted (cf. *FWM* 1796, 3.151, 1). This life, too, ran under the header "useful biography," although here, the precise usefulness of the biography was elusive. Whereas the nameless farmer's virtue might have been useful as an example, Bakewell's biography was informative, but not a guide to either husbandry or virtue, except in the most general sense.

11 Cf. *Gazette of the United States*, January 25, 1796. This is the earliest instance of biography I could find in the United States, but it was later widely reprinted.

Perhaps the most intriguing piece of biographical writing offered by the *Museum* before Dennie's editorship was a biography printed in March, 1796, just weeks before the redesign of the paper. The "Account of Thomas Topham" (cf. *FWM* 1796, 3.152, 1) was a mere curiosity, an assortment of anecdotes from the life of an English strongman, retelling the various feats of strength he had accomplished. It was a widely-published article, initially appearing in the London-published *History of Derby*, and quoted in the *European Magazine*'s January 1792 review thereof. It had a brief currency in April and May 1792 in the United States, probably corresponding to the arrival of editions of the *European Magazine* (the first re-publication was in a Philadelphia paper, the port of entry for much foreign literary production in the Early Republic), appearing in a small number of papers. It was apparently rediscovered early in 1796 and found its way into newspapers from Philadelphia to Boston. One of those papers was the *Farmer's Weekly Museum*. Its own version probably came from one of its fellow contemporary journals in the United States, rather than from the original source; the 1792 versions all included a final paragraph on Topham's death, a paragraph also in the London original, while all the 1796 versions made do without it.

Dennie's accession to the editorship changed the type of biography which the *Museum* exhibited, but what he, at least publically, considered useful about biography was not very clear. When Dennie commented on the question, he often resorted to vagueness: in September 1798, commenting on a fairly randomly chosen biography of British Major General John Fiske, he suggested that the text "exhibits a picture of a dignified and useful man," whose life "may be usefully studied by a large and operative class of mankind." What made the biography useful, though? Dennie did not answer this question: he resorted again to different adjectives, suggesting the biography possessed a "double interest" because it dealt with a "distinguished character" and exhibited "a pure and elegant style" (*FWM* 1798, 6.283, 2). If this made it a pleasure to read and interesting, it did not speak necessarily to how Fiske's life could be useful to his readers. This question, the particular usefulness and benefits to be had from biography remained potent in the *Museum* throughout Dennie's editorship. The terms never really shed their conceptual obscurity. The epigram to this chapter comes from the editorial preface to a biography of Henry Fielding. Strikingly, here Dennie seems to argue that his readers, the "loungers," would not be able to make the biography "useful," an operation that is only possible for the members of Fielding's "country," with instruction left for the rest of the world.

One of the favorite men for Dennie's effusions on biography was Edmund Burke, perhaps the closest Dennie came to an idol. In December 1798, he prefaced a life of the British politician as "so useful" that its materials "are not easily exhausted." Burke, Dennie wrote, offered a model from which readers could "copy his virtues" for their own improvement (*FWM* 1798 6.297, 1). A life of Burke was also one of the last biographies that Dennie printed. Here, an editorial note reminded readers that the magazine had "frequently dwelled" on "the utility of this pleasing portion [i.e., biography] of general literature" and suggested that "the benefit resulting from the biography of literary men cannot be too frequently inculcated upon young and aspiring readers" (*FWM* 1799 7.324, 1). Here, for once, Dennie also stressed the uses he believed would chiefly derive from the perusal of biography: "industry, temperance, perseverance, and every praiseworthy and virtuous habit," Burke's chief characteristics, might find their way into the youth who reads the biography. Conversely, biography could also instruct and be useful by being worthy of imitation, but rather by being an example to be avoided, as he noted the biography of Joseph Mawbey in March 1799 was (cf. *FWM* 1799 6.311, 3). Likewise, the biography of the French revolutionary painter David, whom the editorial introduction calls a "ferocious and sanguinary citizen," whose biography seems chiefly useful for Dennie as "another proof of the savageness of France" (*FWM* 1798 6.293, 1)—and because it came out of a volume of French biographies which Dennie had liberally used for a considerable while. But for all these possible ways in which biography could be useful, the biographies which were printed in the *Museum* rarely offered any hint at how any of Dennie's readers could genuinely make 'use' of them, or benefit from them beyond finding in them amusement for their leisure hours.[12] For Dennie, as indeed for the majority of authors, editors, and publishers making use of the terms, "useful and instructive" was a necessary trope to be invoked, but not necessarily one to be taken seriously. The expansion which the editor offered in the comment on Fielding is an example of the casual modification, which in the last analysis carried no real meaning anymore, of Horace's injunction: the amusement for the lounger, the usefulness for the country, and the instruction for the world offer a rhetorical parallelism that neatly parcels out the benefits of the text. It is a tacit admission of the need to know that the periodical, and with it, its biographies, require amusement, usefulness, and instruction, but at the same time it also recognizes the ultimate meaninglessness of the phrases. The life of Fielding is "instructive to the world" and "useful to his country" not because of empirical fact or theoretical deliberations, but because instruction follows usefulness in the Horacian stock phrase just as the world follows the country in the rhetorical progression from smaller to bigger.

Perhaps, even though it was published prior to Dennie's editorship, it is the 'biography' of Thomas Topham which best suggests the usefulness of biography for the *Museum*, if not in the ways discussed above or admitted to by its editor. The *Museum* was the only paper to carry this text under the header biography. That it did so indicates the broadness of the category biography as the *Museum* understood

12 It is perhaps useful to repeat here Dennie's suggestion that it is primarily the young who could still benefit from the reading of the lives of virtuous men, and to wonder how this belief related the known subscribership—usually, well-settled professional men, merchants, artisans. Did those people subscribe for their children? Sometimes, indeed, they did, as a letter received by Dennie in 1803 indicates. Here, a subscriber acknowledges he had been ordering the *Port Folio* for his sons, away at college, who now no longer desired the paper. This was unlikely to be the norm, nor do college students necessarily seem to figure among the youth to be improved (though, given Dennie's own experiences at Harvard, it may have seemed evident to Dennie that there was much room for the improvement of students' virtue).

it—an understanding which Dennie also subscribed to, as his own choices of biography indicate. The so-called biographies of Topham, Bakewell, and the unnamed farmer indicate just how useful that category was specifically as a category. It was similarly suitable for the publication of entertaining and popular anecdotes such as the episodes in Topham's life, for the dissemination of the didacticism and celebration of virtue that was the farmer's life, and for the re-publication of the numerous short biographical sketches of a whole host of people without any specific qualities worthy or capable of emulation. This was true even when their lives were not in the last instance as entertaining, or the biographies themselves as morally useful, as these two, like the kind of text exemplified by the Bakewell biography. Biography, as a category, lent orderliness to the *Museum* by subsuming a vast variety of different types of writing. This orderliness was a requisite for a paper which needed to advertise the kind of productions it proposed to put out every week: by claiming, as the *Museum*'s editorials and prospectuses did under Dennie's editorship, that biography would constitute a major part of its output, the paper was to no small degree bound to deliver. The broad conception of biography which is not only evident in the texts which were published before Dennie, but also in those which Dennie himself selected as editor, helped fill the self-set requirements for the *Museum*.

Dennie's assumption of the editorship of the *Farmer's Weekly Museum* coincided with the increased use of biography in the journal, but the process was slow. A short biography of Napoleon Bonaparte graced the July 19, 1796 edition of the paper. On November 15, the *Museum* began publishing a long biography of Valentine Duval, an article copied from the *British New and General Biographical Dictionary* which occupied the *Museum*'s biography section for two weeks and which Dennie changed in no respect. On December 6, Dennie made use of another source, the Edinburgh *Lounger* edited by Henry Mackenzie, to publish the "Memoirs of William Strahan, a late celebrated printer." Here, at least, Dennie did some editorial work. Mackenzie's article in the *Lounger* No.29, of August 20, 1785, had meandered towards the biography of Strahan from a more general meditation on the uses of biography, noting that "there are few even of those comparatively insignificant lives, in which men of a serious and thinking case do not feel a certain degree of interest" (113). Mackenzie recognized that William Strahan's claim to biographical fame was rather minor, but included him anyway for sentimental reasons: Mackenzie and Strahan had both contributed to the London *Mirror*. Eliminating the two pages of prefatory material on biography, and of necessity also the personal elaborations of Mackenzie, in Dennie's paper the biography of Strahan carried the title "Memoir of William Strahan, a late celebrated Printer" (*FWM* 1796 4.192,1). Otherwise unchanged, the life of William Strahan may have been made modestly palatable to Dennie's readers by its occasional reference to Benjamin Franklin, but overall must have been a text of only limited interest. It was, however, both obviously available and obviously fitting for the rubric.

From January 31, 1797, to February 21, the *Museum* carried lives of Shakespeare, Spenser, Milton and Cowley, courtesy of two volumes (No.2 and 5) of Robert Anderson's seminal 1795 *The Works of the British Poets*. For the first time, Dennie made sure that some hint of the source existed. He prefaced the first biography

(Shakespeare's) with an editorial comment recommending the "splendid edition of the British Poets" from which he had culled the texts, and explains that "these brief Biographies are written with great neatness, manifest much accuracy, and contain numerous particulars, not generally known to the bulk of readers" so that he would "occasionally adorn the Museum with an extract" (*FWM* 1797 4.200, 1). It became much more than an occasional adornment. For four weeks, every issue of the *Museum* carried a biography from Anderson's collection, and the biographies were given front page place and stood with the essays from the "Shop of Mess Colon & Spondee" and the "Hermit" essays, original productions of Dennie's and his contributors which were the primary attractions of the magazine. But four weeks of unleavened poetical biography must have seemed to Dennie insufficiently varied for his readership's taste. On February 28, he printed a biography of Marie Antoinette, to which he again appended an editorial preface. "The Editor," Dennie wrote, "studious of variety, and fearing lest his readers should tire of the lives of the Poets, presents this week, Memoirs of the Late Queen of France" (*FWM* 1797 4.204, 1). Once more, Dennie made public his editorial guidelines: variety remained the life-blood of his paper. The sympathetic portrayal of Marie Antoinette which leavened late February's *Museum* was suitably direct about its advocacy of virtue to be moderately 'useful;' its measured analysis of France's descent into Revolution was, however, hardly the kind of pro-Federalist, anti-Jacobin message which Dennie's publisher Carlisle had so insisted upon only ten months earlier. But the Queen's life had broken the monotony of poet's lives sufficiently for Dennie to start with them again and keep them going throughout April: he proceeded to publish biographies of Butler (Vol. 5 of Anderson's *Works*), Carew (Vol. 3), Waller (Vol. 5), Drayton (Vol. 3), Suckling (Vol. 3), and Donne (Vol. 4) up to April 18, 1797 (and other texts would soon follow at irregular intervals). As before, Dennie felt no need to make changes to the biographies. From the three volumes of the *Works of the British Poets* which Dennie had ransacked, he had not made use of the lives of Davies, Hall, and Denham; yet no clear pattern emerges in Dennie's selection of biographies. More likely than not, space dictated some of the choices, and certainly the relative fame of some of the biographees, especially Shakespeare, Milton, and Spenser, had influenced Dennie. His poetical series concluded the fourth volume of the *Museum*. Major changes stood before.

That Dennie's role at the *Farmer's Weekly Museum* had grown more central with time became evident in April 1797, if direct evidence was even still needed. A week under a year since the *Museum* had first appeared under his editorship, he offered a first editorial announcement "To Patrons," a role which he would then assume in the *Port Folio* to come. His note accompanied a thorough revamping of the journal: Dennie moved the literary matter, which had hitherto been somewhat liberally and opportunistically spread through the paper, to the last page, which he titled the "Dessert;" at the same time, for the first time, he noted that biography would constitute front-page matter. It had already been exclusively on the front pages so far, of course, but now Dennie situated it explicitly in relation to the other content. Biography would share that space with "Politicks [...] Economicks, Morals, and Daily Detail" (*FWM* 1797 5.209, 1). Although the selection of front-page matter was broad, Dennie here clearly distinguished biographical texts from the literary *belles lettres* of the "Dessert" and placed it among the texts which were generally supposed to be 'useful': information relevant for the creation of republican citizens, such as political and economic events, for virtuous private life, such as morals, and for the immediate community in which the paper was read, the daily sales notices, death notices, and paraphernalia which marked the *Farmer's Weekly Museum* as still very much centered on the region in which it was printed, despite its success in attracting readers further afield. Dennie's reorganization of the *Farmer's Weekly Museum* re-emphasized the role that belles lettres played in the *Museum*, just as had been done earlier by the change in motto. That motto, too, changed again: a Bunyan quote, "…would'st though remember / from New Year's Day to the Last of December? / Then read," replaced the slightly more frivolous one with which the *Museum* had worked a year. Compared to the previous mottoes, this new one, which the *Museum* would use for two years, was quite bare of any ulterior value in its rather random affirmation of the benefit of reading.

Much as the outline of the *Museum* changed, the biographies which Dennie printed in this newly revamped *Museum* were still from the same source: in April, he printed the lives of Suckling and Donne, having apparently obtained the fourth volume of Anderson's *Works*, which he had not previously excerpted texts from; he then again changed the biographical tune to publish a biographies of Alexander Selkirk and Charles Linneaus in early May. This latter text is interesting: it was a stereotypically mediocre biography, stressing the most mundane details of the Swedish scientist's life and person. The reader is informed that Linnaeus was "a little below the common size," that his "eyes were brown and fiery," that "his memory […] became at last as weak as formerly it had been strong," and that he "was not fond of the phonology of words" (*FWM* 1797 5.214, 1). This was precisely the kind of biography which the *Farmer's Weekly Museum* itself, four months later, would severely criticize. In a short note in the section "Nuts" of the "Dessert," Dennie published a complaint about "British Biography".[13] The note decried the genre's propensity for "trifling particulars:" as examples, it cited the information that Matthew Hale was "fond of green turtle baked whole in the shell," that James Thompson, the Scottish poet, was accustomed to "walk two miles in a fair evening, in order to procure an appetite for his supper," or that Bishop Sherlock would go to bed every evening precisely at ten o'clock (*FWM* 1797 5.228, 4). That these complaints were diametrically opposed to the kind of biography which the *Museum* published week after week should not be overemphasized, of course: the "Nuts" section was a place for humorous short notes, for

13 The same article appeared a day later, August 15, in Philadelphia's Democratic newspaper *Aurora*. It seems unlikely that the *Aurora* could have copied the *Farmer's Weekly Museum*'s text in this instance, given the difficulties of transportation; but no original of the text has been discovered so far. Some of the particulars point to the text's origin in the United States—the final anecdote is about Ezra Stiles, president of Yale College—rather than Great Britain.

anecdotes and jokes (many of them original to the *Museum*, as apparently, this note was, too), and indeed, the complaint about British biography ended on a modestly humorous note itself.[14]

The majority of biography published in the *Museum* was British biography, culled from British books and magazines, and the not too distant publication of the Linneaus biography, which conformed almost to a dot to the complaints which Dennie published in the "Dessert," highlights the ways in which Dennie's apparent interest in the form of biography was trumped by other considerations. There was no apparent necessity for Dennie to take sides in the discussion on whether the mundane facts of everyday life should be included in biography, or whether they should not: rather, he could and did have it both ways, as the available room and material dictated. Far from having an overarching ideological goal, Dennie's use of biography and biographical criticism was largely opportunistic. Thus, three weeks after the note in the "Dessert," the *Museum* carried a so-called biography of a "Surinam planter" which echoed the complaints it had offered earlier, while simultaneously, but perhaps coincidentally, standing as a memorial to the violence of slavery. Purporting to illustrate the typical day in the life of, somehwat unsurprisingly, a Surinam planter, the text's satirical treatment of the form of biography stands uneasily besides the casual cruelty which it describes. The piece draws its satirical strength from the juxtaposition of claiming to give a general idea of all Surinam planters' days while offering a wealth of detail which sits incongruously besides this generality. Thus, the biography holds that "His Worship generally begins to yawn about ten or eleven o'clock" (*FWM* 1797 5.231, 2) and makes extensive lists of the clothes worn by the planter at different occasions during the day. With such a fount of trivialities goes hand in hand the choice of subject, with its clear lack of personal or public virtue.

Thus it will not surprise that when Dennie actively solicited his correspondents to supply biography in July 1797, he did not advertise for the useful or instructive: rather, he sought

> the following curiosities: Lives of the Literati in general, and of the later Wits and Poets, in particular. If derived from scarce sources, recent and well written notices of the sentimental Mackenzie, the eccentrick Lyttelton, the fanciful Mrs. Radcliffe, the industrious Charlotte Smith, and Fuseli, author of "Remarks on Rousseau," will be peculiarly acceptable (*FWM* 1797 5.224, 3).

Maybe the "industrious" Charlotte Smith had lived a life it was useful to exhibit to Dennie's readers. By and large, however, not only through the choice of subjects—all writers—but also through his adjectives, Dennie committed himself

14 That all of the *Farmer's Weekly Museum*'s jokes ended on, at best, *very* faintly humorous notes, is a fascinating fact probably owed to today's rougher sensibilities and latent disregard for the finer points of wit than to any inherent deficit of Early Republic humor. Or perhaps the jokes published in the *Museum* were not very good.

firmly to the enjoyable: curiosities, eccentricities, and fancies had no competition from the instructive in this call.

In October and November, 1798, Dennie published two more satirical pieces on biography. The texts were extracted from two April editions of the London weekly *The Looker-On,* run by William Roberts, and Dennie credited them accordingly to "Roberts," even if the precise nature of the reference must have eluded most readers. Indeed, one of the pieces was not by Roberts himself, but rather one of his correspondents, and intriguingly, neither text accurately reflects the circumstances of its initial publication. Roberts's April 14 meditations on biography were in the form of a lengthy essay, to which the fictional dialogue between a biographer and a kennel-scraper, the bit which Dennie published in the *Museum*, was merely an appendix. In Roberts's text, the benefits of biography and the nature of it as an investigation into the private character of the individual concerned are explored, and criticism chiefly levied at the proliferation in biographical essays of what Roberts called "this general extension and simplification of the biographical plan" (LO 1797, 147). Dennie extracted the final fictional dialogue from this lengthy essay, calling it "Satire on the Prostitution of Modern Biography;" in the text, the emphasis on the parallels between the biographer's occupation with "the entertainment and instruction of mankind" and the kennel-scraper's work become the central lampoon. Are not, the kennel-scraper asks, "my old nails and broken horse shoes [...] discoveries as valuable to the world, as those scraps and shreds of immorality, impertinence, and prostitution, you were so earnestly employed in collecting" (*FWM* 1798 6.289, 4)? Against the biographer's indignant query if the kennel-scraper intends to "rank [him]self with Plutarch, and with geniuses of a similar order," the kennel-scraper mischievously suggests that he wishes to "be understood to speak only of the latest biographers;" Plutarch, and other great biographers, "have enough for themselves to keep as distant from you as possible." Standing "in yonder meadow, covered with the bloom of the amaranth, and intersected with amber streams," that is to say, the yellow streams of horse urine, the great biographers keep their distance from the biographers of the 1790s, more at home in the meadows of horse-keeping and the wastes of horses, the likes of which keep the kennel-scraper busy, than in the company of contemporary biographers.

Roberts's paper also supplied the text which Dennie headlined "A Projector's Scheme of Biography in Bags," which had been written by a correspondent of Roberts's in time for *The Looker-On*'s April 21 edition. This piece, too, originally stood at the end of a longer essay on biography, which Roberts had not had the chance to include in his previous edition. This essay was even more supportive of biography, and emphasized the ways in which comparative biographies would yield the reader additional information and a chance to find that "the admirable personages in modern history will often come forth with fairer fame and greener laurels" (*LO* 1797, 168). The extract Dennie provides, written by a correspondent and sometime contributor, instead harkens back to the rather more critical discussion of the previous week. The satirical proposal for a proto-biography machine indeed echoes the suggestion which Roberts had made that "we shall soon buy ready-made lives in our shops" (*LO* 1797, 147): the correspondent suggested that his

> countrymen might be distributed into twelve classes [...] and that for each of these classes might be made twelve little bags, to answer to the months of the year [...] and that in every bag there should be thirty tickets; that on every one of these last thirty tickets, there should be written some suitable and natural event, agreeably to the class to which it belonged. (*FWM* 1798 6.293, 4)

Thus might be produced a system by which "an exhaustless variety" of biography, suitable to a particular class of people, might be produced. "The idea of my bags is classical," wrote Roberts's contributor, "inasmuch as it was suggested to me by the wind bags of which Ulysses talks to Alcinous in the Odyssey" (*FWM* 1798 6.293, 4).

The biographical criticism, whether satirical or editorial, published in the *Farmer's Weekly Museum* during Dennie's tenure as editor spoke with a common voice, against the excesses of contemporary British biography, with its penchant for emphasizing trivialities in the lives of subjects which themselves were of dubious interest. But it did so haphazardly, and there was no apparent interest in conforming the *Museum*'s own publishing practices to this overarching conception of biography. Provided with the material to offer a critique of biography, Dennie gladly edited it in such a fashion as to make the point which he wanted to make, but it remained a point incidental to the availability of material, rather than a point which the *Museum* sought to promote actively, or apply to itself. Furthermore, it was subordinate to the exigencies of the magazine as whole. Dennie's excerpt of the dialogue between the kennel-scraper and the biographer, besides being readily available and having the advantage of offering a perspective on biography which the *Museum* had already previously espoused, fitted the generally whimsical nature of the final pages of the *Farmer's Weekly Museum*, reserved for the reader's "dessert."

Throughout the rest of 1797, Dennie's *Museum* carried the by-now usual selection of lives of poets (he excerpted the character description of Ben Jonson from the fourth volume's lengthy biography of the poet in late May and the complete life of Chaucer from volume 1 in June), politicians, and random worthies from noble ladies to obscure printers. Few of these texts offer much enlightenment, beyond the occasional glimpse at Dennie's thought processes, or, as we shall see later, at least what Dennie sold as his thought processes. In a brief editorial commentary on a biography of William Pitt, he notes his apprehension about the content of the biography, "drawn by a pencil dipt in the harsh colours of faction," but justifies his inclusion of the biography as a "brilliant, rather than a just picture" (*FWM* 1797 5.219, 2). Here again, variety and interest trump usefulness—for how can a false picture be useful? The reader is expected to delight in the brilliancy of the writing, rather than obtain information from the biography; if this remained an unspoken rule for the *Museum*, its selection of texts more than once hints at it. In September, the *Museum* carried a biography of a housewife to an English day laborer. Originally published in London in a text called *The State of the Poor*, the text probably made it to Dennie through the *Lady's Museum* of London. Although it had been called a biographical text before—its original title had been "Village Biography"—it did not seem to fulfill an instructive purpose in Dennie's magazine. Whereas in *The State of the Poor*, it was a damning episode in a book largely concerned with the realistic depiction of, as it were, the state of the poor, for Dennie to place it under the rubric of biography, with its attendant genre expectations, was somewhat frivolous. The "simple annals" of "Dame Strudwick" in fact in many ways contradicted much that biography so often took for granted, or at least presumed to hold true: the importance of private virtue, for example. As the biography notes, "[w]ith all her virtue and all her merit, she was not much liked in her neighborhood" (*FWM* 1797 5.232, 1).

Starting in January, 1798, for two months the *Museum* published biographies extracted from a collection of French biographies of the Revolution, *Biographical Anecdotes of the Founders of the French Republic* (this is also the source for the life of Chamfort, discussed above). Dennie noted as much in the first biography he extracted from the book—although he rather carelessly paraphrased the book's title as "Anecdotes of distinguished Persons connected with the French Revolution" (*FWM* 1797 5.252, 1)—but not afterwards. These French biographies were a curious puzzle, and part of the paraphrase which Dennie offered of his source's title may be owed to the more neutral sound of a vague "connection" versus offering lives of the "Founders". Dennie's still avowedly Federalist paper was a decidedly odd place to find a rather friendly biography of Georges Couthon, one of the members of Robespierre's inner circle, and it was perhaps even odder to find it there without the editorial commentary that Dennie had so frequently used before.

While the rest of the men whose biographies were published were, at least, no Jacobins, they still rested uneasily next to such figures as Edmund Burke, to say the least. What they had in common were two things, again: they were available (Dennie needed only to consult a single source for them) and they were, in the words he applied later to a biography of Mirabeau which he extracted from a different source, "various and striking" (*FWM* 1798 6.285, 2). As Dennie commented in an editorial on the life of Charles Maurice de Talleyrand, "any authentic particulars of the life and adventures of this man will gratify curiosity and extend information" (*FWM* 1798 6.289, 1). It was probably a unique feature of Talleyrand's that people would want to read about him because of his "apostasy [and] cunning craftiness," but, like the biography of David discussed above (also from the *Founders of the French Republic*), all of the biographies could serve the vague purpose of gratifying curiosity. The same interest may have underlain the curious re-publication of the life of Dufriche de Valazé, a decidedly minor character of the French revolution. It had been part of the initial series of lives taken from the *Founders* and was first published there on March 6, 1798; Dennie republished it, with a single minor modification, not even a year later, on February 18, 1799. The life of Valazé, similar to that of Chamfort, ended on a sanguinary and no doubt 'adventurous' note: Valazé, sentenced to death, instead prefers to end his own life—in the courtroom, no less—by a dagger, a suicide so bloody it "covered with the blood of the wise and virtuous man" his judges (*FWM* 1798 6.307, 2); since Dennie did not comment, either in the biography proper or anywhere else in the issue, on the reason for reprinting the text, it would be foolish to argue more than the possibility of this aspect of the story being of importance here. For sure, this ran contrary to the initial notice of Dennie's editorship, back in April 1796, when, over David Carlisle's signature, the *Museum* had avowed that "doleful narrative of bloody murder" (*FWM* 1796 4.157, 1) was not its object at all; but, as with the biography of Chamfort, the Valazé biography had fairly little to recommend it apart from its bloody curiosity.

Conceptually, then, the *Farmer's Weekly Museum* occasionally pretended in theory, but never in practice achieved, a clear line in its biographical articles and biographical criticism. Indeed, it was the very lack of a clear line which defined the *Museum*'s use of biography. Dennie's editorials tailored the *Museum*'s weekly conception to the biographical short text he published in that particular issue, rather than the other way around. Nor was this tendency to conform statements on theory to the exigencies of practices reserved for the day-to-day business of placing British texts in the *Museum*. When the *Farmer's Weekly Museum* set out to 'Americanize' its production, a similar ethos prevailed.

The Abortive Quest for National Lives

On several occasions, the *Farmer's Weekly Museum* attempted to rid itself of its dependence on British biographical productions in filling its columns. What is overall most notable in these attempts is their utter and complete failure: despite Dennie's best attempts, he could neither manage to find writers or apparently interest enough readers in his venture to make continuous pursuit of American biography a major goal.

Dennie first desired his correspondents to submit American biography in July 1797, apropos of nothing in particular. But his wishes were particular: "Sketches of American Biography are much wanted," he announced, and listed a number of men whose lives he wanted to publish. Among these were the American Loyalists Sir Benjamin Thompson and Sir John Wentworth, as well as clergymen and poets: "in brief," as Dennie summed it up, "all distinguished Cis Atlantick characters" would be welcome among his pages. This was a notably loose definition of American biography, and the question whether "men of learned leisure" (*FWM* 1797 5.224, 3) would be willing to laud Loyalist émigrés was not only one of biographical theory—Benjamin Thompson, Count Rumford, was still very much alive at this point, something of a contentious issue in the biographical theory of the day—but also one of politics, of course. As it turned out, it took nine months for a biography of Rumford to appear, and then in a version previously published in an English magazine (cf. Appendix 3).

None of Dennie's other particular requests came to fruition, and Dennie did not renew his call for American lives until November 1798, over a year after he had initially requested his readers' support. This time, he tried a more whimsical tack:

> The Editor implores his correspondents to afford him some literary and political aid. He is timorous, lest his readers should be nauseated with similar dishes, cooked by the same hand. Associates will, in the language of recruiting, meet with kind treatment.
>
> *WANTED,*
>
> A bale of *American* Biography… (*FWM* 1798 6.292, 3, original emphasis)

This time, he was not particular about the biographees he wanted discussed. On the contrary: despite his earlier elaborate attempt to promote biographies, this renewed request found it merely in the company of a broad variety of other texts requested from correspondents at the same time: wit, criticism, "Bundles from the Parnassian Shrubbery," and, for the "dreary dullness of November, two or three sunshine days of American Patronage." What becomes evident again here is the way biography not only becomes subsumed under a number of other texts, but also Dennie's recurrent central concern about variety. the same general purpose of filling the magazine with diversified "dishes." In this reading, the national question did not matter so much: American was not a political term, despite Dennie's implicit claim, but a geographic and literary descriptor which differentiated the kind of biography he sought from the kind he had. To publish American biography would be to publish, new, variegated texts, rather than the conventional reprints of British biography.

Dennie's maneuvering between the political and the practical, between the Federalist ideals espoused by the *Museum* and the materials on hand also found a place in the final attempt made by the *Museum* under his editorship to foreground American biography. In February, 1799, Dennie announced another revamping of the *Museum*. For the moment, he announced, and up until April, "[C]urious Biography and Anecdote" would "continue to diversify its columns," but he had a new idea in sight. Starting in April, when the new volume of the *Weekly Museum* would regularly commence, the paper would be called *Farmer's Museum and Lay Preacher's Gazette*. At the same time, Dennie stressed that there would be a new national bend to the paper, complementing the Federalism that the journal had long emphasized. Not only did the magazine's header now note its publication in the twenty-first year of American Independence and the ninth year of the Federal government, its content, too, would endeavor to reflect more strongly a new American focus. "Critical Speculations, principally upon American works" would be complemented by a new series on "'Federal Biography' containing authentic anecdotes of the principal personages of the United States […] This last article, if well executed, will, from its utility and interest, be worth treble the price of the paper" (*FWM* 1799 6.306, 4).

In this scheme, biography had a dual role: it was, as some of the previous articles published under the header, such as the "biography" of Thomas Topham, had already indicated, an anecdotal form of writing, primarily suitable to fill the requirements of novelty, variety and amusement: thus, general biography shared a department with anecdotes, "diversifying" the magazine. At the same time, Dennie recognized that it was also a suitable genre to further his new apparent goal of Americanizing the *Museum*. Thus, on March 18, 1799, he reaffirmed his desire to shift his biographical productions, and noted in another column to his readers that starting with the coming April, the *Museum* would be enlarged and improved, and would occasionally contain "[a]mong other important improvements, an *American* biography" (*FWM* 1799 6.311, 3, original emphasis). Indeed, when April 1 came, Dennie's paper included an entire rubric called American Biography, in which the editor published the life of John Trumbull. Dennie's lengthy editorial note prefacing the biography is worth quoting at length:

> We do not recollect to have read, in any American newspaper, biographical sketches of the more remarkable personages of our own country. By vanity and national pride it is often asserted, and by truth it is sometimes affirmed, that America can number many, inspired by genius, and many, favoured by learning. But of these worthies how few memorials are to be found: and how little is known of the private life, of the petty habits, of the studies, of the persons, and of the peculiarities of our great men. Inquisitive foreigners smile, when inquiring for the lives of illustrious Americans, they are shown the meager memoirs of a bloated "General," the adventures of a castle convict, and the "experiences and awakenings" of a baptist preacher. The editor of this gazette is proud of the power of commencing a series of the lives of, whose genius
>
> "Has shot a day sprung into distant climes"[15]
>
> He initiates his plan with the life of John Trumbull, Esq., the author of a poem, in copious wit, second only to the cantos of Butler, and in vigour, dignity, and sweetness, superior to the "passing worth of Sir Hudibras"[16] [...] The late Dr. E.H. Smith of New York is alluded to. The editor adds, with a voice not unreproachful, that the following well written life of a brilliant writer was first published in a very recent London Magazine; and that the ingenious biographer either could not find in America a gallery for his portrait, or, which is most probable, despaired of connoisseurs, who would admire, and a M[?] who would patronize. (*FWM* 1799 7.313, 1)

Dennie neither alludes to his own previous efforts at providing his readers with American biography, nor his own success at doing so, the biography of Count Rumford published in April 1798. Surprisingly, for all the Johnsonian language in the editorial introduction, Dennie does not claim instructiveness for the biography but again praises style and biographer, as well as the brilliance of the subject.

Despite this auspicious start, problems loomed for Dennie's new American biography section. In the same issue in which he placed Smith's biography of Trumbull, he requested aid from his readers: "We earnestly request literary gentlemen," he wrote, "to furnish the biographical department of this paper with the lives of the late Doc-

15 Dennie is quoting William Cowper's "Table Talk" (1782).

16 Samuel Butler's best known poem was *Hudibras* (1663-1678), a mock-heroic epic.

tors Clarke and Belknap" (3).[17] But American biography remained a profoundly opportunistic genre in the *Farmer's Weekly Museum*. No one came forward to produce either of these two lives; announced with great fanfare, Dennie's "American Biography" was very much piecework. Throughout the April issues in 1799, the *Museum* carried biographies written by Smith—John Trumbull's, Timothy Dwight's, and David Humphrey's—and finally on April 22, the life of Elihu Hubbard Smith himself. With that, the stream of American lives ended abruptly. Dennie's ambitious project of supplying his readers with genuinely American biography foundered on the rocks of a reality in which he found himself ill-supplied with the necessary texts to fill his little magazine. In September 1799, in one of the final issues of the *Museum* he edited, he prefaced the first American biography in a long time with the regretful reminder of this chapter's epigraph, that he "has repeatedly requested literary men to furnish him with Biographical anecdotes of our domestic character. He is sorry to say that, in no instance, has this requisition been complied with [...]" (*FWM* 1799 7.335, 1). Just as he had noted in February, and "strange as it may appear," this new example of American biography—the subject was Lemuel Hopkins, a notable physician and writer—in the *Museum* came from the *London Magazine*, and, like the biography of John Trumbull, was from Elihu Smith's pen. Smith, Dennie suggested, was forced to turn his writings in to British magazines because "for such modes of writing THERE WAS NO CURIOSITY IN AMERICA" (original emphasis).[18] Dennie profound dissatisfaction with his readership broke through. No longer satisfied to repeat a request for submissions from his readers, he suggested that the evidence now pointed squarely at a lack of literary taste. Why, "if suitable vehicle of communication, numerous readers, and generous patrons abounded, did a subject of the United States send the lives of his own countrymen to a foreign press?" Resignedly, he let his readers know that he was now publishing the life of Hopkins merely "to gratify himself."

Far from being an editorial statement of broad reach, then, his announcements in April 1799 and in the editorial prefaces to Smith's biographies paint the picture of editorial opportunism in which available material was lauded for being generally representative of desirable texts—here, the private lives of eminent Americans—while before and after, the editor had not cared at all for any of the central concerns therein suggested. If none of the biographies previously offered in the *Museum*

17 John Clarke, a New Hampshire born Boston minister, and Jeremy Belknap, also New Hampshire born, also a Boston minister, but most notably the author of the *History of New Hampshire* (1792) and *American Biography* (1794-1798); both had died in 1798 and were widely known in New England and renowned for their literary work.

18 This was not, strictly speaking, true. Smith had determined to publish his lives of American poets in Britain not so much because there was no market for the texts in the United States, but rather for a variety of reasons. One of those reasons, curiously enough, was almost contrary to Dennie's suggestion: Smith wrote his pieces for publication in an English magazine precisely because the English magazines circulated so freely and widely in the United States, thus offering a large American audience; another reason for Smith's choice was his desire to correct some European misconceptions about Americans. Cf. Cronin (1973, 438).

had followed the precepts of Johnsonian biography, with its emphasis on the private life and its insistence that any life, no matter how debased or mundane, could become a biographical life, this was only a momentary concern. The biographies which Dennie wished to publish in April 1799, Smith's short notices of American worthies, did follow Johnson—ergo, in April 1799, this was the biographical mode which fulfilled editorial policy. Dennie's exasperation, however, points to a general problem in Walpole: despite his extensive correspondence, Dennie desperately wanted to leave the town for greater opportunities in the city.

Towards Philadelphia and the *Port Folio*

By 1798, the *Farmer's Weekly Museum* was an undoubted critical but a decidedly modest financial success for Dennie, with his reduced salary and loss of savings. It was not terribly surprising, therefore, that he was on the lookout for other options—and indeed, perhaps more surprisingly, opportunities for other work were offered Dennie on silver platters. Dennie's correspondence between 1798 and 1800 reveals a remarkable side of the periodical business: the efforts of printers and publishers to secure for themselves the services of a successful editor to advance their own newspaper and magazine projects.

It was Dennie himself who made sure word got out that he was looking for a better job. From John Russell, a Boston bookseller and printer, a letter reached Dennie in July 1798 which referred to Dennie's complaints about his current station. As Russell wrote, it

> has been suggested to me by several worthy young gentlemen of this town, who are your friends and admirers; and who, in the assistance they have afforded me, both pecuniary and literary, have proved friendly, liberal and generous; that you were not completely satisfied in your achievements; and that, if a more agreeable situation could be made possible here, you would not hesitate to [?] among the giddy crowd, of this speculative, arithmetical town; besides this suggestion, Sir, they recommended a junction in business with you; and flatter themselves that a union of our industry and abilities, would not only be agreeable but *profitable* [...].

Dennie, Russell went on, would have the editorship, the "compilation, selection, &c with proof reading," while Russell would retain the "commercial, mercantile, and economy of affairs" in his hands. Russell made no suggestion on Dennie's salary, except to note that it should be fixed by a group of people jointly selected by Russell and Dennie. As far as his monetary hopes were concerned, Russell was cheerfully sanguine, "not doubting but that a handsome quantity of Cash might be accumulated by our industry and talents."[19]

19 John Russell to Joseph Dennie, July 10, 1798. Joseph Dennie Papers, Houghton Library, Harvard University, original emphasis, though profitable is underlined twice in the letter.

Although Russell speaks of having submitted to Dennie the "outline of a plan" in his letter, it is notable that this is not the kind of plan which editors would so often advertise in their prospectuses: not an outline of contents, nor a philosophy of the periodical, nor even a rough draft of what Dennie should expect to be publishing—it is not a plan for a paper or magazine. Instead, what Russell offers is a plan to make money, no more or less. While vaguely hinting at the disagreeableness of Dennie's present employment, the nature of an agreeable position remains elusive: the lure of money, however, does not. Russell does not attempt to tempt Dennie with an opportunity to fulfill his literary ambition as a man of letters (although he gives him free reign in his editorial choices); he argues his offer from a strictly pecuniary perspective. That this was a wise choice, Dennie's own correspondence confirms: in a letter to his mother in September, 1799, he noted his reduced salary of 400$ per annum, consequent upon the failure of David Carlisle's firm and the takeover of the publishing (but not the printing) business by Isaiah Thomas in early 1797, and hints at his dissatisfaction with his situation.[20]

Dennie was out to better his financial station. Russell's offer did not apparently tempt him—he never made the move to Boston, and no reply of his is extant—but it was not the last he received in the course of the next year. On November 27, 1798, the Philadelphia printer William Brown made an offer to Dennie. He wanted to sell a share in his paper, the *Philadelphia Gazette*, and offered Dennie the right of first refusal: "previous to a public avowal of my intentions," he let Dennie know, he wanted to let Dennie choose. "[M]y yearly profits [...] exceed 6000 dollars," he noted. To Dennie's obviously speedy reply to his request, Brown replied in turn on December 19th. He clarified his initial offer of a share in the paper to "terms of equal responsibility and profit, for a certain advance of Capital." But Dennie could not take him up, as Brown's disappointed note makes also clear: "I am extremely sorry that your situation is so incompatible with this arrangement." Dennie's suggestion can only be gleaned from Brown's reply: he had apparently offered Brown his services as editor (Brown speaks of an "assistant") but requested a princely salary "nearly equal to the half of my profits," as Brown complains. Brown made it amply clear that there was no chance of this ever happening, and indeed, suggested self-confidently that Dennie was not worth this much money: "In my opinion," Brown noted with the spite of the scorned, "no acquisition of talents can operate so powerfully upon the profits of this paper, as to make them of primary importance to its circulation or value." It was not the talents of the editor but the availability of timely news that made a newspaper worthwhile; on this score, Dennie and Brown were unlikely to see eye to eye.[21]

20 Rather disingenuously, in the prospectus to the *Port Folio*, Dennie would write, in the first footnote, that he, "not without emotion, calls up in review the tranquil pleasures of a studious life, amid the ever-green forests of Newhampshire" (*PF* Prospectus 1). For Dennie, the pursuit of fame and fortune lead him inexorably to Philadelphia; for Dennie's editorial persona, it was, on the other hand useful at least to offer the appearance of sacrifice.

21 William Brown to Joseph Dennie, November 27th, 1798 and December 19th, 1798. Joseph Dennie Papers, Houghton Library, Harvard University.

Brown's offer to Dennie was not the last, but indeed seems to have put some of Brown's publisher colleagues into action. In early February, 1799, a letter reached Dennie from General Lewis Morris from Philadelphia, a long-time correspondent of Dennie's who had for a while kept him abreast of the political developments in Philadelphia (cf. Ellis 1971, 93). "I find that proposals have been made you by Brown," Morris wrote, "I send you enclosed a letter from [John Ward] Fenno making you proposals for Editing the United States Gazette." Fenno's paper, sympathizing with the Federalists, had come to a decline since the death of Fenno's father half a year before in the yellow fever epidemic in Philadelphia. Morris noted that the paper had "fallen off much since the death of the Old Gentleman," and suggested that Fenno wanted to "sell his establishment." Morris's letter wavered curiously between encouragement and caution: "the Editing of a daily paper [in fact, the *Gazette* was a bi-weekly] is a laborious & responsible business—your Talents in that line are much wanted in this City [Philadelphia]."[22] Morris's suggestion that Fenno wanted to sell may be a mistake—Fenno mentions no such thing—or may be an additional caution to Dennie, encouraging him to take great care in his decision. Whatever the case, Fenno's enclosed letter contained a not inconsiderable offer. Like John Russell, Fenno begins his letter by noting that he addresses Dennie only after a conversation with Morris, and comes straight to the point: "[I] offer you the Editorial Department of the Gazette of the United States, [on] the following terms, viz. A salary $800 per annum,--and a percentage (say 20pr Cent) on every additional Subscription, up to the number of 500—12½ per cent, for all after, ad infinitum." The yearly subscription to the *Gazette* was 8$; should Dennie manage to gain Fenno 500 subscribers, then, he would make another 800$, and a dollar for every subscriber above 500 new subscribers. Considering Dennie's salary at the *Farmer's Weekly Museum*, this was indeed a princely sum—and yet Fenno played to Dennie's sense of his own worth by suggesting that

> [t]he sum of 800$ I am conscious is but a trifling consideration to be held out to a gentleman of your acquirements—but I entertain a confidence that the other provision will in a very short time become an object of some consideration. I would not, however, leave the contract on the footing of a contingency, were I not compelled by the very heavy expenses of the Establishment, to confine myself strictly to economy.[23]

Without apparently having heard from Dennie, Fenno wrote again on March 7th, amplifying his offer to include free board and lodging, either by staying with Fenno, or by reimbursing Dennie for his expenses. He also sent Morris to Dennie for a

22 Lewis Morris to Joseph Dennie, February 14, 1799. Joseph Dennie Papers, Houghton Library, Harvard University.

23 John Ward Fenno to Joseph Dennie, February 12, 1799. Joseph Dennie Papers, Houghton Library, Harvard University.

face-to-face talk about the proposal.[24] Dennie did not in the end accept Fenno's proposal, but, as shall be seen, ended up at the *Gazette* for a short time as editor.

Throughout April and May, offers reached Dennie for employment elsewhere. On April 18th, the New York publisher Charles Snowdon wrote Dennie a straightforward suggestion: "Sir," Snowdon began,

> I mean to sell my paper which I believe you have been in the habit of receiving in exchange lately. I offer it to you—If no other attachments bind you to Walpole than the profits of your paper, you would do well I think in taking this offer into serious consideration. For without detracting from yours, it is obvious that mine is superior in profit—being wholly an advertising paper. I ask 20,000$ for the whole establishment.[25]

No doubt various considerations played their part in Dennie's decision, such as it was, not to purchase the paper. It did not fit his editorial persona at all—Dennie would, within two years, denounce advertisements in periodicals—and Dennie certainly did not have the money to spend.[26] But it is telling that Snowdon could both suggest his paper as one which would appeal to Dennie as well as highlight the lack of allure of Walpole beyond the monetary profit. Snowdon does not, apparently, consider Dennie's principles a major sticking point, and does not even attempt to pitch his sale as anything but a profitable venture for Dennie. If the possibility remains, at least latently, that Dennie declined this particular offer because he had, in fact, something to "bind" him to Walpole apart from monetary profit, the following months would lay that suggestion to rest. Dennie received further offers of positions in the publishing world in those months. Late in April, a letter arrived from Baltimore, suggesting the desirability of a newspaper at that place and Dennie's editorship thereof, an unsolicited offer based largely on Dennie's reputation. Having no concrete conception of Dennie's reimbursement in mind, the plan came to naught.[27] In the middle of May, a letter came from Halifax, Nova Scotia, perhaps the oddest of all offers made in those months. The writer, Renna Cossit, noted that upon dropping Dennie's name in conversation with the Governor, that Royal officer had inquired whether Dennie would not desire the editorship of Halifax's *Royal Gazette*—a position in which there "could be no doubt of receiving a handsome income from government and much business here in

24 John Ward Fenno to Joseph Dennie, March 7, 1799. Joseph Dennie Papers, Houghton Library, Harvard University.

25 Charles Snowdon to Joseph Dennie, April 18, 1799. Joseph Dennie Papers, Houghton Library, Harvard University.

26 He had, Dennie wrote to his mother, "In consequence of this bankruptcy [of David Carlisle], [...] lost my whole property" (in Pedder 1938, 171) early in 1797; property which William Warland Clapp has estimated at 500$ (1888, 31).

27 Cf. J. Winchester to Joseph Dennie, April 27, 1799. Joseph Dennie Papers, Houghton Library, Harvard University.

law." Cossit spend much of the rest of the letter discussing the idiosyncrasies of Halifax life, making his note perhaps not altogether well calculated to inspire Dennie's removal to Nova Scotia.[28]

That none of the various suggestions made to Dennie for continued and often considerably more profitable employment in the magazine business came to fruition had a simple reason: concurrently with his grape-vined desire, never directly communicated by him and always passed on as a desire of his by friends, for a change of station in the editorial business, he had solicited, also through Lewis Morris, Secretary of State Timothy Pickering for a secretarial position. The position with Pickering had originally been Morris's idea, but one of which Dennie heartily approved, although he had "yet to learn what the precise duties in the *State* bureau" entailed (in Pedder 1936, 166, original emphasis). For him, the important thing was a place in the government, "if sufficiently renumerated," and if the position was one which he deemed himself qualified for—or perhaps, which he deemed qualified for himself. As he wrote to Morris: "Will you [...] take care that, if an additional officer in the above department be created, he may be invested with the title of confidential assistant, or confidential *Secretary*? The term, *Clerk*, is hardly soothing enough to *my* pride; it might disgust that of my family [...]" (in Pedder 1936, 166-7, original emphasis). Fortune and fame were still going hand in hand in Dennie's thoughts.

It was this plan which finally enabled Dennie to leave Walpole. By mid-May 1799, Dennie had received a positive answer from Pickering to his pleas, requesting him to move to Philadelphia as soon as convenient to take up his new office. Replying to Pickering, Dennie suggested that there might be a delay in his coming to Philadelphia on account of his health and the state of his business affairs. A few days after, he wrote again to Pickering, amending his previous note to admit that he had "neglected, in my letter alluded to, to state, that, when I contracted to conduct a paper in this pace, I stipulated with my principal, that, whenever I should resign that care, I should give the previous notice of three months" (in Pedder 1936, 169-70). It would not be terribly surprising if Dennie had had to be reminded of this by his "principal," his printer and publisher Isaiah Thomas, but that being as it may, Dennie requested Pickering's assent to the change of plans. Pickering replied to the request on June 7, 1799, suggesting that "I should have considered any disposition to neglect the fulfillment of your contract as a disqualification for a public employment" and recommending Dennie not to move to Philadelphia before the "expiration of August, when the weather begins to be more tolerable"—and the city's summerly outbreaks of yellow fever would be

28 Renna Cossit to Joseph Dennie, May 12, 1799. Joseph Dennie Papers, Houghton Library, Harvard University. As David Jaffee notes in *People of the Wachusetts*, Halifax figured in New England relations primarily because, like New Hampshire, it and Nova Scotia as a whole had been a destination in a great migration of New Englanders in the late eighteenth century, leading to extensive commercial contacts (and, later, fuelling the expectation that the War of 1812 would necessarily end with the annexation of much of Canada, Nova Scotia included); cf. Jaffee 1999, 237-8.

over.[29] Dennie would be moving by the middle of September (cf. Ellis 1971, 109; Ellis does not indicate his source). Earning 1000$ a year, Dennie's new position would more than double his yearly income without requiring his literary exertions to pay off in additional subscribers (as the Fenno offer would have), and offered him a chance to escape the by-now undesirable position in Walpole (cf. Pedder 1936, 173). The vital role which money played in his thoughts as he was packing his things together in New Hampshire is indicated by his maudlin epitaph to his service as editor of the *Farmer's Weekly Museum*, included in his long September letter to his family: "be content that I have not tarnished the name of Dennie, and that, if I have not acquired wealth, I am not chargeable, but have, in despite of losses, paid the very heavy expences of four years with the profits of my personal labor" (in Pedder 1936, 174).[30] It is notable that here, as in the entirety of his correspondence with his family, idealistic motivations which could have trumped monetary losses find no mention at all.[31]

Some critics, like Catherine O'Donnell Kaplan, have seen the move to Philadelphia as yet another aspect of Dennie's desire to "support himself entirely from his literary labors," and gloss the move primarily as a means of advancing his literary fame and his correspondents' desire to make his literary fame a vehicle for Federalism: as Kaplan has it, "Federalists [...] were determined to make Dennie more widely read" (1997, 138). Whatever his circle's motivation was, the evidence points to Dennie's desire to become engaged in the political sphere—even if that desire may not have lasted—and that there was no immediate ulterior motive: he took the job with Pickering because he wanted the job with Pickering.[32] Dennie arrived in Philadelphia in Oc-

29 Timothy Pickering to Joseph Dennie, June 7, 1799. Joseph Dennie Papers, Houghton Library, Harvard University.

30 Dennie's "four years" in this letter have been part of the argument by which scholars have argued that Dennie took editorial control of the *Museum* as early as September 1795, half a year prior to the likely date of April 1796. But Dennie wrote in his address "To the Public" of February 11, 1799, of "four laborious years" as well, even though in February 1795, he was still in Boston and unattached to the *Museum*. Perhaps Dennie meant to speak of the entirety of his editorial work, including the *Tablet*, begun in May 1795. In any event, it seems dangerous to base assumptions of Dennie's tenure on his recollections of time.

31 It is, of course, possible to read the developments in 1799 as precisely the form of translation of social and cultural capital into economic capital which is the fulcrum of Bourdieu's field theory. Dennie's work for the *Farmer's Weekly Museum* brought him to the attention of Lewis Morris: he converted, in Bourdieu's terms, cultural capital into social capital, which, in turn, through Morris's agency, could be converted into the economic capital of a gainful employment with Timothy Pickering.

32 Catherine O'Donnell Kaplan suggests that Timothy Pickering's letter, quoted by Dennie in his long letter to his family in September 1799, hints at the Secretary's desire to hire Dennie "as a useful Federalist voice" (1997, 138). Pickering wrote, according to Dennie, "that if, with my genius and taste [...] I could, in some degree relinquish the pursuits of literature, and submit to the drudgery of political business, he would be glad to employ me, and congratulate himself

tober, and his appointment—to the post of "Inspector of Records"—was hailed by the Washington, D.C., *Centinel of Liberty* as "the reward of the literary talents of this gentleman" (1799 October 15, 4.42, 3). This, certainly, is also the interpretation which Dennie put on his new employment. As he noted to his family, his "attention to political topics and [his] known zeal for administration have inspired to advance my hope of fame and fortune," first in an unsuccessful run for a Congressional seat, then in the Federal appointment with Pickering "that I might acquire the diplomatic style." Lest his family assume that he proposed to use the diplomatic to meliorate his often acerbic political style in editing another paper, he assured them of his ultimate goal in Philadelphia: "if, by the success of my pen, and by the confidence of the Government, I should be found worthy[,] my objects were, eiether [sic] a Secretaryship to a Foreign Legation, or a Consulship" (in Pedder 1936, 172).[33] It is especially notable that Dennie saw the secretaryship in the State Department merely as a stepping stone, but not one into a more extensive literary business.

Aside from evidence in his own writings, however, he clearly communicated his privileging of the government position over other offers, and was willing to forgo literature for the well-salaried governmental position. In May 1800, William Cobbett wrote him, replying to Dennie's note that he would not be able to come to New York to see Cobbett again. Cobbett was saddened, but consoled by Dennie's suggestion that the exigencies of office required his remaining in Philadelphia (or rather, Pickering's threat of firing Dennie if he departed): "I feel a consolation," Cobbett wrote, "on your account, from your being influenced by the threat; because it proves to me, that your office is valuable and that you have prudence and fortitude to preserve."[34] Dennie's literary work while in Philadelphia remained sec-

upon being the instrument in availing the public of my talents" (in Kaplan 2007, 138). Given the content of Pickering's letter as reported by Dennie, Kaplan's interpretation seems somewhat farfetched. Pickering stresses Dennie's becoming a public servant precisely in so far as he is willing to give up literature, rather than his usefulness as a man of letters. Indeed, if Pickering had, with open eyes, hired Dennie as a Federalist voice, his letter to John Marshall, his successor as Secretary of State, is slightly puzzling: "Mr. Dennie's habits and literary turn [...] render his service as a clerk less productive than the labours of many dull men" (in Kaplan 2007, 138) If Dennie's Federalism certainly played a role in getting him hired by Pickering—through the intercession of Federalist luminary Lewis Morris—it is by no means clear that he was supposed to play a political role in Philadelphia literary society. It was his job with the Department of State was primarily responsible for getting him to move, including the 1000$ salary. As Harold Ellis notes, "Dennie probably had a pleasant life" (1971, 112) at the Department of State; his rather generous salary offered him incentive enough, to which he added, however, in a letter to his family, "rank, respectability, high opportunities of political preferment" as additional emoluments of the new position (in Pedder 1936, 173).

33 In his belief that he could transfer to a diplomatic post abroad, Dennie may have been influenced by the example of his contemporary Joel Barlow, consul at Algiers in 1795-7.

34 William Cobbett to Joseph Dennie, May 7th, 1800. Joseph Dennie Papers, Houghton Library, Harvard University.

ondary to his duties at the State Department, as he himself acknowledged, both in terms time and pecuniary compensation. He continued contributing to the *Museum* and supplied John Ward Fenno of the *Gazette of the United States*, "occasionally," with "a few speculations for which I can obtain a respectable addition to my salary" (in Pedder 1936, 175). That Fenno paid him for contributions is confirmed by his political opponents: "Joe Dennie [...] is paid for writing in Fenno's Gazette," wrote Samuel Parker of Boston's arch-Republican *Constitutional Telegraphe* in April of 1800 (1800 April 5, 1.54, 3). Dennie had found a comfortable niche in Philadelphia, one which he hoped to leave only for a more lucrative post abroad, but events conspired to prevent his leaving the republic of letters.

Although he had clearly not set out with the purpose in mind, in Philadelphia, Dennie would attempt to make more of a mark, and still more money, as publisher and editor both. By early 1800, Dennie had already reset his sights and was hoping to return to publishing a paper. Now, however, he would not be content with being a salaried editor: he wanted his own paper.[35] This shift in his outlook was owed to a decline in his prospects at the Department of State. In February, he wrote to his longtime friend Roger Vose that he had been "following the fortunes of the Secretary," a phrase which indicates Dennie's awareness that Pickering's position in the Adams cabinet was growing weak-

35 The genesis of the *Port Folio* is difficult to determine in detail (an attempt at this has been made below), and we are not much helped by the conclusions reached by Harold Ellis and Laura Pedder on Dennie's job situation in early and mid-1800. Ellis suggests that Dennie took over the editorship of the *Gazette of the United States* in May, 1800 (Pedder misreads Ellis to say April; cf. 1936, 178), but bases this estimate only on the style of a single note published consequent to the *Gazette*'s sale to Caleb P. Wayne, a Philadelphia printer. Style, however, is a notoriously shaky base for textual ascription. More than this circumstantial and largely idiosyncratic evidence only comes to the fore in June, when the *Gazette* announced it would be edited by the "sometime Editor of the Farmer's Museum" (cf. *Gazette of the United States* 1800, June 20, 17.2413, 3). At this point, Secretary of State Pickering had resigned, and Dennie's position at the State Department, as Private and Confidential Secretary, was becoming tenuous, despite the support of President Adams. Pickering's letter to his successor Marshall could not have been a great help in securing Dennie the job again under the new secretary; it is therefore not surprising that he sought employment elsewhere in June; but it would be somewhat surprising if he sought the editorship of the *Gazette* under Wayne in April, when he had declined the extremely liberal offer which Fenno had made a year earlier, and he was still employed in the State Department. A trial balloon had in fact been floated by Fenno in December, 1799, in which subscribers were informed that, if sufficient additional subscriptions could be obtained, Oliver Oldschool [Dennie] would accept the editorship of the *Gazette*—nothing came of it, as additional subscribers did not accumulate, no doubt leading to Fenno's decision to sell the paper. Why Dennie should accept the paper's editorship from Wayne remains mysterious; that he had it by June, however, is also attested by a letter he wrote to Timothy Pickering on June 19th, enclosing several texts culled from the *Gazette*; cf., on the entire discussion, Ellis 1971, 129-131; Pedder 1936, 171-188; and Joseph Dennie Papers, Houghton Library, Harvard University.

er, as the conciliatory politics which Adams pursued towards the French increasingly conflicted with Pickering's Hamiltonian desire to take a stronger stance, and the secretary's general penchant for disloyalty towards the President (cf. McCullough 2001, 529-31, 537-9). President Adams fired Pickering in May, 1800. Dennie, however, had already put plans in motion for an alternative employment. He told Vose: "I meditate and shall shortly execute a literary scheme, not unmingled with a dash of politics, which uniting the stipends of Clerk and Gazetteer, will place me on the rock of Independence" (in Pedder 1936, 178). This characteristically cryptic line has been read by Laura Pedder to suggest that Dennie was speaking of becoming the editor of the *Gazette of the United States*—but this seems unlikely and is in fact contradicted by evidence. Stressing the "union" of clerk and gazetteer, Dennie was clearly implying a position in which the elements of both would accrue in one single employment, especially with regard to income; but more importantly, the editorship was not a position of independence. Serving at the pleasure of Caleb Wayne, the new proprietor, and having already had to realize that the imprint Oliver Oldschool did not apparently reach out to subscribers terribly much, the position at the *Gazette* was hardly the significant step which Dennie suggested to Vose as imminent. What Dennie was working at was his own paper, a project that he was actively engaged in as early as February 1800. On the 25th of that month, the Philadelphia printer Hugh Maxwell wrote Dennie a long letter which makes clear that Dennie was seeking to establish himself with a paper of his own. Maxwell came right to the point: "To you Sir," he wrote in his first sentence, "it would be unnecessary to describe the difficulties attendant on the publication of a periodical book."[36] To read the letter feels like an intrusion into an ongoing discussion, but several points become evident: Dennie had floated the idea of publishing a paper himself in Philadelphia and asked Maxwell to serve as his printer. In May, William Cobbett, the New York editor and printer, wrote Dennie to note that he had heard that Dennie had "actually conceived the idea of a new *magazine*" (original emphasis).[37] It was a venture he had conceived with Asbury Dickins, a Philadelphia bookseller whom Dennie probably met through William Meredith, with whom Dennie lodged, and Meredith's brother-in-law Thomas Armat, who was Dickins's attorney later. It was Dickins who had written to Cobbett originally and from whom the New Yorker had had first intelligence of Dennie's scheme. The process of creating the paper that was to become the *Port Folio* was on.

What, then, do we take away from three and a half years in which the *Farmer's Weekly Museum* was under Joseph Dennie's editorship, and from the first steps from which the long walk of the *Port Folio* would develop? As will

36 Hugh Maxwell to Joseph Dennie, February 25, 1800. Historical Society of Pennsylvania, Meredith Family Papers 1509, Box 99.

37 William Cobbett to Joseph Dennie, May 1, 1800. Joseph Dennie Papers, Houghton Library, Harvard University.

become evident in the next section, the *Museum* was very like a microcosm of what Dennie later, at the editorial helm of a magazine by no means of "minor form," would do in the *Port Folio*. On the four pages of the *Museum*, Dennie exercised as much editorial control as the need to serve his publisher's requirements, his own limited selection of material, a vague and shifting sense of his role as editor and the purpose of his periodical, and the constraints of weekly publishing allowed him. He exhibited a notable capacity to adapt his conceptions of editorship and biography to the exigencies of the momentarily available material. Dennie could be, and was, educator one week and "traiteur" the next, humble servant of his customers and straightforward about his own desires and wishes in alternating issues, at once the "Lay Preacher" and the "canny professional" (Jaffee 1999, 227). Dennie's suggestion that there existed an "imaginary being, called an Editor" (*FWM* 1797, 5.224, 3), as he wrote in a note to his readers and correspondents, was tongue in cheek, but there was a fundamental truth to it: the single man who needed to be immediately concerned with the business of obtaining subscribers' money, with supplying material for the paper and at once a workman and an artist, a servant and a guiding spirit, certainly did not exist. Dennie was, as David Jaffee has suggested, a salesman of literary products in the burgeoning marketplace for cultural commodities (cf. 1999, 227), but at the same time he was an employee at the *Museum*, and, if a salesman, a salesman who sold wares not his own. This is the central difference between the "Lay Preacher" who Jaffee stresses was the central persona for Dennie and the editorial persona established in the *Museum*: whereas, for the collected sermons of the Lay Preacher, a single voice sufficed, the *Museum* needed to bring together in a single form the highly miscellaneous texts it united every week, and consequently its editor assumed shifting personae. The editor was, more metaphorically, imaginary in other ways also. Dennie's announcement of American biography is a case in point here: however often and determinedly he made sure in 1799 that he wanted, indeed planned with, American biography, the failure to obtain any besides the six pieces he published made all his best laid plans superfluous. Dennie could imagine himself the sovereign (autonomous!) lord over the content of his magazine if he so desired, but in the end, he would repeatedly be hamstrung by his inability to obtain sufficient material. Opportunistic in its choice of what it would publish—the availability of material dictated the regularity with which Dennie could offer his readers biography far more strongly than any concept of editorship or biography—the *Museum*'s success was remarkable nonetheless, and despite all the strictures and difficulties under which he labored, this was a success that was largely owed to Dennie—as the numerous attempts to hire him attest. In Walpole, Dennie made his first sustained acquaintance with the necessary malleability of the editorial stance in the face of limitations, opportunities, and the weekly struggle to publish a periodical. In Philadelphia, he proposed to try his hand (on a very similar plan) as an entrepreneur himself. It would remain to be seen whether the *Port Folio* would have a similar success.

"A Politico Literary Paper": The *Port Folio,* 1801-1812

Ten years after the initial publication of the *Port Folio*, Joseph Dennie reminisced: "In the winter of 1801, the editor of the *Port Folio* commenced the publication of a politico literary paper. He then deemed it expedient to adopt a fictitious name [...]" (*PF* 1811, 87). Despite the twists and turns in content and in form which the *Port Folio* experienced over the first decade of its existence, the magazine had remained lastingly popular. The *Port Folio* had for a long time been the preeminent magazine in the United States, and its editor had received the honor of becoming the "American Addison" to his readers. As Oliver Oldschool, Dennie had published the *Port Folio* for ten years, almost to the day, and now, early in 1811, he decided to drop the pseudonym. Henceforth, he would edit the magazine under his own name. The decision was symptomatic of the many changes which had occurred in the *Port Folio* since 1801. The magazine was not in any meaningful way political anymore: it had "retreat[ed] into literature," as William Dowling has phrased it (1999, 50)—or had it? Certainly, the Oldschool pseudonym had lost its value as a revealing mask, metaphorically circumscribing the ideology of the imagined editor even as it provided a modest protection against the likelihood of politico-legal prosecution for libel and sedition to its actual editor. But the fundamental narrative of the *Port Folio* has probably overstressed politics as a decisive factor. In its first year, politics played an ultimately neglectable role, despite the incoming Jefferson administration's inacceptability to the Federalist Dennie. Dennie's hiding behind the Oldschool pseudonym had not become pointless as far as the question of political protection is concerned, it had always been pointless on this ground, as Dennie's 1803 indictment for seditious libel attests. This chapter seeks to refocus the attention away from political and ideological readings of the magazine towards one that emphasizes the heteronomous production conditions under which it was produced.

From the get go, as we have seen, the *Port Folio* had been a project designed to make money, and indeed, for the most part, it made enough money to sustain Dennie easily—even as he loaned money freely and spent it lavishly on drink and friends. Not everybody had been so sanguine about the *Port Folio*'s prospects. William Cobbett, still hopeful in June of 1800 that Dennie might yet choose to join a common venture in New York City, mischieviously suggested that "[t] he magazine would not yield you ten dollars a month [...]."[38] Even such a bleak outlook, however, did not stop Dennie from persevering at his project. Cobbett correctly identified what drove Dennie: "the road to competence, comfort, and fame," a road which Cobbett believed he could offer to tread with Dennie in New York, but which Dennie thought he could just as easily follow in Philadelphia.

The *Port Folio*'s history has still not been adequately analyzed.[39] I will selective-

38 William Cobbett to Joseph Dennie, May 1, 1800. Joseph Dennie Papers, Houghton Library, Harvard University.

39 The only book-length study of the *Port Folio* as a whole is an unfortunately unpublished dis-

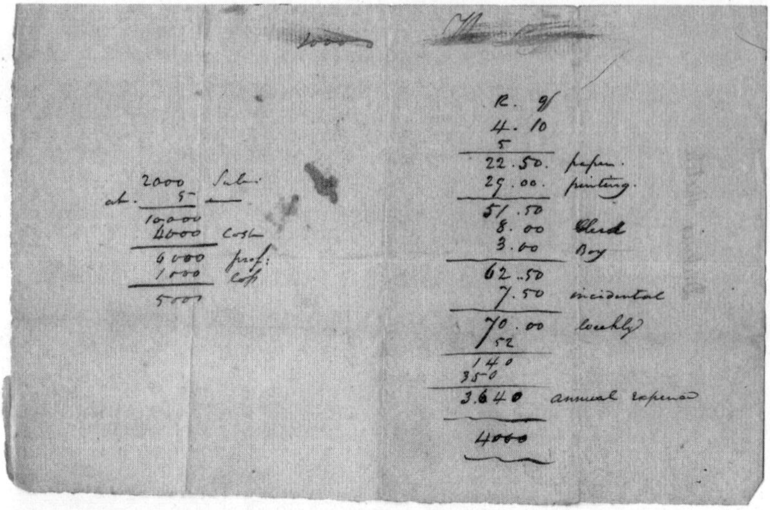

FIG. 3: Calculation marked "A. Dickins Sketch" in Joseph Dennie's handwriting. The left column indicates the profit calculation Dickins made for the *Port Folio*: at 2000 subscribers (about the number the rural *Farmer's Weekly Museum* had in its heyday), Dickins calculated 5000$ profit for Dennie and himself. The right hand column shows the expected annual expenses, including printing costs paid to Hugh Maxwell and weekly "incidental" expenses, perhaps authors' fees or similar costs. Historical Society of Pennsylvania, Meredith Family Papers 1509, Box 99.
Courtesy of the Historical Society of Pennsylvania.

ly highlight and examine four significant points in it: the period of the magazine's inception, from early 1800, when the initial plans were laid, to late 1801 and into the early months of 1802; when Asbury Dickins, the first publisher, left the country and retired his publishership; the years 1806/07, when Hugh Maxwell, the magazine's printer for the first six years, stopped working for the magazine, a new series was begun (with corresponding changes to layout and content), and the first serious problems appeared with Dennie's role in the venture; 1809, when the *Port Folio* was sold to the Philadelphia-New York publishing house of Bradford & Inskeep, changed to a monthly octavo format and seriously shifted its character in other ways as well; and finally, 1812, when, with Dennie's death, Nicholas Biddle's assumption of the editorship, and the War of 1812, the magazine again redefined itself. What unites these datum points is at once their centrality to the history of the *Port Folio*, the availability of copious primary material revealing

sertation (Queenan 1955). Queenan's study is mostly hampered by not being an actual chronological history, but rather an episodic study, centering on editors and content. Even though it is episodic, however, it reveals much about the behind-the-scenes goings on, especially after 1812, and certainly does much with the remarkably thin stratum of archival material.

much about the events behind the scenes, and the relevance of the changes in ownership structure and editorial plan for the printing of biography. Biography's role in the *Port Folio* was never to be central, but always to be present, even as subtle changes occurred in the course of the magazine's history, and representative of the ways in which the Port Folio's editorial processes developed. Yet more importantly, the *Port Folio*'s history at the datum points I have selected highlights the stages of professionalization which the magazine underwent from 1801, when it emphatically foregrounded ideological readings, through 1805, when it first most clearly differentiated the positions of editor and publisher, to 1809, when it became one venture among many for a new proprietor-publisher. On the way, the story of the *Port Folio* reveals the continuities of the business of periodical production more than anything else: the sharp eye for profit and the urgent need to satisfy the magazines' customers.

The Beginnings of the *Port Folio*

When the first volume of the *Port Folio* appeared on January 3rd, 1801, Joseph Dennie was 32 years old; his publisher, the Philadelphia bookseller Asbury Dickins, was just twenty. Dickins had taken over his father's stationery and book shop after the latter's death during the 1798 yellow fever epidemic, running the business for his mother. Fairly successful at what he was doing, Dickins was nevertheless not cut out for bookselling, but saw his genuine calling in publishing. Dickins knew Hugh Maxwell, a Philadelphia printer with whom Dickins worked in the publication of Charles Brockden Brown's final three novels, and who, starting in 1800, lodged with Dickins. Dickins himself was also a satirist whose works were printed by Maxwell. He had inherited some of his father's connections with booksellers far afield, but, as Peter Parker notes in the only biographical sketch of Dickins, his "business was definitely an urban enterprise" (1970, 475). It was from Dickins that William Cobbett had received the first hint in May 1800 that Dennie was planning on launching a magazine venture. The intended new publication, although centered on Philadelphia, had every aspiration of obtaining a similarly Union-wide readership as the *Farmer's Weekly Museum* had. Dickins and Dennie had every sort of reason to expect the venture to be a success, and every sort of incentive to attempt it. For Dennie, Secretary Pickering's demission and the likelihood of Thomas Jefferson succeeding John Adams in the presidency rendered his hopes for political advancement, certainly the lucrative post of a consul abroad, negligible. For Dickins, the chance to advance his reputation was impossible to pass up (cf. Parker 1970, 769).

Over it all, however, loomed the chance to make considerable amounts of money. Dickins himself calculated the possible profits to be made from the venture (cf. fig. 3). Although the note bears no date and is not explicitly marked as relating to the *Port Folio*, it is obviously about a weekly paper, and Dickins shared no other periodical project with Dennie, in whose handwriting the note is attributed. The sketch reveals the considerable hopes which Dennie and Dickins shared for their venture. The two assumed that they could end up with the same amount of subscribers which Dennie had acquired for the *Farmer's Weekly Museum*: 2000, not an unreasonable assumption on the grounds that Philadelphia offered a vastly greater subscriber base than Walpole, New Hampshire. Many of those subscribers, too, would be locals, thus making it easier to supply them with papers and collect their money. Dennie was a known quantity by now, and Dickins could rely on the vestiges of a literary network he had inherited from his father. They acknowledged the possibility that there could be unexpected losses (1000$ would cover 200 defaulting subscribers); at the same time, Dickins calculated 3640$ actual costs, but made his profit calculations with 4000$ cost. Dickins was being careful with his estimates, but he still estimated a net yearly profit for Dennie and himself of two and a half thousand dollars each. For this, he was willing to assume, as Dennie put it in the prospectus, the "cares and risque" of the venture (*PF* Prospectus 1801, 1n5). Indeed, as his correspondence proves, for the duration of the first year of the *Port Folio*'s existence, Dickins was handling subscription lists, payments for paper and printing costs, and other business-related questions, such as the number of off-prints for each number, a question which he, however, sometimes needed to be reminded to address.[40]

Besides Dennie and Dickins, a third man played a vital role in the *Port Folio*'s early years: the Philadelphia printer Hugh Maxwell. Maxwell was young and aspiring, but he also knew his business. Neither Dennie nor Dickins had yet successfully published a periodical, although Dennie was justifiably proud of his editorial record. Maxwell was both interested in cooperation with Dennie and prepared to be himself more involved in the business than just filling in as an executor of print jobs. Dennie received a number of hints for running the new venture in a letter Maxwell sent in February 1800. Maxwell suggested why Dennie, Dickins and he would succeed where others had failed before. Since the demise of James Watters's *Weekly Magazine*, no other attempt to publish a magazine in Philadelphia had flourished; but, Maxwell wrote Dennie, "one great cause of failure in the city is that no person has yet appeared as the conductor of such a publication of sufficient literary character."[41] Dennie would bring this character to the new magazine, and Maxwell also realized that it was important for an editor that "his name should stand high in the public estimation"—a feature Dennie certainly possessed. "That illiterate and obscure bookbinders and printers have not succeeded in any of their various attempts, is not to be wondered at: They perished not from a want of public and public liberality they sunk beneath the weight of their own insignificance," Maxwell suggested. That Dennie's presence would not be sufficient, Maxwell also

40 Cf. Hugh Maxwell to Asbury Dickins, n.d. [January 1801]. Historical Society of Pennsylvania, Loudoun Papers 1791, Asbury Dickins Correspondence,

41 All quotes in the following identified as being Maxwell's from: Hugh Maxwell to Joseph Dennie, February 25, 1800. Historical Society of Pennsylvania, Meredith Family Papers 1509, Box 99. This document is fully reprinted in Lanzendörfer (2012).

understood. He emphasized what he believed to be "not a little advantageous" changes to the magazine forward.

> [A] due attention to the tastes of readers has not been paid. Too profuse a use is generally made of any uninteresting matter which a numerous body of readers do not understand and for those who do, a light portion will suffice. Humor and light reading seem to me to be peculiarly adapted to the tastes of Magazine readers. I do not mean that Philosophy & Morality should be excluded. It is as necessary for the future existence of a work as its present prosperity, that it should stand high in the opinion of those who consider themselves judges of literary merit.

Differences between the British and American models of periodical publishing also made Maxwell doubtful of the foreign news department.[42] Leave that to the newspapers, Maxwell suggested: the *Port Folio* should be a more durable repository. "A magazine may be so conducted as to form a kind of history of our country during the period in which it was conducted," containing public records questions particularly concerned with the United States. Maxwell's argument was not one from public utility, though: as when he wished that someone would pay "attention to the tastes of readers," Maxwell realized that he could translate readers' interest and the magazine's lastingness to increase profits. Make the *Port Folio* lasting, he enjoined Dennie, "so that at a future day the work may become estimable and the copies which remain on hand be sold to advantage. In this lies the great profit of a magazine. Without this advantage it is never worth prosecuting." Maxwell's insight into publishing realities here is interesting. Maxwell's accounts for the period 1801-1806 indicate the frequency with which he reprinted individual issues and complete volumes (i.e., half-yearly editions) for Dennie. *Port Folio* back issues were advertised as early as February 1803 by Ezra Sargeant, a New York bookseller with whom Dennie was frequently in correspondence. For the duration of the magazine's existence, back issues, usually from the commencement, were available at booksellers.

Maxwell's ideas about the periodical business did not grow out of thin air. He had been James Watters's printer for the *Weekly Magazine* as well, and obviously possessed considerable behind the scenes knowledge about the workings of that periodical.[43] To Dennie, he suggested that several of the men who had contributed

42 In this section of the letter, Maxwell showed himself impressively well-versed in the publication differences between American and Great Britain. Maxwell noted that stamp taxes in England made newspapers far more expensive, and considered Americans generally richer. He concluded that magazines therefore could offer rural communities with a cheaper way of obtaining news and other information; the same held not true in the United States. Maxwell's assumption that British consumers were generally less well off than Americans opens questions about the relationship between the British magazine consumership discussed in Chapter 1 in its relation to the American experience.

43 Benjamin Lewis's *Register of Editors, Printers, and Publishers of American Magazines, 1741-1810*

to the *Weekly Magazine* might be interested in also contributing to the *Port Folio*. Among the names were several whom Dennie already knew: Charles Brockden Brown, now running his own magazine in New York; the pseudonymous "Beri Hesdin," whom Maxwell identified as "Mr. Hay" but who was actually Isaac Story; Charles Caldwell; and William Duane.[44] How Maxwell expected William Duane, the acerbic editor of the Republican *Aurora* newspaper, and Dennie to cooperate on a publication remained his secret, however.

In Maxwell's suggestions to Dennie, the periodical business as it was conducted at the turn of the nineteenth century is laid out with great clarity—and at the same time, the major shift which periodicals underwent in the following years is already hinted at. Maxwell's recognition that, apart from Watters, conductors had insufficiently appreciated the importance of playing to the interests of their readership, would play a major role in the conduct of the *Port Folio* during its heyday. Time and again, Dennie would acknowledge the importance of precisely the mixture of a light portion of serious matter and a strong helping of 'interesting' and 'useful' content, and the specificity of the magazine's readership. This came to the fore most strongly after the *Port Folio* turned itself into a monthly, when news and politics took a backseat to the lighter muses. Maxwell also realized the role which morals could play in a successful magazine, and even as he seemed ready to acknowledge its relevance, he also noted that its purpose was all smoke and mirrors. Magazines, Maxwell pointed out to Dennie, did not publish moral tales and high philosophy because their readership required it, or, even less, because it was a virtuous deed for an editor to attempt to educate his readers. Rather, magazines published moral tales because those readers who considered themselves arbiters of literary quality—and note that Maxwell is clear in stressing the term "consider themselves" over the possibility of acknowledging that they actually "are"—deem it their role to highly rank only those magazines which included morals. Moral education, then, as seen through the printer's eyes, as explained to the editor, and no doubt as an opinion shared by the publisher, was a nod towards the clientele and a means to an end—not an end in morality, however, but an end in present and future prosperity for the editor, publisher, and printer. Maxwell's letter is businesslike, clearheaded, and entirely unromantic about periodical literature. In this, it mirrored Dennie's private thoughts on why he was in the periodical business; the public presentation was, of course, different.

In the course of the summer of 1800, even as he started stop-gap work as the editor of the *Gazette of the United States*, Dennie pursued the *Port Folio* project. As with most magazines of the period, the *Port Folio*'s official life commenced with the publication of a prospectus, announced as impending in the *Gazette of the United States* in September and probably available to readers as early as Novem-

(1957) says as much (cf. 23); Maxwell had taken over from Watters himself in May 1798, when the latter reverted to being merely the publisher and editor.

44 For the identification of Isaac Story, cf. Isaac Story to Joseph Dennie, n.d. [1797], Joseph Dennie Papers, Houghton Library, Harvard University.

ber 1800. The *Port Folio*'s prospectus offers invaluable insights into the conception of the periodical and the almost schizophrenic editorial persona which Joseph Dennie sought to create for his new venture. It is a document at once overly precise and maddeningly vague, meticulously crafted to seem to say much and really say very little. In style and form, it stands out among the prospectuses produced by magazine editors and publishers during Early Republic: copiously footnoted and annotated, erudite and eloquent, it presented readers with an editorial persona that was destined to become as famous as the "Lay Preacher." His name, "Oliver Oldschool," was "indicative of his moral, political, and literary creed," Dennie announced. The name also promised safety: Dennie, proclaiming himself a "dissident Editor," felt the "machinery of a fictitious title […] convenient," a chance, if ultimately not a certainty, to avoid the threat of indictments for political libel. The new paper, the prospectus announced, would be published "every Saturday, on a super-royal quarto sheet"

Bits and pieces of the prospectus clearly echoed Hugh Maxwell's influence. The *Port Folio* would "reject the minuteness of foreign and domestic detail" even was it would "communicate, with accuracy, the most interesting and important State papers" (*PF* 1801 Prospectus, 2). Dennie did not entirely heed Maxwell's injunction to delete the department of foreign news, but reduced the space he wished to devote to it to that minimum which might end up doing what Maxwell had so bluntly enjoined him to keep in mind: as a repository of the most momentous events, the *Port Folio* might see long-term sales and lasting presence in people's households. Even as he was worrying about the standing of literary editors in the United States, Dennie noted that in Europe, magazines were "preserved long" (3), echoing Maxwell's desire to have the *Port Folio* something of a repository of historical information.

The main body of the *Port Folio* explicitly stressed a form of virtuousness in editorial principles that went ill with the ultimate goals Dennie had privately announced. In the prospectus, he sought to downplay his expectations as much as Dickins's and his own calculations had positively estimated their potential profit in private. "[U]nder every disadvantage of a narrow subscription, he is resolved to persevere," he announced (1), even as though editorial stamina could stand in for financial security. But the argument in due course becomes a different one. Dennie puts himself at the monetary mercy of his contributors and distances himself from outrights claims to monetary compensation: while Dickins, the "publisher[,] *must* be compensated," and Maxwell, the "compositor[,] *must* be requited" (1, original emphasis), Dennie, the "conductor," merely can put his faith in his audience's willingness to provide a "'quiddam honorarium,'" a Roman law term for a gratuity to which a counselor had no legal right, but which was freely given by his client. Anything else, Dennie claims, would make him a "*Hireling*" (1, original emphasis). Money and literary work are constantly intertwined in the prospectus, but in such a fashion as to obscure all clear lines: Dennie does not make a claim on his readership's money for himself, but emphasizes that literature, and literature alone, is his profession and sustenance, and expects that readers will understand themselves morally bound to support his work: where literature "renders actual service, gives harmless pleasure to some, and new ideas to others, it confers at least a species of obligation, which any code of ethical precept will teach men to repay" (1). For Dennie, if anything, money can only be an objection to literary labor if the sums paid are too small; offering English examples, he asks not to let "writers be rashly censured for *vending* the fruits of mind. Authors, far elevated above the mire of low avarice, have thought it debasement to make Literature *common and cheap*. The affluent lord Lyttleton made his history of Henry II a booksellers [sic] property at the price of three thousand pounds [...]" (1, second emphasis is my own). If even the affluent gentry could sell their writings, why should Dennie not? In seeming to eloquently deny more than a mere voluntary compensation with what is left after Dickins and Maxwell have been paid, Dennie makes the case for paying the editor and his authors for their work. The prospectus never makes the case outright, though, carefully maneuvering in classical allusions: "Literary industry," Dennie suggested, "usefully employed has a sort of draught upon the bank of opulence, and has the right of entry into the mansion of every Maecenas" (1); a draught, at that, that was more than "only a servant's price of labour," the "paltry wages of the vulgar hireling," a "mercenary fugitive." Dennie laid claim to "the generous stipend for mental efforts" that could prevent the editor from simply abandoning his project, feeling unappreciated and underpaid.

All this could work only, of course, because the editor was a virtuous citizen, aiming not for the most profit, but rather a "volunteer-editor" who had forsaken the "tranquil pleasures of a studious life, amid the ever-green forests of Newhampshire" for something quite akin to a public service in Philadelphia (1). In the final lines of the prospectus, Dennie again pulled almost all the stops to portray himself a humble servant of his readers and the miscellaneous muse: he had, Dennie reminded his readers, "[a]t an early season of life" forsaken "the path of ordinary business, for a lowly seat in the Muses' bower," a choice which had "not enriched, or advanced him, yet of its propriety he has never doubted" (4). Dennie's persona in the *Port Folio* prospectus was driven by a passion for literature, but here, again, after couching his socialization in the republic of letters in the virtuous terms of a man who had long been "laboriously employed" chiefly in providing beneficial literature to his contemporaries, lest readers become too convinced by his professions of indifference to monetary gain, Dennie changed tack. He had "long been deluded by the visionary whim, of making literature the hand-maid to Fortune, or, at least, of securing something like independency, by exertions, as a man of letters" (4). The prospectus thus highlighted the constant tension between two opposing goals: to avoid being seen as a mere mercenary compositor, and failing to make a profit off the *Port Folio*. Nor was this, at heart, an idiosyncrasy of Dennie's; rather, the tension was owed to the difficulty of reconciling the vestiges of classical republican theory with the private necessities and desires underlying the project of the *Port Folio*, a manifestation of the mutual illusions under which Early Republic magazines were produced.

His readers, attentively perusing the prospectus, were clearly not inclined to ignore Dennie's footnoted allusions to the classical ideals under which Dennie purported to labor. One wrote to Asbury Dickins, having read the prospectus in February, 1801, that Dennie's "literary industry shall entitle him to a draught on my small bank" even though he did not have "the mansion of a Maecenas."[45] Voluntary quasi-public service entitled "Oliver Oldschool" (as distinct from Joseph Dennie) to compensation, and at the same time ensured that this compensation was not a fee, but rather a freely-given emolument—freely-given, but at the same time impossible not to give, necessary recognition of public service rather than mere salary for labor. Here, maybe, as William Dowling has suggested for the philosophical underpinnings of the *Port Folio* in general, lay "a vision of civic virtue as disinterestedness or unselfish commitment to the community as a whole" (1999, 32), but only if one took Dennie at his public word. As Joyce Appleby has noted, classic republicanism looked askance at the promotion of private monetary interest and considered it anathema to the virtuous citizen serving the public good. The emphasis on disinterested virtue which Federalists held high required that personal interest take a back seat to such public service (cf. Appleby 1984).

Having selected an audience of men whose self-understanding was deeply influenced by classical republican ideals, Dennie could not but tread carefully on the issue of monetary compensation. We might argue, with David Dowling, that underlying the prospectus's notion of the relationship between Oldschool and his readers was a "positive conception of human nature," where the civic industry of autonomous writers and editors was appropriately honored by equally autonomous readers. But this was Oldschool, not Dennie, propounding a sense of virtuous service entirely belied by the material calculations which Dennie, Dickins, and Maxwell had already made way in advance of the crafting of the prospectus. Even as the prospectus and, as Dowling notes, much of the later writings in the *Port Folio*, denied crass monetary interests, emphasized the virtues of classical republicanism, and seemed to frame "the ceaseless pursuit of material interest as decomposing society into a mere aggregate of isolated individuals" (Dowling 1999, 15), there echoed Dennie's letter to Roger Vose through everything the *Port Folio* did: the hopes for pecuniary safety and the "Rock of independence." Dennie was already practicing what Dowling has called with a view to the 1840s the production of a "kind of escapist fantasy from the strictures, and anxieties over commercial, industrial and technological innovations hurtling the nation toward the future" by "exud[ing] a carefully crafted rearguard indifference to the frenetic scramble for capital" (2010, 24) for the benefit of a readership increasingly at odds with the changing economic and social landscape. At the heart of this façade lay a relationship between editor and readership in which both ended up accepting the public necessity of the fantasy of the virtuous, unselfish editor writing for an audience of people who would not accept his services otherwise.

If in his relationship with his readers, Oliver Oldschool highlighted the Federalist philosophy of public service and virtue merely as a front, contrastingly if a lit-

45 Ralph Wormely to Asbury Dickins, February 5, 1801. Historical Society of Pennsylvania, Loudoun Papers 1971, Box 27

tle more clearly positioned, Dennie's treatment of his magazine's political leanings sought to obscure, or at least alleviate, Dennie's genuine Federalist impulse in order to at least potentially open a broader consumer base. Never explicitly avowedly Federalist in the prospectus, Dennie's highlighting of the name "Oldschool" and his paralleling of "the philosophy of the French [...] and the uproar of anarchy" (*PF* 1801 Prospectus, 2) implied, to anyone who was even modestly versed in the political discourse of the Early Republic, that the *Port Folio* would not be a great support to the incoming Jefferson administration; yet at the same time as he emphasized that he "*will not* publish an *impartial* paper" (2, original emphasis), he also stressed his "indifference [...] to the acrimony of our party bickerings, and to the universal eagerness for political *texts*, and their *commentary*" (1, original emphasis). Dennie rendered political information as a public service, suggesting that the *Port Folio* needed to provide "something of Politics to interest Quidnuncs, and something of literature to engage Students" (1). Politics was a topic among others, its inclusion designed to broaden the possible subscribership even as Dennie refused to outright declare for Federalism.[46]

The point here is not to deny that Joseph Dennie was an outright Federalist, to suggest that his later arraignment for seditious libel (a startling irony coming from the Democrat-Republicans!) was a misunderstanding of his own personal convictions, or that the *Port Folio* in its actual practice did not in fact do much to emphasize and perpetuate "party bickerings." Rather, Dennie's rhetoric sought as much as possible to keep an appearance that could appeal to a variety of readers, even recognizing that his own political leanings were clear. Dennie emphatically attempted to differentiate himself from the common newspaper and its all-too-obvious party politics. Party allegiance as a consequence of "education or habit, [...] chance or interest" determined whether a newspaper editor "professes himself a republican, or a federalist" (2), and this and a lack of even the most basic talents for the editorship meant that American newspapers were a very sorry bunch. Variously dragging politics into the foreground and subtly denigrating the subject, Dennie achieved a no doubt desired effect: he could with all justification say that the political principles of the *Port Folio* had been laid out, even as he would be able to attract readers who paid more heed to his pronouncements of being political only in such measure as readers were interested in it. Indeed, he suggested that the *Port Folio* would be "principally devoted to moral instruction, and polite literature" (3), rather than politics.[47] For the most part, this was a sound estimate. The *Port Folio*'s contents

46 Asbury Dickins and Hugh Maxwell, also in 1800, joined in publishing and printing the pamphlet *The Claim of Thomas Jefferson to the Presidency*, which purported to be a help answering the question "Shall Thomas Jefferson be the chief magistrate of these states?" Their joint answer was a resounding "God Forbid!" (8).

47 For a discussion of the *Port Folio*'s political writings and Dennie's Federalism, cf. Dowling 1999. Dowling's readings of the *Port Folio* content are indisputably interesting, but, considering the wealth of material which the *Port Folio* published, maybe a little too selective. With a bit of tongue in cheek, it would seem likely that just about anything can be proven about Dennie from the pages

during its first years were usually about equally divided between politics and fine-arts, but Dennie recognized that there were limits to the political writings he could offer his readers; likewise, however, the contingencies of available material limited the *Port Folio*'s potential to regularly supply the same kinds of material. Its content, accordingly, varied greatly. Some weeks, it carried absolutely no political material at all; sometimes, it carried so much that Dennie felt himself obliged to comment and explain himself. As early as June 6, 1801, in one of his notes "To Readers and Correspondents," Dennie admitted that there was a surfeit of political material in the issue and asked his readers' indulgence: "We hope for the pardon of those, who read merely for diversion. All must be gratified. We must furnish strong meat for statesmen, and 'milk for babes'" (*PF* 1801, 175).

The *Port Folio*'s prospectus showcased the public rationales underlying the magazine; the private correspondence between Joseph Dennie, Asbury Dickins, and Hugh Maxwell, by contrast, provides insights into the respective private motives which the team pursued. The actual *Port Folio* would have to negotiate between these two motivations. Examining the *Port Folio*'s use of biography makes visible this struggle between the public rationales and economic considerations, and again highlights the possibilities of the periodical texts to fulfill a wide range of functions within the magazines of the Early Republic.

From Context to Text: The Role of Biography in the *Port Folio*, 1801-2

What was the role biography was supposed to play in this new magazine? The genre rates mention in the prospectus, if only fleetingly: In describing the prospective contents of the new magazine, Dennie offered a tour-de-force survey of nearly everything that could possibly be expected (cf. Appendix 4 for the complete list). As everywhere else in the prospectus, he negotiated between precision and vagueness, suggesting that the *Port Folio* would print "Articles of American biography"—"and of memoir writing in general" (4). In echoing the *Farmer's Weekly Museum*'s late and unsuccessful call for genuinely American biography, the *Port Folio* gave voice to the high hopes Dennie had for original compositions on a variety of topics. In noting that it held "memoir writing in general" in just about equal esteem, on the other hand, the prospectus acknowledged that much of its material would probably not be able to fulfill those great expectations at all. What the prospectus ended up saying, then, was that the *Port Folio* would include biography—as broadly conceived as possible.

The third number of the *Port Folio* carried its first biography and made the magazine's engagement with the genre as inauspicious a start as possible. What Dennie pub-

of the *Port Folio* alone, given enough selectivity. Of Dennie's own political leanings there can be little doubt, as a letter from Gertrude Meredith to her husband, in which she notes that as late as 1809—the *Port Folio* had long since foresworn politics in favor of literature—Dennie believed "his bitterest foes [to be] fanatical Democrats." Gertrude Meredith to William Meredith, June 8, 1809. Historical Society of Pennsylvania, Meredith Family Papers 1509, Box 51 lished was not only not American biography, not original, it was not even new to a Dennie publication: he himself had already published it, in the June 16, 1795 edition of his Boston weekly, the *Tablet*. It presented a four-paragraph life of an Irish dramatist, John O'Keefe, and violated almost all the basic conceptions of biography, many of which Dennie himself had already espoused. O'Keefe was still alive; the text gave virtually no information at all about O'Keefe himself (not even a date or place of birth), and merely described his dramatical productions; and concluded with the stereotypically bad biographical observation that O'Keefe's eyesight had been declining for fourteen years. More problematically, the biography carried a line which ran wholly counter to the conception of the *Port Folio*: "he, who pleases many, must have merit," the article quoted Samuel Johnson. For a magazine whose prospectus had declared that it would emphatically "not strive to please the populace" (2), this was a surprising assertion to condone by publishing it in an article. It was not the last time, however, that publishing practice disavowed publishing philosophy. The prospectus had been a lure; now, the question was one of justifying the material available, of retroactively attempting to create an editorial coherence from highly disparate material. [48]

For five months, the *Port Folio* did not publish biography; then, in March, 1801, Dennie offered a first glimpse at a philosophy of biography for the magazine. In an editorial note preceding the life of John Henderson, Dennie suggested that few texts were as suitable to periodicals like the *Port Folio* as biographies. The lives which biography could present were "splendid models for the most salutary imitation" by younger readers, and Dennie especially stressed the value of the lives of poets, whose examples might bring forth in readers an ambition to follow in their footpaths, notwithstanding the admitted difficulties of the literary profession (*PF* 1801, 89). If something of Dennie himself echoed through this description of writers "fighting with fortune, and triumphing in literature," precisely what it was that suited biography for miscellanies, Dennie did not explain. Biography was "useful and pleasant," like all suitable texts for periodicals—this was the extent of explanation. Throughout 1801, the underlying conception of biography was never more fully explained. Dennie himself claimed that he "delights in perusing the biography of ingenious men" and suggested he "believes it a mighty incentive to useful exertion," when justifying the inclusion of the biography of the English poet Edward Lovibond (*PF* 1801, 297-8).[49]

48 Both Dennie's incestuous relationship with his own productions and the question of how to justify a text that seems to run counter to earlier stated intentions combined in the March 7 publication of the "Notices of Thomas Coryate." These, too, had already been published in the *Tablet* (on July 14, 1795), and were of questionable value as tools of public instruction. The short text noted that Coryate "had learning, but wanted judgment," possessed an "ill-timed zeal for christianity," and was overall a quaint and odd person (*PF* 1801, 76). Only the second biography published by the *Port Folio*, like the O'Keefe text it possessed none of the qualities Dennie would later consider key to periodical biography—or, for that matter, had considered key while still at the *Farmer's Weekly Museum*.

49 Like so many other lives published in the *Port Folio*, Lovibond's biography came from Robert

Something of Dennie's motivation for the inclusion of biographies can be gleaned from his editorial commentary nonetheless. Biography in periodicals promised shortness, gratifying to a readership which, as Dennie, Dickins and Maxwell were clearly aware, could not be expected to devote genuine study to the *Port Folio.* Of all the roles the prospectus had envisaged for the magazine, it was clear to the editor and his team that its success depended not so much on its instructiveness, as in the pleasure it would bring readers. Maxwell had said as much, very straightforwardly, in his February 1800 letter: "Humor and light reading seem to me to be peculiarly adapted to the tastes of Magazine readers,"[50] and despite his public avowals of morals and good sense, the truth which shone through the *Port Folio*'s public self-representation echoed Maxwell. "Something from this paper is constantly required for the *amusement* of the city" (*PF* 1801, 39, original emphasis), Dennie noted as early as January 31, 1801. The danger of verbosity and the need to amuse his readership remained at the forefront of Dennie's public announcements. In early February, he felt the need to "caution our correspondents against *prolixity*, a *deadly* sin in miscellaneous composition," writings which "the public eye always surveys, with the coldest indifference [...] so aptly and classically characterized by the beautiful American word—*lengthy*!" (*PF* 1801, 46, original emphasis). In late February, he again noted that "'Amusement reigns man's great demand'" (*PF* 1801, 69, quoting Edward Young), encouraging the supplier of a humorous poem to write more of the same; in April, he begged his readers' indulgence for the biography of William Pattison (from Anderson's *Works*), noting that he "hope[d] the prolixity of the following life [...] will not deter the volatile from a perusal" (*PF* 1801, 129). "A prolix essay, in a fugitive paper, terrifies Indolence, and is not always perused by Powers of a higher order, and of the most patient perseverance," he admonished the writers of lengthy political essays in June (*PF* 1801, 191), and in December, Dennie concluded the first year's run of the *Port Folio* by suggesting that "every species of literary and amusing intelligence, will, in future, form articles of regular recurrence in the Port Folio" (*PF* 1801, 414). Biography clearly formed part of this spectrum of articles which were short and amusing, and thus came up regularly—especially since Dennie had found sources enough for biography in general, if not for that seemingly unreachable goal, American biography.

Anderson's *The Works of the British Poets*, and was included in the 11th volume of that useful anthology. The *Port Folio* thus neatly continued the *Farmer's Weekly Museum*'s practice of justifying what content it already had at the ready for inclusion. Dennie was not the only writer who copied verbatim from Robert Anderson: so did Anderson himself. The introduction to his life of Lovibond largely paraphrased and at times copied outright from his own "Life of Hamilton" in volume nine. It must have been a happy coincidence indeed that "[l]ittle attention has been bestowed by the anonymous editor of [both Lovibond and Hamilton's] poems, in transmitting the incidents of [their] lives" (Anderson 1795, 577 and 1794, 411). The *Port Folio* printed Hamilton's biography on July 11, 1801 (cf. *PF* 1801, 221), and Dennie noted that he was "an excellent, though neglected writer" as a modest justification for the biography's inclusion.

50 Hugh Maxwell to Joseph Dennie, February 26, 1800. Historical Society of Pennsylvania, Meredith Family Papers 1509, Box 99.

It is a notable feature of the *Port Folio*'s use of biography in the first year of its existence that while it failed to make much headway with the prospectus's hopes for American biography (the only American's life published in 1801 was that of Alexander Hamilton, and this was a copy from a British publication[51]), it did offer a broad selection of subjects to readers. Writers and poets took the top slot, but the *Port Folio* also published lives of manufacturers, divines, military men, and, perhaps most surprisingly, two biographies of "*bizarres*" (*PF* 1801, 76) and an "eccentric, and unfortunate youth" (*PF* 1801, 129). As in the *Farmer's Weekly Museum*, however, the *Port Folio*'s selection of biographical texts owed far more to their ready availability than to their fitting into any systematic understanding of the role of biography in the periodical. In fact, in practice the *Port Folio* printed biographical texts in spurts, three in March, in August, in September, and in November, four in October and in December, while missing out on February and May, and supplying just two in April, and one in January, June, and July. From September 12 onward until late November, only two issues of the *Port Folio* did not carry a biography. Dennie's main source for most of 1801 was, still, Robert Anderson's multi-volume *Works of the British Poets*;[52] to that, starting in the summer, he added a steady supply of texts from John Aikin et al.'s *General Biography*, a much broader work which enabled Dennie to provide the *Port Folio* with some variety in its biographical department, including German and French authors, British divines, and Italian writers.

Only one of the biographies published in 1801 gives any indication of the processes by which Dennie found the material he used in the *Port Folio*, and that not a particularly flattering one. In June, 1801, he published what he called a "Character of Dr. Samuel Johnson" (*PF* 1801, 198-9). This was an extract from a monograph, Robert Bisset's *Life of Edmund Burke*. Burke was a favorite of Dennie's; if it is likely that he did not own a copy of the *Life of Edmund Burke* in 1801, he was clearly reading the book, benefitting no doubt from his relationship with two booksellers, Dickins and Maxwell, whose stocks may well have included the volume. [53] What he publishes as a character sketch in the *Port Folio* is a more or less random note hidden deep in Bisset's biography of Burke, and no doubt, a coincidental discovery that made its way into the magazine. Between the ready availability of short texts in the

51 The provenance of this work is difficult to establish. The text appears in William Cobbett's May 1801 volume of *Porcupine's Works*, but this seems rather tightly calculated to have made it across the Atlantic in time for publication in the August 1801 *Port Folio*; perhaps not, or perhaps Cobbett, who, as we have seen, was a friend and correspondent of Dennie's while still in the United States, had sent the tract individually to Dennie.

52 A shipping notice in the Asbury Dickins papers indicates that Dennie would have had easy access to the Anderson work. Dickins had purchased two 13-volume sets of the work in December 1801; if this is obviously too late for Dennie to have made use of it in the previous year, at least it points to the availability in general of theses volumes.

53 Hugh Maxwell's day book notes that Dennie purchased a copy of the book in 1803 for 6$; Historical Society of Pennsylvania, Meredith Family Papers 1509, Box 99.

anthologies that were accessible to Dennie, either because, as is likely with Robert Anderson, he owned them, or because, through the various bookseller friends and his bookseller-publisher Dickins, he had access to them, and the occasional coincidental catches that could easily be made ready for publication, clearly the *Port Folio*'s biography department was a haphazard operation.

When Dennie published the life of William Cowper, in April 1801, his rationale was the alleged public clamoring for more information about a well-regarded writer whose previous life narratives had not revealed much about his private life. It was explicitly public curiosity which Dennie emphasized to justify publishing the life of Cowper, noting that the biography was "curious and novel" (*PF* 1801, 125) and that he had seen fit to "select and compress the most striking circumstance" it contained. In October, the *Port Folio* carried the biography of an obscure Scottish poet, John Armstrong, who, as the biography itself admitted, had most produced "pieces scarcely above mediocrity" (*PF* 1801, 322). Armstrong may have appealed to Dennie because, like Dennie himself, he was a professional whose chosen profession—medicine—appealed less to him than the literary engagements with which he had chosen to spent his time. But such modest justifications for the inclusion of particular biographies were few and far between. In late November, whether motivated by public complaints or inspired by his own conscience striking him, Dennie commented on the practices by which he obtained and selected biographical material. Biography, he assured his readers, was not dead filler, or old material, but rather brand-new: "for the first time, published, in the present year" (*PF* 1801, 375). This was not the whole truth—Aikins's first volume of *General Biography*, from which many texts were excerpted, had appeared in 1799, though his second volume had indeed only been published in 1801[54]—and it certainly also obscured the fact that while true for the "recently published" biographies, immediately before, and immediately after, Dennie resorted again to the more familiar and rather more widely known work of Anderson. What biography could be expected to do, and what it apparently seemed to him to threaten, Dennie noted immediately after:

> The life of Blum, though a *German* poet, need not alarm the sprightly reader. It is light and amusing, and will edify him, who loves to dwell on the adventures of a literary enthusiast, struggling through the shades of obscurity, into the sunshine of patronage, and the blaze of day. (*PF* 1801, 375, original emphasis)

Dennie was finding echoes of himself in an inordinate number of the biographies he printed during 1801, explaining, perhaps, why any particular biographical short text came into a closer selection when works such as Aikins's provided a host of alternatives.

54 Explaining, in point of fact, why the biographical short texts published in 1801 had a tendency to offer up men with names between A and C, which was the whole extent of the Aikins volumes published up to that year—how might have fared the public fortunes of Aldrich, Armstrong, Arkwright, Blum, Baretti, Churchill, Brooke, Chaulieu, and Carey, if Dennie had had available an entire alphabet's worth of Aikin's biographies?

Billed in the prospectus as one among a whole host of different genres to be published in the *Port Folio*, biography was a steady presence in the *Port Folio* during its first year. It never became a main focus of the magazine, nor did it ever support the *Port Folio*'s announced political stance. But then, the *Port Folio* frequently indulged its contributors in publishing texts that, no doubt, held only a minority appeal. John Quincy Adams's 44-part "Journal of a Tour Through Silesia," for instance, which ran uninterruptedly from the first number until November 7, 1801, certainly violated any claim to variety that Dennie had made, but allowed him to proclaim occasionally that he had put out an entirely original paper. Otherwise, what determined his choices in the *Port Folio* was availability and suitability of size more than anything else.

The New Series of 1802, and an 1801 Retrospective

By the end of 1801, the *Port Folio* was shaping up into both a critical and a publishing success. Throughout the year, Maxwell's printing press ran off as many as 2000 issues of the *Port Folio* each week, at a considerably smaller cost than he had initially estimated to Dennie. Maxwell charged Dennie and Dickins 30,50$ for each issue, less than he had suggested 1000 copies would cost.[55] By July, the paper's success had led to Dennie and Dickins requiring reprints of the first dozen numbers at 23,20$ each, suggesting something on the account of 1500 further copies per issue printed. And the *Port Folio* proved a steady source of income for Dickins and Dennie throughout 1801. By October, Dennie had cleared 1012,69$ in profits, delivered him with great regularity by Asbury Dickins.[56] This was sufficient to keep Dennie in bread, and, if it did not yet reach up to the maximum reward that John Fenno had offered him in 1800, it was a promising start to the young magazine's endeavors. The magazine had obtained some agents far afield, such as George Hill in Baltimore, who alone had a list of 56 subscribers by November.[57] From their dues of 255$, Hill detracted 10% fees for his agency and postage costs.[58] 23 subscribers were

55 Invoices to Dickins and Dennie, Historical Society of Pennsylvania, Meredith Papers 1509, Box 99. Between the invoices, Maxwell's ledgers, the personal notes of Dickins and Dennie, and the assorted correspondence between Maxwell, Dennie, and their attorneys, information can be found that shows the fluctuations in the prices Maxwell charged for his services. The print runs were surprisingly irregular, and it is not at all clear why that should be the case. The March 21, 1801, edition, is explicitly noted to have been 2000 copies, for which Maxwell, as noted, charged 30,50$; the August 8 issue, however, had 1500 issues "on small paper" cost 36,50$ to print. In 1802, Maxwell's account book suggests, 2000 copies were the regular print run—at 30,50$ each.

56 Joseph Dennie Memorandum ["Account of monies received from AD 1801"]. Historical Society of Pennsylvania, Meredith Family Papers 1509, Box 99.

57 George Hill to Asbury Dickins, November 16, 1801. Historical Society of Pennsylvania, Loudoun Papers 1791, Asbury Dickins Correspondence, Box 27

58 William Hill to Asbury Dickins, August 25, 1801. Historical Society of Pennsylvania, Loudoun Papers 1791, Asbury Dickins Correspondence, Box 27

managed in Savannah, Georgia; numerous individual requests for subscriptions are to be found among the remaining papers of Asbury Dickins.

Other aspects of the business did not go so well. In the fall, Asbury Dickins departed from Philadelphia for Liverpool on the packet *John & Alice*. The passage, worth 138$, was paid by Thomas Armat, Dickins's lawyer and friend, to whom Dickins wrote from shipboard: everything was well, he had successfully and easily made the ship and was looking forward to a pleasant journey. By late October, Dickins had begun to pay Maxwell not in cash, but in promissory notes;[59] this note Maxwell did not receive until Dickins had embarked for England. Evidently, something was amiss, even though Dickins does not seem to have been altogether aware of the problem as he left Liverpool. On October 26, a man by the name of Samuel Blodget brought suit for 15.000$ against Dickins—apparently in a business unrelated to the bookstore or the *Port Folio*. Blissfully unaware that anything untoward was happening, Dickins wrote Armat from Liverpool on December 2nd: "I hope the business in Philadelphia goes on well and prosperously, as I doubt not but that my brother with the assistance you will afford will manage properly—as soon as I go to London, I shall send out something for the store." Dickins suggested that the bookstore should advertise his presence in London to obtain additional orders.[60] The reply from Armat came as a shock. A surprised Dickins wrote Armat from London in February 1802—deeply surprised that "after a profitable business of some years there should remain nothing?" He assured Armat that he had believed "the business to be in a flourishing state," and worried about the individual claims that people laid on him—including one by John Ward Fenno of 1700$, which Dickins protested could impossibly be true.[61]

Asbury Dickins's demission to London and the subsequent shakeup in the *Port Folio* management seem to have made it desirable to begin a "new series" with the

59 Asbury Dickins note, October 22, 1801. Historical Society of Pennsylvania, Loudoun Papers 1791, Asbury Dickins Correspondence, Box 27.

60 Peter J. Parker suggests that Dickins's departure for Liverpool was a result of the suit, and several documents post-dating the suit (including a power of attorney dated the 27th of October) would seem to confirm the possibility, but there is some evidence that Dickins had already departed when the suit was brought apart from his apparently obliviousness in the December 2 letter. He had written from aboard the *John & Alice* on October 3, just passing Cape Henlopen, the southern edge of the Delaware estuary, according to his own handwritten dating; yet by November 6, the *Pennsylvania Gazette* was still listing the vessel as due to depart. The *Gazette* does not note when the *John & Alice* finally left, but it seems difficult to reconcile all the dates available in the files. Transatlantic passages west to east were on the order of forty days; November 6th thus seems late if the arrival at Liverpool was no later than December 2nd, while October 3rd appears slightly early, except if Dickins took his time writing from Liverpool; cf. Parker 1970. Asbury Dickins to Thomas Armat, December 2, 1802. Historical Society of Pennsylvania, Loudoun Papers 1791, Asbury Dickins Correspondence, Box 27.

61 Asbury Dickins to Thomas Armat, February 22, 1802. Historical Society of Pennsylvania, Loudoun Papers 1791, Asbury Dickins Correspondence, Box 27.

new year 1802.[62] Elizabeth Dickins, Asbury's mother, and Dennie would serve as publishers; Maxwell continued as printer. When 1801 ended, the *Port Folio* had made Dennie money, but it had not sufficed to help out Asbury Dickins. By September 1802, with Dickins still in England and his estate in foreclosure, William Fry assumed the publisher's role and took over the Dickins bookstore; Dennie took over Dickins's outstanding debts on the *Port Folio* venture.[63] Dickins played no further role in the *Port Folio*, and William Fry's own part (he was publisher from September 1802 to October 1803) probably never amounted to anything much. Dennie's relationship with Hugh Maxwell, by contrast, remained close. Although the printer found it necessary to address himself to Dennie in June of 1802, noting that he was still being owed 400$ he could ill spare and requesting a quick payment thereof, by November, the two men's relationship was, again, more than cordial.

Dennie had left Philadelphia in the fall of 1802, avoiding the annual yellow fever epidemic. Even though not present, neither was he idle: replying to a letter from a New York subscriber accusing him of dilatoriness and complaining about the "tardy appearance" of the *Port Folio*, he noted that even if there might be a small delay in individual numbers, at the end of the year, the volume would certainly been complete (cf. *PF* 1802, 311). That Dennie could be so sanguine about the likelihood of fulfilling his promise was owed to the availability, in Hugh Maxwell, of a subaltern editor at Philadelphia. In mid-November, 1802, Maxwell wrote to Dennie at the "Sign of the Ship" on the road to Lancaster, where Dennie was spending his time away from the city. He noted that he had "made use of all the materials supplied" and urged Dennie to produce more. That Maxwell and Dennie were at this point the major figures in the venture, Maxwell's letter made clear. It went straight to the heart of a business matter one would find to be more in the publisher's job description to deal with: paper supplies. "[H]ave you contracted for paper for the ensuing year?" Maxwell asked, "It is now almost too late, if you have not already made the necessary arrangements." Maxwell's usually clear handwriting has three misprints and erasures in the three lines it takes him to ask those questions, indicating, perhaps, a certain agitation about the

62 John Hall, writing a retrospective of the *Port Folio* in 1816, was puzzled by this change, and the ones which followed: "Why the distinctions of a new series, second series, &c. were ever introduced, is not easy to discover" (*PF* 1816 2, 274). The *Port Folio* opened a new series nearly every time the publisher changed: in 1802, when Asbury Dickins left the business of publisher nominally in the hands of his mother Margaret, and actually in the far more able ones of Hugh Maxwell; in 1806, when Maxwell handed over the publisher's role to William Fry (opening another "new" series, starting with the volume count at 1); in 1809, when Bradford & Inskeep took over as publishers; and in 1816, when Harrison Hall became publisher and John Hall editor. On the other hand, in 1807, when Dennie himself became publisher again, the series begun in 1806 continued; and when the next new series began, in 1813, no major change in owner- or editorship had occured at all. Aside from the shift in 1802, however, it seems that there was a convenience of publishing involved.

63 Memorandum (probably written by William Meredith) 1806, Historical Society of Pennsylvania, Meredith Family Papers 1509, Box 99.

topic.[64] Ten days later, Maxwell sent Dennie a large manuscript for his perusal and an editorial decision on whether to include the piece or not. Maxwell was now in good spirits overall: he told Dennie that he had "no complaint to make on the score of copy—I have a large quantity in reserve and am happy to find very many choice articles—such as must give satisfaction to the friends of Mr. Oldschool—I send you the poetical department for this week—I am sure you will be highly pleased with it."[65] Although John Queenan suggests that Dennie did not hold Maxwell in high regard as co-editor (cf. 1955, 11), it is clear that Maxwell's work in Dennie's place did not result in adverse reactions from the readers, or from Dennie himself. Despite Queenan's belief that the material plenty Maxwell had mentioned in his second letter meant that Dennie had sent him all this material, this is not necessary from the formulations which Maxwell chose and somewhat illogical: would not Dennie know what amount of material he had sent Maxwell? And why would he want to see what contents were in the poetical department, if he had chosen them himself? By late November, Dennie noted to his correspondents via his "To Readers and Correspondents" rubric that "[t]he pestilence which rageth at noon day, has grievously checked, but has not entirely arrested our business" (*PF* 1802, 367); indeed, there is no telling at all that Dennie was not in full editorial control in the fall months of 1802, even though such a large part of his actual work had devolved on Maxwell.[66]

64 Hugh Maxwell to Joseph Dennie, November 16, 1802. Historical Society of Pennsylvania, Meredith Family Papers 1509, Box 99.

65 Hugh Maxwell to Joseph Dennie, November 26, 1802. Historical Society of Pennsylvania, Meredith Family Papers 1509, Box 99.

66 No period of the *Port Folio*'s existence is so difficult to unravel as regards the editorial efforts as the late months of 1802. The question is exactly as Gertrude Meredith put it in a letter to her husband on August 29, 1802, with the yellow fever season beginning to start and Dennie already absent from Philadelphia: "who carries on the paper in the absence of its Editor" (Historical Society of Pennsylvania, Meredith Family Papers 1509, Box 51). As many as four men may have held editorial sway over the magazine between September and December 1802: Dennie, Maxwell, Thomas Boylston Adams, and Charles Brockden Brown. The evidence for the last two is limited to a letter written by T.B. Adams to John Quincy Adams, dated November 30, 1802 (cf. TBA to JQA, November 30, 1802. Massachusetts Historical Society, Adams Family Papers, Reel 401), in which Thomas Adams notes that he had forwarded a contribution by John Quincy to "the temporary editor of the Port Folio [...] his name is Brown, & he criticized your translation of Genty in the New York magazine called American Review, whereof he is a coadjutor." Thomas Adams goes on to note that Brown suppressed the contribution for "four or five weeks," before he published. Adams then notes that the "last two numbers are revised by me, and I shall continue my superintendence until Dennie returns to the City, which I think will be in a few days." Henceforward, Adams proposed to deal with the business details of the venture. There is no immediate reason to doubt his veracity in this letter, but it opens more questions than it answers. Brown was in Philadelphia in October and through December, as he noted in a letter to Rebecca Linn, his future wife's sister, in October, where "the total suspension of

By this time, too, Dennie had apparently concluded that the *Port Folio* should leave its ambivalent self-description as "not quite a gazette, nor wholly a magazine" behind it. Replying to complaints from his "'Boston subscribers'"—possibly the Adamses—about a lack of punctuality, he on the one hand argued, as he had with his New York correspondent, that ultimately, there would be no loss of *Port Folio* matter, as he would definitely supply all the matter promised. On the other hand, he noted, punctuality was a feature of good newspapers, but the *Port Folio* "is not a *newspaper*, but is composed of materials not essentially fugitive;" thus, "it is of trivial moment at what time it may be perused" (original emphasis). At this point, of course, it was very much in the editor's interest to downplay its weekly punctuality—and the fact that the *Port Folio* was still carrying a small, but noteworthy amount of foreign news—in favor of its durability and lastingness. His further explanations, however, must have been puzzling to a whole number of readers: "The political events of the flying hour must be *instantly* contemplated, or they fade in the distance; but miscellaneous papers may be read to-day or to-morrow" (*PF* 1802, 319, original emphasis). Certainly, political events as such had never been the material from which the *Port Folio* drew, but this outright denial of political material as relevant to a magazine was both expedient and striking. Nor did it remain his only comment on politics in the yellow-fever fraught October of 1802.

Two issues later, on October 23, Dennie commented on "[a] very general objection to the plan of this paper [...] occasioned by our sometime neglect of Political Disquisitions" (*PF* 1802, 335). Despite the grandiose announcements of his prospectus, as John Queenan has noted, politics played a conspicuously minor part in the *Port Folio* during 1801 and 1802, with a spike in 1803 and a return to the low standards afterwards. Dennie failed to obtain materials, despite his best efforts (cf. 1955, 97-8); and consequently his commentary on the allegedly general objection—perhaps more of an imagined objection than anything else—sought to emphasize how misplaced politics would be, anyhow. Politics, Dennie wrote, was "a subject adapted to raise the passions, engross the thoughts of most men, yet Reason informs me a community may be most permanently and importantly served by the peaceful labors of the Student" (*PF* 1802, 335). Politics was fleeting: literature lasted: by this simple formula, Dennie explained, justified, and rendered laudable that which he could not avoid at any rate: the production of a miscellany that was wholly dependent on external support, offering a "mere rationalization" (Queenan 1955, 99) for his work. It was perhaps

business [due to yellow fever] will leave me nothing to do here" (Dunlap 221; identification of Rebecca Linn: personal communication by Matthias Köhler); but no extant communication from Brown mentions such an engagement, or indeed, any stronger connection with Dennie. The letters from Maxwell to Dennie, extending into November, make no mention of Adams, Brown, or any perceived mismanagement, something that Thomas Adams highlighted when he argued his reasons for assuming control of the *Port Folio*'s business details. Adams is listed on a number of receipts penned by Maxwell for money relating to the *Port Folio*, always in company with Dennie; but as with William Meredith later, whose name also appears, it is not at all clear that any formal relationship between the *Port Folio* and Thomas Boylston Adams existed.

a bit more than that: a justification for leaving out materials explicitly advertised in the prospectus, and thus the acknowledgment of a promise made and broken.

The *Port Folio*'s first year set the tone, and the future trajectory, of the magazine, even though many changes still lay ahead. It had found a stable subscriber base, and made sufficient money for all participants—unless otherwise caught up in financial troubles—to stay attached to it into the following years. It had weathered serious problems with the departure of Asbury Dickins and Joseph Dennie's absence from Philadelphia late in 1802; and it had found a sort of literary voice, one which is especially revelatory as to the processes by which the magazine functioned. If we have only looked more deeply into the case of biography, Dennie's 1802 justifications for not including political writings are evidence that biography can be used almost prototypically to understand the strictures of the periodical business: just as he wished to publish American biography, Dennie wished to publish political writings, but his contributors did not oblige him. Just as he justified the inclusion of particular biographical texts in spur of the moment fashion, with due disregard to consistency, so he attempted to frame the lack of political contributions as editorial policy. In either case, the question of reception, the audience's willingness to entertain one text over another, trumped all more ephemeral considerations.

Perhaps in slight contrast to the discussion of biographical short texts, however, Dennie's argument that the *Port Folio* was a magazine, unsuitable for the momentary, but rather ideal for the enduring, may have had conceptual consequences. These were not sudden: for another three years, nothing in the format and style of the *Port Folio* changed, and it continued to produce a fair mixture of texts. It was not until 1806 that something major changed again: when it did, though, it proved major indeed, when Hugh Maxwell's tenure as publisher came to an end and the ensuing claims and counterclaims allow us to look more fully into the business side of the *Port Folio*.

1806-1807: The *Port Folio* Becomes a Magazine

The initial phase of the *Port Folio*'s existence between 1800 and 1802, its nascence and establishment as a major force on the magazine market, already marked many of the issues which the magazine would struggle with during its subsequent existence. The period from late 1805 to early 1807 marks a second key era: with its literary reputation firmly established, the *Port Folio* found itself involved in increasingly complex publishing questions which it was ultimately unable to solve. On the way, it self-consciously reinvented itself as a magazine, switched publishers and printers, and realigned its contents. Despite these changes, however, the years 1805-1807 are most interesting not for the superficial alterations of the magazine proper, but the events surrounding them, playing out in the background between the men primarily involved with the magazine: Dennie as editor, Maxwell as publisher and printer, and Maxwell's successors as publishers, William Fry and then Dennie himself. The events of 1806 reveal much about the vagaries of the periodical business, and the attempts to cope with the problems existing at the *Port Folio* highlight the centrality of the business aspects of the magazine.

For outsiders to the *Port Folio*'s affairs, very little of the problems which the magazine was dealing with by late 1805 was evident. In November 1805, the *Repertory*, a Boston paper, published an announcement by Oliver C. Greenleaf, a local bookseller and agent for the *Port Folio*. It was short and very much to the point. "The Lovers and Patrons of Polite Literature," it read, "are informed, that with the beginning of the 6th volume, in January, the Port Folio will be improved both in form and substance" (*R* 1805, November 5, 2.90, 3). Behind this simple announcement lay a more fundamental change in the complex relationships behind the publication of the magazine. The basic changes to its format were easily enumerated: 1806 saw it shrink from its former royal quarto size[67] down to octavo, the number of columns per page decrease to two, and the number of pages increase to sixteen per issue. This also necessitated a split of the annual run into two volumes, each of which would be collected as a single, bound book, complete with index and table of contents.

If the beginning of 1806 marked these formal structural changes to the *Port Folio*, their roots lay in the previous years. Ever since Dennie and Maxwell had settled into their grooves as editor and publisher, in October 1803, the magazine's running had been more or less smooth. Dickins's failure in late 1801 still cast its shadows over the venture up until the middle of 1804. In November 1802, Maxwell, writing Dennie, asked the editor for his opinion on the Dickins case and noted having heard that the former publisher's affairs "will speedily brought to a crisis."[68] In June, 1803, Dickins's lawyer Thomas Armat had managed to make the creditors foreswear further action against the *Port Folio*, leaving the magazine's proceeds free from interference; by December, 1803, he had managed to make Hugh Maxwell and another friend of Dickins's go about selling the stocks left to Dickins in order to further reduce the private debt.[69] In July 1804, the remaining possessions of the Dickins'—some stock either not sold by Maxwell or independent of it—were being put under Armat's care to sell.[70] If this concluded the sad tale of Dickins's participation in the *Port Folio*, up to the middle of 1803, at least, the financial insecurity of the venture, owed to the debts which lay on it, must have made the business far less enjoyable than in the heady days of 1801.

67 A rough and tumble size comparison might be that between a tabloid newspaper and a contemporary illustrated magazine such as *The New Yorker*.

68 Hugh Maxwell to Joseph Dennie, November 16, 1802. Historical Society of Pennsylvania,, Meredith Family Papers 1509, Box 99

69 Cf. [Note] dated June 27, 1803, Historical Society of Pennsylvania, Loudoun Papers 1791, Asbury Dickins Correspondence, Box 27; Thomas Armat Note, December 31, 1803, Historical Society of Pennsylvania, Loudoun Papers 1791, Asbury Dickins Correspondence, Box 27.

70 Cf. Thomas Armat Memorandum, July 21, 1804. Historical Society of Pennsylvania, Loudoun Papers 1791, Asbury Dickins Correspondence, Box 27.

Precisely what these debts amounted to is difficult to establish. Dennie himself had never been a particularly careful account keeper—in keeping track of Dickins's payments to him in 1801, he had started out noting the dates of his receipts but stopped doing so after two entries, leaving the rest of the record a mere list of sums and rendering it impossible to determine when he was paid for what. This was perhaps less of a problem in personal finances than it was in the records of the magazine itself. Even modern scholars will be puzzled by the various surviving receipts, account sheets, and other records of the business venture. Linda Kerber and Walter Morris suggest that in November 1802, the *Port Folio*'s printing bills were still unpaid (Maxwell does not seem to have complained about this; cf. 1966, 463); yet William Fry's accounts for the year indicate that the *Port Folio* had a 465$ balance in its favor at its publisher's office.

Hugh Maxwell had taken over the publishing of the magazine at the same time that he took over William Fry's (formerly the Dickins's) bookstore on Philadelphia's North Second Street, opposite Christ Church, in late September 1803.[71] He would continue as publisher until the end of 1805, guiding the financial fortunes of the magazine. "During all this time M[axwel]l had the entire management—he received & *expended*," William Meredith noted in 1806 (original emphasis).[72] Large parts of the expenses were Maxwell's own charges for printing, but there were also paper purchases, costs of correspondence, and assorted miscellaneous charges that Maxwell handled. Things seem to have gotten off to a smooth start in 1804, but, as it soon turned out, the responsibility for full financial control may have been too much for Maxwell to handle alone. On January 9, 1805, Maxwell wrote to William Meredith, Dennie's attorney, in the matter of a financial conflict with Dennie concerning the costs Maxwell had charged the *Port Folio*. Maxwell had previously agreed to let James Humphreys, another Philadelphia printer, inspect his accounts and decide what the financial situation between Dennie and Maxwell was—"examining the printing and fixing the price," as Maxwell put it—but now retracted his agreement to have Humphrey examine the accounts. Maxwell was

71 Cf. Meredith Memorandum, n.d. Historical Society of Pennsylvania, Meredith Family Papers 1509, Box 99. William Fry is listed as the owner of the bookstore at 25 North Second Street on the title page of the 1802 volume of the *Port Folio*, and Maxwell's name appears as the owner of that store on a December 1803 advertisement for a book sale in the *Gazette of the United States* (GUS 1803, 24.3485, 3). One of the more fascinating aspects of the business history of the *Port Folio* is this progression in the ownership of the bookstore at 25 North Second Street. Owned at first by Asbury Dickins's father, it passed on to Asbury on his father's death; when Dickins was forced to remain in England to avoid being sued for debt, the bookstore was managed by his mother—for whom Asbury had only stood in, anyway—until William Fry bought it in September 1802. Fry sold the store afterwards to Maxwell. In each of these cases, the ownership of the 25 North Second Street bookstore and the publisher's role in the *Port Folio* went hand in hand; Dennie, consequently, always had a bookstore as a "home base" in his search for publishable material.

72 Meredith Memorandum, n.d. Historical Society of Pennsylvania, Meredith Family Papers 1509, Box 99.

anxious to have "disinterested parties, who have not prejudged, or been previously consulted, on the matter, and before whom I may have perfect liberty to defend my accounts, and where you, or Mr. Dennie, may have perfect liberty to make your objections." Dennie and Meredith had clearly left Maxwell some time to get his finances in order before they would see what the *Port Folio* owed, or was owed, an indulgence for which Maxwell professed to be grateful, even as he declined selecting the parties who would judge his accounts himself. He would, he argued, want to conclude their "business upon mutual and fair ground; so that when the matters in dispute are once settled, the parties shall be perfectly satisfied."[73]

Events transpired so as to make Dennie's and Meredith's willingness to wait for Maxwell's accounts impossible to sustain, not the least because Maxwell was apparently tardy submitting them. In March, a letter from John Lundgren reached Dennie. In the letter, Lungren demanded payment for paper delivered to the *Port Folio* in the year 1804 at a cost of 1360$. Lundgren said that he had received only 750$ of that amount, and when he had last inquired with Maxwell, with whom he had made the agreement, Maxwell had told him that he had nothing to do with the problem and to contact Dennie.[74] A month later, the outstanding debts of the magazine induced Maxwell and Dennie to send out Maxwell's clerk Williams to aid in the collection of monies outside Philadelphia, a move which despite assurances to the contrary, indicated the uncertainty about the agents' ability to perform their duties.[75] In June, Meredith wrote Maxwell, noting that one of Dennie's debtors had requested payment and the accounts were now required. Meredith suggested that there would be a good chance now for Samuel Bradford and a second reviewer to check on Maxwell's accounts and to "close the accounts to the beginning of the present year during the week."[76] Nothing came of this. In fact, by the time Maxwell furnished accounts, the publishership had changed.

The difficulties in the *Port Folio*'s financial accounts had amassed slowly. Reporting a conversation with Maxwell, the Philadelphia physician Nathaniel Chapman—another close acquaintance of Maxwell's and Dennie's both, who lived for a time at the 113 Walnut Street residence which Dennie and Thomas Adams had occupied in 1803-4—noted that Maxwell believed "the Debts of the Establishment were one to Mr. Levis [a provider of paper] of 1300 Dollars, another to himself of 600 Dollars, and a third to a paper maker of 400 Dollars." Despite these debts Maxwell was estimating that Dennie himself probably had a balance in his favor with Maxwell, and "supposed that there were owing to the Port Folio about 6000 Dollars" and "more money had been rec[eived] by Mr. Dennie than he expected, that he believed the Debts would

73 Hugh Maxwell to William Meredith, January 9, 1805. Historical Society of Pennsylvania, Meredith Family Papers, Box 99.

74 John Lundgren to Joseph Dennie, March 5, 1805. Historical Society of Pennsylvania, Meredith Family Papers, Box 99.

75 Joseph Dennie commission to Mr. Williams, April 13, 1805. Historical Society of Pennsylvania, eredith Family Papers, Box 99.

76 William Meredith to Hugh Maxwell, June 18, 1805. Historical Society of Pennsylvania, Meredith Family Papers, Box 99.

be found, not to amount to so large a sum." Clearly, despite the ostensible division of responsibilities between him and Dennie, Maxwell supposed that Dennie himself also received subscription monies. Maxwell placed the number of subscribers in January 1806 at "13 hundred, 11 hundred of which, might be considered as good." He had cleared another 1000 dollars on stock sales, but was worrying about further sales of this sort. "[I]n future," reported Chapman, Maxwell believed that "the Sales would be much less, without a new Series were commenced."[77] In what is possibly a stock list, drawn up in January 1806, Maxwell listed 400 copies each of four of the five previous volumes, which, at 6.00$ a volume, came to an inventory worth 10,000$.[78] This bandying about of figures could not detract from the fact that Maxwell's role as publisher had produced a magazine that was unsure of what it was still owed. Nor did Maxwell's unofficial communication to Chapman square with his official one, as became clear when the accounts finally became available.

By January 1806, the problems with record keeping, and the increasing difficulty of getting anything out of Maxwell, had evidently multiplied to such an extent that Dennie was forced to seek another publisher to help him with the financial side of the magazine. The split from Maxwell, however, was not an easy one. As soon as the relationship between Maxwell and Dennie was dissolved, increasingly acrimonious letters went from Maxwell to William Meredith and back. On January 27, 1806, Dennie had William Meredith join him to go to Maxwell and force him to hand over the *Port Folio*'s financial accounts. The duo met only with Maxwell's clerk, who denied them access to the books, but showed them the remaining stocks of the *Port Folio*. Meredith noted, slightly incredulously, that the printer's cellar contained "a great number tied up in bundles." Returning the next morning, Meredith, Dennie, and Maxwell exchanged "warm words," since Maxwell refused to hand over his books. After some discussion, Dennie

77 Nathaniel Chapman Memorandum, January 28, 1806. Historical Society of Pennsylvania, Meredith Family Papers 1509, Box 99. The problem here seems to have been that the continuing second series of the *Port Folio*, which had commenced in 1803, meant that Maxwell had to keep reprinting earlier issues in order to complete sets which were missing single issues; reprint costs are charged in Maxwell's accounts to Dennie. A letter from Ezra Sargeant to Dennie in February 1806 requests between two and a dozen single issues from the three previous volumes of the *Port Folio*, putting considerable pressure on the publishers to either keep them in stock or be ready to reprint them at will, leaving Maxwell with the necessity of keeping fully typeset plates ready for reprints. Either would have been unfortunate for Maxwell; it is possible that by commencing a new series, Maxwell hoped to be able to forestall requests for back issues. In January 1806, Maxwell presented Dennie with an invoice of 10.835$ for reprints of between 400 and 500 copies of all five annual volumes published so far, a clear indication that the magazine still sold well, or that there had been a request for a final print run of the *Port Folio* before a new series commenced (Ezra Sargeant to Joseph Dennie, Historical Society of Pennsylvania, Meredith Collection 1509, Box 99; Maxwell to Dennie, January 16, 1806. Historical Society of Pennsylvania, Meredith Family Papers 1509, Box 99.).

78 Hugh Maxwell Memorandum to Joseph Dennie January 24, 1806. Historical Society of Pennsylvania, Meredith Family Papers 1509, Box 99.

and Meredith were able to look at Maxwell's accounts. Meredith noted that "even upon [Maxwell's accounts, Maxwell] appeared to be Dennie's debtor". The meeting dissolved without conclusion since Maxwell was unable to deliver an account of the *Port Folio*'s financial affairs at this point, affairs much complicated by the various entanglements between the parties, such as the fact that Maxwell's bookstore was selling some of Dennie's books, accounts of which sales apparently mingled with the *Port Folio*'s.[79]

As Meredith noted, with something of an understatement, it was only with "considerable difficulty"[80] that Maxwell was induced to offer a statement on the accounts between him and Dennie. Indeed, Meredith and Dennie did not receive a full account from Maxwell until March 4. Even then, they were hardly satisfied: indeed, they were shocked. Maxwell claimed that Dennie owed him about 1500$, but added that there were additional charges on stationary and books obtained which did not yet figure in the account. In a memo taken in preparation for yet another meeting, Meredith notes that Dennie was "obliged to rely on Maxwell's account" of the financial affairs of the *Port Folio*, but now, he found himself completely at odds with Maxwell's statements. Exclamation marks punctuate the exasperation with which Meredith and Dennie commented on Maxwell's account. As Meredith notes, William Fry had been paid 72$ for his publisher's role in 1802—by Maxwell's account, he took in 504$ in 1804 and 600$ in 1805. Maxwell took 20% commission for his sale of Dennie's books, and charged what Meredith regarded as an "inconsistent" amount of money for printing, from 30.50$ in 1801 to 36$ in 1802.

Meredith's memo, entitled "Objections to Account as stated," is a fascinating document of the basis of the *Port Folio*'s business, at least from one side—one would love to hear Maxwell's point of view. Much more than just a list of objections to the facts as stated, it reveals the assumptions and the lack of professionalism which underlay the first years of the *Port Folio*'s business. Dennie and Meredith regarded Maxwell's charge for his services as publisher as frivolous, not so much because of the sum itself—which certainly contrasted with William Fry's—but because they felt Maxwell had had intangible profits from the engagement and greatly benefited from his connection with the *Port Folio*. Meredith called the publisher's role a "[g]reat adv[antage] to [the] young bookseller"[81]—Maxwell—and noted that it was "*little labour*" (original emphasis) due to "few subscribers". Thomas Boylston Adams had taken a similar view of the business end of the *Port Folio*, suggesting that "the mechanical employment appurtenant to the punctual transmission &c of the Port Folio, is not, by odds, so great as fell to my lot"[82] while he was his brother's secretary. This, of course, was a matter of opinion—the number of receipts received by Maxwell in his years as publisher would indicate that, if it was done well, the work involved in

79 William Meredith memo, January 28, 1806, Historical Society of Pennsylvania, Meredith Family Papers 1509, Box 99.

80 Meredith Memorandum, n.d. Historical Society of Pennsylvania, Meredith Family Papers 1509, Box 99.

81 My own emendations, of course; possibly, Meredith means "adv[ertisement]" instead, but in either case, the meaning is clear.

82 TBA to JQA, November 30, 1802. Massachusetts Historical Society, Adams Family Papers, Reel 401

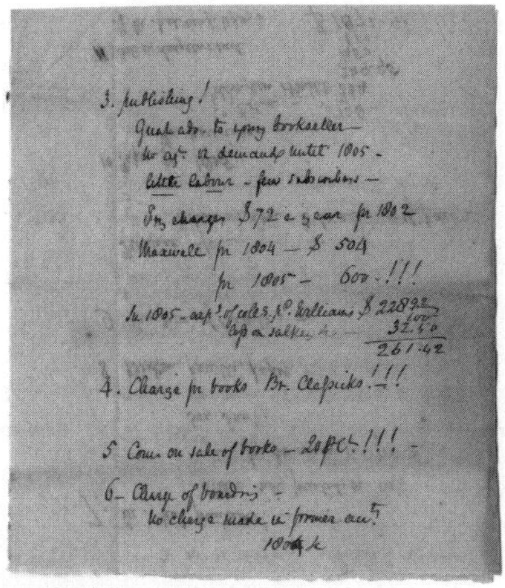

FIG. 4: Excerpt from William Meredith memo, exclamatorically indicating his exasperation with Hugh Maxwell's charges for printing the *Port Folio*. Historical Society of Pennsylvania, Meredith Family Papers 1509, Box 99.
Courtesy of the Historical Society of Pennsylvania

bookkeeping was quite considerable. Indeed, it is clear that Maxwell believed it to be considerable, since his account sheet includes a 400$ charge for "services of Clerk in collecting and attending to the business," added to which were 104$ for "packing and forwarding the paper"—making the total 504$ for 1804.[83]

Meredith and Dennie might well have wondered what exactly they were being charged for here, if Maxwell was in fact handing off the accounting business to someone else, something that arguably would be directly in Maxwell's purview as publisher. Yet perhaps more interesting is the note which Meredith placed next to his second complaint about Maxwell's account, concerning the charges for printing: "*no express contract*" (original emphasis) existed between Maxwell and Dennie, Dickins, or William Fry, on the amount Maxwell was going to be paid for his printing services. For five years, Hugh Maxwell had been printing for Dennie, Dickins, and Fry, without anyone ever formalizing the relations. Already in 1802, Thomas Boylston Adams had complained to his brother that Dennie's "contracts have been loosely and negligently performed."[84] Strikingly, too, Maxwell had consistently underbid his own initial estimate to Dennie on the weekly printing costs, made in 1800. There, he had suggested that it would cost 36$ to print a number, an amount which he only had to charge in 1802, and otherwise never reached, sometimes by a wide margin. Despite this, the Meredith note indicates his and Dennie's irritation at being confronted with the financial calculations of Dennie's printer (cf. fig. 4).

The continual conflict between Maxwell and Dennie, complaints about the lack of punctual delivery, and other affairs took their toll—the separation of Maxwell entirely from the business of the *Port Folio*. In December of 1805, however, Dennie was unwilling to assume the entire control over the venture.

83 Hugh Maxwell account with Joseph Dennie, n.d. (but furnished March 4, 1806). Historical Society of Pennsylvania, Meredith Family Papers 1509, Box 99.

84 TBA to JQA, November 30, 1802. Massachusetts Historical Society, Adams Family Papers, Reel 401

An advertisement in the January 11, 1806 edition of the *United States Gazette* announced that Dennie had "appointed Mr. John Watts, of Philadelphia, his Publisher and General Agent, to whom correspondents, Country Agents, &c. are requested in future to address their letters." Watts, whom William Dunlap called "an Author, scholar & printer" (Dunlap 1930, 397) took over a paper that, despite its strong readership and its continual support from outside writers, was not in good shape, with considerable archives of the magazine unsold and its books in considerable disarray. Nor was John Watts, apparently, a particularly satisfactory choice as publisher. On January 20, 1806, no longer involved in the *Port Folio* business for the past three weeks, Maxwell wrote to Dennie, complaining that Watts had refused to supply the 1806 issues of the *Port Folio* so far published to people who had paid their subscription monies to Maxwell, because Watts felt himself the only person authorized to receive money on the *Port Folio*'s account. Maxwell acknowledged as such, except to note that this was not true for the people he was talking about—who had likely paid before the change in publishers was made. The difficult atmosphere now prevailing was highlighted by Maxwell's fairly direct tone: "this childish affair" should be settled by a personal talk soon. This was a week before Maxwell failed to see Meredith and Dennie on the issue of Maxwell's accounts—childishness, apparently, not being reserved to one side of the debate.[85]

The changes in printer, in publisher, and in external form were not the only ones that occurred in January 1806. The 1806 prospectus proudly reflected the perceived status of the *Port Folio* as "an established literary journal". It also reflected some of the reasoning behind the changes which the *Port Folio* had undergone. Dennie roundly blamed his former "associates" for the "awkward form" the *Port Folio* had hitherto appeared in, and happily reflected on the usefulness of the format changes. While there is no way to be sure of the accuracy of the claim that the format of the *Port Folio* was not decided on by Dennie, it is an interesting comment either way. True or not, it indicates the extent to which Dennie's role in the *Port Folio* was restricted to the weekly editorial decisions, rather than more general decision making on the periodical as a whole, and Dennie's readiness to accept this role. The note preempted any possible criticism, declaring that its "convenience, propriety and taste" had already been acknowledged, as of the January 11 date of the prospectus, by everybody—a clear impossibility, given that the January 11 edition was the first number published in the new format (*PF* 1806 Prospectus, 1).

Dennie's periodical philosophy, if it can be called that, had also evolved again: if in 1801, he had promised entertainment and usefulness every Saturday, and in 1802, had acknowledged that the real value of the *Port Folio* lay not so much in its weekly issues, but rather in its forming a repository of essays that deserved

85 Cf. Hugh Maxwell to Joseph Dennie, January 20, 1806. Historical Society of Pennsylvania, Meredith Family Papers 1509, Box 99. Dennie dated this letter January 30; it is possible he did not receive it until then, though it seems rather unlikely.

a place in the libraries of his subscribers, now, he offered a still more modified view that sought to make clear the possibilities and limitations of the periodical medium. Under pressure to put out a new magazine, now of sixteen pages, every Saturday, he readily acknowledged that at times, entire "[s]ingle numbers may be dull." But his subscribers should be aware that "the whole series of six months' speculation may afford something for the amusement of the idler, and something for the edification of the man of business. For Variety is the motto of this paper, and our object is still to mingle and contrast its ingredients" (*PF* 1806 Prospectus, 1). Indeed, from its first number to its very last in 1825, the *Port Folio* ran with the motto "various that the mind / Of desultory man, studious of change, / And pleased with novelty, may be indulged," on the masthead, from William Cowper's *The Task*, in the initial, softly mock-epic section "The Sofa". The motto, of course, had affirmed much more than the quest for variety: it also outlined the kind of reader that the *Port Folio* was conscious of having to cater to, a very unflattering description of men who could not and were not expected to devote their intellectual faculties to the study of the *Port Folio*.

Dennie went on to pay due thanks to his contributors, defending his previous political vociferousness and himself against the charge of being unpatriotic, and then segued into yet another general complaint about his subscribers' financial morals and another attempt to render himself as a humble servant without monetary interest:

> If his sole object were the acquisition of property, by the profits of publication, the number of munificent or punctual patrons would be insufficient to fill even his tiny coffers. But, though anxious for a competency, he confesses that Wealth is not so glittering to his eye as another splendid and dazzling Power, which often impels him
>
> "To scorn delights, and live laborious days."[86]
>
> Even a sprig from the chaplet of Fame he would often prefer to the gold of the penurious. (*PF* 1806 Prospectus, 5)

Dennie here recurred again to his original editorial self-conception, as suggested in the 1801 prospectus: gold, if grudgingly given, was not the free remuneration of which the public servant was deserving of. That little of this particular self-fashioning was true was a different matter. Dennie's work ethic had never been impressive, and he was not the type to forego fun in favor of long working hours.[87]

86 From John Milton's "Lycidas".

87 William Dunlap gives an impression of Dennie, whom he met for the first time at a dinner at the Conrads' house on January 10, 1806: "Denny [sic] is a small, neat man, an entire contrast to [Thomas Green Fessenden]. He appears to be about 45 years old & is well bespater'd [sic] with grey hairs. Tho' a Masacusets [sic] man he has freed his conversation from yankeeism's [sic], and

If anything, however, the 1806 prospectus offered a positive outlook for the *Port Folio*'s future, one which increasingly devoted the magazine to variety and light reading, addressed to "all classes of his readers" and which highlighted the liberal endowment of the magazine with original contributions. Much of the prospectus was standard fare, dedicated to extolling the virtues of the magazine, the genteelness of its readers, their readiness to offer their patronage, and outlining, now very basically, the prospective contents. It was John Watts, the new publisher, who took the opportunity to condensing the central aspects of the new plan into an advertisement. In a "new and improved form," the *Port Folio* would now focus on literature, and Watts explicitly targeted booksellers and book readers. The *Port Folio* would "advance the cause of domestick Literature," and make sure to "assist the aims of the whole body of Booksellers." To that end, it would expand its advertisements: although there would still be no advertisements in the body of the text, there would now be "some extra pages" devoted to them, and booksellers were enjoined to avail themselves of the opportunities for advertisement thereby offered, including the "moderate terms" (*USG* 1806, January 11, 30.4176, 3) which the *United States Gazette* advertised. Watts no longer included politics prominently in the new setup of the *Port Folio*, a change which did not go unnoticed. In March, the Hartford *Connecticut Courant* succinctly summarized the effect of the changes in a notice by the local *Port Folio* agent, William Watkinson, a local bookseller. "The Port Folio," it announced, "is now a Magazine, devoted to Science and Polite Literature" (*CC* 1806, March 12, 42.2146, 4).

It is not a coincidence that party politics' growing lack of importance to the *Port Folio* was recognized by contemporaries as a shift from newspaper- to magazinehood. Newspapers were the domain of party intrigue—witness William Duane's *Aurora*—and certainly not the kind of refined medium that the Union's men of letters would look to for virtuous instruction (cf. Tucher 2010, 389). When Dennie had called, back in the very first prospectus, the *Port Folio* "not quite a gazette, nor wholly a magazine," the part that was a gazette was the political one. Now, with politics on the way out, observers were justified to deduce that the *Port Folio* henceforward would be a magazine, with all the moral emoluments that went with the designation. The exclusion of politics in the new series was nothing so much as a reaction to the changing fortunes of the Federalist party. If the *Port Folio* had actively set itself up as a magazine devoted, not to Federalism, but to the acquisition of a Federalist audience sharing its professions of classical virtues, and offered an exile at home for the party after the 1801 ascension of Thomas Jefferson to the presidency, the President's re-election and the steadily declining national fortunes of the Federalists indicated that here was an audience that was growing steadily weaker.[88] As Federalist fortunes declined, so

speaks with as much facility and correctness as he writes. He is polite in his address, attentive to the etiquette of conversation and studious so to suit it to those with him as to elicit those sparks which might other wise lie dormant, with all this, I confess I did not hear those brilliant things which I expected from the mouth of the editor of the portfolio." (Dunlap 1930, 368-9)

88 *Port Folio* contributor John Quincy Adams, later the Democratic-Republican Secretary of State

did the *Port Folio*'s interest in Federalists as an audience, and so followed its attempt to reposition itself as a magazine first and foremost interested in literary discussions.

The beginning of the new series of 1806 was more hopeful than events could finally bear out. Watts evidently found the *Port Folio*'s financial records in a deplorable state, and himself very much unable to effect a positive change, despite some efforts. Late in January 1806, newspapers began carrying a carefully phrased note to *Port Folio* subscribers, admitting that "[o]wing to the transfer of this Establishment into the hands of another publisher, and the confused state of the lists of subscribers delivered to him, some delay as arisen in sending the Port Folio to the different towns in the United States" (*NYEP* 1806, February 17, 1320, 4). Crucially for the financial well-being of the magazine, confused subscriber lists meant not only that subscribers might miss out on numbers, but more importantly, that the *Port Folio*'s proprietors had no clear idea of who owed them money. Dennie's and Maxwell's haphazard record keeping had already forced the pair to resort to such broad requests as the one he placed in the November 23, 1805 issue of the *Port Folio*, concurrently with a note that he would commence a new series in the spring. Dennie enjoined "*all manner of persons*, indebted to this Journal" to "remit to him, *on, or before the thirtieth of December next*, in letters, *post paid*, the amount of his claims" (*PF* 1805, 367, original emphasis). Even if Dennie had wanted to address his debtors directly, he could not have done so, given that at this point, he still did not possess Maxwell's statements on the accounts of his subscribers.

The difficulties existing with the subscription list were not abated on John Watts's takeover as publisher. Indeed, the volume of correspondence reaching Watts during 1806, commenting on issues of the *Port Folio* not reaching subscribers, money paid but never acknowledged, and other problems to be laid squarely at the feet of the new publisher, was a clear indication that the business was still not running smoothly. Throughout 1806, the *Port Folio* resorted to the by-now well-known open letters to subscribers printed in the magazine itself and enjoining them to remit their payments for the magazine. Yet, as Dennie himself put it, by the fall of 1806, it was necessary to admit that total success had eluded the publisher and editor in their quest to obtain payment. They therefore adopted a more direct approach, one which Dennie was worried had been unhappily couched in the "discordant dialect of a creditor" as he phrased it in a later note "To Agents and Subscribers" printed on the wrapper of the January 3, 1807 edition of the *Port Folio* (*PF* 1807 1, [1]).[89] The new effort consisted of a printed letter sent to every subscriber of the *Port Folio* who had a balance against himself in the accounts. By this time,

to James Monroe and President of the United States, was perhaps the best manifestation of this shift: in 1808, supporting Thomas Jefferson's embargo act, he had been recalled from his senatorial position by the Massachusetts legislature, and shifted his allegiance to the Democrat-Republicans.

89 An unfortunate consequence of this printing on the wrapper is the loss of this note in most bound editions of the *Port Folio*. The wrapper itself is paginated 1 through 4, and the magazine itself also starts at one; page numbers referring to the wrapper are therefore in brackets.

Dennie and Watts had probably already agreed to dissolve their short-lived partnership: "by mutual consent, and for mutual convenience" (*PF* 1807 1, [4])—Watts having, as Dennie noted, many other things to do that were more important for his business—the two men went their different ways. Dennie himself took over the job of publisher in January 1807, leaving the business of printing the magazine to two young printers with a shop near Washington Square. Dennie had hired an accountant to help him with the books by early November 1806;[90] that same month, letters went out, delineating each subscriber's debts (as far as Dennie and his accountant could work it out) and a longish note, admitting his uncertainty about the process, his willingness to accept his subscribers' word for any deduction they would want to make, and his readiness to accept any form of bank note whatever as a means of payment. Dennie's letter underlines the dire nature of the request: "nothing but an immediate attention to my claims, by every one of my subscribers, can relieve me" (*PF* 1807 1, [2]). It is always necessary to take Dennie's public pronouncements concerning his own financial affairs with a grain of salt, but whatever the true state of the *Port Folio*'s finances, it is clear that the problem was one of record-keeping, rather than patronage.

And, remarkably, the letter campaign, by Dennie's own estimation, worked. In a long paragraph of effusive praise in the 1807 wrapper note, he acknowledged that "this measure has exceeded our most sanguine expectations," with no word of

90 The identity of this person is unclear. John Queenan suggests that it was William Meredith who was dealing with business details of the *Port Folio* in late 1806 and 1807, based on correspondence between William and Richard Peters, as well as several memos in the Historical Society of Pennsylvania's collection (cf. Queenan 1955, 34). However, the record on this ground is far from transparent. All letters and memos deal with legal issues, rather than straight up financial questions, and William, a lawyer, may very well have had interests tangentially touching on the *Port Folio* but otherwise separate from it. By contrast, Dennie began living with William's brother David Meredith early in 1807, and David's signature is on a letter from John Gray, editor of the *New England Republican*, sent in September 1806, in which the latter subscribed to the *Port Folio* and enclosed five dollars to so. David Meredith initialed both the date of the receipt of the letter, as well as the note "Entered," suggesting that David was at least by then keeping the *Port Folio*'s books (cf. John Gray to Editor of *Port Folio*, September 1, 1806 Historical Society of Pennsylvania, Meredith Family Papers, 1509, Box 99). But again, any firm answer to the relationships behind the *Port Folio* are made complicated by the odd bookkeeping practices at the magazine. An account sheet between Dennie and David Meredith involved a balance against Meredith on the *Port Folio* cash book, indicating a close entanglement of indefinite nature between the magazine and David Meredith (cf. Note signed David Meredith, January 26, 1807. Historical Society of Pennsylvania, Meredith Family Papers 1509, Box 99). It is much more likely overall that the person assisting Dennie was David Meredith: the two men lodged together, David not only resided, but also worked in Philadelphia (unlike William, who was very frequently absent on business), and David's work at his family's tannery had always involved finance. William, however, was very likely retained by Dennie as his attorney in the conflict with Hugh Maxwell in the early months of 1806.

complaint from the subscribers. The measure also, as far as was possible, balanced Dennie's books, leaving the *Port Folio* to start 1807 with a clean account. Even in his wrapper-published note, Dennie found it necessary to ask readers who had not yet abided by his request for remuneration to do so immediately; but overall, the financial outlook of the *Port Folio* going into 1807 was perhaps more bright than at any time before. It may have been the success of the letter campaign that induced Dennie to try to be his own publisher for the first time in the *Port Folio*'s history. "The department of publication is now under the immediate superintendence and control of the Editor: all applications on office business must, in future, be made to him, or his clerk" ([4]). That clerk—David Meredith—boarded with Dennie, continuing a tradition in the *Port Folio* business starting with Thomas Bolyston Adams, who also had shared rooms and a business relationship with Dennie.[91] The note addressed to agents and subscribers briefly laid out the ground rules under which the magazine would be published from now on: Philadelphians and anybody living in a city or town without one of the agents the text helpfully listed would apply to Dennie for all publishing questions; everybody else should engage himself with the agent in his hometown, or home state, respectively, if there was only one agent in the state.[92] At once candid, grateful, imploring and optimistic, Dennie noted that

91 The interweaving of business and residence, and of the old property of the Dickins bookstore and the *Port Folio* business, can be traced in the Philadelphia directories for 1801-1811. Up to 1805, with the exception of a part of the time in 1802/3, Dennie lived at 25 North Second Street, the location of the Dickins bookstore, with Elizabeth Dickins, the "Clergyman's widow" whom he mentioned in a letter to his mother (in Pedder 1936, 190, who misidentifies the woman, however); he only moved out for a time to live with Thomas Boylston Adams at 113 Walnut Street (cf. also Pedder 1936, 191), perhaps because William Fry had purchased the Dickins store and needed the rooms for himself. From 1803 to 1806, Hugh Maxwell lived and worked at 25 North Second Street, having purchased the bookstore off of Fry; he lived at the corner of Spruce and 11th Street (fairly far outside the main commercial areas of 1800s Philadelphia) in 1801-2; at that time, Maxwell had only been listed as a printer and had evidently not yet begun his bookstore business. From 1807 onward (he is not listed in the 1806 directory), Dennie resided again at 113 Walnut, this time with David Meredith. In 1809-10, Dennie and the *Port Folio* moved to the long established stationery and book shop of Bradford & Inskeep at 4 South Third Street, where Dennie apparently lived until his death.

92 The list of agents included a large number of names well-familiar to the editor through years of epistolary contact: Ezra Sargeant of New York, David Ogden of Montreal, Oliver C. Greenleaf of Boston, George Hill of Baltimore, William Pritchard of Richmond, all booksellers. The *Port Folio*'s reach extended throughout the United States and Canada, but not into the territories—at least as far as agents were concerned. Several of these agents Dennie had solicited himself, via letter. D.A. Leonard, the postmaster of Bristol, Rhode Island, wrote Dennie in August 1806, acknowledging that he would be glad to serve as agent for Bristol upon Dennie's request, and offered to seek out an agent in Providence. No agent for Providence is listed in the 1807 note—perhaps Dennie did not want to hire anyone whom he was not personally acquainted with; cf. D.A. Leonard to Joseph Dennie, August 2, 1806. Historical Society of Pennsylvania, Meredith Family Papers 1509, Box 99.

FIG. 5: Title page of Robert Anderson's 11th volume of *The Poets of Great Britain*, from which Dennie se-lected dozens of lives for inclusion in both the *Farmer's Weekly Museum* and the *Port Folio*. The life of James Graeme, twice printed by Dennie, is included in this volume.

"the buttresses of business will not hereafter be shaken" (*PF* 1807 1, [4]), suggested that with 200 or 300 names more on his subscription list, he would be entirely satisfied, and laid out the editorial plan for the new year: "Let him have no care but to please the publick, and no occupation but the pursuits of literature" (*PF* 1807 1, [3]). At once hopeful that the publisher's work in finances would prove less arduous than heretofore and relegating more ambitious goals for his magazine to a back-burner, Dennie began 1807 with a magazine greatly changed behind the scenes, somewhat modified in format, but almost unchanged in content.

Notwithstanding its bright outlook in 1807, the next two years were hardly the *Port Folio*'s best, partially owing to Joseph Dennie's increasingly difficult battle with the consumption that would kill him in 1812, but also because a large number of earlier contributors was no longer prepared, either from considerations of time or from a growing disillusionment with the magazine, to devote themselves to it (cf. Ellis 1971, 193-4). But it is important to note that none of the protagonists, not even Hugh Maxwell, on whom the majority of the work and much the expenses had clearly devolved, believed the magazine to be responsible for their financial woes. Certainly, bad bookkeeping and other issues which fell squarely on the shoulders of the publishers were a considerable problem for the *Port Folio* throughout the first decade of the nineteenth century. As Thomas Boylston Adams had it in a letter to his brother in 1802, "Dennie has never had a man of business, either as a partner or a subordinate; the detail of the concern has consequently been neglected, shamefully and many think impardonably."[93] This was a harsh conclusion—especially so since Adams's own involvement in the management after December 1802 does not seem to have had a major impact on the business's financial records—but one which time bore out. But strikingly, it does not seem to be the case that the main reason for the frequent changes in publishers, and afterwards, in printers, was a failure of the *Port Folio* as such, or, as Ellis has it, "the uncertainty and delinquency of subscription payments" (1971, 179).

Despite the editor's often vociferous and frequent complaints to his subscribers that subscription money, although required in advance, was often not paid at all, it is not at all clear from the available sources that the *Port Folio* was a money pit. As early as November 1801, a year in which the *Port Folio* probably cleared as much as 2000$ in profit for its editor and publisher together, Dennie reminded delinquent readers of their duty to pay him for services rendered; a similar note, in June 1802, even went so far as to threaten to have to cancel his work: "Unless the Editor receive more liberal aid, he must, at the close of the present year, *lock up* his Port Folio" (*PF* 1802 175, original emphasis). But this form of complaint continued and continued, as apparently without abatement, subscribers defaulted, failed to pay, and fell between the cracks of bad bookkeeping. None of this detracted investors, such as the publishing firm of Bradford & Inskeep, from finding the *Port Folio* an attractive venture—and neither did these complaints apparently reflect a recurring danger of actual discontinuation of the magazine, even though the events of 1806 may have come close to that.

Too much should therefore not be made of the large turnover especially in publishers: Asbury Dickins left the magazine for unrelated, and, apparently, surprising debts; William Fry left the publishership at the same time as he sold his bookstore in Philadelphia, and it is hardly possible to determine if either factor influenced the other, or if Fry had entirely unrelated problems; John Watts, according to Dennie, found the additional work for the *Port Folio* to be too much, rather than despairing of financial success;[94] and Hugh Maxwell, as we have seen, even if the growing problems with the *Port Folio* were hardly conducive to his financial well-being, finally did not retire his double position as publisher and printer because the *Port Folio* did not pay him enough but because his service as publisher had led to so much uncertainty about the financial well-being of the magazine that Dennie found it necessary to dissolve the relationship.

The shifts in the business background of the *Port Folio* which I have outlined at length above suggest the troubles which attended the haphazard conduct of a magazine. None of the publishers which ran the business side of the *Port Folio* during 1801-1809 fully came to grips with the best way of profiting from the magazine.

93 TBA to JQA, November 30, 1802. Massachusetts Historical Society, Adams Family Papers, Reel 401

94 Cf. Queenan 1955, 32-4 for a short account, partially hypothetical, of the difficulties John Watts experienced during his short stay as publisher.

Even the changes of 1806-1807 were, in retrospect, a doomed attempt to keep a project afloat whose best days were already behind it, a project whose reliance on voluntary submissions and chance finds in other magazines and books could not ultimately produce the kind of periodical that made full use of the potentials of the market. The weekly format put a great strain on a man who had, upon occasion, failed to fully fill his role when merely the editor; now, as editor and publisher both, even with the help of friends, the workload necessarily became too much. Dennie was sick and dispirited, certainly not in a condition to bring the *Port Folio* back to its old glory. More drastic and vastly more successful changes awaited the magazine in1809.

Biography in the New *Port Folio*, 1802-1809

When the major changes to the production structures of the *Port Folio* occurred in 1806, very little had changed since 1802 in the *Port Folio*'s use of biography, but the department had gained a certain prominence, owed, no doubt, to the profuse amount of material Dennie had at hand in the various biographical dictionaries.[95] By late 1802, Dennie had evidently decided to profit from the readily available materials, emphasizing the role of biography in the magazine. On September 25, he promised his readers over a life of William Gifford, taken from the Englishman's new translation of Juvenal's satires, that "Biography shall constitute a regular department in the Port Folio," and reiterating his belief that "none can be more delightful, or more useful." Gifford's autobiography—which Dennie re-categorized as a biography—was brand new and in and of itself therefore worthy of inclusion, but Dennie found the opportunity helpful, as he had in 1801, to link the life he was printing to his own situation—and the classical allusions of his prospectus. It "will not escape the moral reader," Dennie hinted, that Gifford, "a man of genius, struggling with adversity," and benefitting from the support of a British nobleman, was to "be discerned that there is *one*[96] *country, where when a Virgil appears, he never*

95 One of the more important and difficult results of analyzing the biographical department in the *Port Folio* in this time frame is the recognition that it is problematic to use Randolph Randall's "Authors of the *Port Folio* Revealed by the Hall Files" (1940) as a source for ascriptions. The operative word here, of course, is "revealed," which implies the verity of John E. Hall's annotations; but Hall erred. Thus, in May 1802, Dennie printed a life of William Windham, which Hall ascribed to Dennie. But the piece is explicit in naming its source as the *Public Characters for 1802*, an annual British publication Dennie used increasingly. Therefore, hereonafter, even though Randall's ascriptions will be given where possible, the possibility that they are wrong should be borne in mind.

96 "A country truly great and *free*, where Bounty follows Service. Where *ingratitude* is no part of the national character. Where, when a WASHINGTON, or an ADAMS, a HAMILTON, or a PICKERING, are lavish of life to promote public welfare, there are none so detestably base, so meanly penurious as to withhold from them the rewards of honest fame. *Note, by the Editor.*" [Dennie's note and emphasis].

wants a Mæcenas" (PF 1802, 299, original emphasis). Dennie's belief in his own Virgilian right to the kind of public sponsor (or rather, in his case, to being sponsored by a subscribing public) remained prominent in his now more frequent commentaries on the biographies he published. In October 1805, he used the occasion of copying a biography of Benjamin West from the *London Universal Magazine* to ironize his own position. West was happy, successful, and admired in Europe—did he sigh "to return to a country, free to discern, and sovereign to reward merit" (*PF* 1805, 331)? For Dennie, the answer was clear: the sovereign who could reward merit freely was not the American people, or at any rate, they were not going to do so; rather, West had found the right place for the honored artist in the European courts. Biography here offered Dennie a chance to reemphasize what he sought to establish as the best description of the *Port Folio*'s ideal relationship between reader and editor. At the same time, the biographies which he reprinted, and his own editorial duties, were hardly in the same league as Virgil's poetry—and certainly not original.

Dennie's relationship to the question of originality was also frequently highlighted by his editorial commentary. For the duration of 1803, it was evident that Dennie had caught an interest in the Latin poets, publishing a biographical piece on Horace in July 1803, extracted from a recent translation, to complement his reading of Juvenal, which he commented on at times; but the mainstays of his biographical department remained Robert Anderson and, increasingly, the annual publication of the *Public Characters*. In July 1803, he printed a biography, written by John Quincy Adams (cf. Randall 1940, 386) of the French writer Florian, and briefly suggested that it might be presumed to have additional interest on account of being original (cf. *PF* 1803, 228). But despite the fact that he could boast of a truly original text, written for the *Port Folio*, he made less of this text than he did, three months later, of a life of the Portuguese poet Camoens. Here, he noted that to "obtain Original articles of biography for this paper, has always been a favorite object of the Editor"—where original meant texts written for the *Port Folio*. Such texts were becoming more common. In January 1804, the *Port Folio* ran biographies of Joannes Secundus, a Dutch poet, under the heading "For the Port Folio. Original Biography," which a helpful hand initialed "Z." had pieced together (cf. *PF* 1804, 27), and a life of Pascal which Dennie prefaced with a large editorial note. "It is so uncommon," he admitted, "for the Editor to receive an *original* article of our Biographical department, that the following is like certain medals, valuable for rarity as well as splendor," and readers would agree that it was even more valuable for having been written by "an *American* Biographer" (*PF* 1804, 3, original emphasis). Indeed, the *Port Folio* printed original biographies more frequently in early 1804 than at any time before, although it did not note the authors of the pieces it printed. Nor did this trend continue: early in January 1805, the magazine spent four months on the biography of Samuel Richardson, reproduced from the just-published *Correspondence of Samuel Richardson*. If there was any need to remind us of the fact that originality, while desirable, could never be a central criterion in the selection of the *Port Folio*'s material, here was as good a one as any.

The obverse of the quest for originality was the frequent carelessness which the selection process of the biographies revealed. If the *Port Folio*'s financial bookkeeping was horrendous, its literary bookkeeping was nearly as abysmal. Relying, perhaps overmuch, on Robert Anderson's *Works of the British Poets*, Dennie repeatedly printed texts which he had published before in the *Farmer's Weekly Museum*. In September 1805, he re-published the "Life of Graeme," which the *Museum* had run, in parts at least, as the "Character of James Graeme" in July 1799. If in this case, the fact that he had made major cuts of the character piece in the *Museum* may have justified a full inclusion of the biography from Anderson's volumes in the *Port Folio*, other texts were more problematical. In January 1806, Dennie published, under the misleading heading "For the Port Folio," the life of John Donne. Ironically, Dennie found himself in need to defending the choice of the person of Donne for a biography: "But, exclaims the fastidious hunter after novelty, why fatigue your readers with the memoirs of an old divine, whose satires, like his sermons, are rumbling, quaint and austere" (*PF* 1806 1, 21)? The better question to put into his readers' mouths would possibly have been: why fatigue us with a biography that has already been published, especially since the editor had by no means exhausted the possibilities offered by Anderson's *Works*? The "Life of Donne" had already appeared, in full length, in the April 18, 1797, edition of the *Farmer's Weekly Museum*. Other texts which the *Port Folio* repeated verbatim, and without reference to any previous appearance or original source, were the lives of John Suckling (*PF* 1806 1, 308ff and *FWM* April 4, 1797) and Thomas Carew (*PF* 1806, 362ff and *FWM* March 14, 1797). Strikingly, these last two lives were placed between consecutive installments of the translated life of Racine, a text whose irregular appearance Dennie felt forced to comment on late in June 1806. He assured readers that it was not the translator's or his own fault that the biography had been interrupted, but rather the "great press of matter" which lay as backlog in the *Port Folio* offices. His translator, he stated, could be certain that he had not been willfully neglected. That reprints of Suckling's and Carew's biography had preempted an original translation should have been the cause of much embarrassment, and perhaps was; it also spoke to the often haphazard way in which Dennie, in June 1806 also busy with his problems with Maxwell and the growing awareness that John Watts was not doing too great a job as publisher, ran the editorial department.

The Donne biography was the most brazen example of the way in which the *Port Folio* recycled; it also highlights the almost sly way in which Dennie was handling the headlines for his texts. The lives of Pascal and Joannes Secundus had been both "original biography" and "for the Port Folio;" now, texts came under the heading "for the Port Folio," which carried with it the implicit connotation of originality, that were anything but original. Dennie was not fastidious, but at least somewhat conscientious, at acknowledging his sources for those texts (again, mostly Anderson's *Works*),[97] but this only increased the problem: if

97 Cf., inter alia, the biography of John Logan in the March 22, 1806 issue, explicitly credited to Robert Anderson, and still called "For the Port Folio."

texts could be both clearly taken from other sources, and "for the Port Folio," what happened when the editor failed to identify sources, as he frequently did? The imprint gave the appearance of originality to a broad variety of texts, ranging from such as were specifically written for the *Port Folio*, to those translated or selected for it and original, as Dennie had in the *Farmer's Weekly Museum*'s biography of Edmund Burke, only "in this country," to texts which had no originality whatsoever—except that they had not been published in the *Port Folio* before.

As much as the 1806 prospectus shifted the attentions away from politics and into literature, the biographical department remained largely excluded from changes. It had never been overtly political anyway: just like the *Farmer's Weekly Museum*, the *Port Folio* had emphasized the availability of material over its political value. Its most overtly political biography had been that of Alexander Hamilton, which passed virtually unnoticed in August 1801, with the occasional political commentary interspersed among the editorial introductions, as in the life of Benjamin West. After the 1806 changes. the biographical department kept operating much as it had for the previous five years. Politics in biography remained coincidental: the life of Racine included an editorial insisting once more of the preference Dennie had for the aristocratic mode of literary patronage, and a November life of the French writer Roucher stressed Dennie's disgust with the French Revolution.

Perhaps the most noticeable change was Dennie's now ever more strenuous insistence on the value of biographical short texts and his increasing desire to justify the inclusion of particular texts. In February 1806, he included in the continuing biography of Thomas Blacklock, taken from Robert Anderson's *Works* (Vol. 11), a number of editorial remarks reflecting on what biography meant for the *Port Folio*. Initially, on February 1st, the standard explanation sufficed: Blacklock, the blind English poet, "seems to deserve more than ordinary attention" (although the *Port Folio*'s attention, in bringing forward yet another biography from the by-now common source of Anderson's *Works*, was fairly pedestrian), and his life would prove "incentive to bold action" (*PF* 1806 1, 52). So far, so good: a week later, Dennie elaborated. Biography, another editorial averred, had so much to recommend itself, being a "true, native, and lively representation" of the depicted, that "we assign many hours to [it], particularly of the learned, and assign many pages of the Port Folio to a department of elegant literature, which the public voice has declared is not less agreeable to the humour of our readers, than to our own" (*PF* 1806 1, 66). Dennie at once acknowledged the desire to please the public and himself, suggesting that there existed something of a common bond of taste between him and his readers. To a public that, upon occasion, recognized Dennie as something of an arbiter of good taste, Dennie's own belief that biography, as a genre, was "agreeable" at the same time suggested that readers should find it acceptable, too.

The conflation between the editor's interest and the public's interest continued in Dennie's commentary on biographies. In May, 1806, he again declared that he and his readers shared their sense of the value of biography in commenting on an original translation of the life of Racine that it was "a duty we owe to the public, as well as a benefit and pleasure to ourselves, to pay frequent attention to the lives and writings of the French literati." He believed "nothing in the range of reading" to be "more delightful" than "Literary Biography" (*PF* 1806 I, 291), especially that of the French. Placing his editorial choices between duty to others and his own pleasures, Dennie highlighted again his awareness of the necessity to please. This contrasted with some of his earlier editorial positions. In 1803, for example, over a life of Horace, he had still applied the conditional: "If the readers of the Port Folio derive the same pleasure from the perusal of this article, as the editor has done" (*PF* 1803, 244), he would not regret the time spent in transcribing it. At once unsure of his own taste in relation to the public's, and uncertain whether the simple gratification of his readers could be a commendable goal, Dennie admitted that he hoped for a common opinion, but did not expect it. In 1806, Dennie was more certain of matching his own tastes to that of his readers, not only because he had come to understand his readership better, but because he recognized that the magazine, to an extent, made the taste, even as it responded to it. If the editor in 1803 sounded a least slightly timid, fearful of finding his tastes not compatible with that of his audience, in 1806, he and his audience were more clearly established as a community of equal taste.

The general decline which the *Port Folio* went through in 1807 and 1808 also hit the biographical department. Where, in its heyday, nearly every week had been graced with a life, beginning in January 1807, sometimes months went past without a biography being printed in the *Port Folio*. The editorial justifications remained the same: a biography of Virgil in March, copied from the unlikely source of David Urquhart's *Commentaries on Classical Learning*, carried a note simply stating "Biography [...] in point of importance and moral utility, ranks as high as any" and "[t]he name of VIRGIL is sufficient to ensure the attention of the reader" (*PF* 1807 I, 164, original emphasis). In April, Dennie provided a longish preface to a life of a "late Lord High Chancellor of England" (*PF* 1807 I, 259), Edward Thurlow, suggesting that this was an offering to "the gentlemen of the bar [...i]n conformity with our habitual inclination to render every possible service to the eminent lawyers of our country" (259-60). The article, likely taken from the London *Literary Panorama*, once more highlighted the ways in which the *Port Folio*'s editor made his selections to serve the gratification of an audience.

The dearth of biographical short texts did not go unnoticed, certainly not by the editor himself. Dennie explained the small number of biographies published by the *Port Folio* in his usual eloquent fashion. In February 1808, after a lapse of nearly nine months without any biography, a long comment preceded the biography of Charles Mordaunt, which he had picked from the recently-arrived *Biographical History of England*. Dennie acknowledged his debt to his readers:

> In several numbers of this paper, we have insisted, at considerable length, upon the delight, that a great majority of our readers of an inquisitive humour and delicate taste, always experience, in perusing the lives of distinguished men. At no very remote distance of time, we stipulated with the publick that Biography should form a regular

> article in this Journal. It imports us to *pay our vows*. Indeed, an article so agreeable to the humour of the editor, as well as interesting to the curiosity of his friends, should not have been postponed, for a week, if we could have readily found a choice of valuable articles, sufficiently portable for this miscellany. But Addison could not *hate long speeches* more heartily, than the publick detest prolixity, in a paper of the complexion of The Port Folio. (original emphasis)

This was an altogether surprising admission on several levels. Dennie's insistence on finding texts that adhered to a certain maximum length ran counter to the *Port Folio*'s practice in the previous years, where as many biographies ran over two, three, or even more issues, as finished within the confines of one. From the very beginning of the *Port Folio*, of course, Dennie had been aware, and had repeatedly stressed, the need to avoid the specter of "prolixity," but so far, this had meant that he would not print more than a page or a page and a half of biography, before continuing the text in the next issue. What was more, he still had dozens of short biographies available in the reference works he had so far consulted, such as Robert Anderson's *Works*. Nevertheless, he asserted that "we had found ourselves embarrassed by the copiousness of our materials," and had only lately "found a collection of lives written in a terse style and abounding with anecdote" (*PF* 1808 I, 94). To an extent, the *Biographical History of England* appealed to Dennie because of its inclusion of a large number of poets of Augustan England. At the same time, however, the "abundance of anecdote" which Dennie praised in the new selection was suggestive of a reappraisal of the role that biography might be considered to play. As had been periodically hinted at, the emphasis now lay strictly on the entertainment which anecdotes could bring to the *Port Folio*'s readers. That the substance of the biographies which Dennie would print from the *Biographical History* did not necessarily conform to either the prolixity or the anecdotal style which Dennie emphasized mattered less, as usual, than the aggressive salesmanship that Dennie brought to the front. Dexterously, he turned what was clearly a problematic absence of material which he had repeatedly emphasized as central to the *Port Folio*'s roster of content into a particular strength of his editorial oversight: he had not denied his readers biography so much as he had spared them long and tedious writings while he searched for those kinds of texts which could gratify his readers. These readers, by the by, were now clearly regarded as seeking "delight" above all, justifying in turn the search for anecdote. Gone for now were the days of the useful and amusing; come were the days of amusement for amusement's sake. For the duration of 1808, while the *Port Folio* continued to publish the "little medallions of character" (*PF* 1808 I, 94) that Dennie by and large all extracted from the *Biographical History of England*, no further commentary on the purpose and role of biography would come from the editor's pen: the biographical department, like the magazine as a whole, had accepted its role as a supplier of light and amusing material.[98]

98 The sole interesting piece of biography in 1808 is a life of Edward G. Malbone, a recently deceased Rhode Island painter. This essay may be original to the *Port Folio* (an earlier source could

1809-1812: The Monthly *Port Folio* to the Death of Joseph Dennie

The *Port Folio*'s renewed decline after the short enthusiasm exhibited by Dennie in 1807 had major consequences; and the system under which the magazine operated was clearly broken. Dennie had proven himself an incapable administrator long since, and David Meredith, whatever else he was, had not exhibited great monetary care either (as Gertrude Meredith noted in a letter to her husband in 1804).[99] As Dennie felt obliged to note in October 1807, he was "the sole proprietor of this paper, of which, for years, he has had the absolute direction, and, if any emoluments arise from the subscription, the property is exclusively his" (*PF* 1807 2, 284). The distinction between proprietor and director here was the one between publisher and editor, both of which roles Dennie had re-arrogated to himself. Meredith's clerkship notwithstanding, Dennie's was the guiding hand behind the venture, and that hand became increasingly shaky. Exactly how well things stood financially with the *Port Folio* in 1807 and 1808 is difficult to determine. John Queenan suggests that it was in a "most unhealthy financial condition" (1955, 35), but his evidence—one of 1808's two calls for subscribers to pay him—is somewhat inconclusive. Published in the first issue in March, and the first issue in October, the notes to his subscribers are the common fare which had for seven years, on and off, filled the pages of the *Port Folio*. Dennie suggested in October that he had outstanding claims of 10.000$ on his subscription list, about 1600 subscriptions' worth (cf. *PF* 1808 2, 239); yet clearly these could not be just last year's debts (because if so, just about none of his subscribers would have paid), and, if the sum had any origin in reality, likely was the total of missed subscription monies since 1801—averaging to about 200 subscribers failing to pay each yearly installment for the magazine (and, incidentally, only a little above the 1000$ "losses" calculation Asbury Dickins had made in 1800). This, at any rate, was the calculation other periodicals, notably Hezekiah Niles's *Weekly Register*, made when they claimed large sums of money as outstanding credit.

Whatever the financial situation of the magazine, Dennie's health was declining; his contributors were getting fewer; and the work of the publisher, it would seem, was not at all to Dennie's liking. He still possessed the remarkable versatility and readiness to adapt his writings to the changing circumstances of the day that had seen the *Port Folio* transform with relative ease away from a Federalist paper into a largely apolitical literary magazine, however: in late October 1808, he again eloquently justified his editorial course to his readers, commenting on why he had refused inclusion to a religious debating paper. In his explanation, he carefully positioned himself away from mere levity, but acknowledged that "the amusing and cheerful departments of polite literature principally command his care, and Experience shows that they *almost exclusively* gain the publick attention" (*PF* 1808 2,

not be found), but was not, as had been customary, given the "for the Port Folio" headline.

99 Cf. Getrude Meredith to William Meredith, May 3, 1805. Historical Society of Pennsylvania, Meredith Family Papers 1509, Box51

255, original emphasis). He could hardly have put the process of his own growth as editor more clearly. Far from being, as John Queenan has suggested (cf. 1955, 36), an attempt to blame his readers for his inability to put out the kind of literature he wanted to publish, his note was a matter of fact summation of some twelve years' experience in the editorial trade. Nothing that he said about the "amusing departments" was new as such: all of it had studded editorial commentary for years. What was new was the idea that such light writing could sustain the *Port Folio* almost by itself: the *Port Folio* had officially reneged on providing a balance, "something of Politics to interest Quidnuncs, and something of literature to engage Students," as the *Port Folio*'s first prospectus had it. Where Dennie had previously spent much time arguing that those interested in the lighter muses should excuse the difficult dissertations, and those interested in those dissertations should kindly skip the light reading, because the magazine required the patronage of all, by 1808, Dennie had concluded that this was clearly not the case: "if the Editor indulged himself [...] in the lavish expenditure of queries respecting the figures of Homer's shield, or in journalizing the squabbles of fanaticks [...] our readers would soon dwindle to the narrow catalogue of Persius." He concluded on a related note, which clearly stressed the emphasis of the *Port Folio*: "But, above all, if our correspondents should engage in the *unprofitable contest* of religious controversy they would drive away both our smiling and our serious subscribers" (*PF* 1808 2, 255, original emphasis). Religious controversy was, indeed, no profitable field for the *Port Folio* to engage in, neither theologically, nor, as was more important for Dennie's purposes, from a monetary point of view.

Given the background of personal problems and his lack of proprietorial ability, the changes which the *Port Folio* went through in 1809 were not surprising, sweeping though they were. Despite all its shortcomings especially in 1808, as John Queenan notes "[t]he *Port Folio* was still a respected name," and a prospectively successful investment (1955, 37, original emphasis). Thoroughly disillusioned with the publisher's role, this time around the reorganization of the property concluded Dennie's attempts at making money through the business side of the *Port Folio*. He sold his ownership to the publishing house of Bradford & Inskeep.[100] The firm of Bradford & Inskeep was no stranger to the *Port Folio*. Samuel Bradford,

100 The precise structure which underlay the joint venture between Samuel F. Bradford and John Inskeep is unclear. The title page indicated a division of responsibilities: "Published by Bradford and Inskeep, Philadelphia; and Inskeep and Bradford, New York" was its imprint until mid-1814. Then, the *Port Folio* added the name of Abraham Inskeep, whose relation to John is unclear, to the title page. Abraham Inskeep was the New York-based part of Inskeep and Bradford, but what influence he had on the business venture and the *Port Folio* especially is uncertain. It is in fact similarly uncertain what the business structure of the *Port Folio* was like prior to the sale to Bradford & Inskeep. There can be no doubt that Dennie owned the magazine—the sales contract says as much. But in the issues for 1808, Thomas Smith and James Maxwell, the firm of Smith & Maxwell, are listed as having "printed and published" the *Port Folio*. Their publishing role is and remains mysterious, as it clearly did not entail possession of the subscribers list.

printer, publisher, and bookseller, and the active partner in Philadelphia, had been one of the intermediaries during the difficulties between the *Port Folio* and Hugh Maxwell, and had had insight into the *Port Folio*'s finances. He was also a member of the Tuesday Club, the informal gathering of friends that had been involved in supporting Dennie and the *Port Folio* since 1801 (cf. Koschnik 2007, 165). Bradford's relationship with Dennie influenced their dealings, but despite their comparatively close acquaintance, was not particularly to Dennie's benefit.

The *Port Folio*'s sale, quite unlike much of its previous business dealings, was put to notarized paper. In their contract, Bradford & Inskeep agreed to "defray all the expences which may be incurred in the printing & publishing, collecting the subscription money [… & to] perform all the duties insuing out of the undertaking, those of the Editor only excepted," which last job Dennie himself would retain. The contract explicitly specified that Dennie would be expected to hand over "the present subscription list." Dennie's efforts in 1807 to establish precisely who owed what, and withal, who was still on the subscription list in the first place, certainly paid off here. Much of the value of the *Port Folio*, aside from its name, resided, of course, in the known stock of willing subscribers. Instead of being "editor and proprietor," Dennie would from now on be a salaried editor again only, at the not inconsiderably salary of 800$ the first year, to be paid in equal monthly payments,[101] and 1000$ thereafter, until Bradford & Inskeep should decide to discontinue the publication of the magazine. At that point, the contract stipulated, the *Port Folio* would be "retransferred" to Dennie, along with the "list of Subscribers that may then be and all benefit that may hereafter arise therefrom."[102] Curiously, the detailed contract between Dennie and Bradford & Inskeep made no mention of the *Port Folio*'s debts; whether these had accrued to Dennie personally or whether there were none to take over is impossible to decide. But whatever the *Port Folio*'s debt situation, clearly Bradford, who was reasonably well acquainted with the magazine's business side and the publishing business as a whole, "saw it as a good investment" (1955, 37), as John Queenan has suggested.

Dennie's friends were sometimes not particularly cheerful in their estimation of Dennie's new role at the *Port Folio*. As Gertrude Meredith wrote to her husband,

> The truth is, he has been so long accustomed to use his pen at intervals when the fit of bright inspiration was on him, that he groans beneath the necessity of the kind of clerkship he now endures, and finds his muse not as easily confined eight hours a day to the desk, as he is himself.[103]

101 Of, apparently, $66,\overline{6}$$ per month.

102 Contract between Joseph Dennie and Bradford & Inskeep, n.d. [1809]. Historical Society of Pennsylvania, Samuel W. Woodhouse Papers, Collection 1386, Box 4.

103 Gertrude Meredith to William Meredith, June 8, 1809, Historical Society of Pennsylvania, Meredith Family Papers 1509, Box 51

Such opinions notwithstanding, Dennie himself seems to have brightened considerably in his new position. In July, he wrote his mother from the Philadelphia Philosophical Society, painting an almost bucolic picture: "This is a delightful and tranquil apartement, surrounded with groves and gardens, where I may enjoy, at once, the advantages of the Town and Country. Here, undisturbed, I read and write for the Port Folio, and here behold the progress of Science, the glories of Art, and the beauties of Nature."[104] Indeed, the salary which Bradford & Inskeep granted him was not an inconsiderable sum, and Dennie's life style could be easily supported on it. In a precise account of his expenditures from May 1806 to April 1807, Dennie noted spendings of 849,90$—for him and David Meredith together. He was boarding together with Meredith and shared the expenses with him, expenses which even then already included not only board and food, but wine, books, furniture, and other luxury items.[105] The increase in his salary to 1000$ in 1810 promised to bring his income up to the profit from the *Port Folio*'s first year, and indicates the kind of profits Bradford & Inskeep expected to make from the magazine.

Dennie's new old role as a salaried editor had vastly bettered his mood, at least as long as he was in the company of friends. He was still at times unhappy, as when he joined Gertrude Meredith on June 8th, 1809, and complained about his low salary to Gertrude—who, rather unsubtly, noted to him that he would only need to spend a year at it, and then go on to "richer reward"—the 1000$ promised in his contract with Bradford & Inskeep.[106] Such dark moods, however, rose as often as they descended. Dennie's better spirits also found echo in his correspondence with his mother, to whom he wrote on July 15 that he felt he was "in a better situation, than formerly [...] neither rich, nor independent, nor any thing like it, but I am not dishonoured, or a beggar" (in Pedder 1936, 196). On June 14, 1809, Dennie dined at the Merediths' house again. As Gertrude Meredith wrote to her absent husband, Dennie was "in charming spirits" and apparently in some hope of obtaining further funds from his employers. He asked Gertrude what she believed he could ask of Bradford & Inskeep for a monthly "Lay Preacher" essay. "[H]e was very anxious to write them," Meredith noted, but unwilling to write them merely as part of his regular editorial salary. He "could not think," Gertrude wrote, "of giving away all his talents for the paltry sum of 800 dollars." She suggested that he should ask the publishers for 50$ to 100$ per essay, and that Dennie should seek further guidance and the next meeting of the "club,"[107]

104 Joseph Dennie to Mary Dennie, July 15, 1809. Joseph Dennie Papers, Houghton Library, Harvard University.

105 Cf. Joseph Dennie Account Book. Historical Society of Pennsylvania, Meredith Family Papers, Collection 1509, Box 99, on the total sum of joint expenses for 1806-7; David Meredith Account with Joseph Dennie, January 26, 1807, Historical Society of Pennsylvania, Meredith Family Papers, Collection 1509, Box 99 indicates that Meredith paid exactly half the expenses.

106 Gertrude Meredith to William Meredith, June 8, 1809 Historical Society of Pennsylvania, Meredith Family Papers, Collection 1509, Box 51.

107 Gertrude Meredith to William Meredith, June 14, 1809. Historical Society of Pennsylvania, Meredith Family Papers, Collection 1509, Box 51.

the Tuesday Club to which Dennie and Bradford, but also William Meredith and many fellow men of letters belonged. Dennie published no more Lay Preachers, suggesting that the issue, if raised, was beaten down by Bradford. The Tuesday Club remained the voluntary and hospitable get together it had always been, but in matters of business, Bradford and Dennie's friendship did not count. Its service as a source for original contributions remained of great importance to the *Port Folio* in its new guise. The *Port Folio*'s title page and prospectus for the new series of 1809 emphasized its support by "an alliance of literary characters" (*PF* 1809 Prospectus, 1) and assistance by "a confederacy of men of letters (*PF* 1809, title page), to which the Tuesday Club certainly belonged, but which was merely a part of the array of contributors that participated in the new series. As Joseph Dennie's regular round-up of commentary on his contributors indicates, correspondents, some personally known, some not, lived far from and near to the *Port Folio*, and not all participated in the Tuesday Club. Indeed, in the prospectus Dennie noted explicitly that his support network had "been recently formed in Philadelphia," hardly a description that fit the Tuesday Club. As before, contributions to the *Port Folio* were to be voluntary and free of recompense, a fact which the prospectus proclaimed was mainly due to the fact that men of wisdom and intellect deserved public recognition above mere monetary reward (cf. *PF* 1809 Prospectus, 4).

Dennie, no doubt following the requirements which Bradford made of him, laid out to his readers the proper way of being a part of the *Port Folio*'s contributor base. In the first *Port Folio* issue of 1809, the column "To Readers and Contributors" "recommend[ed]" that contributors identify themselves at the bottom of their contributions by "certain cabalistical characters" (alliteration sometimes grabbed Dennie and dragged him down obscure pathways), and foreign correspondents should likewise use a "system of appropriate signatures" (*PF* 1809 1, 90); contributors should make sure to submit their writings "seasonably to our Publishers [...] at least twenty days before he anticipates its appearance in this Journal," "in legible penmanship, carefully punctuated, and with the orthography modelled according to the standard of doctor Johnson" (91). Of these timely and carefully crafted texts, the editor expected one from each member of his "confederacy" a month—a mere "*reasonable service*" (91, original emphasis), as Dennie claimed. Lacking monetary motivations, it is hardly to be supposed that there was exceeding pressure on the contributors even with these strict submission guidelines in force; but they spoke to the sense of professionalism that the relationship with Bradford & Inskeep brought to the *Port Folio*. Dennie's tone suggested less supplication, less awareness of his essential dependency on the voluntary submissions to his magazine and more emphatic in asserting something akin to a right to contributions. Partially, the rather forward formulation of what clearly are more the publishers' demands than the editor's was made possible because of the "vast collection" of books and magazines available to Dennie through the extensive network of Bradford & Inskeep, which, as a happy Dennie made sure to note, included "every new production of merit, published at home or abroad," and from which he would be able to select such articles as best fit the new scheme of the *Port Folio*. "We trust it will not be unreasonably imagined by any of the most exacting subscribers, that a work upon such an extensive plan as The Port Folio, shall be entirely original" (92), he noted.

The new prospectus laid out this and many other points of interest to subscribers. Much about the magazine had clearly changed since 1801, and most of these changes of heart the *Port Folio* now carried on its sleeve—the very title page proclaiming that the magazine was

> dedicated, in chief, to original communications in the popular departments of science combined with occasional criticism, classical disquisitions, miscellaneous essays, records of the progress of the fine and the useful arts, with all the extensive and variegated departments of polite literature, merriment and wit.

Where Dennie's latent Anglophilia had previously echoed through the magazine's content, now the prospectus rhymed: "Prize not the skill of foreign realms alone,/ Nor think it Taste to stigmatize your own" (3), emphasizing far more strongly than ever before the periodical's dedication to American literature. Such a shift had been in the offing since Dennie's proclamation late in 1807 that he felt misunderstood when people claimed he disregarded American literature and its national aspirations; but here it was in the prospectus, more than a mere claim, but rather a promise to the readership. The prospectus offered hopes of a vindication of the "literary reputation of America" (4), the "aggrandizement of our empire" (5), and the "rising generation of the Genius of America" (6); yet at the same time, the magazine was to become more decidedly local, contributing as well to the "power of Philadelphia" (5), complimenting the city's libraries and literary talents, and placing itself firmly within the local orbit of correspondents and contributors. Besides these shifts in proclaimed ideology, however, the most signal change to the content of the *Port Folio* was its now overt dismissal of political articles. So important did the proprietors apparently feel this change to be that they gave it pride of place on the prospectus's very first page: the magazine was now "[r]igidly excluding party politics" (3), a change which would assure that "without offence, it may be perused by the most clashing parties;" and although the prospectus ably wove the veils of rhetoric around the fact, it implicitly acknowledged its hopes that the new setup would permit it to expand its subscriber base: "As we affect neither the stooping gait of plebeians, nor the lofty step of the aristocratical buskin, all may greet us as a party of gentlemen, studious to please according to the laws of urbanity" (10). The prospectus here echoed a determination made before the prospectus itself was written: in late January 1809, in an advertisement Dennie was more explicit, and effectively tied the decision to leave politics behind to a set of unspecified "imperfections," "blemishes," and "errors," resulting in the decision "that the thorny topics both of politics and theological controversy shall be MOST STUDIOUSLY SHUNNED" in order that "no party, or religious persuations [sic], may have the slightest motive to shrink from subscription" (*NYCA* 1809, January 21, 12.4258, 3, original emphasis).

Readers were informed of the ongoing changes in the magazine by newspaper advertisement. On January 21, 1809, the *New York Commercial Advertiser* announced that the new *Port Folio* would commence on the first of March following, and offered Dennie's elaborate justification of the "short pause in its publication." Roundly denouncing the "crippled form of a weekly Journal," he acknowledged the magazine's dilapidated state and suggested that it was mainly due to his own ill-health, "Negligence and Despondency" (NYCA 1809, January 21, 12.4258, 2). Even as he acknowledged that there had been considerable problems with the regularity and quality of the magazine, Dennie suggested in no uncertain terms that he had actively pursued the new publishers to join him in his project. He took credit for the new situation, asking his readers to note that he had not been "unmindful of his duty or their rights." Neither, however, did he fail to make clear that business interests now determined the *Port Folio*'s fate. "Messrs Bradford & Inskeep," Dennie noted, "have A DIRECT INTEREST IN ITS SUCCESS" (original emphasis). Bradford & Inskeep's reputation would assure that they, as "proprietors and publishers" would guarantee for the "punctuality of its appearance" (3). Together with the new contributors, the outlook painted by the advertisement, which was reprinted in whole or in part through the end of February by various newspapers, offered a self-critically optimistic image of the past and future of the *Port Folio*.

The intended remodeling of the *Port Folio* from a weekly into a monthly was a major undertaking. No issue of the *Port Folio* was published in January and February; only on March 7 did the first issue reach subscribers and book vendors in New York and Philadelphia, and more distant agents, such as Oliver Greenleaf in Boston, had to wait until the end of the month until the magazine made its appearance (cf. *R* 1809, March 31, 6.26, 4). A comment to "Readers and Correspondents" in the January 1809 edition (not published until March), gives a tantalizing glimpse at what may have been arduous discussions between Dennie and Bradford on the nature of their new venture. Even though the January number appeared in March, Dennie apologized for the "hasty composition" of this first issue, and noted that readers would pardon him, knowing that "our final plan of arrangement was not settled until nearly the close of February" (*PF* 1809 1, 89). Its prospectus had heralded a broad consumer base ("the Gentleman, the Scholar, the Philosopher, the Merchant, the Manufacturer, and the Man of the World;" *PF* 1809 Prospectus, 10) and a wide sweep of potential subjects for inclusion, from biography and sketches of the times to trial reports, moral and physical science (the latter a complete novum to the magazine), "Levity, Merriment, Wit and Humour" (11). In the prospectus's formulation, the *utile* was clearly taking a backseat to the *dulci*, the scientific department notwithstanding. That there were tensions due to this setup between Bradford and Dennie became obvious in the January note to "Readers and Correspondents," where Dennie used the editor's privilege of addressing his readers to stress his own predilection for contributions in the style of "Addison, Johnson, or Goldsmith" (*PF* 1809 1, 91), and foregrounded, more than the prospectus did, the inclusion of useful writings. Hashing out the precise formulation to be adopted in the prospectus and the very practical concern for what texts ultimately should find inclusion in the new *Port Folio* must have taken much of January and February; but Bradford's "ruling spirit" (1955, 38), as John Queenan has called it, can be detected behind most of the new setup. Scientific papers, never even remotely touched upon in the old *Port Folio*, were now defended by Dennie as being entirely in the spirit of the *London Magazine* (93). In May 1809, while still not entirely sticking with the prospectus's thorough emphasis on entertainment, he announced that the *Port Folio* would henceforward carry a section called "Variety," which would "afford the most diversified entertainment to the reader." He explained:

> Of those departments of a magazine, which are devoted, principally, to the amusement of the loungers, who by the bye, form the great majority in a metropolis, this kind of medley, which may be called small talk, or table talk, or variety, or by any title, which sufficiently indicates its light and heterogeneous character, has always proved highly acceptable.

He went on to note that "although grave essays *may* have their turn [...] the laconic pages in a miscellany are always the first to be perused" (*PF* 1809 1, 459, my emphasis). Unspoken was the corollary that the oft-cited man of limited literary leisure who would scan the *Port Folio* of a Sunday afternoon or four might end up skipping the arduous and instructive scientific papers and instead opt to indulge himself with the variegated amusements of the entertainment section alone.

That there was something of a dissonance between Dennie and Bradford in terms of the envisaged content was palpable, but it was impossible to deny that the new publishers brought remarkable business acumen to the venture. They were already a presence throughout the United States—according to Henry Carey, they even owned a branch in Charleston, South Carolina, one of a handful of publishing ventures who operated in the South (cf. *American Literary Gazette* 1863, 130)—and made sure that the *Port Folio* would not suffer from a lack of publicity. When Bradford & Inskeep took over the publication of the *Port Folio*, they immediately began a campaign designed to improve the public's awareness of their new magazine. Every month, Abraham Inskeep in New York advertised the appearance of the new magazine; these announcements were usually short and to the point: one, published in the *American Citizen* in a number of its January editions, was a five-line affair which simply read "THE PORT FOLIO./No.1—Vol. III./For January./IS THIS DAY PUBLISHED BY INSKEEP & BRADFORD, No. 128 Broadway" (*AC* 1810, January 22, 10.3056, 1, original capitals). Only rarely did Inskeep & Bradford publish the entire table of contents in a one of their publication notices, such as in the one for April 1812 published in the *Evening Post* (cf. *EP* 1812, April 15, 3038, 1). If this did not constitute a major publicity campaign, it was more than the *Port Folio* had experienced before.

Bradford & Inskeep's takeover of the *Port Folio* proved a success. As Dennie wrote to his mother in the middle of 1809, "[t]he circulation of the Port Folio augments" (in Pedder 1936, 198). A month before, Dennie had poetically summed up the first half-year under the new proprietorship, imagining himself on a "public path, sometimes perplexed and obstructed, and sometimes smooth and flowery." He "enjoy[ed] the prospect around us, with signal satisfaction" (*PF* 1809 1, 549).

Dennie's fondness of metaphor found its way also in his compliments to his contributors, seguing into a military metaphor that framed him as an officer of the line promoted on account of "seniority," rather than merit, a spokesman to "THANK THE NATION FOR GOOD QUARTERS AND GOOD PAY." He would, he assured readers and contributors alike, continue his service "as long as our GREAT COMMANDER graciously requires us to remain in the service, obey the word, and do our duty" (*PF* 1809 1, 550, original emphasis). Perhaps Dennie was offering a military-religious metaphor here, suggesting he would follow God's plan for his life; perhaps the great commander was Samuel Bradford. At any rate, Dennie's spirits in public as well as his more mixed, but generally positive messages in private indicate the success with which the *Port Folio* managed to perform in the first years of the Bradford era. Throughout 1809, 1810, and 1811, not a single request for subscribers to pay their dues appeared in the magazine, a striking fact given that the *Port Folio* had so frequently in the past insisted on having its subscription monies paid.

Instead of complaints, Dennie's editorials now emphasized the great public favor in which the magazine found itself. In May 1809, he commented on suggestions that he should include more foreign materials selected from British magazines and proudly noted that he had and hoped to continue to receive a "mass" of original writings for publication, leaving him little reason to select from foreign sources (*PF* 1809 1, 457). Dennie complained in December 1809 that much of these submissions were poetry, rather than prose, at a ratio of ten to one; notwithstanding the fact that so much of this material was "trash," as Dennie himself acknowledged, he took the large amount of it as a positive sign (*PF* 1809 2, 579). Even this form, however, he sought to bend to the requirements of the periodical. He hailed the "lighter deportments of poetry" as "indispensably necessary," emphasized, with a nod towards his contributors, that if well done, they would yield "as much reputation to their authors" as lengthy epics, and suggested for them something of a palate cleansing effect: "we turn from them to prose with so much the more pleasure, after having experienced the difficulty of being constrained and fettered by numbers" (*PF* 1809 2, 581).

In the overflow of exultation over his new riches, which ran contrary to expectations voiced in the prospectus, Dennie may have gone a little far; in August 1809, he backtracked, noting that while he possessed a wealth of communication, these were of decidedly mixed quality, so that he felt himself obliged to return to putting foreign articles in his journal (cf. *PF* 1809 2, 171). Three pages later, in a rather abrupt turn, he suggested that the amount of "meritorious" papers meant that there would be delays for correspondence to see themselves in print. With "many claims to adjust, many departments to fill, many tastes to please, and many criticisms to deprecate," Dennie suggested, it was impossible to always please all contributors. Then, strikingly, he couched his critique of his contributors in entrepreneurial terms: he could not publish pieces immediately which came too close to the deadline that he and Bradford had explicitly laid out in their prospectus. Such submissions and claims to immediate inclusion stood, Dennie exclaimed, "in perfect mockery of all the rules of business" and would lead to "the utter confusion of the printer" (*PF* 1809 1, 175). The changed relationship between the *Port Folio*'s contributors, no longer essentially volunteers, but rather pressured by their commitment to the magazine to contribute, became again apparent here.

The magazine had also become more responsive to the tastes of the day. In September 1809, the changing fortunes in the Peninsula War, where British General Arthur Wellesley, later the Duke of Wellington, was slowly advancing into Spain against the Napoleonic French, induced the *Port Folio* to publish papers on Spain. Wrote Dennie: "As at the present junction, men are peculiarly solicitous about every thing respecting Spain, we feel an extreme desire to make this country better acquainted with the other" (*PF* 1809 2, 282). No major effort was ultimately put into translating this desire into a lengthy engagement with Spain—too much variegated material, as Dennie did not tire to point out, remained in need of being printed in the magazine—but even this one issue's connection between a genuine political development abroad and its own contents differed from the usual attempts to justify by generalities the inclusion of any particular text. Knowledge about Spain was not just "amusing and the instructive"—it was something predicated on the need for information about the real world.

By 1810, the *Port Folio*'s publishers felt financially strong enough, and had a sufficient subscriber base, to print 3000 copies per issue, a high that the magazine never before or after reached (*PF* 1816 2, 73). In January 1811, after the most successful year of *Port Folio* history, Dennie proudly announced to the public that his correspondents grew greater in number, their contributions steadily more valuable, and his hopes for the *Port Folio* ever more sanguine. Here, perhaps, was the high point of Dennie's career as an editor. By now, he was drawing the 1000$ salary promised him by his contract with Bradford & Inskeep, a sum which, at a much lower risk, equaled his gains in 1801, and which he probably never really exceeded before. The *Port Folio*'s public standing was high and his own critical reputation excellent. The contrast between the success of the *Port Folio*'s new monthly format and other papers published within its sphere is illustrative. Robert Walsh, a contributor to the *Port Folio* before 1811 and afterwards an editor of the *Analectic Magazine*, attempted his own quarterly about this time, published in 1811 and 1812. *The American Review of History and Politics* was ultimately a political repository mainly written by Walsh himself, and—unsurprisingly given the success which the *Port Folio* had in moving away from politics and towards the lighter muses—failed somewhat miserably. John Queenan's charitable suggestion that it failed as a consequence of the War of 1812—a war which numerous other magazines survived—seems farther off the mark than the easier supposition that interest in a political quarterly was not capable of sustaining even a largely self-edited magazine such as Walsh's (cf. Queenan 1955, 44). The *Port Folio* had made its shift away from politics in time.

If there were any dark clouds on the horizon, they were personal, not professional. Joseph Dennie was ill, which often made it impossible for him to dedicate enough time to work on the magazine and which forced him to avoid the yellow fever season in Philadelphia even more than others. The prospectus of the new series had already indicated the safeguards which Bradford & Inskeep had installed to make sure that Dennie's sicknesses and absences would not signally interfere with the publication of the magazine: besides the confederacy of the "club," unnamed "assistants" were working for the *Port Folio*. These men included (in fact, may have been confined to, through 1811) Paul Allen, who served as editorial assistant to Dennie. These safeguards had kept disruptions of the *Port Folio*'s publication to a minimum. In December 1809, Dennie noted that "indisposition and the calamities of the times" had caused him to neglect some of his editorial duties, especially his timely correspondence with contributors (*PF* 1809 2, 577); his own frequent absences from the editorial chair made him understanding of delays, but it was increasingly evident that Dennie himself was not going to be up to the task of editing the *Port Folio*. In January 1811, he again complained publically of his "habitual indisposition," which had rendered the *Port Folio* less agreeable than it could have been. Nor were all of Dennie's problems purely medical. He had become such a heavy drinker that William Dunlap, admittedly from the first meeting no great friend of Dennie's, noted with some disgust in his diary for March 29, 1811, after spending a night drinking with Dennie, that "the american [sic] Addison" was "a driveller & a sot," and was giving money freely to anyone who applied because "he has not firmness to refuse." Dunlap was already highly critical of Dennie's performance at the *Port Folio*, which, he noted, had become a mere "ruin" of a once "tasteful & polish'd edifice" (Dunlap 1930, 430), but his estimate of Dennie was seconded by Nicholas Biddle, who noted that Dennie's "regard for his own appearance & situation seemed sadly declining" by the summer of 1811 (in Govan 1951, 39). Biddle's memoir speaks of an attempt to "wean him from his present habits" with their "dreadful effects on others" (40-1); scarcely veiled suggestions of Dennie's increasing intemperance.

It was the recognition that between his drinking habits and habitual illness Dennie was not a reliable person to work with that must finally have lead Bradford & Inskeep to suggest to the fellow Tuesday Club members Nicholas Biddle and Robert Walsh the purchase of one-half interest in the *Port Folio* sometime in 1811. The agreement drawn-up stipulated that Biddle and Walsh would pay 9000$ for half a share in the *Port Folio*'s profits, and co-edit the work with Dennie. The sum paid for their share would at the same time function as something like a loan to Bradford & Inskeep, for which the publishers would pay interest until Biddle and Walsh's profits had amounted to exactly that sum; Bradford & Inskeep promised that they would pay at least 1,500$ every year to the two other men, in order to ensure a complete repayment of the 9000$ within six years. Then came the most vital part: "The profits of the work are now about six thousand dollars per annum."[108] This was an amazing sum. The *Port Folio* had cleared 2000$ profit in 1801, assuming Dennie and Dickins had split those profits equitably; it had always sufficed to

108 Cf. Queenan 1955, 45. The memorandum containing the details of this suggestion was later deposited at the Historical Society of Pennsylvania, where, unfortunately, it could not be located in 2011. Placed either in the "Nicholas Biddle deposit" (Govan 1951, 40) or the "Charles Biddle depository" (Queenan 1955, 45), a subsequent re-ordering of Historical Society of Pennsylvania's holdings seems to have mislaid the piece.

sustain Dennie thereafter. Yet now it was making more than even the fairly optimistic estimate which had induced Dennie and Dickins to begin their venture in 1801, a full 1000$ more. There is little reason to doubt the veracity of the figure: as we have seen, sales of magazines usually entailed a thorough vetting of their books, as happened to Hugh Maxwell in 1806. At about this time, not only Robert Walsh's quarterly was failing: the venerable *Monthly Anthology*, which even Dennie admitted was a paragon of periodical culture (cf. Kaplan 2008, 219), was just then going under. The *Port Folio*, as John Queenan, slightly underselling the achievement, notes, "under the type of competent financial management that it apparently got from its new owners, would have been quite successful in the financial sense almost from the beginning" (1955, 45).

None of this success helped Dennie, however. In the summer of 1811, with yellow fever rising and his own health once more severely depressed, he moved up the Delaware River to spend the summer at Bristol, leaving, in Nicholas Biddle's words, "the journal to its fate" (in Govan 1951, 39). Not only his ill health apparently gnawed at his spirits, but also the mounting private debts that he incurred, notwithstanding his augmented salary; in September, his father Joseph Sr. died after a long illness, adding to the gloom. That same month, Bradford came up to visit him and enjoin him to return, even proposed to take over the private debts, and finally induced him to return to Philadelphia in time to edit the January 1812 edition of the *Port Folio* in the course of December. Even as he was guiding Dennie back to the editorial post, Bradford, "fearing that the aid of Mr. Dennie would be at all times irregular," again contacted Nicholas Biddle about taking a more active role in the *Port Folio* business. This time, Biddle acquiesced. He would become the *Port Folio*'s co-editor with Joseph Dennie, working out the financial arrangements by the middle of December (cf. Govan 1951, 40-1).[109]
Working through December, Dennie prepared what would be his last editorial note in the *Port Folio*. In it, he acknowledged that he had been forced to relinquish the duties of the editor in the autumn of 1811, spending two pages of print on a lamentation of his own sickness and the consequent impossibility of editing, or even writing for, the magazine. Feeling slightly recovered, Dennie gave a friendly nod to the "deputy editor" (Paul Allen, as Dennie himself acknowledges in a footnote) who conducted the *Port Folio* in Dennie's absence—even as he makes clear that "no deputy editor [...] can possibly, at all times, supply the place of the *Principal*. From the very nature of his office, the latter must have more experience in editing, and more *technical* knowledge, with respect to the *details* of literary labor" (*PF* 1812 1, 92, original emphasis).

109 The details of the arrangement are unclear. As we will see below, Biddle received 2500$ a year from Bradford & Inskeep after taking over full time as editor in February 1812; his agreement with Bradford did not include the half-share discussed earlier in 1811, something we know because in 1813, Biddle was offered that half-share again (cf. Queenan 1955, 64-5). An educated guess might suggest that Biddle was supposed to be paid the difference between Dennie's salary and his own later remuneration, 1500$.

Dennie once more offers tantalizing glimpses behind the scenes of the *Port Folio* enterprise. Having managed to come to an accord with Nicholas Biddle, Samuel Bradford's role as proprietor stands out in stark relief again. In late December, Dennie notes, Bradford had decided to keep publishing the *Port Folio*; even though Dennie merely suggests that Bradford's resolve was that "the Port Folio shall be augmented, its spirit quickened, and its POPULARITY PERPETUATED" (*PF* 1812 1, 93, original emphasis), the unmistakable undertone is that the *Port Folio*'s sheer continuance was already a lucky stroke for Dennie. Nor does he fail to acknowledge the benefit that Nicholas Biddle, whose name, however, he leaves out of the announcement, was bringing to the magazine. He admitted to the public that the vaunted "club" of contributors to the magazine no longer existed—even though his claim that the club's demise that come "almost as soon as they convened" contradicts some of his earlier claims—and that he had once more found himself dependent on voluntary submissions and his own pen. From Biddle, he expected signal help with these arduous writing duties; he would be "a *colleague*, who should have a *direct interest* in the enterprize" (*PF* 1812 2, 94, original emphasis). His disingenuous claim that Bradford had given his "joyful acquiescence" neatly hid the fact that it was Bradford's initiative to hire Biddle; but no matter. The outlook which Dennie painted for the new joint venture was bright: "the Proprietors and Conductors of this Journal are not without pleasing prospects" (95).

The January 1812 issue probably reached subscribers in Philadelphia on Saturday, January 4; it was not available to more distant subscribers, such as Oliver C. Greenleaf's Boston customers, until January 10. By that date, Joseph Dennie was dead. He had been, Nicholas Biddle noted, "indisposed" even as he worked on the final note in the January edition, going so far as to suggest to Biddle that he write it instead, something Biddle had not wished to do. Dennie had ended up writing "in a paroxysm of pain". On January 3rd, Biddle dined with Dennie; on January 6th, a Monday, he did not come to a scheduled meeting between the principals of the *Port Folio*. Biddle went to see him, found him sick in bed, but not apparently in any immediate danger, and was shocked to find himself awoken at one in the morning on Tuesday by Dennie's physician to be informed that Dennie was dying—succumbing three hours later to what Gertrude Meredith called "cholera morbus" (in Ellis 1955, 211), a form of gastroenteritis. His sudden death left Nicholas Biddle in sole editorial charge of the magazine (cf. Govan 1951).

1809-1812: Monthly Biography, American Renaissance

For the new series of the *Port Folio*, biography was a crucial genre. The magazine's new prospectus gushed that "[t]han biography, nothing is more fascinating, nothing more instructive, nothing that is perused with greater avidity, or that excites a stronger interest. The lives of the illustrious of our country, and the mighty mass of foreign biography, will always furnish excellent entertainment to the most fastidious reader" (*PF* Prospectus 1809, 11). Not only was it "more fascinating," "more instructive," and read with the greatest avidity and interest: it also offered the now avowedly anti-partisan, national magazine a ready means of advancing this new agenda in print. Perhaps the most striking aspect of this shift in biographical content is the apparent readiness with which it was suddenly found possible to produce American biography. At numerous times before, not only the *Port Folio*, but other magazines had endeavored to print American biography, usually defined as lives of eminent Americans, written by Americans for American audiences; we have seen as much in Chapter 1. Now, the *Port Folio* began a sustained period of publication of American biography.

The breadth of contributions, as far as biographees were concerned, was immense: even the first issue of the new series in January 1809 carried two separate lives, both of which would run over two separate issues. The first was a biography of Commodore Thomas Truxtun, complete with an engraving of a medal struck for the officer in honor of his achievements; the second was a life of John Blair Linn, a Tuesday Club member and brother-in-law of Charles Brockden Brown. Brown was also the author of Linn's biography; Truxtun's life was possibly written by Nicholas Biddle, who had ready access to the naval officers of his time through his brother James, a junior naval officer. While the biography of Truxtun was new, the Linn biography had previously appeared in 1805 in a posthumous collection of Linn's poetry. It served the *Port Folio* as an exhibit of American biography, which, as Dennie noted, "has not been very often pursued in this country, and with the exception of the late Dr. Belknap and of Judge Marshall, we do not remember many names, who have distinguished themselves in this delightful department of composition" (*PF* 1809 1, 21). Both biographies were exhaustive, taking full advantage of the *Port Folio*'s new format. Indeed, it may very well have been precisely this format which now necessitated a more frequent recurrence to original contributions, since most of Dennie's habitual sources for biography offered too short lives now to fill the *Port Folio*'s pages.

Yet if the format of biographies changed, other things did not. If anything, the *Port Folio* after 1809 became more dependent on justifying its editorial choices, the inclusion of particular biographies, given that its sources as well as the number of its issues were now fewer. Dennie prefaced the second part of the biography of John Blair Linn by noting that "the formation and progress of character[,...] still more useful in professional, than in general subjects" (*PF* 1809 1, 129) was the chief advantage of biography; a month later, he repeated this belief verbatim when the *Port Folio* published the life of William Penn. By December 1810, in the long delayed second part of a biography of naval officer Edward Preble, Dennie re-emphasized instead the amusement, entertainment, beauty, pleasantness, and delight which readers could obtain from the study of this life (cf. *PF* 1810 2, 530). Stylistically, the new longer biographies differed very little from what the *Port Folio* had published before: they were the standard kind of mostly public lives, of the life-and-character variety that enabled writers, despite their frequent personal acquaintance with the biographees, to address their topic through a mostly historical eye, sometimes more, as in the biography of Penn, which contained almost nothing personal about the Quaker, sometimes less, as in the biography of Linn. That such a focus impaired the emphasis on the 'formation of character' which it otherwise stressed did not concern the *Port Folio* terribly: indeed, its emphasis with the military and naval biographies was rather to pay homage to those who "invigorated the commerce, extended the fame, and emblazoned the flag of America" (*PF* 1809 1, 361), in other words, to advance a national agenda.

For this national agenda, Dennie avowed particular partiality. In October of 1809, Nicholas Biddle provided the *Port Folio* with a life of his uncle and namesake, the Revolutionary War naval officer Nicholas Biddle, a fairly pedestrian piece. Two months later, Dennie was effusive in his praise of the biography, calling it in his column "To Readers and Correspondents" a "composition so pure and chaste" that it easily bore comparison with similar efforts in foreign papers, and had been received by the public with more admiration than most papers in Dennie's editorial career. Dennie's addresses to his readers were frequently interspersed with hopeful solicitations for further contributions. In April 1809, the *Port Folio* had printed a rather eclectic biography of the Georgia physician Edwin McCall, an otherwise unremarkable member of the medical community whose biography the author justified by suggesting that, having died young, he would be a closer example to emulate for the "youth of the United States," merely one of whom to educate would be sufficient reason for the melodramatic author not to have "lived in vain for his country" (*PF* 1809 1, 299). Dennie commented on this biography in September, five months later, apparently not having received any further submissions from the unknown writer. He encouraged him to provide any "interesting facts or anecdotes" on physicians that he could. In December 1809, Dennie commended the "splendid genius and indefatigable industry" of the author of the life of General Horatio Gates, published a month earlier. This praise—which Dennie notably bestowed on two biographers, and in the final issue for 1809, at a time when the magazine's subscribers were up for renewal of their subscriptions—served a number of functions: it extolled the quality of *the Port Folio* and national literary—and military—glory; it ensured that authors would feel the value of their contributions; and it emphasized the value of the *Port Folio* as a repository for articles that continued to be valuable: "repeated perusal" had kept the biography perfectly satisfactory (*PF* 1809 2, 578). Between the value of the engravings and the value of the biography, the *Port Folio* was marketing itself as a lasting archive, and more so than it had before.

The incidence of naval and military officers among the biographies printed between 1809 and 1812 was remarkably high. Naval officers Thomas Truxtun, Edward Preble, and Nicholas Biddle, and Generals Anthony Wayne, Henry Knox, and Horatio Gates were the first military men whose lives the *Port Folio* described, if one excepts such people as Alexander Hamilton and George Washington, whose lives were usually accorded more praise for their political work than their military. All of these were locally produced biographies: Dennie took great care to keep readers apprised of the often halting progress of their writing as well as to leave authors aware of his great happiness with their work. Justifying their inclusion brought to light once more the broad range of options which biography offered the editor. In April 1809, after praising the life of Truxtun, Dennie used biography as advertisement by suggesting to his readers that a life of Preble was almost finished. The life of Edward Preble was finally published starting in May, 1810, and not concluded until December. In his commentary on the biography, Dennie suggested in May that it had the "power of interesting and delighting thousands" (*PF* 1810 1, 353); in December, he specified that it would be "perused with equal delight, by the gallant tar, and the ardent patriot" (*PF* 1810 2, 530). Biography, in this context, did not fulfill an instructive function, despite Dennie's repeated suggestion that the genre in general was instructive. To be sure, the low incidence of sailors and naval officers among the subscribership sharply limited immediate instruction, yet for Dennie's editorial persona, it was ultimately a nationalist impulse that justified the inclusion of the military heroes, both contemporary and of the Revolution. As he phrased in in the life of Preble, the "Triumph and Fame of American still intertwist his laurels" (*PF* 1810 2, 531).

In the same December issue, once more at the end of a year and subscriber cycle, Dennie again took the opportunity to reiterate his opinions on biography, and to reaffirm that he was "determined to devote to her airs and graces a very liberal share of this Journal" (*PF* 1810 2, 529). Late in the year, and offering an advertisement for the next, Dennie noted again that it was "our intention, with periodical punctuality, to publish according to the extent of our materials, a domestic and a foreign biography" (*PF* 1810 2, 530) and suggested that he himself had already written a fair number of such compositions for inclusion in the *Port Folio*. Since September 1810, however, American biography had become more and more scarce. In that issue, the magazine carried a life of the Prussian general Schill; if it continued its biography of Preble in the next issue, it did not provide another American life until February 1811, written by Charles Caldwell, and then, for the duration of 1811 and into the summer of 1812, made do entirely with foreign lives, mostly British, and the lives of French painters (original contributions for the *Port Folio*), French Marshalls (taken from the new edition of the *Lives of Remarkable Characters of the French Revolution*), and miscellaneous others. In August 1812, the *Port Folio*, now under the editorship of Nicholas Biddle, published a life of the Revolutionary War general Daniel Morgan; but by then, the United States were at war with Great Britain, and conditions for American biography had signally changed. None of Dennie's promised biographies of Americans appeared.

Despite this slow decline in American biography, its high incidence during the first year of the 1809 series and its frequency in 1810 contrasted strongly with the desultory efforts which had been made before. If Luthor Mott's suggestion that "American worthies [had] supplanted Englishmen as subjects for biographers" (1957a, 239) pays insufficient attention both to the more eclectic actual selection of lives and to the problem that many of the texts published in earlier volumes indicated not so much a choice of subjects for biographers as a choice of already-written biographies, it is certainly true that of the efforts made so far in the *Port Folio*, this last one to promote American biography was by a large margin the most successful. Without much doubt, it was Samuel Bradford's network that mainly contributed to the availability of such material, and the selection was much determined by geographical proximity. Thomas Truxtun, whose biography appeared in January 1809, was at that time resident in Philadelphia; Nicholas Biddle, the naval officer, had obvious connections at the *Port Folio*; William Penn was something of an obvious choice for the Philadelphia magazine, as was Edward Shippen, the commonwealth's Chief Justice; William Bradford, a Philadelphia lawyer, was likewise probably included because his biography became available from local sources. Against these local choices were arraigned the national military and naval heroes, the choice of whom depended clearly on the submission of materials by contributors. But in the very fact of their inclusion, the *Port Folio* established itself as a genuinely apolitical, and avowedly national work. The naval and military officers were at once easy choices and interesting material, readily available articles and fulfillment of the prospectus's emphasis on nation, American biography, and the praise of distinguished citizens.[110]

At the same time, despite the major investment of the *Port Folio* in American biography in 1809 and 1810, its subsequent decline once more indicated that a more sustained effort in American biography depended strongly on more people willing to write those biographies—and a readership with a clear interest in such lives. The haphazard collection of Americans that made up the *Port Folio*'s American Biography series—Revolutionary War officers, naval officers on the beach since the Quasi-War with France (Truxtun), private citizens whose particular characteristics as 'American' were of decidedly minor import—was still a far cry from the sustained effort at publishing American biography during the War of 1812 and after. What united them was not so much a sustained effort at nationalizing a discourse as the attempt to give an overarching title to a heterogeneous selection of men of largely local interest, nearly all of whom at connections to Philadelphia, rather than to the nation at large. It would take the War of 1812, and the concomitant rise in American's sense of shared national identity—or at the very least, publishers' belief in the existence of such a rise—to fully establish American biography as the leading type of biography in Early Republic periodicals. Joseph Dennie would not see this, however: his death in January 1812 came at the end of the renewed decline of American biography in the face of lacking submissions and public interest.

The *Port Folio* and Periodical Biography

If this was the conclusion to eleven years of *Port Folio* biography publishing under the direction of Joseph Dennie, what conclusions can we draw from that history?

110 If we cannot well establish the influence of the biographies printed in the *Port Folio*, an idea of their value for the integration of disparate segments of the American population under a shared master narrative of national glory and fame can be gleaned from the fact that the German-language *Amerikanischer Beobachter* translated and published the lives of Thomas Truxtun, William Penn, and Anthony Wayne. That lives of men with no discernable connection to the German immigrant community found their way into a German-language newspaper may easily be considered an indication of their integrative value.

Does biography lend itself to being studied as an exemplary genre, not so much in the sense that it was especially good, wholesome, exciting, or original, but rather in that it can stand as a genre capable of showing the relations between content and production conditions, between editorial choices and proprietorial demands? Certainly the *Port Folio*'s selection and use of biography does not support any of the claims to a coherent, even if merely implicit ideological foundation to its choice of content through the years. If it is impossible to state concretely what the *Port Folio*'s stance on race, on women, on nation, and a host of other issues was (cf. Kaplan 2009, 182-3), it is similarly impossible to state with firmness what its stance towards biography was, what it deemed biography's purpose, purview, and ideal form. Bound within the strictures that determined its financial well-being, the *Port Folio* never evolved a coherent idea of biography. In this, it was hardly alone: in fact, no American magazine managed to produce a biographical practice during the first decade of the 1800s that conformed to any particular biographical theory. The availability of sources, more than anything else, decided what texts were put into the magazine, and justifications came afterward, as the texts' structures demanded, to emplace these texts firmly in a post-facto editorial conception of the magazine.

It is especially noteworthy that some of the sources for the biographies stayed with Dennie for a decade or more, chiefly Robert Anderson's *Works of the British Poets*, a series which he used at the *Farmer's Weekly Museum* and the *Port Folio* both. Dennie did not, as far as it is possible to tell, buy a set of Robert Anderson's *Works of the British Poets* until February 26, 1806, from Hugh Maxwell.[III] The reason for this purchase may have been that Maxwell's store was no longer the *Port Folio*'s editorial office, requiring him to purchase what materials he required for his editing, as far as they were unavailable at John Watts's store, now the editor's home base. If that was the case, it points again to the contingency of Dennie's selections, as well as to the inner workings of the *Port Folio*'s selection process.

The dependency of the biographical department on available and accessible material necessitated that Dennie editorially justify the inclusion of specific texts, making the magazine's biographical 'philosophy' subordinate to practical considerations. However, at the same time the repeated forays into American biography, despite their almost total failure to produce a sustained engagement with genuinely American subjects until 1809-10, indicates that Dennie's pro-British stance never totally submerged his belief in providing local—in the widest sense national—texts to an audience that he hoped would both support his professed interest in this form of biography, as well as provide him with it. That ultimately, these attempts did not come to fruition until the *Port Folio* received the backing of a highly professional organization in the publishing house of Bradford & Inskeep indicates in turn the importance of such institutional support for the magazine. It also indicates the limits of the editor's ability to influence the content of his magazine. Dependent, if he did not want to write every piece in the magazine himself, on the submissions offered him by contributors, themselves sometimes mere

III Hugh Maxwell account book, Historical Society of Pennsylvania, Meredith Family Papers 1509, Box 99 collators of writings published in different sources, or his own selections from other magazines and books, the editor's role was the justification of selections as much as the making of them. Biography functioned here as one of the most readily available genres, offering a wealth of options for Dennie to conform, with little effort, to the contents promised by the *Port Folio*'s prospectuses.

Virtually none of the biographies printed in the *Port Folio* between 1801 and 1812 is capable of sustaining scholarly attention as a literary text. To read them for passages in need of interpretation, of meaning beneath the surface of facts about life dates and character bullet points is to be sorely disappointed. Like other texts genres, it could offer authors and readers more, if the circumstances were right; but for the most part, it sufficed if it performed the role which Joseph Dennie had early identified for it and which he kept in the foreground throughout his tenure. Periodical biography in the *Port Folio* was entertainment to the mass of readers who did not wish to tax themselves unduly with heavy reading: light, often largely pointless, short, and only rarely instructive to anyone who could be expected to actually read the *Port Folio*, biography found its niche in the magazine on the strength not of its possibilities, but rather of its limitations. As the next chapter will show, however, this was not a necessary fate for periodical biography.

The Death of Joseph Dennie and the Continued Life of the *Port Folio*

Joseph Dennie has been accorded a front center place on the *Port Folio* stage, as his editorial pronouncements and decisions, his correspondence, and his undeniable centrality for the *Port Folio* in the minds of his contemporaries almost naturally put him in the spotlight. Yet for all that exposition, it is evidently a mistake to center too much on the person of Dennie, versus the persona of the editor, Oliver Oldschool; and to emphasize too strongly the editor's personal predilections and mooted political and ideological viewpoints in attempting to come to terms with the history of the *Port Folio*.

Does the admittedly "untimely death of Joseph Dennie" really constitute, as William Dowling has it, "a sudden unexpected close" (1999, 70) to an entire period in the life of the *Port Folio*? In a very pedestrian sense, Dowling is of course correct: Dennie's death concluded that period in which Dennie was the editor of the *Port Folio*. In a different sense, however, Dowling's phrasing highlights the problems periodical studies encounters when it places too much emphasis on the editor. The slow decline of Joseph Dennie himself had long since left much of the daily business of the *Port Folio* in the hands of other people than him, people who have too often remained behind the scenes or off in the wings. By Dennie's own admission, much of the second volume for 1811 was done by Paul Allen, and Nicholas Biddle's note that there had been a meeting scheduled the day before Dennie's death between Biddle, Dennie, Bradford and Allen "for the purpose of concerting about the materials of the next Port Folio" (in Govan 1951, 42) suggests that much of the *Port Folio*'s editorial business had already become a common enterprise between all those men who had a "vested interest" in the magazine. Therefore, when the *Port Folio*'s editorship passed to Nicholas Biddle, changes in the magazine were few and far between. Biddle reassumed the appellation Oliver Oldschool, which Dennie had dropped; but neither did he publish a new prospectus nor noticeably move from the policies which had been determined and continually reaffirmed since 1809. In a curious twist, Dennie's professionalization as editor—the shift away from multiple ill-performed roles to being a salaried editor concentrating exclusively on the selection of content—had made him a commodity himself.

If anything, what Dennie's death ultimately showed was that he, indeed any editor, was replaceable even as he might be valuable to a given magazine. The editorial position had become, in the hands of Samuel Bradford and John Inskeep, an executive organ for policies laid down elsewhere.[112] Catherine Kaplan, somewhat disingenuously, ties Dennie's renunciation of the Oliver Oldschool pseudonym directly to the devaluation of the political agenda in the *Port Folio*'s post-1809 iteration (cf. 2008, 218); yet Dennie did not fact retire the pseudonym in 1809, as Kaplan suggests, but only in January 1811.[113] When he did so, and chose to stand 'revealed' as Joseph Dennie before an audience who at no point in the history of the *Port Folio* could very well have been in doubt about his identity (it was not for nothing that Dennie faced a libel suit in 1805), he suggested that it was the lack of a political agenda that finally made him willing to reveal himself. But he had been in charge of an apolitical journal for two years at this point, suggesting a different interpretation. Rather than throwing off a veil that had shielded him from vengeful opponents, the important point was to tear down one barrier between himself and his readers, and to counteract the effect of his own absences from the editorial chair by an assumption of direct responsibility. The Oliver Oldschool pseudonym hid, for example, the work which Paul Allen did for the *Port Folio* in Dennie's absences—editorial agency lay with a persona behind which anybody could do the actual work. Yet to Bradford, and to Dennie himself, the necessity to establish Dennie as the ultimate director of the periodical's content was a crucial element of their business. Starting in January 1811, it was Dennie, not Oldschool, the actual person, rather than the editorial persona, who stood "fairly pledged to his patrons," and who pledged to be "on the alert with respect to the invention, the selection, and the disposition of his materials" (*PF* 1811 1, 87). The Oliver Oldschool pseudonym had not offered safety from persecution; but the name of Joseph Dennie stood as the advertisement of ten years of *Port Folio* history, even absent any meaningful work on Dennie's part. Bradford's own decision to stick with Dennie, even as he recognized that it was unlikely that Dennie would be regularly working on the *Port Folio*, and even as he was prepared to hire someone else as a co-editor, indicates that the recognizability of Dennie's name had, by the beginning of 1811, become a commodity in itself. What Dennie himself called "the habitual and inveterate partiality of his Booksellers" (*PF* 1812 1, 92) to his person was wholly dependent on that good

112 For the identification of John Inskeep, a Philadelphia merchant, cf. Remer 1996, 71.

113 As, incidentally, Kaplan must be aware, since she quotes the article in which he does so.

name. Tellingly, Bradford's offer to assume Dennie's debts to encourage him to return to Philadelphia did not extend to Dennie's mother after his death; rather than any particular partiality towards Dennie on the part of Bradford, the suggestion that he would assume Dennie's debts in return of receiving him back as editor was a business decision that depended very much on the person, or rather on the ability to lay claim to the name, of Dennie.

Nicholas Biddle's resumption of the Oliver Oldschool name was, in turn, the next best thing to having Dennie's name on the masthead: a way of ensuring readers of the continuity of the *Port Folio*'s editorial principles in the absence of its original editor. How far these principles had themselves evolved, Dennie's almost literally final lines in the *Port Folio* indicated in the January edition of his regular "To Readers and Correspondents" column. For the first time in its history, the *Port Folio* not just implicitly acknowledged that it sometimes paid for contributions (as it had in 1801), but came straight forward and pledged the *Port Folio*'s money to contributors. "He, who writes for fame, shall be strenuously supported. He, who writes for gold shall, if his productions be deemed meritorious, receive, from the Proprietors, a liberal remuneration" (*PF* 1812 1, 99). It is curiously symbolic that this change was the final one which Dennie, so often styled as the defender of the voluntary association of a literary public sphere, presided over as editor of the *Port Folio*. The magazine had shed nearly all of its oftenpublicized foundational principles: it no longer took sides in the political debate, it no longer sought to give equal voice to instruction and amusement, it no longer even insisted on voluntary submissions. Instead, it had transformed itself with a shifting market into a periodical that catered to a wholly different audience from that which it had set out to please, but it did so well: so well, in fact, that it would last another fifteen years.

In Dennie's public statements as Oliver Oldschool, a rhetoric of dejection continuously reinforced his image as a selfless servant of the public weal. After eight years of living off the proceeds of the *Port Folio*, still in 1809, the new prospectus could melodramatically claim that

> [h]itherto the success of The Port Folio has been of no brilliant complexion. Commenced at a sinister epoch, and pushed through all the thorns of perplexity, exposed to the cavils of party, though pure of any but honest purposes, and neglected, in consequence of the bad health and misfortunes of the editor, ill supported, and worse paid, still he made it a point of honour never to abandon it ingloriously. (*PF* 1809 Prospectus, 7)

Dennie's remarkably ungrammatical complaints should not be read, however, as "the self-pity of the valetudinarian" (Queenan 1955, 39); rather, they were essential constitutives of the public perception which Dennie desired for his persona. Dennie was fond of portraying himself as a selfless, principled, virtuous servant of the public. Thus, in 1802, in one of his periodical announcements "To the Public," he thanked his readers, "who have aided him in the conducting of a paper, partial to political truth, and elegant literature, and who will never cease to cheer him, though he forsakes the latent tracts of vulgar popularity, and assumes a higher, though, perhaps, a perilous station" (*PF* 1802, 182). If this was the position he preferred to adopt for himself publically, and which allowed him to publically promulgate politics that he himself no doubt subscribed to as well, it was not necessarily an unpopular, and certainly not a perilous station. It was rather a position which resonated with the Federalist audience that he had in mind. Embittered by the defeat of 1801, increasingly at odds with the direction in which the country was going, Dennie's disavowal of "vulgar" popularity and his stress on a "higher" station resounded with Federalists.

The modesty of the Oliver Oldschool persona in his claims for financial remuneration, always content with a modest competency, rather than publically avowing the pursuit of financial fortune, as Dennie did in his letters, also echoed Federalists' unease with the Republican insistence on wealth and luxury for all (cf. Appleby 1984, 90-1). Dennie thus emphatically aligned himself with his consumer base: his professions of disinterested public service in the high realm of literature echoed the Federalist sense of their own position in the republic. The *Port Folio*'s arrival on the public scene was fortuitous: just as Federalists lost the presidency, just as the ascendancy of the 'vulgar' electorate of the Democrat-Republicans was beginning to make its dominance felt, just as Federalism was beginning to seem like a "perilous" choice of political alignment, Dennie's magazine reassured its intended readership of the lasting validity of their old-fashioned values. To this extent, perhaps, it is possible to subscribe to Catherine O'Donnell Kaplan's thesis of the "cultural community" (2009, 127) which participation in the *Port Folio* marked. As we have seen, it would be difficult to understate the extent of this participation: vastly more people were passive recipients of Dennie's work than were actively involved in making it. In a sense, in the time during which the *Port Folio* was avowedly and even in its textual productions at least partially political, Dennie was preaching to the choir: Federalist contributors were writing for an audience itself largely Federalist, under the direction of an editor whose avowed Federalism was at least as genuine a conviction as it was a useful commercial tool. Dennie's reassurances that the beliefs held by Federalists were correct, were good, were ultimately the proper form in which to conduct oneself, placed his readers in a form of community in which the inside, the *Port Folio*, was safety; the outside, where Democrats and the mob ruled, was "perilous". In its political and ideological statemetns, the *Port Folio* created an ideal insider-outsider typology, creating community by othering those who did not read it. Consequently, when the *Port Folio*'s political motivations dimmed in favor of a more broadly acceptable attention to literary and scientific matters, so declined the participation of some of those of its contributors whose reasons for lending their free time to the production of original matter for the *Port Folio* were more overtly political; but at the same time, the dimming of the *Port Folio*'s political motivations has due a more general decline in the fortune of the Federalist politics that had proved so commercially helpful.

What Dennie was producing was a façade, erected for the benefit of a readership which expected or at least rewarded such self-representations. To put it slightly facetiously, "the profit [of b]eing seen [...] as one who is not searching for profit" (Johnson 1993, 15) was profit: money could be made publishing a magazine for an audience which appreciated being seen as liberal patrons of deserving worth, rather than as customers, and giving freely to one who regarded himself as in the service of literature, rather than in the service of his customers. Through the years, as Federalist political fortunes declined, the *Port Folio*'s customers' interests increasingly became the public yardstick—and with that change, the *Port Folio*'s editor and the content he selected for the magazine became more and more devoted to supplying the *Port Folio* with matter that would place it firmly on the side of the leisured readership's interest in amusement.

The important thing about that readership, as the history of the *Port Folio* shows, is that it did not at all require those Federalist politics in order to remain willing to pay for the magazine. In this sense, what William Dowling has called the "great paradox" (70) of the *Port Folio*'s continued survival after 1809, when it very directly abdicated any political perspective, never was an actual paradox. Contemporaries, too, had been puzzled by the *Port Folio*'s survival. John Quincy Adams wrote in 1811 to his brother Thomas, now a circuit judge in Massachusetts, wondering: "How the Port Folio under all its metamorphoses has lived so long is to me unaccountable" (qtd. in Queenan 1955, 43-4). To Adams as to Dowling, the basic truth that the *Port Folio* had survived precisely because of its many metamorphoses was apparently unintelligible. The *Port Folio* never was the quasi-mythical repertory of genuine Federalism, of Augustan classicism and republican virtue that Dowling—and Dennie initially—wished it to be seen as. Dowling's interpretation of the *Port Folio* falls victim to a false monolithicization of a complex arrangement in which political ideology played, ultimately, a minor role, and a role no different from its other publically professed beliefs. Catherine O'Donnell Kaplan is right to say that "[p]olitical engagement furthered Dennie's career as a man of letters," by offering just "enough Federalist rhetoric and argument to make the newspaper acceptable to those who saw it as a party organ" (2009, 132-3). The implicit distinction here is between the *Port Folio* as a means of advancing the political agenda of Joseph Dennie, and the *Port Folio* as a means of advancing a political agenda to which Dennie subscribed, but which, more importantly, he recognized as offering a clientele capable of supporting the *Port Folio*. But there is a countervailing view which contemporaries also offered, and whose importance for the *Port Folio*'s success should at least be entertained as a possibility. When Dennie first announced the *Port Folio*'s imminent publication, Charles Brockden Brown's *Monthly Magazine* positively reviewed its plan and suggested that "[p]olitics [...] will operate, perhaps, favourably to its success." So far, so good, but Brown offered a twist.

> Curiosity is the *all-desirable* on such occasions, and *that* is a principle which acquires from *dis*approbation as well as from approbation. Those who approve, will read, of course, for they want to see their favourite tenets well defended, and those who disapprove, will yet unfold the obnoxious little volume with a—"Come, let's see what the

> rascals have to say for themselves!" Admiration is a delicious sentiment, but scorn has likewise its pleasures, and he merits some gratitude who affords us an opportunity of railing. (*MM* 1800 2, 312, original emphasis)

Politics, Brown shrewdly observed, need not in fact exclude any group, regardless of which ideological leanings the magazine espoused. The *Port Folio* may not have actually attracted the kind of masochistic Republican readership which Brown suggested might find it equally valuable, but clearly, the suggestion that overt Federalist tendencies would most certainly exclude large swathes of readers was not subscribed to by everybody—and as the example of biography has shown, it is hard to say that the *Port Folio* was at all times concerned with politics, anyway.

The ease with which the *Port Folio* mastered the shift away from politics in 1809 is explained not, then, as William Dowling does it, by suggesting that the magazine found an "unaccountable" survival of classical republican virtues in the public sphere and absented itself from political discussion because it discovered the only viable remaining grounds for republican virtue in literature, especially literary history (cf. Dowling 1999, 69-88), a view most recently repeated by Jared Gardner: "Dennie's retreat ultimately has more to do with his inability to accept the compromises and correspondences inherent in periodical publication" (2012, 129). Yet, as I have noted, even the very notion of the 'retreat' misperceives the complex of motivations which underlay everything Dennie did, everything Oliver Oldschool said, and everything the *Port Folio* in its entirety aimed at. The kind of interpretation which, in Stephen Shapiro's words, composes a "lapsarian tale about the retreat of 'intellectuals' from public involvement with commercial nonspecialists and into the cloisters of a solipsistic university" (2008, 152) comes full circle here, where even the intellectual retreat is no longer acceptable.

Rather than seeing the *Port Folio*'s audience as "not only a set of sensibilities to be tutored but also a market" (Kaplan 2009, 170), it seems more apt to say that the magazine's subscribers were, at least in part, a market of people willing to pay to be tutored—but who did not absolutely require political tuition in their magazines. Similarly, it is helpful to see the ostensible dichotomy identified by Bruce Weiner between the market and the enlightenment of readers not as a dichotomy at all. Instead, we should recognize that enlightening readers could be, and to some extent was, a market as well, one which periodicals addressed quite directly. Such a formulation stresses more clearly the commingling of idealism and financial aims: the *Port Folio*'s subscribers were not a target for ideological tutoring *and* a market that could be described and addressed in separation. Rather, they were inescapably both at once. Kaplan correctly notes that "Dennie used partisanship to gain attention and subscribers," rather than making the *Port Folio* a vehicle for Federalism as such, but even the conclusion that there were "deeper concerns" (181) which the *Port Folio* pursued instead is difficult to entirely subscribe to. The deepest concern for the *Port Folio*'s editor Dennie, as for his printer and publisher in 1801, as we have seen, was the question of which materials would constitute the matter for a magazine published to be profitable in the tangible sense of putting money into everyone's pockets. If Dennie indeed imagined himself, as Jared Gardner suggests, as "the man of genius at the head of his periodical society" (2012, 132), this is on the one hand a public imagination of the editor catering to a specific audience and, on the other, an ideal that Dennie, pragmatically, never set above the business of making his living from the magazine, and which he did not let himself distract from in the main publishing articles designed to please and amuse. In this sense, there was no retreat from politics, but a shift from politics to a different, equally and perhaps more profitable focus—and even such a reading unduly privileges Federalist politics in a magazine that had always offered a far broader selection of content. In fact, Dennie was full well aware, certainly in private but every so often also in public, that the *Port Folio* needed to fulfill a wide variety of purposes for a large number of different subscribers. The reason why Dennie could write cheerfully to his mother in 1809 that he had finally found himself ensconced in a situation where he was "powerfully supported" by the most distinguished literary characters of the country was not chiefly because he could, at long last, "feel at home among a community of like-minded peers" (Gardner 2012, 133; after all, the Tuesday Club had been steadily evolving as precisely such a community since Dennie's first arrival in Philadelphia in 1801), but rather because for a short time in 1809 and 1810, the new arrangements at the *Port Folio* had more firmly than before tethered that community to the actual work that went on at the magazine and promised that future numbers would more easily exhibited that requisite variety of content which the *Port Folio*'s financial well-being demanded. Dennie's cheerfulness thus was not one of private satisfaction with public recognition or ideal company, but rather of a steady improvement of his business.

It thus comes as no surprise that when the *Port Folio* carried a public memorial to Joseph Dennie in February 1812, the expectedly panegyric notice carefully avoided mentioning his political leanings, or the *Port Folio*'s insistence on its own political principles in its early years. Dennie had successfully transformed himself, and been transformed by his friends, into a virtuous benefactor of the country's morals and fine arts. The easiness with which Dennie's editorial persona Oldschool slipped into an emphatic affirmation of the American nation and its native genius, not just after 1809, but even in direct address to his readers in 1807, indicates the fragility of interpretations which stress Dennie's desire to find himself accepted into the old world's, England's, literary society (cf. Gardner 2012, 133). The problem which an overly great reliance on editorial pronouncements in the pages of the *Port Folio* creates is precisely the negation of the difference between the editorial persona, Oliver Oldschool, and the editor and sometime publisher, Joseph Dennie—and the impossibility of determining at any point if any particular flight of rhetoric was a genuine statement of sentiments or a sales pitch to the reader. Dennie's repeated insistence on classical Roman relationships between the creator of literature and his liberal patron were probably not too far removed from Dennie's ideal self-conception, but they were at the same time designed to appeal to the envisaged subscribership. In a very basic sense, of course, Catherine O'Donnell Kaplan is right to suggest that Dennie "longed to escape the demands of the marketplace"

(2009, 171)—he certainly feverishly hoped to escape the uncertainties of daily business for a well-salaried position with prospects of advancement, as he had indicated when he accepted Timothy Pickering's offer of a secretaryship. Joseph Dennie, for all his genuine interest in the republic of letters, was not going to sacrifice himself, at any point in his career, for a higher goal: indeed, as his decision to move to Philadelphia in 1800 suggests, he was more prepared to sacrifice literary work for the security which salaried government employment at home or abroad could bring.

The *Port Folio*'s history between 1801 and 1812 thus offers a fascinating glimpse at the inner workings of periodicals in the Early Republic; and at the role which individual genres, here biography, could play in it. If the final verdict must emphasize the contingencies which determined the processes of text selection, the limits to editorial control and creativity, and the banal nature of many of the biographical texts which stood so high in the official estimation of the *Port Folio*'s editor, this is an admittedly one-sided view of biography and the autonomy of editorial agency. Events could conspire to permit the production of texts with which it is still possible to engage in depth for us today. The biography of Edward Preble, for instance, with its lengthy authorial introduction discussing the value of national biography, was an early example of such writings. Still, it would take major external events to place periodicals in a position to produce a large body of texts which deserve a closer look at as artistic texts, beyond whose surface of biographical writing lies a more complex argument about American national identity and the value of periodical biography. The War of 1812, with its resultant flood of original submissions of lives of American heroes, was a key period in the development of American periodical biography and the American periodical business as a whole. Even as the by-now familiar process by which proprietors, interested in exploiting momentary interests in the readership into tangible profits, determined what texts should take precedence in their periodicals and employed their editors to select, to procure, or even to write them, editors and authors themselves found that even a genre such as biography could offer them the freedom to offer different visions about the American nation.

3 Periodicals, Biography, and the War of 1812

> […] [D]ifferent individuals construct or rather develope [sic] their characters, in different ways; some by actions, and others by words, expressed through the medium of conversation or writing. Of the former description are heroes, of the latter, individuals devoted to literature. Many of the most distinguished gentlemen of the sword, both in the land and naval service, have conversed but little, written less, and never dropt a wise or a witty expression. Their lives consisted entirely of action.
>
> Charles Caldwell:
> *The Author Turned Critic; or the Reviewer Reviewed.* 13.

Late in September 1816, Charles Caldwell, the former editor of the *Port Folio* and now among other things a freelance writer, published a thirty-four page reply to a review of Joseph Delaplaine's *Repository of the Lives of Distinguished Americans*, a biographical compendium to which he had contributed the biographical short texts. He was defending his writing against a scathing attack, published in the September 1816 issue of the *Analectic Magazine*, and written by Ezekiel Sanford.[1] Sanford had

1 Scott Casper suggests (1999, 43) that the author of the *Analectic*'s review was Samuel Stanhope Smith, president of Princeton College, a reading which the signature "S.," which Smith had used in the *Analectic* before, supports. However, other evidence makes it clear that Smith could not have been the author: Caldwell's lengthy reply haughtily suggests to the reviewer that he had "engaged in a kind of writing exceedingly improper for you. The task of criticism is unsuitable to your youth and standing in letters" (30). In 1816, Smith was 65, Caldwell 44, so that criticism based on the reviewer being too young would appear a bit unseemly. Granted that Caldwell might have been induced to assume the wrong person to have been the author, more specifically, the October 23 issue of the *Baltimore Patriot* explicitly commented that the review was written by a "Mr. Sandford" (*BP* 1816, 8.96, 2); the *Patriot* was clearly not proof to misprints (it spelled Delaplaine's work "Respository" in the same article), so that the slight alteration in the name does not mean much. In 1819, the *Analectic Magazine* praised Sanford's *History of the United States, before the Revolution*, noting that Sanford was "a very young man, uncommonly well educated; devoted to the most liberal studies and animated by a lively desire of winning distinction for himself and his country in the world of letters" (*AM* 1819 1, 304). The same review also suggests somewhat cryptically that Sanford "conducted this magazine," an editorship

taken Caldwell to task for many things, most notably among them Caldwell's conception of biography. Biography, Sanford suggested, "pursues [...] individuals from the public office to the private station—watches them in their dealings with themselves, and can tell you whether they play with pebbles on the beach, or whether they are subject to intermittent fits of tardy and rapid perambulation" (*AM* 1816 2, 195). History, by contrast, "is conversant with individuals merely in their public capacity [...] perhaps with a little admixture of national character" (194)—a thoroughly conventional critical attitude, as we have seen. The *Repository*'s biographies had none of those virtues: they were entirely devoted to the public lives of the biographees, and thus, were not biography proper. Caldwell's defense, as suggested in the epigram to this chapter, was simple: the men whom he portrayed in the *Repository* could not be shown in their "private station" because they had only really shone in the "public office."

As the *New England Galaxy and Masonic Magazine* pointed out in January of 1818, Sanford's criticism rang a bit oddly for being published in the *Analectic Magazine*. The *Galaxy* criticized Moses Thomas, the *Analectic Magazine's* Philadelphia publisher, rather than Sanford himself, or the editor, Robert Walsh,[2] as the person responsible for the negative review, and came straight to the point: "Mr. Thomas would, probably, wish to have us think [these desirable traits of biography are]

which would have escaped scholars so far. Sanford co-published the *Lives of the British Poets* in an American edition with Robert Walsh, himself a former editor of the *Analectic*; chances are, therefore, that he was indeed both a part-time editor of the magazine, as well as the author of the review of *Delaplaine's Repository*.

2 The editorship of the *Analectic Magazine* has been frequently misattributed. Luther Mott notes as much in his history of American magazines. He recognizes Washington Irving's well-known tenure 1813-1815, and his succession by Thomas Isaac Wharton, but also that the point of Wharton's departure is unclear (cf. 1957a, 279); as the *Port Folio*'s John Hall noted in 1819, Wharton was in fact succeeded by Robert Walsh, who had been involved in the *Port Folio* in 1811 and 1812, and Walsh, in January 1819, by Edward Ingersoll, brother of Charles Jared Ingersoll, also connected with the *Port Folio* for a considerable time. The timing of Robert Walsh's succession remains unclear, but would most likely have been with the first issue of 1817, giving each of the editors a two-year tenure. That there should be misattributions is not surprising, however. Moses Thomas himself, in an advertisement in the second series of *Salmagundi* (1819-20), offered back volumes of the *Analectic* for sale and noted that it had been edited by Irving and Walsh, but also by Gulian C. Verplanck and James K. Paulding. Especially the latter was unlikely to have served in this position, since he was employed as secretary to the Board of Navy Commissioners from April 1815, spent much of 1816 on a journey through the southern states, and served in his Washington post throughout 1817 (cf. Aderman and Kime 2004, 52-82). There is little time for him or Verplanck to have edited the *Analectic*. Mercenary considerations, however, may have induced Thomas to claim so: Verplanck had been a contributor to the original *Salmagundi* and was a well-regarded man of letters; and Paulding was the editor of the second *Salmagundi*. Thomas may have concluded that subscribers to that paper might be more inclined to purchase material from the same authors and editors.

contained in the Analectic Magazine." But, the *Galaxy* believed, that was hardly the case—it noted that the *Analectic Magazine* "has continually reiterated the promise of producing, but has never yet produced" (*NEG* 1818, 1.12, 2), the kind of text which it was now complaining about in the *Repository*. Rather, the *Analectic Magazine*'s considerable reputation in 1816 rested precisely on the form of life writing which Sanford was criticizing in the *Repository*: public lives of eminent Americans distinguished for the things they did in the arena reserved, as far as Sanford was concerned, for historical writing.

It is not surprising that the *Analectic Magazine* should be heavily involved in a discussion of the nature of biography. Originally published as the *Select Reviews*, in 1812 it was bought by the Philadelphia bookseller and publisher Moses Thomas, who hired Washington Irving to edit it. The *Analectic Magazine* quickly became famous for its series of lives of American military, but especially naval, officers, with which it filled many of its pages during the War of 1812. The magazine's publisher was well aware of the prominence which these biographies gave his magazine. More to the point of this chapter, however, was the recognition which the biographical texts published in the *Analectic*—especially those which were written by Washington Irving—received for their literary quality, by the publisher, the audience, and contemporary critics both. Throughout the War of 1812 and beyond, the naval biographies which the *Analectic Magazine* published figured prominently in newspaper advertisements. While most of these notices emphasized the engravings which the *Analectic* also printed—and which Thomas and Irving clearly considered to be the greater draw—the biographical short texts were also advertised quite frequently (cf. *Voice of the Nation* 1.8,1; *Daily National Intelligencer* 1.61, 4; *Repertory and General Advertiser* 10.16, 1; *Daily National Intelligencer* 1.226, 4), suggesting that the publisher was well aware that the biographies could draw new readers in. Indeed, their popularity was difficult to miss. The texts were widely regarded very favorably: by 1818, even the *London Literary Gazette* in faraway and often haughty England could note that the *Analectic Magazine* contained "able essays, [and] well-written biography" (in *A* 1818, 447). In the United States, too, the biographies garnered critical attention. When the *Port Folio* in 1825 reviewed Washington Irving's career up to that point, it explicitly commented on the "manly and masterly style" (*PF* 1825 1, 438) of his biographical writings. And transatlantically, a year earlier, *Blackwood's Edinburgh Magazine* had carried a long series of articles by American expatriate John Neal on American writers—in which, under the pseudonym "X.Y.Z." and pretending to be a British writer, he rather lavishly praised himself—that claimed at least for Irving's biographies that they were "eloquent, simple, clear, and beautiful" (*BEM* 1825 1, 62). As late as 1834, a rambling list from memory of significant American magazines included the *Analectic Magazine* specifically for its naval biographies (cf. *NAR* 1834, 39.85, 291).

It is unsurprising, therefore, that some critics have foregrounded the biographies' role in the *Analectic Magazine*: They were "the greatest success of Irving's tenure" and "certainly did much for the magazine by capitalizing on a wave of popular nationalism and by making it virtually a service journal for naval officers" (Greene

1970, 31). Yet there existed a disparity between Sanford's claims for biography and the biographical practice followed by the wartime *Analectic Magazine*. Upon occasion, the *Analectic* itself recognized and commented on this problem. Gulian C. Verplanck, writing a biography of Brigadier General Winfield Scott, wounded hero of the Battle of Lundy's Lane, noted that it "may [...] be doubted whether [living] subjects come at all within the proper province of Biography," and added that he would therefore "speak of [Scott's] character and exploits in the plain language of history" (AM 1814, 465-6). Likewise, a November 1815 correspondent's letter to Thomas Wharton, since early 1815 the editor of the *Analectic*, supported the *Analectic*'s general policy of displaying public figures in their public capacities, and indeed went so far as to suggest that the

> truth is, most of our great men have been either statesmen or warriors who have rendered themselves conspicuous upon the theatre of public affairs, and whose lives have been in general, marked by few incidents worthy of record, except so far as they are connected with the general history of the country. (*AM* 1815, 377).

Slightly uncharitably to poor Patrick Henry, whose biography the letter writer took as occasion for his commentary, the correspondent announced that the former Virginia governor's "life was nothing until he became a public figure" (381).

The clear disparity between the public biographies written in the magazine and the critical reception accorded the *Repository*—a critical reception in which the *Port Folio* and the *Portico* joined—has been read as being primarily an issue of conflicting conceptions of the idea of biography. Scott Casper has noted that Caldwell's, Verplanck's, and the anonymous *Analectic* correspondent's commentary on biography "squared with the overwhelming mass of biographies in the early republic" (1999, 43) in a dispute over what Casper suggests was essentially a question of "sketches of the public lives of public men, against the Johnsonian vision of [private] biography" (44). But, as we have seen in the discussion of biography in the *Port Folio*, this is an argument that is difficult to sustain. Not only was the overwhelming mass of biography in the Early Republic, the many sketches and short texts which filled the pages of the magazines, not at all interested in theoretical disputes over the relative value of the private over the public life. The vast majority of texts did not at all inscribe themselves in any debate, and certainly not in what Casper has called "[c]ultural nationalism" (45). How could they: the amount of biography written by Americans for an American market was comparatively small, dwarfed by the number of imported biographies of men and women whose relationship to the United States was vanishingly minor.

Casper's generalization causes him to miss a vital point about the biographies about which Caldwell, Sanford, and others specifically argued. He is no doubt correct when he says that "[b]etween 1790 and 1820, American periodicals repeatedly called for biographies of illustrious Americans, which could announce the new nation's place" (1999, 21), as we have also seen exemplarily in the *Port Folio*'s case. Yet both in the response from their contributors as in the nature of their calls, the periodicals in this thirty year period underwent considerable changes. In the first twenty years of the nineteenth century, no event so notably changed the usage and writing of biography in U.S. periodicals as the War of 1812. For all of the genre's prominence as a matter for prospectuses and semi-frequent public avowals of interest in the magazines of the Early Republic, it was the War of 1812 and the resultant upsurge in patriotic feelings which finally made American biography a viable prospect and ultimately a successful venture for American magazines; it was also the added interest in American biography, impossible to fill from existing sources, which led to the writing of many new American lives and the expansion of the authorial autonomy possible within the boundaries of the heteronomous periodical market.[3]

Two aspects go together in my argument about American periodical biography as published during the War of 1812, and for some time after: first, it is necessary to amend previous suggestions about the nature of nationalist biography in the Early Republic. Far from being monolithic, it displays a great variety of approaches to national identity, oscillating between strong attachment to Americans' British heritage and autochthonous readings of American history that emphasized emotional and political independence. This, I suggest, is an important corrective to prevailing views of biography as a genre which existed at two opposite poles, as a didactic instrument to instill private virtue with no regard for nationality, or one to instill national feeling in the reader, with no regard to the biographees' private life and character.

Secondly, I am arguing that these different approaches to national identity and, in fact, the entirety of biographical production during this time, must not be seen primarily as an expression of national sentiment in an effort to further the national idea. Rather, as a close look at the chronology indicates, we need to understand the production of nationalist biography during the War of 1812 as a reaction to an already existing upswing in national sentiment, which periodicals latched onto in an attempt to profit from it. Not only periodicals sought to benefit from the popularity of the national idea: anthologies, monographs, and

3 The following chapter will assume some background knowledge, especially with regard to military and naval history: Anderson and Cayton (2005) situate the impact of war in the general history of the United States. Howarth (1991) and Miller (1977) offer broad overviews of the history of the U.S. Navy. The Revolutionary War naval and military operations are treated in Royster (1981) and Volo (2006); subsequent naval operations (in chronological order) in Toll (2006), Leiner (1999), Palmer (2000), Daughan (2008) and Budiansky (2010). General overviews of the War of 1812 are in Borneman (2004), Hickey (1989 and 2007), Latimer (2009), Lawson (1966) and Taylor (2010). Studies of aspects of that war are in Ellis (2009) and Lord (1972). Modern naval biographies of some of the same officers discussed here (I am only offering a selection) are Brown (2011), Callo (2009), DeKay (2004), Ferguson (2000), Maloney (1986), and Norton (2000), and are often helpful as counternarratives to the texts printed in contemporary periodicals. Budiansky's and Toll's books on the naval aspects of the War of 1812 are especially readable and succinct overviews of the war at sea.

graphic representations all sought to inject themselves into the discourse, professing idealism for the national cause even as they sought a share of the money people were willing to spare for news of the national victories.

These two aspects must be understood to interact, of course: the expression of diverse formulations of national identity could not have happened without the publishing interest that did not foreground any particular formulation, but rather any form of biographical writing that could be profitably placed in the market. Conversely, the success of the nationalist biography which ultimately reached publication in the magazines certainly reinforced nationalist sentiment, as readers' commentaries indicate—there was, in other words, some ideological effect to periodical writings, notwithstanding its essential sales orientation. At the same time, however, it is clear that national American biography had outlasted its welcome even before it stopped being published: in this, as in its inception, it followed, rather than created, shifts in the prevailing ideological conception of the United States, and, what is more important, it could not of itself sustain the national impulse when exterior factors changed. This, I suggest, is exemplary of how magazines in the Early Republic worked. Rather than actively creating ideological change, they became increasingly adept at noticing and profiting of momentary shifts in the interests of their readerships. They ultimately lagged behind that readership, however: just as the publication of naval biographies celebrating the Navy's achievements took some time, so did the post-war realization that interests had once more shifted. The ways in which the magazines reacted to the opportunities presented in the market are still revelatory of the processes which underlay periodical production in the Early Republic.

The heteronomies of the periodical field determined the kinds of texts to be produced—naval biographies, military biographies, descriptions of battles, of campaigns, celebratory poetry, engravings of naval and military officers, obituaries and panegyrics of deceased heroes. Magazines adapted to these demands with a will. At the same time, however, and slightly surprisingly, the heteronomous demands of the historical moment had something like a liberating effect. To be sure, not everybody by far submitted cheerfully to the demands of the time: Washington Irving, for example, was entirely horrified by his publisher's plans to profit off of the War of 1812. All the same, writing naval biographies permitted Irving to exercise a relative autonomy of authorship, creating texts which greatly exceeded the demands of the market and instead offered national imaginaries which were not required by texts merely playing to either the demands of his publisher, his audience, or even the nationalist moment. This is the second aspect which I will discuss in this chapter, and which I suggest is similarly exemplary: even within the increasingly heteronomous medium of the periodical, momentary glimpses of authorial autonomy can be detected, if the circumstances were right.

Ultimately, none of these changes lasted, as competing demands on the periodicals ensured that the possibility of a sustained engagement with the nationalist impulse of the moment was fleeting at best, and dissolved with the return of what might be called business as usual after the end of the war. Yet the war had also by this point catalyzed changes in the production of periodicals, from the relationship between editors and publishers to the question of periodical distribution. These steps on the road of professionalization had been taken before, but had been rendered surer by the war. Nationalism, biography, and the business of periodicals need to be read together for us to be understood each individually; this is the final argument which this chapter makes, bringing the overall argument of this study full circle.

The Ideal Figures of American Nationalism

It is easy to find Early Republic examples of cautionary words seeking to encourage Americans to come together as a nation. Many of these, like Washington's "Farewell Address," have been quoted quite often for their reminder that there existed competing loyalties well-recognized by contemporaries which they actively sought to overcome in an effort to nationalize the federal union. It is also tempting, especially in light of later events and of interpretations of American history which stress the disjunctions, the differences, and the near-secessions of the sixty-odd years prior to the outbreak of the Civil War, to emphasize those almost prophetic-seeming calls for national unity as evidence for the latent lack of nationhood exhibited by Americans. Yet it must not go unremarked that it is nearly as easy to find matter of fact statements which either simply imply the existence of a nation, of national identity, or of national character. If, as Trish Loughran writes, "[m]ore than one new American was puzzled, after 1776, about what it might mean to feel 'nationly'" (2007, 12), others were happy to recognize nationality in their shared independence and confederation: "We have just taken our station among the nations of the earth, as a free, sovereign, and independent people" (*CM* 1786, 1.4, 172) announced a correspondent of the *Columbian Magazine* in December 1786. The discourse on the American nation was not a one-sided quest seeking to establish an as-yet non-existent nation: indeed, it possessed many faces, one of which, certainly, was the fact that the United States was among those polities which "self-consciously defined themselves as nations" (Anderson 2006, 46), even as they struggled to determine what precisely that meant. Even before the successful conclusion of the American revolution, Hector St. John de Crèvecœur's question, "What then is the American, this new man?" (1997, 43-4), had been the rhetorical overture for a lengthy exposition on the peculiar character of Americans—although Crèvecœur ultimately did not totally divorce American colonists from their British ancestry. Instead, he believed in the possibility that the new "race" of men, the Americans, would at some future point become "distinct by the power of the different climes which they inhabit" (44)—that is to say, they would yet develop a unique national character. Together, these comments indicate a fundamental disagreement among Americans in the aftermath of their revolution as to the terminology they were to employ in speaking of their new political system and the form of their mutual attachment.

Americans' puzzlement has carried over into the critical engagement with American nationalism in studies of the Early Republic. Nationalism and its assorted cognates, nation, national identity, national character, among others, are frequently used—indeed, I have used them above without bothering to tell you what I mean by them—but amazingly difficult to pin down, especially when applied to the Early Republic. The difficulties become evident in David Waldstreicher's seminal *In the Midst of Perpetual Fetes*, in which he analyzes American public celebrations and ceremonies in the aftermath of the Revolution for their potential in the making of American nationalism. Waldstreicher himself highlights the paradoxical complexity of American nationalism as he conceives it.

> By the summer of 1776, Independence had been in the air for at least a year, and the Continental Congress had already declared two national fast days, July 20, 1775, and May 17, 1776. Yet on sending out the printed Declaration, the congress did not recommend fasting, mourning, bell ringing, or any other observance. Congress would not—could not—order the nation to celebrate its own birth. The new nation could not exist until the people spontaneously celebrated its existence, until evidence of this nationwide celebration appeared in print. (1997, 30)

Waldstreicher suggests that the nation cannot exist until its existence is spontaneously celebrated by its citizens—a hen-and-egg paradox which remains unresolved. Yet the difficulties with his argument, and indeed with many of the arguments about American nationalism in the Early Republic, are not limited to this particular paradox. Rather, they must be framed in terms of a more central question: when we speak of nationalism in the Early Republic, do we mean to speak about contemporary American conceptions of the idea, or our own critical ones? If the latter, can we be sure that our concepts realistically apply? And if the former, what did Americans conceive of when they spoke of the nation?[4]

4 Numerous books have dealt with the question of American nationalism, and nationalism in general, and have influenced my own views of the nature of American nationalism, even if I have not cited all of them specifically in the text. These sources include Dangerfield (1965); Gellner (1983); Anderson (2007 [1983]); Smith (1986, 1991, 2001); Beeman et al., eds. (1987); Hobsbawm (1990); Greenfeld (1992); Connor (1994); Balakrishnan, ed. (1996); Hebel (1999); Bender (2006); Brückner (2006); Chávez (2009); Kramer (2011). Studies of American nationalism in particular exhibit a broad variety of usefulness. Knud Krakau's 1997 conference volume *The American Nation – National Identity – Nationalism* spares itself the trouble of attempting to come to terms with that difficult question by simply ignoring it. Although providing two thought-provoking essays on proto-nationalist impulses in colonial New England, the collection then leaps clear across the entire post-colonial period until the turn of the nineteenth to the twentieth century. One of the earliest studies of American nationalism still cited today is George Dangerfield's *The Awakening of American Nationalism 1815-1825*. Even in its title, Dangerfield's book opens questions: If American nationalism only awoke in 1815, what was the state of the nation before? Readers of Dangerfield find no real explanation of what constituted American

Most of the studies which have specifically dealt with American nationalism, rather than with the question of how to define the term in general, have in fact avoided an all-too-stringent attempt at definition. What is today still the dominant line of thought on Early Republic nationalism harkens back to the by no means unproblematic though persuasive argument brought forward by Benedict Anderson and generally reduced to the idea of the "imagined community." For Anderson, nations were communities which literally came into existence in the imagination of the newspaper reader, in "the almost precisely simultaneous consumption ('imagining') of the newspaper-as-fiction [...] each communicant is well aware that the ceremony he performs is being replicated simultaneously by thousands (or millions) of others of whose existence he is confident, yet of whose identity he has not the slightest notion" (2006, 35). Anderson's sacral language, the communions and ceremonies, acknowledge his argument that nations replaced religious imagined communities (as Anderson notes, Hegel had observed that the newspaper had replaced morning prayer). His theory has, however, always been problematical for the United States, since his insistence on the role of a vernacular print language, and the community of readership, presents obvious problems in any attempt to distinguish America and Great Britain, specifically in the late eighteenth century.[5] Metropolitan culture determined the American community's reading list to a large extent, both in books and in magazines; and what Anderson emphasizes as the "fatality of human linguistic diversity," an element "essential" to his theory of the development of nations, runs into obvious problems with the British colonies, sharing the same print-language as Britain itself. "[P]rint-languages laid the bases for national consciousness," Anderson avers (44), but at the same time, he recognizes that "language was never even an issue in [the American Revolution]" (47).[6] Anderson's con-

nationalism, and what would differentiate it from federalism or from unionism. Dangerfield's contention that the nationalism of "southern leaders [...] rose and fell with this sense of control [of the central government]" (1965, 15) suggests the expendiency with which the national constitution—an aspect to which we will recur to below—and its basis in anything but political union, was viewed.

5 Americans, of course, could and did read newspapers; the most frequent objection to Anderson's thesis, namely that it "does not always fit well to circumstances in which very large numbers were illiterate" (Day and Thompson 2004, 91) is therefore fairly irrelevant for the Early Republic. Although estimates vary, probably as many as 90% of New Englanders in 1790 were literate, a number that did not significantly fluctuate for the first decade of the nineteenth century. Numbers may have been smaller in the Southern states, possibly by as much as ten percent, and some figures, such as those for Army recruits, lower still by a significant margin, but overall, American literacy was high compared to most European countries; cf. Gordon and Gordon 2003, xvi; Monaghan 2005, 384.

6 Martin Brückner's *The Geographic Revolution in Early America: Maps, Literary, and National Identity* (2006), despite never really coming to define what is meant by the term national identity, offers a suggested amendment to Anderson's thesis. Brückner notes that "[a]fter the Revolutionary war, it was a bitter irony for Anglo-Americans, eager to sever all representational ties

sequent analysis of why we should emphasize the role of print in the creation of an American national imagined community becomes correspondingly problematical. That he draws explicit connections between nascent nationalism and "the relationship between the newspaper, *as a form of book*, and the market" (2006, 30, my emphasis) has led to an almost reflexive adoption of Anderson's theory in works which deal with literary nationalisms, seeking to find the community imagined in, most frequently, the novel. While it is undoubtedly true that American authors in the Early Republic frequently sought to establish a genuinely American literature and to influence the political discourse through their fictions, it is likewise the case that contemporary interest in these American productions was often decidedly modest. A case in point may be *The Algerine Captive*. Royall Tyler's 1797 novel, as Jörg Richter correctly notes, is an "aesthetic declaration of independence," (2004, 61) but whatever Tyler's intentions when writing the novel, or our reactions to it and interpretations of it today are, its nationalist impact at the time of writing was negligible.[7] In

with the former imperial power, that their discussions about Independence and self-government were by necessity conducted in the very language of the former oppressor" (98). Some issue may be taken with the language here, especially in the generalizing of Anglo-American attitudes to their British heritage and the notion of the "oppressor;" but Brückner correctly identifies the problem with Anderson's thesis for the United States. He suggests, without tying this idea back to Anderson, that Americans invested heavily in what Brückner calls "geographic literacy" (100), which substituted geographic representations of American identity for linguistic ones, and thus created a quasi-print language by which Americans could separate themselves from Britain—an effort which ran in parallel with, but, as Brückner suggests, was more successful than, attempts to Americanize the English language (cf. 100-104). Brückner's interpretations sometimes run a little broad—as when he suggests in reference to Noah Webster's American speller that "Just as the written word 'Masschusetts' implied a larger territorial unit by being stretched across the face of a map, so too did the pronunciation of 'Mas-sa-chu'-setts' imitate the territorial form of the geographic referent" (106)—but the basic argument is persuasive enough. If his only reference to Anderson is to his notion of the "map-as-logo[s?]" (134) (I am restoring here the Derridean punportunity which Brückner passes up!), the possibility of revivifying Anderson's thesis for the U.S. context through geographical language seems intriguing.

7 For Richter's own criticism that Anderson's imagined communities rests partially on what Richter calls the "researcher's fiction of identifying reading" (2004, 16), by which he means to imply that not all readers will identify with the national myth presented them, is well taken. It misses Anderson's point, however. Anderson, after all, notes that the imagined community of reading depends on the reader's imagination of himself as being part of a reading community, rather than the contents of the texts read per se—indeed Anderson does not make any point about "reception," as Richter avers (Richter 2004, 15). On the other hand, Richter's charitable concern to have readers seen as more than just willing identifiers with whatever fiction of the nation is presented to them does not extend to "the reception of periodicals of the 18th and early 19th century" (2004, 16)—in other words, Richter acknowledges that that readers or periodicals might well have dumbly identified themselves with the texts they read therein, while readers of novels apparently did not. Precisely why that should be the case, Richter does not say.

1802, the *Port Folio*'s Joseph Dennie—with whose erstwhile publisher David Carlisle Tyler had originally published the book—sought to effect its resurrection from the recent literary dead in calling, unsuccessfully, for a second edition (cf. *PF* 1802, 8); in 1803, noting the re-print of Tyler's novel in England, Dennie bemoaned the fact that "more attention is paid to American productions abroad, than at home" (*PF* 1803, 181); by 1804, Dennie's exasperation about his fellow countrymen's neglect of Tyler, "a favourite friend of the Editor of the Port Folio," was evident. "It must be truly grateful, it must be a soothing *triumph* to the ingenious author to learn that his book is perused in the country of his *ancestors*. In his *native country*, his motley fellow *citizens* were too much occupied in the shallow devices of an infamous democracy [...]" (*PF* 1804, 134, original emphasis). Tyler's aesthetic declaration of independence went largely unnoticed and unheralded by Americans, and was not greeted with much discouragement in England, as might have been expected: after the first American edition, Tyler's book was twice re-printed, once in serialization, in England, and did not see a second American edition until 1816 (cf. Cook 1970, 24).[8]

Anderson himself is studiously evasive about the development of United States nationalism. He suggests that the increase in the number of newspapers created—as "appendages of the market," lest it be forgotten! (2006, 62)—a localized imagined community within each paper's own sphere: "the newspaper of Caracas quite naturally, and apolitically, created an imagined community among a specific assembled of fellow-readers, to who these ship, brides, bishops and prices belonged" (62) which were mentioned therein. If this seems persuasive enough, problems arise in attempting to tie these local newspapers—none of which, whether in Caracas, Concord, or Charleston, had a more than local readership—into a nationalizing network. Somewhat blithely, Anderson suggests that "[t]he newspaper-readers of Mexico City, Buenos Aires, and Bogota, even if they did not read each other's newspapers, were nonetheless quite conscious of their existence" (63). Although Anderson claims that in the case of the future United States, the smaller geographical spaces made it easier for them to gain access to (intercolonial) print matter, the empirical problem remains: there existed no genuinely 'national'—we should probably say 'pre-national' or inter-colonial—newspaper in the American colonies that could have created a community of readers; moreover, such more widely-spread readerships as some papers may have had would not have been able to conclude that they were in a simultaneous reading experience, simply because the vagaries of postal delivery would prevent the imagined-communal reading of the Sunday morning paper on Sunday morning. And if we take Anderson to suggest that the point is not so much a shared experience of reading the same news at the same time, but, rather, of having an imagined communion with other readers of other newspapers, within the continental

8 Oliver Scheiding (2003) makes the point that early reviewers of Tyler's novel did not regard it as an example of national literature, but rather emphasized its inherent 'New England-ness,' as it were; the novel operated as much against the British (against whom Richter sees it as mainly directed) as it did against the Southern plantation society and especially, of course, against slavery.

confines of the American colonies, the argument becomes circular. If newspaper readers in Boston were aware that there existed newspaper readers (or even just newspapers!) in Charleston, so certainly they were aware that newspaper readers existed in London and Edinburgh, and possibly even of the newspaper readers in Bogota.[9] As Charles Clark has noted, the editorial decision to copy London news in American newspapers was not just a politically innocuous function of the need to fill space, but "a way of overcoming the cultural and geographic boundaries that separated outlying peoples from the metropolitan center of their empire" (2000, 353).[10] The shared communion of readership's delimitations, therefore, remain unfortunately vague. In the end, Anderson's argument for the American colonies, whether North or South, boils down to suggesting that their marginalization at the colonial periphery—in the case of the Spanish colonies, the individuals' "shared fatality of extra-Spanish birth" (63)—had already created an imagined community of 'Americans;' otherwise, there could be no boundary to the shared community of reading experience.[11]

9 Charles E. Clark has suggested that what tied American newspapers together was the practice of copying from one another even colonial news, so that "readers in Philadelphia, for example, became accustomed to reading scraps of news and articles of opinion from Boston, Annapolis, and Charleston" (2000, 258), but that up to the middle of the 1760s, much of the news was "still copied from London" (360). Clark subtly inverses the roles between nationalism and newspapers, suggesting that "the proven role of the newspaper as the best existing *instrument* of a shared community consciousness, a function that took on a new meaning now that the community was beginning to define itself as a nation" (361, my emphasis) led to the pre-revolutionary increase in newspapers, rather than the other way around, as Anderson's argument would have it!

10 Trish Loughran makes the point that print culture "did not, in the American case, simply reinforce a sense of simultaneity. On the contrary," she suggests, "it actually worked in many cases to register the failures of such simultaneity and the consequent lack, in Jefferson's word, of 'consanguinity' across the sweep of British empire." This is certainly also a backhanded affirmation of Anderson's thesis, relying on demonstrating that a lack of perceived simultaneity could operate to distance communities from each other. Yet Loughran recognizes that the same operations also were meaningful on the smaller scale of the colonies: "It would be a mistake [...] to think that the scale of the nation was more conducive to a sense of shared, or simultaneous, experience than empire had been." Instead, it was a large number of smaller collectives, most importantly perhaps the state, which engaged American conceptions of self-identity (2007, 12). Empirically, at the very least, there seems to be little evidence to conclude that Americans perceived the simultaneity of communal readership when a Savannah merchant was finally able to peruse a two-week old Boston paper.

11 In a similar vein, fifty years after the Revolution, Alexis de Tocqueville suggested that "[t]he thirteen colonies [...] possessed [...] the same religion, the same language, the same customs, and almost the same laws; they were struggling against a common enemy; and these reasons were sufficiently strong to unite them one to another, and to consolidate them into one nation" (91). That they also shared all of these features—certainly to the debatable extent to which they indeed did share them, especially customs and language—with the British mother country, Tocqueville nicely

Anderson's theory, at least for the case of the United States, thus recurs to a conception of the national idea as pre-existing—a problem which persists in much of the study of American nationalism.[12] The problem becomes more evident when we explore a little deeper the claims that David Waldstreicher makes. He suggests that Congress had "already declared two *national* fast days" (my emphasis), implying that the imagined construct which Congress had applied to its declarations was one which was already conceived of in terms of nationality. But the original fast day proclamation of March 16, 1776, declaring May 17 of the same year as fast day, does not in fact mention a nation, any nation, at all. Instead, it explicitly speaks of "these hitherto free and happy colonies" and the "liberties of America" and, far from declaring, merely "recommend[s]" fast and prayer to the colonies in hopes that doing so will bring divine blessing upon "Continental arms by sea and land" (*Pennsylvania Evening Post*, 1776, March 19, 2.181, 139). Similarly, the June 1775 resolution merely "recommends that Thursday, the 20th day of July next, be observed by the inhabitants of all the *English Colonies* on this continent" (Washington 1775, my emphasis). The intercolonial body of the Continental Congress thus recommended to the colonies the proclamation of two fast days. But were these 'national' fast days in any sense of the word? The question is more than just academic, because it pinpoints the difficulty in coming to terms with the question of American nationalism in the Early Republic.

Even in David Waldstreicher's paragraph as quoted above, 'nation' and 'national' seem to mean two different things: the fast days are 'national' by virtue of their transcoloniality—even before the 'birth' of the nation as a result of the Declaration of Independence. Strikingly, however, now that the nation is birthed, apparently the Continental Congress lacks the power to further nationhood by simply declaring national celebrations. Even in this short paragraph, irreconcilable conflicts of interpretation obfuscate the question of American nation-ness: if the nation was born on July 4th, 1776—how could anything national exist prior to that date? If the nation could not exist prior to being celebrated—how could it be celebrated? Furthermore, is it enough to simply equate intercolonial celebrations, even if they occurred simultaneously in all thirteen colonies, with nationalism—a nationalism which would later be applied to the United States alone, even as the Congressional fast days hoped to include Nova Scotia and New Brunswick, among other non-U.S. British colonies? Is it enough to equate even post-Constitutional celebrations of federalism, of the federal union, with nationalism? Waldstreicher's

elides. Indeed, there is considerable reason to doubt the validity of Tocqueville's allegation as well as Anderson's easy assumptions.

12 For another critique of Anderson's thesis for the United States, cf. Ed White (2000). I do not agree with White's suggestion that the Indian 'nation' should be privileged in our discussion of American conceptions of the nation (cf. 64); while there is indeed a common suggestion in American writings of the period that the Indian tribes constituted 'nations,' none of the conceptions of nationhood which Americans applied to the Indians—specifically, they shared traditions and history—were not also applied to various other peoples and states.

assertion that "[r]eports of celebrations elsewhere demonstrated the simultaneity of national action and the pervasiveness of national sentiments" (1997, 34) hinges on a definition of 'national' that is ill-supported by contemporary usage; crucially, Waldstreicher, but by no means he alone, conflates Americans' attachment to common cause and common country, their patriotism, with a difficult-to-define and difficult-to-trace nationalism, while ignoring the overt rhetoric of a purely geographic 'continentalism' (as in 'Continental Army' or 'Continental Congress') in favor of assuming a national idea behind merely transcolonial events, or political nationalism behind merely patriotic events. Americans not necessarily tied the concept of the nation to a certain, or indeed any, form of polity; rather, as Anthony Marx has suggested more generally, they "perceived themselves [and others] to be members of varying 'imagined communities,' [which] did not neatly overlap with political boundaries" (2005, 19).

Central figures of the new republic agreed with this assessment: as Gordon Wood points out, "Washington did not believe that the people of the United States had become a nation," and "spent much of his time devising schemes for creating a stronger sense of nationhood" (2009, 37-8). Washington's concern that the newly established political boundaries of the United States did not correspond to a communal sense of national belonging was well founded. Especially in New England, the immediate revolutionary and post-revolutionary period saw national feelings directed at the new states, rather than the confederation of states which was struggling for independence and cohesion (cf. Murrin 343). There was no discrepancy apparent to Americans between Fisher Ames's calling New England (in 1801!) the "most assimilated, to use the modern jargon, nationalized" part of the United States, and "the most interesting to America." The object of New England nationalism was not the ostensible American nation, not even political entities such as the state of Massachusetts, but a "people, whose spirit is as lofty as their destiny" (1856, 134) united by their common character, especially in their relation with the sea. Twenty years earlier, in 1781, the Massachusetts legislature had addressed a circular to the inhabitants of the newly-independent state, in which it noted (even as it was preparing to ask Massachusetts citizens for money) that the "animated struggle of six years [sic] successful warfare, has enhanced your national character" (*Providence Gazette* 1781, 18.902, 1). Six years later, the *Worcester Magazine* complained about both the lack of a national—meaning confederate—revenue as well as noting about Bay Staters that they "have no national character: No just pride in the glorious distinction of freemen, which elevates a Massachusetts beggar above the despots of Asia" (*WM* 1787, 633). In 1788, Massachusetts Governor John Hancock unequivocally noted how fragile the national idea was, and how little constitutive force it held for his contemporaries. In a speech to the Massachusetts General Court in February 1788, presenting the legislature with the Constitutional Convention's draft for a new U.S. constitution, he exhorted the senators and representatives to understand that "[w]e can be known to the world, only under the appellation of the *United States*; if we are robbed of the idea of our Union, we immediately become separate nations, independent of each other" (original emphasis). Hancock stressed that nationhood was consequent to and dependent upon the "power to coerce" (*WM* 1788, 292), and thus tied nationhood firmly to a certain form of polity. As John Murrin notes, "[i]n a word, the Constitution became a substitute for any deeper kind of national identity. American nationalism is distinct because, for nearly its first century, it was narrowly and peculiarly constitutional. People knew that without the Constitution, there would be no America" (1987, 346). Yet even the Constitution, Murrin suggests, "was to the nation [...] a way of buying time [...] an ingenious contrivance that enabled a precarious experiment to continue for another generation or two with the hope that the salvation unobtainable in the present might bless the land in better times" (347-8). The institutional approach to building a nation, in other words, could only be a stop-gap measure in an ongoing contest, in which events worked to heighten and to lower again American nationalist impulses.[13]

John Hancock's speech shows at the very least that Americans in the Revolutionary Period and the Early Republic did not sharply divide between nation and state, between people and polity. As the *Literary Magazine* suggested in 1804, in beginning an extensive analysis of the states which made up the political Union, "[t]he inhabitants of the several states differ as much from each other, in their customs, manners, and genius, as they are distinguishable from their ancestors" (252). In other words, what Hector St. John de Crèvecoeur had claimed was an entirely "new man,"[14] the *Literary Magazine* denied existed: the states shared little of a common,

13 A measured analysis somewhat sympathetic to both Murrin and Greenfeld and echoing the idea that nationalism is a matter of recurrent processes, rather than something that can be ontologically realized, is Susan-Mary Grant's: "Americans neither entered nor exited the Revolution with a uniform sense of civic identity [...]. As Connor observes, 'nation formation is a process, not an occurrence', a point which Smith reinforces, in a slightly different context, with his argument that the process of national construction is never 'a once-for-all affair', but is taken up anew by each generation (Connor 2004: 45; Smith 1993: 206) The American Revolution may be regarded as the beginning of the process, although the evidence that some version of nationalism pre-dated the emergence of America as a separate nation is compelling" (Grant 2005, 162).

14 Although the forefather of investigations of American identity, Crèvecœur's Letter III–"What is an American?"–is ultimately not much concerned with political dimensions. Being an American is a curious mixture of simply being well-off, especially when compared to one's humble origins, and simply being in a new place, and having felt the consequences of being in that new place: "by the power of transplantation" (43) alone, the changes wrought in the poor of Europe made them Americans. Variously described as "a new race," a "mixture of English, Scotch, Irish, French, Dutch, Germans, and Swedes" or "neither an European, nor the descendant of an European" (42, 44), it is hardly difficult to become 'American.' Strikingly, perhaps, for Crèvecœur becoming an American is easy, a mere matter of taking one's life into one's own hands, and a feat independent of national origin, indeed a feat easily managed within the confines of an explicitly British America. For all of Crèvecœur's oft-repeated assertions on the new American man, neither the American farmer himself nor the Americans he is talking about have an American national identity. There is no American nation, not even American nationality, in the *Letters*. Crèvecœur's new American man is the same "from Nova Scotia to West Florida" (41). The distinction between be-

national, character; especially the southern slave states differed fundamentally from the industrious northern states. The *Literary Magazine* finally concluded that

> Americans can possess no other national character than what our common ancestors might be supposed to have had immediately after the succeeding irruptions of the Saxons, Danes, Romans, and Normans; and, in all probability, never will, as there is no less a difference between the northern and southern states, than betwixt the Hebrides and the West Indies. (254)

The paradox of these lines, and indeed of the whole essay, is an echo of David Waldstreicher's, namely that it could speak of the generalized 'American' even as it denied him the kind of national coherence, the shared national identity, which would have signaled the political union to be approaching a national union as well, based on the kind of shared character traits which most contemporaries identified with nationality. The unified American who, in the *Literary Magazine*'s phrasing, "is naturally grave, deliberate, and temperate" (256), had at the same time no national character. The *Literary Magazine*'s paradoxical conclusion points to the difficulties which Americans had in deciding how to see themselves.

Any of the terms which Americans favored to describe the nature of their nationhood labored under the problem that there was not much agreement on the precise delineation of those terms. Hans-Ulrich Wehler suggests that "Anglo-American usage equated 'nation-building' and 'state-building'" and used 'nation' in the sense of 'body-politic'" (2001, 25), but this suggestion is similarly incomplete. Contemporary dictionaries instead point to the already-noted lack of distinction between nation and state, but end up with a far broader definition, one so broad, in fact, that it hardly remains a definition at all. Noah Webster's 1806 dictionary defines a nation as "a body of the people united under one prince or government, or their state or kingdom" (199), and Samuel Johnson's English dictionary, in defining 'national' as "publick, general, not private" also hints at the foundations of the nation in a state capable of offering a 'public;' yet Johnson also defines the 'nation' as "a people distinct from others" (2005, 147), a definition which does away with any kind of governmental organization whatsoever and becomes a rather more ethnographical than political reading of nation. In the French-speaking world, the *Encyclopédie* did not explicitly highlight the equivalency between nation and state, but noted that in comparing "the genius of nations," it was necessary to compare "the differences of climate, sustenance, and education of the people" as well as "the constitution of the governments" (385).[15]

ing American as either a mere geographical denominator, a description of belonging to a particular civic society, and being part of a nation, is an important one that is all too frequently ignored.

15 The French original reads: «Pour bien juger du génie des Nations, il faut les comparer les unes aux autres, & ne pas s'arrêter à la seule constitution des Gouvernements. La différence du climat, des aliments & de l'éducation des hommes établit une différence totale entre leur façon de vivre & de penser.»

And even the *Encyclopédie* itself then took recourse to the simpler equivalency of nation-as-its-people: "levity and inconstancy make up the character of that nation" (386), the Encyclopedists wrote about the French, also implying a broadly ethnic definition of nationality.[16]

The problem is certainly not helped by modern theorists' inability to come to an agreement about the nature of American nationalism in its first couple of decades. As Joyce Appleby has noted, "[i]t would be surprising if scholars were able to agree upon the meaning of a word that contemporaries themselves used in such disparate contexts" (in Nord 1988, 44). Appleby is talking about the term "republicanism," but her point remains valid. Is it true that "[t]he American Union, and the spirit of American nationality that underlay it, were the creation of the eighteenth century." (Ratcliffe 2000, 4), when it is by no means clear that Americans possessed the "explicit and peculiar character" (Breuilly 1993, 2) which John Breuilly notes as a distinguishing feature of a nation, specifically because they were not easily distinguished from their fellow British subjects? Americans spoke English, followed British customs of political protest, and well into the nineteenth century filled their magazines and newspapers with articles culled from British publications, as previously noted. Liah Greenfeld's chapter on the United States in her study on nationalism and modernity highlights the extent to which scholars disagree about the American experience of nationalism.[17] Greenfeld suggests that Americans' largely English political heritage already included a latent sense of national identity. Although Americans did not begin to see themselves as Americans until after the revolution, the ability to identify with a nation was part of their political upbringing. Americans, Greenfeld argues, from the outset possessed the "firm conviction that the American society [...] was a *nation*" (1992, 402; original emphasis). This strong allegation proves problematic, however. Although Greenfeld suggests that the settlers in early colonial America possessed a sense of English nationality (whatever their idea of nationality finally was), their conception of themselves as peculiarly American is not so easily established; indeed, she notes that "Crevecoeur [sic] was as firmly convinced of the English-

16 Even the term nationalism itself has a more complicated history than is usually realized, and must be historicized in any study of American nationalism. Despite Anthony Smith's throw-away claim that "in English, its first use, in 1836, appears to be theological" (2001, 5) not only can American statements be found from that same year in which nationalism clearly is used in an entirely political meaning, as in the *Southern Literary Messenger* (cf. 2 1836, 684), but far earlier instances of the term can be easily discovered. As early as 1811, *Poulson's American Daily Advertiser* noted that Frenchmen in Louisiana had "encreased this nationalism," by which it meant the realization that Frenchmen in Louisiana, although by then nominally American, retained their "very deep rooted prejudice" (1811, 2) against the English and Americans, i.e., remained Frenchmen.

17 In fact, Greenfeld's study is exemplary of the divisions within the field of nationalism studies: her argument is that nationalism preceded and was a prerequisite for modernity; by contrast, Ernest Gellner argues that nationality was a consequence of modernity.

ness of America as any American of British descent" (408). Likewise, Greenfeld suggests that American nationalism was tightly linked to federalism. This meant, however, that American nationalism was neither natural, nor self-evident. Proponents of a tighter national union advanced the idea that only in federal union could the nation exist— like John Hancock, Thomas Paine claimed, "we have no other national sovereignty than as United States" (in Greenfeld 1992, 426). The American sense of nationhood, Greenfeld argues, was focused on "a unified inclusive polity" (431), rather than individual but shared traits.[18]

Claims such as Greenfeld's and Ratcliffe's, which attempt to emphasize the national cohesion of the United States even at the Revolution's start are, as we have already seen, problematical. The language of the Declaration of Independence emphatically makes "these United Colonies [...] Free and Independent States" (Jefferson 1950, 432) and adroitly avoids use of the term 'nation' with regard to either the newly-independent states or the former colonies' connection with Great Britain. "[T]he administrative unit that would later come to be called the 'thirteen colonies' had a different set of political squabbles with Britain" (2007, 13), as Trish Loughran points out, but all the 'national' events in 1775 and 1776 could not hide the fact that "1776 produced not a nation but a confederation" (12) of states, each of which inspired identification processes that were much stronger than the nationalist impulses. "The American Revolution was not the logical culmination of a broadening and deepening sense of separate national identity among the settlers of North America" (Murrin 334)—instead, it was the political culmination of a series of latently nationalizing, but ultimately transcolonial grievances. As Anthony Marx has noted, it is vital to clear about the distinction between nation and state, and the consequent distinction between the nationalist attachment to the nation, and the patriotic attachment to the state:

> Nationalism as a collective sentiment of bounded solidarity or identity may or may not be determined by the institutionalized power of states to which it is or seeks to be tied. It may exist among a populace before or without corresponding states being established, and then it may inspire the attempted creation or reconfiguration of such a state. (2005, 6)

This also echoes Timothy Jenks's argument, that understanding that "[t]he political nation and the patriotic nation were never equivalent" (25) in the eighteenth, and I would add the early nineteenth, century, and may help solve the underly-

18 Despite the argumentative flaws stemming from her initial, and unproven, assumption that American society 'was' a nation from the outset, rather than that Americans could conceive of themselves as belonging to a nation and therefore were apt to conceive of themselves as a separate nation when push came to shove, Greenfeld's argument provides a number of crucial distinctions that some later discussions of American nationalism and national identity have failed to allow. Notably, her point that being 'American' at no point prior to the revolution meant more than a geographical distinction is frequently overlooked.

ing dilemma. Jenks is on the right track, but I would like to follow Marx and Walker Connor in suggesting that it is important to differentiate more strictly between nationalism and patriotism, between the attachment to one's group of common descent and to the state within which one lives. As Connor suggests, "the fundamental dissimilarities between state loyalty and nationalism should not be glossed over by employing the noun nationalism to refer to two quite different phenomena" (2004, 38).[19]

At the same time, however, there is no denying that there existed an interest in promoting the concept of nationality, and that this interest recurred to different practices to further different forms of the nation. As far as dictionary makers are concerned, 'nation' at least meant something fairly concrete, even if it did not mean anything particularly distinct. Where Connor's, Hobsbawm's and Appleby's suggestions of a latent terminological indeterminacy gains most weight is in the various semantic constructions connected with nationality that were used widely in the Early Republic, most specifically national character and national identity.

The Character of American Nationalism, and American National Identity

Contributors to American periodicals in the Early Republic spent much time alternatively arguing one of two points: that Americans possessed a national character and had in fact always possessed one, a national character that specifically differentiated them from their English motherland—whether conceived of in terms of actual character traits, as the blunt *Freeman's Journal* suggested in 1781, arguing that the British, "in their national character [...] are the same brutes and savages they were when Julius Cesar [sic] invaded them" (in *Boston Evening Post* 1781, November 17, 1.5, 4); or merely in point of political reality, as Pennsylvania Governor Thomas McKean emphasized was the case when he noted in 1808 that it had been his "lot to witness the progress of our country, from a colonial to a national character" (*G* 1808, 88). Alternatively, magazines opined that Americans did not possess a national character, and that it was either incumbent upon them to create one or that they were, specifically during the War of 1812, witnessing the creation of such a national character.

But what was national character? The concept harkened back to Montesquieu, who had written in his exhaustive *Spirit of the Laws* (1748) about what he called the "general spirit" that "[m]any things govern men: climate, religion, laws, the maxims of the government, examples of past things, mores, and manners; a general spirit is formed as a result" (Montesquieu 1989, 310). Even in Montesquieu, it was by no means clear that there were clear boundaries between nations, as the Baron also held that there was a general spirit of the *times* (cf. 693); but whatever its precise constitution and delimitations, nobody doubted the national char-

19 Cf. also Connor 1994, 90-117, on the "terminological chaos" which underlies many studies of nationalism.

acter, as it came to be known, existed, and was a crucially part of human social existence. "[E]very people," wrote Jean-Jacques Rousseau in 1765, "has, or must have, a character; if it lacks one, we must start by endowing it with one" (cited in Smith 2001, 27). Its nature was disputed, however. James Boswell quoted Samuel Johnson as saying that "there is no permanent national character: it varies according to circumstances" (1791, 381), and, as Johnson elsewhere noted, could be found only in them "whose aggregate constitutes the people [...] collectively considered" (1801, 232), i.e., not in the elites of the country, but rather the masses and their behavior. "Instructive information concerning the national character" of Americans, the unnamed author of the *Port Folio*'s ambitious overture to a never-completed series on the United States noted in 1802, in extension of Johnson, must come from history, the political constitution of a people, as well as the "general usages of manners, opinions, and sentiments, the modes of social intercourse, the general taste and public amusements, the judicial proceedings and characteristic anecdotes." The *Port Folio* believed in the centrality of the climate and "natural constitution of the country" for shaping the national character (*PF* 1802, 132), just as Hector St. John de Crèvecoeur had. Yet in 1812, on the death of Joseph Dennie, the *Port Folio*'s new editor could assert in Dennie's obituary that "such is the power of a single mind in awakening the talents of a whole nation, so easily may the pliant materials of public opinion be moulded by the plastic hand of genius" (*PF* 1812 1, 187) that Dennie's career had ushered in a new era in American literary history. This may charitably be called an unconsciously dialectic approach to nation and national character, always dependent on one another, but probably highlights more the pliable nature of the idea of national character.

As an analytical term, national character is too deeply situated within a nineteenth century conception of race and national constitution to be of much help. In the following, I will suggest that the concept of a national identity will help us understand more precisely what was happening in American periodicals and biography around the War of 1812. To an extent, as Anthony Smith notes, the contemporary term national identity has merely "replaced earlier terms such as 'national character'" (2001, 17). In saying so, however, it is necessary to add that Americans, too, spoke of national identity in the eighteenth and nineteenth centuries, and did so with a similar broad range of meanings as they did when they addressed the national character. In 1790, in a Congressional debate on the assumption of Confederation debts by the newly-constituted United States, James Madison employed the term national identity to mean the identity between the two successive national governments, at least with regard to its incurrence of debts: the new constitutional government, Madison averred, was a government of the same nation as the old confederate one; accordingly, it must take over national debts, based on the national identity of the its constituents (cf. *AMU* 1790, 466). Identity here meant precisely that: the sheer fact that the same people who constituted the citizens of the original confederation were now the citizens of the Federal republic.

Yet this was not the only way Americans conceived of national identity. In 1803, the *Port Folio* carried a commentary on Talleyrand's memoirs, in which the French foreign minister had apparently derided Americans. The *Port Folio*'s response was scathing, and not a small part of it dealt with what it perceived to be Talleyrand's denial of American identity. Talleyrand, the article suggested, had lambasted the American character in order "to prove that this contemptible character is, in truth, no character at all, or at best, that, in habits, opinions, and attachments, we are English." Indeed, this was probably one and the same: likely Talleyrand, so the Port Folio supposed, meant to say that Americans had no unique character, so that either way, he deemed Americans Englishmen. The *Port Folio* rose to the defense: "This branch of the memoir," it declared, "is most important [...] because if we are English, *we have parted with our national identity*" (*PF* 1803, 251, my emphasis). For the *Port Folio*, then, if national character is not equivalent to national identity, clearly a unique national character *makes* national identity. Unlike Madison, the *Port Folio* suggested that national identity was ephemeral, constituted by distinguishing character traits, a metaphysical conception of an overarching emotional link between the individuals making up the nation.

Other suggestions on national identity made a yet different case: "Obvious radical affinity in language is, in most cases," a correspondent of the *Christian Observer* wrote in March, 1815, "the plainest evidence of national identity" (*CO* 1815, 142; original emphasis); and in 1825, the *Religious Intelligencer*, in an essay on the Araucanian Indians, noted that "no people in the world have, for nearly three centuries, maintained so perfectly their national identity." The *Intelligencer*'s conception of national identity was dependent on ancestry and heritage, which the Araucanians, it was suggested, had always had and "yet retain;" and they defined themselves from the "perfection of the customs handed down" (322). Nor did these customs necessarily need to be native, as *Niles' Weekly Register* noted in 1821:

> I am sensible that attempts have been made to excite great prejudices against the common law, as a barbarous system, and a relict of foreign authority. This law is, however, not otherwise an English system, than as our language, which is an essential part of our national identity, is the English language, or than as the laws of nature are English, because Newton, their great discoverer, was an Englishman. (*WR* 1821, 218)

What must be clear from the discussion above is that there cannot be a sensible discussion of American nationalism on the basis of contemporary conceptions of 'nation' and its derivatives—not even of national identity, which, as I will argue, offers the clearest idea of what American biographies did during the War of 1812. Nor does it seem likely that the answer of how American nationalism was 'truly' constituted, allowing us to answer such questions as Susan-Mary Grant's "when was" the American nation, or even Liah Greenfeld's "what was, or whether there was" an American nation, will ever be satisfactorily answered. In fact, there seems very little reason to worry about the truth of Walker Connor's slightly provocative single-word answer to the question, "[i]s there an American [...] nation? No" (2004, 37). A different definition of nation from Connor's would have resulted in a different answer. What is interesting is not, in fact, the question of the existence of the nation, but rather the process of its mediation.

Anthony Giddens has suggested a four-fold division for any account of nationalism: between political character, ideological characteristics, psychological dynamics, and symbolic content (cf. 1985, 215-6); what I will be discussing below is exclusively symbolical in the sense that Giddens proposes:

> Whatever their differences, nationalist ideals tend to tie a conception of the 'homeland'—a concept of territoriality, in other words—to a myth of origin, conferring cultural autonomy upon the community which is held to be the bearer of these ideals. (216)

It is precisely this myth of origin that features most prominently in the discussion of national identity offered by Anthony Smith. As Smith has noted, "the sense of 'whence we came' is central to the definition of 'who we are:'" the mythical histories of descent, the "myths of common ancestry" (1991, 22), shape national identity. For Smith, what he calls a "Western" conception of national identity is constituted by some form of political community as well as a form of homeland. This homeland, Smith emphasizes, does not have to be the land of origin—rather, it needs to be regarded as a place where "terrain and people have exerted mutual, and beneficial, influence over several generations" and which becomes a "repository of historic memories and associations" (1991, 9). Smith's own preference is for an ethnic conception of national identity, constituted not by territory but by descent; in this, the "nation is seen as a fictive 'super-family', and it boasts pedigrees and genealogies to back up its claims" (10). His suggestion is that national identity must necessarily contain elements of both of those points of view: on the one hand territorially bounded and constituted as a polity, on the other hand aware of presumed ethnic and genealogical commonalities of descent. Crucially, it is "myths of common ancestry, not any fact of ancestry" (22) that is the basis of ethnic and genealogical identification: such myths, of course, had their own origins in the imaginary, or alternatively in historical memories played up sufficiently to form the core of a common identification with them.[20]

20 In the terminology of recent critical theory, such a reading of the 'nation' and its various cognates might be analogous to 'empty signifiers'. Although not as such part of nationalist theory, Ernesto Laclau's notion of the empty signifier may be a helpful idea to keep in mind here. It is probably unnecessary to go into the structuralist and psychoanalytical considerations underlying Laclau's idea. In Laclau's example, a society resembling the Hobbesian 'state of nature' needs 'order.' But the term 'order' does not in and of itself signify anything–there is no universally apparent 'order' to be striven for. Instead, the empty signifier 'order,' which merely signifies a number of disparate lacks in the existing social fabric, can be subscribed to by any party in the struggle for a change in the existing situation, whatever their *particular* desire for change and conception of consequent 'order' (cf. Laclau 2007, 43-5). This severe shortening of Laclau's argument does not do it full justice, of course, especially because it ignores the political implications of the empty signifier, certainly Laclau's main concern. But it will serve to illustrate the connection with nationalism: as Laclau notes, the role of the empty signifier can be filled by "[a]ny term which, in a certain political context, becomes the signifier of the lack" (44).

Whatever the ontological status of nation: national identity means to identify oneself with a certain number of fundamental features: a homeland, common myths of origin and historical memories, a common public culture, legal rights, and a common economy (cf. Smith 1991, 14).[21] 'National' identity is one of many identities which individuals may assume and which they may simultaneously have. Periodically throughout the nineteenth century the centrality of American national identity was challenged by the particular interests of sections, individual states, and individual persons, all of which, in addition to religious, to class, and to gendered identity, Americans found they at one time or the other could foreground (cf. Elwert 1995 for a take on switching situationally between various "we-groups").[22] These shifts were momentary and contingent.

21 Smith's emphasis on national symbolisms, "a repertoire of shared values, symbols, and traditions" (16) and the mythic, rather than actual, nature of the genealogical ties presumed by nationalist endeavors, is what I would like to emphasize here. Smith's premordialist impulse to declare that "the idea that nations exist from time immemorial" (19) is problematical, however, and I do not wish to be understood to make any such claim. Smith's argument (and Anthony Giddens's argument above) is a useful corrective, however, to Ernest Gellner's modernist assertion that "the actual formulation of the idea or ideas" of nationalist endeavors "doesn't matter much" (2006, 121). The modernist suggestion, as outlined by Gellner, that nationalism "springs directly and inevitably from basic changes in our shared social condition, from changes in the overall relation between society, culture and polity" (119), and that the precise ideologies purportedly existing among nationalist movements are of no impact on the final outcome may or may not, empirically, be true; it does not allow us to understand, at any rate, the processes of negotiation of nationalism and national identity which certainly took place.

22 Indeed, as John Murrin notes, the Revolution had created "two distinct polities: the United States and Canada," and a "century later the Civil War nearly added a third" (1987, 334). Up to the Civil War, efforts to nationalize the political union, that is to foreground the national identity of the people in the Union over the mere conventional union of the polity, competed with efforts to dismantle the union from political expediency; if the Hartford Convention's readiness to suggest New England secession in 1814 has been overemphasized, the subsequent political turmoil surrounding the Missouri Compromise of 1820, the Nullification Crisis of 1832, the Compromise of 1850, and finally the secession of the Southern states in the aftermath of Abraham Lincoln's election, point to the fragility of national sentiment. The Civil War highlights how easily any incipient nationalist feeling could be overcome, even as the political idea of the Federal Union stayed powerful throughout. It was the political bonds through a common government that American and Southern revolutionaries in 1776 and 1860 found easy to sever, unhindered by too rigid attachments to a common national idea; and it was the partners in that union, rather than the co-nationals, which Horace Greeley famously spoke about when he said that "[i]f the Cotton States shall become satisfied that they can do better out of the Union than in it, we insist on letting them go" (in McPherson 1988, 252). It was patriotism, the attachment to the Union, which made Northerners take the field against the South; and conversely, it was the belief that there was nothing to tie the South to the North but the Lockean social contract, subject to revocation, which allowed Southerners to justify their secession from the political

Naval heroes offered American writers the opportunity to establish this ethnic nationalist moment, to create "authentic, native historical moments" (Smith 2001, 86, in Connor 2004, 37) capable of figuring as incipient myths from which to date the creation of an American national identity. Americans already were largely in agreement about their shared name, the extent of their territory, which if not historic was certainly rather firmly established by 1812, and they had a shared legal and public culture which bound them into a polity. What I will argue is that the biographies I have selected contest the particulars of the common myths of origin and offer different national genealogies. The War of 1812, with its rekindling of the conflict with Great Britain, permitted the voicing of a variety of approaches to national genealogy, from the admission of lasting genealogical ties with the mother country to a complete denial of such a transatlantic family history and the development of an autochthonous national origin in the War of 1812 itself. To understand the novelty of this sustained approach through biography, it is necessary to briefly retrace the history of previous endeavors to do so, and to highlight their ultimate shared fate: failure.

American Biography Revisited

Twice during the 1790s and then in the early 1800s, as we saw in Chapter 2, Joseph Dennie had sought his readers with great emphasis to supply American biography. The quest for American biography as I have outlined it in all its vicissitudes played out similarly in other magazines throughout the period. "[W]e have solicited for [American biography], now, nearly four months, but in vain [...] if we have no American *biography* sent to us, in the course of this month, we shall be under the disagreeable necessity of proclaiming, that all the people, in *this* country, *are dead*" (*MR* 1807 1, 253, original emphasis), wrote Stephen Carpenter, the New York *Monthly Register*'s often-mercurial editor, in January 1807. Inadvertently punning on bios in his exasperated philippic against his unsuspecting (and largely undeserving!) subscribers, by 1807 he was only the most recent of a number of magazine editors whose plans for American lives had foundered on the disinterest of his contributors. Carpenter had only recently moved the *Monthly Register* from its original location in Charleston, South Carolina, to the bustling metropolis of New York, finding the south to be inimical to the success of his magazine. Settled in the city, Carpenter had made clear that while he absolutely assumed the desirability of American biography for his magazine, the production of such texts he would leave wholly to the wherewithal of his correspondents: the fourth section of the *Register*

Union. Against this tendency for political separation stood ongoing efforts to nationalize the polity, efforts which found their expression during the War of 1812 in different contestations of national identity in periodical biographies of naval and military officers. The goal of the next section is to uncover the rhetorical strategies by which biographers of naval officers in the Early Republic sought to give shapes to the elusive concept of the nation.

he would have consist of "Communications from correspondents, consisting of anecdotes, scarce and valuable American biography" (*MR* 1807 1, 2), this section being the only one explicitly reserved for outside contributions. Against this background, Carpenter's surprise and dismay about not being offered biographical texts for his magazine may be considered slightly excessive, but Carpenter was giving voice to a problem which almost all of the magazines who sought out American biography in the first decade of the nineteenth century faced.

The *Monthly Register* never got around in its final year of existence (it folded late in 1807) to publish any kind of biography, whether American or not, and as far as American biography was concerned, few of its competitors had any more luck. The anti-Unitarian Boston *Panoplist* stepped out of its religious doctrinarianism to comment, in December of 1808, in its emendations of the previous years' articles, on American biography. "We are not satisfied," it noted, "that the American publisher takes sufficient pains to obtain American biography" (*PN* 1808, 321), an analysis no doubt owed less to its intimate knowledge of the exertions undertaken by its fellow magazines and the Republic's book publishers, but rather the evident lack of results: few American biographies were in circulation. Publishers' exertions were not wholly to be blamed for this lack, however. As early as 1788, Matthey Carey's *Columbian Magazine* carried a series of American lives, explicitly designed to remember and celebrate "the lives and characters of the founders of these American States" (*CM* 1788, 2.1, 3), written by Jeremy Belknap. Belknap only managed to write three lives, called the "American Plutarch," before the series stopped again. This was the usual phenomenon encountered by all of the series of American lives before the War of 1812. Especially when conceived as running explicitly under the header "American Biography" or its derivatives, none of the series managed to produce more than four or five lives of distinguished Americans. Editors squarely laid responsibility for this problem—when they conceived of it as a problem in the first place—at the feet of their contributors. Joseph Dennie, like Carpenter, saw the lack of American biography as a failure. While the regular changes from one set of lives to another was always framed as a matter of offering his readership greater variety, his lack of American biographies stung the editor severely. Evidently, readers did not often share editors' belief that Americans required the lives of their illustrious compatriots, at least not to the extent of being driven to supply such lives.

There was a disconnection, evidently, between the variously expressed editorial desire to publish American biography and the readership's lukewarm response. In 1804, the *Monthly Anthology* of Boston began the publication of a series called "Biographia Americana," communications for which, it emphasized, "will be extremely acceptable to the Editor" (*MA* 1804, 458). The biographees included a wide and disjointed range of men from William Penn to the recently deceased Harvard professor David Tappan, and by and large were difficult to call biography: the life of Penn was a mere half-column in length, a character sketch only, and filled up considerable space with a letter reprinted from the London *Mirror of the Times* (cf. *MA* 1804, 458-9). The *Anthology* did not receive any original submissions on the topic, and was reduced to copying from British and American newspapers and magazines, a fact not lost on its correspondents, who complained loudly, even as they did not supply original texts themselves. The biography of General Richard Montgomery, wrote "Historicus" in a letter published in November 1804, was "more adapted to fill a column of a newspaper, than to be preserved in a work valuable for its biographical sketches" (*MA* 1804, 591); in reply, "Clemens" wrote, in a note published a month later, that the biographical sketch of Montgomery read like it was more suitable for a newspaper because it came from a newspaper: "You acknowledged that you took the sketch, because you quoted it, from a newspaper, and I suppose, were glad to find it any where" (*MA* 1804, 638). There is little doubt that "Clemens" lightly spoke a striking truth: not only did the *Anthology*'s series depend on outside material, none of its sources supplied more than one biography, making almost any source desirable and rare, no matter how offensive to its readers. American biography was a tedious business. The *Monthly Anthology*'s seven short, newspaper-worthy lives of Americans was in fact the high-point of its experience with American biography. In 1807, as part of a modest reorganization of the magazine, the *Anthology* announced again that it "hope[d] to furnish American Biography" (*MA* 1807, 4)—it ended up publishing none. In 1810, the short-lived New York *Theophilanthropist*, praising the genre's ability to inculcate the wisdom of the sages in its readers, concluded a brief note on biography with its own hopes to further the cause: "We shall in future numbers endeavor correctly to delineate the biography and character of some of the most conspicuous American patriots" (*TH* 1810, 78). Before the magazine concluded its run in September, it had not published a single item in this category.

The only thing as frequent as calls for American biography in magazines of the Early Republic, to put it slightly facetiously, was the failure to publish any. American biography as a separately-named genre, but also as a descriptive category for the kinds of biography published in periodicals, remained an exceedingly minor factor. The *Repository and Ladies' Weekly Museum*, in reprinting the *Polyanthos*'s sketch of Jeremy Belknap in March 1806, tagged onto the text the headline "American Biography," but made no effort to make a series of this category, reducing it to look like an altogether haphazard idea. The question of how Americans perceived American biography, what they believed it should be like and why it should be written, becomes somewhat less important when one realizes that American lives written by American authors and published in American magazines were a vanishingly small subset of the huge number of biographies published otherwise.

Even what little 'American' biography existed (in books or magazine articles) was rarely national in the sense that it described men or women who served as more than local heroes. William Wirt's letter to Dabney Carr cited in an epigram in Scott Casper's *Constructing American Lives* is instructive here. While Casper suggests that there existed a "multifaceted effort to create a national identity and culture" through a rhetoric of "national assertion" (1999, 19, 21), Wirt's comments highlight "the honor of the state" (19)—Virginia!—rather than suggesting a truly national perspective of American biography. By January 1817, after the War of 1812 had concluded, the dichotomy between nation and state shone forth again prominently in biographical sketches. The Baltimore-based *Portico* prefaced a biography of Colonel Jacob Hindman noting that it had promised "Biographical sketches of some of our distinguished Officers." What it meant by 'our' in this endeavor became clear a sentence later: "Maryland has borne an ample share" in the war, and "our fellow-citizens of that state will participate, in the satisfaction which it affords us, to be enabled to commence this series, with one of her most distinguished sons" (*PO* 1817 1, 38). The *Portico* published the life of another Marylander in March, after which the "series" ceased. In the waning of the nationalizing experience of the War of 1812, the *Portico*'s concern for its Maryland-based readership finds its expression precisely in the re-affirmation that 'our' could mean the state's. As my argument will develop more fully in the following, Wirt's and the *Portico*'s stances towards a preference of the state over the nation are bookends to an upswing of national American biography centered on the War of 1812.

If, from time to time, articles on Americans written by Americans appeared in various magazines—the *Polyanthos*, the *Port Folio*, and others—other forms of biography prevailed over the 'genuinely' American. Thus, the *Polyanthos*, which reliably printed biography in its first run 1806-7, and which had so clearly emphasized the suitability of the genre for periodicals, found itself obliged in early 1807 to lament the insurmountable difficulties of providing readers with the kind of biography it wished to offer, and ended up, instead of providing its readership with original communications of American worthies, with the common hodgepodge of British-written and published lives reprinted with editorial commentary emphasizing their usefulness (cf. P 1807 1, 146). Only the *Port Folio*'s post-1809 volumes did sustained work in American lives (cf. ch. 2). Between 1807, when both the *Monthly Register* and the *Monthly Anthology* failed in their quest for American biography, and 1812 when the war finally revived a moribund genre, American biography—whether marked as such, or merely to be defined as such by its content—did not manage to really get off the ground. Certainly it did not manage to monopolize itself in the biographical discourse: its place was as one subset among the entirety of the lives published in American magazines, rather than in a privileged place that would bespeak an interest in the promotion, specifically, of American nationalism. Religious magazines highlighted their cosmopolitan worldview by publishing the lives of divines no matter their nationality; literary journals advanced their biographical sections with lives of Shakespeare and Goldsmith. The point here is not that American magazines published no American lives, but rather that, apart from the *Port Folio*, few magazines undertook a sustained effort to provide their readers with a genuinely American biography, and if they did so, they found themselves hamstrung by a pronounced lack of interest.

The eventual (re-)turn to American biography was not one which was based on the ideologies of editors any more than the previous attempts at establishing the genre had been. Indeed, it is fair to say that it was not based on editorial decisions at all. Rather, American biography's resurgence had its origin in the

War of 1812, the upsurge of patriotic, and indeed, nationalistic feelings engendered by the war in those sections of the populace who subscribed to the magazines that successfully established series of American biography, and, last but not least, a new ascension to considerable authority over content by the periodical publishers. As American biography went through its ups and downs in the early decades of the Republic, it highlighted the limits of its symbolic potential for national identity. "[N]ationalist sentiments tend to surge and decline; they are not so much a part of regular day-to-day social life as those symbols connected with smaller groups," suggests Anthony Giddens (1985, 215). Much of the nationalist potential of biography was actually an after-effect of an already far more receptive state: biography was capable of contesting different forms of national identity only at those moments, and only became viable at those moments, when external influences made for a receptive audience. This is especially true of periodical literature: it could not produce the condition under which readers would accept nationalist biography. Rather, it could only *be* produced with a nationalist cast when the conditions were already ripe for the reception of such nationalizing texts. What it could do, however, was take up the new context and attempt to inscribe its own interpretation of the prevalent national sentiments. It is within this new role of the national hero that I propose to read periodical biography: as the "single most powerful device for fabricating a strong sense of nationhood in a hurry" (Zelinsky 1988, 39), the biography of military and naval officers, themselves already quite directly in the service of the nation, paid by the national government and, despite the various accusations that their service benefitted one or the other regional or social division more than the other, was eminently suitable for fostering the idea of the nation. The War of 1812 suddenly offered a chance to actively promote a new national pantheon, specifically in order to unite the entire Union behind men who, by virtue of having spent so much time on the literally bound(ary)less oceans, had been effaced from regional and state affiliations. As will become evident later, in many cases American military and naval biographers seem to have quite consciously sought to turn their biographees into avatars of the nation, as symbolic representations of a new-found national unity. In this, the biographies, especially those of the *Analectic Magazine*, exceeded the limited goal of writing heroes' lives for an audience that desired them. If reacting to the a newly-heightened patriotism was a sound business decision—especially for any magazine which disavowed party spirit—and often indeed grounded in business, it was also an opportunity to offer diverse readings of what American nationalism could be founded on, and what it could be like. Recognizing the momentary interest in the exploits of national heroes, publishers were ready to exploit the opportunity by playing to the audience's interests, and thus the market's wishes, and thereby granted authors an opportunity to exercise their limited autonomy in the production process of the Early Republic periodical. The two most prominent examples for the editorial subservience to the considerations of the proprietors which pulled their strings in the background are the two leading magazines of their day, the *Port Folio* and the *Analectic Magazine*.

The War of 1812 and the Progress of Naval Biography

In September 1813, the *The Port Folio* published a biography of James Lawrence, an American naval officer who had died on June 1st in the first frigate action that the U.S. Navy had lost during the war. His death and the lost fight had occasioned much mourning, and the *Port Folio* was not alone in deeming it "a national duty… to contribute our efforts to extend and perpetuate" Lawrence's "fame" (*PF* 1813 2, 235). Yet what the *Port Folio* produced was more than biography. It kept its reportage of Lawrence's life before the War of 1812 short, extensively reported on the action itself, and commented on proper behavior in wartime. Most strikingly, however, it meditated on American national origins and offered a vision of American national identity. The article denied that any damage to American pride could result from the loss of Lawrence and his ship; far from it, indeed, because the defeat, bought at great cost for the British, could not efface earlier victories: "even a series of naval losses now cannot control" the recognition that "in all the qualities essential to success on the ocean, the American seamen are not equal, but superior to the British seamen" (254). The reason for this was simply Americans' habitat: "Nature and circumstances have made them so […]. The warm and variable climate of the United States has, to a certain degree, melted the original English constitution of our ancestors" and produced a different "race" of men. This new American man still derived, the *Port Folio* suggested, genealogically from the English, but he had been changed by his new habitat into a superior specimen. Three years later, James Kirke Paulding, in a biography of Commodore Thomas Macdonough written for the *Analectic Magazine*, would offer a radically different take: here, the transatlantic journey has effaced, if not the fact of English ancestry, then certainly its relevance in a new national mythology. "[F]ew of us can trace our ancestry," writes Paulding, but no matter: "obliged to build up a name for ourselves," Americans are forced to invent their own origins and their own original heroes, particularly the naval officers of the War of 1812.

Dozens of original biographies of American naval officers appeared during the time from early 1813 through 1817, monographs, anthologies, and single essays in periodicals. While some attention has been paid to the monographs, studies of biography as well as of the War of 1812 have passed over the biographical work done in periodicals or dismissed it as intellectually minor. Usually, such attention as the texts have received was usually more owed to their authors than to themselves. The biographies are regarded as thoroughly conventional and unequivocal statements in a continuity of American nationalist assertion. Such a view, however, fails to fully appreciate either the production conditions of the texts or the texts themselves. Not by chance does the discussion of nationalism during the War of 1812 involve an interaction between the periodical form, the genre of biography, and Navy (and Army) officers as biographees. In the periodical biographies produced for and printed in magazines from 1812 until the years immediately after the War of 1812—up until 1816 at least—publisher's concerns for making money off of the popular figures of naval, and somewhat later also army, heroes, editors' concern with navigating the often difficult waters of popular opinion between their own editorial policies and the feelings of the populace, and authors' abilities to make periodical biographies more than mere lives of famous men combined to produce a literature that created competing conceptions of American national identity.

I am not trying to argue, however, that any of the rhetorical strategies which American periodicals adopted in their naval and military biographies around the War of 1812 can be read with causal relationships in mind that would establish what effects these texts had on the political development of the United States. The point is not whether or not these texts actually ended up 'creating' or 'influencing' a national identity—or indeed, to what extent national identity is a suitable concept to talk about the Early Republic at all, that is to say, whether it is valid to speak of contemporary Americans as conceiving of themselves in terms of national identity. Rather, I intend to investigate what these texts do—what ideas about America and Americans they propagate, how they create them, and what the significance of these ideas is as elements of a particular rhetoric, rather than as causes of fundamental changes in American identity. The most relevant aspect of these statements, whether in the form of text or engraving, is not their ultimate effect but that they were made at all, and the way in which they fit into the production context of periodicals as a whole. Rhetorically, the brilliant stroke which almost all of these texts insisted upon was that Americans' accession to British glory, whether on a par with Britain or actually in excess of Britain's, was irreversible. They simply claimed victory upon a narrowed field—the frigate actions of 1812 and 1813, and the victories on the lakes—and then expanded their view again to claim these victories' symbolism for a more general American ascendancy, against which they declared the British essentially helpless. Rather than accepting that they would have to reaffirm, over and over, their new found ascendancy, thereby compromising their independence, the periodicals took for granted that once Americans had shown that they could beat the Royal Navy, they needed no longer feel inferior in any field.

It is specifically in this use of periodical biography that the relative autonomy of the genre, under the right circumstances, manifests itself. Nothing in the heteronomous demands on the genre, whether such demands were external to the periodical—such as public demand—or internal—such as those made by publishers on editors and by editors on their contributors—necessitated the writing of such complex meditations on American national identity as the texts which the *Analectic Magazine*, especially, produced. In the field of periodical production, therefore, editors and authors could shift their position towards the autonomous pole at least a little. This opportunity produced remarkable texts, but it remains necessary to stress that their autonomy was relative: they could not, despite the praise which was heaped on them, ultimately prevail in creating an ongoing interest in nationalization when the mood of periodical consumers shifted back to more pedestrian concerns in the aftermath of the War of 1812.

Naval Biography and the British-American Conflict

For a number of reasons, naval officers were well suitable for the nationalizing impulses suddenly prevalent with the beginning of the War of 1812. Certainly, the most important single reason was their success: unlike the struggling U.S. Army, which had opened the campaign season 1812 with the most ignoble defeats on the Northwestern frontier, the Navy had surprised most by repeatedly gaining signal victories over the seemingly invincible Royal Navy, a force which was not only vastly larger than the U.S. Navy, but looked back on a string of victorious naval wars going back for centuries. As Joseph Dennie had commented in the *Farmer's Weekly Museum* in 1798,

> [i]n nautical skill and glory on the ocean, no nation has rivaled England: Her marine officers, with few exceptions, have ever deserved and received the general applause of their countrymen. From the time of Elizabeth, the first dawn of Britain's maritime greatness, to the reign of the present majesty, a series of gallant admirals has convinced hostile fleets of the impenetrability of that 'wooden wall,' the firm rampart of a favoured Island. (*FWM* 1798, 6.294, 1)

Since that time, the Royal Navy had only added to its luster, sweeping the Revolutionary and Napoleonic French fleets away at the Battle of the Nile and at Trafalgar, and establishing itself as the uncontested ruler of the oceans (cf. Mostert 2009).

It was therefore hardly surprising that at the beginning of the war, Secretary of State James Monroe had advocated retaining the fleet in port; the most the Madison administration was prepared to countenance was the creation of two squadrons to protect its own coastal commerce, which was also the most Secretary of the Navy Paul Hamilton was willing to actively support (cf. Borneman 2004, 80; Ellis 2009, 4). Against all odds and all the administration's desire, the Navy's victories had resounded all the more forcefully, and, perhaps more importantly, they were impossible to ignore or brush aside. The *Analectic Magazine*'s biography of Captain Lewis Warrington, published a year after the conclusion of the war, observed as much in its opening paragraphs. "We have selected," it noted, "the distinguished officers of our navy as subjects for biography, not only because they naturally came under the notice of this work [the *Analectic Magazine* carried the additional title "*and Naval Chronicle*" during 1816], but because their actions are not liable to doubt or misconstruction, and their victories when gained are unquestionable." Whereas in battles on land, doubts might remain as to who had carried the victory, at sea, "no denial, or opposite claim, on the part of the beaten enemy" (*AM* 1816 1, 8) could negate the fact that he had had a ship captured from him, or sunk, or, alternatively, that both ships remained afloat and under their own banners, thus making the fight a draw. Of course, American and British newspapers and magazines engaged, instead of debating the reality of victories, in disputes over their meaning; American magazines' ingenious solution to the question of what American victories meant will engage us in detail below.

The second way in which naval biographies were suitable to reflect national identity formation was that naval issues had played a critical role in the run up to war, both with regards to foreign policy as well as domestic politics. The political struggle between Republicans and Federalists was reflected in their conceptions of the role of the navy. The navy's huge overhead made the taxation-wary Republicans seek it out as an ideal target for spending reductions. Thomas Jefferson's first administration proposed major cuts in expenditure to reduce the federal union's debt when it came into office in 1801. Finances and politics combined to lead the Democrat-Republicans to seek cost savings in the armed forces. They laid up the ocean-going frigates which had been the U.S. Navy's mainstay in the Quasi-War with France, at once reducing spending and advancing the anti-navalist cause, with Jefferson himself seeking "such a naval force only as may protect our coasts and harbors from such depredations as we have experienced; and not [...] a navy, which, by its own expenses and the eternal wars in which it will implicate us, will grind us with public burthens, and sink us under them" (in Toll 2006, 162).[23] By the beginning of his second term in office, Jefferson's administration sought the construction, instead of the large frigates, of a force of local gunboats, capable of service inshore, but incapable of involving the U.S. in transatlantic adventures. Federalists were aghast and remained so (cf. Toll 2006, 280-7). In February 1807, Thomas Green Fessenden's Federalist *Weekly Inspector* thundered: "Where, my fellow-citizens, is our once highly respected national character? Where the applause and respectability once attached to the name of an American citizen? *Where its once flourishing navy*? Sold and dispersed, in dry docks, and pop-guns and rattles introduced as a substitute" (*WI* 1807, 270, my emphasis). In March, the *Inspector* approvingly printed a "spirited" resolution put forward by a Federalist Congressman: "Resolved," the text reads,

> that from the want of such protection to the valuable and extensive commerce of the United States, property has already been permitted to be violently and unjustly captured from our enterprising merchants, and to the essential injury of our national revenue, not only on the high seas, but to the disgrace of our national character, in the vicinity of our coast, in the mouths of our harbours, by foreign armed vessels, to an amount that would have furnished a navy capable of effectually guarding our coast and saving our useful and respectable race of seaman from foreign impressment, and of commanding respect from all foreign nations. (*WI* 1807, 59)

23 In fairness to the Democrat-Republicans, it must be said that the original downsizing of the fleet had been ordered by the outgoing Adams administration. Jefferson had found himself interested in using transatlantic naval force to force the Barbary States to abandon their privations of American commerce in the Mediterranean, a fairly successful but immensely costly venture (cf. Toll 2006, 170-253), and had acceded to the necessity of keeping frigates present even after concluding peace with Tripoli (cf. Maloney 1986, 115). But more important than those facts is the political perception of Jefferson's policies.

Federalists actively tied Jeffersonian anti-navalism to anti-nationalism. This fundamental domestic political dispute came into even starker relief when read in the international context. In June 1807, H.M.S. *Leopard* fired upon and boarded the U.S. frigate U.S.S. *Chesapeake* and forced her to surrender four sailors which had recently escaped from British service and enlisted in the American. Federalist publications again voiced their disgust at the consequences of Jeffersonian naval policy for the national character. The *Monthly Register*, discussing Thomas Moore's review of American literature, used the opportunity in July 1807 to simultaneously defend George Washington and bash the Jeffersonian gunboat policy: "[O]ur present ministry have done quite the reverse of all that Washington did,—they have destroyed our navy, annihilated the American naval flag—weakened the resources and lowered the spirit of the people" (MR 1807, 103). Throughout the following five years, it was the Royal Navy's readiness to utilize its material superiority and control of the seas to the fullest that irked Americans. In 1811, the *Little Belt* incident, in which a U.S. warship had fired on a weaker British vessel, once more brought the two nations to the brink of war. Seaborne trade, too, was an issue: The British orders in council hindering American trade with France, reflecting British disregard for neutral rights at sea, and enforced by the Royal Navy, irked American merchants and administrators alike.

All three of these issues were connected with the greatest American grievance towards the British: impressment. The British, hard-pressed for seamen in their ongoing war with Napoleonic France, claimed the right to seize British subjects from American ships for service in the Royal Navy. Since they did not recognize the possibility of relinquishing British subjecthood, this regularly meant that they seized American nationals. American naval officer biographies during the War of 1812 explicitly picked up on the question of impressment as critical elements in the individual identity of the officers they talked about, a feature most notable in Washington Irving's biography of John Cushing Aylwin, which I will discuss briefly below. Personalizing the problem of impressment in a figure capable of offering a martial model, a national icon, for the readership of the *Analectic Magazine*, allowed biography to suggest a broader national significance to Aylwin's own quest to repay the insult of impressment with the injury of defeating the British at sea. By the War of 1812, the "war within the war" (Taylor 2010, 176) between the moribund Federalist Party and the ascendant Democrat-Republicans, territorialized in a Federalist New England, a Republican South, and a small number of battleground states in between effectively precluded a closer national tie between the opposing factions.

The naval heroes of the War of 1812 could stand as national icons in a way that the post-Washington generation of politicians could not. Amongst the men whom Wilbur Zelinsky lists as being part of the "second generation of heroes," the names of naval officers Stephen Decatur and Oliver Hazard Perry stand out. Men such as Albert Gallatin, John Marshall, and John Calhoun, also listed by Zelinsky, could perhaps represent aspects of the "character of the rising nation" (43), but their political roles precluded their use as genuinely national icons. The

American experience squared, in this regard, with the British. The "internal complexities of […] political culture […] worked to prevent any easy process of heromaking, and any simple experience of patriotic culture" (301), Timothy Jenks has noted for the British. Not surprisingly, victorious Republicans, interested in putting the war in the best possible light, after the war emphasized the struggle's importance for American nationhood. President Monroe suggested that the "Union has gained strength […] and the nation character, by the contest" (in Taylor 2010, 420); the former Secretary of the Treasury, Albert Gallatin, commented in an 1816 letter to Matthew Lyon that "[t]he war has renewed and reinstated the national feelings and character which the Revolution had given, and which were daily lessened. The people have now more general objects of attachment with which their pride and political opinions are connected. They are more American; they feel and act more as a nation" (Gallatin 1960, 700). If so, however, it was a peculiar nationhood, one almost solely based on party unity, an 'Era of Good Feelings,' in which the demise of the Federalist Party papered over, for a very short time (until the disputes leading to the Missouri Compromise), the fragility of the national idea in the United States (cf. Howe 2007, 124, 147-163).

Certainly a figure as divisive as Albert Gallatin could hardly have been expected to become a contemporary national icon. Indeed, when the Republican leadership spoke of the nation, party echoed through their conceptions. Thomas Jefferson was perhaps the most prominent Republican when he wrote to Philadelphia editor William Duane in March 1811. Seeking to emphasize the necessity of unity to the "friends of the country," he noted that "[i]f we schismatize on either men or measures, if we do not act in phalanx […] I will not say our *party,* the term is false and degrading, but our *nation* will be undone. For the republicans are the *nation*" (Jefferson 1853, 576, original emphasis). The war helped Republicans by furthering this conception of a party-less United States. By the outbreak of the war, Republicans had become convinced that the honor and survival of the nation had become indivisible from the honor and survival of their party, and conversely assumed that a Federalist revival would ultimately result in a revocation of the Revolution (cf. Hickey 1989, 27; Wood 2009, 668-70). Madison and Gallatin were thus celebrating the triumphant vindication of the Republican party as much as a genuine nationalization of the "loose confederation of regions" (Taylor 2010, 138) which had begun the war in 1812. Indeed, the war had brought the political Union close to the breaking point. "In late 1814," Alan Taylor notes, "national dissolution seemed plausible because Royal Navy commanders were already pressuring vulnerable American coastal communities to drop out of the war" (2010, 415). But December's Treaty of Ghent, ratified by Congress in March, ended the struggle before the stability of the union could truly be put to the test, and news of the successful Battle of New Orleans effectively killed New England's latent anti-union aspirations. As Stephen Budiansky has summarized the political landscape in which the naval victories became so notably capable of providing unexpected national rallying points: "[T]he Federalists had opposed the war, the Republicans had opposed the navy, and so the one thing they could agree on after it was all over was how gloriously the tiny American navy had triumphed" (2010, xi). "Americanus," a correspondent of the *Analectic Magazine*, wrote editor Thomas Wharton in 1816 that the magazine's national cast was severely disturbed by a biography of Senator James Bayard in a previous volume, a biography which was "tinged with strong party feeling" (*AM* 1816 1, 422). To "Americanus," the *Analectic Magazine*'s apparent reputation as a national publication depended, then, in large part on its refusal of party: "Let the Analectic Magazine aspire to preserve the reputation of being a national work—devoted to support the national honour—to advocate the national interest—to correct the national taste—and to inspire a nationality of feeling" (424).

Finally, unlike the Army, whose fighting strength and numbers was not in its regular component, a force of only about 7000 men (cf. Wood 2009, 659), but rather in the state militias that were federalized in the course of the war, the Navy was already something of a national force.[24] In the selection of its officer corps, the Navy Department had a formal requirement for fair geographical distribution of appointments, an endeavor which "implied an active attempt to encourage applications from states and regions that might be underrepresented" (McKee 1991, 44). If in the end, owing to a shortage of applications from New England and Western states, the actual officer corps tended towards favoring sailors from the middle states, especially Maryland, Pennsylvania, and Virginia, this did not diminish the basic understanding of the Navy as a national force. This national role for the Navy, as Christopher McKee has noted, spurred "the country's imagination" in the course of the War of 1812: "the enhanced sense of national identity" (65), and, consequent upon the war, resulted in an upsurge of requests for midshipmen's warrants from regions hitherto underrepresented, allowing the Navy Department to balance out its enlistments (cf. 59-65).

And fourthly, as Washington Irving put it in the biographical sketch of Oliver Hazard Perry, naval victories and the officer with whom they were at all times connected were peculiarly suitable to the requirements of periodicals, and in more way than one. "There is [...] a distinctness of character about a naval victory, that meets the capacity of every mind," he suggested; and, not content with an as yet not insulting formulation, elaborated that

> there is such a simple unity in it; it is so well defined; so complete within itself; so rounded by space; so free from those intricacies and numerous parts that perplex us in an action on land, that the meanest intellect can fully grasp and comprehend it. And then, too, the results are so apparent; a victory on land is liable to a thousand

24 Russell F. Weigley, in his seminal study *A History of the United States Army*, gives the authorized strength of the U.S. Army at the beginning of the war as 35.000 and its as-is strength as 6,686, with an additional 30,000 Federal volunteers (that is to say, to reinforce the Regular Army) and 80,000 militia to be called up for Federal service by Congressional authorization. These authorized strengths were never reached. The Army's regular complement remained below 20,000 men by all counts, and at its height the Army's strength was 38,000 men; cf. Weigley 1967, 118-9, 566.

> misrepresentations; retreat is often called falling back, and abandoning the field called taking a new position; so that the conqueror is often defrauded of half the credit of his victory; but the capture or destruction of a ship is not to be mistaken, and a squadron towed triumphantly into port, is a notorious fact that admits of no contradiction. (*AM* 1813 2, 506).

Easily interpreted and neatly compact in description, naval victories, even if there were a choice of land battles as well, were eminently suitable for a medium that had long recognized the nature of its readers and their unwillingness to invest too much intellectual energy in their reading, and it was in reading in general, too, that the contestation of national identity could truly come to the fore.

Despite all the obvious benefits which the naval forces of the United States had as carriers of a message of national identity, and despite the enormous length of the eastern seaboard, and the large number of people who lived in coastal cities, still the Navy may never have managed to become a focal point of nationalizing interest if not for magazines and newspapers. For a country in which something like 90% of people were farmers, where rural towns and single farms dominated the few larger cities on the coast, and knowledge of the sea must have been severely limited in the majority of the population, it may be considered strange to suggest any ambitions to read American national identity through naval officers. Yet, as Timothy Jenks's analysis of the role of the Royal Navy in arguments about British nationhood has shown, the national identification with a successful fleet could easily transcend the coastal areas, thanks to the communicative powers of print. Quoting none other than William Cobbett remembering his childhood experiences of first seeing the British fleet at anchor, Jenks notes that "'talk of' the navy's 'glorious deeds' and 'memorable combats' was a major vehicle for the articulation of national identity" (2) for the British. The example of Britain, especially the example of Cobbett, is striking for its parallels with the United States. Cobbett is speaking as a rural visitor, a "country boy" (Cobbett 1796, 17) to the coast, where he sees the Royal Navy for the first time—after having only heard of it before in 'song and story,' as it were. Being thrown back on his memories of stories told and retold over and over about the glorious deeds of the fleet, his "heart was inflated with national pride" (Cobbett 1796, 18, quoted in Jenks 2006, 1). "[S]urely," Cobbett remembered thinking, "I had a part in it, and in all its honors" (1796, 18). The mythologization of the Royal Navy and the mediated experience of the "honors" it had won through story become the basis for an individual's identification with the fleet in a genuinely national experience, and identification which is triggered by, but predates, the actual encounter with it. As Jenks suggests, what gets created here "is clearly an imagined community, where naval knowledge constitutes a kind of patriotic catechism and where collective belonging is culturally conferred. The rustic inhabitants of Cobbett's village of memory identify with an ocean, a navy, a fleet, and sailors that many of them have never seen" (2).

Jenks's suggestion that the Royal Navy "had the advantage in its comparative ability to articulate symbolically the national interest" (4), much more so than the

Army, certainly also holds true for the U.S. experience, which, as noted, could connect several of the issues which it went to war about with the nautical domain. The naval conflict could stand synechdochically for the entirety of the U.S.-British relationship: British dominance expressed itself equally in economic power, in cultural metropolitanism, and in naval success and strength. Both British and Americans realized this connection between American weakness at sea, British dominance of the oceans, and the different other domains in which similar relationships prevailed. Timothy Jenks's second anecdote of William Cobbett is enlightening in this regard: Cobbett, now in the late 1790s a bookseller and publisher in Philadelphia (in which capacity he would also correspond with Joseph Dennie, as we have seen in Chapter 2), discovered a print of the British naval victory during the Glorious First of June, where the British had succeeded in bloodying the French fleet. As Jenks relates it:

> He displayed the patriotic print in his shop, where it attracted the attention of two English labourers, who purchased it and an accompanying print at the inflated price of two dollars, having taken out a loan against their wages. These labourers (who were formerly followers of Paine) desired the print in order to lord it over American acquaintances with whom they had quarreled by zealously advocating "the part of their country [Britain]". They purchased the print "by way of defiance" and displayed it to a hostile mob. (22)

It is certainly valuable to note that Cobbett's relation insists on the willingness of even the least well-paid to invest in patriotic paraphernalia, when the opportunity offered and the circumstances warranted it. And it is certainly also interesting to see the Englishman Cobbett essentially defraud his countrymen, charging them a severely inflated price, even as he recognized their patriotic purpose. I will argue in more detail below this capacity of businessmen—especially publishers—to recognize the financial opportunities of patriotic discourses. But more vitally for now, the British laborers were obviously aware that even a print depicting an event rather unrelated to American concerns—a British and French naval battle—could serve to highlight Britain's dominance in American affairs, whether economical or merely emotional.[25] The British laborers in distant lands

25 The U.S. connection to this event is a bit more complicated, but tangential to the issue at hand. Post-revolutionary France had purchased a significant amount of grain in the United States to ward of famine at home, and the French fleet had orders to bring the convoy carrying that grain into Brest. The British, under Admiral Lord Howe, whose brother had been Commander-in-Chief in American during the Revolutionary War and who himself had led the fleet there for a while, was ordered to intercept the convoy. He did not manage to do so and instead engaged the French battle fleet, winning a minor tactical victory but suffering a major strategic defeat in missing the vital grain convoy. For Americans, their involvement in the Battle of the 1st of June then was a commercial one, and one in which they could justifiably say they had not lost a thing; cf. Mostert 2007, 130-152.

identified with their nation by rejoicing in a naval victory; Americans were expected to recognize their national inferiority even by proxy, in British victory over the French—and indeed did so. The symbolism of the naval victories much exceeded their material value, as for all intents and purposes, the British had suffered a severe strategic setback even as they won a minor tactical victory. But the machinery of mythologization worked in a dimension apart from the hard material factors which weighed heavily on strategists. It could transform defeat into victory, both in England and in the United States.

It was on the fertile ground of a latent inferiority complex that American magazines positioned themselves. In the United States as in Britain, "[n]ewspaper and periodical distribution performed a function," in the process of creating a national identity. In Britain, the accounts published by the central organs, Cobbett's *London Gazette* and the *Naval Chronicle*, "were reprinted in the newspaper press and in a number of periodicals," forms that in Britain as in America "had wide readerships" (Jenks 2005, 19). In the United States, especially the *Analectic Magazine* made clear how it felt about American relations with Great Britain. In February 1813, James Paulding suggested in his biography of Captain Hull that there existed in the United States a "superstitious veneration for British naval supremacy" (*AM* 1813 1, 273); in December, Washington Irving noted an "obsequious deference in the minds of too many of our countrymen towards Great Britain, that [...] impairs the independence of the national character" (*AM* 1813 2, 489). As Irving implied and Paulding stated outright, there was a direct connection to be made between British superiority at sea and an at least emotionally dependent America. It is necessary to stress, however, that this was a connection that needed to be actively made and remade and not coincidentally was made by American authors in the context of celebrating precisely those naval victories which, to their minds, had put into question the "obsequious deference" the texts complained about. In their biographical short texts, battle reportage, and other discussions of American naval victories (in poems, for example), American magazines had the possibility of affecting American national identity in a like manner to the British.

At least some periodical editors recognized that the successes of the Navy were capable of raising a national feeling in their audiences. Washington Irving was one of them. In an editorial note which he placed before James Kirke Paulding's biography of Captain Jacob Jones, he announced that he had "omitted several passages of a political nature" (Paulding was a vociferous opponent of rapprochement with Great Britain and a strong Democrat-Republican), and suggested that to utilize the naval officers' biographies for political ends was missing their utility for a greater cause: "we consider," he wrote, "the victories of our navy as so many subjects for national feeling, in the discussion of which the sordid animosities of party should give way to the nobler sentiment of patriotic exultation" (*AM* 1813 2, 75-76). Strikingly, it was this apolitical, national dimension of the naval victories which Congress, too, stressed. Hezekiah Niles's *Weekly Register* printed, no doubt approvingly, a committee report in February 1814. The House of Representatives having queried the appropriate committee for a report on the condition, location, and possible legislative needs of British and French flags taken in the ongoing and previous wars, Congressman Adam Seybert of Pennsylvania replied for the committee much more extensively than was perhaps required. Noting that a considerable number of flags captured during the Revolution and the Quasi-War with France had become lost, Seybert addressed the second part of the query at length: should Congress legislate on the question of the disposal or display of these trophies of war? Seybert and his committee held that it should: it should preserve and display the flags won in successful engagements with the enemy, because "[s]uch trophies excite the spirit of the nation; the result is national character." The war trophies here assumed the same general function as "all [...] representations of our late unparalleled naval victories," and Seybert especially emphasized here the capture of the "three [flags which] belonged to the heavy frigates of the enemy, viz: the *Guerriere*, *Macedonian* and *Java*." As Seybert highlighted, more than any possible captures of regimental standards on land, these naval ensigns were outstanding symbols of U.S. achievement during the war. "It was indifferent whether they consider themselves of the war or of the peace party," Seybert wrote of Americans, "each was ambitious to rank the victor with himself." Seybert's emphasis on Americans attempts to literally identify themselves with the naval officers who had succeeded in besting the Royal Navy is best explained by the extraordinary nature of these victories: "No one can doubt that the government and the people of England would rather we should have taken millions of their merchandise, than that we should have it in our power to exhibit the flag of a single sloop of war, which was gained by equal force" (*WR* 1814, 73). Seybert echoed the metonymical use of the American flag in, for example, Irving's biography of Perry, where it was "tales of our flag insulted" which had set in stark relief the "brilliant successes flashing around the national standard" (*AM* 1813 2, 496), and which ensured that "[o]ur feelings will ever accompany the flag of our country to battle" (497). Pointedly, however, Seybert's aligning of the flags with "all representations" of the previous year's naval victories was a recognition of the value which the periodicals' engagements in biography and other forms of writing had for national identity.[26]

26 The complicated effect accorded biography in this nationalizing venture is well-illustrated in a May 1811 piece from the *Port Folio*. In one of the few Early Republic commentaries on the nature of the national character, the *Port Folio*'s as-customary unnamed author "C" suggests the constitutive role of national pride for national performance. National pride, "so nearly allied to the love of country, that it might almost be regarded as another name for that virtuous attachment," depends in no small part on being "proud of his fellow citizens." Biography's role is to instill pride in the reader, in order to further his patriotic love for his country. But that is not all: it is national pride, the "high-minded emulation of the achievements of his ancestors and countrymen, that nerves the arm of the soldier" (300). As a consequence, "C" argues, Britain's naval prowess alone could not have rendered the Royal Navy mistress of the seas. Britain's national pride, and her sailor's "confident and determined anticipation of victory" (301) were the necessary prerequisite for those victories. The circular argument obviously greatly extends the value of the naval victories: they are now paving the way for even greater victories in the future.

For Seybert and his committee, as for Irving, the full impact of the naval successes could only be adequately gaged if one compared pre-war popular conceptions of the United States and its Navy against their standing now:

> [T]he achievements of that little navy, which a few months ago was the object of derision with the statesmen and the people of England, [are] now the cause of their fears [...]. Our successes on the ocean constitute the pride of our country; they have secured to us the respect of foreign nations. In Europe we again hold that rank which our ancestors had obtained by their many hard fought conflicts, which we had nearly forfeited. (74)

Seybert's analysis also points to a final key question in the argument I am making: why the War of 1812? Did not the Revolution, with its pantheon of men whose greatness few in the Early Republic doubted, supply an adequate number of heroes on which to base one's national identity? Not really, as Joyce Appleby has suggested:

> The Revolution had offered patriots the rhetorical opportunity to treat America's social diversity as a summons to new kind of nationhood, but a successful War for Independence did not supply the shared sentiments, symbols, and social explanations necessary for an integrative national identity. (240)

As David Waldstreicher has shown, the Revolutionary heritage which could have figured prominently in the production of truly national icons was in fact hotly contested between the country's sections (cf. 1997, 257-67). Virginia's dominance in the Revolution (Patrick Henry, Thomas Jefferson, and George Washington especially were all Virginians) and then in the politics of the Early Republic (especially Thomas Jefferson's and James Madison's presidencies) had failed to produce any truly national heroic figure, aside from Washington. William Wirt's interest in Patrick Henry was a Virginian interest, rather than a national one (cf. Casper 1999, 21), as I have already noted. The thirty years since the end of the Revolution had seen, then, too much political strife and too much of a debate over the meaning of American independence for the Revolution to still be able to offer enough unifying potential.

> That would take fresh experiences and opportunistic experiments—not the "mystic chords of memory" that fifty-four years later Abraham Lincoln summoned to the cause of the union, but rather the rooting out of sensibilities acquired in the colonial past. (Appleby 2000, 240)

As the evidence of the naval biographies published during the War of 1812 shows, however, Lincoln was not wrong to situate American national identity in myth: this is precisely where many of the naval biographies written during the War of 1812 were situating it as well. Here was precisely the rhetorical opportunity by which Americans might be stimulated to feel themselves attached to national icons and a new American myth might be calculated absent British influence. It is important to recognize, however, that the authors who exploited the rhetorical opportunity were not free agents, submitting, more or less at will, nationalizing texts to periodicals who obediently printed them. A closer analysis of the production side of biography in the periodicals reveals the underlying heteronomies which structured and permitted the production of the biographies. I will discuss these interdependencies in greater detail below.

The Production of American (Naval) Biography

On April 2, 1812, Nicholas Biddle, since Joseph Dennie's death earlier in the year the editor of the *Port Folio*, wrote to James Monroe, Secretary of State in the administration of President Madison, with a two-fold mission. He needed to secure appointments in the Army for two young friends of his, a task which he completed successfully. But more importantly and at greater length, he wished Monroe's help in writing a biographical sketch for the *Port Folio* on the Secretary. Biddle was straightforward: "The *proprietors* of a literary Journal of some celebrity 'The Port Folio' have been making arrangements for an extensive plan of American biography" (my emphasis).[27] The proprietors since 1809, of course, had been Samuel Bradford and John Inskeep; Biddle was following their wishes in using his connections to politics, specifically to James Monroe, looking for information with which to draft national biographies.

On his own, maybe Biddle would not have so readily adopted the idea of a national biography. Even now, the *Port Folio* seemed ready to catch an early start to its lives of Americans: Bradford & Inskeep's record from the years before, publishing a number of American biographies, gave them a head start here. The war had not yet broken out, even though it loomed ever larger on the horizon. But in fact, under Biddle, there had been something of a retrenchment: since his takeover of the *Port Folio*'s editorship with the February 1812 issue, much of the magazine had been given over to a long term project, a series on the progress of the fine arts with original biographies of the painters, including engravings, while other short biographies were of French marshalls and Russian emperors. Up to the time that the United States declared war on Britain in June, 1812, the *Port Folio* carried no more American lives, although its June edition included the biography of the New York-born British General Samuel Auchmuty. Still, so much of the *Port Folio*'s biographical department was given over to the history of painting, and more especially the lives of painters, that John E. Hall forwarded a complaint to Nicholas Biddle in January 1813—at which point the series had run nearly a year—from a mutual acquaintance that was straight to the point: "'oh hang the painters.'" Hall added that he meant to forward this comment "by way of hint that some folks think this gentry occupy

27 Nicholas Biddle to James Monroe, April 12, 1812. Historical Society of Pennsylvania, Gratz Autograph Collection 206b, Case 8, Box 6.

too much of your canvas," although he himself felt "quite willing that all tastes should be gratified."[28] At that point, the gentle hints from readers merely served to reinforce something that determined Biddle's editorial policies for the entirety of his career at the *Port Folio*.

Variety continued to dominate Biddle's thoughts in all things. To a correspondent (possible the same whom he encouraged and addressed as "Alexis" in a note to readers and correspondents in October 1812; cf. *PF* 1812 2, 436) he wrote an explanatory letter in June 1812, noting that he had not published the author's last submission because the previous numbers had already carried too much about his subject, Russia. It was, Biddle explained, "therefore deemed proper to give variety to the plates" and not to put the submitted engraving and article into the magazine just yet.[29] Similarly, variety and accessibility combined to make Biddle address himself to the Secretary of State: Biddle had been Monroe's secretary for a short while in 1807, when the latter was minister to the Court of St. James: now he utilized their familiarity to request the secretary's assistance in fulfilling his editorial tasks (cf. Govan 1959, 19-20). Biddle's close relation with the secretary certainly played a major role, but Biddle added another, well-familiar reason: "your life abounds with more variety than that of any other public man."[30] For Biddle as for Dennie, the need to offer variety as an antidote to boring monotony remained a central concern in his choice of subjects, his editorial responsibility in fulfilling the wishes of his publishers, and, as John Hall reminded him, also a central aspect of his readership's desires. Bradford & Inskeep's rough outline of a "plan" for American biography as a central feature in the *Port Folio* left leeway for Biddle to seek out the right people—and here, the right people were both those with a genuinely American relevance as well as accessibility of information—while making clear the division of roles within the *Port Folio*'s editorial-proprietorial system. Within the general conception of the magazine demanded by Bradford & Inskeep—a conception which no doubt was reacting to the immediate readers' interest in American lives—Biddle could procure such biographies as he might. However, the supply side was still not working quite as smoothly as the editor had hoped. In December 1812, he apologetically noted his chagrin at having to print a portrait of John Randolph without an accompanying biography, for example.

Like Biddle, his successor, Charles Caldwell, who began his tenure at the *Port Folio* in May 1814, found himself obliged to foreground the newly-nationalized form of the *Port Folio*. Caldwell accepted Samuel Bradford's overture to take over

28 John E. Hall to Nicholas Biddle, January 13, 1813. Historical Society of Pennsylvania, Meredith Family Papers 1509, Box 99.

29 Nicholas Biddle to G., June 22, 1812. Historical Society of Pennsylvania, Meredith Family Papers, Box 99. It is not clear that the engraving, which Biddle returned with a note of thanks and hopes that it would prove useful to the author elsewhere, ever appeared in the *Port Folio*, despite Biddle's public call to his correspondent to keep submitting material.

30 Nicholas Biddle to James Monroe, April 12, 1812. Historical Society of Pennsylvania, Gratz Autograph Collection 206b, Case 8, Box 6.

as editor readily, and fully agreed with the set policy of nationalizing the magazine, and the usefulness to the magazine of emphasizing the ongoing war on its pages. Caldwell himself suggests that the *Port Folio*'s circulation increased by 25% during his two years on the job; while the figure cannot be corroborated, it gives an indication of the success of Bradford & Inskeep's initial decision to focus on American lives and events (cf. Caldwell 1855, 323-4). What Biddle had not done—offer his readers a thorough statement of editorial intent—Caldwell did provide. American biography, now explicitly so-called, would be honored with what Caldwell called "the foremost place" in the *Port Folio*. Caldwell highlighted the role of the periodical in the process of creating a "Biographia Americana" by suggesting that only here, if contributors with access to the requisite information contributed to the best of their knowledge and ability individual biographies, could such a truly national work be created. Indeed, the editor notified his readers that he would occasionally ask for specific lives to be written (cf. *PF* 1814 I, 395-6). And, as Caldwell also noted, the *Port Folio* was clearly ambitious to become a national magazine. "[E]very native of the United States" should find himself represented in and inspired by the figures which the *Port Folio* would aim to portray in its biographies. This was not an idle notion: In June, Caldwell requested lives of General William Henry Harrison and Colonel George Croghan, who had both excelled in recent fighting against Indians and British on the western frontier. His request for the biographies of two Westerners indicated the *Port Folio*'s determination to expand its readership, and indeed it succeeded. By early July, via a convoluted exchange and forwarding of letters, Caldwell obtained the support of a Frankfort, Kentucky, lady who sent him a brief life of the colonel. Together with a second letter, Caldwell printed that text as a "biographical sketch" in the March 1815 edition of the *Port Folio*, suggesting that he had kept the texts while he was waiting for an engraving that never materialized.[31]

31 By this time, the proprietorship of the *Port Folio* had once more changed. Bradford & Inskeep had suffered as serious monetary setback in early 1815. The firm had collectively assumed some 7000$ in debts for customs duties on imports they had made, In early January, the firm surrendered its estates and effects to their creditors, including, no doubt, the proprietorship of the *Port Folio*. From their creditors, that proprietorship devolved upon Thomas Desilver, a Philadelphia publisher; Caldwell called this a "mere transfer of copyright," and indeed nothing major changed in the year in which Desilver held the proprietorship of the *Port Folio*. He in turn sold his property to Harrison Hall, older brother of John E. Hall who at that point became the last editor of the *Port Folio*. Bradford & Inskeep's failure also hurt Moses Thomas, who had given his surety for the bonds which they had failed to repay. Glimpses at the financial troubles underlying Bradford & Inskeep's failure are in *Reports of Cases Determined in the Circuit Court of the United States, for the Third Circuit, Comprising the Districts of Pennsylvania and New Jersey, Commencing at April Term*, 1803. Vol. III. Philadelphia: Philip E. Nicklin, 1827, 508-514. The case file concerns a subsidiary court case in which the United States government was suing Bradford & Inskeep's debtors, rather than the firm itself. The editors of Washington Irving's letters suggest (1978, 386n1) that the ultimate reason for the failure of Bradford & Inskeep was the suspension of specie payments, i.e. the payment of bills of exchange in gold, by American

Underlying Bradford & Inskeep's turn to American biography (a turn which did not preclude, incidentally, the publication of a biography, during the War of 1812, of the British Admiral in Chief of the American station, John B. Warren; cf. *PF* 1812 2, 489-500), executed by their editors Biddle and Caldwell, was their realization that there was money to be made by publishing American lives to an audience finally getting attuned to an increasingly national sentiment. As a correspondent wrote, whose life of William Ladd, a Rhode Island poet of middling reputation, the *Port Folio* printed in November 1813, the readership of the *Port Folio* "very much approve[d]" of the "plan of giving to your valuable miscellany something of a national cast" (*PF* 1813 2, 454). By this time, the *Port Folio*'s American biographies had mainly included military men, leading Biddle's correspondent to suggest that he might also wish to include men of letters.

This was also one of the notions which Charles Caldwell latter offered when he took over as editor. Perhaps the correspondent misunderstood the purpose behind the *Port Folio*'s publication of biography: to follow the mood of the country and its interests, rather than set them. But Caldwell also full well recognized that the times required attention to the military men who were winning victories. In his own efforts to find biographical material, he addressed himself in July 1814 to David Porter, just returned from his cruise in the *Essex* to the South Pacific. Caldwell was pointed both in acknowledging that he wanted to make the magazine a "national work" as well as in emphasizing his reasons for doing so: "At the present time, instances of *American Gallantry* are much sought after and highly prized by American readers."[32] Caldwell's letter to Porter recognized the value in purely commercial terms, as popular reading material, of the biography which it asked Porter to provide material for. It was not just such correspondents, however, who were apprised of the *Port Folio*'s recognition of the public desire for access to its naval officers. In its biography of Captain Alexander Murray, it noted: "As the present war has turned the public attention almost exclusively towards our naval officers, we have occasionally endeavoured to enliven our pages with sketches of characters so brilliant" (*PF* 1814 1, 398). Indeed, the *Port Folio* offered naval biography much more than merely "occasionally:" seven front page biographies in 1814, out of a total of eleven, were of American naval officers; and public commentary clearly indicated the special position which these lives had on account of their timeliness. The September 1813 issue of the *Port Folio*, which contained a biography and portrait of Captain James Lawrence, was advertised precisely for this text in the *Salem Gazette*

banks. On the other hand, Irving himself describes the situation of Bradford & Inskeep as a "very shameful one," and suggested that one of the reasons for the failure was the way American booksellers conducted their business (cf. 1978, 385). On the identity of Thomas Desilver, cf. Queenan 1955, 76; his profession can be traced through database searches for advertisements in his name.

32 Charles Caldwell to David Porter, July 25, 1814. Historical Society of Pennsylvania, Gratz Autograph Collection 250b.

(cf. 1813, September 17, 27.75, 4), as was a life of Bainbridge in the Richmond *Enquirer* of December 1813 (cf. 1814, January 15, 10.80, 4).

The general sense that American biography was an attractive prospect to the readership of the *Port Folio* led Biddle as early as March 1812, before he had even written Monroe, to apprise his readers that there were biographies of "eminent Americans" preparing for future issues of the *Port Folio*. Nor did this growing impetus at Americanization apply only to biography. The same address to his readers also noted that the magazine would seek submissions for a series on "American Gallantry," which, as Biddle suggested, sought to follow the English practice of recording the actions of individual officers, whose exploits might be lost to more general history, and would foreground soldiers and sailors who had performed intrepid service during the late American wars of the Revolution and against France. With similar aims in mind, the March issue also included the poem "Battle of Tippacanoe [sic]," noting of it that while it was clearly not a poem worth critical attention, it was "cheerfully inserted, because it describes American events and actions, and has the hardihood to mention the names of American officers" (*PF* 1812 1, 298). The *Port Folio*'s Americanization of its content already recurred to the belief that military and naval exploits served its aim well, a recognition to which the proprietors had clearly come as early as 1809 in printing the life of Edward Preble. It did not yet stress national identity so much as it did the connection between "countrymen" (*PF* 1812 1, 306), and, given that it was looking principally at historical events, it did not differentiate as much as it would later between the opportunities of naval victories over land victories. Yet with the coming of the war, and consequently to the different martial fortunes of Army and Navy, the *Port Folio*'s rhetoric increasingly emphasized the Navy's particular suitability to its now slightly refocused agenda. In January 1813, an installment of the "American Gallantry" emphasized the Navy's role in the current conflict and the differences between the Army's role and the Navy's—as well as the 'great awakening' of national identity in consequence not of the victories themselves, but rather of the war proper. "The present war has again awakened the energies of the nation," Nicholas Biddle wrote in the editorial preface of the article. "It is [...] on the navy of the United States that our national pride, and our hopes of glory, at this moment repose," precisely because, as we will encounter over and over in the naval biographies, it had "triumphed over the veteran science, and the disciplined valour, of the habitual conquerors on the ocean. They have retrieved all our disasters—they have shed new lustre on our arms, and sustained even in the midst of mortifying reverses, the loftiest tone of national enthusiasm" (*PF* 1813 1, 86-7). This emphasis on the nationality of the new enthusiasm for the Navy was important, as was the stress on the renewal of American military success. Biddle's editorial commentary here summarized all the factors behind the periodicals' ability to stress the national identity of Americans through biography: the unexpected success against the British, the apparently undefeatable rulers of the oceans and erstwhile colonial overlords and the renewal of an explicitly national consciousness through a national military glory which had been forgotten since the Revolution.

The *Port Folio*'s engagement with American biography had progressed early 1813 into an increasing engagement with the nation as an idea that could be supported through biography, thanks, largely, to the public's growing readiness to identify with the nation in the course of the War of 1812. As Hezekiah Niles at the *Weekly Register* phrased it, "war, dreadful as it is, will not be without its benefits in giving us a national character" (*WR* 1812, 160). Nor was it without benefit to publishers. Magazines profited from the public interest in the events and personages of the war, and not just such magazines as the *Military Monitor*, whose short-lived existence began in August 1812 and concluded with the war's end.

The *Port Folio* used American biography because it offered increased patronage and public applause, yet its texts hardly engaged with the possibilities offered by the genre. This was left to another magazine, which, like the *Port Folio*, would make it a top priority to publish the lives of American naval officers during the War of 1812: the Philadelphia monthly *Analectic Magazine*. By contrast with the *Port Folio*, however, the *Analectic Magazine* was almost explicitly created to benefit from the national sentiments engendered by the war through the publication of naval biography, and expanded the possibilities of autonomous expression in periodical biography.

The history of the genesis of the *Analectic Magazine* indicates as much. In November 1812, the Philadelphia bookseller and publisher Moses Thomas (whom we have encountered above as a surety of Bradford & Inskeep's) bought Samuel Ewing's two-year old eclectic repository *The Select Reviews*. Thomas had begun his career as a bookseller and stationer. Twenty-five years old in 1812, he managed to become a reputable bookseller and later, auctioneer.[33] The *Select Reviews* which he bought in 1812—not his first periodical venture—was a magazine dedicated to reprinting British periodical articles, and Thomas set out to hire Washington Irving, the New York author of the *History of New York* and sometime co-editor of *Salmagundi* magazine, to run his new venture as editor.[34] The primary goal which Thomas set his new editor was the publication of naval biographies—an effort which was ultimately both successful and popular. The American novelist John Neal, writing about American authors under the pseudonym X.Y.Z. for *Blackwood's Edinburgh Magazine* in 1825, shrewdly analyzed the situation which Moses Thomas found in 1812 in his sketch of Washington Irving:

> The navy had grown popular, with every body. [...] The Analectic Magazine took fire—with an eye to profit; hunted up materials: employed Irving to write a Biography of these naval captains, one after the other; and gave it out, with portrait after portrait, month after month, to the overheated public. (*BEM* 1825, 62)

Neal's analysis highlights the contingent nature of the *Analectic*'s efforts at avowed-

33 A very short note on Thomas's life and career can be found in his obituary in the *Philadelphia North American and United States Gazette*, August 26, 1865.

34 The obituary in the *Philadelphia Inquirer* (August 26, 1865, 4) suggests that Thomas was "an early correspondent" of Irving's, though Irving's collected letters to not contain any correspondence with Thomas before 1813.

ly national naval biography and stresses the sequence of events which led to the production of biographical short texts. The *Analectic Magazine*'s proprietor was obviously reacting to a larger popular patriotic interest in the naval war. The *Port Folio* recognized in 1825 that "[a]s the war proceeded, and the navy of America rose high in reputation as in utility, the proprietors of the Analectic Magazine prevailed on [Irving] to enrich their periodical with the biography of the most illustrious naval officers" (*PF* 1825 1, 438).[35] "[R]ecent naval victories by U.S. forces," Ralph Aderman and Wayne Kime recognize, "would make those yet unwritten articles timely" (2003, 55): On August 19th, 1812, Captain Isaac Hull had won a spectacular and unexpected victory in a frigate action between his own *Constitution* and the British H.M.S. *Guerrière* off the Canary Islands, news of which had reached the United States in the last days of August; on October 18th, Jacob Jones defeated H.M.S. *Frolic* in U.S.S. *Wasp*; and exactly a week later, Commodore Stephen Decatur defeated H.M. frigate *Macedonian* in U.S.S. *United States*. Even so, Thomas's plan was not something that his prospective editor countenanced. In December, before he had even taken up the job of editing the *Analectic Magazine*, Irving wrote to James Renwick, a long-time friend and fellow Knickerbocker, with loud complaints about his employer Moses Thomas's approach to marketing the magazine and the publisher's plans for the *Analectic*'s content, as well as the implied relationship between him and Thomas. "[M]y publisher," Irving noted testily, "who seems determined to make a comfortable penny out of me, has been advertizing, every day or two, some new addition and improvement [...] of which I have known nothing until I saw the advertisements." The result was, he claimed, a "vile farrago – a congregation of heterogenious articles, that have no possible affinity to one another." Key to Thomas's plan was the publication of what Irving called "a series of portraits of our Naval Commanders with Biographical Sketches" (Irving 1978, 349), an ambitious project of American biography which could only be contemplated by the *Analectic*'s proprietor because he could count on the patriotic fervor of Americans—or, at the very least, enough of his subscribers to please them. Thomas had bought a magazine and reshaped its plan to make money off of the events of the war by "capitaliz[ing] on the public interest" (Aderman and Kime 2003, 55).[36] Irving, as he suggested to James Renwick, was not happy, especially about his publisher's clear belief in setting the magazine's agenda himself. Tes-

35 The *Port Folio* goes on to ascribe a "patriotic purpose" to the *Analectic*'s proprietors, but interestingly, not to Irving, who becomes a mere executive agent fulfilling that purpose.

36 With similar publishing panache, Mathew Carey, the Philadelphia publisher, put out Thomas Clark's *Sketches of the Naval History of the United States* in mid-1813, in order to "capitalize on [popular interest]" in the Navy's victories. As James Green notes, Carey used his "editorial skills" to shape the book "into a persuasive argument for a strong navy and for a naval academy" (Green 1985, 28). Carey's influence on the exact shape and argument of the book is, however, impossible to determine. Stephen Budiansky has noted that John Adams wrote to Carey suggesting the issue of a second edition with additional material suggesting a buildup of the Navy, a proposal which Carey accepted; clearly, then, Carey was not unwilling to add to his author's work (cf. Budiansky 2010, 362-3).

tily, Irving wrote that he "would not consent to have such a fool's cap put on my head; and if they intended to interfere in the conduct of the work, I should decline having anything to do with it" (in Irving 1869, 218-9). Despite his protestations, however, Irving did no such thing (and he had, after all, turned down a similar offer in 1810; cf. Borstein 2007, 95). As the *New-York Mirror* reported in an 1832 biography of Irving, it was due to the "earnest solicitations of the proprietors [sic]" (NYMI 1832, 273) that Irving ended up writing naval biography. A significant motivation must have been the cromulent salary of 1500$, half again as much as Joseph Dennie, a far more experienced editor running a magazine with a larger audience and much greater name recognition had earned in his last years. He would be, as Irving himself recognized, "handsomely paid," especially for work which Irving believed would be something he could do "for the sake of pastime & employment of idle hours" (Irving 1918, 91) and conceived of as an "amusing occupation, without any mental responsibility of consequence" (Irving 1869, 220).

What shines through his correspondence here is what Luther Mott has called Irving's "happy indolence" (1957a, 281), something that was more than just (though it certainly was also) a public persona for Irving, but which did not quite tell the whole story. Irving's notes to Renwick indicate a misconception about the work that he was going to have to do, and indeed, would do, as editor of the *Analectic*—it speaks towards the fact that Irving was anything but a professional editor, although he would develop unexpected talents in the job. Yet Thomas had bought a magazine and reshaped its plan to make money off of the events of the war—he did not need genius in the editor's chair, but he did need precisely what Irving offered him. In his choice of Irving as editor, Thomas indicated how well he understood the periodical business. Just as Bradford & Inskeep in keeping Dennie in a salaried position as editor sought both to profit from Dennie's editorial skill and the name recognition he brought, Thomas looked on Washington Irving as an investment capable of embiggening the worth of his venture. Irving's tenure as editor began in January 1813; in December 1812, the *Port Folio* carried a notice in its "Domestic Literature" section which noted both the change in proprietor as well as emphasizing Irving's editorial role (*PF* 1812 2, 631). More directly, Thomas also took out an advertisement in the *Bureau* of December 23, noting in all-capital letters that Irving would serve as editor.

Thomas thus clearly played on Irving's name recognition. As David Dowling has argued, by 1812, Irving and the New York group of writers known as the Knickerbockers had evolved into a "kind of trademark [...] a moral passport to its audience's hearts, and thus their wallets" (2011, 29). Thomas's shrewd plan brought considerable laurels down on the *Analectic Magazine*, and also on Irving himself. In 1821, the *Port Folio* favorably recommended Irving by noting that to "estimate the value of such a man as Irving [...] we need only remember what was the character of the ANALECTIC MAGAZINE, when his compositions attracted the reader to its pages" (*PF* 1821 1, 131, original emphasis). In 1822, seven years after Irving had ended his involvement with the *Analectic*, the *Port Folio* commented on the generally sad state of American magazines on the occasion of the demise of the *Literary Gazette*, the successor journal to the *Analectic*. It laid blame squarely on the subscribers, suggesting that Americans "wish we had a few more Washington Irvings, [...] and then conclude with a 'well there is nothing like an English magazine after all'" (*PF* 1822 1, 169). Besides the praise heaped onto Irving as editor, these texts also affirm the value which Irving brought to Thomas's new venture. In hiring Irving, Thomas could be sure of both extensive patronage as well as access to the literary talent of Irving's acquaintances, and indeed, Irving lost little time in finding friendly hands to help him. In late November already, he wrote to James Renwick, suggesting that if Renwick could supply a biographical sketch of a recently-deceased mutual acquaintance, he would be happy to print it in the first number of his magazine (cf. Irving 1978, 343). Likewise, fellow Knickerbockers James Kirke Paulding and Gulian Crommelin Verplanck were later hired to write biographies for the *Analectic*.[37]

The usefulness of these connections became evident early on. James Paulding wrote the first three lives of naval officers printed in the *Analetic Magazine*, of Isaac Hull, Stephen Decature, and Jacob Jones. The selection of these officers was determined, on the one hand, by their naval victories; on the other, however, by the availability of material. Stephen Decatur had been an acquaintance of Irving's before the war, and Decatur, Hull, and Jones were all three feted in late December 1812 in New York, where Irving certainly, and Paulding most likely, met all three in person. Much of the life of Jacob Jones Paulding later extracted from the *Port Folio*'s section "American Gallantry" of January 1813, but his personal acquaintance with many of the figures that he drew lives of was a crucial building block of the *Analectic Magazine*'s success with naval biography. Washington Irving himself was deeply involved with several figures in the Navy, including David Porter, whose life he wrote late in his tenure at the magazine,[38] and William Bainbridge, with whom

37 In June 1818, Thomas went so far as to use the wrapper of the *Analectic Magazine* to directly advertise his magazine with authors' names, noting that Robert Walsh and Gulian Verplanck had both "engaged to contribute" to the magazine.

38 I will not be discussing the biography of Porter in the following, since, with the exception of Paulding's biography of Stephen Decatur, it is probably the least interesting life in the magazine—in fact, largely a recounting of his final battle with the British. It may even not have been Irving's text, as the letter to Moses Thomas below amply suggests. Several additional points bear mention: in the middle of July, Irving still wanted to write a biography of William Bainbridge, for which he had been collecting material for at least four months; he did suggest his publisher should find someone to write Porter's biography; Irving does not seem to have had the time for the effort, nor the inclination; the biography of Porter is very different from any of Irving's biographies, having neither a preface nor a postscript; there is no evidence Irving retracted his recommendation to Thomas and acknowledged that he would write the piece himself after all; and the only original source ascribing this piece to Irving is his nephew's collection. We may at the very least doubt the conventional ascription of this piece. There are aspects that favor the interpretation that Irving wrote the piece himself, of course. He knew Porter well, both having been members of the writing club Irving, Paulding and others had formed in New York (cf.

he corresponded by letter and from whom he was collecting biographical material in March 1814 (cf. Irving 1978, 361),

By the time that he was actively researching for a biography of William Bainbridge, Irving had been completely sold to his publisher's commercial aspirations and approach. In July 1814, he wrote to Thomas on *Analectic* business:

> I think it worth your while to get Porters [sic] likeness without delay; and likewise to get a biographical sketch drawn out by some person who can write a neat article. I wish to begin Bainbridges [sic] & therefore will not be able to do Porters [sic] before it would be anticipated & made stale by other writers. His life has been adventurous & would abound with romantic particulars. I would dress up any article that should be furnished; but cannot at present hunt up facts & do the dead colouring. I think it worth your while to pay some job writer for the occasion, as it would be a very taking article at the present moment. (Irving 1978, 363).

Irving reveals his understanding of the role of the editor, as well as the role of the periodical author, in the process of writing biographies. As editor, he would willingly take up the pen to modify such submissions as he received to make them read better—"dress them up," in his parlance—but he did not have the time to either do research on such a text or to do the "dead colouring," a term derived from oil painting meaning a process by which an initial layer of either monochrome or reduced palette paint indicates in broad swathes the outline of the future painting. The process which Irving outlines in none too charitable terms—research, broad strokes dead colouring, and finally, the dressing up—suggest how much hackwork periodical writings effectively were. Irving privileges appearance over substance—and romantic adventure over public usefulness.

Irving's letter also highlights the cooperative nature of the relationship between him and Thomas as it had developed over one and a half years. Thomas was still calling the shots—Irving was merely suggesting possibilities, after all—but left Irving do decide the sequence and choice of naval officers. And the *Analectic Magazine* had most certainly adopted a high degree of professionalism: not only does Irving suggest that Porter's biography should be farmed out to other writers (the choice of which, incidentally, he left to Thomas), but the reason for doing so was commercial to the core: the *Analectic* needed to have such a biography speedily in order to preempt fellow periodicals and to react to the momentary interest of the readership. Irving was particularly well-placed to act speedily in this: news of the event which had brought Porter's name to the fore, his early March fight against two British ships in Valparaiso, Chile, reached the U.S. no earlier than July, when

Aderman and Kime 2004, 40), and might therefore not have required such an extended period of time to assemble material, and the narrative compares Captain Porter to Sinbad, hero of Arabian stories, which was also the nickname Porter had received as a member of Irving's writing club (cf. Irving 1814, 242; Aderman and Kime 2004, 168). As an inside joke, Paulding, Irving, or even Gulian Verplanck, could all have employed the moniker.

Porter himself, paroled by the British, reached New York. Porter wrote the Secretary of the Navy from New York on July 13; Irving wrote Thomas on July 16. Not only was there a temporal and spatial proximity: David Porter was a friend of Irving's and Paulding's from their club, the "lads of Kilkenny," and when Paulding became secretary to the Board of Navy Commissioners in 1815, he lived with Porter in Washington before finding his own place (cf. Aderman and Kime 2003, 40, 63). The close connection which the *Analectic*'s chief writers had with Porter gave them the chance to be first with a life and portrait of the Captain. Nor was Irving's belief in the necessity of timeliness idle. In January 1814, the *Polyanthos* suggested at the end of a brief sketch of the life of Isaac Hull that it had intended the appended portrait for "immediate publication" a year earlier, but that the *Analectic Magazine* had published its own first. The differences between the engravings, the *Polyanthos* suggested, had necessitated a careful check with acquaintances of Hull's until the likeness could be established to be good (cf. *P* 1814, 483).[39]

Similar forms of personal contact, wheedling naval officers and their acquaintances for information from which to fashion biography, prevailed at the *Port Folio*. Nicholas Biddle did not only keep in touch with James Monroe: a letter from Biddle to William Bainbridge of September 1813 indicates the lengths to which the editor was prepared to go. He solicited from Bainbridge a portrait for his engraver, noting that previous portraits of Bainbridge, such as published in the *Polyanthos*, had not been very life-like, and commented on a package of papers which no doubt included material from which Biddle would later that year, in December, be able to publish a life of Bainbridge in his series of American Biography. In June 1814, the *Port Folio* announced proudly to its readers that it had arranged for the publication of "correct and well written biographical notices" of eminent Americans, and requested further assistance on this matter from its readers. The *Port Folio* also received its biographical information from other sources: the Navy Department, from whose files significant elements of the life of Lewis Warrington were drawn, friends of the biographees, and their colleagues (cf. *PF* 1814 2, 1).

Magazines beyond those which commissioned original writings (the *Analectic*, the *Port Folio*, and the *Polyanthos*) sought to benefit from the popular interest in naval and military officers, reprinting a broad variety of texts in order to do so. Not all of these did so to further the national agenda. The *Christian Disciple*, reprinting a newspaper-written life of Captain Thomas Macdonough, emphasized Macdonough's strong religious views, for example (cf. *CD* 1814 2, 351); but the vast

39 The impact of personal contact on the *Analectic Magazine*'s content is also admitted by Irving in a post-script to the Lawrence biography, published a month afterwards. Here, Irving notes: "The facts respecting the battle were almost all taken from notes of a conversation with one of the officers of the Chesapeake, which were afterwards revised and acknowledged by him. Some, it is true, were cautiously selected from the current reports of the day, according as they bore the stamp of probability, and were supported by the concurrence of various testimony. These may occasionally be somewhat misstated, but we believe that in general they are materially correct" (*AM* 1813 2, 234).

majority of reprints, of which there existed a great number, did not mold the biographies to a specific message and rather adopted, in full, those which originally inhered in them. Thus, the New York *Olio*, virtually through its entire run of not quite a year, serialized biographies of naval officers selected from the *Port Folio*, the *Analectic Magazine*, and the *Polyanthos*, usually filling something like a third of its eight pages a week with these texts. At the Baltimore *Weekly Register*, Hezekiah Niles filled much of his supplementary volume for 1814, published in February 1815, with selected naval and military biographies; individual texts made it into numerous magazines and countless newspapers across the Union, from North Carolina to New Hampshire.

Reprints were not either restricted to periodicals: several compendia of biographical short texts also appeared during the War of 1812. Seeking to profit of the immense public interest in the death of James Lawrence during his engagement with the British frigate *Shannon* in June 1813, Lewis Deare, a New Jersey publisher, quickly slapped together the lives of Lawrence printed in the *Analectic* and the *Port Folio*, tacked onto these official papers and eulogies, and had the whole ready for publication by the end of September, suggesting that public interest indicated the need for a collection of materials such as the one he was putting forward. In fact, in this case the *Analectic*'s proprietor seems to have been caught somewhat unawares by the public interest in the life of Lawrence as well as by the possibilities of making additional money through republications, as a note in the *Baltimore Patriot* of September 11, 1813 suggests: Thomas had hurriedly copyrighted the *Analectic Magazine* "to prevent a *republication* of its *original articles*" (*BP* 1813, September 1, 2.57, 3, original emphasis); either this was ineffective, or Thomas stood to make quite some money from the reprints that accrued over the next years. Samuel Brown and John Hathaway's 1815 *American Naval Gallantry*, which openly reprinted the *Analectic Magazine*'s biographies, put it succinctly in its short preface: "A cheap volume of this kind is much wanted" (n.p.), suggesting not only that other compendia already existed, but also that there was considerable demand for the *Analectic Magazine*'s biographies in the populace.

It was by these reprints that the otherwise limited circulation of the *Analectic Magazine* and the *Port Folio* could come to encompass a readership with a national dimension that could function as the audience of the message of national identity these biographies transported in various forms. Aside from extending the biographies geographical distribution, the various forms of reprinting offered chronological expansion, meaning that individual biographies were republished again and again for a considerable time, and with regard to the individual readership, even granting the small circulation of most of the rural and city newspapers of the day. The *Analectic*'s biography of Captain Isaac Hull was republished within two weeks by the Washington D.C. *Universal Gazette* (cf. *UG* 1813, March 19, 1.67, 4); and perhaps more telling is the fate of the biography of Stephen Decatur, published in June 1813 by the *Analectic*, which remained in constant circulation for a year and found publication as late as September 1815.

This précis of the production concerns involved in the creation of periodical biographies of contemporary naval officers gives an indication, if not a complete overview, of the interwoven strands of motivation and organization that combined to produce the possibility of the periodical to intervene in the discussion of national identity in the Early Republic. Based on the publishers clear sighted desire to capitalize off of the naval victories already won in the first months of the War of 1812 and then passed on into the hands of an editor who was tasked with providing exactly those kinds of texts which would fulfill those requirements, the naval biographies proved popular far beyond the most sanguine expectations. Despite their purely commercial origins, and the calumny heaped upon them by modern critics of biography, as I will show in detail in the following, these lives deserve closer critical attention. They reflect periodicals' ability to exceed the limitations usually constricting them, to surmount at least a little the heteronomy of the periodical field and move towards expressions of artistic autonomy. Paradoxically, the pressure to produce commercially successful nationalist biography permitted, within the actual written text, a relative autonomy of expression for writers. The time had come to produce American lives specifically tailored to the momentary upswing in nationalist sentiment—but to do so with a sense of authorial individuality. In making it possible, indeed necessary, that biographies be produced by Americans for Americans—for who would expect complimentary biographies of American naval officers to be published in Great Britain—the War of 1812 allowed the *Analectic Magazine* and the *Port Folio* among other magazines to bring into the genre literary complexities, and indeed complexities in biographical theory, that it had largely avoided before. In very basic terms, there is no need to read periodical biography before the War of 1812, as anything but formulaic, reliable filler. By contrast, the War of 1812 and the biographies produced around it reveal the conditions under which it was possible to produce more than this filler material, to show its potential for relative autonomy within an otherwise completely heteronomous field, and, at that, to engage the question of American nationalism with considerable creativity. When periodicals did so, they produced two similar but not fully coincident types of lives: those which read their biographees into a genealogical continuum that recentered American national identity in an increasingly mythologized present, and those that framed American naval officers as allegories of the nation, in which their individual lives come to represent the larger national struggle.

Indeed, I would like to suggest that latter step as a more basic one, and ultimately if not chronologically a necessary prerequisite for other rhetorical strategies. The first step in mythologizing this present was, for many of the biographies, the transformation of individual officers into allegories of the nation. Such allegorizations brought to the front such aspects of the biographees' lives as corresponded with a national, and particularly national naval, narrative. The parallel reading of naval lives and national history permitted an initial idolization of naval officers, detaching them from their 'real' lives and making them available for a greater purpose—and thus also formed the fundament for the more elaborate discussions of national genealogy and American national identity that other lives offered.

Biographical Allegories of Navy and Nation

Transforming individual naval officers into allegories of the nation, I suggest, laid the groundwork—conceptually if not chronologically—for more complicated rhetorical strategies. The following will discuss two such allegorizations, both published in the *Analectic Magazine* in 1813, and an allegorical engraving which picks up on those biographies and ties them into the genealogies which I am discussing here. Allegorizations were certainly the simplest way of relating the individual experiences of the naval officers which the biographies depicted to the greater concern for the nation as a whole, and permitted readers to identify themselves with the biographees no matter what their own personal experiences were like. To approach what I argue are allegorical interpretations of individual lives in terms of their relevance for the nation, I will start with a life that is not as ambitiously allegorical as my two main choices, but nonetheless illustrative.

In outward form, James Kirke Paulding's biography of Captain Jacob Jones, who had captured the British brig *Frolic* while commanding the sloop *Wasp*, and was one of the men feted on December 26, 1812 in New York, is patently unremarkable. It offers a short summary of the biographee's public career, basically a war history, ending in even shorter general summaries of his outstanding character traits. Jones is "of active mind and vigorous make [...] capable of the utmost vigilance and fatigue [...]. Naturally and habitually temperate himself, he is a great promoter of temperance among his crew" (*AM* 1813 2, 77-8)—a trait no doubt not too endearing to the men under his command. That Paulding reserved a total of seven lines to this character description indicates that the author knew very little of the person he is describing, especially when it is considered that a large part of the piece was simply quoted from the *Port Folio*. The entirety of the description of *Wasp*'s action with *Frolic* was, with slight (uncommented) emendations in the first two lines, quoted (under attribution) from the *Port-Folio*.[40]
Jones's long private history, it turns out, is very much public history as well. Most

40 Indeed, much of the biography, even when it is not explicitly offered as a quotation, may not be Paulding's writing. "The writer of this memoir distinctly remembers also, that in the geographical lessons [Jones] continually bore off the palm, and received, beyond all others, repeated proofs of approbation from his preceptor" (*AM* 1813 1, 71), the biography notes, but Paulding could hardly have known Jones in school. Jones, eight years Paulding's senior, spent his youth in Delaware, Paulding in New York. Who, then, remembered Jones from school? In all likelihood, Paulding had obtained information from a different source and was unwilling to do the necessary editing to remove such odd notes from his copy. Paulding does not indicate the precise source of the article (a January 1813 article entitled "American Gallantry"), nor his reasons to assume that the "account [...] is scrupulously correct". Since we know that Paulding's sources for his biographies included correspondents, the conclusion must be that a certain carelessness pervaded Paulding's work with those sources.

interesting to the biographer is Jones's motivation of choosing, at age 29, a naval life. "[H]e had weighed all the peculiar inconveniences and sacrifices incident to his determination, and had made up his mind to encounter and surmount them all," Paulding wrote, adding that "if courage, activity and hardihood could ensure naval success, Jones was peculiarly fitted for the life he had adopted." Jones is remarkable in providing a model of emulation and national identification in the person of a genuine naval hero who was obviously not 'born' to the profession, as some other biographees were, but determined on his career at a late age and went on to attain his high stature simply by virtue of his "invincible resolution" (73).

Jones, with his difficult and long-winded route to the service, can also work on a different level: though his function remains public, his long search for his public calling and eventual turning to the naval profession can also be read as an advertisement for similar behavior by Paulding's readers. After all, Jones entered "into the service of his country, in the year 1799, when menaced with a war with France," and the U.S. were now at war too; and despite his age of twenty-nine, and despite the supposition that "his friends were dissatisfied at seeing him in a manner taking a retrograde step in life [...]it is probable that they felt some degree of admiration for that decision of character, which, in the pursuit of what he conceived a laudable object, could enable him to make such large sacrifices of personal pride and convenience" (*AM* 1813 2, 72). Paulding's suppositions and imaginings of the hostile reaction of Jones's social sphere to his decision to volunteer for the Navy are, of course, not idle. They attempt to anticipate the possible reactions of the friends of future recruits for the present war, for whom Jones serves as an example. Perhaps even the note that Jones entered the Navy at the age of twenty-nine can be read into this narrative: the War of 1812, breaking out exactly twenty-nine years after the 'birth' of the independent United States in 1783, represents the United States' 'turning' towards a naval career, at much the same 'age' as Jones found his own way.

The biography of Jacob Jones is a modest example of an allegorization of a public figure to refigure him in a larger national context. As the example also makes clear, however, the allegorizations I am talking about are thematically present in the lives, but not overtly spelled out—no "in this he is like the United States itself" to be found anywhere. I regard this as a crucial issue, since it is at precisely this point were my discussion of biography and American periodicals must shift into an exploration of literary strategies. An investigation of the literary strategies employed by the texts which I will discuss below is necessary to fully understand their arguments about national identity, and to recognize the extent and limitations of the authorial autonomy they give evidence for. Much of this chapter so far, like the previous chapters, has insisted on the priority of text-external considerations for the shaping of periodical content, both in my diachronic exemplum the *Port Folio*, as well as in my synchronic look at the production of periodical biography during the War of 1812. The rest of this chapter, by contrast, will shift attention away from evaluations of the extent of heteronomy in the periodical field (so far overwhelming) and towards the autonomous pole. It will investigate the artistry, for lack of a better term, inherent in the naval and military biographies published during the

War of 1812 and their ability to transcend the heteronomous conditions of their production to, in turn, make use of biography for their own often divergent ends, beginning with the two national allegories: Washington Irving's life of William Burrows, and James Kirke Paulding's of John Aylwin.

Washington Irving's biography of Lt. William Burrows, published in the *Analectic Magazine* of November, 1813, came at the heels of a series of naval mishaps since the summer. In June, James Lawrence had been killed and the frigate *Chesapeake* taken off Boston; in August, the brig *Argus* was captured by the British; and since mid-summer, most American naval vessels were being blockaded in port by a growing British naval presence. In this situation, William Burrows's victory in the brig *Enterprise* over the weaker British *Boxer*, during which Burrows was killed, was nonetheless a welcome piece of news: a glimmer of hope on an otherwise dark horizon.

As craftsmanship, Irving's biography of Burrows is remarkable: a text in which Burrows becomes a symbol of America itself. Irving takes the sting out of Burrows's death by arguing that "there is a dearer and more cherished wish that grows closer to the heart" than to receive the praises of one's countrymen: "it is to live in the recollection of those he loves and honours." Irving offers a very practical consideration: "[t]he bravest soldier would not willingly expose himself to certain danger, if he thought that death were to be followed by oblivion [...] human pride shrinks from the darkness and silence of the grave." In publicly affirming the role played by the deceased officers lies another possible application of biography. For the usefulness of this, Irving avers, the very biographee he is portraying is evidence: "In the gallant young officer who is the subject of the present memoir, we shall see these observations verified; he fought with the illustrious example of his brethren before his eyes, and died with the funeral honours of Lawrence fresh in his recollection" (*AM* 1813 2, 396). Irving reaffirms the usefulness of biography, and not the least of his own series of biographies in the *Analectic Magazine*, in just one sentence. While living, the examples the biographies offer must be held up for emulation by their brother officers; when dead, praising their deeds and virtues will make death easier and increase the amount of risk others are willing to take.

More interesting than this slight realignment in the purpose of biography is Irving's effort to make Burrows something more than merely another in a long line of distinguished American naval officers. With great care, he develops character traits in Burrows that resound with the idea of what is typically American. Burrows possesses "a solitary independence of mind" and relies "as much as possible on his own resources" (397), is often accused of "blunt simplicity," but had "an original turn of thought" (399). He is determined to do what he wants and to do what is right: he has a "determined bent" (397) to become a naval officer (as might be argued the U.S. Navy was itself determined to "become a Navy"), but he does not go at it the easy way. "Instead of the puerile vanity and harmless ostentation which striplings generally evince when they first put on their uniform, and feel the importance of command, it was with difficulty he could be persuaded to wear the naval dress, *until he had proved himself worthy of it by his services*" (397, my emphasis). Echoes of Americans and their navy sound throughout this part of Irving's essay. Burrows "felt the novelty of his situation, and shrunk from the exercise of authority over the aged and veteran sailor, whom he considered his superior in seamanship" (397-8). In the first part of this biography, Burrows stands almost allegorically for the U.S. Navy itself: from the shadow of the overbearing Royal Navy, "the aged and veteran sailor," Americans carefully, slowly, only by an earned right, edge out.

Just like Burrows, the U.S. Navy's abilities were first recognized in the Mediterranean during the Tripolitan War – the "zeal and ability" which Burrows here gives evidence for is, also, the U.S. Navy's. The fact that Burrows earns promotion for his ability, rather than the political favoritism for which the Royal Navy's officer corps was infamous, not only marks the difference between the services, but also the inherent differences between the republican ideals of the United States and the monarchical ones of Great Britain, a question which later biographies, especially written by James Paulding, would recur to. The biography of Burrows, in the meantime, continued to ascribe to the lieutenant Burrows, character traits which could just as well—and in later texts, would—be ascribed to the United States itself. Burrows, Irving informs us, "possessed a heart full of noble qualities. He was proud of spirit, but perfectly unassuming; jealous of his own rights, but scrupulously considerate of those of others. His friendships were strong and sincere; and he was zealous in the performance of secret and important services for those to whom he was attached" (399). Whereas, as we shall see, it is the United States that is "proud of spirit" in Irving's biography of Oliver H. Perry and jealous of its own rights ("our ears still ring with the galling terms in which even British statesmen have derided us" (*AM* 1813 2, 495-96)), here these characteristics of a nation in the political sphere are allegorized in an individual of that nation.

Irving makes Burrows a mirror of the young American republic and its navy. Irving knows the navy, like Burrows himself, to be looking for a way to prove itself "worthy" through its services; and Irving had previously shown (in his biography of James Lawrence, below) that through its "zeal and ability", the U.S. Navy had already proved it had become a worthy contender with the Royal Navy. Likewise, Burrows's "jealousy" of his own rights echoes national American concerns from taxation and representation through the impressment that had started the War of 1812. Burrows's noble qualities are the qualities of the American nation.

James Kirke Paulding's biography of Lieutenant Aylwin is perhaps an even more striking example of how a determined biographer could shape the biographical material he had into a statement far beyond the boundaries of mere biography. On its face, Paulding's life of Aylwin is one of the more curious of the naval biographies in the *Analectic Magazine*. Aylwin had never commanded a ship; he had died, in the action between *Constitution* and *Java*, without this action gaining anything in particular from his service. He was, in short, not a notable figure, as the other biographees were; and his death was already a year in the past. Two considerations may have played into Paulding's choice of Aylwin as a biographee: as with Burrows, the lack of any more U.S. victories at sea may have made it seem desirable to return to past glories; and secondly, Aylwin's career and character could easily be adapted by Paulding to serve his political ends.

Aylwin was born a British subject to American loyalists in Quebec. Like many of the other biographees, his early life is of not much interest to Paulding. Aylwin's "father destined him to a naval life," obviously in the British fleet, but the Royal Navy would not be Aylwin's service in the end. The first of Paulding's reasons for adopting Aylwin for a biography interferes: impressment. "Aylwin witnessed [the practice] in the streets of Quebec," notes Paulding, and "[t]he horror excited in his breast at seeing a lad whom he had known, torn from the bosom of his parents by a pressgang, caused an invincible disgust to the English naval service" (*AM* 1814 1, 54). His efforts to enter the U.S. service instead fail, and he becomes apprenticed to a merchant sailor. After several voyages, however, a dispute with his captain leads the captain to have Aylwin "kidnapped by a pressgang" himself. Paulding expounds at length on the situation Aylwin now finds himself in:

> He was immediately sent on board a receiving ship in the Thames; where he found himself surrounded by six or seven hundred individuals, the scourings of a vitious metropolis. All communication with friends was denied him; letters which he wrote were suppressed; hope itself was almost excluded from his breast. From this receptacle of wretchedness he was in a few weeks transferred to a gun brig. Here he was narrowly watched, and endured all the rigour exercised in the English service towards their impressed men, to induce them to enter as voluntary seamen. The great antipathy, however, which he had conceived for their service would not permit him to subscribe to that which he considered would be his own infamy. Threats were unavailing; he had a mind that could not be subdued. (55)

Aylwin's service aboard the British brig lasted, according to Paulding, six years altogether, during which time, while he distinguished himself in gallantry, he never considered joining the Royal Navy for good. Impressment as a practice weighed too heavily on him, even as he was ready to do his duty while he in British service. Through it all, he retained his "honourable sentiment" and "every principle of virtue" (56). Following his release for illness, he became a citizen of the United States, and participated in the two battles fought by U.S.S. *Constitution*, first under Captain Hull, then under Commodore Bainbridge. In the latter action, Aylwin, wounded in the shoulder, suffered a mortal injury and died.

Nothing in Aylwin's naval service, however, could have been called exceptional; and in the manner of the contemporary, republican, nationalist biography, almost any U.S. Navy officer could have become a worthy subject for Paulding. Dead Lieutenants of great ability, frankly, were not in short supply—and, indeed, there were other officers whom the *Analectic Magazine* did not write about which had won signal victories or excelled in subordinate service. But Aylwin's remarkable personal story must have attracted Paulding. Aylwin's own experiences with the pressgang echoed American complaints and returned readers to the reasons for the war that, in January 1814, were not only starting to become relevant in the feelers for peace, but also becoming increasingly obscured by the question of the conquest of Canada. Paulding's graphic portrayal of the horrors not only of impressment itself, but also of the horrors of service in the Royal Navy served to underline the American justification of war. Aylwin's authentic voice is called upon by Paulding to deliver the verdict on the justice of America's war:

> Having been a victim to the practice of impressments, Lieut. Aylwin had strong sensibilities on the subject; and his enlarged philanthropy was excited by the hope that the present war would lessen, if not terminate, the misery occasioned by what he conceived to be a needless and most detestable subjugation of our species. In his last moments it was his frequent ejaculation, in reference to this subject, "I thank God I am dying in so glorious a cause." (56)

Through his life of Aylwin, Paulding is able to reaffirm the moral superiority of the United States in its just struggle to end impressment, emphasizing the horrors of impressed life and neglecting to address the issue that Aylwin, of course, was a British subject, and as such a legitimate target of the pressgang.

Throughout his impressment, Aylwin's resolute and steadfast behavior is praised by Paulding: "[A]lmost his sole resource for amusement and instruction was his bible [...] he would often forget the loss of his liberty and the evils of his situation." (56). The U.S. Navy, which according to Paulding "appeared to him the only proper occupation for one who disliked inglorious ease – the field where his courage and nautical skill would find their reward" (57) was the preferable service. Aylwin's choice of the United States Navy over the Royal Navy, partially due to the horrors of impressment, means choosing the United States over Britain for its moral superiority. He, "having become by adoption, what he almost considered himself by birth, a citizen of the United States," remained at the forefront of the maritime grievances of the United States. "[H]e immediately obtained that employment in our merchant service which his thorough seamanship entitled him to anticipate. For several years he sailed as master of a vessel, experiencing many of those vexations and losses from the respective belligerents to which the commerce of our country has been exposed" (56). Not only impressments, but the problems related to the Orders in Council were directly witnessed by Aylwin. His knowledge of the affronts to American sovereignty at sea made him desirous of seeking actively to improve that situation, in a way that results in him, again, stand in for the Navy and the United States. Accordingly, when war came in 1812, "[t]he regular service appeared to him the only proper occupation for one who disliked inglorious ease – the field where his courage and nautical skill would find their reward" (57). Aylwin's subsequent rise from sailing master on the USS *Constitution* to the rank of Lieutenant is stressed by Paulding as being "the second instance in our navy of promotion from the grade" (58); there is emphasis on the comparative permeability of the U.S. Navy rank system, as there had been in Irving's biography of Burrows.

Jones, Burrows, and Aylwin offer allegorical readings of naval biography which sought to parallel American national character, development, and success dur-

Fig. 6: "This vignette, cut in wood by Anderson, from a design by Sully, represents Columbia seizing the trident of Neptune" (AM 1815 2, 231). The *Analectic Magazine* used this woodcut several times in conjunction with naval biographies, including, in October 1816, before a life of Robert Dundas, Viscount Melville, First Lord of the Admiralty since 1812—a rather nasty twist. Among the interesting aspects of the cut is that a very similar female figure, Britannia, figured in British depictions of naval victory at the time.
Courtesy of the American Antiquarian Society.

ing the War of 1812, with the individual lives the texts portrayed. As such, they made more or less obvious connections between the issues at stake in the war, both such tangible ones as impressment and such intangible ones as the shape of American national identity, and the naval service, its men, and their victories. Naval biography was not by accident the genre of choice for such allegories, given the prominence of naval issues in the run up to the war: who better to symbolize Americans' suffering from impressment and British dominance than those who suffered from it?

It was a small step from reading American naval officers as allegories of the nation to reading American victories at sea as being ultimately much more than naval success and instead heralding a complete change in the relationship between the United States and Great Britain, and their respective roles in the world. The *Analectic Magazine*'s engraving accompanying the first number of its new feature, the "American Naval Chronicle," in September 1815, allegorized this new relationship (cf. fig. 6). An editorial comment stressed how to read the figures for those readers not gifted with interpretatorial talent, but left the interpretation, as in the biographies analyzed above, to the reader. The woodcut shows the figure of Columbia looking towards a lounging Neptune. Columbia's outstretched arm holds Neptune's trident, symbol of maritime power, away from Neptune, who apparently seeks to re-acquire it. Behind her, the waves crest in the form of horses, beneath her, fishes carry the sea shell in which she floats. Neptune's shell, by contrast, is drawn by two white horses, who are orienting themselves towards the left side of the frame. There, the sky is turning ominously dark. To Columbia's right, the clouds are lighter—sunshine can almost be imagined breaking through at any moment. Columbia has taken Neptune's station and tends towards a glorious future. Neptune, by contrast, is reduced to desperate leaps in order to have any hope of escaping the darkness of maritime obscurity.

The *Analectic Magazine*'s engraver allegorized the magazine's insistence on the unalterable ascendancy of the United States. Beating the British on their own domain, American magazines from this read a general American ascendancy into naval victory, figuring that precisely because the British tied their sense of national worth so tightly to their fleet, success at sea was a mere precursor to success elsewhere. Having appropriated the British trident in graphic and in rhetoric, Americans likewise appropriated the rhetoric of national identity from British examples. Ironically, in attempting to re-invent a national identity from the deeds of the U.S. Navy's officers, American authors were adopting and adapting the British strategies which Timothy Jenks has outlined. They were, so to speak, at their most British in asserting their American national identity. While Elsie West commends Washington Irving for "allowing the facts to speak for themselves and [...] eliminating secondary purposes and digressive material" (West 1993, 200), it is in fact precisely those digressions—by no means eliminated at all!—which allowed Irving to make his biographies a means to the greater end of shaping American national identity. In this reading, the specific subjects of the biographies—their biographees—become subordinate to the ways in which their lives can be used as a metaphor for the development of the U.S.-British relationship and specifically to the genealogical relationship between the two nations in consequence of the events of the War of 1812.

The ultimate consequence of American naval victories was that Americans could feel themselves reaffirmed in their independence, and that, perhaps unlike the Revolution itself, in whose aftermath political independence had not been translated into cultural, moral, or in the broadest sense emotional independence, there was now no way back to the old subservience and inferiority. The *Analectic Magazine* neatly illustrated the periodical's insistence that they had taken from the British what would not, could not be returned by rendering naval victories and naval officers as allegories for a general American ascendancy. At the same time, however, the magazine engaged in a mythologization of events that sought to foreground events of the War of 1812 as the point of origin of a national identity, forming a central core of a future mythology for the nation.

Creating Genealogies of National Identity

James Kirke Paulding wrote the first of the *Analectic*'s naval biographies.[41] On August 19, 1812, Captain Isaac Hull, commanding USS *Constitution*, one of the large 44-gun frigates, in a bare half hour successfully fought and captured the British frigate *Guerriere*. Coming two months after the U.S. declaration of war on June 18, Hull's victory over the *Guerriere* was a rude shock for the Royal Navy and amazing news for the citizens of the United States. When *Constitution* reached Boston harbor on August 29, she set off a "ringing and roaring of [bells and guns] all across America" (Toll 2006, 354). American naval forces had fought their first battle against the vaunted Royal Navy, and had come away unexpectedly victorious (cf. Toll 2006, 347-56). Victory catapulted Hull into fame – not least helped by the *Analectic Magazine*, which published the "Biographical Notice of Captain Isaac Hull" in its March 1813 edition; but like many of the successive efforts in the *Analetic*, Paulding's "Biographical Notice of Captain Hull," victor in the fight with *Guerrière*, was much more than just a biography. Only roughly eighty of the 352 lines of the article contain any biographical information on Isaac Hull, and much of that material is more historical in scope than truly biographical. The rest is devoted to a meditation on biography and to offering an interpretation of Hull's victory that firmly established the line the *Analectic* would be taking for the duration of the war, even as it offered a reading of national identity of the United States that provided a first outline of a national genealogy. Concluding his summary of Hull's life, Paulding begins his effort at transmuting the action into something vastly more important than a mere and ultimately inconsequential naval victory. He notes that it was "one of the most important events that has occurred in the history of this country for many years past" (*AM* 1813 1, 270). There had been, he suggests, "a sort of superstitious reverence" for England in existence in the United States, owed chiefly to a sense of history rendered in genealogical terms: America was a young country, with the "fond credulity of a child," which received "the most exaggerated impressions of a nation to whom she had once looked up as a parent" (271).[42] His continued use of the parent-child metaphor extends to a

41 There is some scholarly confusion about the authorship of the naval biographies in the *Analectic Magazine*. William Hedges claims that the "series of brief lives of American commanders in the War of 1812 [was] written by the editor himself and his friends Paulding and Gulian Verplanck" (Hedges 1965, 113). William Cullen Bryant, in his "Address on [Washington Irving's] Life and Genius" (19) suggests Verplanck wrote only one naval biography, unrelated to the eight written during Irving's tenure; Andrew Burstein suggests that Verplanck wrote biographies, but does not say whether these were of naval officers. In fact, the eight naval biographies written during Irving's tenure were written exclusively by him and James Kirke Paulding. Verplanck wrote several political biographies in Irving's second year, which are notable chiefly for their Federalist slant, and sketches of Generals Pike and Scott, but no naval biography (cf. Harvey 1932).

42 Paulding tropes on the parent-child relationship, but complicates it by making Hull's victory into the "parent of a well-founded confidence in ourselves" (269). As we shall see in the following, however, the force of the metaphor remains directed at England as the parent.

life-cycle trope of America as a young nation whose faculties have not yet been tested nor fully developed, and who was as yet influenced by the "opinions implanted early in life" (272), opinions which remained forceful in the minds of Americans even as their basis in fact vanished. Thus, with the United States reaching the end of its metaphorical childhood and standing now "at the very outset of [its] naval career" (273) the habits of "superstitious reverence" had become so ingrained that few could conceive themselves other than outmatched by the British in almost every way. Yet, Paulding continues, in extension of his metaphor, this deference to British naval prowess ignored that Americans were, in point of genealogical fact, "too much [...] of Englishmen [...] to be easily overpowered." It was precisely this English heritage that allowed Americans to succeed so magically (a term Paulding himself suggests), and which enabled it to dissolve "the spectres which had haunted us from the cradle upward" and to "receive [...] a spark, which, at some future period, will animate her to deeds that will realize this first promise of [America's] youth" (273).

Paulding offers his readers a thoroughly conventional view of American identity: They are transplanted Englishmen, now slowly growing out of their dependence on the parent country, but still tied firmly by a transatlantic family history to the British. The victory itself, Paulding notes, is "an object of apparent insignificance," capable neither of denting British naval supremacy nor signally influencing the course of the war. It is by declaring it insignificant in point of fact that Paulding is enabled to make it significant symbolically. Paulding's biography of Isaac Hull renders the victory over the *Guerrière* as a necessary beginning to the growth of a national character, "the only tie now wanting to secure a union of hearts among every class and denomination," a union which Paulding—and by extension the *Analectic Magazine*—clearly considered lacking so far.

Paulding concludes in his biography of Hull that "subsequent instances of similar victories will add vigour [...] and do much to form a national character" (*AM* 1813 1, 274), arguing that what Hull's victory had begun, shattering the myth of British superiority at sea, further such successes might continue. Implicit in this was the idea that it would be necessary to keep winning victories. In his biography of James Lawrence, published with amazing dispatch in August 1813, Washington Irving suggests that no further victories were in fact needed to constantly reaffirm American national identity. On June 1st, Captain James Lawrence, commanding U.S.S. *Chesapeake*, had engaged the British frigate *Shannon* off Boston, and been soundly defeated. Mortally wounded, Lawrence died shortly after the battle. The British rejoiced: "the doubts could be laughed away" (Toll 2006, 417) which had been occasioned by the string of defeats suffered during the previous year, and the right natural order of dominance at sea had been restored. Not so, suggested the *Analectic Magazine*: "The question of naval superiority," which the British now saw reopened, "was in our opinion settled long since, in the course of the five preceding battles [...] the nations are equal on the ocean; and the result of any contest, between well-matched ships, would depend entirely on accident" (*AM* 1813 2, 146). Irving suggests sweepingly that there was no further need to affirm anything at all. Not only because, as Irving argues, the Navy's modest war goals have been achieved in "showing that her maritime power was vulnerable" (139). Rather, whatever would happen in the naval war in the future, any successful effort to redeem British hegemony over the oceans, the redemption of their flag, as Irving has it, required the British to "first obliterate from the tablets of our memories, that deep-traced recollections, that we have repeatedly met them with equal force and conquered" (*AM* 1813 2, 147).

Irving's rhetoric is both a gambit necessitated by events as well as the most important claim the *Analectic* made on American national identity during the war. It persisted in tying the naval war back to the greater question of the nation. If, as Irving indicates, American officers had theretofore been "fighting under superior excitement to the British [...] eager to establish a name, and [...] each has felt as if individually responsible for the reputation of the navy" (*AM* 1813 2, 146) this also echoes the general American desire to achieve emotional independence from Great Britain. Paulding had asserted in "Hull" that the naval victories had effectively tied the national knot by promoting the national character and American national identity as shared benefactors and celebrants of naval heroes. Now, Irving insists that this was in effect an indissolvable tie, independent entirely of future events. In fact, Irving recognizes that Lawrence was as valuable for the construction of a national identity in death as he would have been in life—perhaps more so. "There is a touching pathos about the death of this estimable officer, that endears him more to us than if he had been successful" (*AM* 1813 2, 143). If, as Georg Elwert has suggested, it was "especially the dead [hero]" who could be placed as the "peak element of the prestige pyramid" (1995, §80) which attracted the national populace, Irving seems well aware that Lawrence's death meant that he could now be literarily embalmed as a national icon, as an eidolon in the sense that Wilbur Zelinsky has used the term. "The idea of Lawrence, cut down in the prime of his days, stretched upon his deck, wrapped in the flag of his country—that flag which he had contributed to ennoble, and had died to defend—is a picture which will remain treasured up in the dearest recollections of every American." Lawrence's name, Irving suggests, "will form one of those talismanic names which every nation preserves as watchwords for patriotism and valour" (*AM* 1813 2, 144), and would lastingly unite the nation behind it. Irving's phrasing is felicitous: the "idea of Lawrence" is what counts, rather than the facts of the engagement or, conversely, the ultimate consequences on the course of the war of American naval successes. In transmuting Lawrence into an idea, Irving takes the first steps to make him into a national myth: in death, his name "[will form one of those talismanic names which every preserves as watchwords for patriotism and valor" (136). In a lengthy conclusion to the biography, Irving suggests as much:

> The British may now swarm on our coasts – they may infest our rivers and our bays—they may destroy our ships—they may burn our docks and our ports—they may annihilate every gallant tar that fights beneath our flag—they may wreak every vengeance on our marine that their overwhelming force enable hem [sic] to accomplish—and after all what have they effected? redeemed the pre-eminence of their flag?

> destroyed the naval power of this country?—no such thing. They must first obliterate from the tablets of our memories, that deep-traced recollection, that we have repeatedly met them with equal force, and conquered. In that inspiring idea, which is beyond the reach of mortal hand, exists the germ of future navies, future power, and future conquest. What is our navy?—a handful of frigates; let them be destroyed; our forests can produce hundreds such. Should our docks be laid in ruins, we can rebuild them—should our gallant band of tars be annihilated, thanks to the vigorous population of our country, we can furnish thousands and thousands of such—but so long as exists the moral certainty that we have within us the spirit, the abilities, and the means of attaining naval glory—so long the enemy, in wreaking their resentment on our present force, do but bit the stone which has been hurled at them—the hand that hurled it remains uninjured. (139-40)

Here, Irving picks up Paulding's connection between the naval conflict and its officers, and the future of the nation. American greatness is prefigured in its present naval victories because they confirm the only thing that hitherto has been lacking: American assurance in their own abilities. For this reason, too, Lawrence's defeat may be safely ignored where its ramifications for American self-esteem are concerned. Lawrence has acted boldly, nobly, virtuously, and lost; that, however, is no matter, because Americans had previously assured themselves of their naval prowess, and this knowledge remains. Americans need not in fact claim, as Paulding did, any kind of individual superiority over the British because their forests, their population, in other words, the "future power" of their continental resources and the "future conquests" of their continental and maritime destiny, provide the necessary material superiority to assure Americans of their eventual dominance.

Irving's biography of Lawrence is a most skillful piece of political propaganda. It was hurried into print, as Blackburn acknowledges, "with a precipation that is understandable" (1932, 743): Lawrence's death and the defeat of the *Chesapeake* had created an outpouring of emotions. But the quick publication was owed as much to an entrepreneurial effort to be the first to publish a life of Lawrence as it was an attempt to deflect the demoralization caused by the defeat of the *Chesapeake* (cf. Aderman and Kime 2004, 56) by highlighting not only the reasons for which Lawrence might yet be deemed a successful role model, but also by dismissing the moral importance of the battle. Irving's major recognition in the biography of Lawrence, spelled out in the lengthy final paragraph, is that thanks to the vast resources of the United States, American would at length become dominant, and the question of the individual superiority of Americans was no longer vital.[43]

43 This was also the more practical and level-headed analysis of the Secretary of the Navy, William Jones. Jones, who had shifted American naval operations towards commerce raiding and away from the glorious, but fruitless one-on-one frigate actions, noted in December 1813 to one of his captains that "[t]he Character of the American Navy stands upon a basis not to be shaken" (in Budiansky 2010, 285).

Paulding and Irving suggested in their early biographies that the naval victories won during 1812 had established Americans on one level vis-à-vis Britain, no longer inferior to their erstwhile mother country. In subsequent texts, their thrust became a different one. Now, they began to envisage their relationship with Great Britain as one which moved from equality on the basis of a shared sense of English heritage and began to construct an autonomous American identity grounded in national allegory and incipient national myths. In its own biography of Lawrence, the *Port Folio* had noted that there was no shame in the defeat—it was, the magazine averred, an unequal fight anyhow—and that, in fact, the Americans could consider themselves superior to the British individually. Interestingly, the *Port Folio* also offered a genealogical argument, whose formulation echoed Hector St. John De Crèvecoeur: "Nature and circumstances have made them so" (*PF* 1813 2, 254). The *Port Folio* adapted James Paulding genealogical motive and shaped a different interpretation: although the British still functioned as ancestors, and, indeed, Americans clearly were a "generally younger men," echoing Paulding's family metaphor, the *Port Folio* deemed the British-American relationship an unequal one. Despite the repetition, it may be helpful here to recall again the *Port Folio*'s naturalistic argument:

> The warm and variable climate of the United States has, to a certain degree, melted the original English constitution of our ancestors, till, instead of the broad shouldered and ruddy form of the people of Great Britain, the Americans are a thinner race of men, with less personal strength and stamina, but with more activity, more quickness, more alertness. (*PF* 1813 2, 254)

Here again was the motive of British descent, transmuted into something more: an avowal of a fundamentally different American national identity based in the naturalization of certain imagined physical and psychological traits, proven by the victoriousness of the United States Navy in equal combat and not disproven by the unfair fight between Lawrence and the *Shannon*. However, the *Port Folio* did not offer a way to mythologize the national origins. If Americans are a transmuted race, they are transmuted British. For all its eloquence, this vision was highly conservative. It echoed Paulding's life of Isaac Hull, could trace its intellectual origins back to Jefferson's *Notes on the State of Virginia*, to Crèvecoeur, and to the natural history of the Comte de Buffon. Successive efforts in the *Analectic Magazine*, by contrast, would drift towards offering readers visions of originally American national identity located more explicitly in the War of 1812.

The Hero of Lake Erie and the Future of America

In December 1813, Irving himself supplied the most notable biography printed in the *Analectic Magazine* during the War of 1812. Its subject was Commodore Oliver Hazard Perry, who, in September, had won the Battle of Lake Erie, leading a small squadron of U.S. Navy vessels to victory over a slightly stronger British force and securing the Western theater of the war for the Americans. For the *Analectic Magazine*, Irving crafted a biography which reimagined American national identity by mythologizing the victory on the lake even as he took care to situate the biography in his magazine in such a way as to further emphasize the *Analectic Magazine*'s year-long endeavor to claim America as Great Britain's rightful imperial heir. The biography is the primary example of the confluence of editorial ability and publishing requirements. The text itself proved the possibilities of the biographical genre to offer more than a facile recounting of life events—a literary quality which in turn rendered it an excellent candidate to further the sales of the *Analectic Magazine*. When in 1816, Moses Thomas attempted to sell single numbers of the *Analectic*, it was the December 1813 issue which he singled out. He noted that he had had "additional copies printed" of this particular number, and advertised the biography of Perry as "one of the best written articles in the work" (*AM* 1816, March covers). Thomas's recognition that he had, in the issue in which the Perry article appeared, a number that deserved the printing of additional copies speaks to the regard in which he held the number, a regard he believed justified in assuming could be converted to sales. Indeed, the December issue of 1813, especially the biography of Perry, is a remarkable editorial and authorial effort.[44]

The "Biographical Memoir of Commodore Perry" starts out as had become customary with the *Analectic Magazine*'s biographies not with the life of Perry, but rather with a thoroughgoing meditation on the issue of biography as a means of commenting on the ongoing war. It was for this reason that Irving quickly disclaimed "rigid precision and dispassionate coolness" (*AM* 1813 2, 494) in his narrative, and set out to elaborate his conception of how Americans should behave themselves as a consequence of their victories over the British. He recognized the need, and indeed the propriety, of Americans' exultation over their success, "when the triumphs of the navy are the theme" (494), but also offered a caution: there was, he suggested, a point "beyond which exultation becomes insulting, and honest pride swells into vanity." Americans should avoid crossing that point, because their gains on the field of battle might suffer, if by "fulsome and extravagant paragraphs" in newspapers they were to produce "national arrogance" and thus "lessen our triumphs in the eyes of impartial nations." Irving recognized that his position might not be a popular one, and therefore clarified his purpose. He argued that the point was not to deny "joy [...] in seeing the flag of our country encircled with glory," but rather to be careful in what one ended up claiming. "[W]e make no boastful claims to intrinsic superiority, nor seek to throw sneer or stigma on an enemy, whom, in spite of temporary hostility, we honour and admire." On the other hand,

44 Which, somewhat surprisingly, has not received the deserved attention of scholars. Andrew Burstein in his recent biography of Irving, calls "Irving's biographical sketch of Commodore Perry [...] well written," but thinks it "does not go much beyond being informative, and is typical of the war propaganda others wrote" (2007. 98). As I show here, the Perry sketch was fairly exceptional, as far as its particular form of propaganda went.

however, Irving again took the same line as the previous biographies had done in subsuming the victory on Lake Erie into a long history of public American grievances. The "unexpected and repeated success" (495) of American naval arms rung more resoundingly because "our memories are still sore with the tales of our flag insulted in every sea, and our countrymen oppressed in every port." Irving stressed the national dimension of the struggle:

> He who fancies he can stand aloof in interest, and by condemning the present war, can exonerate himself from the shame of its disasters, is wofully [sic] mistaken. Other nations will not trouble themselves about our internal wranglings and party questions; they will not ask who among us fought, or why we fought—but how we fought. The disgrace of defeat will not be confined to the contrivers of the war, or the party in power, or the conductors of the battle; but will extend to the whole nation, and come home to every individual.

He considered the ongoing struggle affirmatively a "war awfully decisive of the future character and destinies of the nation." Yet, as the following essay made clear, Irving was not prepared to let the course of the war decide the destinies of the nation without mediation. The biography of Perry became an effort to shape the character of the future nation itself, by offering it a new conception of its national identity. As Irving summarized in the final paragraph of his lengthy introduction, "in writing these naval biographies, it is our object not merely to render a small tribute of gratitude to these intrepid champions of our honour; but to render our feeble assistance towards promoting that national feeling which their triumphs are calculated to inspire" (497).

The biographical sketch of Perry proper, very much like those already published by the *Analectic Magazine*, spared few words for business unrelated to the Battle of Lake Erie, for whose commemoration the text was certainly written in the main. After a page recounting the first fifteen years of Perry's service, the biography finds him in command of a gun-boat flotilla at the beginning of the War of 1812. Irving took the opportunity to criticize the Jeffersonian anti-navalist policies, noting the unpleasantness of gun-boat duty for "ardent and daring minds […] obliged to skulk about harbors and rivers," and highlights Perry's desire to be transferred to a more active station. Here, in describing Perry's departure from the "the comforts of home, and the endearments of a young and beautiful wife and blooming child" (499), Irving's greater conception of the biographical essay is introduced. In this description of Perry's leave-taking from his family, Irving begins an implicit connection between Perry and British Admiral Lord Horatio Nelson, a connection on which Irving grounds his conception of American succession to British domination. Nelson, Britain's foremost naval hero, is transfigured into Perry's predecessor—and both come to stand, synechdochically, as the *pars* which indicate the transfiguration of the *toto*, by which America comes to succeed Britain as the foremost power of empire in America.

The reference to Nelson in Perry's departure requires some previous knowledge of Nelson's life—I will come to that later—but Irving does not gamble it all on this

Fig. 7: Oliver Hazard Perry. This engraving preceded the biographical sketch in the *Analectic Magazine*. Perry's right hand is tucked (in the style of Napoleon) into his left coat breast; an echo, perhaps, of the empty sleeve Horatio Nelson pinned to his breast.
Courtesy of the American Antiquarian Society.

item. Describing Perry's letter announcing his victory on Lake Erie, Irving notes that it "has been called an imitation of Nelson's letter after the battle of the Nile; but it was choosing a noble precedent, and the important national results of the victory justified the language" (508). The explicit connection here between the British officer and the American commodore highlights the similar importance accrued both events, as well as the prospect of more signal victories still to come: if the Battle of the Nile was Nelson's first true independent victory, his grand triumph at Trafalgar was yet to come; an echo of greater glory for Perry, too, sounds through the phrase. This late explicit paralleling of Perry and Nelson gives force to the previous allusion in the description of Perry's departure for the lakes; and here, strikingly, the editorial possibilities of the periodical are used to the fullest. If the Perry biography requires knowledge of Nelson's life, the *Analectic Magazine*'s December 1813 edition itself provided it: its review section carried a lengthy discussion of Robert Southey's *Life of Nelson*, a review initially published in the *London Critical Review* of July, 1813. As was customary for the times, the review included large sections copied verbatim—as examples of the prose—from the book itself. Nelson's career is summarized, and his status as a great naval officer amply honored, but the review-sketch concludes with his affair with Lady Hamilton. The reviewer's stance is critical but understanding, acknowledging that "his infirmity has been that of many noble minds," and posing the question "whether Nelson would have been altogether more estimable if the ingredients of his character had been mingled in different proportions" (471-2). Nelson is a hero in the fleet but a flawed man in private life, an issue which the reviewer does not take to be, in the last resort, critical. It becomes important only in connection with Perry: not only is the implicit contrast between the ways in which Nelson left his wife for a mistress evident, but Irving emphasizes the contrast, without naming names, in the biography of Perry. "It is pleasing," Irving writes, "thus to find public services accompanied by private virtues; to discover no drawbacks in our esteem; no base alloy in the man we are disposed to admire; but a character full of moral excellence, of high-minded courtesy, and pure, unsullied honour" (509). Where Nelson, then, combined martial prowess with moral failure, Perry does not; where Perry tears himself from the bosom of an intact family, Nelson's final departure is from his mistress and their daughter. The Nelson connection is reinforced wherever possible: Irving explicitly notes that Commodore Barclay, the British commander whom Perry beat, had himself fought at Nelson's great last victory at Trafalgar; and if it would be too much to claim that the engraved portrait (cf. fig. 7) which preceded the biography was playing on Nelson's empty right sleeve, devoid of the arm which he had lost in the Battle of Santa Cruz (1797), in showing Perry with his right hand tucked into his coat, it would perhaps not be too much to say that the allusion would have been willingly accepted by Irving if it had been pointed out to him.

In juxtaposing biography, portraiture, and review, Irving editorially connects Nelson and Perry; in writing about Perry with implicit reference to the life of Nelson, he places them in relation authorially. By contrasting Nelson and Perry in the two biographical articles, Irving establishes a central figure in the myth of British naval dominance in contrast to an American figure whom he wants to refigure as Nelson's successor. The effort to contrast and compare the two men leads from the similarity of their victory letters and the contrasting private lives to more obscure but telling references and produces a form of hereditary succession: Perry, "yet in the prime of youth," is variously marked as the successor of Nelson, and in succeeding Nelson, becomes a metonymical stand-in for the United States that succeeds Britain.

Irving's editorial and authorial work on a new conception of American national identity does not end with the Nelson parallel. In between the review of the biography of Nelson and the sketch of Oliver Hazard Perry, Irving placed an original article called "Hints on the Navy of the United States." Much as discussion in the magazines prior to the war had emphasized the role which a strong navy could play in cementing American independence and national character, the "Hints" highlighted the ways in which Americans would be able to make use of their natural resources and ingenuity, and actively considered the "means by which [the country's] glory may be perpetuated and its successes continued" (*AM* 1813 2, 475). Largely a factual analysis of the va rious options and opportunities were open to a future U.S. Navy, the article's humble conclusion, that if its remarks should "awaken a discussion that will bring to light any of the naval energies of the nation," they would "attain the end proposed" (486), echoed again the pre-war reflections on the synchrony between naval power and national character, and, for readers who went through the magazine front to back, highlighted once more the importance of Perry's victory, even as Perry's victory validated the conclusions of the "Hints".

The *Analectic*'s editor Irving was primarily responsible for this juxtaposition of texts with a similar outlook; the Perry biography's author Irving was responsible for the conclusion of the biography. For the past nine months, the Analectic Magazine had had to deal with a simple problem: whenever it had claimed that American naval victories had shown American equality, if not superiority, at sea in a one-on-one fight, the British had responded derisively that American frigates, heavier, stronger, and armed with more guns, had always outclassed the British ships. Now, Irving gleefully noted that "[i]n this battle, incontrovertible proof is given [...] that the success of our navy does not arise from chance, or superiority of force" but rather from the sheer ability of American seamen. The Battle of Lake Erie had shown Americans able "to face the foe in squadron, and vanquish him even though superior in force." The December issue of the Analectic Magazine thus neatly concluded the narrative which had begun with the sketch of the biography of Captain Hull, by removing from the British "every excuse in which [they] sought to shelter" (506) themselves.

Irving did not just present a summary of the value of Perry's victory for the immediate circumstances of the War of 1812, and a fitting conclusion to the series of biographies published during 1813, but rather offered his readers a proleptic view of future American grandeur; in that future, the present victory on Lake Erie has been transformed into a mythical past, where Perry plays the role of the "warrior" in a "heroic story," streaming like a meteor through the fight, and working wonders with his single arm" (506)[45], and where the historical legacy of the Battle of Lake Erie becomes much more than a momentary shift in control of a body of water. "Naval warfare," Irving writes, "has been carried into the interior of a continent," and American victory on Lake Erie turns out to have been "the expiring note of British domination" (509). The lakes, Irving's vision suggests, will soon "be embosomed within a mighty empire," no longer "be the separating space between contending nations," thanks to the "ocean warriors that came from the shores of the Atlantic" (510). Irving's striking romantic prose reads Perry's victory, apart from the real-world consequences for the War of 1812 which he had already enumerated, as the prefiguration of a new American empire, in which Canada belongs to the United States. The movement into the wilderness of Lake Erie from the Atlantic re-imagines the westward movement of empire, and the peal which sounds over English domination not only rings out British control over Lake Erie. Through the metaphorical connection between Perry and Nelson, between individual naval victories and a general assumption of the role of Britain's successor, rings in a myth of origin for the American empire. Irving constructs a metaphorical form of genealogy, one which at the same time seeks to reaffirm good relations with Great Britain as it conceives of American victory, and especially American victors, as symbolic of

45 The reference here to a single arm is, no pun intended, mystifying. Irving had previously spoken of captain Barclay, who had indeed lost an arm in battle; but the paragraph now is clearly speaking of Perry, who remained uninjured throughout the action. Irving is probably suggesting here that the hero in the story is usually working with a single arm—a sword, or a spear—and not actually referencing Perry. But, of course, the echo of Nelson is unavoidable.

America's superseding of Great Britain. Even as it does so, it also constructs a form of mythical origin of the United States in the present of the War of 1812: "In future times," Irving notes,

> when the shores of Erie shall hum with busy population; when towns and cities shall brighten where now extend the dark and tangled forest [sic]; when ports shall spread their arms, and lofty barks shall ride where now the canoe is fastened to the stake; when the present age shall have grown into venerable antiquity, and the mists of fable begin to gather round its history; then will the inhabitants of Canada look back to this battle we record, as one of the romantic achievements of the days of yore. It will stand first on the page of their local legends, and in the marvellous tales of the borders. (510)

In the Battle of Lake Erie and the figure of Oliver Hazard Perry, Irving finds suitable material for a mythical construction of national identity: his proleptical musings on the effects of the Battle of Lake Erie immediately transpose the events of war into the diction and realms of the mythical. The inhabitants of Canada, who have, as we have seen, already been integrated in a vaster American empire in succession to the British, will make this battle their *fons et origo*, and themselves stand synecdochically for a future United States whose shape and identity as heir to Britain's empire stems directly from the Battle of Lake Erie, and with it, the personified heir to Britain's naval glory, Oliver Hazard Perry. Yet even as future Americans are able to draw on this mythical past, a past which they are permitted to share in through the medium of the magazine and the unifying power of the national navy, and thereby create a myth sufficient to identify an origin for a national identity, so can contemporaries benefit. They, after all, are the ancestors of those Americans whose national identity can be traced from the shared inaugural, quasi mythical victory on Lake Erie, and who are looking back for their national origins to the time of the War of 1812. Contemporary Americans were therefore enabled to see themselves as the forefathers of those Americans who drew on them for their mythical genealogy, and thereby constitute their own national identity through their descendants. It was towards this goal that the mildness of the biography's rhetoric was chiefly directed: Irving's methodical essay neatly recognized that its efforts to establish a new American genealogy would suffer if Americans persisted in viewing themselves as naturally superior while ridiculing their enemy. American naval triumphs could only be valuable against an enemy who was not intrinsically inferior—to claim a naturalized superiority would in fact devalue the victory. When Irving wrote of the "national feeling" which the naval victories were "calculated to inspire" even as he attempted to reign in precisely those national feelings which the victories *had* inspired, the "vulgar joy and coarse tauntings of the rabble" (495), he indicated the complicated nature of the particular construction of American national identity which he sought to install. Americans could at once consider themselves the legitimate heirs of Great Britain, fairly beaten on its own element; and take their own mythical origin precisely from the time of this victory over the erstwhile motherland. With a bit of cheek, Irving fully acknowledges the ulterior motives which prompted the writing of the biography:

> We have seized this opportunity to express the foregoing sentiments, because we thought that if of any value, they might stand some chance of making an impression, when accompanied by the following memoir. And, indeed, in writing these naval biographies, it is our object not merely to render a small tribute of gratitude to these intrepid champions of our honour; but to render our feeble assistance towards promoting that national feeling which their triumphs are calculated to inspire. (490)

Here, biography becomes a vehicle for editorial policy, in which the biography, ostensibly the article proper, comes to merely "accompany" the political statements, and its value for the production of national identity is explicitly affirmed. Americans could at once consider themselves the legitimate heirs of Great Britain, fairly beaten on her own element, and take their own mythical origin precisely from the time of this victory over the erstwhile motherland, an origin which implied a lack of direct antecedents. This was the approach which James Kirke Paulding would pursue in 1816.

For all that it is billed as a biography, and indeed seeks to appear like a biography, it is worth pointing out that out of the fourteen pages which the memoir took up in the *Analectic Magazine*, eight were devoted not to Perry's life, but to the preliminary and concluding remarks that reflected on the war, on the battle, and on the purposes of biography; Perry's life pre-war was granted a scant paragraph; and the remainder of the text was devoted more to the Battle of Lake Erie, rather than to Perry's life as such. Part of this is no doubt owed to a simple question of where the necessary information on Perry's life was going to come from; yet Irving himself had already hinted at the emphasis of his text in calling it a memoir. Despite its biographical sound, Irving meant the term here to mean simply as, in the definition of Johnson's *Dictionary*, an "account of any thing" (1769, n.p.), and "biographical" as a modifier. Perhaps Irving's "Biographical Memoir of Commodore Perry" is best understood not as a biography accompanied by a considerable amount of introductory and concluding material; rather, it might best be considered a political essay, for which biography serves as the canvas.[46]

Genealogies of National Identity in the *Analectic Magazine* after Washington Irving

Washington Irving left the editorship at the *Analectic Magazine* in February 1815. The magazine then passed into the hands of Thomas Isaac Wharton, a long-time contributor to the *Port Folio*, whose editorial policies did not correspond with

46 Cf. also Scheiding (2010) for a different type of political essay/biography written by Irving during his *Analectic* tenure, the sketch "Philip of Pokanoket."

Irving's, although they were genial to James Kirke Paulding. After Irving had exercised his editorial prerogative to reign in Paulding's political stance in the biography of Jacob Jones, Paulding had not written anything resembling the political essay that was the biography of Hull. Irving played his role as the *Analectic Magazine*'s editor as a mediator between the ultra-nationalist position that assumed the victories of 1812 to be evidence of inherent American supremacy and the British opinion that they signified nothing at all. Unlike, for example, the *Port Folio*'s biographer of Lawrence, Irving cautioned his readers not to assume anything more than parity with Britain, despite the victories attained in 1812. While James Paulding was on a "literary campaign against the British" (Aderman and Kime 2004, 57), Irving moderated Paulding's vicious attacks in his direct editorial influence on the biography of Jacob Jones and in his own writings. Irving realized Paulding's stance towards the British full well, writing to Henry Brevoort with friendly irony in August 1815 that Napoleon's defeat at Waterloo and the French Restoration "will be sore blows to Jims [sic] plans – they will materially delay the object of his life – the overthrow of the British Empire" (Irving 1978, 418). There can be little doubt that Irving was chiefly responsible for reigning Paulding in: Soon after Irving's departure, Paulding's biographies of Commodore Thomas Macdonough and Lieutenant John Templar Shubrick showed what Paulding thought of America's British relations, and how he purported to reframe American genealogy and, echoing Irving, to re-orient Americans mythology towards the heroes of the War of 1812.

Biographical theory became the opening gambit in the biographies. Paulding's biography of Thomas Macdonough starts out by setting out a theory of biography which contrasts the practice in "legitimate monarchies" and in "a simple republic" (AM 1816 1, 201). Monarchical biography, Paulding avers, has an advantage over republican, since a monarchical biographer, if he finds his subject unsuitable for lack of "any thing worth recording," can resort to describing the lives of his subject's ancestors, "to whose exploits [the biographee] is fully entitled by the theory as well as the practice of hereditary succession" (202). This makes it "worth a man's while to perform great actions, since he thereby not only ennobles himself and his wife, but all the rogues and blockheads in his posterity forever and ever" (202). Paulding's acerbic commentary then turns to the question of what biography is worth in republics: Here, honors are "exclusively paid to his own merit," so that biography need not consider family history, an argument which he had already previously made in a biography of another naval officer, John Shubrick. In that piece, the lowly lieutenant's biography is justified by the simple formula that "honour should be paid where honour is due," since words of praise would render it possible to "gain them individual distinction" (*AM* 1816 2, 247-8).

The notion that honoring the individual through the publication of a biography was the only adequately republican form of paying homage to deserving individuals was a common one in the early Republic, but in the essay on Macdonough, Paulding expands it into a theory of genealogical descent. Even if American biographers were inclined to reduce their subjects to the achievements of their forebears, such an effort is impossible, rather than merely undesirable. Aside from the mythico-religious origins of the Bible, in which "few of us can trace our ancestry higher than Adam" (*AM* 1816 1, 203), Americans do not even have a heritage which they could possibly be reduced to. "Family trees," Paulding notes, "are exceedingly scarce [...] containing not more than three or four generations. Our ancestors unluckily forgot their pedigrees" (203). Emigration to America for Paulding becomes the crossing of a Lethean stream, a journey at whose end lies a new identity:

> Not one of our ancestors, that we know of, came over with William the bastard to conquer England [...] We are consequently obliged to build up a name for ourselves, as the first settlers of this country were obliged to build houses [...] It is believed [...] that this undignified republic cannot boast of a single man the merits of whose ancestors can make amends for his own want of spirit. (203-4)

The motive of memory is present here too in Paulding's qualification "that we know of," but more importantly, he denies a shared mythical origin with the British by rejecting any connection with the events of 1066. This is best understood not as a refusal of Norman heritage only, which would still allow Americans to trace their origins back to Angle-Saxon roots, but as a refusal of heritage as such. The Norman invasion of 1066 functions here as the marker of British mythic national origin—mythic not in the sense that it is not a historical event, but mythic in the sense that it anchors the historical national awareness in England. This historical dimension Paulding combines with a fictional, actively myth-making reference: he notes that "[w]e cannot trace back to those glorious times when a man was [...] immortalized, like young Lochinvar" (203), an allusion to Walter Scott's popular poem *Marmion,* set in a mytho-historical Scottish past, a past, in fact, which Scott was actively creating to offer a sense of historical continuity and of national origins. Paulding thereby distances himself from imported mythologies per se, whether based on historical data or contemporary efforts to create them anew. Instead, for Paulding, as previously for Irving, the here and now becomes important, in which Americans are "undignified" by the titles of which the British boast, and each and every deserving individual can come to serve as an example for building "a name for ourselves". Instead of figuring as colonial Englishmen, the first settlers from which Paulding traces American heritage are first and foremost the ancestors of current Americans. Their pioneering work of constructing physical shelters for themselves is a type for American's contemporary achievement of establishing their national identity, their "name". America has granted both the "first settlers" and their descendants, from who Paulding claims descent instead of more distant readings, a chance for a new myth of origin, and an original national identity.[47]

The uniqueness of Paulding's outlined in vision becomes especially noticeable when contrasted with the *Port Folio*'s biography of Oliver Hazard Perry, published in March 1814. The *Port Folio* began its biography precisely with the kind of biographical

47 On Paulding and his national rhetoric, cf. Scheiding (1993).

backdrop which Paulding denied. It emphasized the "reflected splendor from his ancestry," especially highlighting the distinguished pedigree which reached back to the first Perry to emigrate to America, his grandfather's public service in the and stressing his father Christopher's service in the Navy as well. The *Port Folio* then produced a detailed life concentrating on Perry's naval service. The *Port Folio* framed Perry as an exemplary hero, but never reached the more ambitious conclusions which James Paulding offered his readers.

Not until after the War of 1812 did the *Port Folio* manage to frame individual lives in explicitly national terms. When it published a second biography of James Lawrence in January 1817, it recognized that at times, the "efforts of a life [...] become so identified with the events of a nation, that to tell the story is among the duties which it owes to its own history." Thus, it argued, there existed an obligation from selfishness to write about its most prominent men, an obligation which it, too, phrased in genealogical language. It suggested that to portray distinguished eminence in biography should be done with all the "solicitude for a faithful resemblance that a parent feels for a portrait, in which he may survive to his children" (*PF* 1817 1, 4). Yet here again, it bears pointing out that the *Port Folio*, like other magazines before it, made claims for national biography that were descriptive rather than prescriptive, they suggested what the role of a particular piece of writing was, referenced *toto pro pars*, rather than what the mission of the genre of national biography ought to be. Such claims did not so much seek to encourage and explain the need for more national biography, published for the express purpose of actively creating a national identity, than they sought to highlight a justification of the particular text they were attached to. Thus is also explained the limited number of programmatic statements on national biography in the era.

Among the magazines which produced original biographies of American officers during the War of 1812, only the Boston *Polyanthos* came close to the *Analectic*'s efforts at placing the events of the war in a future historical continuum. In 1813, its biography of William Bainbridge proclaimed the lasting effect of the naval victories, and situated the naval officers which had previously won successes—Bainbridge, Jones, Decatur, Hull, and Lawrence—in a similar allegorical relationship as the *Analectic*'s biographies. Great Britain's insistence on naval dominance heightened the impact of these officers' victories: "Memory instantly supplies materials for volumes at the mention of their names. Their exploits, the causes and effects of them, will be recorded by some American Sallust on the imperishable tablets of History" (*P* 1813 1, 282).

Constructing National Identity Through Biography

The most striking aspect of the naval biographies' rhetoric is how they can modify our understanding of constructions of national identity. They are not "[l]ooking to the legitimacy of past generations as supplying cultural autonomy" (Giddens 1985, 216), but instead seek to establish the future pastness of the current generation. Explicitly, as we have seen, Irving's life of Oliver Hazard Perry proleptically projects an American future, but this future is already looking back at Irving's contemporary scene as the origin of its history. Precisely because it is the descendants of his contemporaries, of the current generation of Americans, who will find themselves in this new nation, Irving's readers are enabled to draw their national identity from their shared relationship to the future United States. This play with the relative positions of progeny, of current events, of future and history informs not only Irving's life of Perry, though, but most of the biographies I have discussed above. "[T]hou shalt have a noble memory," as Gulian Verplanck promises Zebulon Pike, a General whose death had occasioned much mourning, and "when our children and our children's children shall read the story of patriots and heroes" (*AM* 1815 1, 395), they would be able to note happily that the United States, too, possessed its stock of characters that could lend mythical depth to the national idea.

Publishers and editors recognized, of course, that in writing biographies, they perpetuated a national message, and recognized, too, that such a national message to a large part in fact depended on their writings. As Charles Caldwell noted in his introductory address when he took over the *Port Folio* in 1814, "unstable and transitory would be the column of fame" which could be erected on the basis of American achievements in war, "were there no poet to court the muse, no orator to thunder on the rostrum, in the forum or the senate chamber, or to immortalize by his praises the achievements of heroism" (*PF* 1814 1, 389). While thoroughly conventional, these beliefs echoed the ultimate purpose of biography as a means of giving narrative to national glory. So defined, however, the biographical texts in periodicals could hardly aspire to autonomy: rather, they picked up on the existing trend and fashioned biographies which supported that trend. There existed a lag of several months after the outbreak of the war and after its end in which periodicals had not yet reacted to a rising, and then still were reacting to a declining sense of the importance of the national identity of the United States which clearly circumscribes this heteronomy, the ultimately reactive nature of the periodical and its orientation towards the consumers' existing desires. Such autonomy as the periodicals achieved lay in their shaping of the materials that they found themselves in need of handling, and here, the different readings of American national identity which especially Washington Irving and James Paulding offered their readers stand out. Surprisingly, within the boundaries of a single magazine, even if under different editors, Paulding and Irving offered their readers different conceptions of American national identity. Both visions emphasized the constitutiveness of the present war for mythical conceptions of American national identity, but while Irving was happy to assure his readers that their relationship with Great Britain remained important, by 1816 James Kirke Paulding was ready to imagine an American identity which denied any transatlantic origins and relied solely on Americans' own, autochthonous history. The texts which I have discussed above thus must be read simultaneously as heteronomous productions of a particular commercially exploitable moment as well as relatively autonomous expressions of different conceptions of national identity. They thus highlight the fact that even at a period of heightened nationalism, Americans were hardly in agreement on what precisely constituted their national identity. Even within the confines of one magazine, and one genre of text, written by just two authors, periodicals offered their readers various conceptions of American national identity, constructed through myths of origin, covering a broad spectrum of different ways for American to see themselves. Some reflected their British heritage and avowed the lasting and profound ties of parent and child, coequal friends, or, at the very least, equals in ability and spirit, while others firmly disavowed any remaining connection with Britain. Even as these texts shared a general sense of American nationhood, they contested the particular form which that nationhood should take. Indeed, as we have seen, Democrat-Republicans at the very least thought that the best form of the nation coincided with an identification with their own party—and magazines were praised for writing without party lines.

The naval biographies merely inscribed themselves in a fleeting moment of national upsurge, rather than as constitutive elements of an American national identity in an ontological sense: we cannot say, indeed, that after the War of 1812, there 'was' an American national identity, or that Americans 'were' a nation. Many histories of the War of 1812 have emphasized the incomplete nationhood of the United States in the aftermath of the American Revolution, and sought to identify in the subsequent decades the progress of American nationalism. Yet, as Jack Green suggests, "[t]he powerful state identities inherited from the colonial era and the deep-seated provincial loyalties, habits, and prejudices they expressed represented a formidable challenge for those who hoped to create a durable national union" in the direct aftermath of the revolution and beyond (2006, 77). This chapter has framed national identity as a rhetorical trope, a contingent figure within a discourse that waxed and waned in importance compared to those other identities which existed in the Early Republic.

By early 1817, the public interest in naval officers' biographies had clearly waned so far as to make it increasingly unprofitable to keep publishing and writing them. Indeed, as early as January 1816, the *Analectic*'s author of the biography of Lewis Warrington had noted that as it was "probable that for some time to come there will occur but few opportunities of gaining distinction in the service [...] our biographical labours may possibly be brought nearly to a close" (*AM* 1816 1, 7). The *Analectic* did not wish to continue publishing naval biographies, now of insignificant officers, because it did not wish to cheapen its former praise of deserving men. The purpose of biography was to herald "distinction in the service of [the] country," advancing the heroic individuals who could figure as public eidolons, and whose ability to do so depended in no small part on the external enemy capable of genuinely uniting the disparate communities of the United States. War had catapulted American nationalism and American naval officers into public interest. Peace relegated those officers to their "ordinary duties" (*AM* 1816 1, 7) and Americans' national identity to one affiliation among many, and by no means a *primus inter pares*.

As Alan Taylor has recently summarized, the war had not been fought because of American nationalism. Rather, it had at best engendered a fleeting nationalism which post-war histories extended backwards and transmuted from a result into a cause (cf. 2010, 458), and which modern histories too often essentialize as a more-than-momentary, lasting impact of the War of 1812. Symbolic of this merely momentary interest in the national dimension of biography is the *Portico*'s already quoted contribution to the biographical productions of the time. The Baltimore magazine had only begun publication in January 1816 and thus missed the War of 1812, but, nevertheless, had promised its readers in late 1816 that it would supply biographical sketches of what it called "our" officers, some of which had already been received and others which it would be glad to have (*PO* 1816 2, 342). When, in January 1817, it published the first of these biographies, of Colonel Jacob Hindman, the meaning of "our" became clear: "*Maryland* has borne an ample share, in the dangers and honours of the late arduous struggle; and our fellow-citizens of that state will participate, in the satisfaction which it affords us, to be enabled to commence this series, with one of her most distinguished sons" (*PO* 1817 1, 38, original emphasis). The Baltimore magazine had effectively denationalized military biography by emphasizing the importance of Maryland's own share in the glory as against a view which would clearly acknowledge an American national struggle against Britain. The *Portico* was by no means anti-national: it advocated the cause of a national literature and even explicitly discussed the future of the Union on its pages. Yet it had to recognize, as the other magazines did too by 1817, that readers were not supplying them with national military lives anymore, and they themselves were giving up the interest in national biographies in the face of readerly indifference.

Scott Casper has suggested that "[b]iography helped Americans understand themselves and their national identity as they manufactured a new culture to match their new polity" (1999, 3), and, in a slight variation, that it was "part of the multifaceted effort to create a national identity and culture" (19). These two interpretations of biography's relation to national identity are, of course, mutually contradictory (was there a national identity to understand, or was there an effort to create one?), and, more importantly, neither fully explains what periodical biography looked like during the War of 1812. Neither did the periodicals explain to readers a single national identity which could be aptly described as "American," nor did they actively engage in making "a" national identity—and indeed, it might be wondered if they created any at all. I have emphasized above that I consider the ways in which especially the *Analectic Magazine* reacted to the War of 1812 and the rhetoric with which it filled its biographies an expression of the relative autonomy granted magazine authors in the course of the War of 1812 to utilize an existing genre's popularity to write texts which exceed the conceptual and literary boundaries of the genre and the medium. These texts prospered in the repeated reprints and anthologizations and found a wide and lasting readership and critical recognition long after the war had ended. The broad republication of the texts which I have discussed above may have helped diminish an effect, of periodical writing, critically investigated by Robb Haberman, namely the creation of several distinct publics, rather than one, common, national public. Haberman notes that periodicals certainly managed to establish "dense local and regional networks for literary exchange" (2009, 3), and that these stood in opposition to larger national identities. Americans could use the naval biographies to identify themselves with the victorious heroes, explicitly presented to them as examples of American virtue. They could identify the individual struggles and victories of the naval officers as synecdoches for the nation, and thus themselves with the nation. These representations of the nation through naval officers, however, were largely contingent, in that they did not function as the end point of a larger movement towards the nation, but were merely one moment in the burgeoning history of the United States where, owed to war-induced patriotism, a momentary upsurge of national feelings could be sustained. Beneath this upsurge lay conflicting and incompatible conceptions of how Americans should see themselves, as evidenced by the contrasting genealogies the *Analectic Magazine* and the *Port Folio* offered their readers during the War of 1812 and in the two years afterwards. Not that it mattered: as the glory of the naval war vanished into the hazes of the past, politics, section, and racial and social strife reared its head again. As Maurizio Viroli has suggested, "[t]he only kind of commitment that is compatible with the pluralism of American society is a commitment to the republic; it is a political allegiance" (1995, 179), rather than the kind of ethno-mythical national identity envisaged in the biographies in the *Analectic Magazine*. With the diminishing of the patriotic fervor that had fueled nationalist politics for two or three years after the War of 1812, Americans found themselves back in a union of separate states, whose individual goals, and later sectional goals, trumped the national spirit and all conceptions of national identity.

Periodical Production after the War of 1812

The period of the War of 1812 shows the possibility for periodical writing to momentarily expand the narrow boundaries of the production heteronomies of the periodical business and to produce texts which functioned as more than just filler material. At the same time, however, the developments which led to the writing and publication of naval biography, specifically the professionalization of the relationship between editors and publishers and the payment of contributors, were crucial for the future of the magazine business, changes which signaled the future development of the periodical.

When Samuel Lorenzo Knapp, editor and proprietor of the *Boston Monthly Magazine*, advertised his new venture on the first pages of the first issue in 1825, not only did he put his own full name proudly on the front page. He also suggested some general points about the reading culture of the United States: "We are a reading people, and must have a large supply of periodical literature for the demands of the market [...] in England [...] there are an hundred magazines issued monthly from the press, or oftener, to satisfy the reading community of Great Britain." Knapp was not so far removed from his editorial predecessors to not mention the usual platitudes of the editorial trade—the desire to "blend amusement with instruction" or to include "as much variety as possible" (*BMM* 1825, 1)—but there is at least some symbolic significance to the sequence of Knapp's statements, in which the satisfaction of the demand of the reading community came befor the editorial principles of instruction, amusement, and variety. Whether or not the market demanded Knapp's or indeed any other periodical is less important than Knapp's obvious belief that it was perfectly sensible to apply not to the inherent value of any magazine in being instructive or amusing, but to the people's acceptance of the demands of the market as a sufficient justification for commissioning a new magazine. Knapp's ability to plainly emphasize market determinations, to be, as it were, blunt about his heteronomy, was not a sudden turn in periodical production, neither an end point of the 'early' periodical nor the beginning of the 'new,' nor "now a space apart from the fray" of political or ideological considerations, as Jared Gardner has suggested (2012, 167). Such suggestions miss the point, made explicit in the foregoing chapters, that the development which saw Knapp propose in 1825 to publish a magazine at the service of an imagined market demand was continuous. Ultimately, Knapp's announcement was another waypoint in the course of a professionalization of the American magazine, which was part of what Charles Sellers has called the "new world of the untrammeled market" (1991, 82). Knapp foregrounded the market publically, but the process which led to that foregrounding, as we have seen, had its origins much earlier: throughout the entire periodical history of the Early Republic, the periodical market had increasingly determined the content of magazines. The professionalization of the periodical business went hand in hand with the possibility of actively and openly pursuing market-oriented goals.

It is important to realize that there was no sharp break with the past. Vestiges of the old and so frequently publically-voiced conception of periodical editing remained. The *Portico*'s editors, whose magazine ran from 1816 to 1818, were fully in the way of the ostensibly disinterested editors of the 1790s when they noted that they "neither expect nor wish to make money, by this undertaking" (*PO* 1817, covers)—something which the short-lived magazine certainly achieved, but paid for by its demise after a modest three years of publication. By contrast, Knapp's *Boston Monthly Magazine* existed until Knapp himself moved from Boston and founded a new magazine. Certainly, it would be false to suggest that there was necessarily more than a symbolic relationship between the one magazine's public anti-commercialism and the other's overt market-orientation, and their respective successes in the periodical field, but the development is suggestive, and it would be logical to at least suggest the possibility of a connection. The *Portico*'s way of doing business clearly diverged from the increasingly professional models that existed around it, while Knapp's model was fully involved in the process of professionalization. Their respective fates, then, may stand as examples of possible outcomes of placing a magazine in the periodical field after the War of 1812, like the *Monthly Anthology* and *Niles' Weekly Register* did in more general terms in Chapter 1 for the time before the war. Whereas the *Monthly Anthology* had a fairly good run with its anti-commercial, morally-educative conception up until its final demise in 1811, a similar approach in 1817 was much more quickly doomed to failure; and whereas the *Weekly Register*'s editor Niles did not until 1819 find it possible to overtly pronounce his desire to make money off of the paper, the *Boston Monthly Magazine* was able to set out from this very premise. Something, then, clearly had changed, if ever so modestly and in ever so small steps.

Few other aspects symbolize so clearly the success of professionalizing the periodical business as the demise of the *Monthly Anthology* in 1811 and the simultaneous 6000$ profit of the *Port Folio,* and its subsequent adoption of a system of paid contributions. While there is some truth to the belief voiced by Catherine O'Donnell Kaplan that the *Anthology* "led the way toward a new, nineteenth-century vision of letters in America, and the wicked, daring *Port Folio* had in the end fallen in line" (2008, 219), and while the *Anthology*'s literary learning and erudition, as well as its exclusion of politics and its decidedly national cast (if hardly national success) were to some extent adopted and refined by the post-1809 *Port Folio,* the full story is more complicated—and reaffirms the notion that we cannot understand the Early Republic periodical without an in-depth investigation of its business backgrounds. The trailblazing *Monthly Anthology* was a dead end, not because of its contents so much as because of its insistence on old-fashioned practices and a lack of business acumen, something that, despite their partnership's ultimate collapse from unrelated business problems, the firm of Bradford & Inskeep brought to the *Port Folio*. At the heart of the issue, as I have suggested, lies the question of money. Relations based on money increasingly substituted for relationships based on collegiality, on shared sentiments, on friendship, and on community—relationships which themselves never exclusively carried a periodical, of course, as even the *Monthly Anthology* was dependent for being printed on the business relationships which lay outside the realm of the Boston Athenaeum. Thus decommunalized—not fully, to be sure, as there were still relationships which did not depend on money, or on money alone—periodicals increasingly became professionalized.

It bears pointing out that some magazines did well despite not professionalizing across all the aspects that I have outlined above. *Niles' Weekly Register*, for example, ran for thirty-eight years as essentially a one-man business, with first Hezekiah Niles and then his son chiefly responsible for editing and publishing it (cf. Luxon 1947, 2). Niles, as I have argued in Chapter 1, had a more professional operation than, for example, the *Monthly Anthology*, and a literally more professional reason for publishing—the *Weekly Register* was his main source of income, after all—but, as far as can be ascertained, he never hired an editor to do his work, never paid for contributions, and never managed to get away from subscription as the sole method of distributing his work. Likewise, the *Port Folio* ended up renouncing many of the professional changes that Bradford & Inskeep had instituted during their proprietorship: under John E. Hall, whose brother Harrison was the publisher from 1816, it was especially the editor's role which suffered. John Hall did not manage to keep up the *Port Folio*'s large number of contributors—presumably, given the *Port Folio*'s 1818 complaint about the practice, because it did not wish to pay for contributions. Its content was increasingly provided by the Hall family alone, and even this effort faltered by the 1820s, when the magazine was almost entirely a selection of second-hand papers. In 1820, the *Port Folio* began a two-year period as a quarterly, rather than a monthly, a shift in publication format being frequently an indication of enduring sickness. (As the magazine had felt when it changed to the monthly format in 1809, and as the *Analectic Magazine* suffered in 1821. Then under the proprietorship of James Maxwell, also its printer—almost always, as we have seen, a bad combination—it changed to a weekly format that barely managed to last out the year.) The *Port Folio* returned to the monthly format in 1822, absorbing the *New York Monthly Magazine*. By 1823, John Hall himself admitted that the magazine had only 900 subscribers; part of the reason may have been that Hall had not fully come to terms with the marketplace of periodicals. He treated, as John Queenan notes, the extremely successful and very dangerous *North American Review* as a fellow in fight for an American literature; the *Port Folio*, for its part, was wholly unable to keep track. More and more, it fell apart, spent the last two years of its existence only partially in print and publication, and finally failed with the December issues of 1827, probably only printed in 1828 (cf. Queenan 1955, 78-91). Even in its demise, however, the *Port Folio* can highlight aspects which speak to the professionalization of the magazine business in those years. It did not drag down Harrison Hall's company with it: the *Port Folio* was one venture of Hall's among many others, and Hall no doubt made sure that whatever subscription monies subscribers were still indebted for, they could not ruin him; and, as the final act of proprietorship, Hall sold the *Port Folio*'s subscriber list, that bone of such contention in 1806/07, to the *Museum of Foreign Literature and Science*, a Philadelphia magazine edited by Eliakim Littell (cf. Queenan 1955, 91). The end of the *Port Folio* thus signals both the problems which plagued magazines which failed to successfully cater to an audience capable of sustaining its production, and suggests how the basis of the entire venture, the business potential, here vested in subscriber lists (as much in 1806 as in 1827), remained the same throughout the period.

Professionalization was a process that shifted not the actual basis of periodical production, but rather the public presentation of the underlying economic motivations. I have suggested that three aspects of periodical production especially underwent a form of professionalization in the first two decades of the Early Republic: the relationship between publishers and editors, the relationship between magazines and their contributors, and the relationship between magazines and their readers, who were increasingly given the chance to be something else than subscribers only.

Much had changed at the *Port Folio* by the time the magazine finally folded in 1827, and much of this change was unexpected, especially the unfortunate role of John E. Hall—for initially, it had seemed that Hall was the exemplum par excellence of the new relationship between publisher and editor that slowly took over much of the periodical business. When Hall took over the running of the *Port Folio*, his predecessor was explicit in situating Hall as a professional, that is to say, full-time, editor. Charles Caldwell, in drawing the figure of his successor in his final address to the patrons of the *Port Folio*, announced that Hall would give his full devotion to the "regular business" (*PF* 1816 1, 87) of the *Port Folio.* Nor was Caldwell insensible to the fact, and the belief shared, as he had been forced to admit in the summer of 1814, by his readers, that his editorship was sometimes unsatisfactory. He begged a measure of indulgence for the faults which the combined workload of his medical practice and the editorial office had caused in the editing of the *Port Folio*, but also giving tacit recognition to the shift in professionalism which the mid-1810s witnessed in periodicals.

Both the *Port Folio* and the *Analectic Magazine* found that their work could not effectively continue with part-time editors. One of the men who recognized that the time of part-time editors was drawing to a close was Washington Irving himself. Having joined the militia of New York in the summer of 1814, Irving did not attend to his duties at the *Analectic Magazine* with as much dispatch as might be hoped for by Moses Thomas, and realized as much. Even as he was still discussing editorial matters with his publisher, Irving told Thomas that he would forego payment in part for the last few months in which he had not devoted his full attention to the *Analectic* and noted that he should "have to give up all formal agency in the work after the close of the year" (1978, 382). Thomas replaced Irving with Thomas Isaac Wharton, a lawyer. Wharton's energy enabled him to keep up the *Analectic*'s reputation despite being an amateur, like Irving; under his editorship, the magazine sought to keep profiting from its reputation as a pro-naval journal and became, from 1816 to 1818, a quasi-service journal under the name *Analectic Magazine and Naval Chronicle* for which James Paulding and Gulian Verplanck kept writing. While Hall's taking over of the editorial role with the March 1816 edition of the *Port Folio* also saw the end of the front page existence of military and naval news, the *Analectic* found its niche precisely in this section of the market. When Moses Thomas left the business of publishing in 1819 to pursue a different career as a marketer of books—organizing a book fair in the 1820s—James Maxwell took over as publisher, with Edward Ingersoll as editor. Just as the *Port Folio*'s take over by the Halls precipitated a steady decline in the magazine, so did Maxwell's of the *Analectic*. While the precise reasons for its decline are uncertain, again it may be surmised that similar reasons contributed to the *Port Folio*'s decline.

As the changes in proprietorship and editorship indicate, magazines themselves were increasingly becoming commodities, or in the modern parlance, brands, which could survive changes in personnel with ease, if they themselves remained financially sound. Such soundness, as we saw in the discussion of the *Port Folio*'s sale in 1806/07 and then again in 1809, depended to a large extent on the existence and viability of a subscriber list—which was valuable even if the 'brand' name was retired, as happened with the *Port Folio* in 1828, and it was no doubt one of the basic reasons why Moses Thomas in 1812 did not simply found a new magazine, but rather bought the *Select Reviews*, a magazine whose plan was nothing like that envisaged by Thomas for the *Analectic* which it became. This was only one aspect of the shifting relationship between proprietorship and editorship. For Bradford & Inskeep as for Moses Thomas, to stay with our examples, periodicals were investments, and only some investments among many: both publishers not only continued to publish books and to sell books at their stores, but they also published other periodicals at the same time. Thomas published, during the War of 1812, a map of Lower Canada, a *Naval History of the United States*, James Kirk Paulding's *John Bull and Brother Jonathan*, chemistry handbooks, and assorted other volumes, but also the *Theological Magazine*, a quarterly devoted to religious instruction. Inskeep & Bradford, the New York branch of the publishing house, for another example, co-published the *Analectic Magazine* in New York; Bradford & Inskeep, while also publishing a variety of books, were the publishers of the *Mirror of Taste and Dramatic Censor*, a magazine devoted to the theater.[48] What is important in this regard, again, is to note that the *Analectic Magazine* for Thomas, and the *Port Folio* for Bradford & Inskeep, were not original ventures that the publishers had conceived of and begun *ab ovo*, but rather were properties which they bought with the clear intention of profiting from them; and that at the same time, they offered a diverse array of publications to the public, each tailored to a different and specific, and usually not overlapping, interest. This is especially striking in the example of Moses Thomas, whose *Analectic Magazine* must have been little competition to the *Theological Magazine*, and vice versa. This arrangement demanded, however, the hiring of editors specifically for each magazine, especially since Thomas was determined to advertise the *Analectic*'s new editor for additional public interest. Would anyone have bought the *Theological Magazine* edited by Washington Irving? The question is more than just tongue in cheek, since its answer indicates the ways in which magazine publishing had become more professional in the first decades of the 1800s. Matching editors and prospective magazine content; publishing a wide variety of magazines to benefit from a steadily segmenting market (cf. Gardner 2012, 159); and reacting even within the confines of one magazine to the recognizable shifts in the readership's interests were not only done with greater frequency over the decades following 1790. They also became increasingly publicized stances which periodicals could adopt.

The second crucial development which professionalized many magazines during the period of the Early Republic is the increasing differentiation between contributors and editors, owed, in part, to a growing willingness of publishers to pay contributors for submissions to their magazines. Underlying these developments is the steadily increasing relevance of commercial considerations, which undermined the understanding of the periodical business as an extension of the coffee-house meeting grounds of the literati of the Union. The possibility to openly avow what for the most part was frequently silently condoned before struck one aspect of periodical production with especially great force: the possibility of paying for contributions. Clearly, in the ordered world of Anthology Societies and Tuesday Clubs, where the ideal of sociability and the belief that one's writing could genuinely contribute to an ongoing public discourse stood above the mere mercenary consider-

48 Wrappers for the *Analectic Magazine*, including advertisements, and the *Mirror of Taste*'s cover page give identification of the various projects undertaken by the two publishers during 1809-1816, or thereabouts.

ation of making money, the idea that a magazine's content might be determined by the production of made-to-order articles whose sole value was not the furtherance of public discourse but rather the supply of amusement to a passive audience was problematical, to say the least. Yet even here, it is important to recognize the continuities in the periodical market: while it is no doubt at least theoretically possible to identify the first magazine to take up the practice (indeed, Mathew Carey's *Columbian Magazine* has a certain claim to the distinction), it is less helpful to seek to pin down when the practice started as to see when the practice became publically avowable, a practice which indicates the permeation of the field of periodical production by the ideals of the market.

Catherine O'Donnell Kaplan has succinctly summarized what may be called the editorial economy of the 1790s: the editor's ability to "earn money from literature [...] was entirely dependent on the eagerness of others to remain amateurs" (2007, 125). If this is not entirely correct—given the counterexamples of paid contributions even in the 1790s—it is certainly the case that the larger amount of content produced for periodicals in the 1790s and first decade of the 1800s was produced voluntarily and without recompense, a fact which helped the editor/proprietors' margins—assuming, of course, that enough material was produced, of a high enough quality, and in a sufficient frequency, as to render a magazine capable of putting out an issue a week or a month. This, as we have seen, was a considerable problem even for the large, well-known, and popular *Port Folio*, which by 1809 probably, and certainly by 1812, had resorted to a far less voluntary system. Throughout the War of 1812, the periodicals' desire to obtain topical materials relevant to a readership interested in the war, and anxious for texts describing naval and military victories and heroes shifted this accent still more, by permitting editors to commission texts for publication in their magazines, as the *Analectic Magazine* did. Rather than leaving content to the chance submission of relevant texts, the *Analectic* thus placed its emphasis on marketability, and was prepared to pay the price for this marketability by paying its contributors. With paying for contributions came an increasing awareness that the paid contributor could as it were repay his commission by dropping his anonymity—if not in each and every of his articles, than at least generally.[49] Thus, Moses Thomas's advertisements for the *Analectic* named the names of men who had previously contributed to the magazine and would continue to do so, especially Gulian Verplanck and James K. Paulding.

Given Thomas's professionalized outlook on the magazine, it does not come as a surprise that the *Analectic Magazine*'s proprietor was in the forefront of those publishers which actively advertised a system of submissions by which anybody who supplied a text which Thomas was willing to print would be paid. On Sep-

49 As I have already noted elsewhere, the pseudonyms of Paulding ("P.") and Verplanck ("V.") were usually but not always affixed to their writings. While it is not possible to decide if this information sufficed for readers to identify the two men (and the others who likewise subscribed themselves by initials only), it is clear from many examples that readers were often well aware who the contributors were.

tember 28, 1816, the *Washington City Weekly Gazette* offered its readers that astounding piece of news: "The proprietors of the Analectic Magazine propose publishing a Quarterly Journal in Philadelphia, and offer three dollars a page for all such original communications as they shall deem worthy of notice." Four months later, the new quarterly had vanished, as the *Boston Daily Advertiser* noted, because Moses Thomas had concluded to "devote his attention exclusively to the Analectic Magazine." With that new emphasis on his existing publication came a transfer of his willingness to pay for contributions as well, so that the *Analectic Magazine* was now preparing to pay the three dollars a page for communications. Thomas's prose spoke volumes about the value of appealing to a contributor's idealistic pride as the sole motivation to participate in the periodical business. "He hopes," Thomas wrote, "that such a proposal, joined to the motives of literary exertion arising from a just sense of national pride, will be sufficient to rouse the ablest writers." Positively rephrased, money and national pride should be sufficient for anybody to contribute; negatively put, national pride and idealism alone could not hope to rouse anybody to exertion. Given that, Thomas's appeal to the pride of his contributors rang hollow against the purse he held out for any valuable piece of writing. But Thomas's care not to emphasize money alone, the necessity to couch its new official policy in the careful terms of an offer which merely added to a pre-existent sense of national pride, rather than being a salary that divorced the contribution to magazines completely from the long-professed idealism of its writers, soon became evident. In 1818, the *Port Folio* reviewed James Kirke Paulding's *Letters from the South,* whose final chapter was a snarky commentary on American literary critics. As the *Port Folio* noted, it found itself in need to accept Paulding's description of American critics, by and large working for the large literary magazines, as being, in the *Port Folio*'s own words, a "hapless race of men who are doomed to drudge for a task master" (*PF* 1818 1, 139), little different from Virginia's slaves and incapable of forming any original thought. The *Port Folio* found its reason for this general decay in the authorial calling in precisely the sort of overt business-relationship which the *Analectic Magazine* had offered in its willingness to pay its contributors. "We shall never forget the sensations which this order [the *Analectic*'s willingness to pay] excited," the *Port Folio* wrote. In mock-apocalyptic tones, the magazine painted a picture of Philadelphia's streets overrun with money-grubbing amateurs seeking paper and ink, lessons in grammar, in languages, and in handwriting; "and in the surrounding country scarcely a goose was to be found with feathers enough to warm her nest" (140).

The *Port Folio*'s scathing sarcasm on the matter of paying for contributions, however, was clearly a case of too much protest. It had itself, at least since 1812, regularly paid its contributors for writings, and not merely those which it had solicited, but rather for anything which it had printed, as noted in Chapter 2. Perhaps more than that: as Nicholas Biddle noted in a letter to a supplicant, James Elliot, in May 1813, the *Port Folio*, where he held the "general superintendence over its material," had several people around who were "by stipulation engaged to furnish regular contributions."[50] Biddle's hint suggests that there was something of a staff available to Bradford & Inskeep to keep regular contributions going. Indeed, Thomas himself had noted in his advertisement that he was not starting a new practice: "He believes the price now offered to be greater than was ever before paid for a similar work in this country, and equal to the compensation received by the writers of the Edinburgh and Quarterly Reviews" (*American Mercury* 1817, February 18, 33.1703, 4). There was, evidently, a common, if not regularly openly admitted, practice of paying for contributions.

The *Port Folio*'s criticism of the *Analectic*'s open admission of paying for its contributions throws some light of the business practices at the magazine after its purchase by Harrison Hall. John E. Hall found himself much less well-endowed with contributors than his predecessor Caldwell. John Queenan's suggestion that part of the reason why the Hall brothers found their *Port Folio* less successful in getting contributions was the Hall's "snobbery" (1955, 207) is well-taken and might well be true; but the *Port Folio*'s complaint about the *Analectic Magazine*'s paid contributors suggests that the Hall's problem was mainly that they themselves were unwilling to pay, or possibly unable—in other words, that they had, as it were, dialed back the professional setup which Biddle, Caldwell, and Bradford & Inskeep had used to make the *Port Folio* so successful in 1812-1816. If that is so, we may conclude that Hall's snobbery merely meant that he did not believe that literary productions should be paid for by the publisher, an opinion which, while perfectly in tune with decades of periodical history, was increasingly coming to be sidelined by a professionalized periodical business.

Hall's criticism of the *Analectic Magazine* was also somewhat surprising as the *Port Folio*'s own paid contributions were an open secret: Washington Irving wrote to a correspondent in April 1814, declining his offer of literary anecdotes and noting that while Moses Thomas could not afford to take him on, the *Port Folio*'s proprietors were also "in the habit of paying for original writings" (1978, 362). Nor was the *Port Folio*'s staff likely to have been unaware of the fact that notwithstanding Thomas's open admission in 1816, the *Analectic Magazine* itself had been paying for contributions regularly, as Washington Irving's correspondence also clearly indicates. Thomas certainly paid James Kirke Paulding and Gulian C. Verplanck for their contributions to the *Analectic Magazine* long before 1816. While the details of his arrangement are unknown, and it is especially unclear if any other contributors to the *Analectic* were paid, Irving wrote Thomas in October 1814 that he needed a settlement of accounts, in order that "I may pay Paulding according to my agreement with him" (Irving 1978, 382). Similarly, in January 1815, as he was preparing to leave the magazine, Irving wrote to Verplanck noting that Thomas has suffered insolvency as a consequence of the failure of the publishing house of Bradford & Inskeep, with which Thomas had kept intensive business relations, as we have seen in parts above. Irving sought to calm Verplanck, who was apparently facing going unpaid for his contribu-

50 Nicholas Biddle to James Eliott, May 13, 1813. Nicholas Biddle Papers, Library of Congress.

tions: "For the sums which Thomas is indebted to you, You [sic] will have your chance with the other creditors" (387). This was probably small consolation to Verplanck—his relationship with Thomas, though, ultimately was not hurt, as the publisher quickly recuperated and returned to the *Analectic* with a new editor in charge—but indicates the ways in which business relations underlay the respective roles of editor, publisher, and contributor, in the professionalizing magazine of the 1810s.

Neither were these two magazines the only ones who paid. Perhaps the first public notice of a magazine willing to pay for contributions appeared in the New York *Examiner*, whose editor Barent Gardenier offered two dollars a page for each well written communication that he resolved to print in the magazine—though only if the author paid the postage, otherwise he would not be entitled to payment (cf. *E* 1814 2, 2). The *Examiner*'s efforts did not apparently lead anybody to complain or comment. The 1820s saw a steady increase in the public advertisement of magazines prepared to pay their contributors, and, what was more important, the gradual acceptance of the practice. The Philadelphia *American Monthly Magazine* offered two dollars per page in 1824 (*Cincinnati Literary Gazette* 1824, January 10, 1.2, 14); the New York literary journal *American Monthly Magazine*, then still advertised as *The Legendary*, published by Nathaniel P. Willis, was noted in early 1828 to offer a dollar a page for contributors (*Philadelphia Album* 1828,J anuary 2, 2.28, 245). By 1831, the *Casket* advertised its rate of one dollar per page for contributions more prominently than any other aspect of its venture (*Atkinson's Saturday Evening Post* 1831, July 23, 10.521, n.p.). Such sign posts merely indicate the development of feeling regarding the payment for literary production which had occurred in the decade and a half since the War of 1812. "It is no longer the reproach of Philadelphia," noted the *Yankee and Boston Literary Gazette* in a lengthy review of *The Legendary*'s plan, "that they have more money than wit, because they offer to exchange the former for the latter at three dollars a page." As this and other reviews noted, it was increasingly becoming a matter of both national literary prestige as well as the individual survival of American magazines that pushed both the acceptance of as well as the need for paid contributions. James McHenry, of the Philadelphia *American Monthly Magazine*, was recognized to have used monetary compensation to attract such literary greats as Henry Wadsworth Longfellow and Sarah Josepha Hale (author of "Mary Had a Little Lamb") to his magazine even as he himself lacked the talent to sustain the magazine solely by his own literary efforts or those of his uncompensated friends. As the *New Bedford Mercury* noted with unvarnished scorn, the "editor is a very common-place writer [...] The non-fulfilment of the articles of the prospectus relative to payment will inevitably cause the Magazine to drop" (*NBM* 1824, September 17, 18.10, 2). In June of the same year, the *Yankee and Boston Literary Gazette* connected the issue of payment for articles in periodicals with the increasingly tempestuous problem of literary copyright and noted with straightforwardness that if the United States meant to have "a literature of our own, we must pay for it" (1.25, 196). A month later, what was probably the same critic used the opportunity of reviewing the *American Quarterly Review* to conclude that "it is better for native authors to get two dollars a page for writing heavily about what nobody will ever take the trouble to read, than to publish more sprightly and powerful things, and give them away at their own charger. They who are willing to spend five dollars a year now, for the encouragement of anything native, will soon be ready to double or treble that sum" (*YBLG* 1828 1.30, 233). All of this echoed a comment which Washington Irving had made in a letter to Gulian Verplanck as early as January 1815. Commenting on the failure of the firm of Bradford & Inskeep and the consequent financial demise of Moses Thomas (he got better), Irving worried that these "failures […] will sensibly affect the interests of literature, and deter all those from the exercise of the pen who would take it up as a means of profit—" (1978, 386). Unsurprisingly, for Irving there was no stigma attached to the use of writing for the purpose of making money; he was ahead of his time only by a very little.

If periodicals can be said to have functioned as the printed equivalent of the sociable community of the coffee house (or the tavern, as Jared Gardner points out; cf. 2012, 46), it was a coffee house to which entrance was strictly controlled on the basis of quality and of correspondence to the professed positions of the prospectus. It was also a coffee house which teetered at all times precariously on the brink of foreclosure. The metaphor, indeed, is faulty: the interest of the coffee house owner is the sale of coffee, and whether the customer freely interchanges ideas and socializes or sullenly droops in a corner is of no immediate consequence to him. The owner does not charge his customer an entrance fee, or pays him to provide other customers with coffee; the magazine, in effect, did both. Periodicals made money not from facilitating the interchange of ideas, from providing a forum for the publication of texts; they made money off the ideas and the texts themselves, and consequently guarded access to their pages.[51] And furthermore, Americans, as Andie Tucher sums it up, "were not panting for the opportunity to write for a magazine" (2010, 397). It is the most striking fact, for which the *Port Folio* may stand as a prime example, that few contributors lasted beyond single submissions, and fewer of these submissions still were, in any shape, political. The often-invoked "virtual salon" of the periodical, in which "the editor could organize the best and brightest the nation had to offer to do the vital work of steering the ship of state, as early republican periodical editors and serial authors from Webster to Dennie had imagined" (Gardner 2012, 169), saw the best and brightest submit frivolous poetry and humorous anecdotes, random satirical essays on the

51 Stephen Shapiro's analysis of the role of the coffee house (2008, 66-7) must also be noted here. Shapiro points out that the communities of the coffee house frequently functioned as predecessors of strongly commercial operations, such as the New York stock exchange and the insurance company Lloyd's of London. "The coffeehouses became amplifiers for the market's expansion as magnetic zones where a mass of small capital could be drawn into the market;" here, with "credibility as their initial commodity," what Shapiro calls the bourgeoisie used "their own behavior as a monetarizable object" (66). In other words, Shapiro reads the intellectual exchanges and sympathetic bonds created by the *actual* coffee house as precursors to and facilitators of financial goals. Seen in this way, the 'virtual' coffee house may retain at least some analytical validity despite the serious flaws of the metaphor.

thoughts of the day, pastorals, and literary and dramatic criticism, in vastly greater numbers than political essays. The galley of state's editor-steersman was missing his rowers, the bark of state its wind, and the virtual salon was crowded with people who were more likely to lift their mug and laugh at the raucous humor of their fellows than they were likely to soberly listen to a lengthy political speech.

As we have seen, while large numbers of individuals contributed to the magazines, the even vaster weekly and monthly requirements made it impossible that the ultimately slim number of interested volunteers could fully satisfy the periodicals. Alternatives to the wholly voluntary commitment which dominated the first decade of the 1800s were needed. The *Port Folio*'s post-1809 system, in which a distinct group of people was put under moral pressure to support the magazine continuously, failed as quickly as it had begun; ultimately, a more reliable means of obtaining material was required. Paying for contributions was ultimately a necessary step, and also the most clearly successful step, as the enumeration of the increasing number of magazines which were willing to pay for articles indicates. The third question which played a role in the professionalization of periodicals about the War of 1812 was the other side of the medal: how could money be made in selling the magazines to prospective readers? Of the three points I have identified above as being symptomatic of the increasing professionalism of American magazines in the period after 1815, the mode of getting the magazine to the reader was perhaps the least obvious. There is no doubt, and I wish to raise no doubt, that the vast majority of magazines throughout the years of the Early Republic were 'sold'—the term is slightly misleading here—by subscription. Subscription, as I have noted in Chapter 1, carried with it certain benefits and certain burdens, the most frequently commented-upon of which was certainly the need to publish and then adhere to a prospectus, and the greatest ostensible benefit the regularity and calculability of income. The problems with subscription had hamstrung the vast majority of periodical projects during the Early Republic, and caused the demise of countless magazines. Agencies promised one way out of the problematic relationship between publishers and readers, substituting locally-known and respected men, often booksellers, for the distant and impersonal relationship to the publisher via letter. Yet agencies, too, did not solve the problem: often, individual agents were responsible for the entirety of a state or territory, and themselves were not as reliable as the publishers would have wished, and a costly venture to boot, since they skimmed off a portion of the money made. There exist, however, contradictions between some business practices employed by periodicals and the underlying idea of the subscription periodical. Why, for example, should anybody advertise the contents of an individual issue of his magazine, if, as Hezekiah Niles but by no means he alone emphatically suggested, "this paper cannot be sold, or given away, except to regular subscribers, on any pretence whatever" (*WR* 1811, 240)? Subscribers were already tied to the magazine anyway—new subscribers might of course be attracted, but could anybody be expected to pay 6$ or so for a yearly subscription, only because they were interested in a particular issue? Likewise, what was the point of advertising future content in the back of an issue, when subscribers were essentially bound to receive that issue anyhow, no matter what its content?

One thing about Niles's comment is striking in this regard: "Frequent applications has [sic] been made at this office to purchase [...] numbers of the REGISTER" (*WR* 1811, 240, original emphasis). In the particular case, this had to do with the particular content of that issue of the *Register*, full of valuable public documents; but the interesting aspect is another one. There existed, obviously, a large enough number of people who, even though they did not subscribe to the *Register*, knew enough about its contents to make 'frequent' requests to Niles for the purchase of single numbers of the magazine. Not only did a significant number of people, then, either read Niles's advertisements in other newspapers and magazines or his magazine itself via friends and acquaintances who were subscribers, but they believed that it must be possible to obtain individual issues of Niles's magazine. Why should they, though? The answer, I suggest, is because despite subscription being the general system by which magazines were published, and certainly the soundest means by which they could be conducted, it was already by the 1810s coming to be regarded as obsolete, and being increasingly if somewhat surreptitiously replaced.

The first point to be made, of course, is that subscription, while overwhelmingly dominant, was clearly not the only way of publishing a magazine, even in the first decade of the 1800s. The Boston *Ordeal* sold individual issues for 10¢, although it gave no information as to the mode by which these individual issues were distributed (cf. 1809 1, 5); the *Massachusetts Baptist Missionary Magazine* likewise sold individual numbers, for 12½¢, and, given its missionizing character, even offered a deal of ten cents for a dozen issues, probably in the interest of preachers and missionaries who might want to spread the good word (cf. *MBMM* 1805 1, 5). Both of these magazines certainly still obtained the majority of their sales from subscription, but they recognized that other outlets for their writings existed. Indeed, I have already suggested a few of these in Chapter 1, but would like to reiterate them here in the larger context. It seems that some booksellers subscribed specifically in order to be able to re-sell individual issues of magazines to local customers—one possible reason for subscriber lists which include dozens, sometimes hundreds of subscriptions with booksellers in more distant locations. While this may be an artifact of the agency system as well, we may trace some of the practice of resale through the advertisements which booksellers took out in local newspapers. Interestingly, in this practice, the value which biography possessed, or was assumed to possess, takes obvious form. In an advertisement which Boston bookseller Charles Williams had published in the March 20, 1813 edition of the *Boston Daily Advertiser*, he announced that the March edition of the *Analectic Magazine* had just arrived at his store. But more than that, the contents of the magazine became the centerpiece of his advertisement. A full table of contents was appended to the initial paragraph, in which, however, one item was specifically stressed: a pointing hand dingbat was set before the entry for the "Biographical notice of capt. Isaac Hull," an entry which was further emphasized by setting it in italics (*BDA*, 1813, March 20, 1.16, 3). Williams also highlighted the presence of a portrait of Hull in the same issue. Advertisements in newspapers of the period suggest that American booksellers were in the business of actually selling magazines by individual number. Mostly, these were booksellers in places distant from the city of publication, who posted advertisements in local papers suggesting they would be "selling" magazines. While not exactly plentiful, such notices appeared time and again in American newspapers, which otherwise were quite reliable in suggesting that magazines had become available for subscribers at the respective bookstores. Perhaps the most interesting of these booksellers' announcements was one which the New York *Columbian* printed on October 6, 1813, and which very directly stated that Inskeep & Bradford themselves (the New York branch of the joint publishing house) were selling the *Port Folio*'s October volume at Abraham Inskeep's Broadway bookstore. There could be no mistaking this advertisement to say anything about subscription. The ad also included a full table of contents and concluded by noting that the *Analectic Magazine*, with a portrait of William Bainbridge, was similarly available at the store (cf. 1813, September 6, 4.1209, 4). The *Alexandria Gazette* carried an advertisement by James Kennedy & Son, booksellers, on March 12, 1813, noting that Kennedy had just received the January, February, and March editions of the *Analectic* and was awaiting subscribers to pick them up (cf. *AG* 1813, March 12, 13.3899, 3). By the middle of June, however, the "present month" of the *Analectic* was explicitly "for sale" by Kennedy. The July edition of the *Analectic Magazine*, and indeed that magazine continually afterwards, was only available by subscription. Did this mean that Kennedy's June advertisement of the *Analectic* for sale was a misprint, or an aberration? Possibly; but there exist numerous other, equally clear statements to the effect that the possibility of buying individual issues existed. Kennedy, for example, similarly advertised the *Port Folio* for sale in March (cf. *AG* 1813, March 19, 13.3906, 4), and a wider range of examples exists. One more example might suffice. The booksellers Van Winkle & Wiley had been the agents for the *Analectic Magazine* in New York City (or at least two of its agents, given that a competitor also held that he was the magazine's agent) since January 1815, and for two years, regularly announced in New York's newspapers that they had the magazine ready for subscribers. However, in January 1817, their announcement suddenly shifted to a different formulation. Now, they explicitly had the magazine "for sale" (cf. *Courier* 1817, January 3, 2.609, 3), and their advertisements at least did not return to the suggestion that the magazine was only ever available to subscribers. By March 1820, Wiley himself alone carried on selling the magazine, and so did he when going back into a partnership, as the firm of Wiley & Halsted, in July 1820.

Beyond those implicit routes to single issues, the demand for them as communicated to publishers by correspondents broke its way. In March 1816, Moses Thomas noted on the cover of the *Analectic Magazine* a genuine shift in the publisher-consumer relationship. Thomas acknowledged the pressure from persons who found it "inconvenient" to subscribe to the *Analectic Magazine* to be able to obtain single issues. Thomas's choice of wording is intriguing: he acknowledged one good reason for finding subscription problematical, that subscribers might not be stationary, that they might move regularly. More broadly speaking, however, subscription was inconvenient for many others: those who did not wish to take every issue regardless of its content; those who did not desire to pay 6$ in advance every year; those who desired to be able to stop their deliveries of the *Analectic Magazine* at any point they desired. It was in consequence to the pressure from those desiring the chance to buy individual copies of the *Analectic*'s numbers that Thomas "concluded to try the experiment of selling single numbers." These would cost 1$ if including an engraving (virtually no issue of the *Analectic* appeared without one anymore) and 75¢ if not, because, Thomas claimed, "complete sets will thereby be broken," something Thomas found disadvantageous for his further sales practice (Hugh Maxwell's 1800 note that the true profit of a magazine lay in the sales of bound volumes still, apparently, holding true). This was also the reason why the offer did not include the 1813 issues, of which Thomas retained only a small number of complete sets, with the exception of the December issue, whose engraving and biography of Oliver Hazard Perry had apparently been a bestseller and of which additional copies had been printed. Thomas repeated the offer in April and May, but then cancelled it in favor of offering complete sets of all back issues, including a second edition of the 1813 volumes. Mail-order magazine purchases, apparently, were not the way to go; but the effort pointed to the realization that subscription was not the be all and end all of magazine salesmanship.

It was ultimately one particular kind of article, the naval biographies, which induced the belief in the viability of individual issue sales. The demand for these texts, then, directly affected the professionalization of various aspects of the production of periodicals. Publishers found themselves in need of hiring writers to fill the popular demand. The popularity which had accrued the naval biographies, as evident in the reprints, the advertisements and also Thomas's taking out of a copyright on the *Analectic Magazine* itself: all of this cohered to form the idea that given the right content, it might be possible and indeed given the doubling of the price from 50¢ per issue if bought by subscription to 1$ if doubt singly even likely to make a profit off of individual issues. These issues, of course, must carry the kind of topical material that would allow them to be sold quickly and in larger numbers—naval biographies, surfing on the wave of national popularity during 1813-14, were the best examples of such writings, promising precisely the national readership which was desirable. Yet ultimately, none of these alternative mechanisms of distribution caught on in the United States during the first few decades of the 1800s. The problem was evident to publishers and editors, as was the existence of solutions which promised to remove the risks and burdens of subscription from the publisher. As John E. Hall noted in the editorial note preceding the first 1818 issue of the *Port Folio*, "[i]n Europe, booksellers purchase magazines by wholesale from the publisher, and the business of retail being thus scattered among a number, it can be conducted with promptness and punctuality" (*PF* 1818 1, Preface). Hall did not suggest the obvious—that Americans should institute this procedure amongst themselves as well—but rather complained of its impossibility in the United States. Again, this may be more owed to the short sightedness which the Hall editorship exhibited in other cases as well. Even so, there clearly existed alternative distribution routes both in the United States and abroad, tapping which would go far in the future to preserve the viability of the American magazine.

Relatively autonomous texts, the naval biographies, produced in response to the heteronomous demands of the historical moment, thus drove three aspects of professionalization. The production of periodical biography during the War of 1812 thus stands in a unique position: extraordinary by the standards of biographical texts in periodicals of day, it exhibits the literary potential of periodical biography, while simultaneously this relatively autonomous literary expression is directly implicated in the professionalization of the American magazine, helping to prepare the way for paid contributions, individual issue sales, and stricter control of editorial content by the publishers. It is this that makes the synchronic look at periodical biography around the War of 1812 a revealing final step in the study of the road of professionalizing the American magazine.

Conclusion: Professionalizing Periodical Production in the Market Age

Money makes the Press go.

The Casket 1812, 153

In the complex of relations between the periodical as a medium, biography as a genre, and nationalism as a topic and idea, I have sought to trace the development of a growing and increasingly public orientation in the periodical field towards the demands of the market. This study has argued that the evidence that we can accumulate about the production of periodicals and the periodical field in the Early Republic suggests that periodicals moved towards the heteronomous pole of the periodical field throughout the Early Republic, and with an increasing openness about their purposes in the market. That we can more easily explain the publishing choices made by Early Republic periodicals by reference to the market instead of ideologies which foreground periodical's active role in willfully creating a unique American nation in the case of biography and nationalism might come as an especially great surprise given the dominance which ideological readings of the genre and the subject have in scholarship. Such ideological readings, emphasizing periodicals' role in the furtherance of republican virtue, virtual community, and nationalism, are not necessarily wrong if one realizes that they explain only a small segment of the texts published in periodicals—they mirror well the public discussion of the roles of the nation, of biography, and of the periodical at the time. They fall short in explaining the actual manifestations of medium, genre, and theme, however, and, critically, the ways in which the ideas were both transformed in the course of these manifestations and the ways in which the ideas were coopted for market-oriented goals devoid of much ideological content. My own attempt at offering an explanation of these manifestations may not be as neat but is, I believe, at last more plausible in its description of the development of periodicals in the Early American Republic. At the heart of this development lay what the *Casket* so blithely formulated: it was money that made sure the presses ran from week to week, and from month to month. One addition is necessary: as clear as it is that "money made the press go," whether in 1790 or in 1825, as clear is it that between these two dates lay a process during which American magazine producers and consumers alike were reconciled to the fact, allowing them to speak ever more openly about the mercenary causes of American periodicals.

Up to the end of the Civil War and beyond, the structures of the periodical market kept evolving (as a matter of fact, of course, they are still evolving today), working on the issues which have been central to this study. In the process of doing so, as I have already intimated, the periodical business meandered back and forth between positions along the line of professionalization. By 1850, *Harper's New Monthly Magazine* of New York began selling individual issues of its magazine through book stores and street vendors even as it was still available in subscription, a form of distribution which it is still using today—and which, as we have seen, had its beginnings at least as far back as 1805. If, as Leon Jackson has noted, *Harper's* "solved the problem of selling by subscription simply by not selling by subscription" (2008, 174), it did so in a continuity, a broken continuity perhaps, but one nonetheless, of earlier attempts to do the same. Similar points of continuity involve the agency system in the antebellum period and the increasing shift away from what Jackson has called the "world of gifts and gift exchange" (129) towards an increasing commercialization of the business of letters, the writing for and publishing of magazines. When Nathaniel P. Willis, Louis Godey, and even Catherine Maria Sedgwick could, in the late 1820s through the 1830s, "frame literary production in solely economic or quantitative terms" (49), this was certainly a progression from the ways in which early 1800s publishers, editors, and authors circumspectly sought to justify economic profit through idealistic motivations—yet it bears pointing out, again, that it was merely a progression, rather than a completely new development. In this sense, I would suggest that this study both situates itself as a chronological expansion of Jackson's study of the antebellum period and as a necessary qualification and modification thereof. Jackson's suggestion that it "was becoming possible for the first time to imagine the circulation and exchange of writing as no longer something that generated money coincidentally [...] but as, rather, a commercial process defined primarily by the money it could make" (49) is mistaken. Neither the imagination nor the public admission of the monetary dimensions had now become possible where it previously had been impossible. Instead, it was increasingly possible to do both—foreground money in public discourse and conceive of money as the central aspect of periodical publishing without even acknowledging the fantasy of disinterested virtue—in a trajectory of development which went back at least as far, the introduction of this study suggests, as 1775, and as far forward as the late 1890s (cf. Sedgwick 2000).

This interpretation of the periodical business ultimately, I believe, necessitates a reappraisal of the history of ideas in the Early Republic. If, as I have suggested above, there existed something like a shared fantasy of disinterested virtue to which both periodical consumers and producers subscribed, which permitted them to keep submerged that they were not engaging in a free exchange of ideas but rather responded to each other in a market economy ultimately concerned with profit, what is the consequence for our approach to such a history of ideas? Would any of the men and women who formed the complex of relations in which periodicals were produced have been 'duped,' to put it colloquially, by the mutual pretensions of monetarily disinterested editors and voluntary contributors, of magazines seeking the republican education of their readers and readers seeking magazines for instruction? Would they have been incredulous to be told that the editor who addressed his readers with such care to note that he was seeking nothing but their applause and a modest competency was after money, that the readers who applauded the moral instruction of a magazine were happy to find the major part of it devoted to their amusement? Would they have been aghast to find that the editorial investment in laborious explanations of the usefulness of single texts, alleged selected with great care as part of a greater plan, mostly was intended to cover up the haphazard process by which available sources determined, more than anything else, the choice of texts to be printed?

The question here is if we can deduce the importance of such concepts as disinterested virtue, Federalist idealism, incipient nationalism, or a more general republicanism in magazines by concentrating solely on the textual content of those magazines. Certainly, an interest in making money off of magazines does not preclude the use of these magazines for the furthering of ideological goals—even a publisher who wishes to advance, for example, national republicanism may find himself equally interested in financial success. Yet what I have outlined above is the history of a field in which the monetary interest predominated to the detriment of a clearly articulated political message—and, more importantly, in which the political message was itself a means of advancing the monetary interest. This, as I have argued in Chapter 2, was what ultimately makes the twists and turns in the *Port Folio*'s political stances understandable: never more than one aspect among the magazine's various promises to its readers, its ideological stances catered to an audience and rose and fell with the prominence of that audience. Such a reading privileges not only market aspects of the production of periodicals, it also raises the question of magazine influence. And it ultimately must come to ask if a surface reading of texts is not too superficial, as it were. What happens when we read producers and consumers of magazines in the Early Republic as being willing participants in a mutually if implicitly agreed upon fantasy that was slowly dispelled by an ever greater and more open acceptance of the influence of market forces? The "market revolution," the process by which this acceptance took hold among the populace and economic reasoning could be publically foregrounded, in this sense subsumes the aspects of professionalization which I have outlined above.[1]

1 A second point is that Bourdieuan scholarship likewise has moved the attention of scholars away from textualist approaches by noting that shifts in the literary field have had a tremendous influence on the texts themselves and thus complicates the problem of interpreting the resultant texts, putting more emphasis instead on institutional conditions of production. Cf. Leypoldt (2009). A similar point to the one I am making here is also suggested by contemporary Marxist readings, if not in the field of Early American studies. Mark Fisher, in his recent essay on *Capitalist Realism*, has suggested that the alleged postmodernist demystification of the pervasiveness of market forces and the commodification of cultural products is merely evidence of a certain naivety, insofar as it assumes that there existed in the past groups who "*really* believed in the Symbolic," i.e. in the collective fictions shared by producers and consumers of goods about those goods (2009, 50, original emphasis). I would suggest, tentatively, that studies of the Early Republic have frequently fallen into the trap of assuming that the symbolic orders they analyze were 'really' believed by contemporaries.

In this context, the history of periodical production in the Early Republic is significant, because we can here trace the emergence of the kind of professionalization which breaks with the accepted fantasy. That development was not, as I have been at pains to note, without its twists and turns—indeed, as Leon Jackson ably shows, much of what went on even as late as the mid-1830s and 1840s in periodical production looked very much like the kind of socially embedded periodical of earlier periods. Jackson's suggestion that a process of gift exchange was constitutive of much periodical authorship in the antebellum period should perhaps be emphasized more in its assumption that there was a material exchange going on, compared to the often one-sided route which lead from the author of a text to the publisher of a periodical under the conception of virtuous disinterestedness in the virtual coffee house, rather than its distinctness from monetary payment (cf. 2008, 89-141). In offering yet another aspect of writer-publisher-editor relations, the non-monetary payment, even in advance, for contributions thus becomes yet another step on the long road of professionalization. I want to add one final sign post on that road:

> "Money," says the editor of a Frankford, (Penn.) paper, "will raise our ideas, 'twill guide the pen to themes engaging and enrapturing, 'twill direct us to tit-bits of news, and make us ever assiduous to please—'twill save us from many an oath; and what is more, 'twill save us from the cursed, fiend-like, tormenting dun; which daily wastes away our frame, and if not speedily removed must inevitably bring us to the grave." (*C* 1812, 153)

The unnamed Frankford editor and his approving colleague at the *Casket* offer a remarkable view of the value and role of money to the Early Republic periodical, and its 1812 date, about midway between the start and end points of this study and just before the major upheaval I have suggested was precipitated by the War of 1812, seems almost symbolic of the quote's liminality. Here is the past, of Dennie's *Farmer's Weekly Museum* pronouncements and the early *Port Folio*—making money meant that editors could be of an easy mind, as the last lines suggest, that they need not fear for their future or worry about their prospects. Money was a means which permitted editors to do their cherished work, as recompense for which a modest competency would be sufficient. Already, however, the tone of the *Casket*'s quote is much more negative than most early comments: the alternative to making money is not just worries, and then, as most previous texts might have had it, the dissolution of the magazine and loss of its value to society, but rather the editors' deaths. Even at this point, then, the sense that something vital was tied to the financial success of the magazine was brought to the fore. Yet this wholly passive view—a magazine is published, money is made to satisfy the publishers, a new magazine is published; or alternatively, money is not made, and people suffer early death from worry—is augmented here by an entirely more active component: money makes sure things happen in certain ways. The prospect of money makes magazines publish those kinds of writings which are "engaging and enrapturing," it will make editors "assiduous to please." The idea here is not that a safe income will *allow* writers to write texts which then will, thanks to their lack of worries, be amusing, sprightly, pleasant, but rather that the prospect of making money by writing about such topics as are interesting and charming will lead the writer to them—as it will direct the editor to the varieties and shortness of "tit-bits of news" rather than the lengthy virtuous dissertations that fail to interest their readers. This, in all its bluntness about putting the magazine in the service of the reader's amusement and in foregrounding the reaction of the production side of periodicals to the heteronomous demands of the market, is the future of periodicals in the Early Republic then, as projected—correctly—by the *Casket* in 1812.

Beneath all these changes lay the increasing marketization of the United States in the Early Republic. The various aspects of this marketization, the ways in which periodicals increasingly became investments, in which written contributions were commodified, and others I have outlined above, did not happen in all places and among all groups with equal speed, requiring the elaborate systems of proclaimed idealism that we have seen at work. The readiness of periodicals to pay for contributions, for example, preceded the public readiness to openly acknowledge the acceptability of paid contributions. But periodicals still played their part in the process which is usually called the 'market revolution,' by which, in John Larson's words, "[i]ndividual identity dissolved into anonymity, commitment into contract, vocation into work, a living into a wage" (2010, 9). As Larson also points out, it was rather immaterial whether this market revolution described any actual dissolution of community or merely the public belief in such a dissolution: what mattered was that the new market relations between people replaced earlier systems in which friendship and common interests bound them together (cf. Koschnik 2007). In the case of periodicals, the fantasy of common virtue and disinterested editorship, which I described at the very beginning of this study, likewise found itself subdued by the changes in the market, whose liberal mechanisms came to be increasingly accepted as the republic grew older. This was an incremental process, however, and we can detect the traces of that process, its increasing penetration of the periodical field, in the histories I have outlined above. As John Adams recognized as early as 1790: "disinterested virtue is disappearing among us" (qtd. in Appleby 1984, 14). Granted that Adams was a comparative reactionary among the Revolutionaries, it is still notable that even in 1790 he was already bemoaning the loss of public virtue. By 1820, thirty years onward, "a common economic vision" had penetrated "most sectors of a flourishing market elite" (Sellers 1991, 101)—a slow but steady process that deeply influenced the production of periodicals as well. It was with this increasing penetration of the populace by the ideas and ideals of the market that an increasing openness about the market orientation of periodicals went hand in hand. Today, we see nothing problematical in the fact that a magazine such as *The New Yorker* pays its writers, has a salaried editor, is supposed to make a profit for Condé Nast, and ultimately bases even its investigative pieces on the belief that they should be entertaining reading to its subscribers—and those who merely buy the magazine at a higher price in the store. The process by which it became unproblematic to voice these motivations in public is precisely the process of professionalization which we have seen at work in the periodicals of the Early Republic.

Appendices

Appendix 1: *Port Folio* Title Page & Wrapper, March 22, 1807
(Courtesy Library Company of Philadelphia)

THE PORT FOLIO

N° XIII.

PHILADELPHIA, MARCH 28, 1807.

TO BOOKSELLERS.

The leading booksellers in this city and in the other cities and great towns of the Union are very respectfully requested to furnish the Editor with their advertisements; more particularly whenever the publication of a WORK OF STERLING AND ACKNOWLEDGED MERIT is projected. The Port Folio has a circulation so extensive that, if his request be granted, it will redound to individual interest not less than to the advancement of literature. Throughout the wide expanse of the United States, and in all the British dominions in North America, men of fortune, of influence, of letters, and liberality subscribe, with scarcely an exception, to this paper; and it imports every literary merchant that his advertisement be perused by a description of persons alike eager to read and generous to reward.

The Editor will print such advertisements on terms just and moderate, and on a credit the most liberal. Moreover, when CLASSICAL, STANDARD, and VALUABLE books are announced for publication the Editor will, according to the measure of his time and talents, notice such works under the title of Literary Intelligence, without any other bias, than that with which he always hopes to lean towards Genius, Learning, Truth, and Utility.

PORT FOLIO OFFICE,

North-East Corner of Second in Dock-street.

Appendix 2: *The Emporium of Arts and Sciences* title page, showing booksellers; (Courtesy Library Company of Philadelphia)

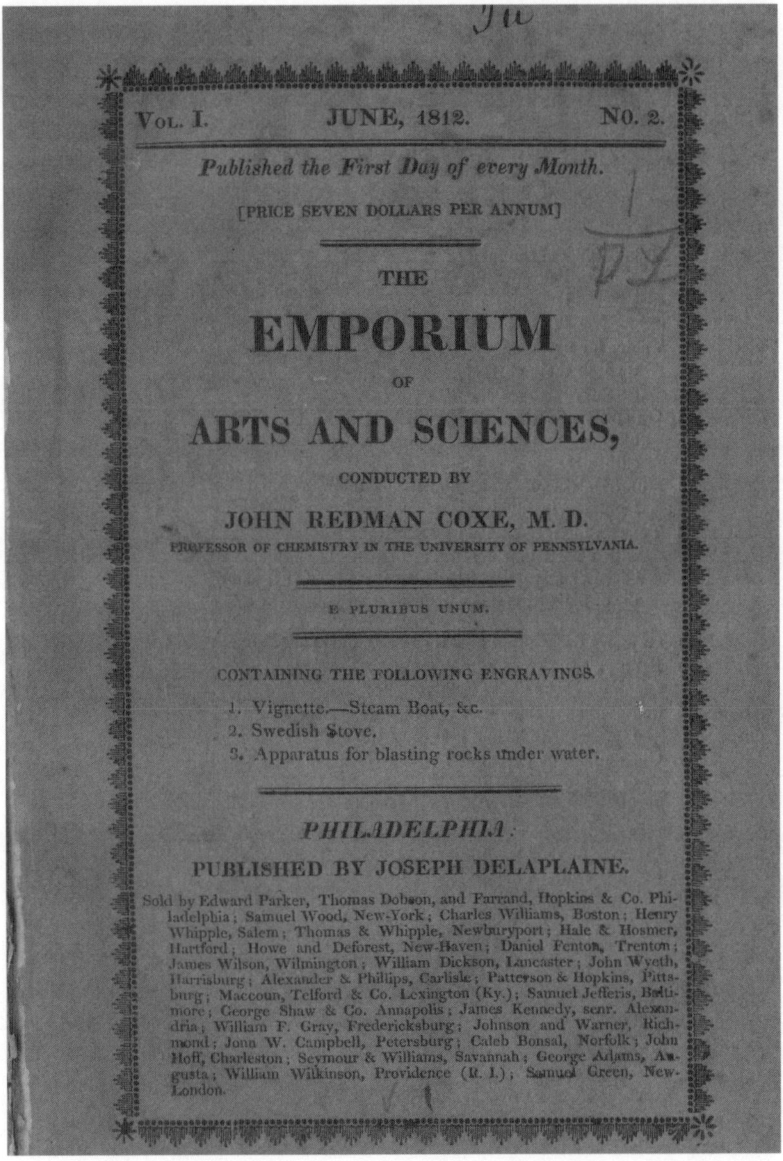

VOL. I. JUNE, 1812. NO. 2.

Published the First Day of every Month.

[PRICE SEVEN DOLLARS PER ANNUM]

THE

EMPORIUM

OF

ARTS AND SCIENCES,

CONDUCTED BY

JOHN REDMAN COXE, M. D.

PROFESSOR OF CHEMISTRY IN THE UNIVERSITY OF PENNSYLVANIA.

E PLURIBUS UNUM.

CONTAINING THE FOLLOWING ENGRAVINGS.

1. Vignette.—Steam Boat, &c.
2. Swedish Stove.
3. Apparatus for blasting rocks under water.

PHILADELPHIA:

PUBLISHED BY JOSEPH DELAPLAINE.

Sold by Edward Parker, Thomas Dobson, and Farrand, Hopkins & Co. Philadelphia; Samuel Wood, New-York; Charles Williams, Boston; Henry Whipple, Salem; Thomas & Whipple, Newburyport; Hale & Hosmer, Hartford; Howe and Deforest, New-Haven; Daniel Fenton, Trenton; James Wilson, Wilmington; William Dickson, Lancaster; John Wyeth, Harrisburg; Alexander & Phillips, Carlisle; Patterson & Hopkins, Pittsburg; Maccoun, Telford & Co. Lexington (Ky.); Samuel Jefferis, Baltimore; George Shaw & Co. Annapolis; James Kennedy, senr. Alexandria; William F. Gray, Fredericksburg; Johnson and Warner, Richmond; John W. Campbell, Petersburg; Caleb Bonsal, Norfolk; John Hoff, Charleston; Seymour & Williams, Savannah; George Adams, Augusta; William Wilkinson, Providence (R. I.); Samuel Green, New-London.

Appendix 3: Biographies Published in the *Farmer's Weekly Museum* During Joseph Dennie's Editorial Tenure, Including Probable Sources.

The sources here indicated for the biographies published in the *Farmer's Weekly Museum*, unless explicitly acknowledged by Dennie, are conjectural. The vary in likelihood between those which have, as far as could be discovered, only appeared in one other source, and those which appeared in a number of places previous to Dennie's selection of them. In all cases, the decision which publication seems most likely as the original source has rested on two considerations: did Dennie copy from this source more than once, and is there any evidence that Dennie had access to one source, but not the other? Articles which are here listed as coming from the *Lady's Magazine* and the *European Magazine* have largely been attributed on this basis, as otherwise, a number of sources would only account for single texts.

Biographee	Publication Date	Original Source	Place & Date Misc. Notes	Source Ackn.?
Lord Chatham	June 28, 1796	Seward, William. *Anecdotes of Some Distinguished Persons Chiefly of the Present and Two Preceding Centuries.*	London, 1795.	
General Bounaparte	July 19, 1796	?	?	
Sketch of the Character of Rittenhouse	August 2, 1796	?	?	
Life of Duval, Superintendent of the Imperial Library in Vienna	November 15, 1796	Owen, William, and William Johnston. *A New and General Biographical Dictionary Containing an Historical and Critical Account of the Lives and Writings of the Most Eminent Persons in Every Nation.*	London, 1784.	
Memoirs of William Strahan, a late celebrated Printer	December 6, 1796	Mackenzie, William. *Lounger No. 29.*	London. August 20, 1785.	

The Life of Shakespeare	January 31, 1797	Anderson, Robert. *The Works of the British Poets*, Vol. II	London, 1795.	
The Life of Edmund Spenser	February 7, 1797	Ibd.		
The Life of Milton	February 14, 1797	WBP, Vol. V		
The Life of Cowley	February 21, 1797	Ibd.		
Memoirs of the Late Queen of France	February 28, 1797	?	?	
Life of Butler	March 7, 1797	WBP, Vol. V		
The Life of Carew	March 14, 1797	WBP, Vol. III		
The Life of Waller	March 21, 1797	WBP, Vol. V		
The Life of Drayton	March 28, 1797	WBP, Vol. III		
The Life of Suckling	April 4, 1797	WBP, Vol. III		
The Life of Donne	April 18, 1797	WBP, Vol. IV		
Notice of Alexander Selkirk, the original Robinson Crusoe	May 2, 1797	Sinclair, John. *Statistical Account of Scotland.*		X
Notices of Sir Charles Linnaeus	May 9, 1797	Stoever, D.H. *The Life of Sir Charles Linnaeus.*	London, 1794	
Notices of Ben Jonson	May 16, 1797	WBP, Vol. IV		
The Life of Chaucer	June 5, 1797	WBP, Vol. I		
Political Life of Pitt	June 12, 1797	?		
Memoirs of the Late Countess of Exeter	July 10, 1797	*Monthly Magazine*	London, March 1797	X
Account of Arthur Young	July 17, 1797	*European Magazine and London Review*	London, December 1795	
The Life of Surrey	July 24, 1797	WBP, Vol. I		
Madame Roland	August 7, 1797	?		

Madame La Fayette	August 14, 1797	Presumably from *Biographical Anecdotes of the Founders of the French Republic.* [...]	London, 1797	
Notices of Thomas Beauclerc	August 21, 1797	*European Magazine and London Review*	London, March 1797	
Notices of Lord Mansfield	August 28, 1797	?		
"A Surinam Planter"	September 4, 1797	*European Magazine and London Review*	London, March 1797	
Dame Strudwick	September 11, 1797	*Lady's Magazine, Or Entertaining Companion for the Fair Sex*	London, March 1797	
		Alt: *Edinburgh Magazine*	May 1797	
An Account of John Baskerville, Printer	September 18, 1797	*New York Magazine*?	April 1791	
The late Right Honorable Edmund Burke	September 25, 1797	*Monthly Mirror*	London, July 1797	
Life of Bishop Horne	October 2, 1797	?		
John Boydell, Lord Mayor of London	October 23, 1797	*European Magazine and London Review*	London, April 1792	
The Life of Mortimer, the Painter	November 27, 1797	*Monthly Magazine*	London, February 1797	
Memoirs of the Life of the Late Robert Burns	December 4, 1797	*Monthly Magazine*	London, March 1797	
Lord Orford	December 26, 1797	*Lady's Magazine* [...]	London, April 1797	
[Unnamed of Edmund Burke]	January 2, 1798	*Edinburgh Magazine*?	Month? 1797	
Malesherbes	January 30, 1798	*Biographical Anecdotes of the Founders of the French Republic.* [...]	Here called "Anecdotes of distinguished Persons connected with the French Revolution."	X

Couthon	February 6, 1798	*Biographical Anecdotes of the Founders of the French Republic.* [...]		
An Account of the Life and Writings of Wieland, a celebrated German writer	February 13, 1798	*Monthly Magazine*	London, June 1797	
Account of Her-ault de Sechelles	February 20, 1798	*Biographical Anecdotes of the Founders of the French Republic.* [...]		
Amar	February 27, 1798	*Biographical Anecdotes of the Founders of the French Republic.* [...]		X
Dufriche de Valaze	March 6, 1798	*Biographical Anecdotes of the Founders of the French Republic.* [...]		X
Fabre De Galantine	March 13, 1798	*Biographical Anecdotes of the Founders of the French Republic.* [...]		X
Account of Mr. Warton	March 27, 1798	*The Scot's Magazine, or General Reposi-tory of Literature, History* [...]	May 1797	
Notices of Count Rumford	April 3, 1798	*European Magazine and London Review*	February 1797	
The Life of Shakespeare	May 22, 1798	Bioren and Medan's *The Plays and Poems of William Shakespeare*	Philadel-phia, 1795	X
The Life of Henry Fielding	August 27, 1798	?		
Character of Major General John Fiske	September 3, 1798	Bentley's "Fune-ral Discourse"	?	X
	September 10, 1798			X
Sketch of Mirabeau	September 17, 1798	John Moore: *A View of the Society and Manners in France, Switzerland and Germany.*	London: 1780	X

Sketch of Charlotte Corde	September 24, 1798	John Moore: *A View of the Causes and the Progress of the French Revolution* [in a footnote]		
The Life of Thomas Otway	October 1, 1798	Theophilus Cibber: *Lives of the Poets of Great Britain*	London, 1753	
Character of Talleyrand	October 15, 1798	*Biographical Anecdotes of the Founders of the French Republic.* […]		
Life of Chamfort	October 22, 1798	*Biographical Anecdotes of the Founders of the French Republic.* […]		
[Thomas Garratt]	October 29, 1798	*Monthly Magazine*	London, March 1798	
[William Enfield]	November 5, 1798	*Monthly Magazine*	London, November 1797	
Anecdotes of David, the Celebrated French Painter	November 12, 1798	*Biographical Anecdotes of the Founders of the French Republic.* […]		
[Adam Duncan, Viscount Duncan of Camperdown]	November 19, 1798	European Magazine and London Review	London, January 1798	
Character of Edmund Burke	December 10, 1798	?		
Some Account of Bisset	December 24, 1798	*Lady's Magazine* […]	London, April 1794	
An Account of Baron Swedenborg	December 31, 1798	?	?	X
The Life of M. Zimmerman	January 7, 1799	*European Magazine and London Review*	October 1797	
Notices of Klopstock	January 14, 1799	*Monthly Magazine*	London, April 1798	
Rev. James de la Cour	January 21, 1799	*European Magazine and London Review*	London, November 1797	
The Life of Schiller	February 4, 1799	*Monthly Magazine*	London, June 1798	
The Life of Goldoni	February 11, 1799	*Monthly Magazine*	London, February 1798	
The Life of Dufriche de Valaze	February 18, 1799	*Biographical Anecdotes of the Founders of the French Republic.* […]		

The Life of Godefroi Izarn, Marquis Da Valadi	February 25, 1799	*Biographical Anecdotes of the Founders of the French Republic.* […]		
Character of a Fine French Woman	March 11, 1799	Jean-Jacques Rousseau: *Emile et Sophia, ou: L'Education*		
Character of Francois de Neaufchateau	March 11, 1799	*Monthly Magazine*	London, September 1798	
Sir Joseph Mawbey	March 18, 1799	*Monthly Magazine*	London, June 1798	
John Philip Kemble	March 25, 1799	*European Magazine and London Review*	London, August 1798	
The Life of John Trumbull	April 1, 1799	*Monthly Magazine*	London, August 1798	
The Life of Dr. Timothy Dwight	April 8, 1799	*Monthly Magazine*	London, July 1798	
The Life of Colonel David Humphreys	April 15, 1799	*Monthly Magazine*	London, September 1798	
Dr. Elihu Hubbard Smith	April 29, 1799	*Monthly Magazine*	London, February 1799	
Account of Joseph Wright	May 6, 1799	*European Magazine and London Review*	August 1797	
Richard Warren, M.D.F.R.S.	May 13, 1799	*European Magazine and London Review*	November 1797	
The Life of Edmund Burke	June 17-July 22, 1799	*Monthly Review*	August 1798	
Character of James Graeme	July 29, 1799	Either WBP Vol 11, or *Monthly Review*	If latter, September 1798	
Lord Nelson	August 19 & 26, 1799	*The Public Characters* 1798	Dublin, 1799	
The Life of Dr. Lemuel Hopkins	September 2, 1799	*Monthly Magazine*	London, November 1798	
Sir George Leonard Staunton	September 9, 1799	*The Public Characters* 1798	Dublin, 1799	
Some Memoirs of the Late Reverend Thomas Alcock	September 16, 1799	*European Magazine and London Review*	October 1798	
The Life of Joel Barlow	September 23, 1799	*Monthly Magazine*	October 1798	

Appendix 4: Excerpt from *Port Folio* Prospectus (Courtesy Historical Society of Pennsylvania)

PROSPECTUS.

Paris. But we can pay homage to beauties of *purer* lustre. We have "of *honorable* women not a few;" who associate study and invention, who unite the *virtues* to the graces, and who are "capable of making the bad good, the inconstant stable, and the giddy wise."

Nor is the Editor of that hermit humour, to be regardless of the innocent wishes of the modish tribe. Though it cannot correctly be expected that he should be a critic of *Coquelicot*, or learned in *laces*; yet, he will not omit to notice sometimes the shop of the milliner, and "watch the wild vicissitudes of taste." Fashionable *dress*, as well as manners, shall be occasionally described; and to please the flaunting belle, he will, with no languid voice, and in the words of Anstey, invoke *her* tutelary power.

"Come then, nymph of various mein,
Votary true of beauty's queen,
FASHION, come,—on me a while
Deign, fantastic nymph, to smile.
Vers'd in science debonnair,
Bowing, dancing, dressing hair,
You gaily trip it o'er the globe,
Clad in party colour'd robe.
Bring, O bring thy essence pot,
Amber, musk, and bergamot,
Eau de chipre, eau de luce,
Sans pareil, and citron juice.
Nor the band-box leave behind,
Fill'd with stores of every kind;
All the enraptur'd bard supposes,
Who to FANCY odes composes;
All that fancy's self has feign'd,
In a band-box is contain'd:
Violets, pinks, Italian posies,
Myrtles, jessamin, and roses,
Aprons, caps, and 'kerchiefs clean,
Straw-built hats, and bonnets green."

It remains for the Editor to indicate to his friends and correspondents, various topics of composition, and to subjoin the conditions to which the purchase of his paper is subjected. He enters copiously into the detail of the *first*; and, he presumes, that to the terms of the *second*, no just and generous man will hint an objection.

Brief reports of the most interesting debates in Congress, *from the notes of members*, friendly to this undertaking.

Political information, and political disquisition from the pens of *Principals*.

Elegant, or interesting speeches, in either house of Congress.

An *early* and *prompt* communication of momentous state papers.

Monthly, quarterly, or semi-annual retrospects of foreign affairs.

Faithful translations from valuable French, Spanish, or German books, pamphlets or papers. But, it must be understood, that the Editor totally prohibits every thing *Jacobinical*.

Economical essays, on the model of count Rumford.

Statistical tables.

Abstracts of the specification of every new patent.

Summary of domestic politics.

Detections of Jacobinical forgery, falshood, and misrepresentation.

Accurate reports of legal decisions, involving important national, commercial, or private interests.

Essays on rural economy.

Scientific papers.

Notices of the useful and fine arts.

Notices of new books, pamphlets, and literary projects of every description.

Information, respecting every species of "lettered worth," in obscurity.

Sketches of tours and journies, either through our own, or foreign territory.

Journals of voyages.

Descriptions of local peculiarities, and characteristical manners.

Review of new, or fashionable musical publications.

Remarks on the manners of the times, and on public amusements.

Descriptions of the fashionable dresses of the season.

Hymeneal register.

Articles for an obituary of remarkable, or distinguished persons, accompanied by anecdotes, after the model in "*The Gentlemans' Magazine*."

Meteorological diaries.

The various tribes of *gay* and useful miscellany; and in this pleasant and flowery walk, the Editor will assume the freedom to particularize the objects, he wishes should be attended to.

Burlesque translations.

Parodies of the poets, particularly of Shakespeare.

Cross readings.

Ship news extraordinary

Advertisements extra.

Humorous and satiric ballads, in the style of John Gilpin.

Tender and pathetic ballads, in the manner of Dr. Percy's "O Nancy wilt thou go with me," and Hamilton's "Braes of Yarrow."

Mock odes, imitations &c. in the manner of "The Rolliad."

Hudibrastic poetry.

Characteristical and humorous diaries.

Dialogues, sentimental, or sportive.

Correct songs, adapted to the taste of the Anacreontic group, or the amateur.

Translations from the classic poets of Spain and Italy.

Epigrams.

Anecdotes.

Articles of levity, wit, and humour.

Articles of American biography, and of memoir writing in general.

Historical documents, or narrative.

Elegant translations of brilliant or useful passages from THE ANCIENTS.

Concise moral lessons.

Criticisms on new books and pamphlets.

Periodical essays, in the manner of Addison, Johnson, or Goldsmith.

Moral Allegories, Tales, and Romances.

Dramatic Sketches of Character.

Extracts from scarce and curious publications.

Extracts from the most *novel* works of celebrity, published abroad.

Extracts from the most *recent* and valuable American publications.

Original poetry.

Scenes of original plays.

Original letters.

Notes, concerning Americans of genius, enterprize, or mechanic skill, resident abroad, and

Literary selections from the London, or Cambridge, Bristol, Bath, Liverpool, Edinburgh, Glasgow, and Dublin newspapers.

Ab [1800]-2

Notes on the Text

Despite the efforts of lexicographers and school teachers' spelling books, in the late eighteenth and early nineteenth century spelling, while not exactly as haphazard as in the sixteenth and seventeenth centuries, was not yet entirely standardized. Most notably, perhaps, what we perceive as British English variants were still overwhelmingly in use in the United States. These variant spellings I leave as they were in the original. Furthermore, words with a regular contemporary variant spelling that is today non-standard or obsolete in any variety, such as "enterprize," "expences," or "publick," I have also left standing without the notation [sic]. That adverb I have reserved for obvious errors of spelling such as "piography" for "biography" or "malecontent" for "malcontent" (assuming no puns were intended, of course). When in doubt, I have left the notation out, and accept the penalty of a misprint.

For the most part, editors and authors of articles in Early Republic periodicals did not sign their names. In some cases it is possible to identify regular contributors ("P." and "V." in the *Analectic Magazine* being James Kirke Paulding and Gulian Verplanck, for example). On occasion, the nature of the material makes it likely that it was editorial matter, and can be ascribed to the current editor of the periodical in question. In every case, an effort has been made to follow these trails of evidence to establish an author, and articles will be given with their author, wherever possible, in the text.

Unless otherwise noted, all quotations from German and French texts are my own translations, although I have endeavored to provide the original French for the reader's safety. Quotations from Latin, by contrast, I supply in translation from sources.

For ease of reference, I have adopted parenthetical citation for this text, with one exception: archival sources are cited in footnotes. This is an inelegant solution to be sure, but it signally unclutters the text proper. I have adopted abbreviations for almost all periodicals cited in the text, a complete list of which follows this note. Some periodicals that I only cite once I opted to cite in full in parenthesis.Magazines, which usually numbered pages consecutively over a year's issues, are cited by date and page, e.g. "*PF* 1802, 243;" where this format cannot be followed, because each issue in a given year had its own consecutive page count, I note whether the first or second half-yearly issue is cited: "AM 1815 I, 152". Newspapers, which do not usually carry a running page count, or indeed any count at all, are cited by date, volume, issue, and page, with the exception of the *Farmer's Weekly Museum*.

Bibliography

List of Abbreviations

I have opted to cite periodical articles by abbreviations; a full list of articles can be found in the bibliography sorted by journal abbreviations. A list of abbreviations follows below in the alphabetical order of magazines names, inclusive of publication location and publication dates, as some magazines carried the names of previously ventures (such as the *American Magazine*). Newspapers are not included in this list.

AMA	*The American Magazine*, Albany. 1815-1816.
AMU	*The American Museum or, Universal Magazine*, Philadelphia. 1789-1892.
AR	*American Review, and Literary Journal*, New York. 1801-1802.
AM	*The Analectic Magazine*, Philadelphia. 1812-1820.
A	*The Athenaeum*, New Haven. 1814.
AT	*The Atheneum; or, Spirit of the English Magazines*. Boston. 1817-1833.
BCR	*Balance, and Columbian Repository*, Albany. 1802-1807
BOW	*Boston Weekly Magazine*, Boston. 1803-1805.
C	*The Casket*, Hudson. 1811-1812.
CD	*Christian Disciple*, Boston. 1813-1818.
CO	*Christian Observer*, Boston. 1802-1842.
CM	*Columbian Magazine*, Philadelphia. 1786-1790.
EAS	*Emporium of Arts and Sciences*, Philadelphia. 1812-1814.
EF	*Evening Fireside*, Philadelphia. 1804-1806.
E	*Examiner: Containing Political Essays on the Most Important Events of the Time*, New York. 1813-1816.
FWM	*Farmer's Weekly Museum*, Walpole. 1793-1810.
F	*Floriad*, Schenectady. 1811.
G	*Gleaner; or, Monthly Magazine*, Philadelphia. 1808-1809.
LH	*Lancaster Hive*, Lancaster. 1803-1805.
LC	*Literary Cabinet*, New Haven. 1806-1807.
LMS	*Literary Miscellany*, Philadelphia. 1795.
LM	*The Literary Magazine, and American Register*, Philadelphia, 1803-1807
LT	*Literary Tablet*, Hanover. 1803-1807.
LWM	*Ladies' Weekly Miscellany*, New York. 1806-1810.
MAM	*Massachusetts Magazine*, Boston. 1790-1796.
MBMM	*Massachusetts Baptist Missionary Magazine*, Boston. 1803-1816.

MMM	*Massachusetts Missionary Magazine*, Boston. 1803-1808.
MER	*Medical Repository*, New York. 1797-1824.
MM	*Merrimack Magazine and Ladies' Literary Cabinet*, Newburyport. 1805-1806.
M	*The Miscellany*, Trenton. 1806.
MA	*The Monthly Anthology*, Boston. 1806-1811
MR	*Monthly Register, Magazine, and Review of the United States*. Charleston, SC. 1805-1806; New York. 1806-1807.
NEG	*New England Galaxy and Masonic Magazine*, Boston.1817-1836.
NEQR	*New England Quarterly Magazine*, Boston. 1802.
NYM	*New York Magazine*, New York. 1814.
NYMI	New York Mirror, New York. 19
NYMR	*New York Magazine, or Literary Repository*, New York. 1790-1797.
N	*The Nightingale*, Boston. 1796.
NWR	*Niles' Weekly Register*, Baltimore. 1815-1837.
NAR	*The North American Review*, Boston. 1815-1940.
O	*The Olio*, New York. 1814.
OG	*Omnium Gatherum*, Boston. 1810.
PN	*The Panoplist*, Boston. 1805-1820.
PRP	*Philadelphia Repertory*, Philadelphia. 1810-1812.
P	*The Polyanthos*, Boston. 1805-1807, 1812-1814.
PO	*The Portico*, Baltimore. 1816-18.
PF	*The Port Folio*, Philadelphia. 1801-1827.
PR	*Prospect*, New York. 1803-1805.
RI	*Religious Intelligencer*, New Haven. 1810-1837.
T	*The Tablet*, A Miscellaneous Paper, Boston. 1795.
TM	*Theological Magazine*, New York. 1795-1799.
TH	*Theophilanthropist*, New York. 1810.
TP	*The Time-Piece; and Literary Companion*, Philadelphia. 1797-1798.
UACM	*Universal Asylum, and Columbian Magazine*, Philadelphia. 1790-1792.
WG	*Western Gleaner*, Pittsburgh. 1813-1814.
WI	*The Weekly Inspector*, New York. 1806-1807.
WM	*Weekly Magazine*, Philadelphia. 1798-1799.
NWR	*Weekly Register*, Baltimore. 1811-1814, thereafter *Niles' Weekly Register*
WOM	*Worcester Magazine*, Worcester. 1786-1788.

Primary Sources (Periodicals)

AM *Analectic Magazine*

(1813 1, 264-74). Paulding, James K. "Biographical Notice of Captain Isaac Hull." [Essay-Biography]. *The Analectic Magazine* 1, March 1813. 264-274.

(1813 2, 70-78). Paulding, James K. "Biography of Captain Jacob Jones." [Essay-Biography]. *The Analectic Magazine* 2, July 1813. 70-78.

(1813 2, 122-141). Irving, Washington. "Biography of Captain James Lawrence." [Essay-Biography]. *The Analectic Magazine* 2, August 1813. 129-141.

(1813 2, 233-4). "Captain Lawrence." [Editorial]. *The Analectic Magazine* 2, September 1813. 233-234.

(1813 2, 396-403). Irving, Washington. "Biographical Notice of the Late Lieutenant Burrows." [Essay-Biography]. *The Analectic Magazine* 2, November 1813. 396-403.

(1813 2, 494-510). Irving, Washington. "Biographical Memoir of Commodore Perry." [Essay-Biography]. *The Analectic Magazine* 2, December 1813. 494-510.

(1814 1, 54-61). Paulding, James K. "Biographical Sketch of the Late Lieutenant Aylwin." [Essay-Biography]. *The Analectic Magazine* 3, January 1814. 54-61.

(1814 2, 465-86). Verplanck, Gulian Crommelin. "Original. Biographical Sketch of Major General Winfield Scott." [Essay-Biography]. *The Analectic Magazine* 4, December 1814. 465-86.

(1815 2, 376-82). "Remarks on the Character of Patrick Henry. To the Editor of the Analectic Magazine." [Letter to the Editor-Biography]. *The Analectic Magazine* 6, November 1815. 376-382.

(1816 1, 1-10). "Biographical Sketch of Captain Lewis Warrington." [Essay-Biography]. *The Analectic Magazine* 7 (37), January 1816. 1-10.

(1816 1, 201-216). Paulding, James K. "Biographical Sketch of Captain Thomas MacDonough." [Essay-Biography]. The *Analectic Magazine* 7, March 1816. 201-216.

(1816 1, 422-5). "Strictures on the Biography of Mr. Bayard. To the Publisher of the Analectic Magazine." [Letter to the Editor]. *The Analectic Magazine* 7, May 1816. 422-425.

(1816 2, 193-209). Sanford, Ezekiel. "Original. A Repository of the Lives and Portraits of Distinguished Americans [Review]." [Essay-Review]. *The Analectic Magazine* 8, September 1816. 193-209.

(1816 2, 247-52). "Biographical Sketch of Lieutenant John Templar Shubrick." [Essay-Biography]. *The Analectic Magazine* 8, September 1816. 247-252.

(1819 1, 304-15). "Art IV. A History of the United States, before the Revolution, with some account of the Aborigines, by Ezekiel Sanford. Philadelphia, 1819." [Essay-Review]. *The Analectic Magazine* 9, April 1819. 304-315.

AMA *American Magazine*

(1815, 177-83). "Biographical Sketch of the Late Baron Steuben." [Essay]. *The American*

Magazine, A Monthly Magazine 1 (5), October 1815. 177-183.

AMU *American Museum*

(1790, 457-72). "Second Session." [Reportage]. *The American Museum, or, Universal Magazine* 7 (6), June 1790. 457-472.

AR *American Review, and Literary Journal*

(1801, ii-v). "Preface." [Editorial-Prospectus]. *The American Review, and Literary Journal* 1.n.d. 1801. ii-v.

AT *Athenaeum*

(1814). "Prospectus." [Prospectus]. *The Athenaeum* 1 (1), February 12, 1814. 1-4.

ATS *Atheneum; or, Spirit of English Magazines*

(1818 1, 445-9). "American Resources." [Essay.] *The Atheneum; or, Spirit of the English Magazines* 3 (12), September 15, 1818. 445-449.

BCR *Balance, and Columbian Repository*

(1804) "Literary Notice: Prospectus." [Advertisement-Prospectus]. *Balance, and Columbian Repository* 3 (37), September 11, 1804. 292-294.

BEM *Blackwood's Edinburgh Magazine*

(1825 1, 48-69). Neal, John. "American Writers. No. IV." [Essay]. *Blackwood's Edinburgh Magazine* 17 (96), January 1825. 48-69.

BOW *Boston Weekly Magazine*

(1803, 71). "To Readers and Correspondents." [Editorial]. *Boston Weekly Magazine* 1 (17), February 19. 71.

C *Casket*

(1812, 153). "Editor's Garret." [Editorial]. *The Casket* 1 (13), February 29, 1812. 153.

CD *Christian Disciple*

(1814 2, 351-2). "Commodore Thomas MacDonough." [Essay-Biography]. *Christian Disciple* 2 (11), November 2, 1814. 351-352.

CM *Columbian Magazine*

(1786, 172-5). "For the Columbian Magazine. Thoughts on the Present Situation of the Fœderal Government of the United States of America." [Essay]. *The Columbian Magazine* 1 (4), December 1786. 172-175.

(1788, 3-5). "The American Plutarch. The Life of John Winthrop." [Essay-Biography]. *The Columbian Magazine*, January 1788. 3-5.

CO *Christian Observer*

(1802, 120-1). "The Origin, Advantages, Disadvantages, and Importance of Literary Journals." [Essay]. *Christian Observer, Conducted by Members of the Established Church* 1 (2), February 1802. 120-121.

(1815, 141-3). "To the Editor of the Christian Observer." [Essay-Letter to the Editor]. *Christian Observer, Conducted by Members of the Established Church* 14 (159), March 1815. 141-143.

E *Examiner*

(1814 2, 1-2). "The Examiner." [Editorial]. *Examiner: Containing Political Essays on the Most Important Events of the Time* 3 (1), November 5, 1814. 1-2.

EAS *Emporium of Arts and Sciences*

(1813, i-iv) "Subscribers' Names." [Editorial]. *The Emporium of Arts & Sciences* 2, April 1813. i-iv.

(1813). "Prospectus of the Emporium of Arts and Sciences (New Series)." [Prospectus]. *The Emporium of Arts & Sciences* 2 (12), April 1813. 1-14.

(1813, 481-484). "Subscribers Names." [Editorial] *The Emporium of Arts & Sciences* 2 (12), April 1813. 481-484.

EF *Evening Fire-Side*

(1804, 1). "Prospectus." [Prospectus]. The Evening Fire-Side, or Weekly Intelligencer 1 (1), December 15, 1804. 1.

F *Floriad*

(1811) "The Editors of the Floriad to its Patrons." [Editorial]. *The Floriad* 1 (1), May 24, 1811. 1-5.

FWM Farmer's Weekly Museum

(1793, 1.1, 1). "To the Public." [Editorial]. *Newhampshire Journal: Or, The Farmer's Weekly Museum* 1 (1), April 11, 1793. [1].

(1795, 2.102, 1). "Useful Biography." [Essay-Biography]. *Newhampshire and Vermont Journal: Or, The Farmer's Weekly Museum* 2 (102), March 17, 1795. [1].

(1796, 3.151, 1). "Useful Biography. Mr. Bakewell of Dishley." [Essay-Biography]. *Newhampshire and Vermont Journal: Or, The Farmer's Weekly Museum* 3 (151), February 23, 1796. [1].

(1796, 3.152, 1). "Biography. Account of Thomas Topham." [Essay-Biography]. *Newhampshire and Vermont Journal: Or, The Farmer's Weekly Museum* 3 (152), March 1, 1796. [1].

(1796, 4.157, 1). "To the Public." [Editorial]. *Newhampshire and Vermont Journal: Or, The Farmer's Weekly Museum* 4 (157), April 5, 1796. [1].

(1796, 4.159, 3). "Acknowledgment to Correspondents." [Editorial]. *The Newhampshire and Vermont Journal: Or, The Farmer's Weekly Museum* 4 (159), April 19, 1796. [3].

(1796, 4.192, 1-2). "Biography. Memoirs of William Strahan, a Late Celebrated Printer." *The Newhampshire and Vermont Journal: Or, The Farmer's Weekly Museum* 4 (192), December 6, 1796. [1-2].

(1797, 4.200, 1-2). "Biography. The Life of Shakespeare." *The Newhampshire and Vermont Journal: Or, The Farmer's Weekly Museum* 4 (200), January 31, 1797. [1-2].

(1797, 4.204, 1-2). "Biography. Memoirs of the Late Queen of France." *The Newhampshire and Vermont Journal: Or, The Farmer's Weekly Museum* 4 (204), February 28, 1797. [1-2].

(1797, 5.209, 1). "To Patrons." [Editorial]. *The Farmer's Weekly Museum: Newhampshire and Vermont Journal* 5 (209), April 4, 1797. [1].

(1797, 5.214, 1-2). "Biography. Notices of Sir Charles Linnaeus." [Essay-Biography] *The Farmer's Weekly Museum: Newhampshire and Vermont Journal* 5 (214), May 9, 1797. [1-2].

(1797, 5.219, 2). "Biography. Sketch of the Political Life of Pitt." [Essay-Biography]. *The Farmer's Weekly Museum: Newhampshire and Vermont Journal* 5 (219), June 12, 1797. [2].

(1797, 5.224, 3). "To Readers and Correspondents." [Editorial]. *The Farmer's Weekly Museum: Newhampshire and Vermont Journal* 5 (224), July 17, 1797. [3].

(1797, 5.228, 4). "[British Biography.]" [Essay]. *The Farmer's Weekly Museum: Newhampshire and Vermont Journal* 5 (209), August 14, 1797. [4].

(1797, 5.231, 2). "Biography. A Surinam Planter." [Essay-Biography]. *The Farmer's Weekly Museum: Newhampshire and Vermont Journal* 5 (231), September 4, 1797. [1].

(1797, 5.232, 1). "Biography. Dame Strudwick." [Essay-Biography]. *The Farmer's Weekly Museum: Newhampshire and Vermont Journal* 5 (232), September 11, 1797. [1].

(1797, 5.244, 3). "To Readers and Correspondents." [Editorial]. *The Farmer's Weekly Museum: Newhampshire and Vermont Journal* 5 (244), December 4, 1797. [3].

(1797, 5.252, 1-2). "Miscellany. Biography. Malesherbes." [Essay-Biography]. *The Farmer's Weekly Museum: Newhampshire and Vermont Journal* 5 (255), January 30, 1798. [1-2].

(1798, 5.255, 3). "Notice." [Editorial]. *The Farmer's Weekly Museum: Newhampshire and Vermont Journal* 5 (255), February 20, 1798. [3].

(1798, 6.268, 1-2). "Biography. The Life of Shakespeare." [Essay-Biography]. *The Farmer's Weekly Museum: Newhampshire and Vermont Journal* 6 (268), May 22, 1798. [1-2].

(1798, 6.282, 1-2). "Miscellany. Biography. [Life of Henry Fielding]" [Essay-Biography]. *The Farmer's Weekly Museum: Newhampshire and Vermont Journal* 6 (282), August 27, 1798. [1-2].

(1798, 6.283, 1-2). "Miscellany. Biography. Character of Major General John Fiske." [Essay-Biography]. *The Farmer's Weekly Museum: Newhampshire and Vermont Journal* 6 (283),

September 9, 1798. [1-2].
(1798, 6.285, 2). "Biography. Sketch of Mirabeau." [Essay-Biography]. *The Farmer's Weekly Museum: Newhampshire and Vermont Journal* 6 (285), September 17, 1798. [2].
(1798, 6.289, 1) "Miscellany. Biography. Character of Talleyrand." [Essay-Biography]. *The Farmer's Weekly Museum: Newhampshire and Vermont Journal* 6 (290), October 15, 1798. [1].
(1798, 6.289, 4). "Satire on the Prostitution of Modern Biography, in a Dialogue Between a Biographer and Kennel Scraper." [Essay-Satire]. *The Farmer's Weekly Museum: Newhampshire and Vermont Journal* 6 (290), October 15, 1798. [4].
(1798, 6.290, 1-2). "Biography. Life of Chamfort." [Essay-Biography]. *The Farmer's Weekly Museum: Newhampshire and Vermont Journal* 6 (290), October 22, 1798. [1-2].
(1798, 6.292, 1-2). "Miscellany. Biography [of William Enfield]." [Essay-Biography]. *The Farmer's Weekly Museum: Newhampshire and Vermont Journal* 6 (292), November 5, 1798. [1-2].
(1798, 6.292, 3). "To Readers and Correspondents." [Editorial]. *The Farmer's Weekly Museum: Newhampshire and Vermont Journal* 6 (292), November 5, 1798. [3].
(1798, 6.293, 1). "Miscellany. Biography. Anecdotes of David, the Celebrated French Painter." [Essay-Biography]. (1799, 6.306, 4). "To the Public." [Editorial]. *The Farmer's Weekly Museum: Newhampshire and Vermont Journal* 6 (293), November 12, 1798. [1].
(1798, 6.293, 4) "A Projector's Scheme of Biography in Bags." [Essay-Satire]. *The Farmer's Weekly Museum: Newhampshire and Vermont Journal* 6 (293), November 12, 1798. [4].
(1798, 6.294, 1). "Miscellany. Biography. Adam Duncan." [Essay-Biography]. *The Farmer's Weekly Museum: Newhampshire and Vermont Journal* 6 (294), November 19, 1798. [1].
(1798, 6.297, 1-2). "Biography. Character of Edmund Burke." [Essay-Biography]. *The Farmer's Weekly Museum: Newhampshire and Vermont Journal* 6 (297), December 10, 1798. [1-2].
(1799, 6.306, 4). "To the Public." [Editorial]. *The Farmer's Weekly Museum: Newhampshire and Vermont Journal* 6 (306), February 11, 1799. [4].
(1799, 6.307, 1-2). "Biography. The Life of Dufriche de Valaze." [Essay-Biography]. *The Farmer's Weekly Museum: Newhampshire and Vermont Journal* 6 (307), February 18, 1799. [1-2].
(1799, 6.311, 1-2). "Biography. Sir Joseph Mawbey." [Essay-Biography]. *The Farmer's Weekly Museum: Newhampshire and Vermont Journal* 6 (311), March 18, 1799. [1-2].
(1799, 6.311, 3). "To Readers and Correspondents" [Editorial]. *The Farmer's Weekly Museum: Newhampshire and Vermont Journal* 6 (311), March 18, 1799. [3].
(1799, 7.313, 1). "American Biography. The Life of John Trumbull." *The Farmer's Weekly Museum: Newhampshire and Vermont Journal* 7 (313), April 1, 1799. [1].
(1799, 7.313, 3) "To Readers and Correspondents." *The Farmer's Weekly Museum: Newhampshire and Vermont Journal* 7 (313), April 1, 1799. [3].
(1799, 7.324, 1-2). "Biography. The Life of Edmund Burke." [Essay-Biography]. *The Farmer's Weekly Museum: Newhampshire and Vermont Journal* 7 (324), June 17, 1799. [1-2].
(1799, 7.335, 1-2). "Miscellany. American Biography. The Life of Dr. Lemuel Hopkins." [Essay-Biography]. *The Farmer's Weekly Museum: Newhampshire and Vermont Journal* 7 (335), September 2, 1799. [1-2].

G *Gleaner*

(1809). "On News-Papers or Political Journals." [Essay]. *The Gleaner; or, Monthly Magazine* 1 (11), July 1809. 499-502.

GUS *Gazette of the United States*

(1800, 17.2413, 3). "[Editorial Note]." [Editorial]. *Gazette of the United States* 17 (2413), June 20, 1800. [3].

LC *Literary Cabinet*

(1806). "Prospectus." [Prospectus]. *Literary Cabinet* 1 (1), November 15. 1.

LH *Lancaster Hive*

(1803, 17-8). "Inconvenience of a Learned Wife." [Essay-Editorial]. *The Lancaster Hive*, 1 ory (5), July 20. 17-18.

LM *Literary Magazine*

(1803). "The Editor's Address to the Public." [Editorial]. *The Literary Magazine , and American Register* 1 (1), October. 3-6.
(1804 2, 252-7) "For the Literary Magazine. The American Character. To the Editor, &c." *The Literary Magazine , and American Register* 2 (10), 252-257.
(1806, 265-6). "Duty of Periodical Essayists." [Essay]. *The Literary Magazine , and American Register* 6 (37), October. 265-266.

LMI *Literary Miscellany*

(1795, 23-33). "Subscribers' Names." *The Literary Miscellany* 16, n.d. 23-33.

LMS *Literary Miscellany, or Monthly Review, a Periodical Work*

(1811, 38-42). "On the Advantages of Periodical Publications." [Essay]. *The Literary Miscellany, or Monthly Review, a Periodical Work* 1 (1), May. 38-42.

LT *Literary Tablet*

(1803, 1). "To the Public." [Editorial]. *Literary Tablet* 1 (1), August 6, 1803. 1.
(1803, 15). "[Editorial Apology]." [Editorial]. *Literary Tablet* 1 (4), September 17, 1803. 15.
(1804, 103). "To the Public." [Editorial]. *Literary Tablet* 1 (15), August 9, 1804. 103.
(1806, 71). "To Correspondents." [Editorial]. *Literary Tablet* 3 (18). May 21, 1806. 71.

LWM *Lady's Weekly Miscellany*

(1808, 253-5). "[The editor of this miscellany tenders grateful acknowledgements…]." [Editorial]. *Lady's Weekly Miscellany* 6 (16), February 13, 1808. 253-255.

M *Miscellany*

(1805, 2). "On the Advantages Resulting From Periodical Publications." [Essay]. *The Miscellany* 1 (1), June 10. 2.

MA *Monthly Anthology*

(1804, 458-60). "Biographia Americana. Or Anecdotes of Professional, Learned, or Distinguished Characters in America. William Penn." [Essay-Biography]. *The Monthly Anthology, and Boston Review* 1 (10), August 1804. 458-460.

(1804, 591-2). "Biographia Americana; or Memoirs of Professional, Learned, or Distinguished Characters in the United States. Richard Montgomery." [Essay-Biography]. *The Monthly Anthology, and Boston Review* 1 (8), November 1804. 591-592.

(1804, 638-9). "Biographia Americana; or Memoirs of Professional, Learned, or Distinguished Characters in the United States. Richard Montgomery." [Letter to the Editor]. *The Monthly Anthology, and Boston Review* 1 (9), December 1804. 638-639.

(1805, 170-4). "Observations on the Literary Miscellany." [Essay]. *The Monthly Anthology, and Boston Review* 2 (4), April 1805. 170-174.

(1805, 405-6). "Thoughts on Plagiarism." [Letter to the Editor]. *The Monthly Anthology, and Boston Review* 2 (8), August 1805. 405-406.

(1807, 1-4). "Address of the Editors." [Editorial]. *The Monthly Anthology, and Boston Review* 4 (1), January 1807. 1-4.

(1808, 259-68). "Article 13. [Review of the Life of George Washington]." [Review]. *The Monthly Anthology, and Boston Review* 7 (5), May 1808. 259-268.

(1810 2, 145-161). "For the Anthology. A Discourse, Intended to Have Been Delivered…" [Essay*]. The Monthly Anthology, and Boston Review* 9, September 1810. 145-161.

(1811 1, 261-5). "Address of the Editors." [Editorial]. *The Monthly Anthology, and Boston Review* 10, June 1811. 261-265.

MAM *Massachusetts Magazine*

(1794, 708). "To the Public." [Editorial]. *The Massachusetts Magazine; or, Monthly Museum*. 708.

(1795, 3). "On Periodical Publications." [Essay]. *The Massachusetts Magazine; or, Monthly Museum* 7 (1), April 1795. 3-4.

MBMM *Massachusetts Baptist Missionary Magazine*

(1805, 5). "Conditions." [Editorial]. *The Massachusetts Baptist Missionary Magazine*, 1 (1), September 1805. Covers: 5.

MER *Medical Repository*

(1797, 9-16) "List of Subscribers." [Editorial]. *The Medical Repository* 1, January 1797. 9-16.

MM *Monthly Magazine*

(1799, 1-3). "On Periodical Publications." [Essay-Letter to the Editor]. *The Monthly Magazine, and American Review* 1 (1), April 1799. 1-3.

(1799, 282-7). "American Review, Article XV; [Review of American Biography]." [Review]. *The Monthly Magazine, and American Review* 1 (4), July 1799. 282-287.

(1800, 96-9). "Dialogues of the Living. Dialogue II." [Essay]. *The Monthly Magazine, and American Review* 2 (2), February 1800. 96-99.

(1800 2, 311-2). "Domestic [Literary and Philosophical Intelligence]." [Essay]. *The Monthly Magazine, and American Review* 3 (4), October 1800. 311-312.

MMM *Massachusetts Missionary Magazine*

(1803, 3-5). "Introduction." [Editorial]. *The Massachusetts Missionary Magazine, Containing Religious and Interesting Communications* 1, May. 3-5.

MMS *Merrimack Miscellany*

(1805, 71). "To Our Patrons." [Editorial]. *Merrimack Miscellany* 1 (18), October 5. 71.

MR *Monthly Register*

(1806 1, 1-3). "Introductory Essay." [Editorial]. *The Monthly Register, Magazine, and Review of the United States* 1, December 1806. 1-3.

(1806 1, 33-7). "Fourth Section. Communications. Biography." [Essay]. *The Monthly Register, Magazine, and Review of the United States* 1, December 1806. 33-37.

(1807 1, 253). "Fourth Section. American Communications." [Editorial]. *The Monthly Register, and Review of the United States* 2, March 1807. 253.

(1807 2, 91-106). "Third Section. American Litrature [sic] Reviewed. Epistles, odes, and Other Poems, by Thomas Moore, Esq." [Review]. *The Monthly Register, and Review of the United States* 3, July 1807. 91-106.

N *Nightingale*

(1796, 57-8). "To the Editors of the Nightingale." [Letter to the Editor]. *The Nightingale; or, a Melange de Literature: A Periodical Publication* 1 (5), May 19, 1796. 57-58.

NAR *North American Review*

(1834 2, 277-301). "Art. I—Periodical Literature of the United States. The Republic of Letters; being a weekly Republication of Works of Standard Literature." [Review]. *The North American Review* 39 (85), October 1834. 277-301.

NEG *New England Galaxy and Masonic Magazine*

(1817, 1-2). "Biography. Cursory Thoughts on Biography." [Essay]. N*ew England Galaxy and Masonic Magazine* 1 (1), October 10, 1817. 1-2.

(1818, 2-3). "Literary Review. Delaplaine's Repository and the Analectic Magazine." [Essay]. *New England Galaxy and Masonic Magazine* 1 (12), January 2, 1818. 2.

NEQ *New England Quarterly*

(1802, 25-7). "On Natural History." [Essay.] *The New England Quarterly Magazine* 2 (1), April-June. 25-27.

NYM *New York Magazine*

(1814, 1-3) Hardie, James. "Prospectus.—To the Public." [Prospectus]. *The New-York Magazine and General Repository of Useful Knowledge* 1 (1), May. 1-3.

NYMI *New York Mirror*

(1832, 273-4). "Original Biography. Sketches of Distinguished Characters. Washington Irving." *The New York Mirror* 9 (35), March 3, 1832. 273-274.

NYMR *New York Magazine, or Literary Repository*

(1791, 635-7). "On the Advantages of Periodical Performances." *The New York Magazine, or Literary Repository* 2 (11), November 1791. 653-655.

O *Olio*

(1813, 1). "To the Public." [Editorial]. *The Olio, a Literary and Miscellaneous Paper* 1 (1), Jan 27, 1813. 1.

(1813, 19-20). "On the Utility of Periodical Productions." [Essay]. *The Olio, a Literary and Miscellaneous Paper* 1 (3), February 13. 19-20.

OG *Omnium Gatherum*

(1810, 336). "To Readers and Correspondents." *Omnium Gatherum, a Monthly Magazine*, May 1810. 336.

P *Polyanthos*

(1806 1, iii-iv) "Editorial Address." [Editorial-Prospectus]. *The Polyanthos*, December 1805. iii-iv.
(1806 1, 5-15). "Sketch of the Life and Writings of the Rev. J. Belknap, D.D." [Essay-Biography]. *The Polyanthos*, December 1805. 5-15.
(1806 1, 18-24). "On the Advantages of Periodical Performances." *The Polyanthos*, December 1805. 18-24.
(1806 1, 72). "To Readers and Correspondents." [Editorial]. *The Polyanthos*, April 1806. 72.
(1806 1, 144). "To Readers and Correspondents." [Editorial]. *The Polyanthos*, May 1806. 144.
(1806 2, 72). "Editor's Notes." [Editorial]. *The Polyanthos*, August 1806. 72.
(1813 1, 281-8). "For the Polyanthos. Biographical Sketch of Commodore William Bainbridge." [Essay-Biography]. *The Polyanthos* 1, March 1813. 281-288.
(1813 1, 64). "Periodical Publications." [Anecdote-Essay]. *The Polyanthos* 2, May 1813. 64.
(1814 1, 176-82). "Characteristic Sketch of Capt. Isaac Hull, of the United States Navy." [Essay-Biography]. *The Polyanthos* 3, January 1814. 176-182.

PF *Port Folio*

(1801 Prospectus, 1-7). "Prospectus of a New Weekly paper, Submitted to Men of Affluence, Men of Liberality, and Men of Letters." [Prospectus]. *The Port Folio* 1 (1), January 3, 1801. [1-7].
(1801). "To the Public." [Editorial]. *The Port Folio* 1 (3), January 17. 23.
(1801, 38-9). "To Readers and Correspondents." [Editorial]. *The Port Folio* 1 (5), January 31, 1801. 38-9.
(1081, 46). "To Readers and Correspondents." [Editorial]. *The Port Folio* 1 (6), February 7, 1801. 46.
(1801, 69). "To Readers and Correspondets." [Editorial]. *The Port Folio* 1 (9), February 28, 1801. 69.
(1801, 76). "Biography. Notices of Thomas Coryate, An Eccentric Traveller." [Essay-Biography]. *The Port Folio* 1 (10), March 7, 1801. 76.
(1801, 83). "For *The Port Folio*." [Letter to the Editor]. *The Port Folio* 1 (11), March 14, 1801.
(1801, 89-90). "Biography. Sketches of the Character of John Henderson." [Essay-Biography]. *The Port Folio* 1 (12), March 21, 1801. 89-90.
(1801, 123-4). "For *The Port Folio*." [Letter to the Editor]. *The Port Folio* 1 (16), April 18. 123-124.
(1801, 125-6). "Biography. [William Cowper]." [Essay-Biography]. *The Port Folio* 1 (16), April 18, 1801. 125-126.
(1801, 129). "Biography. William Pattison." [Essay-Biography]. *The Port Folio* 1 (17), April 25, 1801. 129.
(1801, 175). "To Readers and Correspondents." [Editorial]. *The Port Folio* 1 (22), May 30, 1801. 175.
(1801, 191). "To Readers and Correspondents." [Editorial]. *The Port Folio* 1 (24), June 13, 1801. 192.
(1801, 198-9). "Biography. Character of Dr. Johnson." [Editorial]. *The Port Folio* 1 (25), June 20, 1801. 198-199.

(1801, 221-2). "Biography. [The Life of Hamilton, a Scottish Poet, and an Excellent, Though Neglected Writer]." [Essay-Biography]. *The Port Folio* 1 (28), July 11, 1801. 221-222.
(1801, 297-8). "Biography. The Life of Lovibond." [Essay-Biography]. *The Port Folio* 1 (38), September 19, 1801. 297-8.
(1801, 322). "Biography. The Life of Dr. Armstrong." [Essay-Biography]. *The Port Folio* 1 (41), October 10. 322.
(1801, 375). "To Readers and Correspondents." [Editorial]. *The Port Folio* 1 (47), November 21, 1801. 375.
(1801, 414). "To Readers and Correspondents." [Editorial]. *The Port Folio* 1 (52), December 26, 1801. 414.
(1802, 8). "Literary Intelligence." [Essay]. *The Port Folio* 2 (1), January 16, 1802. 8.
(1802, 135). "To Subscribers." [Editorial]. *The Port Folio* 2 (17), May 1, 1802. 135.
(1802, 138). "The Republic of North-America, in Its Present Condition." [Essay]. The Port Folio 2 (18), May 8, 1802. 138.
(1802, 175). "To the Public." [Editorial]. *The Port Folio* 2 (22), June 5, 1802. 175.
(1802, 182). "To the Public." [Editorial]. *The Port Folio* 2 (23), June 12, 1802. 182.
(1802, 299-300). "Biography. Sketch of the Life of William Gifford, Esq." [Essay-Biography]. *The Port Folio* 2 (38), September 25, 1802. 299-300
(1802, 311). "To Readers and Correspondents." [Editorial]. *The Port Folio* 2 (39), October 2, 1802. 311.
(1802, 319). "To Readers and Correspondents." [Editorial]. *The Port Folio* 2 (40), October 9, 1802. 319.
(1802, 335). "To Readers and Correspondents." [Editorial]. *The Port Folio* 2 (42), October 23, 1802. 335.
(1802, 367). "To Readers and Correspondents." [Editorial]. *The Port Folio* 2 (46), November 20, 1802. 367.
(1803, 55). "Conditions of *The Port Folio*." [Editorial]. *The Port Folio* 3 (7), February 12. 55.
(1803, 167) "List of Agents for *The Port Folio*." [Editorial]. *The Port Folio* 3 (21), May 21. 167.
(1803, 176). "Delinquent Subscribers." [Editorial]. *The Port Folio* 3 (22), May 28. 176.
(1803, 181). "Literary Intelligence." [Essay]. *The Port Folio* 3 (23), June 4, 1803. 181.
(1803, 229-30). "Biography. For *The Port Folio*. Life of Florian." [Essay-Biography]. *The Port Folio* 3 (29), July 15, 1803. 229-230.
(1803, 234-6). "Biography. For *The Port Folio*. Life of Florian. (Concluded)." [Essay-Biography]. *The Port Folio* 3 (30), July 23, 1803. 234-236.
(1803, 244-5). "Biography. Life of Horace." *The Port Folio* 3 (31), July 30, 1803. 244-245.
(1803, 250-1). "Politics. For the Port Folio. Genuine Memoir of Talleyrand." *The Port Folio* 3 (32), August 6, 250-251.
(1803, 319). "To the Public." [Editorial]. *The Port Folio* 3 (40), October 1. 319.
(1803, 383). "To Subscribers." [Editorial]. *The Port Folio* 2 (48), December 4. 383.
(1804, 3-4). "Original Biography. For *The Port Folio*. Life of Pascal." [Essay-Biography]. *The Port Folio* 4 (1), January 7, 1804. 3-4.
(1804, 27). "For *The Port Folio*. Original Biography. Life of Joannes Secundus." [Essay-Biography]. *The Port Folio* 4 (4), January 28, 1804. 27.
(1804, 134). "Miscellaneous Paragraphs. For the Port Folio." [Notes]. The Port Folio 4 (17),

April 28, 1804. 134.
(1805, 75-77). "Literary Intelligence. For *The Port Folio*. Proposals for Publishing by Subscription, in Monthly Numbers, A Work Entitled, Amoenitates Graphicae." [Advertisement-Prospectus]. *The Port Folio* 5 (10), March 16, 1805. 75-77.
(1805, 118). "To Readers and Correspondents." [Editorial]. *The Port Folio* 5 (15), April 20, 1805. 118.
(1805, 277). "Literary Intelligence." [Advertisement]. *The Port Folio* 5 (35), September 7, 1805. 277.
(1805, 331-2). "Biographical Sketch of Benjamin West, Esq. President of the Royal Academy, &c. &c." [Essay-Biography]. *The Port Folio* 5 (42), October 26, 1805. 331-332.
(1805, 367). "Due Notice." [Editorial]. *The Port Folio* 5 (46), November 23, 1805. 367.
(1806 Prospectus, 1-8). "New Prospectus of *The Port Folio*. An Established Literary Journal." [Prospectus]. *The Port Folio* 1 (1), January 11, 1806. 1-8.
(1806 1, 21-4). "Biography. For *The Port Folio*. The Life of Donne." [Essay-Biography.] *The Port Folio* 1 (2), January 18, 1806. 21-24.
(1806 1, 52-5). "For *The Port Folio*. Biography. Life of Blacklock." [Essay-Biography]. *The Port Folio* 1 (4), February 1, 1806. 52-55.
(1806 1, 66-7). "For *The Port Folio*. Biography. Life of Blacklock (Continued)." [Essay-Biography]. *The Port Folio* 1 (5), February 9, 1806. 66-67.
(1806 1, 83-7). "For *The Port Folio*. Biography. Life of Blacklock (Continued)." [Essay-Biography]. *The Port Folio* 1 (6), February 15, 1806. 83-87.
(1806 1, 99-102). "For *The Port Folio*. Biography. Life of Blacklock (Continued)." [Essay-Biography]. *The Port Folio* 1 (7), February 22, 1806. 99-102.
(1806 1, 114-7). "For *The Port Folio*. Biography. Life of Blacklock (Continued)." [Essay-Biography]. *The Port Folio* 1 (8), March 1, 1806. 114-117.
(1806 1, 132-5). "For *The Port Folio*. Biography. Life of Blacklock (Concluded)." [Essay-Biography]. *The Port Folio* 1 (9), February 22, 1806. 132-135.
(1806 1, 109). "Carpe Diem!" [Editorial]. *The Port Folio* 1 (7), February 22. 109.
(1806 1, 291-3). "For *The Port Folio*. Biography. Memoirs of the Life of John Racine." [Essay-Biography]. *The Port Folio* 1 (19), May 17, 1806. 291-293.
(1806 1, 308-10). "For *The Port Folio*. Biography. Life of Suckling." [Essay-Biography]. *The Port Folio* 1 (20), May 24, 1806. 308-310.
(1806 1, 362-4). "For *The Port Folio*. Biography. Life of Carew." [Essay-Biography]. *The Port Folio* 1 (23), June 14, 1806. 362-364.
(1807, [1-4]). "To Agents and Subscribers." [Wrapper] *The Port Folio* 3 (1), January 3, 1807. 1-4.
(1807, [4]). "New and Correct List of Agents." [Wrapper] *The Port Folio* 3 (1), January 3, 1807. 4.
(1807 1, 164-70). "Biography. [Virgil]." [Essay-Biography]. *The Port Folio* 3 (11), March 14, 1807. 164-170.
(1807 1, 259-63). "Biography. Considerations on the Character of Lord Thurlow." [Essay-Biography]. *The Port Folio* 3 (17), April 25, 1807. 259-263.
(1807 2, 127-8). "To Readers and Correspondents." [Editorial]. *The Port Folio* 4 (8), August 22, 1807. 127-128.
(1807 2, 240). "To Readers and Correspondents." [Editorial]. *The Port Folio* 4 (15), Octo-

ber 10, 1807. 240.
(1807 2, 284-7). "To Readers and Correspondents." [Editorial]. *The Port Folio* 4 (18), October 31, 1807. 284-287.
(1808 1, 94-96). "Biography [Charles Mordaunt]." [Editorial]. *The Port Folio* 5 (6), February 6, 1808. 94-95.
(1808 1, 160). "To Agents and Subscribers." [Editorial]. *The Port Folio* 5 (10), March 5, 1808. 160.
(1808 2, 239). "To Our Readers." [Editorial]. *The Port Folio* 6 (15), October 8, 1808. 239.
(1808 2, 254-6). "To Readers and Correspondents." [Editorial]. *The Port Folio* 6 (16), October 15, 1808. 254-256.
(1809 Prospectus, 3-11). "Prospectus, &c." [Prospectus]. *The Port Folio* 1 (1), January 1809. 3-11.
(1809 1, 21-31). "Biography. Sketch of the Life and Character of John Blair Linn." [Essay-Biography]. *The Port Folio* 1 (1), January 1809. 21-31.
(1809 1, 129-34). "Biography. A Sketch of the Life and Character of John Blair Linn. (Continued from page 29.)" [Essay-Biography] *The Port Folio* 1 (2), February 1809. 129-134.
(1809 1, 89-95). "To Readers and Correspondents." [Editorial]. *The Port Folio* 1 (1), January 1809. 89-95.
(1809 1, 298-304). "A Biographical Notice of the Late Edwin LeRoy M'Call, M.B." [Essay-Biography.] *The Port Folio* 1 (4), April 1809. 298-304.
(1809 1, 358-64). "To Readers and Correspondents." [Editorial]. *The Port Folio* 1 (4), April 1809. 358-364.
(1809 1, 455-60). "To Readers and Correspondents." [Editorial]. *The Port Folio* 1 (5), May 1809. 455-460.
(1809 1, 546-50). "To Readers and Correspondents." [Editorial]. *The Port Folio* 1 (6), June 1809. 546-550.
(1809 2, 170-6). "To Readers and Correspondents." [Editorial]. *The Port Folio* 2 (2), August 1809. 170-176.
(1809 2, 282-4). "To Readers and Correspondents." [Editorial]. *The Port Folio* 2 (3), September 1809. 282-284.
(1809 2, 577-81). "To Readers and Correspondents." [Editorial]. *The Port Folio* 2 (6), December 1809. 577-581.
(1810 1, 353-65). "Biography—For *The Port Folio*. Life of Commodore Edward Preble." [Essay-Biography]. *The Port Folio* 3 (5), May 1810. 353-365.
(1810 2, 529-48). "Domestic Biography-For *The Port Folio*; The Life of Commodore Edward Preble." [Essay-Biography]. *The Port Folio* 4 (6), December 1809. 529-548.
(1811 1, 87-8). "To Readers and Correspondents." [Editorial]. *The Port Folio* 5 (1), January 1811. 87-88.
(1812 1, 89-97). "To the Public." [Editorial]. *The Port Folio* 7 (1), January 1812. 89-97.
(1812 1, 185-91). "Mortuary. Joseph Dennie, Esquire." *The Port Folio* 7 (2), February 1812. 185-91.
(1812 1, 298-300). "Battle of Tippacanoe." [Poem]. *The Port Folio* 7 (3), March 1812. 298-300.
(1812 2, 436-7). "To Readers and Correspondents." [Editorial]. *The Port Folio* 8 (4), October 1812. 436-437.

(1812 2, 489-500). "Biographical Memoir of Rear-Admiral Sir John Borlase Warren, Bart. K.B." [Essay-Biography]. *The Port Folio* 8 (5), November 1812. 489-500.
(1812 2, 628-31). "Domestic Literature.—For the Port Folio." [Review-Advertisements]. *The Port Folio* 8 (6), December 1812. 628-631.
(1813 1, 86-91). "American Gallantry.—For the Port Folio." [Essay]. *The Port Folio* 1 (1), January 1813. 86-91.
(1813 2, 235-55). "For the Port Folio. Biography of Captain James Lawrence." [Essay-Biography]. *The Port Folio* 2 (3), September 1813. 235-245.
(1813 2, 454-60). "American Biography.—For the Port Folio. [Dr. William Ladd]." [Essay-Biography]. *The Port Folio* 2 (5), November 1813. 454-460.
(1814 1, 203-19). "American Biography.—For the Port Folio. Life of Commodore Perry." [Essay-Biography]. *The Port Folio* 3 (3), March 1814. 203-219.
(1814 1, 383-98). "To the Patrons of the Port Folio." [Editorial]. *The Port Folio* 3 (5), May 1814. 383-398.
(1814 1, 399-410). "American Biography.—For the Port Folio. Life of Commodore Murray." [Essay-Biography]. *The Port Folio* 3 (5), May 1814. 399-410.
(1814 1, 499-516). "American Biography.—For the Port Folio. Biographical Memoir of Commodore Dale." [Essay-Biography]. *The Port Folio* 3 (6), June 1814. 499-516.
(1814 2, 1-7). "For the Port Folio. Biographical Notice of Captain Warrington." [Essay-Biography]. The Port Folio 4 (1), July 1814. 1-7.
(1815 1, 99-102). "To Readers and Correspondents." [Editorial]. *The Port Folio* 5 (1), January 1815. 99-102.
(1815 1, 195-7). "For *The Port Folio*.- A New Plan for Writing Lives." [Essay]. *The Port Folio* 5 (2), February 1815. 195-197.
(1816 2, 273-7). "Bibliography. For *The Port Folio*." [Editorial-Essay-History]. *The Port Folio* 2 (4), October 1816. 273-277.
(1817 1, 3-22). "For the Port Folio. The Life of James Lawrence, Late Captain in the United States' Navy." [Essay-Biography]. *The Port Folio* 3 (1), January 1817. 3-22.
(1817 2, 2). "To Readers and Correspondents." [Editorial]. *The Port Folio* 4, July 1817. 2.
(1821 1, 131-6). "Art. XX. Washington Irving, Esq." [Essay-Biography]. The Port Folio 11, March 1821. 131-136.
(1822 1, 169-71). "Literary Intelligence." [Essay-Editorial]. *The Port Folio* 1 (3), February. 169-171.
(1825 1, 436-40). "Memoir of Washington Irving, Esq." [Essay-Biography]. *The Port Folio* 277, May 1825. 436-440.

PM *Pennsylvania Magazine*

(1775) "For the Pennsylvania Magazine. Useful and Entertaining Hints." [Essay]. *The Pennsylvania Magazine; or, American Monthly Museum*, February 1775. 53-57.

PMM *Philadelphia Monthly Magazine*

(1798 1, 71-4). "Farther Remarks on the Utility of Periodical Performances." [Essay]. *The Philadelphia Monthly Magazine; or, Universal Repository of Knowledge and Entertainment*

1 (2), February 1798. 71-74.
(1798 2, 7). "On the Advantages of Miscellaneous Reading." [Essay]. *The Philadelphia Monthly Magazine; or, Universal Repository of Knowledge and Entertainment* 2 (7), July 1798. 7-8.

PN *Panoplist*

(1808, 319-21). "Vol. IV. Part I." [Essay]. *The Panoplist, and Missionary Magazine*, December 1808. 319-321.
(1812, 199-201). "To Patrons." [Editorial]. *Panoplist & Missionary Magazine*, November 1812. 199-201.

PO *Portico*

(1816, 1-4). "Prospectus." [Prospectus]. *The Portico, a Repository of Science & Literature* 1 (1), January. 1-4.
(1817, 38-53). "Miscellany. Biography. Biographical Sketch of Colonel Jacob Hindman, of the United States' Army—(with a Portrait)." [Essay-Biography]. *The Portico, a Repository of Science & Literature* 3 (1), January 1817. 38-53.
(1817 1, 211-22). "Biography. Sketch of the Life of Lt. Col. Nathan Towson." [Essay-Biography]. *The Portico, a Repository of Science & Literature* 3 (3), March 1817. 211-222.

PR *Prospect*

(1803, 8). "To Subscribers." [Editorial]. *Prospect, or View of the Moral World* 1 (1), December 10, 1803. 8.

PRP *Philadelphia Repertory*

(1810, 224). "Prospectus of the Philadelphia Repertory, A Literary and Miscellaneous Paper, published weekly, by Dennis Heartt, Assisted by Gentlement of Learning and Talents." [Prospectus]. *The Philadephia Repertory, Devoted to Literature and Useful Intelligence* 1 (28), n.d., 1810. 224.
(1812). "To the Subscribers of the Repertory." [Editorial]. *The Philadelphia Repertory. Devoted to Literature and Useful Intelligence* 2 (50), May 2, 1812. 399.
(1812, 400). "Proposals For Publishing by Subscription a Weekly Paper Entitled the Bureau, or Repository of Literature, Politic, and Intelligence, by S.C. Carpenter." [Advertisement-Prospectus]. *The Philadephia Repertory, Devoted to Literature and Useful Intelligence* 2 (50), May 2, 1812. 400.

RI *Religious Intelligencer*

(1825 2, 320-2). "The Araucanian Indians." [Essay]. *The Religious Intelligencer* 10 (21), October 22, 1825. 320-322.

T *Tablet*

(1795, 1-2). "The Farrago No. 1." [Essay]. *The Tablet. A Miscellaneous Paper, Devoted to the Belles Lettres* 1 (1), May 1795. 1.

TM *Theological Magazine*

(1795, 3-4). "Preface." [Editorial]. *Theological Magazine* 1 (1), 3-4.
(1795, 5-14). "Biography. Sketches of the Life of Joseph Bellamy." [Essay-Biography]. *Theological Magazine* 1 (1), January 1795. 5-14.
(1796, 31-34). "Remarks on the Several Classes of Readers." [Essay]. *Theological Magazine*, September 1, 1796. 31-34.

TH *Theophilanthropist*

(1810, 76-8). "Biography." [Essay]. *The Theophilanthropist: Containing Critical, Moral, Theological, and Literary Intelligence* 2, February 1810. 76-78.

TP *Time Piece*

(1797, 1). "To the Public." [Editorial-Prospectus]. *The Time Piece; and Literary Companion* 1 (1), March 13, 1797. 1.
(1798, 1). "The Wanderer No. I." [Essay.] *The Time Piece; and Literary Companion* 2 (86), April 3, 1798. 1.

UACM *Universal Asylum and Columbian Magazine*

(1790, 268-72). "History of the Life and Character of Benjamin Franklin, L.L.D. &c. &c. &c." [Essay-Biography]. *The Universal Asylum and Columbian Magazine*, May. 268-272.

WG *Western Gleaner*

(1814 2, 52). "Miscellanies. To Readers and Correspondents." [Editorial]. *The Western Gleaner; or, Repository for Arts, Sciences, and Literature* 2 (1), June. 52-55.

WI *Weekly Inspector*

(1806, 1-2). "Prospectus of the Weekly Inspector." [Prospectus]. *The Weekly Inspector* 1 (1), Aug 30, 1806. 1-2.
(1806, 81). "To the Public." [Editorial]. *The Weekly Inspector* 1 (11), Novebmer 8, 1806. 81.
(1806, 89). "To the Public." [Editorial]. *The Weekly Inspector* 1 (12), November 15, 1806. 89.
(1807, 58-9). "Article No. 5 [Resolutions]." [Speech]. *The Weekly Inspector* 2 (30), March 21, 1807. 58-59.
(1807, 270-1). "For the Weekly Inspector. The Times." [Essay-Politics]. *The Weekly Inspector*

1 (24), February 7, 1807. 270-271.
(1807, 414-5). "Exit of the Inspector." [Editorial] *The Weekly Inspector* 2 (52), August 22. 414-415.

WM *Weekly Magazine*

(1798). "To the Editor of the Weekly Magazine." [Letter to the Editor.] *The Weekly Magazine of Original Essays…* 1 (5), March 3, 1798. 140-141.

WOM *Worcester Magazine*

(1787, 613-5). "From the Independent Chronicle, printed at Boston." [Essay]. *Worcester Magazine, Containing Politicks, Miscellantes, Poetry, and News* 2 (50), March 1787. 613-615.
(1788, 291-293). "Governour Hancock's Speech." [Speech]. *Worcester Magazine, Containing Politicks, Miscellantes, Poetry, and News* 4 (23), March 1788. 291-3.

WR *Weekly Register*

(1811, 2-3). "Something New." [Prospectus]. *Weekly Register* 1 (1), September 7. 2-3.
(1811). "Agents for the Weekly Register." *Weekly Register* 1 (10), November 9. 175-176.
(1811). "The Editor's Department." [Editorial]. *Weekly Register* 1 (13), November 30. 240.
(1812 1, 47). "To Agents and Readers." [Editorial]. *Weekly Register* 2 (29), March 21. 47.
(1812 1, 159-60). "Things as They Are." [Essay]. *Weekly Register* 2(36), May 9, 1812. 159-160
(1814 1, 72-4). "National Trophies." [Essay]. *Weekly Register* 5 (130), February 26, 1814. 72-74.
(1815 2, 205). "Handsome Compliment." [Editorial-Letter to the Editor]. *Niles' Weekly Register* 9 (221), November 25. 205.
(1815, 235). "Letters to the Editor." [Letter to the Editor]. *Niles' Weekly Register* 8 (196), June 3.
(1816 1, 381-2). "Niles'Weekly Register." [Editorial]. *Niles' Weekly Register* 9 (230), January 27. 381-382.
(1816 2, 98). "Letters to the Editor." [Letter to the Editor]. *Niles' Weekly Register* 10 (241), April 13. 98.
(1817, 369). "New Arrangement and Prospectus." [Editorial-Prospectus]. *Niles Weekly Register* 12 (310), August 9. 369.
(1817). "End of the Volume." [Editorial]. *Niles' Weekly Register* 11 (286), February 22. 432.
(1818). "[The Terms of the Weekly Register]." [Editorial]. *Niles' Weekly Register* 15 (365), xiv.
(1819 1, 2). "Terms of the Register." [Editorial]. *Niles' Weekly Register* 16 (391), February 27. 2.
(1820 2, 449). "[The Close of the Editorial Year.]" [Editorial]. *Niles' Weekly Register* 18 (468), August 26 1820. 449.
(1821 1, 212-21). "Legislature of Connecticut. Governor's Message." [Speech]. *Niles' Weekly Register* 20 (508), June 2, 1821. 212-221.

Primary Sources (Excluding Periodicals)

Ames, Fisher (1856). “Falklands II.” 1801. *Works of Fisher Ames. With a Selection from his Speeches and Correspondence*. Ed. Seth Ames. Boston: Little, Brown & Co. 131-6.

Bailey, Isaac, ed. (1815). *American Naval Biography*. Providence: Isaac Bailey.

Belknap, Jeremy (1794). *American Biography: Or, An Historical Account of Those Persons Who Have Been Distinguished in America*. Boston: Isaiah Thomas and Ebenezer Andrews.

Boswell, James (1791). *The Life of Samuel Johnson, LL.D.* London: Henry Baldwin.

Buckingham, Joseph Tinker (1852). *Personal Memoirs and Recollections of Editorial Life*. 2 Vol. Boston: Ticknor, Reed, and Fields.

Caldwell, Charles (1816). *The Author Turned Critic; or The Reviewer Reviewed; Being a Reply to a Feeble and Unfounded Attack on Delaplaine's Repository in the Analectic Magazine and Naval Chronicle, for the Month of September 1816*. Philadelphia: n.p.

— (1855). *The Autobiography of Charles Caldwell, M.D.* Philadelphia: Lippincott, Grambo, and Co.

Clifford, James L. (1962). *Biography as an Art: Selected Criticism 1560-1960*. Oxford: Oxford University Press.

Cobbett, William (1796). *The Life and Adventures of Peter Porcupine, With a Full and Fair Account of All His Authoring Transactions*. Philadelphia: William Cobbett.

Cooper, James Fenimore (1846). *Lives of Distinguished American Naval Officers*. 2 Vols. Philadelphia: Carey and Hart.

D'Alembert, Jean Le Rond, and Denis Diderot, eds. (1765). *Encyclopédie, ou Dictionnaire Raisonné des Sciences, des Arts et des Métiers. Vol 11, N á Pari*. Neufchastel: Samuel Faulche.

Deare, Lewis (1813). *Biography of James Lawrence, Esq., Late A Captain in the Navy of the United States*. New Brunswick: Lewis Deare.

Delaplaine, Joseph (1817). *Delaplaine's Repository of the Lives and Portraits of Distinguished Americans*. Philadelphia: Joseph Delaplaine.

Dunlap, William (1822). *Memoirs of Charles Brockden Brown, the American Novelist*.1815. Londn: henry Colburn.

Dunlap, William (1930). *Diary of William Dunlap (1766-1839). The Memoirs of a Dramatist, Theatrical Manager, Painter, Critic, Novelist, and Historian*. 2 Vol. New York: New York Historical Society.

Folsom, Benjamin, ed. (1814). *A Compilation of Biographical Sketches of Distinguished Officers in the American Navy, with Other Interesting Matter*. Newburyport: Horatio G. Allen.

French, Benjamin F. (1825). *Biographia Americana; or, A Historical and Critical Account of the Lives, Actions, and Writings of the Most Distinguished Persons in North America; from the First Settlement to the Present Time*. Philadelphia: D. Mallory.

Gallatin, Albert (1879). *The Writings of Albert Gallatin*. Vol. 1. Ed. Henry Adams. Philadelphia: J.B. Lippincott.

Goldsmith, Oliver (1770). *The Deserted Village: A Poem*. London: W. Griffin.

Hogan, Edmund (1795). *The Prospect of Philadelphia and Check on the Next Directory, Part I*. Philadelphia: Francis & Robert Bailey.

Hogarth, William (1772). *The Analysis of Beauty, Written with a View of Fixing the Fluctuat-*

ing Ideas of Taste. London: William Strahan.

Horace (2007). "Ars Poetica." Transl. S.P. Bovie. In: Richter, David H., ed. *The Critical Tradition: Classic Texts and Contemporary Trends*. New York: Bedford/St. Martin. 84-94.

— (2010). "Ars Poetica." Transl. D.A. Russell. In: Leitch, Vincent B., et al., eds. *The Norton Anthology of Theory and Criticism*. 2nd Ed. New York: W.W. Norton. 121-133.

Hutcheson, Francis (1729). *An Inquiry Into the Original of Our Ideas of Beauty and Virtue*. London: J and J. Knapton et al.

Irving, Washington (1978). *Letters. Vol. 1: 1802-1823*. Ed Ralph M. Aderman et al. Boston: Twayne.

Jefferson, Thomas (1853). *The Writings of Thomas Jefferson: Being His Autobiography, Correspondence, Reports, Messages, Addresses, and Other Writings, Official and Private*. Vol. 5. Ed. H.A. Washington. Washington, D.C.: Taylor & Maury.

— (1950). *The Papers of Thomas Jefferson, Vol. 1: 1760-1776*. Ed.Julian P. Boyd. Princeton: Princeton University Press.

Johnson, Samuel (1793). *The Rambler, in Four Volumes*. Vol. 2. London: T. Longman, et al.

— (1812). *Johnson's Dictionary of the English Language, in Miniature*. 1755. London: Thomas Tegg.

— (2005). *A Dictionary of the English Language*. 1755. Oakland, CA: Octavo.

McBride, James, ed. (1815) *Naval Biography, Consisting of Memoirs of the Most Distinguished Officers of the American Navy*. Cincinnati: Morgan, Williams, & Co.

Montesquieu, Charles de Secondat, Baron de (1989). *The Spirit of the Laws*. 1748. Ed. Anne M. Cohler, et al. Cambridge: Cambridge University Press.

Patterson, R. (1815). *Naval Biography: Or, the Lives of the Most Distinguished American Naval Heroes of the Present Day*. Pittsburgh: R. Patterson.

Pope, Alexander, transl. (1796). *The Odyssey*. With additional Notes by Gilbert Wakefield. London: Wye and Law.

Reports of Cases Determined in the Circuit Court of the United States, for the Third Circuit, Comprising the Districts of Pennsylvania and New Jersey, Commencing at April Term, 1803. Vol. III. Philadelphia: Philip E. Nicklin, 1827.

Robinson, James (1810). *The Philadelphia Directory for 1810, Containing the Names, Trades, & Residence, of the Inhabitants*. Philadelphia: William Woodhouse.

Tocqueville, Alexis de (2007). *Democracy in America*. 1835-40. Ed. Isaac Kamnick. New York. W.W. Norton.

Washington, George (1775). "General Orders, Head Quarters, Cambridge, July 16, 1775." URL: http://etext.virginia.edu/washington/fitzpatrick/ Last Accessed: 10.05.2012.

Webster, Noah (1806). *A Compendious Dictionary of the English Language [...]*. New Haven: Sidney's Press.

Wilmer, James Jones (1811). *The American Nepos: A Collection of the Lives of the Most Remarkable and the Most Eminent Men [...] of America*. Baltimore: A. Miltenberger and John Vance.

Wilson, Thomas, ed. (1819) *The Biography of the Principal American Military and Naval Heroes; Comprehending Details of the Achievements During the Revolutionary and Late Wars*. 2 Vols. New York: John Low.

Secondary Sources

Adams, Donald R. Jr. (1986). "Prices and Wages in Maryland, 1750-1850." *Journal of Economic History* 46 (3), September; 625-645.

Adams, Douglas N. (1988). *The Long Dark Tea-Time of the Soul.* London: Heinemann.

Aderman, Ralph M. (1964). "James Kirke Paulding's Contributions to American Magazines." *Studies in Bibliography* 17. 142-153.

Aderman, Ralph M., and Wayne R. Kime (2003). *Advocate for America: The Life of James Kirke Paulding.* Selinsgrove: Susquehanna University Press.

Amory, Hugh (2000). "Printing and Bookselling in New England, 1638-1713." In: Amory, Hugh, and David D. Hall, eds. *The Colonial Book in the Atlantic World.* Vol. 1. of *A History of the Book in America.* Cambridge: Cambridge University Press. 83-116.

Amory, Hugh, and David D. Hall, eds. (2000). *The Colonial Book in the Atlantic World.* Vol. 1. of *A History of the Book in America.* Cambridge: Cambridge University Press.

Anderson, Benedict (2006). *Imagined Communities.* London: Verso.

Anderson, Fred, and Andrew Cayton (2005). *The Dominion of War: Empire and Conflict in America, 1500—2000.* London: Atlantic Books.

Appleby, Joyce (1984). *Capitalism and a New Social Order: The Republican Vision of the 1790s.* New York: New York University Press.

— (2000). *Inheriting the Revolution: The First Generation of Americans.* Cambridge: Belknap Press of Harvard University Press.

Balakrishnan, Gopal, ed. (1996a). *Mapping the Nation.* London: Verso.

— (1996b). "The National Imagination." *Mapping the Nation.* Ed. Gopal Balakrishnan. London: Verso. 198-213.

Balleisen, Edward J. (2001). *Navigating Failure. Bankruptcy and Commercial Society in Antebellum America.* Chapel Hill: University of North Carolina Press.

Barrow, Clayton R., ed. (1973). *America Spreads Her Sails: U.S. Seapower in the 19th Century.* Annapolis: U.S. Naval Institute Press.

Beetham, Margaret (1989). "Open and Closed: The Periodical as a Publishing Genre." *Victorian Periodicals Research* 22 (3), Fall; 96-100.

Bender, Thomas (2006). *A Nation Among Nations. America's Place in World History.* New York: Hill and Wang.

Berube, Claude, and John Rodgaard (2005). *A Call to the Sea: Captain Charles Stewart of the USS Constitution.* Washington, D.C.: Potomac Books.

Blackburn, P.C. (1932). "Irving's Biography of James Lawrence – And a New Discovery." *Bulletin of the New York Public Library*, 36. 742-745.

Borneman, Walter R. (2004). *1812. The War that Forged a Nation.* New York: HarperPerennial.

Bourdieu, Pierre (1993). *The Field of Cultural Production.* Ed. Randal Johnson. Columbia University Press.

— (1995). *The Rules of Art. Genesis and Structure of the Literary Field.* Stanford: Stanford University Press.

— (2008). *Outline of a Theory of Practice.* Cambridge: Cambridge University Press.

— (2011). "The Forms of Capital." 1986. In: Szeman, Imre, and Timothy Kaposy, eds. *Cul-*

tural Theory: An Anthology. Chichester: Wiley-Blackwell; 81-93.

Brake, Laurel, and Anne Humpherys (1989). "Critical Theory and Periodical Research." *Victorian Periodicals Review* 22 (3), Fall; 94-5.

Breuilly, John (1994). *Nationalism and the State*. Chicago: The University of Chicago Press.

Broadberry, Stephen, and Bishnupriya Gupta (2008). "Lancashire, India and Shifting Competetive Advantage in Textiles, 1700-1850: The Neglected Role of Factor Prices." URL: http://www2.warwick.ac.uk/fac/soc/economics/staff/academic/broadberry/wp/cotdiv20a.pdf. Last Accessed: 07.06.2011.

Brückner, Martin (1999). "Lessons in Geography: Maps, Spellers, and Other Grammars of Nationslism in the Early Republic." *American Quarterly* 51 (2), June; 311-343.

— (2006). *The Geographical Revolution in Early America: Maps, Literacy, and National Identity*. Chapel Hill: University of North Carolina Press.

Budiansky, Stephen (2010). *Perilous Fight: America's Intrepid War with Britain on the High Seas, 1812-1815*. New York: Knopf.

Burstein, Andrew (2007). *The Original Knickerbocker: The Life of Washington Irving*. New York: Basic Books.

Brown, Gordon S. (2011). *The Captain Who Burned His Ships. Captain Thomas Tingey, USN, 1750-1829*. Annapolis: Naval Institute Press.

Caine, Barbara (2010). *Biography and History*. Basingstoke: Palgrave MacMillan.

Cairns, William B. (1976). *On the Development of American Literature from 1815 to 1833, with Especial Reference to Periodicals*. 1898. Madison: University of Wisconsion Press.

Callo, Joseph (2009). *John Paul Jones: America's First Sea Warrior*. Annapolis: U.S. Naval Institute Press.

Cappon, Lester J. (1978). "Jared Sparks: The Preparation of an Editor." *Proceedings of the Massachusetts Historical Society* (90). 3-21.

Casper, Scott E. (1999). *Constructing American Lives: Biography and Culture in Nineteenth-Century America*. Chapel Hill: University of North Carolina Press.

Chamberlain, John (1991). *The Enterprising Americans: A Business History of the United States*. Tyler: Institute for Christian Economics.

Chartier, Roger (1992). *L'Ordre des Livres. Lecteurs, Auteurs, Bibliothèques en Europe Entre 14eme et 18eme Siècle*. Aix-en-Provence: Editions Alinea.

Chávez, John R. (2009). *Beyond Nations: Evolving Homelands in the North Atlantic World, 1400-2000*. Cambridge: Cambridge University Press.

Chielens, Edward E. (1975). *The Literary Journal in America to 1900. A Guide to Information Sources*. Detroit: Gale Research Company.

Christadler, Martin (1968). *Der amerikanische Essay 1720-1820*. Heidelberg: Carl Winter Universitätsverlag.

Clapp, William W. (1880). *Joseph Dennie: Editor of The Port Folio and Author of the Lay Preacher*. Cambridge: John Wilson and Son.

Clark, Charles E. (2000). "Periodicals and Politics. Part One. Early American Journalism: News and Opinion in the Popular Press." In: Amory, Hugh, and David D. Hall, Eds. *A History of the Book in America. Vol. 1: The Colonial Book in the Atlantic World*. Cambridge: Cambridge University Press. 347-366.

Colclough, Stephen (2007). *Consuming Texts. Readers and Reading Communities, 1695-1870*.

Basingstoke: Palgrave Macmillan.

Commager, Henry Steele (1975). *Jefferson, Nationalism, and the Enlightenment*. New York: George Braziller.

Connor, Walker (1994). *Ethnonationalism. The Quest for Understanding*. Princeton: Princeton University Press.

— (2004). "The Timelessness of Nations." *Nations and Nationalism* 10 (1/2). 35-47.

Connors, Linda E. and Mary Lu MacDonald (2011). *National Identity in Great Britain and British North America, 1815-1851. The Role of Nineteenth-Century Periodicals*. Farnham: Ashgate.

Cook, Don L. (1970). "A Note on the Text." Tyler, Royall. *The Algerine Captive, or, the Life and Adventures of Doctor Updike Underhill: Six Years a Prisoner among the Algerines*. 1797. Ed. Don L. Cook. New Haven: College & University Press. 24.

Crèvecœur, J. Hector St. John de (1997). *Letters from an American Farmer*. Ed. Susan Manning. Oxford: Oxford University Press.

Cronin, James E., ed. (1973). *The Diary of Elihu Hubbard Smith (1771-1798)*. Philadelphia: American Philosophical Society.

Dangerfield, George (1965). *The Awakening of American Nationalism, 1815-1828*. New York: HarperTorchbooks.

Daughan, George C. (2008). *If by Sea: The Forging of the American Navy.From the Revolution to the War of 1812*. New York: Basic Books, 2008.

Day, Graham, and Andrew Thompson (2004). *Theorizing Nationalism*. New York: Palgrave MacMillan.

De Kay, James T. (2004). *A Rage for Glory: The Life of Commodore Stephen Decatur, USN*. New York: Free Press.

Dowling, David (2011). *The Business of Literary Circles in Nineteenth-Century America*. New York: Palgrave MacMillan.

Dowling, William C. (1999). *Literary Federalism in the Age of Jefferson: Joseph Dennie and The Port Folio, 1801-1811*. Columbia: University of South Carolina Press.

Edgar, Neal L. (1975). *A History and Bibliography of American Magazines, 1810-1820*. Lanham: Scarecrow Press.

Eldrige, Herbert G. (1982). "The Paper War Between England and America: The Inchiquin Episode, 1810-1815." *American Studies* 16 (1), 49-68.

Ellis, Harold M. (1971). *Joseph Dennie and His Circle: A Study in American Literature from 1792 to 1812*. 1915. New York: AMS.

Ellis, James (2009). *A Ruinous and Unhappy War. New England and the War of 1812*. New York: Algora.

Engerman, Stanley L., and Robert E. Gallman, eds. (2000). *The Cambridge Economic History of the United States, Vol. II: The Long Nineteenth Century*. Cambridge: Cambridge University Press.

Fergus, Jan (2006). *Provincial Readers in Eighteenth-Century England*. Oxford: Oxford University Press.

Ferguson, Eugene S. (2000). *Truxtun of the Constellation: The Life of Commodore Thomas Truxtun, U.S. Navy, 1755-1822*. 1956. Baltimore: The Johns Hopkins University Press.

Ferguson, Robert A. (2004). *Reading in the Early Republic*. Cambridge: Harvard University Press.

Fetz, Bernhard, ed. (2009). *Die Biographie: Zur Grundlegung ihrer Theorie*. Wien: De Gruyter Verlag.

Fetz, Bernhard, and Wilhelm Hemecker, eds. (2011). *Theorie der Biographie: Grundlagentexte und Kommentar*. Wien: De Gruyter.

Fetz, Bernhard, and Hannes Schweiger, eds. (2006). *Spiegel und Maske: Konstruktionen biographischer Wahrheit*. Wien: Paul Zsolnay Verlag.

Fisher, Mark (2009). *Capitalist Realism: Is There No Alternative?* London: Zero Books.

Fortune, Brandon B. (1987). "Portraits of Virtue and Genius: Pantheons of Worthies and Public Portraiture in the Early American Republic, 1780-1820." Dissertation. University of North Carolina at Chapel Hill.

Fowler, William M. (1984). *Jack Tars and Commodores: The American Navy, 1783-1815*. New York: Houghton Harcourt Mifflin.

Gardner, Jared (2012). *The Rise and Fall of Early American Magazine Culture*. Urbana: University of Illinois Press.

Garraty, John A. (1957). *The Nature of Biography*. New York: Alfred A. Knopf.

Gellner, Ernest (2009). *Nations and Nationalism*. New York: Cornell University Press.

Giddens, Anthony (1985). *The Nation-State and Violence*. Vol. 2 of *A Contemporary Critique of Historical Materialism*. Berkeley: University of California Press.

Gilje, Paul A., ed. (1997). *Wages of Independence. Capitalism in the Early American Republic*. Madison: Madison House.

Gilmore, William J. (1989). *Reading Becomes a Necessity of Life. Material and Cultural Life in Rural New England, 1780-1835*. Knoxville: University of Tennessee Press.

Gordon, Edward E. and Elaine H. (2003). *Literacy in America: Historic Journey and Contemporary Solutions*. Westport: Praeger.

Govan, Thomas P. (1951). "The Death of Joseph Dennie: A Memoir by Nicholas Biddle." *The Pennsylvania Magazine of History and Biography* 75 (1), January; 36-46.

Grant, Susan-Mary, and Brian Holden Reid, eds. (2000). *The American Civil War: Explorations and Reconsiderations*. Harlow: Pearson Education Limited.

Grant, Susan-Mary (2005). "When Was the First New Nation? Locating America in a National Context." *When is the Nation: Towards an Understanding of Theories of Nationalism*. Ed. Atsuko Ichijo and Gordana Uzelac. London: Routledge.

— (2000). "From Union to Nation? The Civil War and the Development of American Nationalism." *The American Civil War: Explorations and Reconsiderations*. Ed. Susan-Mary Grant and Brian Holden Reid. Harlow: Pearson Education Limited. 333-357.

— (1997). "Making History: Myth and the Construction of American Nationhood." *Myths & Nationhood*. Ed. Geoffrey Hosking and George Schöpflin. New York: Routledge.

Greene, Theodore P. (1970). *America's Heroes: Changing Models of Success in American Magazines*. New York: Oxford University Press.

Greenfeld, Liah (1992). *Nationalism: Five Roads to Modernity*. Cambridge: Harvard University Press.

Gross, Robert A., and Mary Kelley, eds. (2010). *An Extensive Republic: Print, Culture, and Society in the New Nation, 1790-1840*. Vol. 2of *A History of the Book in America*. Chapel Hill: University of North Carolina Press.

Guiberneau, Montserrat, and John Hutchinson, eds. (2001). *Understanding Nationalism*.

Cambridge: Polity Press.

Haberman, Robb K. (2009). "Periodical Publics: Magazines and Literary Networks in Post-Revolutionary America." Dissertation. University of Connecticut.

Habermas, Jürgen (1989). *The Structural Transformation of the Public Sphere. An Inquiry into a Category of Bourgeois Society*. London: Polity Press.

Hankins, Richard (1975). "Puritans, Patriots, and Panegyric: The Beginnings of American Biography." *Studies in the Literary Imagination* 9 (2), Fall; 95-109.

Harris, Christopher (1985). "Character Portraits of American Military Heroes of the Revolution, 1782-1832." Dissertation. Brown University.

Harvey, Sara King (1936). "A Bibliography of the Miscellaneous Prose of Gulian Crommelin Verplanck." *American Literature* 8 (2), May; 199-203.

Hebel, Udo, ed. (1999). *The Construction and Contestation of American Cultures and Identities in the Early National Period.* Heidelberg: Winter.

Hedges, William L. (1965). *Washington Irving: An American Study, 1802-1832*. Baltimore: Johns Hopkins Press.

Heidler, David and Jeanne (2004). *Daily Life in the Early American Republic, 1790-1820: Creating a New Nation.* Westport, CN: Greenwood.

Heilbronn, Günther (1996). "Horace in ultima Hesperia." In: Schmidt, Ernst A., ed. *Zeitgenosse Horaz: Der Dichter und seine Leser in zwei Jahrtausenden*. Tübingen: Günther Narr. 344-370.

Herold, Amos L. (1966). *James Kirke Paulding. Versatile American*. 1926. New York: AMS Press.

Hickey, Donald R. (1989). *The War of 1812: A Forgotten Conflict.* Chicago: University of Illinois Press.

— (2007). *Don't Give Up the Ship!: Myths of the War of 1812.* Chicago: University of Illinois Press.

Hobsbawm, Eric J. (1990). *Nations and Nationalism since 1780: Programme, Myth, Reality.* Cambridge: Cambridge University Press.

Howarth, Stephen (1991). *To Shining Sea: A History of the United States Navy, 1775-1988.* New York: Random House.

Ichijo, Atsuko, and Gordana Uzelac, eds. (2005). *When is the Nation: Towards an Understanding of Theories of Nationalism*. London: Routledge.

Irving, Pierre (1869). *Life and Letters of Washington Irving.* 3 Vol. New York: G. Putnam & Son.

Jackson, Leon (2008). *The Business of Letters. Authorial Economies in Antebellum America.* Stanford: Stanford University Press.

Jansen, Christian, and Henning Borggräfe (2007). *Nation – Nationalität – Nationalismus.* Frankfurt/M: Campus.

Jenks, Timothy (2006). *Naval Engagements. Patriotism, Cultural Politics, and the Royal Navy 1793-1815*. Oxford: Oxford University Press.

John, Richard R (1995). *Spreading the News: The American Postal System from Franklin to Morse*. Cambridge: Harvard University Press.

Jones, Brian Jay (2008). *Washington Irving: An American Original.* New York: Arcade Publishing,

Kammen, Michael (1978). *A Season of Youth: The American Revolution and the Historical Imagination*. New York: Alfred A. Knopf.

Kaplan, Catherine O'Donnell (2003). "He Summons Genius to His Aid: Letters, Partisanship, and the Making of the Farmer's Weekly Museum, 1795-1800." *Journal of the Early Republic* 23 (4), Winter; 545-571.

— (2007). *Men of Letters in the Early Republic: Cultivating Forums of Citizenship.* Chapel Hill: University of North Carolina Press.

Kaser, David (1957). *Messrs. Carey & Lea of Philadelphia: A Study in the History of Booktrade.* Philadelphia: University of Pennsylvania Press.

Kerber, Linda K., and Walter J. Morris (1966). "Politics and Literature: The Adams Family and *The Port Folio.*" *The William and Mary Quarterly* 23 (3), July; 450-476.

Kielbowicz, Richard B. (1983). "The Press, Post Office, and Flow of News in the Early Republic." Journal of the Early Republic 3, Fall. 255-280.

Kirsch, George B. (1982). *Jeremy Belknap: A Biography.* New York: Arno Press.

Klein, Christian (2002). *Grundlagen der Biographik: Theorie und Praxis des biographischen Schreibens.* Stuttgart: Metzler.

—, ed. (2009). *Handbuch Biographie: Methoden, Tradition, Theorien.* Stuttgart: Metzler.

Kohn, Hans (1957). *American Nationalism: An Interpretative Essay.* New York: The MacMillan Company.

Koschnik, Albrecht (2007). *"Let a Common Interest Bind Us Together." Associations, Partisanship, and Culture in Philadelphia, 1775-1840.* Charlottesville: University of Virginia Press.

Krakau, Knud, ed. (1997). *The American Nation – National Identity – Nationalism.* Münster: Lit.

Kribbs, Jayne K., ed. (1977). *An Annotated Bibliography of American Literary Periodicals, 1741-1850.* Boston: G.K.Hall.

Laclau, Ernesto (2007). *Emancipation(s).* 1996. London: Verso.

Laclau, Ernesto, and Chantal Mouffe (2001). *Hegemony and Socialist Strategy: Towards a Radical Democratic Politics.* London: Verso.

Lanzendörfer, Tim (2012). "From the Archives: Joseph Dennie, the Value of the Editor, and the Creation of *The Port Folio.*" *American Periodicals* 22.1 (Spring 2012). 94-106.

Larson, John Lauritz (2010). *The Market Revolution in America. Liberty, Ambition, and the Eclipse of the Common Good.* Cambridge: Cambridge University Press.

Latham, Sean, and Robert Scholes. (2006) "The Rise of Periodical Studies." *PMLA* 121 (1). 517-531.

Latimer, Jon (2009). *1812: War with America.* Cambridge: Harvard University Press.

Lawrence, Paul (2005). *Nationalism: History and Theory.* Harlow: Pearson Education Limited.

Lawson, Don. (1966). *The War of 1812. America's Second War for Independence.* New York: Abelard-Schuman.

Lawson, Russell M. (1998). *The American Plutarch. Jeremy Belknap and the Historian's Dialogue with the Past.* Westport: Praeger.

Lee, Judith Yaross (2005). "From the Field: The Future of *American Periodicals* and American Periodicals Research." *American Periodicals* 15 (2). 196-201.

Leiner, Frederick C. (1999). *Millions for Defense: The Subscription Warships of 1798.* Annapolis: U.S. Naval Institute Press.

Lewis, Benjamin (1957). *A Register of Editors, Printers, and Publishers of American Magazines, 1741-1810.* New York: New York Public Library.

— (1961). *An Introduction to American Magazines 1800-1810.* Ann Arbor: University of Michigan Department of Library Science Studies.

Leypoldt, Günter (2009). *Cultural Authority in the Age of Whitman. A Transatlantic Perspective.* Edinburgh: Edinburgh University Press.

Little, J. Frederick, and Leo Groarke (1989). *Good Reasoning Matters. A Constructive Approach to Critical Thinking.* Toronto: McClelland & Stewart.

Lora, Ronald, and William H. Longton (1999). *The Conservative Press in Eighteenth- and Nineteenth-Century America.* Westport: Greenwood Press.

Lord, Walter (1972). *The Dawn's Early Light.* New York: W.W. Norton.

Loughran, Trish (2007). *The Republic in Print. Print Culture in the Age of U.S. Nation Building, 1770-1870.* New York: Columbia University Press.

Luxon, Norval Neil (1970). *Niles' Weekly Register: News Magazine of the Nineteenth Century.* 1947. Westport: Greenwood Press.

Marx, Anthony W. (2003). *Faith in Nation. Exclusionary Origins of Nationalism.* Oxford: Oxford University Press.

McCollough, David (2001). *John Adams.* New York: Simon & Schuster.

McKee, Christopher (1991). *A Gentlemanly and Honorable Profession: The Creation of the U.S. Naval Officer Corps, 1794-1815.* Annapolis: U.S. Naval Institute Press.

Maloney, Linda M. (1986). *The Captain from Connecticut: The Life and Naval Times of Isaac H*ull. Boston: Northwestern University Press.

Mann, Bruce H. (2002). *Republic of Debtors. Bankrupcty in the Age of American Independence.* Cambridge: Harvard University Press.

Matson, Cathy, ed. (2006). *The Economy of Early America. Historical Perspectives & New Directions.* University Park: Pennsylvania State University Press.

Merrill, Dana K. (1932). *The Development of American Biography.* Portland, ME: The Southworth Press.

— (1957). *American Biography: Its Theory and Practice.* Portland, ME: The Bowker Press.

Miller, Nathan (1977). *The U.S. Navy. A History.* Annapolis: Naval Institute Press.

Monaghan, E. Jennifer (2005). *Learning to Read and Write in Colonial America.* Amherst: University of Massachusetts Press.

Mott, Frank L. (1957a). *A History of American Magazines 1741-1850.* 1930. Cambridge: Harvard University Press.

— (1957b). *A History of American Magazines 1850-1865.* 1938. Cambridge: Harvard University Press.

Müller, Markus Jens (2006). *American Literary Nationalism in the Early Republic.* Hamburg: Verlag Dr. Kovac.

Murrin, John M. (1987). "A Roof Without Walls: The Dilemma of American National Identity." *Beyond Confederation: Origins of the Constitution and American National Identity.* Ed. Richard Beeman, Stephen Botein, and Edward C. Carter III. Chapel Hill: University of North Carolina Press. 333-347.

Mussell, James (2009). "Cohering Knowledge in the Nineteenth Century: Form, Genre, and Periodical Studies." *Victorian Periodicals Review* 42 (1), Spring; 93-103.

Nord, David Paul (1988). "A Republican Literature: A Study of Magazine Reading and Readers in Late Eighteenth-Century New York." *American Quarterly* 40 (1), March; 42-64.

Norton, Louis Arthur (2000). *Joshua Barney: Hero of the Revolution and 1812.* Annapolis: U.S. Naval Institute Press.

O'Neill, Edward H. (1961). *A History of American Biography 1800-1935*. 1935. New York: A.S. Barnes.

Oates, Stephen B. (1986). *Biography as High Adventure: Life-Writers Speak on Their Art*. Boston: University of Massachusetts Press.

Oberholtzer, Ellis P. (1906). *The Literary History of Philadelphia*. Philadelphia: George W. Jacobs & Co.

Officer, Lawrence H. (2010). "Dollar-Pound Exchange Rate From 1791," MeasuringWorth. URL: http://www.measuringworth.com/exchangepound/. Last Accessed 03.07.2011.

Okker, Patricia, et al. (2007). "From the Field: Periodical Studies and Access. A Research Soceity for American Periodicals Forum." *American Periodicals* 17 (1), 114-125.

Palmer, Michael A. (2000). *Stoddert's War: Naval Operations During the Quasi-War With France, 1798-1801*. Annapolis: U.S. Naval Institute Press.

Parke, Catherine N. (2002). *Biography: Writing Lives*. London: Routledge.

Parker, Peter J. (1970). "Asbury Dickins, Bookseller, 1798-1801, or, the Brief Career of a Careless Youth." *The Pennsylvania Magazine of History and Biography*, 94 (4). 464-483.

Pasley, Jeffrey L. (2001). *The Tyranny of Printers. Newspaper Politics in the Early American Republic*. Charlottesville: University of Virginia Press.

Pedder, Laura, ed. (1935). *The Letters of Joseph Dennie, 1768-1812*. Orono: University of Maine Press.

Pitcher, Edward W.R. (2000). *An Anatomy of Reprintings and Plagiarisms: Finding Keys to Editorial Practices and Magazine History, 1730-1820*. Lewiston: The Edwin Mellen Press.

Pykett, Lyn (1989). "Reading the Periodical Press: Text and Context." Victorian Periodicals Research 22 (3), Fall; 100-108.

Queenan, John T. (1955). "*The Port Folio*: A Study of the History and Significance of an Early American Magazine." Dissertation. University of Pennsylvania.

Randall, Randolph C. (1940). "Authors of *The Port Folio* Revealed by the Hall Files." In: *American Literature* 11 (4), 379-416.

— (1973). "Joseph Dennie's Literary Attitutes in *The Port Folio*, 1801-1812." In: *Essays Mostly on Periodical Publishing in America. A Collection in Honor of Clarence Gohdes*. Ed James Woodress. Durham: Duke University Press.

Ratcliffe, Donald (2000). "The State of the Union, 1776-1860." *The American Civil War: Explorations and Reconsiderations*. Ed. Susan-Mary Grant and Brian Holden Reid. Harlow: Pearson Education Limited. 3-37.

Remer, Rosalind (1996). *Printers and Men of Capital. Philadelphia Book Publishers in the New Republic*. Philadelphia: University of Pennsylvania Press.

Richardson, Lyon N. (1966). *A History of Early American Magazines 1741-1789*. 1931. New York: Octagon.

Richter, David H. (2007). *The Critical Tradition: Classic Texts and Contemporary Trends*. New York: Bedford/St. Martin's.

Richter, Jörg (2004). *Nationalität als literarisches Verfahren: Der amerikanische Roman (1790-1830)*. Paderborn: Ferdinand Schöningh.

Rilling, Donna J. (2006). "Small-Producer Capitalism in Early National Philadelphia." In: *The Economy of Early America. Historical Perspectives & New Directions*. Ed. Cathy Matson. University Park: Pennsylvania State University Press.

Robertson, Andrew (2001). "Look on This Picture... And on This!" Nationalism, Localism, and Partisan Images of Otherness in the United States, 1787-1820." *American Historical Review* 106 (4), Oct 2001. 1263-1280.

Robertson, Ross M. (1973). *History of the American Economy*. New York: Harcourt Brace Jovanovich.

Royster, Charles (1981). *A Revolutionary People at War: The Continental Army and American Character, 1775-1778*. New York: Norton.

Scheiding, Oliver (1999). "The Nation's Remembrancer and the Rhetoric of Rededication: James Kirke Paulding's *The Puritan and His Daughter*". *The Construction and Contestation of American Cultures and Identities in the Early National Period*. Ed. Udo Hebel. Heidelberg: Winter. 221-236.

— (2003). *Geschichte und Fiktion: Zum Funktionswandel des frühen amerikanischen Romans*. Paderborn: Schöningh.

— (2010). "The Indian Chief as Federalist Icon: Washington Irving's Refigurations of Philip of Pokanoket." In: Leypoldt, Günter, and Bernd Engler, eds. *American Cultural Icons: The Production of Representative Lives*. Würzburg: Königshausen & Neumann.

Seavoy, Ronald E. (2006). *An Economic History of the United States. From 1707 to the Present*. New York: Routledge.

Sedgwick, Ellery (2000). "Magazines and the Profession of Authorship in the United States, 1840-1900." *The Papers of the Bibliographical Society of America* 94 (3), September; 399-425.

Sellers, Charles (1991). *The Market Revolution. Jacksonian America 1815-1846*. Oxford: Oxford University Press.

Shakespeare, William (2003). *Hamlet: Prince of Denmark*. Ed. Philip Edwards. Cambridge: Cambridge University Press.

Shapiro, Stephen (2008). *The Culture and Commerce of the Early American Novel. Reading the Atlantic World-System*. University Park: Pennsylvania State University Press.

Shipton, Clifford K. (1948). *Isaiah Thomas. Printer, Patriot and Philanthropist, 1749-1831*. Rochester: Leo Hart.

Simpson, Lewis P. (1954). "A Literary Adventure of the Early Republic." *The New England Quarterly* 27 (2), June; 168-190.

Smith, Anthony D. (1986). *The Ethnic Origins of Nations*. Oxford: Basil Blackwell.

— (1991). *National Identity*. Reno: University of Nevada Press.

— (2001). *Nationalism: Theory, Ideology, History*. Cambridge: Polity Press.

— (2008). *The Cultural Foundations of Nations: Hierarchy, Covenant, and Republic*. Oxford: Blackwell.

Smith, Gene A. (2000) *Thomas Ap Catesby Jones: Commodore of Manifest Destiny*. Annapolis: U.S. Naval Institute Press.

Smith-Rosenberg, Carroll (2010). *This Violent Empire: The Birth of an American National Identity.* Chapel Hill: University of North Carolina Press.

Smyth, Albert H. (1970). *The Philadelphia Magazines and Their Contributors 1741-1850*. 1892. Freeport: Books for Libraries Press.

Stokes, Melvyn, and Stephen Conway, eds. (1996). *The Market Revolution in America. Social, Political, and Religious Expressions, 1800-1880*. Charlottesville: University of Virginia Press.

Tassin, Algernon (1916). *The Magazine in America*. New York: Dodd, Mead, and Company.

Taylor, Alan (2010). *The Civil War of 1812: American Citizens, British Subjects, Irish Rebels & Indian Allies*. New York: Alfred A. Knopf.

Tebbel, John, and Mary Ellen Zuckerman (1991). *The Magazine in America, 1741-1990*. Oxford: Oxford University Press.

Thomas, Evan (2003). *John Paul Jones: Sailor, Hero, Father of the American Navy*. New York. Simon & Schuster.

Toll, Ian W. (2006). *Six Frigates. How Piracy, War and British Supremacy at Sea Gave Birth to the World's Most Powerful Navy.* London: Michael Joseph.

Torsella, Joseph M. (1988) "American National Identity, 1750-1790: Samples from the Popular Press." *The Pennsylvania Magazine of History and Biography* 112 (2), April; 167-187.

Tucher, Andie (2010). "Newspapers and Periodicals." In: Gross, Robert A., and Mary Kelley, eds. *An Extensive Republic: Print, Culture, and Society in the New Nation, 1790-1840*. Vol. 2 of *A History of the Book in America*. Chapel Hill: University of North Carolina Press. 389-408

Turner, Mark W. (2006). "Time, Periodicals, and Literary Studies." *Victorian Periodicals Review*, 39 (4), Winter; 309-316.

Viroli, Maurizio (1995). *For Love of Country. An Essay on Patriotism and Nationalism*. Oxford: Oxford University Press.

Volo, James M. (2006). *Blue Water Patriots: The American Revolution Afloat*. Westport: Rowman and Littlefield.

Waldstreicher, David (1997). *In the Midst of Perpetual Fetes. The Making of American Nationalism, 1776-1820*. Chapel Hill: University of North Carolina Press.

Walton, Gary M., and Hugh Rockoff (2010). *History of the American Economy*. Mason: Southwestern.

Warner, Charles D. (1968). *Washington Irving*. Port Washington: Kennikat Press.

Warner, Michael (1991). *The Letters of the Republic. Publication and the Public Sphere in Eighteenth-Century America*. Cambridge: Harvard University Press.

Waterman, Bryan (2007). *Republic of Intellect: The Friendly Club of New York City and the Making of American Literature*. Baltimore: The Johns Hopkins University Press.

Wehler, Hans-Ulrich (2001). *Nationalismus: Geschichte, Formen, Folgen*. München: C.H. Beck.

Weigley, Russell F. (1967). *History of the United States Army*. New York: MacMillan.

Weiner, Bruce I. (2009). "The Democratic Exchange of Reading and Writing: Americanization and Periodical Publication, 1750-1810." *Cercles* 19; 102-113.

West, Elsie (1993). "Washington Irving: Biographer". In: Tuttleton, James, ed. *Washington Irving: The Critical Reaction*. New York: AMS. 197-205.

Wolff, Michael (1971). "Charting the Golden Stream. [Response to 'The Creation of Social Myth: Journalism and Empire']." *Victorian Periodicals Newsletter* 4 (1), February; 9-16.

White, Ed (2000). "Early American Nations as Imagined Communities." *American Quarterly* 56 (1). March; 49-81.

Wilke, Jürgen (1978). *Literarische Zeitschriften des 18. Jahrhunderts (1688-1789)*. Stuttgart: J.B. Metzlersche Verlagsbuchhandlung.

Williamson, Samuel H. (2010). „Seven Ways to Compute the Relative Value of a U.S. Dollar Amount, 1774 to present," *MeasuringWorth*, April 2010. URL: www.measuringworth.com/uscompare/ Last Accessed: 15.07.2011.

Wodak, Ruth, et al. (2009). *The Discursive Construction of National Identity*. Edinburgh: Edinburgh University Press.

Wood, Gordon S. (2009). *Empire of Liberty: A History of the Early Republic, 1789-1815*. Oxford: Oxford University Press.

Wood, James P. (1949). *Magazines in the United States. Their Social and Economic Influence*. New York: Ronald Press.

Woodall, Guy R. (1968). "The Relationship of Robert Walsh, Jr., to *The Port Folio* and the Dennie Circle: 1803-1812. *The Pennsylvania Magazine of History and Biography* 92 (2), April; 195-219.

Wright, Carroll D. (1885). *History of Wages and Prices in Massachusetts*. Boston: Wright & Potter.

Zelinsky, Wilbur (1988). *Nation into State: The Shifting Symbolic Foundation of American Nationalism*. Chapel Hill: University of North Carolina Press.

Index

67644465R00204

Made in the USA
San Bernardino, CA
26 January 2018